917.6889
MCH

S GREAT
SMOKY M

Dick

Mit

DATE DUE	
APR 1 7 2001	
MAY 1 9 2001	
JUN 2 8 2001	
JUL 2 4 2001	
AUG 3 0 2001	

D1065815

The Insiders' Guide®
An imprint of Falcon® Publishing, Inc.
A Landmark Communications company
P.O. Box 1718
Helena, MT 59624
(800) 582-2665
www.insiders.com

•

Sales and Marketing: Falcon Publishing, Inc.
P.O. Box 1718
Helena, MT 59624
(800) 582-2665
www.falcon.com

•

FIRST EDITION
1st printing

•

©2000 by Falcon Publishing, Inc.

•

Printed in the United States of America

•

Front cover photo: Spring Mountain in the Great Smoky Mountains, Pigeon
Forge Department of Tourism. Back cover photos, clockwise from top left:
waterfall, Pigeon Forge Department of Tourism; Dolly Parton, Dollywood;
Ober Gatlinburg tram, Ober Gatlinburg; bucolic Sevier County, Sevierville
Chamber of Commerce; Cherokee man, Cherokee Tribal Travel &
Promotion Office; Cherokee Orchard-Roaring Fork Motor Nature Trail,
Gatlinburg Department of Tourism. Spine photo: Sevier County
Courthouse, Sevierville Chamber of Commerce.

917. 6889   •

Publications from *The Insiders' Guide®* series are available at special discounts for bulk purchases for sales promotions, premiums or fundraisings.
Special editions, including personalized covers, can be created in large
quantities for special needs.
For more information, please contact Falcon Publishing.

ISBN 1-57380-106-2

Preface

So you've got the Smokies on your mind. Good thinking! With upwards of 10 million people coming to visit this enchanted place every year, and more than a thousand of them deciding to stay in the area, you're in good company. If you're among the one-third of our visitors who come here at least once every three years, you've probably noticed that changes are afoot everywhere you look lately. And change is not something most of you come here to see. Take heart—what you came here for is still here. It's just that attitudes and appetites are changing, and a place that depends on tourism for its own survival has to make adjustments.

The difference between evolution and revolution is time. Evolution is an on-going process that occurs naturally enough that no real change is noticed when things go along at their normal pace. Our mountains are a product of evolution; among the most ancient on Earth, the Great Smokies were once as tall as the Swiss Alps and rockier than the Rockies themselves. They were also at the bottom of a vast ocean.

As the rest of the planet changed to what it is today, so did the Smokies. Shaped and molded by nature's awesome hand for eons, the Smokies have been rounded into a beautiful, peaceful, accessible wilderness paradise that's yours to explore and fall in love with in a different way every time you enter it. The foothills at the northern edge of the Smokies are another story: Unprotected from the whims of capitalism and the entrepreneurial talents of the most progressive society in the history of the planet, what's going on in east Tennessee is anything but evolution. It isn't really a revolution, either; it's more of an explosion.

If you remember the Smokies of the 1970s and before, when people dropped in for a few days of rest beside a river, treat the memory like a child grown up: Cherish it... and let it go. You can still come to the Smokies and relax beside a river for a few days, but what you have to go through to get to that river has changed in ways you probably never imagined. The gentle folk of east Tennessee's Great Smoky Mountains, once a bastion of tranquility, have made some major concessions to the fact that today's American vacationer is looking for more than rippling water and breathtaking scenery. The biggest product of those concessions is that the big, open spaces you used to see on your way into Gatlinburg and Pigeon Forge are now filled with attractions and accommodations that make it possible for you to enjoy a week or more of your vacation time without getting within 10 miles of the mountains that used to be the primary attraction.

The mountains haven't changed. Great Smoky Mountains National Park is still at the end of the trail leading into the area, and so are those cool rippling streams in those friendly mountains that seem to want to enfold you in their warmth. The natives are still the same folks you can't quite forget when your stay ends. And the new residents, who used to be visitors like you, are still doing their best to emulate the friendliness of the natives.

East Tennessee's Smokies are a growing, happening place. Sevierville is awakening to the tourism market in ways that change for the better every day; Pigeon Forge is firmly established as a first-rate family destination; and Gatlinburg's world-famous craftspeople abound in greater numbers than ever before. And Great Smoky Mountains National Park is still the nation's most visited. What used to be, still is; there's just a whole lot of what's new in front of it, and more to come. You have a choice: Come to the new Smokies that's alive and throbbing to the beat of a new millennium, or come back to the Smokies that have always made you feel welcome and comfortable and sent you back home rested and at peace.

And if that Smoky Mountain smoke gets in your eyes, as the old song says, welcome back again. You'll love being here for the rest of your lives, and we'll see what we can do to help make your transition as smooth and easy as your decision to stay.

About the Authors

Dick McHugh

When "the smoke" got in Dick McHugh's eyes during a vacation in 1974, most of it was blown there by his wife, Joan. Happily employed as a technical writer and diverted as a hockey player and golfer, McHugh felt right at home in his native Michigan. Except that doggoned smoke just wouldn't go away. So in August 1975 the McHugh family uprooted and headed south, saying goodbye to the security of 20 years at General Motors, a nice home in the suburbs, and all of their family and friends, and hello to the sleepy city of Gatlinburg, tucked snugly in the bosom of the Great Smoky mountains.

They didn't know it at the time, but the McHughs were in the vanguard of a migration that would double the population of Sevier County by 1985, and triple it again in the following decade. The massive growth of the area in general, and in the cities of Gatlinburg and Pigeon Forge in particular during the 1980s, was significant enough to Dick that he started keeping track of developments in a journal in 1981. That journal formed the foundation for his contribution to this book.

Gatlinburg was a small town when the McHugh family moved there in 1975, and it remains so to the natives and pre-1980 immigrants. Sliding easily into the 1975 mountain culture, which was a lot like the post-World War II world they both grew up in, Dick and Joan opened a craft shop outside downtown Gatlinburg and settled into the production of toys and the raising of their two children. As parents are wont to do, they also got involved with the various programs children get into, and Dick found himself coaching Little League baseball and football, helping administer both programs, handling the public address chores, and writing stories for the local newspaper. In the manner of small towns everywhere, Gatlinburg's citizens were happy to let Dick do all the writing and talking he wanted, and a second career as a free-lance writer and microphone wielder was born. It grew eventually to include a talk show on the local cable channel, three books on the history and culture of the mountains and their people, and innumerable tourism-oriented articles in magazines and newspapers.

When the children grew up and left home, the McHughs closed their business and sought other niches. Joan expanded her prodigious talents into several handcraft disciplines, and now produces wood carvings, baskets, fabric wall hangers, and her own line of recycled paper products to several craft shops. Dick has pursued his love of writing and worked as a bowling center manager, motel desk clerk, and custodian to keep bread on the table. It seems both McHughs will do whatever is necessary to stay in their adopted home, but that's a story you'll hear from anybody who lives in the Smokies but wasn't born there. And don't look for them to wipe their eyes while they're talking; they know the smoke won't come out.

Mitch Moore

Mitch Moore lived his first eighteen years in a place as much unlike the Smoky Mountains as can be imagined. In the flat, rural farmlands of northeast Arkansas, he watched the evening sun disappear behind a level, distant horizon, not mountain peaks and hill tops. In fact, the only vertical deviation in the area's landscape was the man-made levee that protected his hometown from the floodwaters of the Mississippi River. That same river, though, instilled in Mitch a respect for nature's size, power and magnificence, a reverence that would later be rekindled when he put down roots near the overwhelming presence of the Smokies.

The journey to East Tennessee was a gradual one. Mitch attended Vanderbilt University in Nashville, where he wrote for the student newspaper and was also heavily involved in the theater department, appearing on stage in a number of major productions. In 1984 he received a B.A. in political science, put his sheepskin on display in a bookcase and returned to the stage, promptly pursuing a career in stand-up comedy. He spent the following seven years as a professional comic, touring the nation and sharing the bill with such performers as Tim Allen, Drew Carey and Jeff Foxworthy.

By the early '90s, Mitch found that life on the road was wearing thin, and he began keeping an eye out for the right moment to step away from the grind. Employment opportunities in the Smoky Mountains led him farther east and steadily uphill. He spent several years in the publishing industry, working as a writer and production artist for a real estate magazine, and later, an arts and entertainment journal.

Today, Mitch is a freelance writer with regular assignments for several Smoky Mountain area tourism publications as well as *The Knoxville News-Sentinel*. He lives with his 11-year-old son, Paul, and has absolutely no spare time.

Acknowledgments

Dick McHugh

I'm fortunate to have discovered this area a few years before most of the rest of the world, and to have adopted it as my home on its merits as a place in which to live and raise children. Because I got here when Gatlinburg was a small town and Sevier County was an insular community, I am privileged to know a few more people than those who followed me, and to share the belief that it's still a tight society if you want it to be. To that end, the best way to express my gratitude on a personal level would be to refer the reader to the 1976 Sevier County telephone book, where most of us have friends and family on every one of its 37 pages.

In the case of this particular book, I'm particularly grateful to a large group of friends and acquaintances who came forward with information when they learned about the project. That saved a lot of wear and tear on the little fat guy. Specifically, and with full and apologetic knowledge that somebody's going to be left out, I particularly thank two groups: On the professional side, thanks to David McCarter and Molly Harrison, my Insiders' Guide mentors, for getting Mitch and me off to a better-directed start than I would have myself; and to John Harrington, who may be the best friend I've never met, for his remarkable editing skills; to my good friend and frequent co-conspirator Gordon Brugman, whose photographic skills saved me a lot of footwork, and whose outrageous sense of humor keeps me on as even a keel as I can maintain; to Betty Webb, my longtime friend at Gatlinburg's splendid Anna Porter Library, for her untiring patience in helping me find a lot of really obscure information, and her encyclopedic memory that filled in a lot of gaps; to Angie Trentham, secretary to Gatlinburg's City Manager, and Janet Whaley, receptionist at the Gatlinburg Visitors and Convention Bureau, who pointed me in the right direction every time I needed municipal assistance; to Jack Schneider, who has seen Gatlinburg's post office grow from a three-man operation to a modern service, and has kept me abreast of the changes; and to Kay Powell, Pigeon Forge's indefatigable tourism director, who actually knows what's going on in that amazing city from day to day. Personally, and here's where I'm probably going to drop more balls than I catch, I'm grateful to my Saturday night poker gang—Mac and Susie Macdonell, Marilyn and sometimes Bob Gosse, Betty and Cecil Posey, and Harry Maloney, for passing along every tidbit of information and gossip so that I knew what was happening locally; to Connie and Arne Walker, Jerry McCarter, Barry and Karen Jinks, Lori Tierney, and a bunch of others who never lost faith that someday I'd finish this job; very importantly, to my partner and new friend Mitch Moore, whose marvelous talent for putting words on paper is combined with a finely tuned sense of the absurd that allowed him to work with the likes of me; and, finally, to Joan, my life partner of 40-plus years, who brought me to this enchanted place, and who has rightfully maintained that we couldn't find a better place to grow old together.

Mitch Moore

I presume that one of the reasons I was selected for this project was that I already knew quite a bit about this area. Having lived here for seven years, I also had the advantage of a unique perspective—that of both newcomer and entrenched local. Regardless, I'm sure there are those around these parts who would balk at the notion of ever calling me a true "insider." After all, there is the school of thought that if you're not born and raised in the Smokies, you're not a local and you never will earn that status. Despite what any naysayers might claim, I think I've been here long enough to know what's what about a few things. But in the process of researching this book, I discovered there was still a whole lot I didn't know about this area. To those who helped me with those gaps in my Smokies education, I express my sincere thanks.

A few people and organizations that I would like to single out are: the various departments of tourism and chambers of commerce in our cities of Sevierville, Pigeon Forge and Gatlinburg (Jon Elder, Kay Powell and Tony Smith, respectively), whose assistance was valuable to me on a number of chapters; Kathy Leedy of Select Real Estate, Bill Stevens and the staff of Great Smoky Mountains Association of Realtors for help with the real estate related chapters, and for knowing that real estate is a subject near and dear to my heart (insert sarcasm here for that last remark!); Patsy Bradford of the Sevier County Heritage Museum for valuable information and folklore surrounding the history of the area; and every hotel, motel, restaurant, wedding chapel, go-cart track, attraction, real estate company, music theater and retail shop that I peppered with my relentless questions.

I would like to thank Insiders' Guides, not only for giving me a regular writing gig for the better part of two years, but for the opportunity to get out there and really explore my home in the Smokies. Within the Insiders' organization I would like to extend my appreciation to our editor, John Harrington, for his patience and cooperation. Finally, I must extend my most sincere sentiments of gratitude to my co-author and partner in crime, Dick McHugh. We had never met before teaming up for this book, and along the way we discovered that our respective areas of expertise complemented each other nicely—he being a Gatlinburg resident, knowledgeable of that end of the county, and I being the Seviervillian, quite familiar with that territory. Between the two of us, we hopefully did some justice to Pigeon Forge. Every step of the way it seemed that when one of us was lacking in one area, the other was able to take up the slack. The fact that we also share similar writing styles and a mutual admiration of the semicolon (much to the dismay of our editor) hopefully has made for a smooth, informative, entertaining read.

And thanks to you who have purchased this first edition of *The Insiders' Guide to the Great Smoky Mountains.* My wish is that through it, you'll be able to discover a quite unique little corner of America, just as some of us have managed to rediscover it.

Table of Contents

Directory of Maps

SMOKIES OVERVIEW

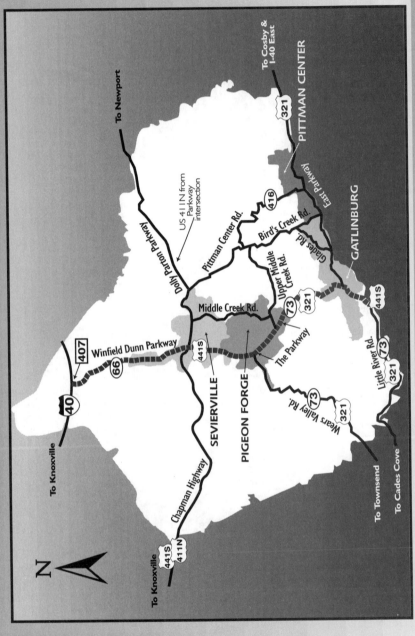

SEVIERVILLE

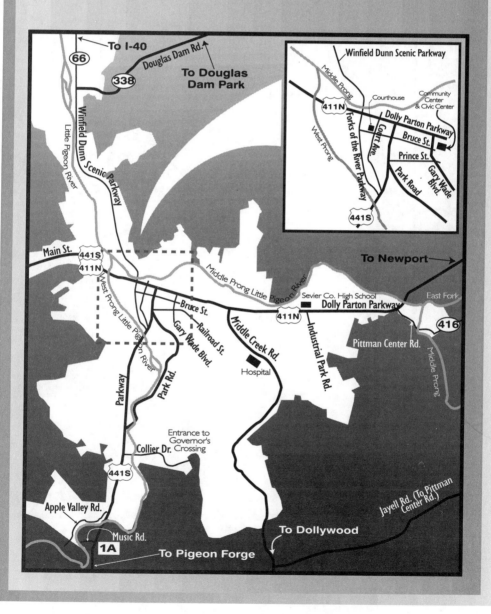

PIGEON FORGE

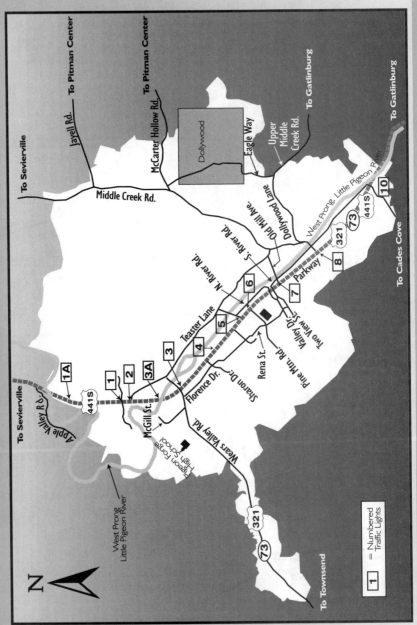

GATLINBURG

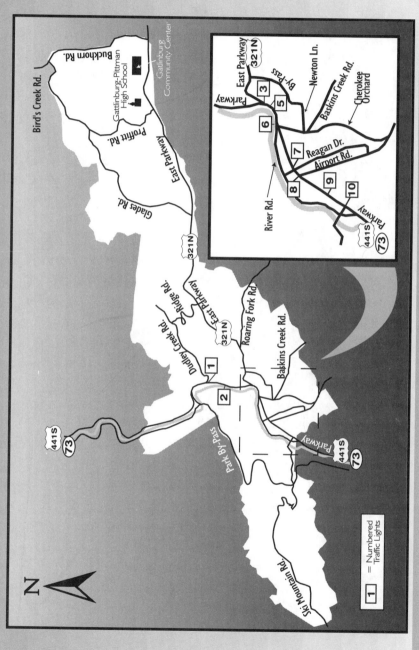

GREAT SMOKY MOUNTAINS NATIONAL PARK

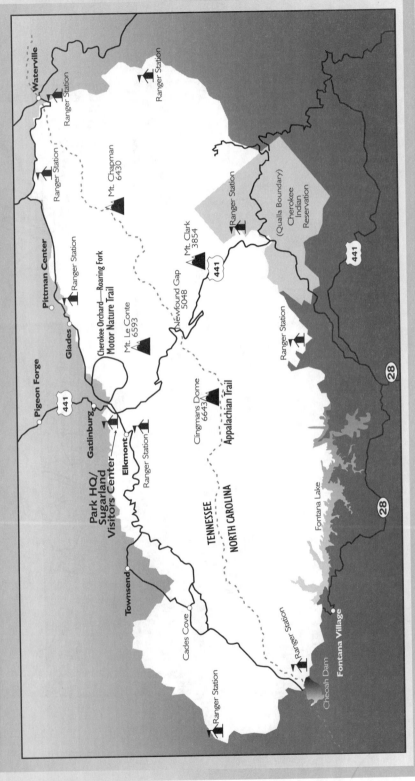

How To Use This Book

The Great Smoky Mountains and their environs have been one of America's most popular tourist destinations for more than half a century, and it suddenly looks like the whole world has discovered the place all at once. The growth that's taken place in the Gatlinburg-Pigeon Forge-Sevierville area in the last five years is so rapid and so widespread that even the residents are losing track of it. There's so much to see and do in the Smokies that you can blow half your vacation trying to figure out what to do while you're here, and you probably didn't come to this peaceful place to get stressed out trying to cram all the enjoyment the place has to offer in the short time you've got. That's why we wrote this book.

Don't be intimidated by the size of this volume. A place that has as much going for it as the Smokies area takes a lot of explaining. Remember, this is a guide. You should carry it with you in your travels to help bring the kaleidoscope of things to do in the Smokies into focus. If you need help finding anything, look in the index under the subject heading that fits your question, then go to that chapter and you'll find the subject arranged from north to south, always starting with Sevierville and going southward through Pigeon Forge and Gatlinburg. We've also included a chapter on Cherokee and the area in North Carolina immediately south of the national park. (For much more information on beautiful western North Carolina, we encourage you to pick up a copy of *The Insiders' Guide to North Carolina's Mountains*.)

The Great Smoky Mountains National Park is pretty well covered in its own chapter, but things that are as common to the park as they are to the cities, like campgrounds and annual events, will also be mentioned in the appropriate chapters. If you're looking for a specific place or business, flip to our comprehensive index to see where it's mentioned in the book.

We'd also like to point out rather proudly that the maps in this book are the most up-to-date available. Road construction is one of the biggest growth industries in the Smokies right now, and the changes are happening almost faster than the map producers can keep up with. What our maps show is current as of January 1, 2000, and we already know they'll be changing in our first update. The chapters on Getting Here, Getting Around; Accommodations; and Attractions should be particularly helpful in showing frequent visitors what's new each year—if you haven't been here since 1996, there's a few new places that'll blow you away!

Even if you live here or come often enough to qualify as a part-time resident, it's tough to stay abreast of the changes taking place along the northern half of the Smokies corridor, from Interstate 40 to Pigeon Forge's northern city limits. We're taking special pains to document those changes as they occur.

As you travel through the Smokies corridor, we hope you'll be impressed by the efforts of the municipal and park managers to provide directional signage. Sometimes it almost seems like overkill, but the prevailing attitude that too much is better than too little is characteristic of the local knowledge that tourism is the lifeblood of this area. The folks who built this industry did that on purpose, and they have a personal stake in seeing that you enjoy your stay, come back often, and tell your friends. This book is another link in the chain of information that supports the local efforts, and it's the only one we know of that encompasses the entire area as exhaustively. As the area continues to grow, we'll update this Insiders' Guide annually to stay abreast as best we can.

Your help will be appreciated—if you see something in the Smokies that we've omitted, or something we might have done a little better, let us know. Write to us at *The Insiders' Guide to the Great Smoky Mountains,* P.O. Box 1718, Helena, MT 59624, or access our Website at www.insiders.com with your comments (good or bad—we can take it), and your input will be part of our update efforts.

Area Overview

LOOK FOR:
- **Sevierville**
- **Pigeon Forge**
- **Gatlinburg**
- **Pittman Center**

Sevier County, Tennessee, home of Great Smoky Mountains National Park, is whatever the visitor or the prospective resident wants it to be. As the host area for the most-used entrance to America's most-visited national park, Sevier County has become a center for tourism, with all the advantages and disadvantages that attend such a circumstance. As a mostly rural county in some of east Tennessee's most beautiful and fertile countryside, it's a place where the family values generated by an agricultural lifestyle are still practiced and considered socially important. And as an area leader in light industry, Sevier County is undergoing significant change to attract new industrial business and new people to run it.

What it really boils down to is that Sevier County, Tennessee, originally occupied by white settlers around 1781 and established in 1784 as a part of Greene County in the ill-fated state of Franklin (see our History chapter), is a combination rarely found east of the Mississippi anymore. It's a settled area with a rich history that's world-famous for what it is today, and is just beginning to realize and develop its own potential. And for all that the Smokies corridor is that makes it attractive to upwards of 10 million visitors annually, the future would be scary if it weren't planted in such a solid past.

At 660 square miles, Sevier County is among the largest in Tennessee, but the settled area this book deals with takes up less than 10 percent of that space. There is also the little matter of about 240 square miles of wilderness at the southern end of the county that's not available for any kind of development, and hopefully never will be—it comprises about 30 percent of Great Smoky Mountains National Park. It's as much a matter of topography as any other consideration that the corridor itself, described by the route of Winfield Dunn Parkway (Tennessee 66) south from Exit 407 on I-40 to its merging with U.S. Highway 441 in Sevierville, and then south through Pigeon Forge and Gatlinburg to the national park entrance, bisects the county from top to bottom. The Smokies corridor does, however, encompass all four of the incorporated cities in Sevier County, and includes about two-thirds of its 62,000-plus permanent population.

Sevier County is politically divided into four cities and a whole lot of unincorporated communities. The unincorporated areas, spelled out in our Neighborhoods and Real Estate chapter, depend on the county for educational services (see the Education chapter), police protection by the county sheriff, fire control by volunteer departments, ambulance service and electric service. An elected commission of representatives from 15 civil districts oversees the operation of those facilities and departments necessary to govern any county; day-to-day operations are supervised by an elected County Executive. While the influx of new population is bringing profound change to the political and economic face of the Smokies corridor, it's still not a very good idea for anybody but a Republican to seek elected office in Sevier County.

The cities take care of their own police and fire/emergency services within their city limits, and each city also provides public works services at various levels. The cities deliver their refuse to a county-owned facility for disposal, and unincorporated areas have convenience stations where residents and businesses take their trash. The lone airport is jointly owned and operated by the cities of Gatlinburg and Pigeon Forge, and is located within the city limits of Sevierville.

The three principal cities that make up the corridor (the fourth is a very special case that we'll deal with shortly) are still controlled primarily by the descendants of the original settlers of the area. Each is uniquely different from the others because of what it took to tame the land in the late 18th and early 19th centuries. The chapter on the county's history will cover in greater detail their individual development, but the differences in the roles the cities of Sevierville, Pigeon Forge, and Gatlinburg played in the evolution of the county are central to an understanding of how Sevier County operates. As usual, we'll start with Sevierville and proceed south, with one significant exception from the norm: This chapter will include the town of Pittman Center, an incorporated area east of Gatlinburg on U.S. Highway 321. Pittman Center is one of Tennessee's newest cities, incorporated in 1974, and so dedicated to the preservation of its mountain heritage that it officially discourages commercial development.

The definitive visitor to Sevier County is a tourist family. Mom, Dad, and the kids are here to have a good time in the middle of enough variety to satisfy everybody, and Tennessee's Great Smoky Mountains are going to see that enough satisfaction is delivered to keep the family coming back for generations to come. And if that tourist family happens to include a cleverly-disguised industrial scout, we'll convince them that Sevier County has everything necessary to bring their business in: Good roads, plenty of land to build a business and new homes, and a place to raise a family with strong roots.

Sevierville

Compared to its neighboring cities, the most unusual thing about Sevierville is its normality. While Pigeon Forge and Gatlinburg are hopelessly synonymous with the tourism industry, Sevierville has managed to retain much of the virginal character of Small Town U.S.A. In fact, the local Chamber of Commerce bills it as "Your Hometown in the Smokies," and there's a lot of truth to that. If it were plucked out of the county and placed in another part of the state, Sevierville would likely sustain itself as it has for over two centuries—with farming and industry as well as small businesses that are locally owned and cater to the townsfolk.

To be sure, Sevierville has begun to reap the economic benefits of tourism, as Pigeon Forge did in the 1980s and Gatlinburg before that. Accommodations, restaurants, shopping centers and even music theaters have gradually become familiar fixtures on the Sevierville landscape. But even today, the town has its own distinct personality that, rather than being defined by tourism, has merely been complemented by it. Economically, the town is viable, not so much because of the influx of dollars from the Johnny-come-latelies, but because it has always been one (see the History chapter).

Much of Sevierville's flavor has as much to do with politics as it does economics. When the city was chosen to be the county seat in 1795, the stage was set for it to become a hub of governmental and commercial activity. Today, the network of offices and agencies that has grown and spread from Sevier County's first rudimentary government not only employs hundreds of residents, but naturally draws to it the rest of the county's citizens that receive its services. From court appearances to license plate renewals, Sevierville is the place you have to go.

Geographically, the town is laid out like many of its size and background. The historic downtown area is wedged between the east and west forks of the Little Pigeon River. Just a few blocks from downtown you'll find most of the

INSIDERS' TIP

According to one marketing survey conducted on behalf of the Sevierville Chamber of Commerce, the average visitor to that city is between the ages of 45 and 64, earns between $35,000 and $60,000 per year and has had at least some college education. The number one reason cited for visiting Sevierville was "Vacation." Tied for second were "Shopping," "Scenery" and "Entertainment/Theaters."

Handmade country crafts are a major drawing card for visitors to the Smokies.

Photo: Courtesy Maplewood Country Stores

city's schools, the new police station, the city's community center and a former movie theater turned civic center. From its central core, the town has expanded in all four directions with balanced concentrations of residential, commercial and municipal growth. Although the Smoky Mountains dominate Sevierville's southern horizon, much of the city is actually characterized by relatively flat terrain, with the occasional undulation or foothill dropped in for character.

Radiating from downtown, Forks of the River Parkway, then the Parkway (U.S. 441; it's just named "Parkway") lead south to Pigeon Forge and feature much of the city's commercial and tourist-oriented development. Traveling north on Winfield Dunn Parkway (Tenn. 66), you'll also find rapid growth in residential areas as well as accommodations, shops, restaurants and attractions geared toward the vacationer.

Chapman Highway (U.S. Highways 411 and 441 concurrently) leads west toward Seymour and Knoxville; its surrounding areas primarily remain a mixture of residential neighborhoods and undeveloped farmland. As Dolly Parton Parkway (a.k.a. U.S. 411) takes you east, away from downtown, you'll notice that much of the old and new growth alike has a more local flavor to it. Fast food restaurants, retail stores and service-oriented businesses have seemingly sprung up overnight in an effort to serve the growing numbers of Seviervillians who have moved eastward to escape entanglements with heavy tourist traffic.

One only has to take a drive through the county's three main towns to see how Sevierville is "mundanely unique" to Sevier County. It's the only city in the county that has a movie theater, new car dealerships, a hospital, factories, an airport and a good ol' small town main street. Churches, schools and banks are in abundance, and although Wal-Mart has taken a healthy bite out of the retail pie, mom-and-pop businesses generally hold their own.

As mentioned earlier, tourism has been both directly and indirectly responsible for much of Sevierville's recent growth; a growth that is unmistakable. Of the roughly 1,600 businesses that call Sevierville home, about 50 percent of them are in some way linked to the tourist trade. These include hotels, outlet centers, restaurants, music theaters and attractions. Looking at the statistics provides a fairly reliable litmus test of this contention. For example, the number of available hotel and motel rooms has increased more than 500 percent since 1988. Today over 2,200 rooms are in existence, compared with only 443 ten years ago (see our Hotels & Motels

The Ober Gatlinburg Tramway is one of the Smokies' more recognizable manmade landmarks.

Photo: Courtesy Ober Gatlinburg

chapter for details). Between 1991 and 1999, city hotel-motel tax revenues increased from $163,781 to over $500,000.

Local manufacturing is another good barometer of Sevierville's economic health. Another substantial chunk, about 20 percent, of the city's economy is accounted for by local industry. Along sections of Dolly Parton Parkway, you'll find three industrial parks that are home to over a dozen national and local manufacturers. These thriving companies turn out products such as textiles and high-tech electronics as well as lights, magnets and valves that wind up in automobile assembly. One of the most fundamental indicators of Sevierville's growth is its increase in population. The current estimated population is about 9,000 year-round residents. Compare that with only 4,556 back in 1980. Projected estimates for the year 2010 place the city's population at nearly 14,000.

As Sevierville continues to feel its oats, it regularly faces issues that naturally accompany growth. One issue is the city's liquor laws. Be aware (or should we say "beware?") that there are no liquor stores in Sevierville. The only alcohol sold over the counter is beer, which can be found in most local supermarkets and convenience stores. Until just a few years ago, no alcohol of any kind was sold by the drink, ostensibly to preserve the town's "family atmosphere." Changes in city law now allow for beer to be sold by the drink in restaurants that have a seating capacity of at least 150 and where at least 50 percent of sales are from food. Also, beer can be sold at city golf courses, special events and at the new minor league baseball stadium. Right now there are only a few "wet" restaurants, but that number is growing in an ongoing effort by restaurateurs to please the tourists. Oh, the times they are a changin'!

INSIDERS' TIP

The record for the highest single-day traffic count in Sevierville is 106,000 cars. Jaywalkers and small animals beware!

Pigeon Forge

For over 100 years, Pigeon Forge was a sleeping giant, a rural farm community nuzzled peacefully against Smoky Mountains' majesty. Unlike its northern neighbor, Sevierville, which had developed sturdy economic legs of its own from Day One, and its southern neighbor,

Gatlinburg, which began to prosper in the '40s and '50s because of the National Park and mountain crafts, Pigeon Forge suffered from an identity crisis until about 25 years ago. Until then, Pigeon Forge was nothing more than rolling farmland dotted by the occasional restaurant or hotel that lined the Parkway in the hopes of sporadically snagging vacationers on their way to and from the mountains (see our History chapter).

During the '80s, Pigeon Forge reaped benefits from the Knoxville World's Fair and the opening of Dollywood Entertainment Park. Then, the benevolent giant awoke and today stands as tall (in a figurative sense) as the mountain peaks which serve as its backdrop. Since then, Pigeon Forge has made up for lost time, generating gross sales tax revenues surpassing those of Gatlinburg (nearly $8 million in 1998-99) and even surpassing that town in permanent residents (it's right at 4,000). In the summer, the town's daily population swells to over 40,000.

Today, Pigeon Forge is almost Las Vegas-like in appearance, with a "main drag" that's packed full of hotels and motels, restaurants, attractions, music theaters and shopping outlets. Sign after neon sign pulses brightly in the night, promising more fun, more entertainment and more value than the guy next door. One interesting aspect to all of this (a frightening aspect to some) is that the benevolent giant is still growing!

Unless you are a local, familiar with the residential areas and side roads (see our Real Estate chapter), the axiom "what you see is what you get" stands as a fair assessment of the city's geography. Pigeon Forge is laid out pretty much along the steady course of the Parkway (U.S. 441), running for approximately four miles from the abrupt cut off of Sevierville's city limits near Apple Valley Drive to The Spur, which leads to Gatlinburg. The Parkway is frequently intersected, either by small side streets with finite lengths or by roads leading into the more rural sections of the county. Along these paths is where you'll find most of the city's residences as well as many of its churches, small businesses and government offices.

Needless to say, the distilled essence of today's Pigeon Forge is largely a product of tourism, an industry in which serving the visitor is a priority in all sectors. The indisputable facts are that the town as a whole has grown and prospered, experienced low seasonal unemployment rates

Many visitors choose to enjoy the area's abundant scenery on horseback.

Photo: Sevierville Chamber of Commerce

and has generated close to a half-billion dollars in gross business receipts in each of the past four years.

Now, the different spins you can apply to these facts vary, according to whom you ask. City administrators and promoters as well as business owners and upper level managers are, no doubt, thrilled with the state of affairs. Those who work on tourism's front lines often present a different picture. While jobs are plentiful in season, the market tapers off from late fall through early spring, and layoffs are a standard operating practice. Also, a great number of the jobs available are service-oriented positions (hotel and motel housekeeping, food service, retail, etc.), which pay at or slightly above minimum wage and offer few benefits.

By the way, "union" is a dirty word in Sevier County. Past efforts to rally hotel and motel workers have failed; today, most employees realize that business owners can readily draw replacements for them from a large and eager pool. While some may go so far as to demonize the economic powers that be, most local citizens are willing to live with the negatives of seasonal employment and moderate wages for the sake of working in a vibrant economy in a beautiful mountain setting.

In defense of this situation, we can say that things used to be worse. There was a time when "seasonal employment" meant working the summer months only; these days, the off-season grows shorter and shorter each year. Also, you'll find that, as in larger cities, many waiters, bartenders and the like are aspiring performers, looking to get a foot in the door of area music and variety theaters. As a case in point, one of the hosts of Dixie Stampede's show started out as a server at that particular Pigeon Forge attraction before working his way up to the show's front man position (see the Music Theaters and Nightlife chapter).

There's also no denying that Dollywood has been an unqualified boon to the city of Pigeon Forge. Much of Pigeon Forge's early success in tourism came from absorbing some of Gatlinburg's spillover with its hotels and restaurants. Soon, entrepreneurs realized that there was a market for developing attractions in Pigeon Forge that would draw people there for its own sake. Enter Dollywood, which was built on a site that had previously been a Silver Dollar City theme park. Since 1986, thanks to the name recognition of and promotion by Dolly Parton, Dollywood has consistently expanded. It is now the state's single most visited theme park, accommodating over 2 million visitors annually, and its parent company, Dollywood Entertainment, is Sevier County's largest single seasonal employer. (See our Dollywood chapter for a more in-depth look at the park.)

Dollywood Entertainment is also responsible, in large part, for the explosion in the Smokies' music theater business. Several theaters had existed in Pigeon Forge, going back as far as 1984, and Dollywood Entertainment itself had started Dixie Stampede in 1988. But with the company's opening of Music Mansion in 1994 and the city's creation of an infrastructure for a multi-theater development known as Music Road, the era of an outright "theater community" in Pigeon Forge was ushered in. Suddenly, visions of the town nipping at the heels of Branson, Missouri, were dancing through the heads of local developers and promoters.

While there are times that growth in Pigeon Forge appears to be unbridled, city planners will tell you that they don't want their city to become another Branson, with too much stuff packed into too little space. So far, the city appears to have stuck to its guns. The Parkway's six wide lanes generally allow for smooth progress through town (except during the town's frequent custom auto shows), and Sevierville's widening of the Parkway up to Pigeon Forge city limits will only help with traffic flow. Considering that the average traffic flow on Pigeon Forge's section of the Parkway in 1997 was around 53,000 cars per day, cautious city planning is probably a wise option.

One subject on which the city has refused to budge is alcohol sales. Like Sevierville, there are no liquor stores here, and only beer can be purchased in supermarkets and convenience stores. However, alcohol can't be served by the drink within city limits. One notable exception to this rule is the Pigeon Forge landmark, Alf's restaurant, which was "grandfathered" in when local alcohol ordinances prohibited by-the-drink sales; yes, you can still get a cold beer at Alf's

INSIDERS' TIP

Gatlinburg's bicycle-riding policemen have become an attraction all by themselves. Tourists are continually stopping the cycle cops to ask for information. The most frequently asked question is, "Why are you riding that bike?" The answer is that the bicycles let the police move rapidly through traffic, increasing their effectiveness at responding to emergency situations.

The Smokies are often a study in contrasts, where modern progress and Mother Nature coexist in harmony.

Photo: Sevierville Chamber of Commerce

(see our Restaurants chapter). Another exception is Mountain Valley Vineyards, where, thanks to state agricultural laws, wine can be purchased by the bottle (see our Attractions chapter).

Gatlinburg

There has always been a certain charm about downtown Gatlinburg, probably because of the intimacy of the city itself. Despite the fact that any day or night can find upwards of 20,000 people browsing the shops and attractions crammed into a half-mile on a couple of streets, there's a relaxed atmosphere that makes Gatlinburg a pleasant place to spend some time. The Parkway strip from the area of traffic light #3 (the traffic lights in both Pigeon Forge and Gatlinburg are numbered) to the Park entrance is full of enough variety shops and amusements to use up whatever part of a day you want to give it, and there's enough variety sprinkled in to keep the kids amused as well.

Gatlinburg today is a city of about 4,000 souls that takes care of a visitor population averaging 35,000 a day. The only way to accomplish this feat is to pretend you're a city of 35,000 that has a single main street less than a mile long. All services provided by any city are provided in Gatlinburg on that basis. That's why the downtown is always sparkling clean and heavily planted with seasonal flowers, and it's also why this so-called small town seems to be crowded with police officers on walking beats, bicycles, motorcycles, and in patrol cars.

Gatlinburg is, in fact, one of the safest places you'll ever visit. With the proper warnings and precautions, young children can be left to their own devices in the downtown area in the same manner you'd let them go their own way in a theme park. In the history of the town, there's no record of a child ever being harmed in downtown Gatlinburg. Ever.

It's also probably one of a very few cities its size that has three fully-operational fire halls, a 150,000 square-foot convention center, and a 50,000-plus square-foot community recreation center, (when you read about it in our Parks and Recreation chapter, you probably won't believe it). A mass transit system consisting of several trolleys on six different routes serves locals going to and from work as well as visitors using it for its convenience.

We'd do well to remember at this point that the downtown business district is a very small part of the corporate package—the city limits of Gatlinburg extend about a mile north of downtown and stretch about 4½ miles out the East Parkway. The Great Smoky Arts & Crafts Community, a few miles east of downtown, is almost entirely within the city limits and is more than ten times larger in area. There are also four residential areas ringing the downtown area that dwarf it in size. Gatlinburg has a lot of vacant land; it just isn't real adaptable to construction. The only property with true development potential is along the East Parkway to the city limits, and it's going fast.

The city government consists of five city commissioners elected entirely at large. Commissioners serve four-year terms, which are staggered so that elections take place every two years. The commissioners elect a mayor from their body every year. The day-to-day operation of the city is directed by a city manager, who is hired by and responsible to the commissioners. Gatlinburg has 355 permanent employees on the rolls today. Citizen participation in local government is unusually high, with more than a dozen advisory boards serving the city's community development and recreation departments, involving the volunteer participation of close to 100 citizens.

Because it's the only city in Sevier County where it's legal to sell liquor, and because state law mandates that all taxes collected on the sale of liquor be used for education, Gatlinburg has its own board of education, which disburses these funds to the city's two schools. Additional teaching positions and equipment purchases provided for by liquor tax monies were prime considerations in a 1998 poll conducted by the *Wall Street Journal,* which recognized Gatlinburg-Pittman High School as the best high school in the South.

Gatlinburg has come a long way in a short time as a center for tourism and as a host city to people looking for temporary gratification. It's also done an admirable job of standing still long enough to attract a growing population of people from all walks of life who become willing participants in the city's ongoing drive to continually reinvent itself without losing touch with its pioneer heritage. Content at this point to concede that its only industry is making people happy, and willing to do what's necessary to reach that goal without compromising its singular brand of integrity, Gatlinburg moves forward still believing that all stories that start with "Once upon a time..." must inevitably end with "...and they all lived happily ever after."

INSIDERS' TIP

One of the many feathers in Pigeon Forge's tourism cap is the distinction of being a shopper's paradise. The city was named "Favorite Shopping Spot in the South" by *Southern Living* magazine readers as well as being voted "Number One City for Outlet Shopping" by *Outlet Bound* magazine in 1995.

Hiking is one of the most popular activities in Great Smoky Mountains National Park.

Photo: Sevierville Chamber of Commerce

Pittman Center

This is an unusual case, and to keep it in perspective we've compressed history and overview into a single statement. Pittman Center is an incorporated city east of Gatlinburg that has no business district, no post office (it's served by Gatlinburg), practically no commerce, and no desire to ever have any of the above. It probably wouldn't even be a city if one of its citizens hadn't gotten crosswise with the Gatlinburg building inspector back in 1974, but we're getting ahead of ourselves.

The community of Pittman Center was established when the Elmira District of the Central New York Conference of the Methodist Episcopal Church established a missionary school in the mountains east of Gatlinburg and named it for their own superintendent, Dr. Eli Pittman. The school was operated by the United Methodist Church until 1955, when the Sevier County Board of Education bought the three-story building for $20,000 and assumed responsibility for the education of the fewer than 100 students. The Methodist Church then donated the 650 acres it had originally purchased to the community. A new school was built next to the original building in the early '60s, and the high school grades were transferred to the new Gatlinburg-Pittman High School when it was built in 1964.

The little mountain community, never wanting anything more than to be left alone, then languished into the 1970s while Gatlinburg continued to grow to the east, slowly annexing land and extending its influence into unincorporated land by enforcing a nebulous "development district" statute that gave it legal control of development within five miles of its own expanding city limits. Things came to a head in 1974, when an un-named Pittman Center man was stopped from building a house on his own land by a zealous Gatlinburg building inspector trying to protect Gatlinburg's "development status" by enforcing Gatlinburg's building codes.

Into the fray jumped the venerable Conley Huskey (1907-94), a Pittman Center native and long-time political giant in the area. Knowing that the only way to stop Gatlinburg from exercising its influence in Pittman Center, and eventually annexing it, was to incorporate the area into a city of its

INSIDERS' TIP

All that lovely greenery in Gatlinburg's hanging baskets and roadside flower beds is grown in the city's own greenhouse, overseen by a full-time horticulturist.

own, Conley Huskey drew up and circulated a petition practically overnight to incorporate a new city. He waited two weeks to file the petition so the two pregnant women in the area could deliver their babies and bring the population to the 365 heads the state laws of the time required. The vote to incorporate was 128 for, 24 against, and Pittman Center became a city in 1974. And Conley Huskey's unnamed friend built his house.

Conley Huskey, a long-time Sevier County commissioner, paid most of the costs of incorporation out of his own pocket (he recalled once that he'd have been $10,000 better off if he'd kept his mouth shut) and was rewarded by being elected Pittman Center's first mayor, an office he held until 1990. The old school building had fallen into disrepair by this time, but it was renovated and is now Pittman Center's city hall. At three stories, it's also the most imposing structure in the city. Pittman Center has gone on record as being dedicated to the preservation of its mountain heritage, and, as such, has resisted any sort of commercial growth.

The city's biggest asset at the time of incorporation was Cobbly Nob golf course (now Sunterra Resort), a privately operated facility on municipal land. Pittman Center sold the golf course to a private developer in 1978, and used the proceeds from the sale to pave every road in the city. Pittman Center today is just about what it wants to be: A protected mountain community of less than ten square miles and a population of about 500. The city is governed by a mayor and board of three aldermen, elected at large every two years. The day-to-day affairs of the city are overseen by a part-time administrator who directs the activities of the city's five full-time employees: A recorder, two policemen, and two maintenance men. The operating budget for fiscal year 1998 was $330,000, generated mostly by a property tax rate of 32 cents per $100 assessed valuation and a 3 percent hotel-motel tax. Fire service is provided by a well-equipped volunteer department.

Getting Here, Getting Around

The area we refer to as "the Smokies" is a large chunk of east Tennessee and a smaller portion of western North Carolina with an irregular and totally arbitrary border. To keep it as simple as possible, we're primarily talking about the corridor that is described by Tenn. 66 and U.S. 441 along a path of about 30 miles from Exit 407 off I-40 to the Great Smoky Mountains National Park entrance at the southern city limit of Gatlinburg. Keep going, and you'll eventually wind through the park and into North Carolina.

We'll start this chapter with a small section on getting here, then concentrate on telling you how to get around once you're here. It can be a challenge, and sometimes we have a little traffic, but trust us to get you where you want to go.

LOOK FOR:
• Airports
• Numbered Traffic Lights
• Shortcuts
• Trolleys

Getting Here

By Air

Gatlinburg-Pigeon Forge Airport
1255 Airport Rd., Sevierville
• **(865) 453-8393**

Let's start off with one vital piece of information. When you land at this airport, you won't be in either Gatlinburg or Pigeon Forge—you'll be in Sevierville. Don't ask us to explain this one. It's probably the same logic responsible for locating the Gatlinburg Municipal Golf Course in Pigeon Forge.

The airport itself is a full service, fixed base operator. Its 5,500-foot runway can accommodate aircraft ranging from small, single engine planes to corporate jets. Although no commercial airlines fly in here, it does frequently receive aircraft chartered by individuals or companies. There are no landing fees, but there is an aircraft parking fee of $5 per night.

Amenities available on site include a maintenance crew, jet fuel and gas for piston-driven planes. The airport does not operate a shuttle service, but there is a rental car office on the premises that can be reached at (865) 453-8918. The service is provided by the local Ford dealership (see "Getting Around"), and a limited number of cars are kept on hand at the airport itself. Of course, you can also leave by taxi, if you wish. See the "Getting Around" section for information on local cab companies.

McGhee Tyson Airport
Alcoa Hwy., Alcoa
• **(865) 970-2773**

This airport is in the community of Alcoa, approximately 15 miles south of Knoxville on U.S. Highway 129 (Alcoa Highway). The airport accommodates 12 airlines providing non-stop flights to 15 major cities including Atlanta, Dallas-Ft. Worth, St. Louis, Chicago, and Washington, D.C. Among the more familiar carriers that fly in and out of Knoxville are Northwest, United, TWA, U.S. Airways and Delta, the latter accounting for roughly 35 percent of the airport's traffic.

McGhee Tyson is undergoing a major terminal renovation, an expansion spurred by the airport's recent growth in popularity. By late 2000, the $53 million facelift should be complete, featuring increased ticket counter space, a single security checkpoint, an expanded baggage handling area and more waiting areas. The renovation adds 140,000 additional square feet to the building and will also increase the number of passenger gates, concession areas, flight information displays and escalators.

Both short- and long-term parking sites are available. Maximum per-day rates are $5 for long-term parking and $10 for short-term.

Entering the main terminal, you'll find the baggage claim areas and a number of rental car agencies on the lower street level. The upper level includes the gates and ticketing areas as well as some typical airport facilities and amenities— restaurants, snack bars and gift shop.

For transportation from McGhee Tyson Airport to the Smokies, there are a number of options available. The following national car rental agencies maintain fleets at the airport. We've listed toll-free numbers as well as local numbers that provide direct access to each company's airport rental office.

Alamo: (800) 327-9633 or (865) 681-3966

Avis: (800) 331-1212 or (865) 970-2985

Budget: (800) 527-0700 or (865) 970-4143

Hertz: (800) 654-3131 or (865) 970-4030

National: (800) 227-7368 or (865) 970-2993

Thrifty: (800) 367-2277 or (865) 970-2277.

If you're driving to the Smokies from the airport, there are two basic ways you can go. Traveling north on U.S. 129 (Alcoa Highway) will take you directly to I-40 near downtown Knoxville. Head east on I-40 to Exit 407 and you'll be at the north end of the Smokies corridor. An alternate, not to mention more scenic, path would be to take U.S. 129 south from the airport for about two miles and bear left, following the signs to Maryville and Alcoa. Tennessee Highway 35 will take you east through those two communities. Once you're in Maryville, follow the signs for U.S. 411 North. That highway will take you north to Seymour

and then east, directly into Sevierville. Depending on traffic, both routes to Sevierville are about a 45-minute to one-hour drive.

There are several taxicab companies that provide transportation from McGhee Tyson Airport. The following taxi services will usually either have cars waiting outside the terminal at street level or can be at the terminal within about five minutes.

AAA Taxi: (865) 679-6962
ABC Taxi: (865) 970-4545
Benchmark Taxi: (865) 567-0035
Sunshine Taxi: (865) 310-7047
Tennessee Taxi Service: (865) 984-8555

All of the companies that service the airport operate on a fixed fare schedule. A one-way trip to Sevierville costs $40; one-way to Pigeon Forge is $45; one-way to Gatlinburg is $50. Prices are based on a one-passenger fare; additional passengers cost $3 each.

Another option is to contact Sassafras Transportation at (865) 971-4075. This company makes trips to Sevierville for $11.50 per person, Pigeon Forge for $12.80 per person and Gatlinburg for $14.10 per person. Fifteen percent discounts are offered for senior citizens and students. Children younger than 5 ride free.

Sassafras Transportation utilizes a 15-passenger van to take riders directly to their hotel or motel in each of the three cities. The company's main drawback is its limited Sevier County schedule. June through August, they make one trip per day, at 1 PM, Monday through Saturday. The rest of the year, trips run Monday through Friday.

By Ground

Greyhound Bus Terminal
100 Magnolia Ave. NE, Knoxville
• (865) 522-5144

Unfortunately, if you plan to get to the Smokies by bus, Knoxville is about as close as you're going to get, since there are no major bus routes that run into Sevier County. Knoxville's Greyhound terminal receives approximately 35 to 40 arrivals daily. Since there

---

INSIDERS' TIP

Interestingly, the new women's restrooms at Knoxville's McGhee Tyson Airport have received what is probably more than their fair share of local media coverage. The toilet seats are covered with a clear, plastic protective material that slides onto the seat rim electronically with each new use, making for more sanitary conditions. It can only be assumed that those in charge of the airport's renovation saw any efforts to provide men with similar seat covers as being totally futile.

Traffic light #8 on the Parkway in Pigeon Forge. All traffic lights on the Parkway in Pigeon Forge are numbered and have illuminated signs.

Photo: Dick McHugh

are no rental car agencies located at the bus station, your best bet for getting to the Smokies is to contact Sassafras Transportation at (865) 971-4075 (see above section). Sassafras Transportation's one-way, per person rates from the bus terminal are $5 to Sevierville, $6.30 to Pigeon Forge and $7.60 to Gatlinburg. Again, the price is right, but they only make one Sevier County run per day.

Getting Around

There is no more beautiful or peaceful place on the planet than the Smokies. There is a serenity here that's simply not available anywhere else, and it comes from a combination of several agreeable factors that don't come together quite so nicely as they might in other places you visit.

You might want to repeat this mantra to yourself a few thousand times if you're sitting in the parking lot that the Smokies corridor is wont to become without notice on any given summer day. Traffic is a problem in any place where upwards of 75,000 people are all trying to go anywhere at the same time. And when 50,000 of them are on the same street at the same time, it doesn't matter how long the street is—you've gotten yourself into a traffic jam that only time will resolve, and you're on *your* time, and it probably didn't come cheap. So let's see what we can do to save a little time and a lot of frazzled nerves. And let's maybe even see if we can make your arrival a little easier.

Handy Hint #1: The roads we discuss are all paved and wide enough for trailers or RVs to pass. Other routes are used by the locals and some of our more knowledgeable visitors, and they'll be glad to share them with you, but we're going to stick with the routes that don't require special handling.

Handy Hint #2: If you're bumper-to-bumper in Great Smoky Mountains National Park, you're stuck—we can't help you. Take whatever comfort you can from the beauty of your surroundings and pray that your gas and your composure hold out until you break free.

First, let's tell you about negotiating the Smokies Corridor. Here's how the corridor lays out: Exit 407 on I-40 is Tenn. 66, also known and labeled as the Winfield Dunn Scenic Parkway. Unless you're coming into the area from the southeast via U.S. 321 into Gatlinburg, or have chosen to forego the Interstate system at a point west of Exit 407, chances are you'll enter the area at Exit 407. It's the way most travel services recommend for travelers coming from the north, south, or west. People coming from the east (the Carolinas and those folks from Georgia and Florida who don't use Interstate 75) usually get off I-40 at the Foothills Parkway (Exit 445) and come in to Gatlinburg on U.S. 321—a route that's discussed later.

A word of caution: There are very few places in the area where roads have only one name or only one state or federal route number. Every road name we use is the one that observation has proven correct. In cases where one road is identified by maps and highway signs as having several route numbers, our maps will show only the numbers that are used by the local gentry. For example, the Parkway, our main stem and primary reference point, can have up to seven different identifications from Sevierville to the Park entrance. We'll use only "Parkway" and "U.S. 441," and our maps are marked accordingly. In the section on bypasses and back roads we'll address the name changes more specifically.

Eight miles south of Exit 407, Tenn. 66 intersects Dolly Parton Parkway (U.S. 411/441—see why we try to use simpler terms?) in Sevierville. You'll probably see the golden dome of the courthouse as you approach Dolly Parton Parkway. More than a century old, the Sevier (pronounced "Severe") County courthouse is one of Tennessee's oldest and one of the prettiest in America (see our Attractions chapter for more). After crossing Dolly Parton Parkway, another mile brings you to the end of Tenn. 66 at U.S. 441 S. Turning right toward Pigeon Forge, you're now on what is locally known as the Parkway, and if you've managed to avoid bumper-to-bumper traffic so far, the honeymoon is about to end.

Remember the intersection where you turned onto the Parkway—it will come up later for visits to a few places. For now, though, you're closing in on your first destination: Your home away from home for the duration of your visit (assuming you're staying in or near Pigeon Forge or Gatlinburg. If you're staying in Sevierville, you've probably already checked in by now).

Proceeding south along the Parkway, you'll notice that the first few miles are sparsely settled with motels, convenience stores and local services, with a few gift/craft shops thrown in. You're still in Sevierville, the county seat, which is just beginning to tap into the tourism market (more on this in our Area Overview chapter).

Keep your eyes peeled for the Wal-Mart megastore on the right and Governor's Crossing resort complex on the left. When you pass these places you're approaching Pigeon Forge, and the landscape will change dramatically. Shortly past the Music Mansion and Louise Mandrell theaters on the right and a clutch of music halls on the left, you'll see the Pigeon Forge Department of Tourism, and if you still thirst for literature and/or more information, it's a good place to stop and get your bearings. Then, welcome to action-packed Pigeon Forge! You actually passed out of Sevierville and into Pigeon Forge when you crossed the river just before Music Mansion, but the sign's hard to see.

The next three miles are a steady stream of motels, restaurants, amusements, and shops strung out shoulder-to-shoulder along both sides of the Parkway. If you're staying in Pigeon Forge, start looking for your lodging place as soon as you cross Apple Valley Road. In average conditions you'll have sufficient time to look, because you're probably going

INSIDERS' TIP

There are only three roads that extend more than a couple of miles east and west of the corridor for its entire length. One (Tennessee Highway 139) is only important to golfers going west, and to those headed for Douglas Dam (see Parks and Recreation and Campgrounds & RV Parks) headed east. The other two are Dolly Parton Parkway (U.S. 411/441), which goes east out of Sevierville to Cocke County and Newport and west to Knoxville, and the East Parkway (U.S. 321N) which heads east out of Gatlinburg.

INSIDERS' TIP

When you make your hotel reservations, ask the clerk if the hotel provides a shuttle service that can pick you up at either the Gatlinburg-Pigeon Forge Airport or Knoxville's McGhee Tyson Airport.

to be in really slow-moving traffic. If you know which side of the road you're staying on, get in the lane you'll be turning out of, and resist every temptation to get out of it. If you're going on to Gatlinburg, stay in one of the two center lanes all the way through Pigeon Forge.

Pigeon Forge used to have only one traffic light. The city's unbelievable explosion into tourism in the late 1980s changed that forever, and now it seems like a traffic light is some kind of status symbol. They may be necessary to help regulate traffic, but it sure seems like there's a lot of them on a straight stretch of highway. Pigeon Forge has numbered its traffic lights on the Parkway. Right now there are 10 traffic lights and 11 numbers, including two with a number and an alphabetic suffix. Here's how they lay out, running north to south:

1A.   The entrance to the parking lots for Music Mansion, the Louise Mandrell Theater, and the Alabama Grill, this intersection will become increasingly popular as the road is developed to wrap around the west side of the Parkway and become Music Row. Several music theaters are in planning and early construction phases along this planned road. This light will get a lot of attention in our next edition.

1.   Henderson's Chapel Road; several new motels are already open here, with more expected as Music Row is built and developed.

2.   Teaster Lane goes off to the left, leading to a spate of music theaters and the largest concentration of outlet malls. Teaster Lane is also the southern bypass around the Parkway, leading to Lower Middle Creek Road and Dollywood Lane (see "Getting Around").

3A.   A traffic regulator (with no cross street—yet), light #3A is at the point where the McGill Avenue connector will eventually lead into Pigeon Forge's educational campus, city park complex and the new community center scheduled to open in late 2000.

3.   Wears Valley Road (U.S. 321S/Tennessee Highway 73W) is no longer the northern terminus of the Forge, but it's where you turn left (east) to go to the largest selection of outlet malls—if that's where you're heading and you missed Teaster Lane at light #2. In the other direction, Wears Valley Road is being developed so fast it's hard to stay abreast, but the Pigeon Forge educational complex of three schools is about a half-mile down on the right. Several campgrounds are on Wear's Valley Road, and are described in our Campgrounds and RV Parks chapter.

4.   Approaching the center of the downtown area on the Parkway, traffic light #4 is a regulator that prevents unbelievable traffic snarls at the entrance to the Pigeon Forge Factory Outlet and Z Buda Outlet malls (See our Outlet Shopping chapter).

5.   Jake Thomas Road goes off to the left (north), leading to Teaster Lane.

6.   Pine Mountain Road goes south (right), leading to the Pigeon Forge city offices and U.S. Post Office.

7.   In what was the center of Pigeon Forge before the boom, the lighted intersection at Old Mill Avenue provides access to the Old Mill shopping area and Patriot Park. This is the original traffic signal in the city, and Old Mill Avenue leads to Middle Creek Road, which is handy to know about as a convenient bypass (It'll come up again in the section on "Getting Around").

8.   The "Dollywood" light is so named because it's where most traffic turns to go the area's biggest single attraction. Note: This is Dollywood Lane where it leaves the Parkway, but when it passes the Dollywood entrance about a mile out of town it becomes Upper Middle Creek Road, confusing even to lifelong locals, and it leads out of town and runs alongside the Gatlinburg Golf Club. Upper Middle Creek is a major "back road," and will be described in depth later on. The traffic light that appears just as you see the golf course is Middle Creek.

9.   There is currently no traffic light #9.

10.   You'll know when you're out of Pigeon Forge by the sudden disappearance of businesses and the equally sudden appearance of wilderness when you pass through the southernmost traffic light. Be aware that the right-hand lane ends at this light. Unless you're planning to go up Conner Heights Road at the intersection, be out of the right lane.

The next four miles pass through federal property, on what's referred to locally as the Spur. With mountains rising from the right shoulder and the lovely Little Pigeon River on the left, this short respite from the hodgepodge of commercialism behind and before you is a preview of the Great Smoky Mountains National Park. This is a flat, twisty road. When you leave Pigeon Forge and when you enter Gatlinburg four miles later, you're traveling almost due south. In between, you'll hit close to 180 degrees of direction changes.

Handy hint: This illustrates one of the local phenomena that makes visiting here such a hoot sometimes. When you get a general direction from a local, like, "Go east for three miles," do what you're told. In the three miles you travel you might think you're going every direction but east, but you'll get where you wanted to go.

As you approach Gatlinburg you'll notice on the right the Gatlinburg/Great Smoky Mountains National Park welcome center. This is another handy place to pick up literature and information, including a lot of park literature that's difficult to get through the mail. Continuing past the welcome center, a broad sweep in the road takes you past the Park bypass and into downtown Gatlinburg. It may also bring you to a screeching crawl as the traffic begins reacting to traffic lights you can't quite see yet. Hello, Gatlinburg!

Gatlinburg usually doesn't have as much traffic as Pigeon Forge, but it seems like more sometimes, because Gatlinburg doesn't have as much Parkway as Pigeon Forge, either. Two miles long and never more than four lanes wide, the Parkway in Gatlinburg provides exactly zero opportunities to pull over to the side and take stock. There's no "to the side"—the buildings come right to the sidewalk, which comes right to the curb. It's helpful to know where you're going at all times in Gatlinburg. If you plan to park, it's so essential that there's a section devoted to that subject below. For now, let's finish the Parkway portion of the Smokies corridor.

From the end of the Spur at the north (upper) end of town to the Great Smoky Mountains National Park entrance two miles later, Gatlinburg, like Pigeon Forge, is punctuated by 10 numbered traffic lights. They are, in order:

1. The Dudley Creek bypass to U.S. 321N.
2. A blinker 200 yards south of #1. If you have any reason to cross the river on the north end of the Parkway (there's a motel there, and some cabins on Laurel Street), this is your only chance.
3. (A Biggie)—U.S. 321 comes in from the left and the Parkway swings right. U.S. 321 is the only road out of Gatlinburg to the east, and leads immediately to a string of motels. Further east are a scattering of businesses, the U.S. Post Office, Gatlinburg's city hall complex, and the Great Smoky Arts & Crafts Community. Note: This piece of road has gone through several name changes in the last decade. At various times it has been Tenn. 73, East Main, U.S. 321 (its current federal designation), and it's current local handle, East Parkway. The locals (except for postal workers and firemen) have given up trying to keep current, and will refer to it as either "73" or "321." This guide will use the latter, along with East Parkway.
4. There is no traffic light #4—nobody knows why.
5. River Road goes off diagonally to the right. It travels roughly parallel to the Parkway for less than a mile, past several motels, restaurants, and attractions, and rejoins the Parkway outside of town, near the Great Smoky Mountains National Park entrance sign.
6. Just a block from #5, Cherokee Orchard Road goes off to the left, leading to another large group of motels and condos in the Baskins Creek area. Cherokee Orchard rises as it continues east and south to its intersection with Airport Road. If you meant to turn onto River Road and missed it, you can recover here by turning right.
7. A flashing light (yellow if you're on the Parkway) at Reagan Drive—handy if Reagan Drive has any importance to you (a few motels, a couple of churches, and the Gatlinburg branch of the Sevier County Court Clerk's office are on Reagan Drive). You can also get to River Road by turning right, but when you get to the River Road at the bottom of the hill, you'll be on Maples Lane.
8. Airport Road goes off and up to the left. The Gatlinburg Convention Center, a few attractions, several motels, and most of the downtown churches. From the intersection at Cherokee Orchard Road, Airport Road passes Mynatt Park and a residential area on the right,

INSIDERS' TIP

Tennessee has recently enacted a very tough drunk driving (DUI) law, and your status as a visitor will not let you off the hook. What it boils down to is this: If you are stopped for suspicion of DUI and fail a field sobriety test, you will then be asked to submit to a breath analysis. If that test indicates a blood alcohol level of 0.1 percent or higher, you are subject to arrest and incarceration for a minimum of 48 hours. You could also lose your driver's license for a year. *Don't test this law!* You can't win unless you're cold sober, and even then it's not a pleasant experience.

and enters the Great Smoky Mountains National Park. We'll deal with it again in the "Getting Around" chapter.

9.   Another blinker at the aerial tramway terminal; forgettable unless you're staying in a motel on the other side of the river.

10.   The last light, at Ski Mountain Road. A right turn will take you through the River Road intersection and up Ski Mountain. Mostly chalets and condos, Ski Mountain Road is the only way a visitor would want to go into the Chalet Village area.

Some hardy souls also think it's the only route to Ober Gatlinburg ski resort. Wrong. The only *sensible* way to get to Ober Gatlinburg is to park in town and ride the aerial tramway. Think about this: Ski Mountain Road goes straight up from town, and straight down from the ski lodge, except for that nifty little double hairpin in the middle, and when it's covered with snow and ice it still goes straight up and straight down. It's a narrow two-lane road with no shoulder for most of its length. Ride the tram to the ski lodge.

If you go through traffic light #10 heading out of town, you're in the woods as quickly as you were when you left Pigeon Forge. The big difference this time is that you're now in 50 *miles* of woods, interrupted only by the Pigeon Forge/Sevierville bypass a mile or so ahead, and the Sugarlands Visitor Center another mile up the road.

That's the Smokies corridor for everybody that used Exit 407 to get here. For those rugged individualists who came a little more overland, here's where you are:

If you came out of Knoxville on U.S. 441, or onto 441 from U.S. 411 in Seymour (a popular route for knowledgeable Georgians), continue east about 12 miles to the traffic light at Tenn. 66 (it's well posted) and hang a right. You're now in the Smokies corridor, and you'll be on the Parkway in a mile.

If you came through the Park from Townsend on Little River Road (Tenn. 73E), turn left at the Sugarlands Visitor Center. You're now on U.S. 441 going north, and if you don't take the bypass to Pigeon Forge you'll be at traffic light #10 in Gatlinburg in about as much time as it takes you to read this paragraph.

If you came into Gatlinburg from the east on U.S. 321S (a favorite route for people coming out of the Carolinas), you will enter downtown Gatlinburg at traffic light #3.

Finally, if you came into Sevierville from the east on U.S. 411S, turn left at the traffic light at U.S. 441 S (If you turn right you'll be in a supermarket parking lot). If you miss the intersection, you've got two more chances in the next two blocks. Take either one and stay on it. Both roads end at the Parkway.

If you got truly crazy and came out of Townsend on Wears Valley Road (U.S. 321 / Tenn. 73 E), turn right at the traffic light after you pass the giant Kroger store. You'll be on the Parkway in Pigeon Forge.

Now that everybody's in the corridor and settled, the rest is remarkably easy. Every direction in the rest of this book will use one of the landmarks previously mentioned (i.e, "From traffic light 7 in Pigeon Forge," or "From the Sugarlands Visitor Center") to get you started. Using this chapter as your guide, go from wherever you are to that starting place, and then enjoy your time in the Smokies. The important thing to note here is that the alphabet soup that makes up the road system in the Smokies corridor consists of only one north-south road (U.S. 441 in all its descriptions) and three major east-west roads (I-40, U.S. 411/441 [Dolly Parton Parkway] in Sevierville, and U.S. 321 [East Parkway] in Gatlinburg). You'll get used to the various descriptions sooner than you think, but remember these simple pointers to make moving around as simple as possible:

• Regardless of what city you're in, the terms "Parkway" and "Main Street" will *always* refer to U.S. 441. In Sevierville, a short portion of U.S. 441 west of the downtown area is actually named Main Street.

• U.S. 411 (note the difference) is Dolly Parton Parkway in Sevierville—it's also Main Street and Chapman Highway on the western end (toward Knoxville), and Newport Highway east of Sevierville.

• What you may hear called "73" in Gatlinburg is actually U.S. 321 N, and it goes east out of town at traffic light #3.

Shortcuts and Back Roads

Now that we've scared you to death will all this talk of traffic, we should let you know that there are ways to get around in the area without using the Parkway. They are known and used by the local population, and the folks who live here are not averse to sharing the knowledge with our visitors—we know where our bread is buttered. The problem is that most of our visitors don't ask about these byways until they've been burned by the traffic, and then they tend to get specific about where they want to avoid. Herewith, a list of handy little back routes on paved, generally level roads.

For openers, let's go back to your introduction to the area coming off Exit 407 from I-40. If you've spent the last 10 minutes or so enjoying the view of the courthouse dome from the Winfield Dunn Scenic Parkway (Tenn. 66) and you haven't seen a traffic light yet, take heart. A light is just around the bend you're creeping up on, but you're probably in a traffic situation that's not going to ease off until you get to Gatlinburg, some 20 miles down the road.

At our daytime average speed of 10 to 20 miles per hour, we're talking an hour or so to Pigeon Forge, and God knows what it'll take to get to Gatlinburg. Here comes a small slice of salvation that can get you to those two towns much quicker. What you want to do is turn left at the traffic signal, so get over as soon as you can.

The traffic light you're approaching is at Dolly Parton Parkway (U.S. 411/441), the main east/west thoroughfare in Sevierville. We're going to take a detour by turning left on Dolly Parton and putting all that traffic in the rear view mirror. Warning: This gambit is for people staying in Pigeon Forge or Gatlinburg. If you're staying in Sevierville, this shortcut isn't much help—you've got to get back into the traffic jam. Do it by turning right at the *second* traffic light you come to on Dolly Parton Parkway. That puts you back on the Parkway (U.S. 441). This intersection is where U.S. 411 and 441 part company; U.S. 411 continues east toward our first bypass road, and U.S. 441 drops southward toward Pigeon Forge and Gatlinburg.

Back to our escapees: If your goal is Pigeon Forge, your target is Middle Creek Road, about a mile from where you fled Tenn. 66. It's clearly labeled and there's a traffic light at the intersection. Also note that Middle Creek goes off only to the right—it's not a cross street (yet—long-range planning projects a new road that will run east off Tenn. 66 south of the French Broad river, and will drop south to meet Middle Creek.). Hang a right on Middle Creek Road.

For the first mile, you'll be in an area of local businesses and professional buildings. After you pass Fort Sanders/Sevier Medical Center, the county's only hospital, you'll pass through four or five miles of farmland. When you see the entrance to Dollywood's parking lot on your left, you're approaching Pigeon Forge. If you stay on Middle Creek you'll merge with Dollywood Lane near the center of Pigeon Forge and renew your acquaintance with the Parkway at traffic light #8. This side trip has cost you about three miles and probably saved you an hour.

If you're headed for Gatlinburg, stay on Dolly Parton Parkway and go through the light at Middle Creek. Less than a mile up the road you'll pass an industrial park on the right and Sevier County High School on the left. A mile or so later you'll reach a traffic signal where your only option is to turn right; take it, and you'll be on Pittman Center Road (Tennessee Highway 416).

Settle back and enjoy the scenery for a while. You've begun a journey of some eight to 12 miles, depending on precisely where you're going, and you're on a road through

INSIDERS' TIP

Sometimes the lure of the roads leading away from the main roads is just too attractive to resist, and you find yourself on a winding mountain or country road with no earthly idea of where you are. The solution is simple: Every back road in the county is paved and leads eventually to a highway. When you come to a highway, don't cross it. Turn on to the highway and stay on it until you get to something that looks familiar. It shouldn't take long.

Gatlinburg's Riverwalk is a popular spot for a summer stroll.

Photo: Dick McHugh

some real pretty farmland. The road itself will change its name two or three times; pay no attention.

Five miles in from your turning point, Pittman Center Road turns left. *Keep going straight,* and you're now on Bird's Creek Road. The road coming in from the right is Upper Middle Creek, which comes out of Pigeon Forge as Dollywood Lane. We'll get back to it shortly.

Continuing on Bird's Creek, you'll enjoy more rural scenery for the next 4½ miles until you come to a stop sign. You're now in the Great Smoky Arts & Crafts Community, which means you're closing in on Gatlinburg. You're also within a mile of the end of Bird's Creek Road.

As you approach the intersection at Glades Road (again, right turn only), notice that Bird's Creek seems to flow on to Glades. If you're headed for downtown Gatlinburg, go with the flow. Glades Road ends at U.S. 321, three miles (turn right) from traffic light #3 in downtown Gatlinburg. If your destination is a lodging place more than five miles east of Gatlinburg on U.S. 321, skip the turn at Glades Road, and bear just slightly left. Now you're on Buckhorn Road.

(These name changes occur a lot around here, and most of them came about when old roads were re-routed in years past to intersect other roads. When the roads came together nobody could see a good reason to change the name of one of them just because the intersection formed a straight line instead of a corner.)

Buckhorn Road continues south about two more miles to U.S. 321, a little more than five miles east of downtown Gatlinburg. A left turn here will take you toward Pittman Center and the condo communities of Cobbly Nob, Brandywine, and Bent Creek.

The two bypass routes described above are the longest alternate routes in the area, but will cut out long waits in Parkway traffic. Used in reverse, they're handy for getting back to I-40 when you leave the Smokies.

Let's go back to Upper Middle Creek Road for a minute. Remember, this is the one that leaves Pigeon Forge as Dollywood Lane at traffic light #8 and runs past the Gatlinburg Golf Club. Upper Middle Creek intersects Bird's Creek Road (nee Pittman Center Road) about midway between Pigeon Forge and the Great Smoky Arts & Crafts Community. If you're out that way and want to get to Pigeon Forge without going back through Gatlinburg, it's the best route. Upper Middle Creek goes left off Bird's Creek just past Caton's Chapel School.

That takes care of the really big shortcuts. Now let's tackle the little ones that make in-town travel a little more palatable, starting in Pigeon Forge. There really aren't any shortcuts in Sevierville to speak of because the city's laid out in a very compact fashion. To keep things in perspective, we're saying the Parkway runs north and south through town:

Skirting Pigeon Forge to the East

Teaster Lane is a bypass around the Parkway on the east side of Pigeon Forge that runs from traffic light #2 just north of Wear's Valley Road to Dollywood Lane/Upper Middle Creek. Coming south on the Parkway (from Sevierville), turn left at traffic light #2 and follow the road as far as you want to go. Note that this is a brand-new road, and doesn't appear in its present form on many maps. The traffic light near the southern end is Middle Creek Road; a left turn will take you to the back entrance to Dollywood and, eventually, back to Sevierville.

You can get to Teaster Lane from the Parkway at Jake Thomas Road (traffic light #5), about halfway between Middle Creek and Wears Valley Roads. Teaster Lane includes most of Pigeon Forge's outlet malls.

The Western Side of Pigeon Forge

These directions take you from north to south; if you're traveling north, use Teaster Lane. Florence Street runs off Wears Valley Road a block west of the Parkway (Mel's Diner is on the corner). Running parallel to the Parkway for about half its length, the street goes through a very nice middle-class neighborhood and a kaleidoscope of name changes. You can get back to the Parkway just about anywhere along the way.

When it passes the Pigeon Forge Civic Center and its name becomes Rena, take the next left. If you don't, you'll wind up out in the countryside and the only way to get back is to backtrack. Pigeon Forge is planning a western by-pass using Florence/Rena as a base, which will run from Wears Valley Road to Conner Heights Road at the southern end of the city. When complete (no real firm date exists), you'll be able to go around Pigeon Forge from Wears Valley Road to the Parkway Spur.

Let's go on to Gatlinburg. As mentioned earlier, the only safe "back way" from Pigeon Forge to Gatlinburg is the Dollywood Lane/Upper Middle Creek-Bird's Creek-Glades route. However, you can take the Parkway Spur south and bypass Gatlinburg on either side before getting into the downtown gridlock.

The park bypass runs off the Spur just past the Gatlinburg Welcome Center, and is highly recommended if the Great Smoky Mountains National Park is where you're going. Two road-side turnoffs provide spectacular views of Gatlinburg on the way over. You'll come off the bypass inside the park boundary, and the Sugarlands Visitor Center (a must-stop for first-time visitors) is about a mile ahead. The bypass is clearly marked on your return.

In Gatlinburg, the Dudley Creek bypass (turn left at traffic light #1 and follow the signs) will put you on U.S. 321 about a mile-and-a-half east of downtown. If you're heading toward Gatlinburg (west) on U.S. 321, look for the Ace Hardware and NAPA Auto Parts stores on the right. Turn right at the traffic light and you'll be headed back to the Spur.

Caution: This route is steep and narrow in some places. Large vehicles and towed loads should think twice.

We come finally to Gatlinburg's in-town bypasses, the Baskins Creek/Newton Lane Bypass and Cherokee Orchard Road. These are convenient anytime you're on the east end of town and want to get around the Parkway in the heart of the business district.

First, the Baskins Creek/Newton Lane Bypass: This one requires alertness at both ends. It's clearly marked, but if

INSIDERS' TIP

From the time you enter the Parkway in Sevierville, think of it as a giant funnel. It starts out as a six-lane road in Sevierville and continues that way through Pigeon Forge (although the outside lanes there are virtually at a standstill during the summer), and narrows down to four lanes on the Spur and through Gatlinburg. At the Sugarlands Visitor Center, the four lanes become two regardless of which way you're going.

you miss it on one end (U.S. 321) there's no turning back, and a whiff on the Cherokee Orchard end could drop you into the busiest intersection in town.

Coming west toward downtown on U.S. 321, the street sign says "Baskins Creek Bypass." It's on the left, about halfway around a sweeping curve, and there's a large earthen breastwork at the corner. If you miss it, the only way to get back is make an illegal U-turn on a hill in heavy traffic. Just go on down to the Parkway at traffic light #3, turn left to traffic light #5, and turn left again. Now you're on Cherokee Orchard Road, two blocks from where you would have come out if you hadn't missed the turn.

Cherokee Orchard climbs rapidly as it goes away from downtown, and curves around to intersect Airport Road at the equivalent of about eight city blocks from the Parkway. A right turn on Airport Road will take you back towards downtown; a left leads out of town.

If you're hurtling down Cherokee Orchard toward town, you'll see two side streets very close together right at the bottom of the hill. The *second* one is marked as the "Newton Lane By-Pass." Take it to the right and you'll go around town to U.S. 321. You might note the Anna Porter Public Library at the corner of Cherokee Orchard and Newton Lane, and the municipal parking lot beside it. Both can be valuable resources if used properly.

Finally, River Road in Gatlinburg is a viable bypass to get to Ski Mountain Road and the Great Smoky Mountains National Park. Bear right at traffic light #6. Because River Road is populated primarily by motels and restaurants, pedestrian congestion is lighter.

The alternate routes described in this chapter can be invaluable in terms of saving time and tempers. Remember that there are even more alternate roads available, but they're not really intended for heavy traffic or unfamiliar drivers. For the most part, the real "back roads" are not really safe to drive on unless you know what to expect in the way of sudden turns, rapid elevation changes, livestock and wild animals in the road, and other obstacles too numerous to mention. Bring this guide with you and use it frequently; it should help you realize the joy you came here seeking.

Parking in Gatlinburg

If you must drive into town, there is some parking available. Several private lots on Airport Road, adjacent to and across the street from the convention center, operate on a sliding rate scale depending on what's going on in town at the time. They usually work on an hourly basis, and sometimes offer an all-day or maximum rate. There are a few private lots scattered along the Parkway behind the storefronts, but they fill up early. During the summer when school is not in session, the Pi Beta Phi elementary school PTA operates the school's parking lot as a fund-raiser. The school is on Cherokee Orchard Road, one block from the Parkway at traffic light #6.

The City of Gatlinburg operates five parking lots and two multi-story decks in and around town. Two of the lots offer free parking:

1.   The Welcome Center park & ride lot on the Parkway spur coming from Pigeon Forge (96 spaces). Parking is free, and the Green route trolley will take you into the center of town for a quarter a head. The lot is unattended.

2.   The north Parkway lot, next to Hillbilly Golf before traffic light #3 (34 spaces). Parking is metered (honor system), and the lot has public restrooms. Convenient to businesses and attractions north of the main business district, it's a hike into town and back if you've got kids to consider. A monthly permit is available at City Hall for $35. The lot is unattended.

3.   Downtown Parking Garage (398 spaces). Gatlinburg's newest parking structure is at the intersection of the Parkway and East Parkway (U.S. 321N), south of traffic light #3. Hourly rates are $1.50 (minimum) for the first hour and 75 cents per additional hour, with a maximum charge of $6 per day. A long-term parking permit is available for $35 a month. The deck is operated by an attendant.

4.   Aquarium Parking Garage (400 spaces): Directly behind the Ripley's Aquarium, this is structure has the same short- and long-term rate schedules as the Downtown Garage. It is also attended.

5.   Anna Porter Library (72 spaces). Turn left at Cherokee Orchard Road (traffic light #6), go two blocks to Newton Lane and turn left again. Entrance is just past the library. Coming in from U.S. 321, turn left at the Baskins Creek By-pass. Lot entrance is on the right just after the

road levels out. It's a short walk to downtown, and the rate is hourly (two-hour minimum). The lot is operated by an attendant.

6.   Reagan Drive (204 spaces). Reagan Drive intersects the Parkway at traffic light #7— look for Ripley's Believe it or Not museum. The lot is two blocks up on the left, just past the Presbyterian Church. It's a moderate downhill walk into town and a strenuous uphill walk back. Payment is honor system with meters; no attendant is present.

7.   City Hall park and ride (84 spaces). Located on U.S. 321, two miles east of downtown, between City Hall and Post Office. Parking is free, ride the Orange route trolley into town. The lot is unattended.

Car Rentals

In addition to the Knoxville-based companies mentioned in the "Getting Here" section of this chapter, there are several car rental agencies in Sevier County. Local companies are good for those traveling in larger recreational vehicles who may want a more manageable form of getting around town. They may also be an attractive option for those who experience car trouble and have to put their personal vehicle in the shop for a day or so.

In Sevierville, you can contact Enterprise Rent-A-Car at (865) 908-3044 or McNelly-Whaley Motor Company at (865) 453-2833. McNelly-Whaley is the local Ford dealership that also maintains a satellite office at Gatlinburg-Pigeon Forge Airport in Sevierville. In Sevierville or Pigeon Forge, you can call Aaron Automotive Rentals at (865) 429-2277. Also in Pigeon Forge, you'll find Affordable Car Rental at (865) 428-7686. In Gatlinburg, call Southland Car & Jeep Rentals at (865) 436-9811.

These rental agencies maintain fleets with as few as seven cars or as many as 50. Fleet sizes will vary from season to season, but you might find it harder to find cars during the peak tourist months. Except for the one Ford dealership, most of the companies keep a variety of makes and models on site, including vans. Most will also deliver their cars to you.

We found that prices range from as low as $28 per day for subcompact models to $80 per day for luxury and sport models. Although credit cards are the standard form of payment, most of the companies will accept cash. In these cases, a more substantial up-front deposit is required. If you live outside Tennessee and wish to pay with cash, you may want to call ahead to verify if a particular company will accept your cash deposit.

Taxis

You will also find a number of cab operators located throughout the county. Don't expect to see the traditional yellow checkered cab pull up to your door, however. Some of these companies, especially the newer ones, utilize late model minivans that accommodate more passengers. Most of the businesses we've included service the entire Sevier County area (and, in some cases, transportation to the airport and bus station in Knoxville). In Sevierville, contact Donald Newman Taxi at (865) 453-6551 or Newman's Taxi (separate business) at (865) 453-3654. In Pigeon Forge, you'll find All Right Taxi at (865) 429-3531. In Gatlinburg, call All Park Taxi and Tour at (865) 908-0911, Burt's Taxi Cab Service at (865) 908-6500, or C & O Taxi Service at (865) 436-5893.

Jeep, Motorcycle and Scooter Rentals

Jeeps, motorcycles and scooters provide alternative means of transportation that are more than just another way of getting from Point A to Point B. On a beautiful day in the mountains, there's nothing like traveling with the wind in your hair and the sun in your face—just for the fun of it. It's also a great way to see the sights.

There are a few area businesses that rent these types of vehicles on an hourly or daily basis: J J Rentals, (865) 436-0308; Lee's Scooter and Jeep Rentals, (865) 436-3060; and

INSIDERS' TIP

Generally speaking, travel in the park and in the immediate Gatlinburg area follows a pattern: East and west are basically flat; north and south usually involve a lot of up and down.

Southland Car & Jeep Rentals, (865) 436-9811. As is the case with regular automobile rentals, these rental fleets are frequently in use during the peak season months, so availabilities are limited. Rental terms will vary from company to company, but in general you can expect to pay an up-front deposit and must be able to show a driver's license and proof of insurance. Some companies will also have minimum age requirements for certain types of vehicles.

Trolleys

Short of having the use of a car while visiting the Smokies, your next best bet is to utilize the trolley systems of Pigeon Forge and Gatlinburg. The trolleys are a dependable, inexpensive way to get around that will take you most anywhere you might want to go. Their combined service routes run from the north border of Pigeon Forge all the way into the national park as well as the Great Smoky Arts and Crafts Community. And if you've been on your feet all day, nothing beats just plunking down your quarter (or more, in some cases), sitting back and taking in the sights while someone else does the driving.

While Sevierville currently doesn't have a trolley system, city officials have been studying the possibility of implementing one in the near future with routes running throughout the city and possibly to Dollywood.

Pigeon Forge Fun Time Trolley
(865) 453-6444

The main office and the fleet for this trolley service are on Old Mill Avenue, at the Patriot Park site, behind The Old Mill. There are three primary trolley routes that cover more than 100 stopping points throughout the city of Pigeon Forge.

The largest route runs the length of Pigeon Forge's Parkway, making turn-around loops at the north and south ends. A second route takes passengers from the trolley office to Dollywood. The third route emanates from the Belz Mall area, running west along Wears Valley Road. From there, the trolley travels south, behind Pigeon Forge Factory Outlet Mall on Florence Drive and Willow View Drive, then heads east on Pine Mountain Road to the Parkway. The route then heads south on the Parkway, east on Old Mill Avenue past the trolley office and finally north on Teaster Lane back to Belz Mall.

There are two transfer points, one at Belz Mall and the other at the trolley office. At the Belz Mall location you can switch from the Wears Valley Road/Teaster Lane trolley to the Parkway trolley. At the main office you connect to both of these routes as well as the Dollywood route.

The Pigeon Forge Fun Time Trolley runs from 8:30 AM to midnight, mid-March through October. In November and December trolleys run from 10:30 AM to 10 PM, except for Thanksgiving Day, Christmas Eve and Christmas Day.

INSIDERS' TIP

The prices for Pigeon Forge trolley tokens are discounted if purchased in volume. Individually, they are 25 cents each; ten tokens cost $2, and 20 tokens cost $3.50.

Trolley fare is 25 cents each time you board. Both coins and tokens are accepted. You can purchase individual tokens for 25 cents each at the trolley office or the Pigeon Forge Department of Tourism. Although the trolleys themselves are not wheelchair-accessible, a special van can be made available with 24 hours advance notice.

Although the trolley system is basically shut down from early January through the middle of March, you can still enjoy the city's lights on its Winterfest Trolley Tours, which run from mid-November through February (see our Annual Events chapter). Tours depart from the trolley office on Monday, Wednesday and Friday evenings at 6:30 PM. Heated buses and informed hosts will guide you through the history of all the light displays. The cost of each trolley ride is $3 per person.

Gatlinburg Trolley
(865) 436-3897

This system services more than 100 locations in Gatlinburg. The trolleys themselves are green and orange, but this is not to be confused with the different color-coded routes that traverse the city. Each trolley has a sign posted on its front and sides indicating which route it follows.

Before we present the different routes, a bit of semantics. Many of the routes described below originate from what we've vaguely described as "downtown" Gatlinburg. Your specific point of origin will depend upon what time of year you visit. Currently at traffic light #6, the downtown departure site will move, upon completion of the Ripley's Aquarium, to the new trolley office behind the aquarium and in front of the new city parking garage.

Orange Route—This trolley originates from the Gatlinburg Convention center, travels up Airport road and through the Baskins Creek neighborhood before circling back to downtown near traffic light #6. It then runs north along the Parkway and out U.S. 321 (East Parkway), all the way to the Gatlinburg Community Center. This route operates from 8 AM to midnight daily, late March through October. The fare is 25 cents.

Green Route—The trolley starts at the Gatlinburg Welcome Center on "The Spur" (U.S. 441) at the north end of the city. It runs south along the Parkway, then onto River Road in downtown Gatlinburg, all the way to the Ski Mountain Road area near the national park boundary. Like the Orange Route, this route operates from 8 AM to midnight daily, late March through October. The fare is 25 cents.

Winter Route—This route is a sort of modification of the Orange and Green routes, and only operates from November through late March. The trolley originates downtown and covers most sections of town, including U.S. 321 (as far as City Hall), The Spur (out to the welcome center), sections of the Parkway downtown, most of River Road as well as Airport Road, Cherokee Orchard Road and Baskins Creek Road. Only one trolley is in operation Sunday through Thursday from 10 AM to 6 PM. Two trolleys run on Friday and Saturday from 10 AM to 10 PM. The fare for the Winter Route is 25 cents.

Yellow Route—These mini trolleys run along U.S. 321, from downtown Gatlinburg out to the Great Smoky Arts and Crafts Community, making a loop around Glades Road and Buckhorn Road through the community itself. The normal operating schedule is from 8

AM to midnight, late March through October. In November and December, these trolleys run daily from 10 AM to 6 PM; January through March, they run Saturday and Sunday only from 10 AM to 6 PM. The cost is $1.

Tan Route—Also known as the National Park Route, this circuit runs from downtown to Sugarlands Visitors Center in Great Smoky Mountains National Park. From there, it continues into the park itself, to the Laurel Falls parking area and Elkmont campground, eventually returning to downtown. The round-trip travel time is 11/2 hours. This route runs June through October only, and the fare is $2.

Red Route—The Dollywood Route, as it is also known, departs from downtown Gatlinburg and takes passengers to the Gatlinburg Golf Course (in Pigeon Forge) and, of course, Dollywood. In season, daily trolleys depart approximately every 50 minutes from both downtown and the theme park itself. In November and December, these trolleys run only on weekends and holidays. The fare is 75 cents each way.

Smoky Mountain Lights Trolley Tours

Not to be confused with the Winter Route trolleys, these special sightseeing trolleys offer spectacular views of Gatlinburg's Winterfest lighting displays. Tours depart from downtown and cost $4 per person. In November and December, they run Sunday through Saturday at 6:30 PM and 8 PM. In January, they run Saturday only at 6:30 PM and 8 PM. However, since tours don't run on Thanksgiving, Christmas and a few other selected days, the city advises calling (865) 430-4148 to verify specific times and dates. See our Festivals and Annual Events chapter for more information about these trolley tours.

As in Pigeon Forge, the Gatlinburg trolleys are not wheelchair-accesible, but Gatlinburg's mass transit department has a specially equipped van available that will provide transportation for the disabled. They can be reached at (865) 436-3897.

INSIDERS' TIP

The prices for Pigeon Forge trolley tokens are discounted if purchased in volume. Individually, they are 25 cents each; ten tokens cost $2, and 20 tokens cost $3.50.

History

And Then There Were Mountains...

LOOK FOR:
* Early Inhabitants
* Settlement and
  Early Government
* Birth of a County

It all started with one drawn-out event, a geological cataclysm that created our very landscape. The Great Smoky Mountains were formed around 200 million years ago during a collision of continental land masses, which geologists refer to as the Appalachian orogeny. As layer upon layer of rock strata and ocean sediment were slowly folded and forced skyward, the face of the earth became permanently changed, and the stage was set for a chain of events that continues to unfold today. After all, history is always being made.

Along with its towering fortresses of stone, nature was busy at work in other areas long ago, carving valleys, leveling pastures and causing rivers and streams to spring forth with water. As was the case with the native inhabitants and early settlers of other uncharted lands, geography played a crucial role in primeval mountain life. Mountain settlements were valued as much for their protection as they were their beauty. And locating near a river was imperative. Running waters were the source of life for drinking, washing, fishing and in later centuries, grinding corn and generating electricity.

It's a given that the many places and things that make up our communities are named after the people who influenced their time. But the legacies of mountain and river are readily apparent in today's Smoky Mountain communities. An old settlement and an existing highway share the name Boyd's Creek. Sevierville was originally known as Forks of Little Pigeon, and today's city of Pigeon Forge takes its name from that same water source. Upper and Lower Middle Creek Roads are important thoroughfares through the county, and the names of countless businesses and streets contain the "M" word, the word that never finds its way far from the local vocabulary—"mountain."

The First Inhabitants

Despite their strong association with Cherokee Indians, the Smoky Mountains were first home to various prehistoric Indians that preceded the Cherokee by as many as 20,000 years, according to some scientists. The earliest documented Native American existence in the area points to the Archaic Period Indians who lived here as far back as 10,000 years ago and as recently as 900 BC. They lived in small nomadic groups of 25 to 30 people and survived primarily off the hunting of animals.

The Eastern Woodland Indians made their homes in the mountains between 900 BC and AD 900. Artifacts like arrowheads, pieces of pottery and crude tools have been recovered from different sites around the county and suggest that the Woodland Period Indians enjoyed a more agrarian, less nomadic lifestyle. This time also marked the advent of the burial mound, the means through which many modern discoveries of Indian relics have been made.

Following the Woodland People were the Indians of the Mississippian Period (AD 900 to 1600). This period saw increases in both tribal populations and the complexity of political organization, and is generally regarded as the peak of prehistoric Indian culture. Existence of their lifestyle has been revealed through several notable local digs: on McCroskey Island in the French Broad River, a site in Pigeon Forge and at the McMahon Indian Mound located along the east bank of West Fork of the Little Pigeon River in the heart of Sevierville. Today, a hotel and a historical marker stand on the McMahon site (see our Hotels and Motels chapter for more).

The Cherokee were descendants of these early Indian civilizations. They primarily made their homes in present day North Carolina and used East Tennessee lands as hunting grounds. As white visitors and settlers made their way into Cherokee territory, years of alternating peace and conflict were the backdrop for Indian existence. The tribe maintained a strong presence in the Smokies until they were marched en masse to the Oklahoma territory in the 1840s on the infamous Trail of Tears. Today, however, a fairly strong Cherokee population still makes its home in western North Carolina (see our Cherokee, North Carolina chapter).

Early White Visitors

One of the Cherokees' earliest recorded experiences with the white man was friendly enough, according to historical accounts. Hernando de Soto journeyed into the area in 1540, likely during a gold expedition, and received a warm greeting from the natives. However, as the years passed, more and more white men, usually traders, infiltrated the region and didn't always receive such warm receptions. In fact, many were killed by the Cherokee, including two Virginia traders named Boyd and Daggett. In 1775, these two men were slaughtered, and their bodies were thrown into a creek. Incidentally, this was the origin of the name Boyd's Creek, a site that would later play an important role in the development of Sevier County.

In 1776, large numbers of white men were introduced to the area as colonial armies clashed with the British and their allies, the Cherokee. That year, Colonel William Christian from Virginia led 1,800 infantry in a punitive expedition against a number of Cherokee Overhill towns located along the Indian War Path, the area's only travel route of the time, which extended from Pennsylvania to Georgia. Many of the soldiers who passed through this area remembered its beauty and resources and returned here to settle in the years following the Revolutionary War.

Two particular battles from that war relate to local history. Colonel John Sevier led a group of men from Washington County, North Carolina (as Tennessee was known at the time) against the British at the Battle of King's Mountain on October 7, 1780. Although the British were defeated in that clash, what was of more local significance was the subsequent Battle of Boyd's Creek two months later. As Sevier and his men returned from King's Mountain, they discovered that their settlements had been attacked by Cherokee Indians during their absence. At Boyd's Creek on December 16, Sevier led 100 men to victory against the Cherokee in what was to be the first of 35 Indian battles in which the colonel would engage over the years.

INSIDERS' TIP

One of the early city ordinances enacted by Sevierville's first city council in 1901 is of peculiar interest. The act was intended to "prevent the teasing, worrying or annoying of persons of unsound mind, imbeciles, idiots, lunatics and fools within the corporate limits of the Town of Sevierville." No one can say that Seviervillians aren't a compassionate bunch!

Settlement and Early Government

At war's end, a number of those who fought for the Continental Armies received land grants in recognition of their service. Many made homes along Dumplin' Creek, just north of the French Broad River, and later along Boyd's Creek and the Little Pigeon River. One of the earliest known of these settlers was Isaac Thomas, a former Indian trader who had been a guide for William Christian in 1776 and was a scout and a guide for John Sevier at Boyd's Creek. He was given 1,000 acres west of West Fork of the Little Pigeon River around 1781 or 1782, making him one of Sevierville's first permanent white residents. He even gave Sevierville its first name, Forks of Little Pigeon.

Over the next couple of years, other notable local fathers made their way toward the Smokies.

In 1782, Major Hugh Henry built a homestead at Dumplin' Creek near the present day community of Kodak. Henry's Station, or Henry's Crossroads as it was known, was typical of the small blockhouses used by settlers in those days; these "forts" were not only used as dwellings but as protection against Indian attack.

In 1783, Captain Samuel Newell settled near what is now the unincorporated town of Seymour in west Sevier County. Newell was a veteran of battles with both the British and the Cherokee; he was to be prominent in the political structure of the area, from its formative years all the way through Tennessee statehood. His home, Newell's Station, would later be the first "county seat" of an infant Sevier County.

Also in 1783, James McMahon, another prominent figure of early Sevierville, settled on 400 acres between the east and west forks of Little Pigeon River, the present day site of Sevierville's downtown district. It was on this land that the McMahon Indian Mound was first excavated in 1881.

During the early 1780s, pioneers were not only faced with the hardships presented by a rugged wilderness existence but by the political goings on of the day. Although North Carolina had passed an act in 1783 reserving much of what we now know as East Tennessee for the Cherokee, it was also issuing land grants and selling land to white settlers in that same territory. Needless to say, this only exacerbated tensions between the whites and the Indians, leading to frequent conflict.

By 1784, the North Carolina treasury was severely drained by the war. It no longer had the resources or the inclination to support and protect its outposts to the west. The settlers of Washington County and the recently formed Greene County had become frustrated with North Carolina's neglect and inability to protect their settlements from Indian attack. In November of that year, the settlers met in Greeneville and organized their own government for a territory they named the State of Franklin, a moniker that they hoped would ingratiate them with the national government in their efforts to achieve statehood. Despite a noble attempt, however, Franklin fell short of its goal, coming within six votes of becoming the 14th state.

Although it failed in those efforts, Franklin did manage to come to more peaceful terms with the Cherokee. In 1785, a delegation from Franklin, led by its governor, John Sevier, met with Cherokee leaders and warriors at Henry's Station near Dumplin' Creek. With the signing of the Treaty of Dumplin' Creek, much of today's East Tennessee was officially opened up for homesteading. Although the Cherokee were well compensated in exchange, not everyone in that nation was in agreement with the peace accord, and numerous massacres were still led against the white settlers.

The Birth, Rebirth and Rebirth of a County

Sevier County was first formed on March 31, 1785, when the Franklin legislature divided existing Greene County into three smaller counties, one of which was named for Franklin governor John Sevier. The first county court was held at Newell's Station. In 1788, however, the state of Franklin collapsed due to dissension among its citizens as well as North Carolina's failure to recognize it as a sovereign entity. The following year, a brief attempt at reorganization was made with the formation of the state of Lesser Franklin, but when John Sevier and other leaders swore allegiance to North Carolina, Franklin ceased to exist once and for all.

Sevier County went through a second incarnation when the former State of Franklin was ceded to the federal government and became part of the Territory of the United States South of the River Ohio. William Blount was appointed its governor, and by 1794, Sevier County was reformed, with its first court being held at the home of Isaac Thomas on November 8. Samuel Newell remained active in this new government, becoming one of the Sevier County court officials, as did Samuel Wear and Mordecai Lewis, both of whom will be discussed in our history of Pigeon Forge.

Finally, in 1796, Sevier County as we know it today came into existence when Tennessee achieved statehood. The new state name was derived from Tenasi, the name for Cherokee villages along the Little Tennessee River. Its first court was held on July 4th in the county's first courthouse, which was located in the heart of Sevierville. Several county notables had represented their home district at Tennessee's constitutional convention, including Samuel Wear, Samuel Newell and Sevierville resident Spencer Clack. Clack had moved to Sevierville around 1788 and settled on 400 acres on the north side of East Prong of Little Pigeon River. He was an active force in local government, education and religion.

Sevierville

Although the legislative act that had reestablished Sevier County in 1794 also called for a commission to locate a county seat, it wasn't until 1795 that the commission finally chose a site at Forks of Little Pigeon; Isaac Thomas suggested the name Sevierville in honor of John Sevier. The commission acquired a 25-acre tract of land from James McMahon, whose centrally located homestead made the property a good prospect. There, a primitive court house along with a prison and stocks were constructed. Also, the rectangular piece of land was parceled off into 50 half-acre lots that were sold to the highest bidders for home construction. The establishment of Sevierville made it the seventh oldest town in Tennessee, and following the planting of those early roots, the fledgling community blossomed into the center of the county's economic and governmental activity.

Sevier County's first three courthouses, all of which were believed to have been destroyed by fire, were located in a section of downtown where Sevierville's two main thoroughfares, Cross Street (now Court Avenue) and Main Street intersected. When a fourth brick courthouse was erected on the site in 1856, this one-acre tract came to be known as Public Square; in addition to having a courthouse and a jail, the site also evolved into the commercial and social hub of Sevier County.

Such was the situation until 1896, when the current courthouse was built on a new site one block away. Shortly after World War I, a major fire devastated several key Public Square businesses, and in 1948, U.S. Highways 441 and 411 (running concurrently) were widened. These events helped usher in a period of general decline during which existing Public Square businesses were either replaced by new ones or eliminated altogether. Today, this section of downtown is unremarkable from a commercial standpoint. Nevertheless, the area is liberally festooned with historical markers and other placards, which remind today's citizens of Public Square's once-strong pulse.

Sevierville was typical of most 19th-century Sevier County communities in that education was a priority among its residents. By 1923, as many as 99 different schools were reported to be in operation throughout the county, most of them being small, one-teacher schools. In 1806, Nancy Academy was founded in Sevierville, one of the city's first wobbly steps in the pursuit of public education. Offering a curriculum based on "the three Rs," Nancy Academy thrived for almost a century until internal conflict, a fire and a theft contributed to the school's demise in 1892.

In 1890, Nancy Academy was succeeded by another secondary school, Murphy College. Although the school was administered under the auspices of the Methodist Episcopal Church, its curriculum was "free from sectarian teachings," according to its catalog. The school folded in 1935 due to the hardships of the Great Depression as well as the county's expanding public school system. The original Murphy College building was renovated and today houses the administrative offices of the county's school system. The larger, multi-building facility that was later used by the college is now home to the Church of God Home for Children, a local orphanage.

Sevierville experienced another period of heavy population growth in the early 1800s. Following the War of 1812, veterans were given land grants in the area, just as they had been following the Revolutionary War. Many of Sevierville's early fathers who had fought for our nation's independence also saw action in the War of 1812, including Spencer Clack and Isaac Thomas. By the way, it was the massive enlistment of area residents in that war that helped earn Tennessee the nickname "The Volunteer State."

Although the Civil War touched the town and the county as a whole, neither were as directly affected as some other regions of the South. One reason was that few slaves were found in the area—because of the hilly terrain, farms tended to be smaller and didn't generate the income necessary for the land owners to purchase large numbers of slaves. There were a few plantations in the county, nonetheless, including Wheatlands, near Boyd's Creek, and Rose Glen, located on today's Pittman Center Road.

HISTORY

Officially, Tennessee was a Confederate state, but most of East Tennessee sympathized with the Union. As such, many who wanted to fight for the Union Army had to make their way across the state line to neighboring Kentucky to enlist. Some even dressed up as women to be able to cross the tightly regulated borders. The only major Civil War battle to take place in the county was the Battle of Fairgarden, about seven miles east of Sevierville. In 1864, a division of Union soldiers attacked a stronghold of Confederate troops and forced them back several miles. Reportedly 65 Confederate soldiers were killed and over 100 were taken captive. Outside of this engagement, the county only saw a few minor skirmishes, and it was used by both armies as a source of food and supplies.

INSIDERS' TIP

When visiting downtown Sevierville, take an hour or so to visit the Sevier County Heritage Museum on Bruce Street. The self-guided tour is interesting, informative and free of charge. See the Attractions chapter for a more detailed description of what the Heritage Museum has to offer.

The turn of the century was an eventful period in Sevierville. One of the darker, but still more colorful chapters of local history (literally and figuratively speaking) was the White Cap era of the 1890s. Not to be confused with the racially motivated Ku Klux Klan, the White Caps were a group that practiced what could best be described as vigilante justice, often stepping in to weed out "lewd" and "immoral" people from the county. Those targeted were first given written notice to leave the county; those who failed to do so were severely whipped by White Caps. At their peak of influence, around 1894, whippings of men and women were almost nightly occurrences.

After several years, however, the White Caps were gradually infiltrated by a more serious criminal element who knew that their crimes would go unpunished as long as they operated within the White Cap ranks. As the vigilantes lost favor with the public, another group, the Blue Bills, were formed to confront them and try to head off their attacks. The Blue Bills were comprised largely of local professionals and businessmen who clashed frequently with the White Caps, often with serious consequences.

Tensions finally came to a head with the murders of Sevierville residents William and Laura Whaley by two White Cap members. The two culprits were convicted and hanged in Sevierville's Public Square in the late 1890s, making them the last to be publicly executed in the city. In the years that followed, legislation and a tough stance by local law enforcement soon turned Sevier County into one of the most peaceful, law-abiding counties in the state. Fortunately, that trend has continued to this day.

The turn of the century also brought a couple of politically relevant changes to Sevierville. The county's fifth courthouse, which is still in operation, was completed in 1896 (see our Attractions chapter), and on April 11, 1901, Sevierville finally became an incorporated town. Several previous attempts to do so had been shot down because the town was divided over the issue of alcohol sales (some things never change!). With the incorporation of 1901, Sevierville became a dry town, and until just a few years ago, alcohol still was not sold by the drink (see Area Overview).

Sevierville continued to thrive in the first half of the 20th century. Its population was still fairly small, but for its size, it was a healthy, self-sufficient community. Over the next 50 years, however, a number of significant events slowly but surely connected it to the rest of the globe. Two world wars were responsible for hundreds of local men either enlisting or being drafted to serve their country. As was the case in many other parts of the nation, young men's lives were changed permanently when they left the safety of their farms to engage in battle halfway around the world. Dozens never returned to their hometown in the Smokies.

In 1909, Sevierville's commercial links with outside markets were expanded with the completion of the Knoxville Sevierville and Eastern Railroad, the first incarnation of what would be generally known as The Smoky Mountain Railroad. Unfortunately, the railroad languished under several owners until its ultimate demise in 1961; the increased popularity of the automobile limited its success. The railroad did enjoy a brief period of profitability in the 1940s during the construction of Douglas Dam, but today, no vestiges of its existence remain in the city (except for a street named Railroad Street).

Douglas Dam itself brought massive amounts of inexpensive public electricity to the Smokies

HISTORY

for the first time. Built on the French Broad River between 1942 and 1943 by the Tennessee Valley Authority (TVA), the dam flooded a lot of good, level farm land, but it helped light up an area that, until then, had either gone without electricity or had relied on small, private companies for power. The TVA was to lay its hands on Sevierville again in the 1960s when it literally rerouted the course of the Little Pigeon River near downtown to help prevent more of the major, destructive flooding that had plagued the city for decades.

It wasn't until the post-World War II era, however, that the rest of the world would finally start to make its impact on Sevierville. After the war, the Interstate highway system and America's intensified love affair with the car brought more and more visitors to the Smoky Mountains. For decades, most of these travelers simply saw Sevierville as a place through which to pass on their way to Gatlinburg and the mountains. When Knoxville hosted the 1982 World's Fair, all of the county's communities prospered from the spillover, including Sevierville. Throughout the 1990s, the city has continued to develop into a tourist destination in its own right (see Area Overview).

Pigeon Forge

By the late 1700s, Pigeon Forge had followed a similar course to that of Sevierville, serving as a place of settlement for soldiers after the war for America's independence. At least this was so until Sevierville became the county seat; from that point on, the two communities followed different paths. Sevierville expanded in every sense while Pigeon Forge remained a small, sleepy mountain village until tourism began to really take root and flourish in the 1970s and 1980s.

In 1781, Samuel Wear became the first permanent white settler in what is now Pigeon Forge. Wear was a Revolutionary War colonel who had been a longtime friend of John Sevier and had served as a captain under Sevier at the Battle of King's Mountain. He was given a land grant of 500 acres and built his homestead near the mouth of Walden's Creek, a tributary of the Little Pigeon River. Wear was a key figure in the formation of the state of Franklin and served as Sevier County court clerk for 27 years, starting with the first county court at Newell's Station in 1785.

During this same period, other settlers who were to play major roles in the development of Pigeon Forge put down roots, including Floyd Nichols, Barefoot Runyan and Mordecai Lewis. It is believed that Lewis probably operated a mill back in those days; it is known that his land occupied the present day site of The Old Mill (see our Attractions chapter) on the banks of the Little Pigeon River. His land also adjoined that of Isaac Runyan, a son of Barefoot and his wife, Margaret Rambo.

Most of these early Pigeon Forge settlements were located along the river, where two primary types of businesses developed: mills and iron works, or forges. Isaac Love, another significant figure of early Pigeon Forge, married a daughter of Mordecai Lewis and inherited the Lewis family mill. By 1820, Love was operating an iron works on the same site, and ten years later, Isaac's son, William, built the present day Old Mill there. Still in operation, The Old Mill may be the oldest existing mill in Tennessee. On May 29, 1841, a post office was established under the name Pigeon Forge, and William Love was appointed postmaster. In those days, this post office was located on the same site as the Love's mill and forge, making it the center of the town's activity.

The name Pigeon Forge was derived from the existing iron works as well as the Little Pigeon River. The river itself had gotten its name from the huge flocks of migratory passenger pigeons which had frequently stopped there throughout the 1700s and early 1800s to feed on the abundance of beech trees. Unlike the town that bears its name today, the passenger pigeon dwindled into extinction. The last one died in captivity at the Cincinnati Zoo in 1914.

In the 1840s, the iron works gradually failed due to the lack of transportation in and out of the area. The Sevier County Turnpike Company had built a "road" which extended into Sevierville, but this was nothing more than a glorified trail. Another factor that led to decline of the forges was the low iron content of the existing ore veins. And when a blast furnace at the Love's iron works exploded, the

INSIDERS' TIP

Back when Gatlinburg was still a one-street town (and it was dirt), barnstorming pilots used to drop in for informal gatherings. They landed on the only level strip of land, which was a lane leading into town from Cherokee Orchard. Locally known as the "airport", this lane grew into a major artery as the town grew up, and its long-time popularity with the pilots made it natural to call the new street Airport Road.

family moved to Missouri, selling their business to John Sevier Trotter, a local miller who later revived the iron works.

When the Civil War broke out, Pigeon Forge was used as a northern stronghold; thirty townsmen joined the Union forces. Although there were no battles or skirmishes in the town, hard times befell those who stayed behind to mind the home front. Schools were abandoned, roads deteriorated and the flow of supplies from the outside dried up.

At the turn of the century, progress slowly crept into this rural Sevier County community. It wasn't until 1890 that the town's second store opened for business, and in 1898, Pigeon Forge's first telephone was finally connected. By 1907, the town's population was still only 154, but the following 30 years brought steady growth—stores, churches and schools would spring up in greater numbers.

In August, 1916, the Pigeon Forge Railroad Company extended the Knoxville, Sevierville and Eastern Railroad line, bridging the Little Pigeon River in Sevierville and then running southeast into Pigeon Forge. Completed in 1920, this extension contributed to KS & E's revenues and aided with the flow of timber and lumber traffic out of the area. However, the growing popularity of large trucks as a means of transportation contributed to the abandonment of the Pigeon Forge rail extension in 1929.

INSIDERS' TIP

The Parkway that runs through Pigeon Forge was built after World War II. Before then, people going from Sevierville to Gatlinburg traveled down Pittman Center Road to Glades Road, and into Gatlinburg on Tenn. 73, a distance of about 20 miles on dirt roads.

The establishment of Great Smoky Mountains National Park in 1934 was ultimately to affect the lives of Forge residents in an irreversible manner. The birth of the park naturally led to larger numbers of visitors passing through Pigeon Forge on their way to Gatlinburg and the Smoky Mountains. In 1946, however, the Pigeon Forge tourism industry began in its own right with the city's first sale of a parcel of land smaller than a farm. The tobacco barn that stood on the land eventually became Pigeon Forge Pottery, located across the street from The Old Mill. The family-run business still thrives today in the heart of the city, and is renowned for its handmade wares (see our Mountain Crafts chapter for more).

As more businesses and accommodations grew to serve the growing tourist traffic, Pigeon Forge found itself being transformed from a sleepy, rural town comprised primarily of farm land into a viable economic community. In response to this metamorphosis, residents voted (by a narrow margin) to incorporate the town in 1961. From there, the snowball effect took over in changing both the character and the physical landscape of Pigeon Forge. Tourist-oriented businesses multiplied exponentially, particularly during the '70s and '80s. The 1982 World's Fair in Knoxville and the opening of Dollywood in 1986 both contributed to making Pigeon Forge an actual tourist destination, rather than a mere stopover.

Today, the large expanses of corn fields have been replaced by restaurants, hotels, attractions and shopping malls which host up to 40,000 visitors per day (see Area Overview). Regardless, the legacies of the Pigeon Forge of old live on in the descendants of the founding fathers who still reside there. Pigeon Forge's permanent population of around 4,000 doesn't have to look too far beyond the gift shops and go-cart tracks to see the green, wooded hillsides that still roll away toward the horizon and remind them of the way things once were.

Gatlinburg

Imagine, if you please, that it's any hour of daylight on a summer day of anytime between 1810 and 1910, and you're vacationing in Gatlinburg, Tennessee, soon to become a prominent national resort. To make it a little easier to visualize, let's say you're standing at the foot of the space needle, the city's tallest street-level landmark, looking back along the Parkway to the Ferris wheel at Fun Mountain. What do you see?

First, you don't see the space needle or Fun Mountain. In fact, you're probably not even standing on or near a road; you're in a field, probably corn, belonging to either a Reagan, a Maples, or an Ogle, depending on the time. Also, depending on the time, you may be at the edge of White Oak Flats. And one more certainty: You can count the number of people you see on your fingers. If you see any people at all.

Like most cities in most everywhere else, Gatlinburg got its start as a farming community when non-nomadic American Indians (the Cherokee in this case) settled here somewhere around 500 years ago and established farms in the fertile bottom land. The biggest mistake these noble citizens made was to invite certain white men to share the bounty of their fields and forests. By the beginning of the 19th century, the land belonged to the white men through various treaties and the granting of Tennessee's statehood in 1796.

Among the white men who had hunted and fished this particular area as a guest of the Cherokee was a South Carolinian named William "Old Billy" Ogle, whose wife was part Indian. He staked a claim on a choice piece of land (very close to the Arrowmont School campus today) and cut and hewed enough logs to build a cabin. He then returned to South Carolina to grow a crop of food large enough to feed his family for the year he figured it would take to move to Tennessee and establish a home. He never made it back.

When Billy Ogle left his Tennessee property and returned to South Carolina, he walked into a malarial flu epidemic that took his life. His widow, Martha Jane, approaching 50 and still tending to seven grown children (and some of their children), left South Carolina and the flu for an "extended" visit with her brother Peter Huskey in Virginia. From there the brood migrated to Tennessee, stopping briefly at Wear's Fort on Waldens Creek (west of Pigeon Forge), and then made their way into White Oak Flats, probably through Wears Valley and Elkmont (history is a little vague on this point, but no other roads existed at the time). Martha Jane's oldest son Isaac built the cabin his father had left the provisions for (there's also some historical disagreement on this point—some historians insist Isaac bought 50 acres of land, but from whom is a mystery), and a new community began its existence. The year was 1805.

It's significant to understand that Martha Jane Huskey Ogle and her family were by no means entering an untamed wilderness. They knew exactly where they were going, and what they were going to find. The immediate area they inhabited was mountainous and previously unsettled by white people, but the region was not. Sevierville was an established city before 1800, and so was Knoxville. And, despite the fact that Big Orange football was almost a century up the road, the University of Tennessee had been in operation for more than a decade when the Ogle family established the White Oak Flats community.

The arrival of Martha Jane Huskey Ogle and her young in this valley established the area known then as White Oak Flats, and, in a naturally expanded form, known today as Gatlinburg. The change of names occurred in the 1850s, when a decidedly unpleasant man named Radford Gatlin arrived and opened a general store. In addition to the rumored possession of a slave (not a social asset in East Tennessee), Radford Gatlin brought with him a sulfurous wife, no children, an attitude that didn't sit well with the locals, and enough government contacts to secure a postal commission, which he used to name the community in his own honor in 1856. By 1859 Gatlin had succeeded in alienating enough of the townsfolk that he was invited to seek his fortunes elsewhere. He agreed to go peacefully if the name "Gatlinburg" would be retained, and the locals bought the deal.

Gatlin disappeared into an uncertain history, but it is known that he worked for the Confederacy during the Civil War. The city was occupied briefly by Confederate troops during the Civil War while saltpeter for gunpowder production was being mined in the mountains. Union forces came in around Christmas in 1863, took over the town without firing a shot, and Gatlinburg's involvement in the war ended. It was significant only in that the Battle of Gatlinburg was the last known "conflict" in which Native Americans were engaged. They were camp followers of the Confederate troops, and their actual status has never been clearly defined.

From its founding as White Oak Flats and the non-eventful involvement in the Civil War, the town remained frozen in time for almost a century. The establishment of the post office in 1856, and the accompanying adoption of the name Gatlinburg, were the only significant changes in the town's basic operation from around 1825 until 1912, when a curious twist of fate occurred that was to change the face of Gatlinburg forever.

Pi Beta Phi Women's Fraternity is a national organization dedicated to education and health care. In the latter 19th and early 20th centuries, the good ladies of Pi Beta Phi worked as American missionaries, bringing the blessings of formal education and basic hygiene to isolated communities. In 1912, Pi Beta Phi considered two locations in east Tennessee as sites for a settlement school; neither site was in Sevier County, but their selection committee chose Sevierville as a central location to meet and discuss the alternatives. During their meeting,

The current Sevier County Courthouse was built in 1896.

Photo: Sevierville Chamber of Commerce

HISTORY

A Rich Family History

As we look at the Smokies from the viewpoint of a new century, it's instructive to understand that more than 90 percent of the explosive growth of the area occurred in its last two decades. It's also interesting to note that for a period of more than 50 years prior to 1980, the only real attraction the area had was a protected wilderness, and only one city really prospered from that circumstance.

The growth of the Smokies corridor has obscured the fact that there are still a lot of people living in Sevier County who grew up without electricity and indoor plumbing. Seems hard to believe when you look around, but these hills are still full of people who remember when their nearest neighbor was "near a mile" away, and

it's fascinating to learn something about how they lived before the tourism boom. It's also interesting to know that very few of these old-timers refer to the old days as "good" times, which ties in with the curious fact that the older folks are the ones who are most accommodating to the visitor population. All of the above considered, it seems natural that a work like this would be remiss if it didn't seek out an ultimate "insider" for a look at the changes wrought by the combination of history and geography that made the Smokies what they are and what they're becoming.

One of the more interesting phenomena about the people of the Smokies is that more of them appear to be known by their middle names than by their given first names. This is true of every generation of natives in this area to date. There's no really consistent reasoning behind any of this, since very few of the natives are named after their parents specifically. It's apparently a local thing that's not particularly strange to these gentle people, but it's a little unsettling when you're talking to one of them and two or three other people in the group use different names to speak to and of the person you're talking with. We'll be careful in this volume to let you know when we're using middle names and local nicknames when we bring up the natives by name.

Leon Owenby (his first name is John, but hardly anybody remembers that anymore) was easy enough to find; he was right there in his lawn chair at the house where he was born in 1926. And he was an easy choice, too; his pedigree is as "pure Gatlinburg" as you can find, going back to Billy and Martha Jane Ogle on both sides of the family, with the names Reagan, Maples, McMahan and Evans also liberally salted through the five generations of Sevier County natives that precede him. Leon's mother was a Reagan, and her mother was an Ogle. His father, Dick, came from a long line of Ownbys (note the spelling difference) dating to 1860 in Sevier County, and Dick Ownby's mother was a Maples. The esteemed Hattie Ogle McGiffin, the closest thing Gatlinburg will ever have to a grande dame, is Dick Ownby's first cousin. Raised primarily by his maternal (Reagan) grandparents, Leon identifies closely with them, but considers himself an Ogle more than anything else because he reminded most of his elders of "Little Noah" Ogle, his maternal great-grandfather, who owned a massive amount of property east of downtown Gatlinburg in the 19th century.

Sarah Allie "Peg" Reagan (1900-56) was the daughter of Elijah Lawson "Laws" and Martha Ogle Reagan. The second of five children, Allie Reagan Ownby was, in the local vernacular, "a pistol ball." She was a gregarious, aggressive business type about half a century ahead of her time, and rumor has it that she never met a party she didn't like. At the time of Leon's birth, Allie was a nationally-known weaver who traveled extensively for the J. C. Penney Company, demonstrating her weaving at their stores. She retired from traveling in about 1928 and came home to found Smoky Mountain Handweavers, one of Gatlinburg's original craft shops. The

Leon and Georgia Owenby at home with Cricket. A copy of the picture behind Leon's right shoulder hangs in Ruby Tuesday's restaurant on the Parkway in Gatlinburg, where the picture was taken when Leon was a boy and the building that now houses the restaurant was his family's home.

Photo: Christine Owenby

building where the Handweavers' shop was established is now Ruby Tuesday's restaurant on the Parkway, and it was also the only other house Leon ever called home. There's an old picture of a family beside the fireplace hanging in Ruby Tuesday's; it's Leon's family, and he's the little boy in the picture. Allie Ownby operated Smoky Mountain Handweavers until her death. She also, for reasons unknown to anybody, changed the spelling of the family name on Leon's birth certificate (but not on his sister's) to Owenby. Allie's father founded the E. L. Reagan Furniture Company in 1918 in its current location on the banks of Roaring Fork Creek. Dependent at the time on the river as a power source (electricity was still a decade down the road), Reagan's Furniture Shop is Gatlinburg's oldest business in continual operation by the same family. The water wheel that provided the power was connected to the tools it ran by a series of leather belts, and one of Leon's early jobs was repairing broken belts. A different series of belts provided power for the homes of E. L. Reagan and his family. The present proprietor is Laws Reagan's youngest son Harlan (first name James), born in 1920.

Horace Richard "Dick" Ownby was born in 1896 in the Greenbriar community east of Gatlinburg that's now part of the Great Smoky Mountains National Park. He was the ninth of 10 children of James "Codger Jim" and Susanna Maples Ownby. Dick met Allie Reagan after serving in World War I (his family's military tradition goes back beyond the Revolutionary War) and married her in 1919. Dick Ownby worked for a while as a groundskeeper at the summer home of an East Tennessee industrialist, but gravitated into the Reagan family industry after the births of his two

(Continued on next page)

children. He worked as an apprentice furniture maker for his father-in-law until his own creative spirit moved him to establish himself as a craftsman in his own right. His skill at inlay and parquet work provided a steady income that complemented Allie's. He also farmed a large piece of land that's now the site of several motels on East Parkway, and he personally built the street leading from East Parkway to his home, the one Leon lives in today, which Dick built in 1922. A talented artisan and decent husband, Dick Ownby was never much of a parent to his children, mostly because he never seemed to be able to stop working. He died in 1964 and is buried next to his wife in the White Oak Flats cemetery in downtown Gatlinburg.

Leon Owenby remembers when Gatlinburg only had two roads. The Parkway (it was Main Street then, also known as Tennessee Highway 71) ran from the mill in Pigeon Forge to the Sugarlands community, and Highway 73 (now U.S. 321N) ran out of town through the Glades to Sevierville, neither in the roadbeds they occupy today. To get to Knoxville, the choices were to go to Sevierville through the Glade or to challenge the "Sand Pike" out of Pigeon Forge. Now Wear's Valley and Walden's Creek Roads, the "Sand Pike" was not for the fainthearted or unprepared-parts of it still aren't. Leon and a group of his buddies used to delight in "borrowing" a parents' car at an ungodly early (or late, depending on your personal viewpoint) hour in the morning and heading out the Sand Pike flat-out to see if they could break the one-hour barrier to the Knoxville city limits. They might as well been trying to break the sound barrier, Leon recalls, because a high-speed drive over the Sand Pike usually meant somewhere around a dozen flat tires that would need repair on the spot. A patch kit and tire pump were absolute essentials on the Sand Pike run, and knowing how to patch a tire real quick didn't hurt. One of Leon's frequent companions on the Sand Pike run was Harry Montgomery, Gatlinburg's current police chief. After a little bit of recollecting on these trips, Leon further recollected that most of the Sand Pike adventures took place "somewheres 'round 1939, maybe 1940," and his friends agree that's about right. We did the math - by Leon's account, he was driving his Daddy's car through this wilderness at breakneck speeds and fixing flat tires on the run at about age 12. Presented with this evidence, Leon and his cronies allowed that was about right, too.

After getting all the education the Pi Beta Phi settlement school had to offer by the time he was 14, Leon knocked around a little (working in the furniture shop when needed, and a short stint with the Civilian Conservation Corps building roads, bridges, and dormitories in the new National Park) until he turned 17, when he entered the U. S. Army during World War II. He spent some time in post-war Germany before coming home in 1949 and marrying Georgia Brackins. They celebrated their 50th anniversary last July in the company of all seven of their children, plus assorted in-laws and grandchildren and great-grandchildren.

Georgia Brackins Owenby appears to be getting short shrift here, considering her importance in the lives of Leon and their family, but that's how she prefers it. A reticent lady who was born in a log cabin in the Gum Stand community between Gatlinburg and Pigeon Forge, Georgia remembers the day when a surveyor from the Department of the Interior asked her to open both doors so he could shoot a survey line right through the middle of the house for a new road the Park Service was going to build. Georgia and her family packed up and moved closer to Gatlinburg "right quick."

Leon remembers clearly the coming of the first tourists, mostly hikers and campers from Knoxville who came to explore the mountains. "They was nice enough folks," he recalls, "and we'd try to take care of 'em as best we could. Andy Huff's hotel (the Mountain View, now gone) put 'em up if they wanted rooms, and the restaurant fed 'em if wanted to stay over." As more and more of the "summer folks" decided to stay over, new restaurants and hotels opened up, and Laws Reagan's crew built the furniture for the new hostelries. "Between Laws, O. G. Ward, and Shirl Compton (the Wood Whittlers, still operating a couple miles out East Parkway}, we all stayed pretty busy from the time the Park opened building furniture," Leon remembers, "and it was nice to have a job in the winter." The quality of work done by the local artisans wasn't lost on the visitors, and the burgeoning crafts industry was helped when the visitors learned they could take home the furniture, quilts, brooms, and even butter churns they saw and used during their stay. As a cabinet maker, Leon's skills were in considerable demand from the 1950s until he retired in the late 1980s. It's tough to put exact dates here, because Gatlinburg's craftspeople rarely ever stop working entirely. Leon's no exception, and he worked sporadically until 1990, when diabetes made it hard to stand up for long periods. The quality of E. L. Reagan's furniture was such that several Tennessee governors chose to sit at desks made by Leon Owenby, and several governors of other states ordered desks that Leon built, disassembled, and shipped in pieces because there wasn't a cartage company around that could handle a full-size desk, some of which weighed upwards of 300 pounds. And when President Franklin D. Roosevelt visited Gatlinburg in 1940 to dedicate the new National Park and took a liking to his furnishings at the Mountain View Hotel, 14-year-old Leon Owenby got one of the biggest assignments of his life: A desk and dresser fit for a President were built and shipped to the White House in the spring of 1941. They might still be there somewhere.

Leon Owenby remembers hearing about his great-grandfather's holdings when it took more than a half-hour to walk home without ever leaving the property. "It ran from Main Street to Glades," Leon recalls, "and along the highway and Dudley Creek. Noey gave a lot of it to his family, and sold most of the land east of Dudley to the Montgomery family. The rest of it stayed in Laws' family (the Reagan side), and that got pretty well divided up 'mongst Laws's kids and grandkids." To give you a better perspective, here's how the land laid out using modern landmarks: Starting at the Parkway where Zoder's Best Western Inn is located on the banks of Roaring Fork Creek, and continuing down to traffic light #3; then along East Parkway about 2 miles to Glades Road, the Ogle property included both sides of East Parkway from Dudley Creek to a ridge line north of East Parkway. The piece of land in question is about six square miles, and now includes every building from traffic light #3 to Glades road, along with several hundred residences. It's bigger in area than downtown Gatlinburg will ever be, and most of Gatlinburg's permanent population lived on this piece of land until the middle 1970s. "Little Noey" Ogle died about a month before Leon was born, but the older members of the family always said Leon was his "spittin' image". The property where Leon and three of his children live with their families are among the last pieces of the original holdings still in family hands, and the biggest piece of undeveloped commercially-zoned property in Gatlinburg. Leon's determined that it'll stay that way so his grandchildren will always have land to live on where they can grow properly. His family has stayed close to home, too; three sons and their families live on or very near the family compound, and three of the other four children live in Gatlinburg.

Also in the family tradition, Leon's kids work in the two family trades: woodworking and public service. Two sons, a daughter, and a daughter-in-law work for the Park Service, and one son works for the City of Gatlinburg. Two other sons are construction workers, building homes and businesses for new residents—both exceptional woodworkers, they also do a little moonlighting as craftsmen.

Historical records going back to 1055 in England testify to Leon Owenby's Ogle lineage, and the Ownby (occasionally Ownbey) line has been traced to 1670, also in England. Like a lot of his local kinfolk, Leon Owenby is a member of one of the oldest English-speaking families on Earth. And he couldn't care less. He's happy he was born in this place he still thinks is one of God's major blessings, and he's content to live out his life in the loving company of his family and what friends he's got left. He has no regrets about the way Gatlinburg has grown, and he's pleased that generations of his progeny will be able to grow up in the small town atmosphere he and his friends have preserved.

someone suggested that they add Gatlinburg to their list of possible sites, and, since it was handy, they decided to have a look. They must have liked what they saw, because Gatlinburg is where they established their school.

The Pi Phis brought an ambitious agenda with them. Their primary goal was to provide formal education to the mountain children, which in turn provided alternatives to subsistence farming as a lifestyle. Beyond that, they also brought consistent medical care and hygiene training to the community at large. They didn't really plan to set the town up in an industry, but not too long after their arrival the Pi Phis found that Gatlinburg had something the nation was crying out for. The handcrafts that had virtually disappeared from America during the industrial revolution that Gatlinburg had apparently slept through were not only still being practiced here, they were still being used for everyday life.

Enter O. J. Mattil and Winogene Redding. Mattil was brought to Gatlinburg as a vocational instructor in 1922. After indoctrinating the locals in the latest farming techniques, he set up classes for the boys in woodworking, basketry, and carpentry. Until he was able to afford a generating plant and woodworking machinery (Gatlinburg didn't have electricity at the time), Mattil's classes worked with hand tools. While all this was going on in Mattil's workshop, the other members of the Pi Phi staff were finding examples of Gatlinburg's native craftsmanship in most of the homes they visited. Knowing the marketability of the items they saw just about everywhere, the Pi Phis started recruiting the local craftspeople to both teach the youngsters their crafts and to produce their goods for sale. In 1926, Pi Beta Phi opened the Arrowcraft shop as a local outlet, and started shipping the crafts of Gatlinburg to other Pi Phi outlets across the country. Winogene Redding organized and managed the whole program. It wasn't long before the crafts of Gatlinburg were in demand all over the United States. In less than five years, Gatlinburg had gone from an isolated farming community to the craft capital of America, and Pi Beta Phi was the driving force that made it happen.

It is possible that Gatlinburg's crafts would have become nationally known without the intervention of Pi Beta Phi. Forces were already at work to create the Great Smoky Mountains National Park in Gatlinburg's back yard, and the natural influx of tourism could have given the city its craft market a decade or so later. It's also possible that by the time the park and its visitors arrived, handcrafts would have disappeared from Gatlinburg like they had in most of the country.

The arrival of the Pi Phis brought about a change in the fortunes of Gatlinburg that is still paying generous dividends. For as long as craftspeople are able to make a living in this industry in this place, the names of Pi Beta Phi, O. J. Mattil, and Winogene Redding should be spoken only in capital letters. Winogene Redding stayed on with Pi Phi through the transfer of the school to the county educational system, and worked as a weaving instructor and author at the Arrowmont School until her retirement in the early 1960s. She died in Nashville in 1981, having made a profound impact on the weaving industry and those she taught to practice and to love it.

In 1928, O. J. Mattil broadened his horizons and those of several thousand craftspeople in nine southeastern states as a prime mover in the formation of the Southern Highlands Handicraft Guild. He remained a dominant figure in that organization until his death 50 years later. In 1945, long after the school they had established in Gatlinburg had become part of the county educational system, Pi Beta Phi and the University of Tennessee established the Arrowmont School of Arts & Crafts on the land it occupies today in downtown Gatlinburg. The Arrowmont School is considered one of the pre-eminent institutions of its kind in the world. It's given the attention it deserves in our Education chapter. The Arrowcraft Shop stands today in

HISTORY

INSIDERS' TIP

Nostradamus, look out! On November 11, 1925, a monument to Colonel Samuel Wear was dedicated in Pigeon Forge. General W. T. Kennedy of Knoxville, who spoke at the dedication ceremony, made a prediction before the assembled group. He foresaw the creation of a national park in the Great Smoky Mountains as well as a "broad concrete highway" which would run from Knoxville, through Sevierville, Pigeon Forge and Gatlinburg all the way to North Carolina via the national park. This speech was made ten years before Great Smoky Mountains National Park and decades before today's multi-lane Parkway every became a reality.

INSIDERS' TIP

Legend has it that Timothy Reagan, the man employed to build Sevier County's first prisoners' stocks in 1795, persuaded the county sheriff to allow himself to be locked in them in order to test them out. Reportedly, the sheriff was left locked in the stocks for a considerable amount of time, much to the amusement of the local residents.

its original location at the intersection of the Parkway and Cherokee Orchard Road in downtown Gatlinburg. Pi Beta Phi sold the shop to the Southern Highlands Handicraft Guild in 1993.

As the older of the sister cities that play host to more than 10 million visitors each year, Gatlinburg finds itself torn between its gentle past and an uncertain future that promises to be anything but gentle. By the mid-1980s, Gatlinburg had pretty much settled into a routine of busy summers and idle winters with an economy fueled mainly by prosperous, middle-aged tourists, when a couple of strange things happened: The face of tourism changed dramatically, and Pigeon Forge reacted quickly and positively to the change. As suddenly as if it had been swallowed by an unseen and unknown force, the conservative Gatlinburg tourist base was engulfed by a tidal wave of younger, livelier people, married and single, who were looking for a good time and had the money to pay for it. And they brought their kids with them. And poor old Gatlinburg, blind-sided by a change it never saw coming and hemmed in on three sides by the Great Smoky Mountains National Park, is struggling mightily to accommodate a whole new population in an area that really wasn't big enough for the old one.

Because new development space downtown is unavailable, any new idea must first decide if existing structures are compatible. If so, fine; if not, the first tool used in new construction is the wrecking ball. Faced with the reality that the new tourist population is not as laid back as the previous generations, Gatlinburg is reinventing itself annually to meet the demand of its new clientele, and is methodically and regretfully destroying its own history to do it. Still an international center for handcrafted merchandise and fine art, Gatlinburg strives to maintain those industries as the primary link to its past while it continues to come up with new ways and new places to accommodate the best guesses it can make for the shape its future will take.

That was Then...

The tiny portion of Sevier County that constitutes the Smokies corridor would be a textbook example of niche development if textbooks were updated monthly. The explosive growth of the Smokies corridor is a direct result of the establishment of Great Smoky Mountains National Park, and the area's identity has been developed by the folks who originally came to the area to enjoy the scenery and the hospitality of the local residents. It's regrettable to some local purists that a lot of people come to the Smokies for a variety of reasons totally separate from the "old days," but the fact that they come in larger numbers each year speaks well for the future. While almost 90 percent of Sevier County's land is still farmland and wilderness, about the same percentage of the population, including a lot of folks from surrounding counties, is involved in the tourism industry. When historians of the future consider the emergence of the Smokies corridor as a principal tourist destination, it will be interesting to see if they're able to figure out why all those people first chose to come to this place.

HISTORY

Hotels and Motels

LOOK FOR:
- Sevierville
- Gatlinburg
- Pigeon Forge

Price Code

Our pricing guide is based on two adults staying in a standard room on a weekend night during the peak season. Although many of the places we've included allow children to stay at no additional cost, there was some variance among the ages at which one was considered to be a "child."

Less than $60	**$**
$61 to $80	**$$**
$81 to $100	**$$$**
$101 to $120	**$$$$**
$121 and more	**$$$$$**

Once upon a time, Gatlinburg had exclusive bragging rights when it came to hotels and motels in Sevier County. For decades, its proximity to Great Smoky Mountains National Park made it the area's dominant visitor destination. Accommodations in Pigeon Forge were built initially just to catch the tourist overflow from Gatlinburg, and lodgings in Sevierville could practically be counted on one hand.

The climate began to change in the 1980s. When Knoxville hosted the World's Fair in 1982, all of the local communities prospered from the spillover, and when Dollywood Theme Park opened in 1986, Pigeon Forge picked up steam as a tourist destination in its own right. These days, the number of hotels and motels in Sevierville is growing rapidly as well, evidence of the entire region's phenomenal expansion.

It's difficult to keep up with the statistics when it comes to charting the growth of the hotel/motel industry in the Smoky Mountains. Seemingly, as soon as city and county officials get an accurate tabulation of the number of lodging facilities and rooms to be found in the area, another foundation is poured at another construction site. To put things in ballpark terms, however, there are nearly 200 hotels and motels representing more than 16,000 individual rooms in Sevier County alone. That's a lot of guest soap. But then again, the supply of rooms usually fights to keep up with demand, and in the Smokies, the demand is high and the supply is both eclectic and broad reaching.

Of course, the properties you'll encounter occupy a wide berth when it comes to factors such as price, amenities and location. What's unique, though, is that when it comes to the types of establishments to be found, there is a distinct pattern in the make-up of each community as you travel south from I-40. The accommodations on the northern outskirts of the county and in Sevierville itself tend to be well-known franchises that are newer and offer a long slate of amenities tailored to the traveler. The tradeoff is that they're often farther away from the bulk of the action in the Smokies. Conversely, the big franchises are less prevalent as you travel through Pigeon Forge and draw nearer to Gatlinburg. That is where you'll encounter more independently owned lodgings, many that have been family-run for generations. While they are closer to the heart of area activities, the range of available amenities can sometimes be narrower. In either case there are certainly advantages, tradeoffs and exceptions to the rules, all of which will be explored in more depth in each city's respective section.

Rules of Thumb

A number of policies, services and amenities are common to the vast majority of the hotels and motels in Tennessee's Great Smoky Mountains. We'll outline them here and leave you to make the assumption that these conditions exist unless otherwise stated. For example, it's safe to presume that most of the rooms provide cable television. Most, but not all, of the TVs are accompanied by remote controls and receive at least one free movie channel. However, call ahead to confirm this when making reservations. Other safe bets are that the properties are open all year, carpeted, air conditioned, provide both smoking and nonsmoking rooms, accept most major credit cards, have at least one swimming pool and don't allow pets. Again, exceptions to these rules will be noted in the individual write-ups.

In most of the descriptions in this chapter, you won't find too much detail about room aesthetics, unless something noteworthy or distinctive warrants its mention. We found that the layouts and decor of most of the standard rooms and suites are fairly consistent from one property to the next. Whether the hotel was brand spanking new or an older facility that had been recently remodeled, we almost always found clean, well maintained, pleasantly decorated interiors.

We also discovered that first impressions of hotel exteriors could be deceiving. In many cases, we came across older motels at which one might ordinarily just give a cursory glance when driving by. However, stopping to look inside the rooms often revealed deceptively plush surroundings. Generally, variances in rates are reflections of a property's location and the number and types of amenities offered, not the cleanliness of its rooms.

As we take you on our guided tour of hotels and motels in the Smokies, we will start at I-40's Exit 407 and head south on Tenn. 66. The facilities we've included are more or less presented in the order in which you'll encounter them, and we'll stick to that plan until we've traveled all the way through Sevierville, Pigeon Forge and Gatlinburg to the entrance of Great Smoky Mountains National Park. In Gatlinburg, we will take detours to check out lodgings on secondary roads and parallel streets, but otherwise, we will remain faithful to our north-south course.

Any Reservations?

One question that inevitably crosses the mind of the prospective Smoky Mountains visitor is "How far ahead should I make reservations?" That mainly depends on the time of year you plan to travel. If your agenda has you staying here during an unusually busy time, like the Fourth of July holiday, you'll want to hit the phones as much as six months ahead of your intended arrival. For the most part, the proprietors with whom we spoke recommended making reservations anywhere from two to six weeks prior to a visit during peak season. During the off-season, it's a buyer's market where you can often arrive in town with no reservations and pick your room (although we never advise doing that!). Major credit cards are generally the most accepted form of deposit when making reservations. Cancellation policies vary from one hotel to another. A few require as much as 72 hours advance notice of cancellation, but the typical time is 24 hours. When it comes to specific reservation information as well as cancellation procedures and fees, we recommend getting the particulars from each of the lodgings that you contact.

Pricing Information

Our pricing guide is based on two adults staying in a standard room on a weekend night during the peak season (traditionally the summer vacation months and October, when the autumn leaves turn). Although many of the places we've included allow children to stay at no additional cost, there was some variance among the ages at which one was considered to be a "child." Where applicable, we've mentioned these specific cutoff ages, but in general they range from 12 to 19 years old. The room rates at many of the hotels and motels we encountered were simply flat fees. In these cases, the customer purchases a room at a single price, no matter how many people occupy it. Keep in mind, though, that many establishments place limits on the number of people allowed in each room and will charge extra for additional adult guests.

There are some exceptions to our price guide that are worthy of noting. While some of the more expensive hotels and motels might be out of your budget during the summer, those same properties can have substantially lower rates during the off-season. It was not uncommon for us to find hotels that charge more than $100 per night in October charging $30 or $40 per night for the same room in April or May. Again, the laws of supply and demand keep things in check.

Another exception comes into play during high-traffic events like major holidays or any of the area's popular custom auto shows. Although these special event periods only pop up sporadically throughout the year, be aware that lodging rates during those periods can be even higher than we've indicated for the typical peak season.

Sevierville

As mentioned previously, each of the three primary communities in our area has its own particular character as it relates to the bigger accommodations picture. Even in the region that we are designating as "Sevierville," a number of factors might influence your selection.

The first seven establishments we've included are all on or near Winfield Dunn Parkway (Tenn. 66), the main route that runs from I-40 to downtown Sevierville (some are officially located in the small, unincorporated community of Kodak). They are almost exclusively franchises of national chains, most of which have been constructed within the past five years. While they are somewhat removed from the lion's share of the area's most visited spots (Pigeon Forge is 8 to 15 miles away, Gatlinburg is 15 to 20 miles), there are advantages to choosing them.

If you've made a long journey to get to the Smokies, the last thing you want to do is sit in bumper-to-bumper traffic trying to reach your hotel. The Winfield Dunn Parkway accommodations tend to be heavy on comfort and amenities, and they can make for a welcome end to what might be a long and tiring drive. Also, these hotels and motels are ideally situated for a vacation that may include outlying areas in addition to the Smokies. Those who have Knoxville or Asheville, North Carolina, on their itineraries will greatly benefit from the uncongested and centrally located Tenn. 66 lodgings. See our chapter on Daytrips to get some suggestions for such excursions.

The remainder of the Sevierville section includes many hotels that are similar in age and atmosphere to those that were just mentioned, but have the added advantage of being within a few minutes' drive of an abundance of shopping, dining and entertainment options. But we'll get there soon enough. In the meantime, buckle up!

Quality Inn Interstate
$$$ • 3385 Winfield Dunn Pkwy., Kodak
• (865) 933-7378, (800) 348-4652

Conveniently located just off I-40 at Exit 407, this hotel is one of the first you'll encounter on the "Smokies Corridor," and it offers a pleasant night's stay for the traveler who's eager to get off the road. In operation since 1992, Quality Inn Interstate is a good pick if you're looking for an attractive room at a price that won't break your pocketbook. The inn's 65 standard rooms and 15 suites are accessible from interior corridors on all three floors. All rooms have two queen-sized beds. Some feature whirlpool tubs and balconies as well. For fun in the water year-round, take a dip into the indoor swimming pool. Children stay free at this Quality Inn, and discounts are available for AARP and AAA members.

Holiday Inn Express
$$$ • 2863 Winfield Dunn Pkwy., Kodak
• (865) 933-9448, (800) 939-9448

Typical of the new breed of hotels found along the road to Sevierville, this franchise exudes comfort and was voted 1998's "Newcomer of the Year" by its parent corporation. Access to rooms is inside, and room keys are required to enter the hotel through doors other than those in the lobby. The hotel's 73 standard rooms feature private balconies and porches as well as computer modems for the traveler who can't leave work at home. Fifteen suites offer a broader amenities package, including sleeper sofas, refrigerators, microwaves, fireplaces, coffee makers and whirlpool tubs.

The property boasts a breakfast bar, guest laundry room, indoor pool and whirlpool. This Holiday Inn Express is totally smoke-free, and presents a light, pleasing decor with accompanying views of the surrounding countryside. Children younger than 19 stay at no cost; AARP and AAA discounts are extended as well. Although the hotel is still several miles out of Sevierville, it's convenient to Lee Greenwood's music theater, shops, restaurants and two golf courses.

Wingate Inn
$$$$ • 2450 Winfield Dunn Pkwy.,
Sevierville • (865) 933-5544,
(800) 243-0560

Luxury, elegance and functionality define the overall character of this Wingate Inn, constructed in 1996. When you enter the lobby, you step into a spacious, airy atmosphere and

Gatlinburg Inn

You may be familiar with the feeling: You're walking along the busy main drag of a tourist mecca, trying to take in all of the sights and sounds around you, and suddenly something is very much out of synch. It's not something wrong, it's just suddenly. . .different. It's like a rock group has started playing Brahms.

What's happened here? Well, if you're on the Parkway in Gatlinburg, you've probably come to one of the truly rare sights in town: A section of street that doesn't have a building hovering over the sidewalk. And then you see it, set back from the

low stone wall that protects its parking area from the sidewalk. Announced by an unpretentious wood sign, the Gatlinburg Inn appears to have been built at the wrong end of the property.

If you're moved to look beyond the parking lot into this strange place that seems so serene among the bright lights and carnival sounds, you cross the parking lot, return the greeting of the security guard who seems to have materialized from thin air, and walk up the stairs, across the wide front porch and through the automatic door that seems out of place until you remember this is a place of public accommodation. The door was installed in the '50s, long before any laws concerning such things were written.

Inside the lobby, you're back in the time warp. The reception desk is at the back, and the smiling people tending it obviously know you're there, but they haven't spoken yet because you're not close enough for their modulated tones to reach you comfortably. The lobby is like an old movie set, but obviously very real. The handblocked wallpaper and matching curtains cover what little of the walls are not taken

(Continued on next page)

The Gatlinburg Inn, est. 1937. Located in the heart of downtown Gatlinburg, the Gatlinburg Inn is an oasis of civility in a busy tourist mecca.

Photos: Courtesy Rel and Wilma Maples

HOTELS AND MOTELS

up with the huge wood-framed windows that look out to the world you just left, and wrought iron plant stands loaded down with various flora in pots of every description seem to circle the room.

Fringed area rugs cover the parts of the slate floor that contain overstuffed couches and chairs surrounding tables that hold various magazines. If you happen not to see it, the Westminster chimes on the grandfather clock will announce its presence every 15 minutes. And a row of rocking chairs invites you to sit and regard the scene outside. If you're very lucky, you learn that the gracious lady sitting in one of the rocking chairs is Mrs. Wilma Maples, the manager. And if you sit quietly and pay attention (this part's easy—for all her old-world charm she's a commanding presence), Wilma Maples will tell you about the Inn from before its beginnings, and about the remarkable, Bunyanesque man who built it as part of his life-long quest to bring a better standard of living to the people of Gatlinburg.

Rellie L. (Rel) Maples (1905-1985) was a Gatlinburg native who was raised to the notion that service was nobler than self, and that monuments were built on a foundation of trust. After graduating from high school at Lincoln Memorial University and attending the University of Tennessee, Rel Maples came home to a city affected by the Great Depression, but not ruined by it. He worked as a cook in the CCC camp while the Great Smoky Mountains National Park was being built, and then built his own cafe on the Parkway in town, on land owned by his grandfather Ephraim Ogle. When the log restaurant burned, Rel Maples started making blocks the next day to rebuild it with more fireproof material. The Village shopping mall stands on the site today.

Rel's parents had a patch of land a little way up the Parkway from the Log Cabin café. In 1937 he harvested the corn and potatoes on it and started clearing the land with a mule-drawn scoop to build a hotel that would house the growing number of tourists coming to visit the mountains. The Gatlinburg Inn opened its doors in 1937, in very much the fashion it appears today.

While its appearance hints that it was built for the gentry of the time, the Gatlinburg Inn was in fact built for the average tourist. It was a coincidence that most of the tourists in the years before and immediately following World War II were well-heeled and traveled with entourages and certain expectations of service, and Rel Maples understood these things and made certain that the Gatlinburg Inn met the standards of its clientele. The 67 rooms and seven suites were designed and furnished for comfort without compromise, and most of the original furniture is still in use. The chairs and sofas have been reupholstered several times (old will do—shabby won't), but the quality built into the Inn endures, and so does its absolute refusal to surrender to any cookie-cutter trends in the lodging industry today. Also in keeping with the fashion of the time, separate quarters in the lower level housed the chauffeurs and domestic staffs of the Inn's visitors.

The dining room of the Gatlinburg Inn was a masterpiece of propriety. The supplier of the hand-painted china, sterling silver finger bowls, and crystal used in the dining room joked that the dining room furnishings cost as much as the rest of the hotel, and he probably was close to right. Wilma Maples remembers the dining room fondly, particularly the Tuesday night dinners, when the guests would gather for dinner and then retire to the tennis courts for square dancing. As the nature of tourism changed with the times following the war, the "new" tourists objected to the idea of dressing for dinner, so Rel and Wilma regretfully closed the dining room in 1972, rather than lower their own standards.

Wilma Miller Maples is not a Gatlinburg native. Born to a large family in Union County, Wilma came to Gatlinburg in 1943 as secretary to the chief ranger in the Park. She worked summers at the Gatlinburg Inn from 1946 to 1950, when she moved to Oak Ridge to work for a research engineer. That job lasted until 1953, when she received a letter from Rel proposing marriage and a return to Gatlinburg. "It came out of the clear blue sky," she recalls, "And I really didn't know what to make of it at first." Wilma returned to Gatlinburg and became Mrs. Rel Maples in 1954 for "the best 31 years of my life."

The Gatlinburg Inn is as important to Gatlinburg's growth as the man who built it. In 1950, Rel Maples persuaded Bill Mills to join him in the establishment of the First National Bank of Gatlinburg, ending the necessity for the city's residents to travel 14 miles to Sevierville whenever they needed change. The Inn hosted the first city offices prior to the construction of the original city hall, and the city's first large-press newspaper was printed in the basement.

Wilma recalls almost wistfully the days when the Inn hosted the cream of American society, from captains of industry to an A-list of entertainment people. Igor Sikorsky, the inventor of the helicopter, was a guest there, and so was Melville Bell Grosvenor, son of the founder of the National Geographic Society. J. C. Penney, who changed America's shopping habits, stayed at the Inn when he visited the area, and so did the parents of Stanley Marcus, who took Penney's concept to a level of luxury still unmatched in this country. Tennessee Ernie Ford brought his parents. Liberace and Frank Fontaine were satisfied guests, as was "Pistol Pete" Maravich, the late basketball superstar. Wilma remembers with particular fondness the frequent visits of Boudleaux and Felice Bryant, the Hall-of-Fame songwriting team, who stayed in room 388 almost every winter for more than 20 years. The Bryants were so much like family that they were given keys to the front door, in case they stayed out past the Inn's closing hour. During their stay in 1967, the Bryants wrote "Rocky Top." The list could go on for a long time, but you get the idea: The Gatlinburg Inn is a haven for travelers who enjoy being sheltered in an air of total civility, regardless of their background or social position.

If the Gatlinburg Inn seems a little out of step today it's only because it has refused to change its pace with the rest of the world. The Inn remains open from April through October, and 95 percent of its clientele are repeat guests who first came as children and are now bringing their own children and grandchildren for a graphic demonstration of how they grew up. And they're greeted by employees who've been there for as long as the guests can remember, especially the redoubtable head housekeeper Grace Bales Barker, who, according to Wilma Maples, "God sent to me in 1969 after Rel's heart attack." And, since the Inn is particularly resolute about record-keeping, the older guests can look back at the old registers and find the dates and rooms they stayed in on every visit.

Wilma Maples continues to operate the Gatlinburg Inn as Rel intended it be run, and she laments the passing of the time when the operation was business as usual. And while she also regrets the passing of Gatlinburg from the friendly little mountain town it was, she understands with crystal clarity what's going on and why. Notwithstanding that, this iron-willed lady will go on as long as she can, operating her hostelry in the gentler fashion of her heart while her feet are planted firmly in the present.

To inquire about staying at the Gatlinburg Inn, call (865) 436-5133.

immediately notice the nearby meeting rooms and large continental breakfast area. Guest rooms are designed with both the business and vacation traveler in mind. Each of the 101 units includes a refrigerator, coffee maker, iron and ironing board, in-room safe, two phone lines and a cordless phone. Sleeping arrangements range from two double beds to one or two queen beds to a single king bed. The health-conscious can stay in shape in a well-equipped fitness center, then relax in the nearby whirl-pool.

This hotel is unusual in that if offers tremendous convenience in an otherwise under-developed section of highway. Wingate Inn is just one element of the Riverbluff Landing development located along Tenn. 66, overlooking the scenic French Broad River. The hotel stands in the shadow of the Lee Greenwood Theater as well as the entertainer's own restaurant, L.G.'s on the River. The quaint shops of Maplewood Country Stores next door are reminiscent of the farmer's markets and general stores of yesteryear (see our Shopping chapter). Wingate Inn offers AAA and AARP discounts, and children younger than 12 stay free.

Clarion Inn Willow River
**$$$$ • 1990 Winfield Dunn Pkwy.,
Sevierville • (865) 429-7600,
(800) 610-0565**

Old Southern charm abounds at this Clarion Inn that opened its doors in 1997. Pulling into the parking lot, you're greeted by fastidiously manicured landscaping and a three-story structure with large, stately columns and an exterior facade awash in white. Inside, the antebellum decor remains consistent. The lobby blends elegance and 19th-century simplicity, featuring accents of ornate lighting fixtures and intricately carved stair railings. Rocking chairs are prominent, and several pieces of *Gone With the Wind* memorabilia adorn the walls and tables.

This Clarion's 89 rooms have either two queen beds or one king bed and a sleeper sofa. Refrigerators, coffee makers and private balconies with porches are standard for these units. Those who desire fireplaces and whirlpools in their rooms can opt for one of 16 deluxe suites. Clarion Inn Willow River sets out a generous morning feast in its continental breakfast area, and has both laundry facilities and meeting rooms at the disposal of its guests. An indoor pool and hot tub are accessible 24 hours a day. The outside pool area is unique in itself with a white gazebo and elevated deck overlooking the water. The entire scene is surrounded by the "Lazy River," a man-made channel, similar to those in water parks. All you have to do is grab one of the small inner tubes provided and shove off with the current.

Those making excursions away from the hotel will find themselves near the Lee Greenwood Theater and only a few miles from Sevierville and Eagles Landing Golf Course. Golf and honeymoon packages are both offered here. The rates at Clarion Inn Willow River are on a per-room basis and allow occupancy of up to six people, depending on the size and number of beds in the room. They honor AAA and AARP discounts and have both group and corporate rates.

Super 8 Motel
$$$ • 1410 Winfield Dunn Pkwy., Sevierville • (865) 429-0887, (800) 800-8000

In keeping with the tradition of Super 8 Motels,

this one is an overall good value. Children younger than 12 stay free and discounts are available to seniors. Sixty rooms make up this property, each with a unique split-bedroom layout. The sleeping areas contain either queen- or king-sized beds and are separated by a common bathroom. All rooms are tastefully decorated and furnished and open on to a private porch or balcony overlooking a scenic, tree-lined stretch of the Little Pigeon River. Each of this Super 8's three floors has a common area—there's a whirlpool spa on the first floor, a porch with rocking chairs on the second floor and an exercise room on the third floor. The motel's location provides handy access to nearby Douglas Lake and Eagles Landing Golf Course. Open since 1995, it is family owned and has received superior quality assurance ratings from its parent company.

Comfort Inn Mountain View Suites
$$$$$ • 860 Winfield Dunn Pkwy., Sevierville • (865) 428-5519, (800) 441-0311

If the comfort and privacy of a suite is what you're looking for, this Comfort Inn is a good selection. Open since 1988, this three-story facility provides exterior entry to most of its 95 two-room suites. Several are accessible from the inside and face the indoor pool and spa area. From others, you'll enjoy pleasant views of the Great Smoky Mountains from your private balcony. The suites can sleep up to six people and offer various combinations of features, including in-room whirlpool spas, woodburning fireplaces, mini bars, microwaves, coffee makers and refrigerators. Each suite is well furnished and has two televisions, one in the bedroom and one in the sitting room.

During your stay you might take in the free continental breakfast in the morning or perhaps unwind at either of the two swimming pools. There is an indoor pool and one outside, complete with waterfalls and whirlpool spa. Comfort Inn Mountain View Suites has meeting facilities and golf packages available on request. AAA and Senior discounts are honored, and children younger than 16 stay at no additional cost. The motel is located adjacent to a small shopping plaza that contains several shops and the Sevierville Chamber of Commerce office. This will allow you access to a wealth of infor-

INSIDERS' TIP
Be sure to check with the desk clerks to see if they have discount tickets to any attractions or restaurants you're planning to visit. Most everybody will have something to save you a dollar or two.

mation about what Sevierville has to offer. Comfort Inn Mountain View Suites has won several beautification awards from the city for its neatly landscaped and often festively decorated grounds.

Hampton Inn
$$$ • 681 Winfield Dunn Pkwy., Sevierville • (865) 429-2005, (800) HAMPTON

This particular Hampton Inn surprised us with its terrific value. Its four interior, security-controlled floors and 42 rooms and suites are housed in a compact, stucco-look structure located just on the outskirts of Sevierville proper. The 32 standard rooms each contain two queen beds and are of elegant and tasteful decor. The 10 suites are spacious and open, featuring king beds and either a recliner or sofa. Fireplaces, refrigerators, microwaves, coffee makers and in-room whirlpool tubs complete the king suite package. For the hearing impaired, there is even a system available in some rooms that allows for outside communication via keyboard.

This Hampton Inn's complimentary breakfast buffet includes a healthy selection of fresh fruit. The health-conscious will also want to take advantage of the exercise room, and kids can give their thumbs and fingers a good workout in the game room. Constructed in 1994, the hotel provides guest laundry facilities, fax services and a meeting room that accommodates 100 people. A variety of discounts are offered for those seeking extra value. Children younger than 18 stay free, and seniors can ask about Hampton Inn's Lifestyle 50 discounts that allow up to three additional guests to share a room at no extra charge.

Landmark Inn
$$ • 401 Forks of the River Pkwy., Sevierville • (865) 453-0318, (800) 548-9038

This long-established, independently owned motel extends comfort, convenience and value in the heart of Sevierville. Its 80 standard rooms are pleasing to the eye and have balconies and porches with direct views of the Great Smoky Mountains and the Little Pigeon River. Landmark Inn's 20 specialty rooms contain ameni-

ties combinations that may include refrigerators, kitchenettes, coffee makers, fireplaces and in-room whirlpool tubs. The motel's proximity to the river makes a number of fun activities immediately available to guests. Kids will enjoy feeding the ducks, and fishermen can drop their lines in the water in search of the big one. For peaceful and scenic strolls, check out the city's Memorial River Trail Greenway, a paved walking/jogging trail that flanks the Little Pigeon River and passes directly in front of Landmark Inn.

The Mize Motel
$ • 804 Parkway, Sevierville • (865) 453-4684, (800) 239-9117

Offering a clean and comfortable room at a great rate, The Mize Motel has been a fixture on Sevierville's Parkway since the days when motels in the city were sparse. Its gray stone exterior is typical of the older mom-and-pop motels, but the interiors of its 42 standard rooms and four efficiency apartments have been nicely remodeled in recent years. The kids will enjoy romping in the shaded lawn in front of the motel or splashing in its heated pool. Although the rooms aren't heavy on amenities, this is a good choice for the vacationer who simply wants decent accommodations in a location convenient to planned destinations. The Mize Motel is closed December through March. They offer AAA and senior discounts, and children stay free.

Sleep Inn
$$$ • 1020 Parkway, Sevierville • (865) 429-0484, (888) 429-0484

This three-story hotel, built in 1996, contains 70 interior-access rooms, each imbued with what could almost be described as an art deco motif. The units are filled with plenty of curves and stylish furnishings; the glass doors in the showers add to the character. Rooms also include coffee makers and are laid out with either two double beds or one king-sized bed. Free continental breakfast, an outdoor pool and meeting/banquet facilities round out Sleep Inn's offerings. This hotel's location puts guests within one mile of the Governor's Crossing development, a multifaceted collective of shops and restaurants and featuring the entertainment of Governor's Palace Theater.

HOTELS AND MOTELS

Many area hotels and motels help warm up winter days and nights with fireplaces.

Photo: Courtesy Ober Gatlinburg

Green Valley Motel North
$$$ • 1544 Parkway, Sevierville
• (865) 453-4066, (800) 426-4066

Green Valley Motel's 52 rooms are split between two buildings, and the rooms are entered from the outside. The original, older structure houses approximately 22 units; the remainder of the rooms are in a three-story addition. The decor of all the rooms is consistent, however, from one building to the other, and the layout offers a choice of either two double beds or one king bed. The newer rooms feature private balconies, and some come outfitted with whirlpool tubs and refrigerators. Green Valley Motel extends discounts to seniors, and children younger than 13 stay free. The motel is closed January through March, but offers handy access to the Governor's Crossing complex as well as Tanger Five Oaks Outlet Mall.

Oak Tree Lodge
$$$ • 1620 Parkway, Pigeon Forge
• (865) 428-7500, (800) 637-7002

Although it's in a rapidly developing area between Sevierville and Pigeon Forge, Oak Tree Lodge benefits from its placement among open, green fields bordered by white fences. This pastoral setting, combined with charming, antebellum architecture, make for a vacation or business stay replete with Southern atmosphere. The three-story structure accommodates 64 standard rooms and 36 suites in a combination of both interior and exterior access. All rooms feature either a double queen bed or single king bed setup, refrigerator and coffee maker, as well as private balconies and porches. In suites, you'll discover fireplaces and whirlpool tubs.

Built in 1990, Oak Tree Lodge boasts both indoor and outdoor pools, an exercise room, continental breakfast, private catering, and they can even help you arrange for babysitting services. In-room VCRs are available for rental if you or your gang are in the mood for a flick. The hotel lies within a short distance (walking distance, in some cases) of outlet shopping malls and restaurants. Other sites of interest that are either on or near the property include tennis courts, hiking trails, a horseback riding stable (see Parks and Recreation) and an on-site meeting facility that can seat up to 100. Oak Tree Lodge recommends making reservations six months in advance.

Comfort Inn Apple Valley
$$$$ • 1850 Parkway, Sevierville
• (865) 428-1069, (800) 228-5150

This Comfort Inn has racked up its share of accolades in recent years, having been named International Comfort Inn of the Year in 1995 and having taken awards from the city of Sevierville for Winterfest Landscaping and Fall Decorations. Inside, the quality continues throughout the hotel's 100 extra large standard rooms and 10 suites. All rooms are located within three, interior-access floors and have either two queen beds or one king-sized bed. Standard rooms feature private balconies, refrigerators and in-room coffee makers. Suites are available with whirlpool tubs and in-room fireplaces.

Comfort Inn Apple Valley offers its guests both indoor and outdoor pools as well as an indoor whirlpool spa. Groups can take advantage of the conference room facilities, and all guests will enjoy the convenient continental breakfast served each morning. This hotel is situated in a handy section of Pigeon Forge. The Apple Valley farms complex is a short walk away, and the majority of Pigeon Forge's music theaters and outlet shopping malls can be accessed with a brief trolley ride. Seniors receive a 10 percent discount.

Pigeon Forge

During the last 10 years, the section of northern Pigeon Forge and southern Sevierville have fused into one continuous band of businesses geared to the vacationer. As such, most people driving south on the Parkway aren't aware when they've crossed from one city to the next. But one particular characteristic of Pigeon Forge's identity is noticeable, if you're aware of it—a heavier concentration of independently owned accommodations. From smaller, mom-and-pop motels to multi-storied, luxury hotels, fewer of the easily recognized franchise names are represented in this mix. As such, this section will help acquaint you with a healthy dose of unfamiliar names and place less emphasis on the franchises. Since there are so many properties in Pigeon Forge from which to choose, we've presented only a sampling (albeit a large one) of what we feel are the better picks.

Keep in mind another premise when perusing these listings. In Pigeon Forge, especially south of Traffic Light #3, almost every hotel or motel is within easy walking distance of restaurants, entertainment, attractions and shopping. In some cases, where we feel a particular lodging is extremely convenient to a local point of interest, such a reference is made. Otherwise, assume that most anything you want is just outside your door. Also keep in mind that Pigeon Forge has a trolley system with numerous stopping points that can take you inexpensively up and down the Parkway. See our chapter on Getting Around for more specifics.

Mountain Melodies Inn
$$ • 1949 Parkway, Pigeon Forge
• (865) 453-2250, (800) 838-9777

This facility is well placed for those with music and variety shows on their agenda. Directly across the Parkway from the Louise Mandrell Theater, Anita Bryant's Music Mansion and the Glasgow Comedy Dinner & Show, it's within a short walk of several other Pigeon Forge music theaters as well. Open since 1995, Mountain Melodies Inn has 60 standard rooms and 25 suites offering queen and king beds. All rooms include private balconies and refrigerators. Fireplaces and whirlpool tubs are available in suites. Their in-room television system provides the latest movie hits on a pay-per-view basis. The hotel is a five-story building that provides interior access to all rooms, and there's plenty of room for the family car in the two-level parking area.

Ramada Limited
$$$ • 2193 Parkway, Pigeon Forge
• (865) 428-0668, (800) 269-1222

This Ramada Limited successfully puts forth a pleasant country decor without slipping into tackiness. The many wooden fixtures and the stacked stone fireplace in the lobby are just some of the elements that help create a cozy, rustic ambience when you enter. When it comes to amenities, however, this property is certainly not primitive. Guests can take advantage of a spacious indoor pool and whirlpool partially surrounded by large and numerous windows. An exercise room, game room and breakfast room are also

INSIDERS' TIP
Although the number of visitors to the Smoky Mountains drops off dramatically at the end of summer, there is always a heavy influx of vacationers in October who come to see the stunning fall foliage, which peaks around the second or third week of the month. We recommend making reservations for this time of the year many months in advance.

on hand for traveling convenience. All of the 126 standard rooms in this three-story, interior-access hotel feature two queen beds, a refrigerator and a microwave. There are also nine suites on the premises that include coffee makers, fireplaces and in-room whirlpool tubs. Overall, the furnishings and trappings combine both elegance and simplistic country charm. All rooms are also equipped with VCRs, and a movie rental center is located in the lobby. This Ramada Limited is in a location central to the Pigeon Forge music theater community (many are within walking distance) as well as an abundance of restaurants and outlet shopping opportunities. They honor both AAA and senior discounts.

Music Road Hotel
$$$$$ • 303 Henderson Chapel Road, Pigeon Forge • (865) 429-7700, (800) 429-7700

Just one block off the Parkway, this hotel goes all out to provide a total vacation experience, on a large scale and at a competitive price, considering all that's available. The beige, seven-story structure towers above lush, colorful landscaping and the peaceful waters of the Little Pigeon River. As a matter of fact, guests can relax in rocking chairs along the lobby level observation deck that runs the entire riverside length of the building. The river isn't the only water to be enjoyed here, however. The outside pool area is like a mini water park, complete with pool, waterfall, fountain, spiral slide and Lazy River ride. Kids will also appreciate the nearby arcade and snack bar. The indoor pool is open 24 hours a day and includes a whirlpool area as well.

The 90 standard rooms and 73 suites also reflect Music Road Hotel's overall attention to detail. All rooms are accessed from inside the hotel and 80 percent of them are smoke-free. The standard rooms are substantially larger than the average hotel room. Each comes with two queen beds and a roster of amenities including a refrigerator, a microwave, a private balcony, and an iron and ironing board. The bathrooms are conveniently equipped with two sinks, a linen closet, a hair dryer and a telephone. The suites are similarly outfitted but also offer fireplaces, in-room whirlpools and king-sized beds.

When you first step into the Music Road Hotel, you're drawn into the large, open lobby by its elegant furnishings, wood floors, and huge stacked stone fireplace. Just off the lobby is a generous continental breakfast area which includes muffins, pastries, cereals, bagels and, of course, coffee. Also found on the first floor are a number of meeting rooms for groups and businesses as well as another arcade. Music Road Hotel offers senior discounts and group rates.

Heartlander Country Star Resort
$$$ • 2385 Parkway, Pigeon Forge • (865) 453-4106, (800) 843-6686

This hotel's central proximity to both outlet shopping malls and music theaters makes it a strategic choice for the vacationer. The multi size conference and meeting facilities offered make Heartlander Country Star Resort a logical option for the business traveler.

Heartlander's 160 standard rooms and eight suites each contain either two double beds or a king bed as well as private balconies for enjoying Smoky Mountain views. This property is five stories tall, provides interior room access, has a large game room with pool table and boasts a shop where guests can pick up gifts and sundries. An outdoor pool, indoor pool and whirlpool spa round out this hotel's guest package. Pets are allowed, but owners are required to pay a one-time, non-refundable fee of $20. AAA and Senior discounts are honored, and children younger than 12 stay free.

Radisson Inn & Suites Pigeon Forge
$$$$$ • 2423 Teaster Ln., Pigeon Forge • (865) 429-3700, (800) 333-3333

At this Radisson property, comfort, convenience and inspiring views make for a winning Smokies vacation combination. The seven-story, coral-hued building is located a short distance off the Parkway on a quiet hilltop, peacefully removed from the bustle of traffic. This site provides a direct "back road" route to Belz Factory Outlet World and Tanger Outlet Mall, both just down the street.

Inside, a number of services and amenities are found, including a game room, meeting rooms, an expanded continental breakfast, laundry facility and exercise room with sauna. There are two swimming pools, both indoor and outdoor; the interior site has a whirlpool. In-room accommodations are consistent among this Radisson's 70 interior units. Each provides a refrigerator, microwave oven, coffee maker and a private balcony that opens your room to memorable mountain views. Rooms come with either a double queen bed setup or have a single king-sized bed and sleeper sofa. Five spacious suites provide guests with the added luxuries of hair dryers, irons and ironing boards, fireplaces and whirlpool tubs. Built in 1995, Radisson Inn & Suites Pigeon Forge offers discounts for AAA members, seniors and allows children younger than 18 to stay at no additional cost.

Econo Lodge Riverside
$$ • 2440 Parkway, Pigeon Forge
• (865) 428-1231, (800) 632-6104

With 201 units on the premises, Econo Lodge Riverside provides clean and spacious rooms in a pleasant setting near the Little Pigeon River. If you're intent is to dive into the music theaters and shopping opportunities in Pigeon Forge, you'll find this motel to be handily situated. Belz Factory Outlet World and Tanger Outlet Mall are a short distance away, as is Ogle's Water Park. When you're not out on the town, you'll find relaxation at either the outdoor pool area or the picnic spot down by the river. For sleeping arrangements, you may select a room with either two double beds or one king bed. Nicely priced, this Econo Lodge honors AAA and Senior discounts and does not charge extra for children younger than 18.

Mountain Trace Inn
$$$ • 130 Wears Valley Rd. West,
Pigeon Forge • (865) 453-6785,
(800) 453-6785

This is, perhaps, one of the best-placed accommodations in Pigeon Forge. Ogle's Water Park, two outlet malls, a supermarket and a coin-operated laundry are all within easy walking distance. It is just off the Parkway on Wears Valley Road, one of the routes to the scenic and historic communities of Wears Valley and Townsend. The building itself consists of four floors and 89 exterior access rooms. All rooms have two queen beds and refrigerators. There are also three family suites and 10 honeymoon suites that are enhanced by amenities such as whirlpool tubs, fireplaces and kitchenettes. The main part of the motel was constructed in 1992, with 42 units added in 1995. Another recent addition was the indoor pool and whirlpool facility that conveniently features changing rooms. Other services which guests might consider a boon include a free continental breakfast and nondenominational worship services held each Sunday morning. Mountain Trace Inn has AAA and senior discounts. Their rates are flat, per-room fees that allow up to five people per room.

Timbers Log Motel
$$$ •134 Wears Valley Rd. East,
Pigeon Forge • (865) 428-5216,
(800) 445-1803

Shopping fanatics, this is the place you want to be! Timbers Log Motel can be found directly across Teaster Lane from Belz Factory Outlet World, Tanger Outlet Mall and other retail finds like Westpoint Stevens (a bed, bath and linen outlet) and Old Time Pottery (housewares galore). While you're shopping, the kids can go nuts themselves across the street at The Track, an amusement center featuring go-carts, miniature golf, bungee jumping and video games (see our Attractions and Kidstuff chapters).

The motel itself, however, offers plenty of its own charms. With an exterior constructed of hewn logs and mortar, this lodging conveys the feel of a mountain cabin, but does so in the heart of Pigeon Forge activities. There are 22 standard rooms that have either two queen beds or one king bed, and also reflect this same rustic approach. Some of the rooms, but not all, include a refrigerator or coffee maker. There are also 20 suites steeped in woodsiness and set up in a variety of configurations, including a two-level layout. Some are tailored to families, with kitchenettes and multi-bed arrangements that can sleep up to six. Some are more suitable for honeymooners, with fireplaces and whirlpool tubs. Timbers Log Motel was built in 1989 and provides three floors of exterior access rooms. Pets are allowed with a one-time $10 fee, and discounts are available for seniors. The rates charged are on a flat, per-room basis.

Days Inn
$$$ • 2760 Parkway, Pigeon Forge
• (865) 453-4707, (800) 645-3079

This Days Inn lies near the heart of the Pigeon Forge "strip" and its highly concentrated mix of restaurants, attractions and shopping options. It also delivers spacious, well-appointed rooms and suites at reasonable rates. The 120 rooms and 23 suites are all exterior-access and spread out over three floors. Standard rooms have two queen beds plus refrigerators, and whirlpool tubs are available in suites. The inn gives discounts to AARP and Days Inn Club members.

Valley Forge Inn
$$$ • 2795 Parkway, Pigeon Forge
• (865) 453-7770, (800) 544-8740

Developed in three phases beginning in 1988, Valley Forge Inn supplies a mixed bag of room layouts and amenities. The inn's 150 standard rooms and 21 suites are divided among three buildings, the tallest of which is four stories; rooms are accessible from the outside as well as interior hallways. In the original structure you'll find that the typical room has two queen beds and a well-remodeled package of furnishings and decor. The second and third buildings, which went up in the early and mid 1990s, contain both standard rooms and suites. Some of the perks to be found in many of these include refrigerators, microwave ovens, coffee makers, fireplaces, whirlpool tubs, and private balconies. Some of the newer suites are big enough to sleep six in a single king and two-queen bed combination. On the top level of the newest building there are even ten, two-level townhouses with two bathrooms in each. Valley Forge Inn is near the Little Pigeon River and extends free continental breakfast, a coin operated laundry, indoor and outdoor pools as well as in-room satellite television. Seniors can look for five percent discounts on rates.

Park Tower Inn
$$ • 201 Sharon Dr., Pigeon Forge
• (865) 453-8605, (800) 453-8605

Standing just one block west of the Parkway, Park Tower Inn is one of the best overall values in this area. There are 113 rooms and nine suites on the property, all of which are entered from interior corridors and are spacious and colorfully decorated. Refrigerators, two queen-sized beds and large, open balconies are the norm for standard rooms. Suites and rooms with kitchenettes offer an expanded range of amenities such as whirlpool tubs, fireplaces and coffee makers. On-site conveniences abound at this hotel, which was built in 1994. Three elevators provide easy access to all six floors, and microwave ovens are centrally located at each level. In addition to the outdoor pool, there is a massive indoor aquatic facility, complete with pool, two whirlpool tubs and a Lazy River ride for inner tube relaxation. Vacationers and business travelers alike will appreciate Park Tower Inn's free continental breakfast, guest laundry, game room and exercise facilities. They can also add an excellent security monitoring system and meeting facilities to their roster of pluses. AAA and senior discounts are available, and quoted rates are good for up to four people per room.

Maples Motor Inn
$$ • 2959 Parkway, Pigeon Forge
• (865) 453-8883, (888) 453-8883

Found on the Parkway, a short hop from Pigeon Forge Factory Outlet Mall, this family-owned inn is a nice place to bring your own family. Providing agreeable rooms at an equally agreeable price, Maples Motor Inn has 57 units in its original building, all of which have refrig-

erators. Another section was built in 1996, in which a selection of large, feature-filled suites can be found. These suites provide whirlpools, fireplaces and kitchenettes in a spacious, well-furnished floor plan. Outside, a large pool is flanked by a smaller kiddie pool. Vacationers with children in tow will also benefit from the picnic area and toddler playground found on the grassy lawn. Maples Motor Inn is closed during January and February and takes all major credit cards except for American Express. Children younger than 3 stay at no additional charge.

Mountain Breeze Motel
$$-$$$ • 2926 Parkway, Pigeon Forge
• (865) 453-2659

This newly remodeled, two-story motel in the heart Pigeon Forge's "main drag" treats guests to a number of in-room comforts at a hard-to-beat price. Rates for two people vary, depending on the number and size of beds required. The rates are lowest for rooms with one queen bed, higher for one king bed and higher still for setups with two queen beds. Efficiencies and suites are available as well. All rooms provide guests with a refrigerator and coffee maker while some have microwaves. There is a heated outdoor pool as well as a kiddie pool and hot tub on the premises. Mountain Breeze Motel gives AAA and senior discounts, and honors Visa and Discover cards only.

Willow Brook Lodge
$$$ • 3035 Parkway, Pigeon Forge
• (865) 453-5334, (800) 765-1380

When you first arrive at this motel, your attention is soon drawn to immaculate land-scaping, a homey architectural style and an exterior color scheme that's very easy on the eyes. Sixty-one rooms and 17 suites offer different floor plans, amenities and sleeping arrangements that have been arranged into six different accommodations packages. Guest rooms have either two queen-sized beds or one king-sized bed and sleeper sofa. All have refrigerators, and some have balcony views of the Little Pigeon River. Four suite combinations offer a variety of configurations of queen and king beds, sleeper sofas, whirlpool tubs, fireplaces, microwaves, coffee makers and refrigerators. Some have private balconies and separate living and dining areas. Constructed in 1991, Willow Brook Lodge provides exterior access to all three floors. Coffee and donuts are provided each morning, and discounts are extended to

AAA members and seniors. Children younger than 12 stay at no extra cost.

Holiday Inn Pigeon Forge Resort Hotel
$$$$$ • 3230 Parkway, Pigeon Forge
• (865) 428-2700, (800) 555-2650

Well-equipped rooms, along with extensive on-site amenities, make this a great headquarters for a vacation or business stay. Approximately 200 rooms and 10 suites are housed in this Holiday Inn's five interior-accessible floors. The typical unit has two extra-long double beds, while a few have king-sized beds. All rooms provide a hair dryer, an iron and ironing board and in-room coffee maker for guest convenience. Some rooms come with refrigerators, and microwave ovens are included in the suites.

While the rooms are certainly comfort-intensive, there are plenty of other treasures to be found on the premises, making a stay at this Holiday Inn Resort virtually a vacation in itself. The lobby is open and features a sitting area next to a large, stone fireplace. Further exploration reveals an open arcade area that's reminiscent of a carnival midway. Kids will love the video games and other coin-operated attractions to be found there. Beyond the arcade lies a large atrium section featuring an indoor pool and whirlpool tub. The pool is flanked by lush greenery and a waterfall that cascades from a high stone wall. Other creature comforts available to guests are a laundry facility and an exercise room. Meeting and conference rooms of all sizes are also located on the premises, able to accommodate almost any group with the services and the facilities they need.

This Holiday Inn Resort is one of the few lodgings in the area that boasts a restaurant in the hotel itself. Louie's Restaurant and Grill delivers a well-rounded menu and serves breakfast, lunch and dinner. One of their acclaimed specialties is their all-you-can-eat steak dinner, which gives guests the option of selecting and cooking their own cuts over Louie's large, open grill. The restaurant also provides room service during its business hours and is available to cater banquets in the meeting facilities.

Attention to service is a priority at this particular property, which was a 1997 recipient of Holiday Inn's Torchbearer Award, designating it as one of the top 25 Holiday Inn hotels in the world. Some pets are allowed and babysitting services can be arranged, provided that the hotel is given advance notification in both cases (preferably at the time reservations are made). AAA and Senior discounts are honored. Although room prices are charged as a flat, per-room rate, rollaway beds can be provided for an additional $6.50 fee.

River Lodge South
$$$ • 3251 Parkway, Pigeon Forge
• (865) 453-0783, (800) 233-7581

Although the lobby, office and a handful of rooms are located on the Parkway, the bulk of River Lodge South's 71 rooms and six suites are situated one block to the east, overlooking the Little Pigeon River. Ground floor rooms open in the rear onto a grassy riverside embankment where picnic tables and barbecue grills allow guests the benefits of cooking out near the water. You can also feed the ducks with food purchased from small coin-operated machines located nearby. Units on the second and third floors of the motel have private balconies. Inside the rooms, two queen beds and refrigerators are standard. Several suite options are presented, including various combinations of kitchenettes, fireplaces and in-room whirlpool tubs. Family units are available with split bedroom floor plans. The outdoor pool is heated, and a limited continental breakfast is served in the mornings. Be sure to ask about AAA and senior discounts.

Valley View Motel
$$ • 111 Valley Dr., Pigeon Forge
• (865) 453-2692, (800) 282-8001

This small motel, tucked away one-half block west of the Parkway, has been part of the Pigeon Forge landscape for many years, but was extensively remodeled in recent years. The motel's exterior is quaint and unassuming. Inside, however, its rooms are of a quality rivaling its larger, better-known counterparts. Valley View Motel's 32 units are found mostly on one level of the building with a few on an upper level. Each room has a refrigerator and either a single king bed, a single queen bed or two double beds. A few have balconies facing the Parkway. There are no smoke-free rooms available, and the motel is closed December through March. Senior discounts are offered, but they don't take American Express.

Vacation Lodge
$$-$$$$ • 3450 Parkway, Pigeon Forge
• (865) 453-2640, (800) 468-1998

When Pigeon Forge's business district consisted of a couple of gift shops, a general store, and a motel all clustered around the city's only traffic light, the Vacation Lodge was the motel. Like the city, the Vacation Lodge grew in all directions during the 1980s to its present size of more than 90 rooms in a variety of sizes. Ample parking and central location make the Vacation Lodge a favorite of people planning to park their cars where they're staying and enjoy Pigeon Forge on foot or by using the Funtime Trolley. The Old Mill area, one of the city's oldest shopping centers and still the place where most of the handcrafts and truly unique gifts are available, is across the Parkway and a block back on Old Mill Street.

River Chase Motel
$$$$ • 3709 Parkway, Pigeon Forge
• (865) 428-1299, (888) 754-3316

Originally built in 1982, the River Chase has constantly upgraded itself to the 105-unit facility that sits at the corner of Dollywood Lane today. The four-story structure has a variety of up-scale rooms and an enviable return rate to attest to its treatment of its guests. From double rooms to super suites with private balconies, refrigerators, and microwave ovens, the River Chase offers a high degree of comfort and convenience, and one of the most exciting attractions around for the kids: The inside and outside swimming pools each have their own water slide! The inside slide is over 100 feet long.

Briarstone Inn
$$$ • 3626 Parkway, Pigeon Forge
• (865) 453-3050, (800) 523-3919

Convenient to most of Pigeon Forge's amusements and restaurants, the Briarstone Inn is operated by one of the city's oldest and most experienced host families. Comfortable rooms with queen beds, in-room coffee, pay-per-view TV, and available Jacuzzi and fireplace suites provide a wide range of choices for any size group from honeymooners to families. AARP and senior citizen discounts are offered, as well as special discounts at local restaurants.

Bilmar Motor Inn
$$-$$$ • 3786 Parkway, Pigeon Forge
• (865) 453-5593, (800) 343-5610

Another of Pigeon Forge's more established motels, the Bilmar was built in 1976 on what was then the southern edge of town. It's closer to the center now, but the 76 rooms at the Bilmar are still as comfortable and welcoming as the folks who have greeted their guests for over 20 years. A large open area in front of the heated swimming pool makes the Bilmar a favorite spot for watching the parade of hot rods and vintage cars that invades Pigeon Forge most

weekends of the summer. And since a good number of the car owners stay at the Bilmar, up-close and personal views that you wouldn't normally get are right at your door.

Norma Dan Motel
$$$ • 3864 Parkway, Pigeon Forge
• (865) 453-2403, (800) 582-7866

Celebrating its 41st season under single-family ownership, the Norma Dan has kept pace with the growth of Pigeon Forge. From its small beginnings as a 12-room motel in 1958, the Norma Dan has expanded to the beautiful 85-room multi-story structure it is today, with one of Pigeon Forge's biggest swimming pools. Because of its popularity with tour groups, the Norma Dan also has one of the biggest and best-protected off-street parking lots in the city. Some of the Norma Dan's earliest couples, who spent their honeymoons in the mountains, are still coming back, and now they take advantage of the AARP discount program.

River's Landing Resort
$$$-$$$$ • 4025 Parkway, Pigeon Forge
• (865) 453- 9081, (800) 345-6799

River's Landing was a landmark when it stood practically alone on the south end of Pigeon Forge back in 1969, but now it's closer to the center of town. 131 rooms with easy access to the on-site restaurant and the biggest indoor swimming pool in the Smokies have made the River's Landing popular with two and three generations of families who come back year after year. A playground for the little ones and the large poolside arcade for the bigger kids will keep everyone occupied while Mom and Dad kick back for a while in the hot tub. Guest laundry service is available as an added convenience.

Capri Motel
$$$ • 4061 Parkway, Pigeon Forge
• (865) 453-7147, (800) 528-4555

Down home southern hospitality is the hallmark at the Capri, and with 80 percent of their guests coming back every year, you've got to figure the Ownbys know how to run a motel. They should—it's all they've ever done. The Capri's spacious front lawn and immaculate landscaping and swimming pool are just an indication that the recently remodeled 106 rooms are going to be the same way. Add the free continental breakfast served every morning and the special meeting facilities for bus-size corporate and family groups, and the covered trolley stop right at the front door, and you know the Capri is going to take good care of you during your stay in the Smokies.

Green Valley Motel
$-$$$ • 4109 Parkway, Pigeon Forge
• (865) 453-9091, (800) 892-1627

The Green Valley Motel was built mainly to lodge families, and its 70 percent rate of repeat visitors indicates it was done right. Ground-floor access to most of the 50 rooms and convenient restaurants and gift shops in easy walking distance have made the Green Valley a popular lodging place for generations of visitors to the Smokies. The outlet store adjacent to the Green Valley is operated by the same family that built it all, and most of the veteran guests do a lot of their shopping without ever leaving the property.

River's Landing
$$$$ • 3929 South River Rd., Pigeon Forge
• (865) 453-4444, (888) 345-6799

No, it's not a misprint or a repeat; River's Landing has opened a new 50-room motel on the Little Pigeon River, just a short distance from its original place on the Parkway. Private balconies overlooking the river and fireplaces in every room make the River's Landing on the river a cozy place to enjoy an evening without any outside distractions. The public hot tubs beside the pool and the same friendly service that made the original River's Landing a big favorite are all present in the new edition. We expect the new River's Landing to enjoy the same lofty level of popularity as its senior sibling up the street.

Creekstone Inn
$$$$ • 4034 South River Rd., Pigeon Forge
• (865) 453-3557, (800) 523-3919

A new standard in gracious living, the Creekstone is a 172-room high-rise hotel on the Little Pigeon River, with a full slate of amenities to please the family, the honeymooner, or the most discriminating guest. Spacious rooms and suites with fireplaces, refrigerators, in-room coffee makers, and Jacuzzis make staying in your room a

INSIDERS' TIP

Each of the primary cities in Sevier County has some type of hotel/motel association which can provide more specific information about its members. You can call each city's Chamber of Commerce or Department of Tourism for the current contact and phone number for each of these associations. The Chambers themselves will be happy to provide you with additional lodging information as well. Sevierville Chamber of Commerce, (865) 453-6411; Pigeon Forge Department of Tourism, (865) 453-8574; Gatlinburg Chamber of Commerce, (865) 430-4148.

pleasure when the pressure of enjoying your vacation starts to wear a little bit. Convenient parking on the ground level, with elevators to the rooms above, takes the hassle out of getting to your car or your room. The private balconies that grace each room provide a great place to watch and feed the resident flock of ducks, and the river running along the back edge is an inviting place to just sit and watch or go down and cool your tired feet.

Gatlinburg

As the progenitor of the tourism industry in the Smokies, Gatlinburg is still a favorite lodging place for veteran visitors. In fact, Gatlinburg's nearly 100 hotels and motels, boasting a total of nearly 6,300 rooms, depend heavily on repeat business. The lodging scene in Gatlinburg runs through the full spectrum of accommodations, from old-fashioned tourist cabins in settled neighborhoods to luxury high-rise hotels in the heart of downtown. The list that follows is a representative sample of the broad variety of hotels and motels in Gatlinburg, most of which are in walking distance of the downtown business district. Those that require more than a 10-minute walk to the Parkway are all within 100 yards of a trolley stop. All of Gatlinburg's hotels and motels provide handicap accessibility with ground-floor entrances to rooms that are specifically designated for smoking or non-smoking use.

Most of the multi-story facilities have elevators, and all have ramps between levels. Most offer AARP and senior citizen discounts; call ahead to be sure.

The facilities listed will be in order as follows, and please remember this is a sampling, not a complete list. First, we'll deal with the entire length of the Parkway, from the entrance to town at the Highland Motor Inn to the Clarion, which is within 100 yards of the Great Smoky Mountains National Park entrance ("On the Parkway"). Next, we'll go back to traffic light #6 and turn left (east) onto Cherokee Orchard Road to look at the idyllic Baskins Creek section. Then, from traffic light #5, we'll travel south and west along River Road and into the Ski Mountain neighborhood west of the Parkway. Our next grouping is on Airport Road (traffic light #8—the Space Needle corner), and includes a mixture of large convention-oriented and small family owned motels. Finally, we'll travel east out U.S. 321N from traffic light #3, where most of the smaller independent facilities and Gatlinburg's biggest independently-owned motel are found.

Parkway

Highland Motor Inn
$$$ • 131 Parkway, Gatlinburg
• (865) 436-4110, (800) 635-8874

The Highland is easy to find; it's the first building you'll see on the right as you enter Gatlinburg on the Spur. Opened in 1962, the Highland has the Parkway at its front door and the Little Pigeon River and North Gatlinburg Park behind it. Pets are welcome at the Highland (limit two, nominal fee). There are several amusements and shops in the immediate area, and the green route trolley stops at the Highland's front door.

Stony Brook Motel
$$ • 167 Parkway, Gatlinburg
• (865) 436-5652, (800) 633-5652

Away from the center of town but conveniently near it on the green trolley route, the Stony Brook Motel has 40 rooms with fireplaces and refrigerators. Several amusements and stores are in sight without going into the downtown area. The Stony Brook is a favorite gathering place for the contestants that invade Gatlinburg every April for a nationally popular Scrabble tournament.

Rivermont Motor Inn
$$$ • 293 Parkway, Gatlinburg
• (865) 436-5047, (800) 624-2929 out of state, (800) 634-2929 in Tennessee

Three floors of private balconies directly over the Little Pigeon River (you can fish from your balcony!) make you forget there's bumper-to-bumper traffic right outside the door. From standard two-bed rooms to luxury suites with fireplaces and Jacuzzis, the Rivermont's spectacular view of the river and the mountains in the background make you forget you're in a city at all. Built before the tourist boom of the 1970s, the Rivermont is a classic reminder of what the Smokies are really all about.

Rocky Waters Motor Inn
$$$-$$$$ • 333 Parkway, Gatlinburg
• 7861, (800) 824-1111

When Ralph Lawson first built the Rocky Waters in the late 1930s, the road ran down the other side of the river. When the new road was built, the Rocky Waters' owners built a bridge and a new building on the new Parkway, and now it's the only motel in town with units on both sides of the river. A hundred rooms and three cabins provide a broad variety of accommodations, all with private balconies on the Little Pigeon River. The on-site launderette is a step-saver for Mom after the kids have enjoyed an afternoon in one of the two pools, or after a relaxing dip in one of the spas.

Best Western Zoder's Inn
$$$$ • 402 Parkway, Gatlinburg
• (865) 436-5681, (800) 528-1234

Wallace Zoder came to the Smokies in 1934 to work as an engineer in the developing national park. Seeing the early potential of the area, Wallace built his motel beside the Parkway (it was called Main Street then) to house the summer guests who were beginning to trickle in. The old building is gone now, replaced over the years by the ultra-modern 90-room structure that pampers today's travelers, but Wallace and Dot Zoder's traditions of service and comfortable, courteous accommodation are being carried on by their children and grandchildren. World-class luxury at surprisingly reasonable rates are the norm at Zoder's. Not content with the continental breakfast you can get most anywhere, the Zoders have added a sumptuous wine and cheese reception from 5 to 7 PM every evening, and a great cookies-and-milk bedtime snack from 8 to 10 PM, all served in the refreshment bar next to the guest lobby. And, as if that's not enough to satisfy anybody, a walk along the creek to the back of the six-acre woodland will wash a whole day's cares away.

Best Western Twin Islands
$$$ • 539 Parkway, Gatlinburg
• (865) 436-5121, (800) 223-9299

How about an island right in the middle of downtown Gatlinburg? Well, there's only two, and the Luther Ogle family built a superb motel that uses up both of them. 109 rooms, all with river views and some with private balconies, surround a central courtyard that makes you feel like you're in a private resort. All of downtown Gatlinburg is just outside the front driveway. Like the rest of the old-line family properties, Twin Islands furnishes the rooms like living rooms instead of bedrooms, with fireplaces and Jacuzzis available in several suites. If you're looking for complete privacy, the Honeymoon Island suites provide isolation without taking you away from the bright lights.

Greystone Lodge at the Aquarium
$$$ • 559 Parkway, Gatlinburg
• (865) 436-5621, (800) 451-9202

If you're in the part of the Greystone that's across the street from that huge construction project, you're looking at one of Gatlinburg's most exciting new additions: Ripley's Aquarium in the Smokies is described in detail in our Attractions chapter. If you're at the other end of the Greystone, you're looking at the west prong of the Little Pigeon River. This is a big complex—260 rooms in all, in several structures that reach as high as five stories along the river and stretch out for more than a quarter of a mile. Continental breakfast is served every morning from 7 to 10 in the refreshment bar beside the lobby. Several room configurations vary from two double beds to queen and king rooms, some with hot tubs and fireplaces.

Riverside Motor Lodge
$$$ • 715 Parkway, Gatlinburg
• (865) 436-4194 • (800) 887-2323

The original Riverside Motor Lodge was built in 1925 by local entrepreneur Steve Whaley, who insisted to his amused friends that "Some day a half-million people a year will visit Gatlinburg!" A commemorative plaque on the front wall identifies the Riverside as Gatlinburg's oldest continuously operated lodging establishment. Steve Whaley lived to see his prediction realized, and much more. The Riverside has undergone a lot of changes in the ensuing 70-plus years, including the establishment of Gatlinburg's first shopping mall as an attachment to the front of the building. Today's Riverside is a combination of old and new, with enough repeat business to make reservations hard to come by in the summer, especially on weekends, when the place is taken over by square dance groups from all over the country. Now in the center of the downtown business district that grew up around it, the Riverside hearkens back to a gentler time with its paneled and carpeted hallways leading to comfortable rooms furnished like sitting rooms of days gone by. Originally built on ground that led to the banks of the Little Pigeon River, the Riverside now has River Road at its back door, where a separate lobby welcomes the trav-

eler. By clinging stubbornly to the spirit in which it was built, the Riverside Motor Lodge has established itself as a living example of how Gatlinburg's original innkeepers felt they should treat their guests.

Ramada Inn Four Seasons
$$$-$$$$ • 756 Parkway, Gatlinburg
• (865) 436-7881 • (800) 933-8678

The Ramada is as close to the middle of everything as you're likely to find, but its unique layout shelters its guests from the hubbub on the street. With 148 luxurious units, plus two cabins, the Ramada offers a variety of accommodations that's hard to match even in Gatlinburg. The indoor swimming pool is one of the city's more elegant, and the on-site convention facility has three good-sized meeting rooms, a full stage, and its own kitchen. The Gatlinburg Convention Center is just a block away, and you'll walk past several restaurants and a full slate of attractions to get there.

McKay's Inn Downtown
$$-$$$ • 903 Parkway, Gatlinburg
• (865) 436-5102, (800) 625-2971

Having celebrated 50 years of lodging visitors in 1998, McKay's Inn Downtown has a pretty good handle on what the tourist is looking for in the Smokies. Seventy-four rooms and suites provide enough variety to satisfy any taste, and McKay's location directly across from the Gatlinburg Convention Center makes it a natural for convention and tour groups. McKay's is affiliated with several major travel clubs, including Encore, and supports several motor coach associations. A set of large rooms with a balcony directly overlooking the Parkway provides one of Gatlinburg's favorite gathering places for parade watchers.

Quality Inn at The Convention Center
$$$-$$$$ • 938 Parkway, Gatlinburg
• (865) 436-5607, (800) 933-8674

If the wall between the two buildings ever falls down, it'll be the Quality Inn *in* the convention center. This beautifully designed motel is literally the Convention Center's next door neighbor—both facilities are built right on the property line that separates them. Convenience is only part of the story here. The unique topography of this motel provides a spectacular view of the mountains out the back and arm's length availability of more than two dozen attractions and restaurants out the front. Most of the rooms are unusually large and well appointed, with comfortable furniture in addition to home-style amenities that tell you this is more than the usual "chain" property.

Bon-Air Lodge
$$$ •950 Parkway, Gatlinburg
• (865) 436-4857, (800) 848-4857

Tucked into a hillside just off the Parkway, the Bon-Air has a stairway leading down to the back yard of the Gatlinburg Convention Center. Recently renovated from top to bottom, the Bon-Air features 74 oversized rooms with a choice of bed configurations, fireplaces, and Jacuzzis. The view of the mountains from the balconies on the back building is spectacular, and the popular veranda on the front building overlooks the Parkway. If you can tear yourself away, downtown Gatlinburg is at your doorstep and the Great Smoky Mountains National Park entrance is just a couple of blocks up the Parkway.

Clarion Inn & Suites
$$$$$ • 1100 Parkway, Gatlinburg
• (865) 436-5656, (800) 933-0777

Luxury is the minimum standard at the Clarion—every one of the 131 rooms, from king and queen bed double units to the penthouse suites with their own elevators, is richly appointed to pamper the most demanding guest. Private balconies in every room provide great views, and the only rooftop meeting and banquet facilities in Gatlinburg give a special flavor to large gatherings. And speaking of flavor, the Clarion's deluxe continental breakfast is renowned as one of the best in a town famous for that sort of thing Several unique gift and sundry shops are located in the building, and the aerial tramway to Ober Gatlinburg is just across the street. The Clarion is just 100 yards from the entrance to the Great Smoky Mountains National Park, and four of Gatlinburg's finest restaurants are in that space, along with the interesting Calhoun's Village, one of the city's newest shopping malls.

Baskins Creek Neighborhood

Jack Huff's Motor Lodge
$$ • 204 Cherokee Orchard Rd., Gatlinburg
• (865) 436-5171, (800) 32-1817

Nobody alive in Gatlinburg can remember when the Huff family didn't operate several lodging facilities, and Jack Huff's is one of the oldest. Located a block off the Parkway and directly across the street from Pi Beta Phi elementary school, Jack Huff's Motor Lodge is another of the many independent motels in the city that reminds us of a different time. Sixty clean, comfortable rooms are maintained in a style that makes the guests feel at home, and it must be working—more than 75 percent of Huff's business is made up of people who've stayed there before. The coffee pot that awaits the guests every morning in the lobby is a gathering spot for what seems to be an ongoing reunion. Downtown Gatlinburg is just outside the door at the rear entrance to the Village, one of Gatlinburg's most popular shopping malls.

Bales Town & Country Motel
$$ • 221 Bishop Ln., Gatlinburg
• (865) 436-4773, (800) 458-8249

Bill Bales' father built the original motel in 1956, and now Bill III and his wife Marsha welcome old and new guests. In addition to standard guest rooms where comfort is the keynote, the Bales Motel also has a couple of townhouses and a cottage on the grounds for larger parties. Long-term rentals are available, and guests paying for six nights will get their seventh night free. Two blocks from downtown Gatlinburg in the secluded Baskins Creek neighborhood, Bales Town & Country offers a glimpse of how the local families live.

Jerry Lee Motel
$$-$$$ • 208 Woliss Ln., Gatlinburg
• (865) 436-5198

You can sit on your balcony at the Jerry Lee Motel and get as good a view of the mountains as you're likely to find anywhere. Stroll a couple of blocks through a quiet neighborhood in the other direction and you're in the heart of the downtown business district. The kids won't be bored while you're gazing at the scenery, either—the Jerry Lee has its own arcade right next to the on-site grocery store and swimming pool. This is another of Gatlinburg's old-line family-owned and operated accommodations, opened in the 1960s by the grandfather of the current manager.

Johnson's Inn
$$$ • 242 Bishop Ln., Gatlinburg
• (865) 436-4881, (800) 842-1930

Originally built in 1946 and constantly improved to keep pace with the times, Johnson's Inn sits within sight of downtown, but not within hearing distance. The four-story tower that contains most of the motel's 48 rooms has an elevator and gently sloped ramps for total wheelchair accessibility. Johnson's customer loyalty is so high and so important to the owners that they publish their own newsletter to keep their guests up to date with what's going on in their home away from home. Jacuzzi suites and fireplaces in selected rooms provide for pleasurable evenings away from the maddening crowds.

Kingwood Inn
$$-$$$$ • 117 Bishop Ln., Gatlinburg
• (865) 436-4509, (800) 637-3143

Tucked into a mountainside at the end of the road, the Kingwood offers seclusion from the hubbub of the business district, three blocks away. Seven cottages on the grounds provide additional privacy for larger groups, and the Kingwood has a launderette for the convenience of its guests. The popularity of the Kingwood as a home away from home is attested to by the fact that 80 percent of their guests have returned annually since their 1964 opening.

River Road & Ski Mountain

River Terrace Resort & Convention Center
$$$-$$$$$ • 240 River Rd., Gatlinburg
• (865) 436-5161, (800) 521-3523, (800) 251-2040

For a place as close to town as it is, the River Terrace offers guests in its 205 rooms an awful lot of good reasons not to leave the grounds. One of the city's favorite restaurants is right in the center, two heated outdoor pools and the spa are convenient, and there's a lounge for the nightlife lover. Toss in the on-site health food store with its own lunch menu and yoga, aerobics, and martial arts sessions, and you might not have time to go anywhere else. The River Terrace's 20,000 square-foot convention center is large enough to attract good-sized convention groups or huge family reunions. Advance notice is requested and a deposit is required if you plan to bring your pets.

Riverhouse Motorlodge
$$$-$$$$$ • 610 River Rd., Gatlinburg
• (865) 436-7821

The Riverhouse believes in pampering its guests. Spacious rooms with a choice of beds and fireplaces (choose wood or gas logs—after Labor Day) have private balconies overlooking the Little Pigeon River. It's hard to stand on the balcony and believe you're only a block from downtown Gatlinburg. And, maybe best of all, the staff at the Riverhouse will deliver a continental breakfast tray to your room every

morning! Long, easy grade ramps make the second floor rooms easily accessible to wheelchairs.

King's Motel
$$-$$$ • 625 River Rd., Gatlinburg
• (865) 436-4396, (800) 762-3914

King's Motel has been owned and operated by the King family since 1939. Thirty-eight reasonably priced rooms with available kitchenettes, and a rental house on the property that will sleep a family of six, have made King's Motel a gathering place for generations of families. King's is convenient to the Parkway by a sidewalk that runs alongside the large parking deck at its side, if you really want to leave the peaceful courtyard and swimming pool. Our Insiders also got a special surprise when we made a second trip back to this place, but you can read about that in our Campgrounds and RV Parks chapter.

Fairfield Inn
$$$$ • 680 River Rd., Gatlinburg
• (865) 430-7200, (800) 228-2800

Laid out in a park-like setting along the Little Pigeon River, the Fairfield's 54 rooms all have fireplaces and private balconies overlooking the water. The hot tub suites and extra large king suites heighten the relaxed atmosphere. The quiet setting on River Road is just far enough away from downtown to shield the bright lights and noise, but close enough to walk in less than five minutes. Ober Gatlinburg's aerial tramway mall is less than a block away, and so are several excellent family restaurants.

Best Western Fabulous Chalet Inn
$$$$ • 310 Cottage Dr., Gatlinburg
• (865) 436-5607, (800) 933-8675

Just across the river from River Road (turn at the traffic light by the Ober Gatlinburg tramway mall), the Fabulous Chalet has a combination of river views and mountain views. Regardless of whether your room has a single king bed or a suite with a hot tub and fireplace, the view is breathtaking. Set back in one of Gatlinburg's nicer residential areas, the Fab Chalet (local parlance) is a short stroll from a couple of truly outstanding restaurants and the Ober Gatlinburg tramway mall, and about two blocks from the entrance to the Great Smoky Mountains National Park. Downtown Gatlinburg is about three blocks in the other direction.

Riverhouse at the Park
$$$$$ • 205 Ski Mountain Rd., Gatlinburg
• (865) 436-2070

At the southwest intersection of River Road

and Ski Mountain Road, Riverhouse at the Park is conveniently situated for a short walk into downtown Gatlinburg or a short hike into the Great Smoky Mountains National Park. There's a trail just across the river that's a great favorite with local exercise walkers at all hours of the day and night. Forty-eight rooms at three levels of accommodation, ranging from merely wonderful to "I don't deserve this" offer spectacular views of the Little Pigeon River and the mountains. Creature comforts, from whirlpool baths to wet bars and fireplaces, abound, and the Riverhouse staff brings your breakfast to your room every morning. The level of pampering at the Riverhouse would make anybody feel guilty that wasn't totally convinced they deserve it.

Grand Prix Motel
$-$$$ • 235 Ski Mountain Rd., Gatlinburg
• (865) 436-4561, (800) 732-2082

With the Park for its back yard, the Grand Prix offers special low-cost lodging for hikers among its 30 rooms. Two kitchen units will accommodate up to eight people each, and honeymoon suites are also available. An on-site laundromat provides real convenience for the family. Pets are always welcome at the Grand Prix.

Watson's Motel
$$ • 426 Ski Mountain Rd., Gatlinburg
• (865) 436-4747, (800) 621-8249

Herbert and Georgia Watson built their original motel in 1948. Daughter Alana Tinker has kept the property under family control and improved it to its present 67-room status, plus a family-size guest cottage. Kitchens are available in almost half of the rooms, and the motel has its own after-hours attraction that's kept a lot of their visitors coming back year after year: Bears and deer come out of the Park wilderness across the street almost every night to eat at Watson's. If you brought your pets with you, keep them in your room during the side show.

Airport Road

Airport Road runs uphill from the Parkway at Traffic Light #8, which is the corner where the Space Needle rises from the street. An eclectic combination of lodging places runs from small (20 rooms and less) family-owned motels to two of the city's largest franchise establishments. The Gatlinburg Convention Center and churches representing most Christian denominations are all convenient to the Airport Road motels.

Gillette Motel
$$$ • 235 Airport Rd., Gatlinburg
• (865) 436-5601, (865) 436-5376,
(800) 437-0815

A block up Airport Road from the Parkway, the Gillette Motel is directly across the street from the Gatlinburg Convention Center. The 80 rooms in an imposing three-story structure are usually filled during the summer by repeat visitors and convention-goers, but the location makes the Gillette worth a look. During the Christmas season the Gillette is a consistent prize-winner for its spectacular lighting efforts.

Bearland Lodge & General Store
$$$ • 305 Airport Rd., Gatlinburg
• (865) 436-4565,
(800) 654-8827 (in Tennessee),
(800) 654-9593 (out-of-state)

Location is only part of the story here. The Bearland is right across the street from the Gatlinburg Convention Center, and a long enough block from the Parkway to feel secluded. The 30 rooms have enough variations to satisfy any taste and most family sizes, and the Bearland General Store is one of the most popular shopping places in the neighborhood. Fireplace units are stocked with unlimited wood in season, and a new fire is laid each morning by the housekeeping staff. Six downtown churches are within a three-block walk.

Rocky Top Village Inn
$$$ • 311 Airport Rd., Gatlinburg
• (865) 436-7826, (800) 553-7738

Named for Tennessee's state song, the Rocky Top is owned by the tune's co-writer, Felice Bryant. Eighty-nine luxurious rooms in several configurations appeal to most tastes, and a guest loyalty rate of more than 75 percent attests to the Rocky Top's hospitable treatment. Bring your pets, too—they're welcome at the Rocky Top (advance notification appreciated).

Alto Motel
$$ • 404 Airport Rd., Gatlinburg
• (865) 436-5175, (800) 456-4336

An intimate 21-unit facility, the Alto specializes in quiet accommodation. Three blocks from downtown and within walking distance of five churches, the Alto maintains an atmosphere of peace and quiet that reflects the mountains. Because 70 percent of its guests are annual repeaters, the Alto suggests all reservations be made in advance.

Gazebo Inn

$$$ • 417 Airport Rd., Gatlinburg
• (865) 436-2222

A lovely front lawn surrounded by flowers greets you at the Gazebo Inn, establishing an air of serenity that carries right through the comfortable 60-room structure. Guests are pampered in the Bavarian ambience that fits the Smokies perfectly. Connecting rooms, fireplaces, non-smoking rooms, balconies, and patios all combine to make the Gazebo a relaxing place when the pressures of travel are at their most pressing.

Days Inn-Glenstone Lodge

$$$ • 504 Airport Rd., Gatlinburg
• (865) 436-9361, (800) 362-9522

This place is definitely not what you expect when you hear the name. If this place leaves a light on for you in every room they'll illuminate a fair stretch of Airport Road, and that only covers about a quarter of what's available. More than 200 comfortable rooms with king, queen, or double beds (you choose) and eight deluxe and executive-type suites surround a central atrium that's totally isolated from the street. Full banquet and catering facilities complement the award-winning restaurant (see our Restaurants chapter) and on-premise meeting rooms, and the Gatlinburg Convention Center is close enough to reach in less than a five-minute walk.

Holiday Inn Sunspree Resort

$$$$ • 520 Airport Rd.,
Gatlinburg
• (865) 436-9201,
(800) 435-9201,
Groups (888) 562-2946

You won't have any trouble finding the Sunspree—just put your shades on and look for the sign that almost renders them useless. It wouldn't be totally fair to call the big pink Sunspree sign garish (it's a nice shade), but it sure is bright.

The Sunspree itself is brilliant. Forget the name "Holiday Inn"—if this place could float it'd be the greatest luxury cruise ship you could imagine. The Holidome, the central part of the complex where you check in and out, has a full-service restaurant, a lounge with planned family and adult activities, a market/deli, a pizza counter, and a pool with extra seating space to eat while you watch the swimmers, and the activities desk, where you can plan a day or a week for the kids or the whole family, including picking up tickets to most of the local attractions. The eight-story tower adjoining the Holidome has interior guest rooms, a 4,800-plus square-foot ballroom, and a pool and spa on the fourth floor big enough to entertain large groups. Lest we forget that it's a lodging facility, the majority of the 400 rooms and suites are in the terrace area at the back of the property, where three multi-story buildings feature views of the mountains in the (near) distance and LeConte Creek practically at your feet. Mynatt Park, one of Gatlinburg's real jewels (see our Parks and Recreation chapter) is right next to the terrace section. The Gatlinburg Convention Center and downtown are a couple blocks the other way. We could go on and on, but you've probably gotten the picture: If you want to go to a resort right in the middle of everything that has everything to offer, the place with the most visible sign in the Smokies is probably what you seek.

Ledwell Motel

$$ • 615 Airport Rd., Gatlinburg
• (865) 436-5304

At the top of Airport Road about four blocks from downtown, the Ledwell is across the street Mynatt Park, Gatlinburg's largest municipal playground. The Motor Nature Trail in the Great Smoky Mountains National Park is short drive up the road, and the orange trolley route stops at the Ledwell's front door for the convenience of the guests. Forty-five rooms offer all the amenities you'd expect, and free coffee is served in the lobby every morning.

Gatlinburg Travelodge

$$$ • 610 Airport Rd., Gatlinburg
• (865) 436-7851, (800) 578-7878

Right at the top of Airport Road, the Travelodge offers luxurious accommo-

INSIDERS' TIP

Airport Road in Gatlinburg is uphill all the way from the Parkway. If you're staying on Airport Road and it's getting late and you're getting tired, walk down the Parkway *away* from Airport Road to the Mountain Mall at the intersection of Parkway and Cherokee Orchard Road, and get on the orange route trolley. You'll ride up Cherokee Orchard Road to the top of Airport Road and then down Airport Road toward the Gatlinburg Convention Center. The driver will be glad to stop just about anywhere along the way to let you off. It's one of the best quarters you'll ever spend.

HOTELS AND MOTELS

Numerous spectacular Christmas displays make the holiday season a popular time to visit the Smokies.

Photo: Courtesy Pigeon Forge Department of Tourism

with discount coupons for lots of local attractions and restaurants. The on-site cafe is a great place to start the day or enjoy a midday snack. Ski packages are available in season.

East Parkway

Following East Parkway (U.S. 321N) east of town from traffic light #3, a succession of smaller, family owned and operated lodging places is within a few blocks. These are mostly places that were built on farmland in the '50s and '60s, and vary in size from intimate to huge. With few exceptions, these are comfortably furnished, moderately priced accommodations in what appears to be the middle of the commodations with extremely high return percentages, where you'll be treated more like a visiting family member than a guest tenant. This strip of road is served by the orange trolley route, and the trolley will stop at, or within 50 feet of, the door to every motel listed.

INSIDERS' TIP

Cultivate the friendship of your desk clerk; they're fountains of information, and can save you many hours of frustration.

HOTELS AND MOTELS

dations in what appears to be the middle of the woods. Gatlinburg's beautiful Mynatt Park is right next door, and one of the most popular sections of the Great Smoky Mountains National Park is just up the road. More than 130 attractively decorated rooms, with beds you really hate to get out of, look out on LeConte Creek and the mountains, and the Travelodge's indoor pool is considered one of the most beautiful in the Smokies. Conventions of up to 500 can be accommodated in the conference section, and the Travelodge prints its own travel guide

Creekside Inn
$$$ • 239 Sycamore Ln., Gatlinburg
• (865) 436-5977

One block south of East Parkway, the Creekside Inn features four stories of rooms with private balconies on beautiful Roaring

Fork Creek. Fireplaces, Jacuzzis, and kitchen facilities are available, and every room's telephone can be dialed directly. Wildlife sightings are common across the creek, and downtown Gatlinburg is a pleasant three-block stroll from the Creekside's front door.

East Side Motel
$$ • 315 East Parkway, Gatlinburg
• (865) 436-7569

Tom and Marlene Trentham built the East Side in 1971 on land that was part of her father's farm. Four-fifths of the East Side's guests come back, most of them annually, and Marlene says running the motel is a lot like having a great big house and a great big family to fill it. The East Side is convenient to both ends of downtown at the same time—traffic light #3 is a short walk or trolley ride from the front door, and the Bishop Lane bypass is just across the street.

Brookside Resort
$$$-$$$$ • 463 East Parkway, Gatlinburg
• (865) 436-5611, (800) 251-9597

The only word to describe the Brookside is huge—six multi-story buildings containing 230 rooms in every imaginable configuration stretch along three blocks of the East Parkway, with Roaring Fork Creek at the back. The Brookside's front lawn, featuring the black bear statue that's a favorite landmark, is bigger than most of the lodging properties in town. With the orange trolley stopping at the front door and Winery Square shopping center right across the street, the Brookside has unmatched convenience. Add the on-site basketball, volleyball, and wallyball courts, and the available riverside pavilion with its own kitchen facility, and

you can park your car at the Brookside and not get back into it until you leave.

Ski View Motel
$-$$ • 602 East Parkway, Gatlinburg
• (865) 436-4768, (888) 808-7967

Charlie Ogle built the Ski View on a pie-shaped point of land in 1964 that was "a sight out of town." Now that the town has moved out to meet it, the Ski View is proving itself to be a popular lodging spot, not only for its reasonable rates but also for the spectacular view it presents. At no time during a stay at the Ski View is the visitor more than one story off the ground, but the unique architecture of the place puts you close to 75 feet above the roads that serve it. An overview of downtown Gatlinburg is available from one side of the Ski View, and the mountains of the national park are on the other. Four blocks from downtown Gatlinburg, the Ski View is adjacent to one of the city's most popular music theaters and just two blocks from Winery Square shopping center and several restaurants.

Virgil's Motel
$$ • 959 East Parkway, Gatlinburg
• (865) 436-4838, (865) 436-5516

Virgil and Mattie Belle Trentham opened their motel in 1948 in what was "way out of town" at the time. They keep the place fresh and new-looking for new and established guests (one guest has rented the same room every year since the '60s). Virgil Trentham is regarded as a living legend among fly fishermen in the area, and Mattie Belle's related to everybody, so a stay at Virgil's is one of the best history lessons you can get in Gatlinburg.

Bed and Breakfasts & Country Inns

LOOK FOR:
- Sevierville
- Wears Valley
- Gatlinburg

Price Code

Our pricing key indicates the average cost of a room for two adults, exclusive of taxes, during the tourist season (April through October). Where two codes are present, the higher code usually applies to guest cottages. Most bed and breakfasts accept credit cards—we've noted the ones that don't.

$	Under $100
$$	$101 to $130
$$$	$131 to $160
$$$$	$161 to $200
$$$$$	Over $200

Changes in America's social mores since the social revolutions of the 1970s led the lodging industry to adopt new standards in tolerance toward the marital status (or the lack thereof) of its visitors. In the Great Smoky Mountains, this liberal attitude is best reflected in the growth of a new niche entry: The bed and breakfast inn.

Other tourist areas accommodated the bed and breakfast crowd by converting big old homes and boarding houses to increase the intimacy of their accommodations, and added a meal or two to hang on to their guests a little longer. That approach didn't fly in the Smokies. First, the few big old homes left in the area are in many cases still in use by succeeding generations of their builders. Secondly, the hotel/motel industry had just about wiped out the very few boarding homes in the area with the on-going explosion of construction that began in the late '70s and continues to this day.

The result of all this is that the bed and breakfast industry in the Great Smoky Mountains is driven by a growing number of great, new, old-*looking* structures that were mostly built in the last decade. Regardless of their location (and some of them are going to give you a whole new appreciation of the term "remote"), the bed and breakfast inns of the Smokies are in the vanguard of a vibrant, growing addition to the established lodging industry. Designed and built with the specific market in mind, the Smokies' bed and breakfast inns are intended to satisfy the demands of a clientele that consists almost exclusively of couples. Children are not actively discouraged, but most of the inns limit the number of occupants in a single room, and the limit is usually three. Several have "couples only" policies, and they'll be mentioned in the individual descriptions.

Being of recent construction, the inns have many of the amenities you'd find at any upscale lodging place: Expect cable television with one or more premium channels, central heating and air conditioning, and some form of hot tub or whirlpool. Telephones are commonplace, and stereo systems are standard fare in most places. The shared bathrooms that always made boarding homes such an adventure are not in evidence in the Smokies. With only a few exceptions that compromise scenery for convenience, the views of the mountains from private or semi-private balconies and full-width porches are absolutely spectacular—every inn can state with some justification that their view is "the tallest," "the widest," "the highest," ad infinitum.

The "breakfast" part of the equation is usually what you'd expect to find in a place like Tennessee, where bacon and sausage are considered vegetables. The three basic Southern food groups (meat, flour, and grease) are served in copious amounts, with some surprising gourmet touches added. Enough fruit, cereal, and whole-grain baked goods are usually available to satisfy the health-conscious, and afternoon and pre-bedtime snacks are commonly offered. Some of the inns will serve lunch and dinner to large groups with sufficient advance notice. Pets are a universal no-no, and please don't ask for any exceptions— the guests that killed off the pet question brought a pot-bellied pig with them.

The unique nature of this segment of the lodging industry makes it almost imperative that reservations be made well in advance. It's more like you're visiting in a very solicitous house than staying in a motel, and the hosts need as much planning time as they can get. Everybody we talked to said they welcome walk-in traffic on the rare occasion when they have vacancies, but "rare" is the operative word here. Conversely, because of the individual planning necessary to take care of guests on a practically individual basis, cancellations usually require about 10 days advance notice for full refunds—specific differences will be individually noted. Check-in times are all mid-afternoon (around 3 PM), and the earliest checkout is 11 AM. Smoking is without exception restricted to outdoor areas.

A word of warning as we begin our journey. Except for a few places convenient to downtown Pigeon Forge and Gatlinburg, the inns described herein (and it's not a complete list—there were some places we simply couldn't send an unsuspecting visitor) are in areas of the county where the average tourist probably wouldn't go for any other reason. We've extended ourselves to provide clear directions to every one, and they're all accessible on paved roads. As usual, we'll begin in Sevierville and move south—please note that *all* accommodations are south of Dolly Parton Parkway (U.S. 411/441).

Sevierville—East

Blue Mountain Mist Country Inn & Cottages
$$-$$$ • 1811 Pullen Rd., Sevierville
• (865) 428-2335, (800) 497-2335

Set peacefully among several prosperous farms, Blue Mountain Mist is a haven of country charm and style. The inn is on a 60-acre farm owned by the Ball family, surrounded by mountains on three sides. The 12 rooms include nine with queen beds and three suites with queen beds and additional bedding for family members. A hearty country breakfast is served family-style in the sun-drenched dining room, and coffee and desserts are offered each evening.

The immaculate grounds invite the visitor to kick back and enjoy a respite from the pressures of the day, or to stroll through the gardens and maybe throw few rounds of horseshoes. The hammock on the corner of the full-width front porch is almost irresistible on a warm summer afternoon. Nestled in the woods behind the inn, five quaint cottages offer privacy with style. Each cottage has a kitchenette and grille and a private yard with a picnic table. Bedside Jacuzzi tubs and fireplaces grace each cottage, and breakfast in the inn is included with cottage reservations.

Traveling east out of Sevierville on Dolly Parton Parkway (US 411N), Middle Creek Road is a lighted intersection about two miles from downtown. Turn right on Middle Creek and go south past the hospital and several professional buildings about 3.9 miles to Jay Ell Road on the left. Turn left about 1.5 miles to Pullen Road, also on the left. Blue Mountain Mist is the huge, turreted farmhouse-style structure on the corner.

The River Piece Inn
$$ • 1970 Pittman Center Rd., Sevierville
• (865) 428-6547, (888) 265-3097

This one's a piece of cake to find; 21/2 miles south of Dolly Parton Parkway, the River Piece is a lovely bright yellow farmhouse style building right on Pittman Center Road in one of the flattest areas of the county. Looking south and east across Mitchell Bottoms, one of Sevier County's original farm settlements, Webb's Mountain and Greenbrier Pinnacle are clearly visible, with a lot of other peaks between them. The middle prong of the Little Pigeon River flows right by the back yard, and you can sit on picnic tables and watch the tubers float by.

The two-story inn has five guest rooms, each named for a prominent ancestor, furnished with antique furniture and hand-carved hardwood mantels over gas fireplaces. The two ground-floor suites have private entrances. Built on land owned by the innkeepers' families since the 1830s, the River Piece offers lush accommodations with old-fashioned elegance for discerning couples. Queen-size beds and whirlpool baths grace every room, and the dining room and parlor have wood burning stacked

The Lion's Den is an exotic master suite with a double whirlpool and private dining at Christopher Place.

Photo: Courtesy Christopher Place

stone fireplaces. The full country breakfast includes homemade breads and jellies. Family-style dinners are available to groups renting the entire inn.

The River Piece's location on Pittman Center Road is central to outlet shopping, all the music theaters, and the Greenbrier entrance to the Great Smoky Mountains National Park.

Sevierville—Parkway

Calico Inn
$ • 757 Ranch Way, Sevierville
• (865) 428-3833, (800) 235-1054

An intimate establishment with three guest rooms, Calico Inn welcomes school-age children, with a limit of three people per room. The attitude and the surroundings are laid back, with a panoramic view of the mountains forming a backdrop for the nearby woods and fields. After the country breakfast has filled you to the brim, you can relax on the front porch and watch squirrels and rabbits at play, or head for the wonders that await you in America's favorite vacation spot. Whatever your choice, the comfort of Calico Inn awaits you at the close of your day. Convenient to all the attractions

on the Parkway, Calico Inn is a rustic structure two miles off the Parkway on New Era Road, just south of the Wal-Mart center.

Wears Valley

The three inns on and adjacent to Wears Valley Road have addresses in both Pigeon Forge and Sevierville. Political boundaries aside, they're described here in the order you would come upon them if you turned westbound on Wear's Valley Road (U.S. 321) from the Parkway in Pigeon Forge.

Hilton's Bluff Bed & Breakfast Inn
$$ • 2654 Valley Heights Dr., Pigeon Forge
• (865) 428-9765, (800) 441-4188

Close enough to the Parkway that you could hear traffic if the woods didn't get in the way, Hilton's Bluff is a 10-room inn with a variety of bed configurations and plenty of space for corporate meetings, church retreats, weddings and rehearsal dinners. Bright and airy rooms and game facilities make Hilton's Bluff an ideal place to relax without ever leaving the property. Three honeymoon-style suites have heart-shaped two-person Jacuzzis. The day begins with a full country breakfast and ends with delicious surprise snacks and refreshments. There's always something to do at Hilton's Bluff: The selection of parlor games is outstanding, the library has several interesting fiction and non-fiction books, and there's enough woods just outside to make for a leisurely stroll. The Pigeon Forge trolley stops at the corner just below the inn. Valley Heights is just a half-mile from the Parkway—it's the second street off the Parkway to the left.

Von Bryan Mountaintop Inn
$$ • 2402 Hatcher Mountain Rd., Sevierville • (865) 453-9832, (800) 633-1459

Von Bryan Inn is a palatial structure that commands an unparalleled vista of beautiful Wear's Valley, with the Smokies rising behind it. Seven rooms with private baths and a choice of king or queen beds enjoy this view, and the swimming pool and picnic area behind the inn are dominated by Bluff Mountain rising in the distance. The log chalet in front of the inn has two queen beds, two twin beds, two bathrooms, a whirlpool bath, and a wraparound deck that provides both of the spectacular views. Hatcher Mountain Road is seven miles from the Parkway on Wear's Valley Road. Von Bryan Mountaintop Inn is 2½ miles up Hatcher Mountain Road. The run up Hatcher Mountain seems a lot longer the first time, but it's paved and worth the trip.

Little Greenbrier Lodge
$-$$ • 3685 Lyon Springs Rd., Sevierville • (865) 429-2500, (800) 277-8100

One of the oldest lodging structures in the area, Little Greenbrier has had a checkered history since it opened in 1939 as a hotel for businessmen and visitors to the national park. When the closure of the railroad to Elkmont took away its clientele, the building went through several changes and several years of vacancy before being renovated and opened in its present form in 1993. Sufficient hardwood and wicker furniture was salvaged to retain the Victorian flavor of the original hotel. The lodge today has 10 rooms, eight of which have private baths. Private balconies and porches are available on both floors of

the Victorian structure, with views of both the mountains and Wear's Valley. Lyon Springs Road is nine miles from the Parkway on Wear's Valley Road, and Little Greenbrier Lodge is 1½ miles east (left) off Wear's Valley Road. Lyon Springs continues into the Great Smoky Mountains National Park through Little Greenbrier Cove, coming out to the Little River Road at Metcalf Bottoms picnic area. At this point Gatlinburg is just five miles to the east.

Gatlinburg

The route through Gatlinburg will be the same one we've used throughout the book: We'll start on the Parkway and head through town and up into the Ski Mountain area north of town. Then we'll go east out U.S. 321 (East Parkway). The eastern side establishments are spread over an area of about 35 square miles, and all directions to them will begin at traffic light #3.

Eight Gables Inn
$$ • 219 North Mountain Tr., Gatlinburg • (865) 430-3344, (800) 279-5716

Ten spacious rooms are furnished with a decidedly feminine touch, each with its own private bath and great view through large windows. The covered porch and grounds provide a relaxed atmosphere, as do the sitting areas inside the inn. The Magnolia Tea Room is the setting for the gourmet country breakfast (you'll love the potato pie au gratin), and is open for lunch Tuesday through Friday. Groups of up to 30 can be accommodated for luncheon meetings. The evening dessert bar for guests only is a big hit with the kids. Eight Gables is situated right between Gatlinburg and Pigeon Forge, and the trolley stop at the Gatlinburg Welcome Center provides service to both cities. Before you even get into Gatlinburg on the Parkway spur, Eight Gables Inn is across the road from the Gatlinburg Welcome Center.

Tennessee Ridge Bed & Breakfast
$$$ • 507 Campbell Lead, Gatlinburg • (865) 436-4068, (800) 737-7369

One of the best combined views you'll ever see is what the Tennessee Ridge offers. Overlooking the entire expanse of downtown Gatlinburg with the full range of the Smokies behind it, this gorgeous seven-room structure offers a symphony for the eyes. And the other senses get their share, too. The five suites with views that match the sitting and kitchen areas have their own balconies to add a dimension of privacy to the scene, and the two rooms with mountain views have a sense of intimacy that enhances the overall charm of the inn. Turn right at Greystone Heights Road (traffic light #5) and just follow it about a mile up to Tennessee Ridge. The inn is open from mid-February through December.

Olde English Tudor Inn
$-$$ • 135 West Holly Ridge Rd., Gatlinburg • (865) 436-7760, (800) 541-3798

Right in the center of downtown Gatlinburg, the Olde English Tudor Inn is an oasis of comfort and serenity. The innkeepers live in the building, so you won't ever be isolated from the kind of service you like to expect. Eight comfortable guest rooms range in accommodation from double beds to king, all with views of the mountains or downtown. The rear patio and flower garden are a welcome break from the downtown hubbub, and the community room is a great place to meet new and old friends. To get to the inn, turn left at traffic light #7 (Reagan Drive), left again at Reagan Lane (the first street) and left one more time at Holly Ridge—the inn is the first place on the right.

Butcher House in the Mountains
$$ • 1520 Garrett Ln., Gatlinburg • (865) 436-9457

Butcher House is a study in elegance that's hard to take in all at once. The living and dining areas are furnished with antiques and museum-quality appointments that the owners actually encourage their guests to use. The dinnerware and linens used to serve the gourmet dishes they call breakfast (along with the hearty fare Tennessee is famous for) would do credit to the finest restaurant, and the furnishings in the five guest rooms are equally posh. The family atmosphere is so strong that the Butchers have built an impressive list of return reservations. As for the view, let's let it suffice to say that it's more than you can imagine, even at 2,800 feet. Butcher House is high in the moun-

tains protecting Gatlinburg's north side, and is best approached from the Park by-pass. Detailed directions will be provided by the innkeepers when reservations are made. Because of the mountainous terrain and uncertain weather, Butcher House in the Mountains is closed in January.

Gatlinburg—East

Our first two establishments are within 100 yards of each other on the edge of Gatlinburg's world-famous Great Smoky Arts & Crafts Community, described at length in our Mountain Crafts chapter. To get there, go east two miles out East Parkway (US 321) from traffic light #3 to the traffic light at Glades Road. Turn left on Glades and go about two more miles to the blinking light at Powdermill Road, where another left turn will lead about two blocks to a fork in the road. Take the *left* fork (John's Branch Road) about 1.2 miles to Tanrac Trail, and turn right. Follow the road up. The first inn is on the right, about a third of a mile. The second is at the end of the road just a stone's throw further.

> ## INSIDERS' TIP
> It would be nice to say that the level of service you get at the bed and breakfast establishments is typical of the rest of the area, but it isn't—it's much better. Don't be afraid to ask for anything that seems reasonable to you.

Timber Rose English Lodge
$$ • 1106 Tanrac Tr., Gatlinburg • (865) 436-5852

Built in the style of a true English lodge, Timber Rose offers lavish accommodations for couples only in five large suites. Each suite has its own private entrance, with every amenity you could wish for: spacious living room, dining room, full kitchen, romantic bedroom, wood-burning fireplace, and a hot tub on the private porch. Opulent furnishings appear throughout the inn, featuring Corinthian statuary and stained glass windows everywhere. The view of the Smokies is almost 100 miles wide, and the feeling is that you'll never want to return to civilization. In fact, it's hard to believe civilization is only a mile or so away.

Fresh-baked pastries and fruits are delivered to the suites every morning, and you'll know the daily chambermaid service has been there when you see yesterday's empty champagne bottle replaced by a full one in a silver cooler. The innkeepers at Timber Rose pride themselves on their ability to pamper their guests in an aura of total civility surrounded by a wilderness that will astonish you.

The Colonel's Lady B & B Inn
$$-$$$ • 1120 Tanrac Tr., Gatlinburg
• (865) 436-5432, (800) 515-5432

Sitting on a buttressed ridge above the Great Smoky Arts & Crafts Community, The Colonel's Lady is a treasure trove of antiques, paintings and heirlooms collected by seven generations of the family that runs the inn. A lovely cottage suitable for up to four people and eight suites with jetted tubs and hot tubs and your choice of king or queen beds make The Colonel's Lady an ideal spot for family reunions, intimate weddings, or special celebrations. The special gourmet additions to the daily country breakfast make the occasion memorable (you won't believe what the chef can do with grits!), whether you choose the family dining room or the covered porch for your meal. Afternoon refreshments are served if you're not busy shopping and sightseeing in Gatlinburg or the Great Smoky Arts & Crafts Community, both just minutes away.

INSIDERS' TIP
Due to the remote locations of most of the establishments in this chapter, you should make certain that you're familiar with the route back to your bedroom if you're out after dark. If you get lost, call your host—it won't be the first time for them.

Buckhorn Inn
$$ • 2140 Tudor Mountain Rd., Gatlinburg
• (865) 436-4668

The only establishment in the Smokies corridor that is considered a true country inn, the Buckhorn Inn has been in business since 1938. Set on 35 acres of woodland in a secluded area six miles east of Gatlinburg, the inn has its own walking trails and lake for the enjoyment of its guests. Breakfast is included in the lodging fee, and lunch and dinner are available to guests by reservation only. The inn is located within the boundaries of the Great Smoky Arts & Crafts Community, providing a unique shopping experience. Special maps prepared by the inn's staff describe nearby hiking trails in the Great Smoky Mountains National Park, and throw in a few secret locations known even to very few locals. The main building contains six guest rooms with private baths, and four guest cottages on the property lend additional privacy in a sylvan setting. The Buckhorn Inn staff are all specially trained to provide whatever information you want to plan your own day, and can usually throw in a few hints to make a good time better. From traffic light #3 in Gatlinburg, take East Parkway

(U.S. 321) about 4½ miles east to Buckhorn Road and turn left. Tudor Mountain Road is about a mile in on the right.

Cornerstone Inn Bed & Breakfast
$ • 3966 Regal Way, Gatlinburg
• (865) 430-5064

Settled in the middle of the mountains near Pittman Center, the Cornerstone Inn offers secluded accommodations within easy driving distance of all of the area's attractions. The full-width porch that spans all three second-floor rooms offers a panoramic view of the mountains surrounding the inn. Wicker rockers and porch swings provide a comfortable place to gaze at the mountains and watch the rabbits play and the hummingbirds feed in the front yard. The guest rooms have queen beds and private baths. Wicker furniture and antiques decorate the bedrooms and great room, where a wood-burning fireplace forms a pleasant backdrop to the dining room and kitchen. The country breakfast on the screened-in back porch is a great way to start the day, and home-baked desserts and beverages in the evening are a nice finishing touch.

From traffic light #3 in Gatlinburg, take East Parkway (U.S. 321) about 5.6 miles east, across the Conley Huskey bridge, to Pittman Center Road (Tenn. 416). Turning left, follow the wildly beautiful middle prong of the Little Pigeon river about 3½ miles to King's Branch Road on the left (you'll cross the river about halfway to King's Branch). Turning on to King's Branch, look for the first street to the left—that's Regal Way. Follow Regal Way to the first driveway on the left, the entrance to the Cornerstone Inn.

7th Heaven Log Inn
$$ • 3944 Castle Rd., Gatlinburg
• (865) 430-5000, (800) 248-2923

You don't have to be golfer to really love 7th Heaven, but it couldn't hurt. Located overlooking the seventh green at Bent Creek golf resort (see our Golf chapter for course details), 7th Heaven Log Inn is a secluded inn with five rooms and a host of activities designed to satisfy and relax you without ever leaving. The natural log and knotty pine guest bedrooms borrow the natural golf theme for their names, but the biggest thing they offer is comfort. In-room coffee served before the special country

A True Work of Art

It is generally agreed that artists are not like the rest of us. Most artists, it's usually conceded, are just enough off-center that they see things differently, and if they don't get real offensive about it we're willing to cut them a little slack. As long as they return the favor by enriching our lives with their art, we'll put up with the fact that they might not have both feet planted on the same piece of ground.

And then there's Vern Hippensteal. Here is an artist who sees things with such clarity that he's able to record them on canvas as accurately as if he'd used a camera, but no camera can breathe life into a scene like Vern can. Maybe that's because Vern Hippensteal is a scientist by education (he's got a degree in physics), a printer by heritage (it's one of the family businesses), and, in his own terms, an artist by the grace of God. The difference between Vern Hippensteal and other truly gifted artists is that Vern lives in a disciplined world, with both feet planted firmly in his native soil. And when Vern and his wife Lisa decided to build and operate their own inn, the first thing they did was design it themselves, to reflect the peace and beauty of their birthplace.

Vern's artistic and mathematical talents came in real handy for the concept and the structural details. Lisa's experience growing up in the famed Mountain View hotel in Gatlinburg, managed for several years by her father, provided the nuts-and-bolts details that separate a classic lodging place from a merely outstanding one. Impeccable taste didn't hurt either, and this couple brims with that. The result is Hippensteal's Mountain View Inn, a monument to good taste and sensibility that has elevated itself to practically legendary status in less than a decade.

Even the location is an exercise in serendipity—Vern was stalling for time to find the right location when a piece of hilltop property came on the market—for about 15 minutes. Acting as their own general contractor and decorator, Vern and Lisa built,

Hippensteal's Mountain View Inn, from the only vantage point higher than itself.

Photo: Courtesy Vern Hippensteal

decorated, and opened their inn in 1990, in a manner so seamless that it seems now like it's always been there. Even the location has a gentle irony—the easiest way to get there is to drive through the Great Smoky Arts & Crafts Community, which is a nice way to prepare you for what's coming. The driveway is a little more than half a mile long, and is straight out of central casting: One minute you're on a gently climbing mountain road, then there you are. As you come around the last turn the inn appears in its entirety, looming over a landscape that most people can only imagine.

A quick look around tells you that this place is going to take a lot of exploring. It starts with a walk up the stairs, across the full-width front porch (try to ignore the rocking chairs—there'll be time for that later) and into the impossibly bright lobby, where the dominant white of the wicker furniture and imposing limestone fireplace is complemented by the alternating black marble floor tile and walls covered with artworks. Everything about the lobby says, "Sit here and enjoy the rest of your life," and you really want to, but there's so much more that you press on. Follow the guide that has materialized beside you (if it's a tall guy with a beard, his name is Vern) up the stairs to the lodging area. At the top of the stairs is the library. Some guests have been known to get past this point only to sleep and eat. The walls are lined with bookcases, and the selection is as eclectic as you'll find anywhere: Stephen King and Mark Twain share shelf space with Norman Vincent Peale, and a stack of jigsaw puzzles on the table invites you to stay. The room at the back is Vern's studio—if he's not your guide, he might be in there doing whatever artists do.

The rest of the second floor consists of nine elegantly furnished rooms, each named for the painting that the room is planned around. Queen beds and comfortable furniture grace each room with enough comfort that leaving isn't easy (notice a pattern here?), but there's still a lot to see. If at this point you're led to the other building, where two guest suites take up the second story, the nice couple on the porch there are probably Tom and Jane Woods, Lisa's parents, who live on the first floor. They're excellent company.

Back in the lobby, the dining room is at the end closest to the stairs. White wicker chairs and glass-topped pedestal tables make the room seem to float like a mirage, but the food served at the morning breakfast is very real, and very solid, and very good. And once again, the natural ability of East Tennessee's natives to serve and nourish you is enhanced by the soul of the artist: Vern and Lisa see to it that your meal is served with the flair that their specialty dishes deserve.

The food prepares you for whatever your day in the Smokies entails. Vern and Lisa are inveterate hikers, and will encourage you to go into the mountains and see why people can't get enough of this place. You may have plans of your own, but if you want to hang around, that's okay, too. There are games to be played and magazines to be read in the lobby, or the library may be softly calling to you. And there are still those rocking chairs on the porch, where the view of the Smokies range exceeds 200 degrees in width, stretching from Greenbrier pinnacle to the east across Mt. LeConte to Mt. Harrison. Vern talks about extending the porch completely around the inn, which would make Douglas Lake visible to the north. Just sitting and drinking in the constantly changing scenery is a pleasant way to pass a day.

To stretch the legs and further calm the soul, a stroll around the seven manicured acres of grass and woodlands will bring new discoveries as you find the gardens and flower beds, and an occasional sighting of the resident animal population is always a delight. If you get hungry or thirsty during the day, you're welcome to go into the kitchen and help yourself to whatever's available. Like always, someone will appear from thin air to help you if you need it; you'll never get used to it, but that's the way they do things here.

It's been lamented here that the face of tourism is changing—that people are in

(Continued on next page)

too much of a hurry these days, and they don't stop and smell the roses as often as they might. Some of that attitude has pervaded the Smokies, and the natives have mixed emotions about it. The money the modern tourist leaves here is good, and the increased security is comforting, but there's still room for people coming here who want to leave the outside world outside for a while and recharge their emotional batteries. Hippensteal's Mountain View Inn was built for those people, by a couple who share their concerns, and who have had the good sense never to leave the place so many others want to visit.

To get to Hippensteal's from traffic light #3 in Gatlinburg, drive two miles east on East Parkway (U.S. 321) to Glades Road (the third traffic light); turn left and follow Glades Road through the Arts & Crafts Community about 2.3 miles to its terminus at Bird's Creek Road. Turn left again, and less than half a mile later you'll come to the first of two forks; take the right one up and over the hill to the second fork, which you also take to the right for about another half mile to the inn's driveway (Taten Marr Way) on the left. For reservations at the inn ($$$), call (865) 436-5761 or (800) 527-8110.

breakfast gets you jump-started for a day that may include a few games of bumper pool or billiards on world-class tables. Or, you might just sit around the great room and decks reading, enjoy friendly conversation and feed the panhandling animals the scraps from your breakfast and the fresh-baked afternoon snacks.

To get to 7th Heaven, drive 8.5 miles east on East Parkway (U.S. 321) from traffic light #3, past the entrance to Bent Creek/Sunterra golf resort, to Butler Branch Road on the left; crossing the golf course, follow the signs to Castle Road. 7th Heaven is the second driveway on the left.

Finally, Something Really Special...

Our intent in this book is to keep you close to the Smokies corridor, but once in a while something comes along that warrants a deviation from that standard. We found a bed and breakfast inn in Newport, about 25 miles east of Sevierville and Gatlinburg, that's so exceptional we decided to suspend the rules. If you go there, you'll thank us.

Christopher Place

$$$$$ • **1500 Pinnacles Way, Newport**
• **(865) 623-6555, (800) 595-9441**
The drive from our main coverage area to Christopher's (see directions below) may have tested your patience a bit, but that will be forgotten before you get out of your car. And you just know you're going to love the person who greets you in the parking lot.

The main house at the inn is a Federal-style mansion with nothing to indicate you're in a lodging place. The three-story vestibule reveals a selection of inviting rooms in almost every direction. To the left, past a peek at the dining room and kitchen, the living room features a grand piano and a selection of comfortable furniture perfect for enjoying the wildflowers outside the picture window. Across the hall the library has books, puzzles, periodicals, and more comfortable places to sit with another attractive scene outside. If you continue through the vestibule and out the front door, you'll be on the full-width front porch. You can stand and gape at the view across the front yard (a lot of the mountains you're looking at are in North Carolina), or you can sit in one of the rocking chairs and just bask in the atmosphere of elegance you've entered. If you're like most everybody who's stayed at Christopher Place, you're already in love with it, and you probably haven't even seen your room yet.

And it doesn't really matter which of the seven suites you're staying in; the room is smashing. Whether it's Mountain Sunrise, the cheery corner room with the brass queen bed and the garden outside, or Camelot, the regal suite with the hand-carved mahogany king bed and the breathtaking mountain view, your room is going to be among the best you've ever spent a night in. And if your choice is the fabulous Roman Holiday suite, you'll dance on the edge of decadence for your entire stay— if you get out of the double whirlpool long enough to dance at all. But don't take

BED AND
BREAKFASTS &
COUNTRY INNS

our word for it—read the guest diary in your room. And add your thoughts to share with the next occupant. Every room has a private bath, a coffee maker, stereo system with compact disc and cassette players, a hair dryer, and snuggly terry robes.

If you decide to come out for breakfast, do it at your leisure: Breakfast is served when you're ready to eat, and the hearty country fare will be supplemented with the personal choices you described when you made your reservation. If it's a birthday or anniversary, a special surprise will be added. And all of the food is hand-picked and brought in fresh by the staff every day—nobody around will make the trip up the mountain to deliver groceries.

INSIDERS' TIP

The bed and breakfast industry in the Smokies probably offers the most intimate experience you'll have with the local population. Don't be surprised if you get emotionally involved with your hosts.

When you've finished breakfast and feel like doing something, or nothing, you'll find you're in the right place for that, too. The three acres of mountainside you're on contains enough to keep you busy if you want to stick around— the swimming pool and tennis court are real handy behind the gym, where a fully-equipped weight room is available for a workout with free weights or exercise machines. The tanning bed, double shower, and sauna are all beside the gym, and a kitchenette with soft drinks will help keep you cool. If something more energetic than a stroll of the grounds is your preference, a hiking trail takes off from the back of the property and goes up the side of English Mountain. The trail will get you closer to nature at whatever level of challenge you want, and local wildlife sightings usually include wild turkey, red fox, gray squirrels, and raccoons. If you choose to seek other pleasures, Gatlinburg is about 45 minutes away to the south and east, and I-40 will take you back to Sevierville and Pigeon Forge in about the same time. The Cosby entrance to the Great Smoky Mountains National Park is 15 miles south on Tennessee Highway 32, the same road that leads to Gatlinburg.

And if you're wondering who's there to take care of you, just wish out loud for something. The entire staff are past masters at the art of domestic invisibility. They are there when you need them; otherwise, they're not around—at least not where you can see them. These are the cream of the crop of East Tennessee natives who have an instinctive feel for service. They love to take care of people, and it shows mostly in the fact that they only show up when you want something they're trained to provide. They're also a great source of local information, and can make arrangements for some unusual trips—ask them about a llama trek. And, no—you can't take the staff home with you.

Christopher Place has won just about every award available to a bed & breakfast, and carries the highest designations available by every rating service that has seen it. The elegance of the accommodations and the effortless grace of the staff are hallmarks of hospitality anywhere at any level, and achieving their goal of providing you with an unforgettable vacation experience is as satisfying to them as it is rewarding for you.

Christopher Place can be tough to find. The key is to get to English Mountain Road on Tenn. 32, and there are three approaches to that point:

From I-40 East (Like from Knoxville or Interstate 81S): Take Exit 435 in Newport and turn south (right) three miles; English Mountain Road is on the right.

From I-40 West (From North Carolina): Take Exit 440 (U.S. 321 -Wilton Springs Road) two miles west to Tenn. 32; turn right 3.5 miles to English Mountain Road on the left.

From Gatlinburg: Take U.S. 321 (East Parkway) to its terminus at Tenn. 32 (about 17 miles from traffic light #3 in Gatlinburg). Turn left (north) on Tenn. 32 about 10.3 miles to English Mountain Road on the left. Christopher Place tries to keep a directional sign at the intersection of Tenn. 32 and English Mountain Road, but their efforts so far have failed. (It's been suggested that a less attractive sign might not get stolen as frequently. An alternative would be to just give a sign to everyone in the county named Christopher.) However, once you're on English Mountain Road, follow it two miles (it'll seem longer) through the rolling countryside of rural Cocke county, until the pavement ends. The next right turn is Pinnacles Way, and it winds a mile up the face of English Mountain to Christopher Place.

Vacation Rentals

LOOK FOR:
• Locations
• Amenities
• Money Matters

For tens of thousands of Smoky Mountain vacationers each year, there's simply no substitute for the comfort and atmosphere offered by overnight and short-term accommodations rentals. Chalet, cabin and condominium rentals are ideally suited for a variety of different vacation scenarios such as family vacations, honeymoons and romantic getaways, company retreats, church outings or other group celebrations.

In a sense, it all boils down to what one wants out of a Smokies experience. One of the primary reasons people cite for coming here is the enjoyment of the mountains and all their natural surroundings. In that respect, vacation rentals are often your best option when it comes to accessing the beauty and the splendor of the environment while at the same time being able to relax in a virtual home away from home. Campgrounds certainly put you in touch with nature, and hotels and motels offer plenty of convenience and amenities, but overnight rentals are generally able to provide the best of both worlds and more.

There is seemingly a countless number of choices when it comes to selecting a rental property. The number of cabins, chalets and condo units here totals in the thousands, and grows larger all the time. In fact, the prospect of narrowing down your vacation lodging site could be a little overwhelming. Don't worry—that's what this chapter is for. We'll present you with a basic overview of what kinds of properties and amenities are out there and where they're located. We'll also provide you with a starting point in terms of prices as well as reservation and payment methods. From there, we'll point you in the direction of a number of rental companies and resorts in the area. Collectively, they'll give you access to just about any type of rental property in whichever area of the Smokies you desire.

What to Choose

Although there are infinite variations when it comes to the styles of Smoky Mountain vacation rental properties, they can loosely be classified under three basic types, which are primarily distinguishable by their architectural differences—chalet, cabin and condominium.

The term "chalet" generally refers to the style of home reminiscent of those in mountainous European villages. The classic chalet's most distinguishing characteristic is its A-frame construction. Typically, you'll also find large and numerous windows for mountain viewing as well as ample outdoor deck space. In Sevier County, the largest concentration of chalets is found nestled in the hilly slopes surrounding Gatlinburg.

When you hear the word "cabin," images of a sturdy, rustic, log dwelling probably spring to mind. While there is surely an abundance of log structures for rent throughout the Smokies, you might be surprised to find that many of them are anything but rustic. Developers have found log homes to be a popular lodging option with visitors, so it's not unusual to see new ones springing up everywhere. And despite their bucolic image, today's log rentals offer plenty of modern conveniences.

Cabins probably offer the widest berth in terms of architectural range. You'll find everything from smaller one-bedroom cabins to sprawling ranch-style structures to multi-story log homes with heavy-duty square footage. Many incorporate some of the popular exterior features common to chalets, like large picture windows and porches. Cabins are found throughout the Sevier County area, but you're more likely to find them in the middle to northern sections where the terrain is generally less steep and more conducive to cabin construction.

Condominiums are the easiest type of rental to separate from the group. Put simply, they most often resemble apartment complexes and are noted for housing a large number of units in a centralized building or set of buildings. They range from multiple groupings of ground-level flats and town homes to interior-access, high rise structures. Condominiums are most prevalent in and around Pigeon Forge and Gatlinburg, but they can be found in Sevierville and outlying areas as well.

You'll notice in the listings of rental companies later in the chapter that some companies market themselves as "resorts." This means that that company's rental properties are centralized and offer common on-site amenities like swimming pools, tennis courts or golf courses. Most resorts are made up of either condominiums or cabins.

One type of resort that isn't addressed in this book is the timeshare. These are vacation rentals that are jointly owned by multiple owners, each of whom gets to stay in the unit a specified number of weeks each year. Since this touches on the concept of ownership rather than renting, we've avoided the subject for the purposes of this chapter.

Selecting a Location

While overnight rentals are more heavily concentrated in Gatlinburg and Pigeon Forge, they can be found virtually anywhere in the county—and beyond. With that in mind, it's up to you to decide what your vacation priorities are when considering where you want to stay. If scenic mountain views are high on your list, you might want to be closer to Gatlinburg. If you want quick access to shopping and music theaters, consider Pigeon Forge. Basing yourself out of Sevierville will help you avoid a lot of the heavier traffic and also allow handier access to surrounding markets like Knoxville or Asheville, North Carolina.

There are a few specific sections of the Smokies that are noted for their abundance of rental choices. When dealing with overnight rental companies (see section below), you'll likely hear some of the following names in addition to the county's three main cities: Walden's Creek, a few miles off Wears Valley Road, outside Pigeon Forge; Wears Valley, about 10 miles southwest of Pigeon Forge; Ski Mountain, the generic name given to the concentration of chalet homes located a couple of miles from downtown Gatlinburg on Mt. Harrison (see our Neighborhoods and Real Estate chapter); and Cobbly Nob, a resort area about 12 minutes from Gatlinburg on U.S. 321.

Amenities

Along with type of structure and location, amenities are always a major factor when choosing a vacation rental. To the good fortune of the overnight renter, Smoky Mountain properties are usually rife with the luxuries and the "little things" that can make an overnight accommodation seem like home.

As a caution, however, we'll tell you that just because a particular property is laden with amenities doesn't mean that the cabin, chalet, or condo unit itself is necessarily attractive or offers good views. It may just be a dump that happens to have a lot of bells and whistles. There are just so many different properties out there, the only way to be sure is to ask your rental agent to e-mail or "snail mail" current photographs to you along with the property's other marketing materials. This type of information is also usually accessible on a rental company's web site.

While there are specific cabins, condos and chalets that are exceptions to this list, most vacation rentals will include furnished linens and towels, kitchens equipped with dishes, silverware, cooking utensils and appliances like refrigerator, stove and microwave oven (you're responsible for the food!), hot tubs/whirlpool baths, fireplaces, washers and dryers (either in the unit or a laundry room) and cable or satellite television. Some places, especially the resorts, have access to other exterior amenities like swimming pools, tennis courts and golf courses.

Money Matters

How much can you expect to pay for an overnight rental? The main determining factor is the size of the unit needed. A small, one-bedroom condo will obviously not be as expensive as a seven-bedroom cabin. You'll be hard pressed to find a price lower than $65 to $85 per night for two people. Prices can go as high as several hundred dollars per night for a multiple bedroom unit.

In most cases, prices are based on occupancy per unit. For example, a one-bedroom condo might be considered to have a capacity of four people (one bed and a sleeper sofa), and a three-bedroom cabin may have a capacity of eight (three beds and a sleeper sofa). Since prices are structured according to a unit's capacity—larger accommodations will cost more because it's presumed that more people will be staying in them. You will also likely be charged extra for additional occupants beyond the unit's limit. Based on information from many of the companies with which we spoke, an average figure is $10 per night per person for anyone over 12 years of age.

While individual policies vary from one rental company or resort to another, there are some general guidelines and procedures that you'll encounter with just about all of them. These will especially be useful if you've never rented these types of overnight accommodations. It's strongly recommended, however, to confirm any particular company's specific policies when shopping around.

It's advisable to make reservations months in advance, especially for holiday or peak season periods. If you haven't already encountered this information in our other accommodations chapters, peak visitation times are during the summer months, October and holidays like 4th of July, Memorial Day, Labor Day and, of course, Thanksgiving and Christmas. Six months out, you'll probably be safe, but many repeat vacation renters will book their regular unit for the following year on departure. It's typical for most companies to have reservations on their books for one and sometimes even two years in advance.

Most places require that you reserve a minimum number of nights. Two nights is an average minimum, especially when you're dealing with weekends. If you're booking for holidays or peak season periods, you're looking more at a three- or four-night minimum.

You will usually have to post a deposit within a certain time period after making your reservation in order to hold it. The amount can range anywhere from the amount of the first night's rental to 50 percent of the total cost of the stay, depending on your rental agency. While credit cards are universally accepted, double-check with the booking agent to confirm which specific cards are accepted. Some companies also accept cash and even personal checks (if they receive your check well enough in advance). The balance of the total is expected on arrival.

INSIDERS' TIP

One term that you might hear tossed about when entering the world of vacation rentals is "cottage." The reason we haven't specifically addressed that classification is because there's not always a popular consensus as to its architectural definition. Some people say "cottage" when what they're clearly talking about is a chalet, and the same goes for cabins. While there are surely structures you could look at and say with certainty, "That's a cottage," you could probably just as easily lump them under the cabin or chalet umbrella.

Cancellation policies also vary from one place to another, but two weeks seems to be a standard cutoff point to safely cancel your reservation (we spoke with companies that allow as few as 72 hours and some that require a month's notice). If you cancel before that cutoff time, you'll probably have a choice of either rescheduling your reservation or receiving a refund. Some places give a full refund, while some keep a nominal administrative fee.

Cancellation within the cutoff period usually results in full forfeiture of the deposit. The same goes for early departure during the time of stay. Most of the agents with whom we spoke, however, did mention that exceptions can sometimes be made if the customer can document a family emergency like death or serious illness.

Overnight Rental Companies

There are some helpful distinctions we'll point out that may deflect confusion when sifting through this section. Earlier in the chapter we made a reference to companies that call themselves "resorts," which are noted for their centralized accommodations and amenities. For the purposes of distinction, resort companies are somewhat unique when compared to the rental company whose inventory is comprised of separate properties located all over the county. In both cases, however, it's common for the individual units to be owned by absentee investors.

Condominiums present their own peculiarities. Some condo units are marketed through rental companies. It's very common to see individual unit listings within a single condominium complex handled by different overnight rental businesses. On the other hand, the management of that same condominium development may also personally handle the marketing and property management for other units in the development. The choice of who manages a particular unit is usually up to the discretion of that unit's owner.

Some of the companies we've included below deal exclusively in rentals, but many are also full service real estate businesses through which you can invest in rental property as well. Refer to our Neighborhoods and Real Estate chapter for information on other area companies through which you can buy, sell and manage vacation rentals.

The addresses below are for each company's business office. This is usually where you go to check in, pay the balance of your rental and get your keys (you also receive specific instructions on how to get to your rental, if it's located at a separate site). We've included web site addresses since they usually include photos of specific properties and pricing information. In most cases, you can even make your reservations from a company's web page.

Sevierville

Oak Haven Resort
1947 Old Knoxville Hwy., Sevierville
• (423) 428-2009, (800) 652-2611
www.OakhavenResort.com

Oak Haven is easily accessible from I-40 and Tenn. 66 (less than eight miles from the interstate), but it still offers its guests a fair amount of seclusion with decent mountain views. On the property are 46 one-, two- and three-bedroom log cabins, each of which is equipped with a hot tub, whirlpool bath, fully equipped kitchen, gas grill and a TV/VCR/stereo combination. An outdoor pool and a picnic pavilion with barbecue grills are available to all guests.

For those who wish to venture away from the resort, Douglas Lake is only five miles away, and Eagles Landing Golf Course is located next door (see our chapters on Parks and Recreation and Golf for more details about both). Several golfing packages are available. The resort is also within easy striking distance of Pigeon Forge and Gatlinburg.

Echota Resort
110 Echota Way, Sevierville
• (423) 428-5151, (800) 766-5437
www.echotaresort.com

Fifty-five new but rustic log cabins and a

> **INSIDERS' TIP**
> Most rental companies require that you book a minimum of at least two nights, but if you've got your sights set on a one-night stay, check to see if your rental office has an odd night that they need to fill between other reservations. Believe us, they won't pass up the chance to book it if you're otherwise dead-set against a longer stay.

central amenities area make up this resort just a few miles from downtown Sevierville. The one- to four-bedroom cabins feature vaulted ceilings, private hot tubs, kitchens with dishwashers and microwaves, washers and dryers, satellite TV and gas grills. On-site amenities include a multipurpose clubhouse, swimming pool and lighted tennis courts. Eagles Landing Golf Course and Douglas Lake are each a short drive away from the resort.

If you're thinking of getting hitched in the Smokies, you should know that Echota is also a wedding provider (see our Weddings chapter). Wedding packages are available to guests, and services can be performed in the clubhouse or even in guest cabins.

Hidden Mountain Resort
475 Apple Valley Rd., Sevierville
• (423) 453-9850, (800) 452-5992
www.hiddenmountain.com

More than 300 cabins, cottages and villas make up this sprawling resort community that gives quick access to Sevierville and Pigeon Forge. Hidden Mountain is divided into two main areas. The west section is made up exclusively of cabins, while Hidden Mountain East is comprised of cabins, Music Mountain Villas and Old Home Place Cottages. In-unit amenities vary from property to property.

There are swimming pools at both the east and west locations, and a clubhouse and exercise room are available to guests at Hidden Mountain East. Hidden Mountain Resort offers a number of dining and entertainment packages (priced separately from the accommodations), ranging from $40 to $375.

Pigeon Forge

Eagles Ridge Resort and Cabin Rentals
2740 Florence Dr., Pigeon Forge
• **(423) 453-2220, (800) 807-4343**
www.EaglesRidge.com

Another of the newer resorts to spring up in the Smokies in recent years, Eagles Ridge is a centralized village consisting of approximately 120 log cabins and chalets just one mile off the Parkway in Pigeon Forge. The accommodations range from one- to four-bedroom units featuring kitchens, fireplaces, hot tubs, whirlpool baths and outdoor grills. Common amenities include a swimming pool and clubhouse. Eagles Ridge offers golf and wedding packages, and can coordinate catering services with area restaurants.

Kimble Real Estate and Rentals
3346 Parkway, Pigeon Forge
• **(423) 429-0090, (800) 447-0911**
www.kimblerentals.com

Take your pick of more than 70 properties found predominantly in the Pigeon Forge area, including cabins, chalets, condominiums and one- and two-bedroom suites. The units are within a half-mile to 12 miles of Pigeon Forge. Those that aren't located in and near the city itself are generally situated east of Pigeon Forge in the direction of Pittman Center. Among the amenities found in Kimble's rental units are hot tubs, fireplaces, satellite and cable TV, VCRs, full kitchens and barbecue grills. Some units have access to a swimming pool.

Laurel Crest Resort
636 Wears Valley Rd., Pigeon Forge
• **(423) 428-8570, (888) 850-1415**
www.bluegreen-corp.com

Villas and townhomes with flexible layouts and lots of amenities make up this Pigeon Forge resort located just a couple of miles from the Parkway off Wears Valley Road. The villas are one-bedroom units featuring well-equipped kitchens and entertainment centers. The deluxe units have whirlpool tubs and fireplaces as well. All units have sleeper sofas that bring the sleeping capacity to four people. You can also combine one-bedroom and one-bedroom deluxe layouts to create a two-bedroom configuration sleeping eight.

The one-bedroom townhomes sleep up to four and have basically the same amenities as the villas, except washers and dryers are included as well. The two-bedroom townhomes feature an upstairs master bedroom suite and can accommodate up to six guests. Both can be combined into a three-bedroom unit that sleeps up to 10 people.

Clubhouse amenities at Laurel Crest include heated indoor and outdoor pools, whirlpool hot tubs, an exercise facility, sauna, game room and reading lounge. Staff coordinators also plan activity programs for children and teens.

Mountain Valley Properties
513 Wears Valley Rd. #2, Pigeon Forge
• **(423) 429-5205, (800) 644-4859**
www.mountainvalley.com

This rental company has an inventory of more than 140 vacation chalets and cabins. The properties are found within a 15-mile radius of Mountain Valley's Pigeon Forge office, located in areas including Gatlinburg, Pigeon Forge, Wears Valley, Waldens Creek, Chalet Village and Sevierville. All units have full kitchens, fireplaces, TVs and VCRs and barbecue grills. Other amenities vary from property to property and include hot tubs, whirlpool baths swimming pools, tennis courts and pool tables. Mountain Valley properties also offers wedding services.

Wears Valley

Although the following companies have Sevierville addresses, they are actually located in Wears Valley, about 10 miles southwest of Pigeon Forge.

Cove Mountain Realty
3174 Wears Valley Rd., Sevierville
• **(423) 429-5577, (800) 245-2683**
www.covemountain.com

Cove Mountain offers more than 60 rental cabins and chalets situated in and around the beautiful Wears Valley community. Guests are afforded wonderful views of mountain, forest or river settings. The properties are a few miles away from the hustle and bustle of Pigeon Forge, offering access to Townsend, Cades Cove and a back entrance to the national park. The cabins and chalets have anywhere from one to five bedrooms, each featuring a hot tub, gas

Despite their primitive exteriors, vacation cabins are usually big on comfort and amenities.

Photo: Courtesy Sevierville Chamber of Commerce

grill, washer and dryer, cable or satellite TV and a VCR.

Valley Realty
3202 Wears Valley Rd., Sevierville
• (423) 453-1171, (800) 833-6258
www.valleyrealty.com

Another well established vacation rental company in Wears Valley, Valley Realty has about 25 log homes of varying styles. Units are scattered throughout the immediate Wears Valley vicinity. Amenities vary among the different properties, but many units have fireplaces, hot tubs and whirlpool baths. Some cabins and cottages have centralized amenities areas with a game room, swimming pool and tennis court.

Gatlinburg

Gatlinburg Real Estate and Rental Company
211 Parkway, Gatlinburg
• (423) 436-5104, (800) 359-1661
www.gatlinburgchalets.com

The company's rental office has the advantage of being one of the first you encounter as

you enter the heart of Gatlinburg from the north on U.S. 441. Their inventory of rental property includes more than 80 chalets and cabins located within four miles of downtown. Amenities vary, but include saunas, hot tubs, whirlpool baths, fireplaces and fully equipped kitchens. Units have from one to six bedrooms.

The Highlands Condominium Rentals
855 Campbell Lead Rd., Gatlinburg
• (423) 436-3547, (800) 233-3947
www.highlandscondos.com

The Highlands' location gives it the illusion of being cut off from everything, but it's actually just off the Gatlinburg Bypass, and it's convenient to the national park and downtown. Guests can choose from 77 one-, two- and three-bedroom condominium units, all of which are managed by The Highlands' on their five-acre site.

Each unit comes with a fireplace, whirlpool bath, kitchen and private balcony. On-site amenities include two swimming pools, sun deck, sauna, indoor and outdoor hot tubs and an exercise room. The views from The Highlands are great. You can see many of the vacation homes on Mt. Harrison in the valley below and other mountains in the near distance.

From time to time, the aerial tramway to Ober Gatlinburg passes by in the foreground.

Ski Mountain Chalets and Condos
416 Ski Mountain Rd., Gatlinburg
• (423) 436-7846, (800) 824-4077
www.skimtnchalets.com

You'll find this rental company as you start driving up Mt. Harrison on Ski Mountain Road. Approximately 100 one- to five-bedroom properties are on its rental program. All properties are located within four miles of downtown on Mt. Harrison. The units come with fully furnished kitchens, TVs and VCRs and barbecue grills. Some have hot tubs, whirlpools, washers and dryers, game areas and stereos.

Mountain Laurel Chalets
440 Ski Mountain Rd., Gatlinburg
• (423) 436-5277, (800) 626-3431
www.mtnlaurelchalets.com

This real estate and rental company offers more than 100 chalets and cabins that are primarily located on Mt. Harrison and are anywhere from one-half to four miles from the main office. Depending on the unit, the views can be memorable. Since Ski Mountain Road meets downtown Gatlinburg at the south end of the city, many of Mountain Laurel's properties provide fairly quick access to the national park. You can rent units with as few as one or as many as 11 bedrooms. Amenities vary from property to property.

Chalet Village
1441 Wiley Oakley Dr., Gatlinburg
• (423) 436-6800, (800) 262-7684
www.chaletvillage.com

Perched along the east face of Mt. Harrison (about halfway to the top), this section of Gatlinburg is where you'll find some of the most memorable views in town. The village itself is a collection of chalets and condominiums built mostly on steep, wooded sites. They're connected by Ski Mountain Road, the main thoroughfare to the top of Mt. Harrison, and a mind boggling network of hilly, curvy side roads. All but the most adroit of navigators will need a map to find their way among the maze, but the views make the trip well worth the effort.

More than 140 units, with anywhere from one to eight bedrooms, are on Chalet Village's rental program. Well-equipped kitchens, whirlpool tubs, cable TV, charcoal grills, fireplaces and balconies, decks and porches are among the properties' features. Be aware that guests planning to stay from December through March are advised to use a four-wheel-drive vehicle or have snow chains available for travel up the mountain. In recent years, however, snowfall has been less than average, and driving up Ski Mountain Road has not been a hazardous venture.

Jackson Mountain Homes
446 Brookside Village Way, Gatlinburg
• (865) 436-8876, (800) 473-3163
www.jacksonmtn.com

For those who want both bountiful mountain views and the convenience of being near Gatlinburg, Jackson Mountain Homes has plenty to offer. Their roster of vacation rentals includes approximately 75 cabins and chalet-style homes in addition to a handful of condominium units. The properties have between one and five bedrooms and can accommodate two to 18 guests. They are located, for the most part, within the Gatlinburg city limits. The amenities vary from home to home, but terrific mountain views, hot tubs and pool tables are commonly found. Approximately one-third of Jackson Mountain's properties have swimming pool access.

Mountain Loft Resort
110 Mountainloft Dr., Gatlinburg
• (423) 436-4367, (800) 991-0002
www.bluegreen-corp.com

This resort lies just off U.S. 321, only a couple of miles from downtown Gatlinburg. It's owned by the same corporation that runs Laurel Crest Resort in Pigeon Forge and offers similar configurations of one- and two-bedroom villas and one-, two- and three-bedroom townhomes. Refer to the Laurel Crest write-up in the Pigeon Forge section of this chapter for detailed descriptions of the various layouts and amenities available. Mountain Loft, however, also has two-bedroom chalets with lofts that sleep up to six. The chalets have amenities similar to those in the villas and townhomes.

At the clubhouse, you'll

INSIDERS' TIP
The state of Tennessee requires that any company in the overnight rental business operate with a vacation lodging license obtained through the Tennessee Real Estate Commission. To be on the safe side, make sure that any overnight rental company you deal with is properly licensed.

find indoor and outdoor pools, hot tubs, an exercise room, sauna and game room. Hiking trails are located nearby, and the resort provides 24-hour security service. Guests might also be interested in Mountain Loft's Courtesy Vacation Planning, whereby staff members help plan activities like golfing, fishing and rafting trips, horseback riding and ski trips. Activities are also planned for children and teens.

Greenbrier Valley Resorts
3629 East Parkway, Gatlinburg
• (423) 436-2015, (800) 546-1144
www.cobblynob.com

You'll have to travel a little out of your way to get there, but the properties you'll find through Greenbrier Valley Resorts offer quality accommodations in a peaceful, secluded notch of the county, well removed from all the hurly-burly of Gatlinburg and Pigeon Forge. This company is approximately 11 miles from downtown Gatlinburg on U.S. 321 and has more than 40 properties from which to choose, including log cabins, chalets and condominiums.

Units have from one to eight bedrooms and amenities that include fireplaces, hot tubs, TVs and VCRs, stereos, washers and dryers, barbecue grills and well-outfitted kitchens. Guests have full use of recreational facilities at The Village Of Cobbly Nob, the residential community in which Greenbrier's properties are

INSIDERS' TIP

If you walk the streets of Gatlinburg long enough, chances are you'll eventually encounter an "off-premises contact." Otherwise known as OPCs, these are timeshare sales people who operate outdoor booths and kiosks on the sidewalks of downtown Gatlinburg. Sometimes they can be downright pushy in their efforts to attract the attention of passersby.

located. Facilities include three swimming pools, tennis courts and 24-hour security. Most of Greenbrier's properties offer views of the Smokies or Bent Creek Golf Course, which is adjacent to Cobbly Nob (see our Golf chapter).

Deer Ridge Resort
3710 Weber Rd., Gatlinburg
• (423) 436-2325, (877) 333-7743
www.deerridge.com

If views are your thing, this scenic vacation resort won't disappoint. Located 12 miles from downtown Gatlinburg, just off U.S. 321, Deer Ridge sits high atop a foothill peak with views of mountains that are so close they take your attention hostage. A little more than 80 one-, two- and three-bedroom condominium units are available on site, all having sleeper sofas and some having lofts. Each unit comes with a woodburning fireplace, TV, VCR, two phones with data ports and a kitchen with plenty of appliances, silverware and dishes.

Clubhouse amenities include indoor and outdoor pools, sun deck, hot tub, sauna, steam room, lighted tennis court, game room and video rentals. The resort's playground area features a child's playhouse, swings, half-sized basketball court, volleyball area, picnic tables, grills and covered pavilion. Bent Creek Golf Course is located less than two miles from Deer Ridge at the bottom of the hill. The resort offers its guests golf packages as well as discount tickets for Dollywood.

Campgrounds & RV Parks

LOOK FOR:
• **Sevierville**
• **Douglas Dam**
• **Pigeon Forge**
• **Gatlinburg**
• **Great Smoky Mountains National Park**

There's something about mountains that makes people who wouldn't normally consider the possibility want to camp. The pioneer spirit embedded in most Americans makes the idea of going to sleep under the stars and waking to a fresh dewy morning, with maybe a babbling brook thrown in, stir the blood. And there's no better place for starry nights, dewy mornings, and babbling brooks than the Great Smoky Mountains.

In keeping with our promise of orderly presentation, we'll lay out the more than 40 campgrounds and RV parks along the Smokies corridor in a north-to-south progression, starting at exit 407 on I-40. Diversions will run away from the Parkway in whatever direction they occur. As usual, geography is on our side—very few of the roads that meet the Parkway actually cross it for any distance, so most turns off the Parkway are in a single direction without doubling back.

From this point forward, we'll use the term "campground" to denote any commercial or government-operated facility that rents space for a temporary shelter that you bring with you. Several of the campgrounds will actually rent you a trailer, and they'll be handled individually.

Naturally, the Great Smoky Mountains National Park proper is a camper's paradise, and four of its campgrounds that are contiguous to the Smokies corridor will be dealt with in detail as the last section of this chapter.

Rules of Thumb

The commercial campgrounds tend to provide creature comforts that hook up to your portable home. Unless otherwise stated, you can expect 30-50 amp electrical service at all permanent sites, and most have cable TV. Water and sewer hookups are common, and those that are more than 5 miles from a downtown area usually have well-stocked stores and well-maintained on-site recreational facilities. Swimming pools are as common-place at campgrounds as they are at hotels, and laundry facilities are usually available. Public bathrooms with showers are pretty standard, particularly in those facilities that feature separate tenting areas.

One of the true advantages of RV-type travel is the ability to bring your pets along. Unless specified otherwise, all of the campgrounds in the area permit pets on leashes.

Because facilities and prices vary based on several factors (convenience to the bright lights is foremost), we'll provide a price breakdown for each campground, based on a single camping space for two people in a single camping unit. (A separate fee averaging less than $5 is charged for vehicles in tow.) Unless stated, all prices quoted are plus tax. Additional person charges run between $2 and $3 for everyone over 5 years old. The practice of including a seventh night free when a six-night stay is reserved and paid for in advance is so prevalent that we'll treat it as normal—if you're planning a week-long stay, check out the possibility of getting your last night free. It's also safe to assume that major credit cards are accepted, unless specifically stated otherwise.

Most of the campgrounds are affiliated with national associations or publications, and every one we visited took pride in showing us their high rating certificates. The competition is fierce, and you are the beneficiary. Expect immaculate surroundings, except in places that cater to the more seasoned "primitive" camper, and don't be afraid to mention problems or shortcomings to the management.

On Reservations

Like any other lodging facilities in the Smokies, campgrounds are at their peak from early April through October, and reservations couldn't hurt. If you plan to be in the area at peak times like July, August, and October, reservations are highly recommended. If you're a seasoned trailer traveler, you know when your fellow RVers are on the road. Cancellations are normally accepted with seven days' notice required for a full refund of deposits, and we'll note exceptions.

Sevierville

Our sampling of seven campgrounds that use the county seat as their mailing address falls into two categories—three are lined up along the corridor, and four are in the vicinity of Douglas Dam Park, a TVA facility about five miles east of Tenn. 66. (See our Parks and Recreation chapter for more on Douglas Dam Park.) We'll deal first with the ones on the corridor and come back to the Douglas Dam facilities.

Smoky Mountain Campground
194 Foretravel Dr., Kodak
• (865) 933-8312, (800) 864-2267

Among the largest in the area, Smoky Mountain Campground is in view of I-40 for a lot of its frontage, though most of its camp-sites are buried in wilderness. Foretravel Road is the first turn left (east) after leaving I-40 from either direction—it's less than 100 yards from the freeway. Stretching back into the woods from the spacious office building are 200 level trailer/RV sites with full hook-ups and 100 tent sites with a choice of services. The large banquet hall seats 500, making this park a favorite for reunion groups and travel clubs. A stage and public address system are included. Smoky Mountain Campground is open year-round. A trailer space with full hook-up is $16 a night; tent sites with water and electric are $12 per night, and a primitive tent site (no hook-ups) is $10. A large RV dealership with complete parts and service facilities is adjacent to the campground.

Ripplin' Waters Campground and Rental Cabins
1930 Winfield Dunn Pkwy.
Sevierville • (865) 453-4169,
(888) 747-7546

Right on the highway about midway between I-40 and downtown Sevierville, Ripplin' Waters is convenient to just about everything, and a short walk from a couple of antique malls and amusements. In five years it'll probably be in the middle of everything you come to the Smokies to enjoy.

Ripplin' Waters is on a level plain with the Little Pigeon River at its back. 155 paved RV sites have full hook-ups, and you can fish directly from the riverside sites. A full hook-up site is $16 per night ($17 riverside), and two furnished cabins are available at $53 per night. Ripplin' Waters is open year-round and offers monthly rental rates.

River Plantation RV Park
1004 Parkway, Sevierville
• (865) 429-5267, (800) 758-5267

Just south of downtown Sevierville, River Plantation has more than 200 total sites, with 163 full hook-ups. Tent sites are available, as are four cabins. A quiet walking trail along the Little Pigeon River provides a nice view of the mountains in the distance. Full hook-up sites range from $18 to $22 in season, while water and electric only sites are $16. Cabins with kitchen and bathroom are $59 per night in season, and primitive tent sites are $12. River Plantation has special monthly rates and year-round storage available. Special consideration is given for groups to provide adjacent sites around the pavilion.

Douglas Dam

When the Tennessee Valley Authority dammed up East Tennessee's rivers to provide electric power, they also created a bunch of pretty cool lakes that became vacation spots in their own right. One such is Douglas Dam in northeast Sevier County, where the TVA improved the situation by building a park around the dam. Two diverse privately owned campgrounds and two government operated facilities resulted from these projects.

First, a word of warning: There are *two* roads named Douglas Dam Road. Both go east off Tenn. 66 (about four miles apart), and they merge in Douglas Dam Park. The northern version is Tenn. 139, and it enters the park below Douglas Dam. The southern road, Tennessee Highway 338, is about two miles outside of Sevierville, and it's the one we'll use to get you to all four of the campgrounds in this section. Tenn. 338 stays above the dam until it crosses the French Broad River right in front of the dam and merges with Tenn. 139.

Douglas Lake View Stables and Cabin Rentals
1650 Providence Rd., Sevierville
• **(865) 428-3587**

About three miles east of Tenn. 66, Providence Road runs east off (south) Douglas Dam Road at a well-marked intersection. Winding inland away from civilization about a mile, Providence Road passes the Providence Missionary Baptist Church (est. 1795) and ends at the stables. This can be a real slice of life in the raw if you're so inclined: For about $7, you can pitch a tent anywhere on the 18-acre ranch. If you want a little more civilized lodging, a variety of camping cabins named for famous cowboys movie stars is available for $49.50 a night (add $10 if you want a Jacuzzi—the Hopalong Cassidy cabin has one). The bunkhouse-sized lake cabin has rooms from $60 (lower level) to $90 (upper level), with special rates for weekly rentals. This place is actually a dude ranch with camping facilities, and has a long list of activities designed to feed and entertain you without your ever leaving the grounds. One of our favorites is the "horseshoe golf" course, where the guests use horseshoes instead of golf clubs. Since it's set in a horse pasture, the "course" has some unusual, pungent ground hazards, and the burro or goat that serves as your caddy is wont to wander off from time to time.

Sevier County Campground
1506 Dyke Rd., Sevierville
• **(865) 453-9111**

The only commercial campground actually on Douglas Lake, Sevier County Campground has about 50 full hook-up sites at $12 a night and 25 water/electric sites for $10. Sites can be used for vehicles or tents, with a limit of one unit per site. The campground is within easy walking distance of a public park, and has its own boat launch. Well-placed signage guides you into the campground from Douglas Dam Road, a little more than five miles from Tenn. 66.

The campground is open from April through October. A "no refund" policy is in effect.

Douglas Lake Campgrounds
Douglas Dam Park, Sevierville
• **(865) 632-3733 (weekdays)**

This listing is actually for two separate campgrounds in the park that operate under identical rules. The headwater campground is on the lake shore right at the dam, and has 54 sites, while the the tailwater camp on the French Broad River directly under the dam has 68 sites. The Douglas Lake Canteen, the only commercial enterprise in the park, is at the entrance to the tailwater camp. Public restrooms are adjacent to both campgrounds. To establish a campsite at either spot, campers are instructed at the entrances (by signage) to find a campsite, fill out the form provided at the entrance, and drop the completed form, with payment, in the deposit vault at the entrance, within 30 minutes of arrival. Campsites with electric service are $16 a night and primitive sites are $11. Camp sites may be occupied for a maximum of 21 consecutive days on a first-come, first-served basis. Holders of Golden Age or Golden Access passports are entitled to a 50 percent discount on rates. No credit cards are accepted for payment, but personal checks are OK. The campsites are patrolled by TVA rangers, who also monitor the deposit vaults.

Pigeon Forge

The campgrounds in Pigeon Forge are set in clustered groups at both ends of the city, with a couple of exceptions. The first group is spread along two miles of Wear's Valley Road (Tenn. 321)—turn right at traffic light #3. The Wear's Valley Road campgrounds are all on the south (left) side going away from the Parkway, and all have camping sites and picnic facilities on Walden's Creek, which forms the back boundary

Deer wandering quietly through a field are a common sight in our rural areas.

Photo: Courtesy Pigeon Forge Department of Tourism

of all of them. The rest are at the southern end of town, and all but one are within sight of or a short walk from the Parkway.

Clabough's Campground
405 Wear's Valley Rd., Pigeon Forge
• (865) 453-0729, (800) 965-8524

About a half-mile from the Parkway, Clabough's is actually two campgrounds bisected by a city street. 170 full hook-up sites include 15 along Walden's Creek. The campground is open April through December. All sites are $19 a night except in October (peak foliage season), when $20 is the going rate. The campground is situated far enough off the road to provide seclusion from the traffic, and the on-site grocery store/gas station/deli is open 16 hours a day. The Pigeon Forge Fun Time trolley stops at the entrance to Clabough's.

King's Holly Haven RV Park
647 Wear's Valley Rd., Pigeon Forge
• (865) 453-5352, (888) 204-0247

More like a city of temporary shelters than anything else, King's has been a family-owned operation since the 11-acre park was part of a farm purchased by the family in 1928. King's is open year-round, with special activities during the summer season. The Friday night gospel sing in the pavilion is a local tradition. Full hook-up rates vary from $16 in January and February to $23.50 June through October. Tent sites with water and electric service are $13 to $18, respectively, for the same periods. Monthly rates are available on request.

Eagle's Nest Campground
1111 Wear's Valley Rd., Pigeon Forge
• (865) 428-5841, (865) 428-8699,
(800) 892-2714

Eagle's Nest is open year-round, and features extra-wide spaces for units with slide-out rooms or awnings. A total of more than 200 spaces covers the spectrum of services, and nine cabins provide rustic comfort. Eagle's Nest also offers trailer storage through the winter, and has a computer connector in the office for those who can't leave cyberspace behind. Seasonal rates are $21 for full hook-up, $19 for limited service, and $17 for tent spaces. Off-season rates are $1 lower across the board. Cabin rates are available on request.

Pigeon Forge KOA Campground
Middle Creek Rd. (P.O. Box 210),
Pigeon Forge • (865) 453-7903,
(800) 367-7903

Opened in what was really an out of the way location in the 1960s, KOA is now the campground nearest to downtown Pigeon Forge. 196 trailer/tent sites and 15 "Kamping Kabins" are arranged near and along the west prong of the Little Pigeon River, with the business district on the other side. KOA is open April through November, with rates varying from $23 for a primitive site to $30 for a full hook-up. The cabins are $39.95 for a single room unit and $47.95 for a two-roomer. The central location and KOA's long history make advance reservations highly recommended.

Z Buda's Smokies Campground
4020 Parkway, Pigeon Forge
• (865) 453-4129

Z Buda's campground takes advantage of the unique topography of the Smokies area by placing their 260 campsites at every level of the 18 acres of wooded mountainside that reaches to the highest elevation in Pigeon Forge. In fact, one group of sites has a panoramic view of the city that's unmatched anywhere else while you're standing on the ground. Several restaurants are at the bottom of the hill near the trolley stop. For the convenience of its guests, Smokies campground has three bathhouses to provide access from all parts of the park. The campground is open from mid-March through mid-November, weather permitting, and all sites are $17.50 per night.

The following three campgrounds are all west (turn right) of the Parkway at traffic light #10. When we finish with these we'll come back to the Parkway and pick up a sizable group on the east side.

Shady Oaks Campground
210 Conner Heights Rd., Pigeon Forge
• (865) 453-3276

About half a mile up Conner Heights Road, Shady Oaks is one of Pigeon Forge's older camping facilities. It was built by the Graham family in 1969, and the shade trees that have grown up around the 107 sites make it seem like you're in the

INSIDERS' TIP

Off-season rates for park model trailers and cabins can sometimes be negotiated to a figure low enough to make it worthwhile for you to leave your trailer home and still come to the Smokies and live in the style you're accustomed to enjoying.

wilderness. The on-site fishing facility deepens the impression. Proximity to downtown Pigeon Forge is enhanced by the appearance of the trolley every 20 minutes or so. The year-round campground offers 87 full hook-up sites and 23 large tent sites $18.50 a night.

Mill Creek Resort Club
449 W. Mill Creek Rd., Pigeon Forge
• (865) 428-3498, (865) 428-4490

The Mill Creek Resort is a sprawling layout with easy access to 72 paved, pull-through sites, available year-round for $19.95 per night. Twenty-five park model trailers and five log cabins, each designed for four to six people, rent for $75 a night when you can get them—there's usually a waiting list in mid-summer and October. The view of the mountains is to die for, and the "back road" access to downtown Pigeon Forge is a real asset in the peak season.

Mill Creek Road departs Conner Heights Road to the right about a half-mile west of the Parkway. It also runs off the Parkway a little north of Conner Heights, but it's in a confusing area. You can get familiar with it when you stay at Mill Creek resort by turning right when you leave the resort and making careful notes when you hit the Parkway.

Li'l Ponderosa Campground and RV Park
909 Little Cove Rd., Pigeon Forge
• (865) 453-5278

Li'l Ponderosa is a perfect example of what two miles can do in terms of civilization in the Smokies. For openers, don't worry about finding Little Cove Road—just turn onto Conner Heights at traffic light #10 on the Parkway and keep going. The road changes names about a half-mile in, and Li'l Ponderosa has a lot of signage to keep you apprised of the mileage yet to go. It seems like more than two miles the first time you drive it, but the distance is deceiving. Once you get there, you know you're in the boondocks when you see various livestock grazing in the fields. Look at the animals carefully—sometimes they're not all domestic or farm animals. In keeping with the rustic setting, Li'l Ponderosa has a choice of posh to primitive in the way of accommodations: 40 full hook-up trailer/RV sites rent for $20 a night, and 32 tent sites, all with electric service, are available for $16. Two primitive cabins sleep four to six at $40. The campground is open year-round.

Returning to the Parkway for the last leg of Pigeon Forge Campgrounds, the final four are

jammed together at the southern extremity of the city in a fashion that could convince the unsuspecting traveler they're in one really huge campground. Despite the different addresses, it is actually possible to drive from the Creekstone Resort through the middle of Riveredge RV Park and into Foothills Campground without going on another street. Alpine RV Park is at the southern end of the line and is set back off the Parkway.

Creekstone Outdoor Resort
304 Day Springs Rd., Pigeon Forge
• (865) 453-8181, (800) 848-9097

Creekstone has an interesting choice of 120 sites, equally divided among the riverside, the woods, and the center of the park. Creekstone is open year-round, with rates ranging from $22.50 for center sites to $26.50 for riverside sites during the peak season. All sites are $12.50 a night December through March, and range from $14.50 to $18.50, depending on location, in April, May, and November.

If you're southbound on the Parkway in Pigeon Forge, the best way to get directly into Creekstone Resort is off South River Road, a block east of the Parkway, before you get to traffic light #10. If you're northbound, go through the traffic light and take Jehu, the first street to the right. This will keep you from driving through another campground to find your spot.

Riveredge RV Park & Log Cabin Rentals
4220 Huskey St., Pigeon Forge
• (865) 453-5813, (800) 477-1205

The entrance to Riveredge is right at traffic light #10 on the Parkway. The resort itself is separated from the Parkway by the Little Pigeon River and a whole lot of trees. Landscaped campsites in the woods and along the river—175 of them—belie the convenience to all of Pigeon Forge's attractions, and the on-site arcade is an attraction in its own right. Complete hook-ups are $22.50 a night April through December and $19.50 during the winter months. Twenty-one cozy camping cabins with full-size beds and bunk beds are $33.50 for two people during the season ($4.00 per additional person over 4 years old). For the ultimate in "roughing it", Riveredge has seven one- and two-bedroom cabins with all the amenities, including gas fireplaces and Jacuzzis. These cabins rent for $115 per night, with a $12 charge per additional guest over 13 years old.

Foothills Campground & Cabins
4235 Huskey St., Pigeon Forge
• (865) 428-3818, (888) 428-3818

A quiet, comfortable, family atmosphere prevails at Foothills Campground, tucked in the woods less than 100 yards from the Parkway. Its 42 full hook-up sites on shady level ground are complemented by 10 A-frame cottages and seven log cabins with great views of the mountains. Foothills is open April through November, with RV/tent sites renting for $18 a night. The one-room cabins have two double beds, central heating and air conditioning, and cable TV for $45 a night for two people. The log cabins have a single spacious room with two double beds and a kitchen area with microwave and refrigerator. The cabins also have outdoor charcoal grills and picnic tables, along with covered porches with rocking chairs. Log cabin rental is $75 a night for two people. Additional people over 6 years old are $5 a head in A-frames and log cabins. Downtown Pigeon Forge is less than a mile up the Parkway, and the trolley stops at the campground office.

Alpine RV Park and Campground
251 Spring Valley Rd., Pigeon Forge
• (865) 428-3285

Just off the Parkway at the extreme southern end of Pigeon Forge, Alpine has a full spectrum of camping possibilities, and is one of the few campgrounds in the area that has RV parts and service on-site. Originally built in the 1960s and constantly improved, Alpine has 80 full hook-up RV sites, four camping cabins, four park model trailers, a pair of two-bedroom cottages, and three primitive tent sites, all in a secluded setting 400 feet east of the Parkway. Alpine is open mid-April through October. Full hook-up trailer sites are $18.50 a night, while tent sites with water and electric service are $16.50. Park model trailers are furnished with one queen and one sofa bed (bring your own linens) at $60, and the fully furnished two-bedroom cottages can sleep up to eight people for $80 ($70 if you bring your own linens). Additional people in the park model trailers and cottages are $5 each. The four camping cabins each have a double bed and two twin beds and will sleep four people comfortably. Air conditioning and cable TV are included, but linens aren't. Nightly rental is $29.50 for two adults, with $4 apiece charged for additional people.

Gatlinburg

Once again, we're looking at the old versus new situation that's so common here: The older, more established lodging places in Gatlinburg are generally smaller and more independent than you'll find in Pigeon Forge and Sevierville. In fact, every campground that's actually within the city limits is independently owned, and all but one is still operated by the family that built it. As we move farther east out of town, some larger campgrounds with franchise affiliations pop up. The last two campgrounds in this section are actually in Cosby, which is in Cocke County. We've included them in the Gatlinburg section because they're on the same road as every property east of the city. The Great Smoky Mountains National Park also has a campground at Cosby, and it's covered in the Park section of this chapter.

Dudley Creek RV Resort & Log Cabins
200 Parkway, Gatlinburg
• (865) 436-5053, (800) 922-6799

You're no more than into Gatlinburg when you come to Dudley Creek. Turn left at traffic light #1, and you're there. Eighty-five spaces are surrounded by woods, with Dudley Creek at the back near the spacious playground and bathhouse. If you didn't know you just turned off the Parkway, you'd never know it's out there. Sites are $22.95 April through December, and $19 in January, February, and March. Groceries, gasoline, some attractions, and a restaurant are in walking distance. The green route trolley stops at the office every 20 minutes for easy transportation into town, less than a mile from the campground. The campground also has 14 fully furnished one-bedroom log cabins available.

King's Motel & RV Park
625 River Rd., Gatlinburg
• (865) 436-4396, (800) 762-3914

This one is such a well-kept secret that it almost slipped by even us Insiders. King's Motel, right smack in the middle of downtown Gatlinburg, has six full service RV hookups behind the motel and next to the swimming pool, and they've been there for more than 40 years. With an extremely high visitor loyalty rating (85 percent of King's

INSIDERS' TIP

Most of the campgrounds that have campfire facilities also have or provide firewood. Check with your operator before foraging for something to burn.

Towing Services

When the best of plans go awry and you find yourself in need of a towing service, here are a few that have specially equipped wreckers and trained drivers to handle RVs and other large loads. All of the services listed accept major credit cards and most of them have affiliations with major road service clubs and RV associations.

Sevierville
Baker's Wrecker Service, (865) 453-9203;
Bradley's Wrecker Service, (865) 453-5005;
Travis Towing and Recovery, (865) 932-0094.

Pigeon Forge
Carr's Auto Service, (865) 453-3152;
McCarter Garage & Wrecker Service, (865) 453-8238.

Gatlinburg and the National Park
Anthony's Wrecker Service, (865) 436-2178;
Cap's Towing Service, (865) 436-9773;
Skyline Wrecker & Service, (865) 436-4653.

customers are repeat visitors), it's tough to get a space at King's, but the call is free. At $20 per night, the spaces are competitively priced, and the lights of downtown Gatlinburg are close enough to read a newspaper by.

Twin Creek RV Resort
114 Low Gap Rd., Gatlinburg
• (865) 436-7081, (800) 252-8077

Tucked into the foothills just off East Parkway, Twin Creeks is, by its own description, upscale.

The park is open from April through October and allows no tents on its large 72-space property. Every RV site is paved, with its own deck and fire ring. The resort is heavily wooded and beautifully landscaped, and features an arcade for the kids and a Sunday morning worship service open to all guests. Site rental ranges from $25 to $30 based on location (all sites are $30 in October). It's hard to believe downtown Gatlinburg is just a mile away, and the orange trolley comes into the campground for fun, convenient transportation. A delightful old stone cottage on the grounds has been completely renovated inside for luxurious living in a rustic setting. It sleeps four people, and is available on a restricted basis.

Trout Creek Campground
1640 East Parkway, Gatlinburg
• No Credit Cards accepted
• (865) 436-5905 in season,
(865) 436-6402 out

Trout Creek was opened in 1966 on a flat space alongside Little Dudley Creek that's not quite as secluded as it used to be, but it still provides a lot of privacy. Seventy-five full-service sites are convenient to the highway, and a separate, primitive camping area right beside the stream takes good care of tenters. The orange trolley stops right in front of the campground, and there's a great family restaurant next door. Gatlinburg is less than three miles to the left, the biggest golf community in the county is about 10 miles to the right, and Trout Creek is within the boundaries of the world-famous Great Smoky Arts & Crafts Community. Open April through October, Trout Creek's sites rent for $17 per night in April and May and $22 the rest of the season. Primitive tent sites are $14 a night.

LeConte Vista Campground Resort
1739 East Parkway, Gatlinburg
• (865) 436-5437

A spectacular panoramic view of the Smokies is the beginning of the good things the Conner family has been offering since they opened LeConte Vista in 1968. A total of 75 shaded, drive-through spaces feature grassy tent sites and concrete pads for RVs. LeConte Vista offers a full slate of on-site activities, including a day camp for the children during the summer. Evening trips into Gatlinburg are simple: The orange trolley stops at the campground office. Picnic tables and fire rings spread liberally throughout the park provide excellent places for socializing and looking at that wonderful view. The 10 PM quiet hour is positively enforced. Full hookups for RVs and trailers are $23 per night; tents and vans are $19. Two one-room camping cabins are available for $30 a night.

Greenbrier Island Campground
2353 East Parkway, Gatlinburg
• (865) 436-4243

Greenbrier Island is exactly what it says it is: An island campground in the pristine middle prong of the Little Pigeon River. Greenbrier Island isn't being immodest when it claims to be the "best campground in town"—it's the only one in the town of Pittman Center. Six miles from traffic light #3 in Gatlinburg, Greenbrier Island takes a lot of wrinkles out of "roughing it" by offering a variety of accommodations. In addition to 46 full-hookup RV spaces available at $15 a night, you can choose from 36 water/electric spaces, 24 improved campsites, or six primitive campsites at $14 each, all prices tax included. "Flint rock," the swimming hole at the north end of the campground, has been a favorite of locals for generations. The entrance to Greenbrier Island is a short distance off East Parkway on Pittman Center Road (Tenn. 416). Greenbrier is open April through October.

Outdoor Resorts of America
4229 E. Parkway, Gatlinburg
• **(865) 436-5861, (800) 677-5861**

The largest facility in the southern section of Sevier County, Outdoor Resorts is a "condo" campground (for lack of a better description), offering permanent sites for members' trailers and RVs, overnight sites for public rental, and public rental of furnished trailers. Sites with and without trailers are also available for sale to interested campers. A total of 376 sites includes more than 100 along the banks of Webb's Creek, and 32 around the lake in the center of the resort. Two swimming pools complement the full spectrum of recreational facilities for all ages. A non-denominational church service is offered Sunday mornings at 11 May through October. A trailer space rents for $26.50 a night for a family of four during the season, $22 November through April. Rental trailers run from $65 to $80 per night, and some restrictions and deposit requirements apply.

Crazy Horse Campground & RV Resort
4609 East Parkway, Gatlinburg
• **(865) 436-4434, (800) 528-9003**

Centrally located for both east- and west-flowing traffic, Crazy Horse is 12 miles from downtown Gatlinburg and 15 miles from the Wilton Springs exit 440 on I-40. The Foothills Parkway exit (443) is closer yet, but not recommended for towed loads. Crazy Horse has 212 camping sites about evenly divided between full hookup and water/electric, six rental trailers, and several cabins in various configurations. To accommodate a usually high population, Crazy Horse has three laundries, three bath houses, a private lake, and the longest waterslide in the Smokies—500 feet of twisting and turning fun. The Jack-Tales Theater, at the back of the park, is a long-standing local favorite, and will give campers and their families a chance to act in a series of plays adapted from fairy tales and local legends. Crazy Horse is open from April through October. Peak season is June through August, and October. Full hookup sites are $26.50 per night, and water/electric sites are $23. Camping cabins with electricity, small refrigerator and heater, sleep six at $45. Rental trailers and one-room cabins sleep four, and are $68 a night. The one-bedroom cabin with all the amenities for up to four occupants is $83.

Arrow Creek Campground
4721 East Parkway, Gatlinburg
• **(865) 430-7433, (888) 382-7769**

Nestled in a heavily wooded area, Arrow Creek is a secluded campground with the convenience of a major highway at its entrance. Sixty graveled and level sites accommodate all types of camping with whatever level of convenience is desired. Each site has its own picnic table and fire ring. The recreation hall, playground, and horseshoe pits will keep everybody occupied in a peaceful setting. arrow Creek is open April through October, with peak-season rates in effect from mid-June to mid-August and throughout October. Full hookups are $20 in peak season, $18 non-peak. Water/electric trailer sites are $18 and $16, respectively, as are tent sites with water and electric; and primitive tent sites are $16 in season and $14 non-peak.

Toolich's Campground & RV Park
4857 East Parkway, Gatlinburg
• **(865) 430-2680, (888) 866-5424**

The newest of the area's campgrounds, Toolich's is set on a large knoll 15 miles east of Gatlinburg. Forty-nine good-sized drive-through sites surround a recreation complex that includes a public hot tub and the social hall. A good selection of arcade games is available in the game room, adjacent to the office. Rental car and jeep service is available, and the owner-operators live on-site to provide 24-hour security. Toolich's opens on Easter weekend

INSIDERS' TIP
If you're towing a trailer or driving a large vehicle, avoid the Dudley Creek and Bishop Lane bypasses in Gatlinburg. Both are steep and curvy, with long downhill approaches to a usually busy U.S. 321.

and stays open through December. Full hook-ups are $24, water/electric sites are $21, and tent/van sites are $15 a night.

Venture Out at Gatlinburg
5355 East Parkway, Cosby
• (423) 217-2205

Venture Out is a privately-owned, members-only campground that has a limited number of campsites available to the general public. Directly across the street from Big Wally's, one of the most popular mom and pop restaurants in East Tennessee, Venture Out pampers its owner-members with a decidedly low-pressure atmosphere. Available sites rent for $21.70 a night, based on availability.

Yogi Bear's Great Smoky Jellystone Park Camp
East Parkway, Cosby
(P.O. Box 282, Gatlinburg 37738)
• (423) 487-5534, (800) 210-2119

Don't let the name fool you; this isn't an amusement park. It's a campground for families who enjoy a place where there's always something going on. Jellystone's back yard is the Great Smoky Mountains National Park, with the popular Maddron Bald hiking trail jumping off right out of the campground. The Maddron Bald trail is a pleasant one-mile walk back to a lovely picnic grove. In-season day camp sessions feature a Yogi breakfast and cartoons and a full slate of children's activities. Bingo, live entertainment, ice cream socials, and wagon rides keep everybody on the go if they don't want to just kick back beside one of the mountain streams running through the park. Jellystone is open from mid-March through October, with 70 trailer/RV sites, one rental trailer, three fully-furnished and one camping (bear bones—get it?) cabin, and 22 tent sites. Most of the trailer sites are on an island surrounded by the stream. Streamside full hookup is $27 per night, water/electric hookup is $23 to $25. Off-stream full hookup is $24, and off-stream water/electric hookup is $20. Tent sites with water and electric service are $21, and primitive tent sites are $15. Rental trailers are $60 for up to four people. The three full cabins sleep six at $80 a night, and the Bear Bones cabin will accommodate six for $43.

INSIDERS' TIP

Coming back and would just as soon leave your trailer here? Check with the campground operator for storage rates. Campgrounds that don't offer storage can usually put you in touch with places that do.

Great Smoky Mountains National Park

As you might expect, the Great Smoky Mountains National Park has a lot of opportunities for camping. The Park Service maintains 10 developed campgrounds with more than 800 total sites, all of which are charitably described as primitive. They're all accessible by RV or towed trailer, but there are no hookups or shower facilities. This section will list four of the 10, including one in North Carolina; the remaining six are all at some distance from the Smokies corridor (four are in North Carolina), and will be described in detail in the section devoted to the national park.

All park campgrounds are open from mid-May through October, weather permitting, and space usage is restricted to six people per site. Two tents or one RV and one tent are allowed per site, with exceptions granted only on-site in the case of immediate family members exceeding the limit. Stays in all national park campgrounds are subject to a seven-day maximum. Reservations are accepted up to three months in advance at Cades Cove, Elkmont, and Smokemont campgrounds by calling the National Park Reservation Service at (800) 365-2267; all other campgrounds are operated on a first come-first served basis. Information on other campgrounds is available by calling (865) 436-1266 for Tennessee campgrounds, and (704) 497-1930 for North Carolina.

Keep in mind that these campgrounds are in otherwise unsettled areas, and the only amenity you'll find is a flat place to park. Regulations vary from place to place, and you can expect to be informed of them in excruciating detail by the rangers in attendance. The following is a list of the four campgrounds in the National Park that are contiguous enough to be considered part of the Smokies corridor, starting with the easternmost and moving west, then south. Telephone numbers at campground descriptions are for ranger stations—not all campgrounds have phones. Check out our chapter on the park for detailed information on some of the recreational opportunities available in the national park.

Cosby Campground
TN Highway 32

Set on the northeast edge of the Park, Cosby campground is just off East Parkway (U.S. 321N) about 20 miles east of Gatlinburg. The campground is accessible to several hiking and scenic trails, and is a good jumping-off point for a hike to Hen Wallow Falls and old-growth forest. Cosby campground is open April through October with 175 campsites. Site rental is $12, and RV length is restricted to 25 feet.

Elkmont
Little River Road (TN Hwy 73)
• (865) 436-1271

Situated 9 miles southwest of Gatlinburg and 5 miles from the Sugarlands Visitor Center, Elkmont is one of the original campgrounds in the Park. Once a thriving settlement, the Elkmont area is being reclaimed by nature in accordance with the Park Service's philosophy of limited development. The surroundings are as wild as you'll find in an area as convenient to a paved highway. Elkmont is open April through November and has 220 single sites at $15, and group sites (maximum 15 people) by reservation only at $23 apiece.

Cades Cove
Townsend, TN • (865) 448-2472

One of the most popular day trip locations in the Park, Cades Cove is also a camping fa-vorite. The cove, with its preserved pioneer farmstead and open grazing for a variety of wildlife, is 27 miles from Gatlinburg on Little River Road. The outdoor amphitheater and pavilion make Cades Cove a favorite for large groups. The campground is open year-round. 161 sites for trailer, tent, and family camping rent for $15. Group sites for 8 to 20 campers are $33; up to 30, $48; and up to 30 with reserved pavilion, $63. Church group usage is very high in the summer, so you'll want to make reservations as early as possible.

Smokemont Campground
U.S. Hwy 441, N.C. • (704) 497-9270

Just about the time Newfound Gap Road (U.S. 441) levels off in its descent from the gap into North Carolina, the Smokemont campground comes into view on the north side of the road (left if you're going south out of Tennessee). Smokemont has an RV-only section with 43 sites, and close to 100 tent sites. Due to its convenience to Cherokee (six miles south), the campground is open year-round. RV sites are $15 a night. Group campsites are $23 for groups up to 20 and $33 for groups of 21 to 30.

Restaurants

LOOK FOR:
- Sevierville
- Pigeon Forge
- Gatlinburg

Millions of people visit the Great Smokies every year, and every one of them must eventually answer that nagging daily question: "Where to eat?" Fortunately, you never have to go too far to find sustenance in these mountains. It takes little more than a casual stroll down the Parkway in any of our cities to come face to face with enough dining options to cover your mealtime decisions for an entire week and more. From massive portions of down home Southern cooking to ethnic flavors from around the world, Smoky Mountain restaurateurs aim to please.

The restaurant business in these parts is fortunate in that it seems to be less vulnerable to seasonal influences than other tourism-based industries like shopping, attractions and accommodations. Rare is the local restaurant that closes down in the off-season. After all, even when visitors aren't in town, Sevier County's 60,000-plus residents need places to go for the "power lunch" or the relaxed dinner out on the town.

Naturally, you'll find an abundance of national chains—not just the fast food giants like McDonald's and Taco Bell, but also familiar "sit-down" restaurants like Shoney's, T.G.I. Friday's and Applebee's. As a matter of fact, newer corporate-owned eateries are well represented and seem to spring up daily. This chapter, however, will take you in a different direction. With a few exceptions, we've culled out the establishments that aren't necessarily household names (but perhaps may be someday). Some are less expensive, hole-in-the-wall cafes while others offer more pricey, upscale dining. Some are favorite local haunts while others are tourist "musts." What they all have in common, though, is that they offer the patron an enjoyable Smoky Mountain dining experience.

One of the best things about eating out around here is that the words "dress code" aren't a part of the local vernacular. No matter how elegant the setting or refined the cuisine, dressing for dinner usually means putting on jeans instead of shorts. Not one of the restaurants we're presenting requires a jacket or tie (although we'll assume that you will wear a shirt and shoes in accordance with state law!). As for reservations, they're usually not accepted because most restaurants receive heavy walk-in traffic; this is especially the case in peak season. What you'll usually have to do is just show up and put your name on a waiting list if necessary. In our write-ups, we will point out the places where you do need to make advance reservations.

Price Code

The following code is based on the price of two entrees from the dinner menu, not including appetizers, desserts, beverages (alcoholic or otherwise), taxes or gratuities.

$	Less than $15
$$	$16 to $25
$$$	$26 to $35
$$$$	More than $35

The subject of parking must necessarily hinge on the city you're planning to visit. If you're dining in Sevierville or Pigeon Forge, you can count on finding plenty of free parking no matter where you go, unless we tell you otherwise. In Gatlinburg, you'll be more dependent on public transportation or lots where you'll have to pay to park. Most restaurants along Gatlinburg's Parkway have limited parking, if any at all. We'll cover parking options within each restaurant's write up in the Gatlinburg section of the chapter.

When evaluating a restaurant's prices according to our code, bear in mind that most places have a less expensive lunch menu as well as a reasonably priced children's menu (the cutoff age is usually between 10 and 12 years old). You can assume that most places serve lunch and dinner, but if a particular restaurant serves breakfast, for example, or is closed for lunch or dinner, we'll mention it. You can also work under the assumption that a restaurant accepts most major credit cards unless we specify otherwise. Traveler's checks aren't a problem, but don't even bother trying to pay with a personal check drawn on an out-of-town bank.

We close with a word about alcohol sales. Outside the city limits of Sevierville, Pigeon Forge and Gatlinburg, restaurants can serve only beer by the drink. Each city, however, has its own different alcohol ordinances, ranging from "anything goes" to "nothing doing." Since we're covering Smoky Mountains restaurants geographically, we'll address each city's laws as we come to them.

Sevierville

Until just a few years ago, restaurants in Sevierville weren't allowed to serve alcohol of any kind. The city's current beer ordinance, however, allows a restaurant to serve beer if it has a seating capacity of at least 150 people and if at least 50 percent of its sales come from food. In the relatively short time since this law was passed, the number of beer-serving restaurants in Sevierville has grown from zero to nearly 10.

L.G.'s on the River
**$$$ • 2530 Winfield Dunn Pkwy.,
Sevierville • (865) 932-6732,
(800) 721-8830**

What does L.G. stand for? Here's a hint: The restaurant is located directly behind the Lee Greenwood theater at Riverbluff Landing on Tenn. 66. Greenwood himself is a part owner of L.G.'s, which opened for business in 1997, and the Grammy Award winner makes a habit out of stopping by the restaurant after his performances to greet patrons.

The menu features a well-rounded sampling of American fare, including steaks and chops, seafood, chicken dishes and sandwiches. Most entrees come with a choice of soup or salad plus a side item (veg-

etable, rice, etc.). L.G.'s is especially proud of its pasta dishes, namely the grilled chicken and portabellas, which features these two items tossed in a Parmesan cream sauce with linguini noodles. Incidentally, the portabella mushrooms stuffed with shrimp and crab also make for a tantalizing appetizer. The seafood entrees aren't always the biggest sellers, but they're well represented and worthy of selection. The Atlantic salmon filet is big on flavor and accented with a zesty hollandaise sauce.

Aesthetically, L.G.'s makes the most of its "riverbluff" setting. The restaurant is situated high atop a steep bluff overlooking the French Broad River. From this vantage point, customers both in the dining rooms and out on the terrace can see broad expanses of river and rolling countryside during the day. The interior ambience isn't too shabby either. Lofty, raftered cathedral ceilings and stacked stone fireplaces create a feel of enormous coziness. Overall, the setting could be described as rustic with a hint of elegance.

There are a couple of other points about L.G.'s worthy of mention. On Sunday, you can sit down to a bountiful brunch from 11 AM to 3 PM featuring carving stations serving roast beef, turkey and ham. You'll find crepes and omelets cooked to order as well as typical breakfast items like bacon and eggs.

L.G.'s is open seven days a week for lunch and dinner. Reservations aren't accepted, but you can call ahead to put your name on the waiting list if you're on your way to the restaurant. Management recommends a 5:30 PM dinner if you're planning on attending the Lee Greenwood Theatre and 7:30 if not. The restaurant is open a little later at night than other area establishments to accommodate the after-show crowds.

Villa Mexico
$ • 127 Forks of the River Pkwy., Sevierville • (865) 453-3858

It's only been open since 1995, but that's long enough to make Villa Mexico one of the few Mexican restaurants in the county with any staying power. It has a limited amount of interior seating, and the decor is fairly non-

INSIDERS' TIP

Since beer sales became legal in Sevierville restaurants, many of the city's newer dining establishments have taken advantage of that ordinance. In addition to some of the "wet" restaurants mentioned in this chapter, there are several others belonging to regional and national chains that can also serve you a cold one. They include T.G.I. Friday's, Fuddrucker's and Texas Roadhouse (all at Governor's Crossing), as well as Damon's and Sagebrush Steakhouse, both of which are located right on the Parkway in Sevierville.

Virgil's has been a downtown Sevierville institution for a decade.

Photo: Courtesy Sevierville Chamber of Commerce

dessert, you'll enjoy traditional Mexican treats like flan, sopapillas and fried ice cream.

Lotus Garden
$ • 131 Forks of the River Parkway, Sevierville • (865) 453-3891

In a way, it's rather interesting that this Chinese restaurant is located next door to a Mexican restaurant (see Villa Mexico above). But then again, it all makes perfect sense when you learn that both restaurants have the same owner (they also share the same restrooms)! Yes, there is apparently an advantage to diversification in the restaurant business.

For more than a decade, Lotus Garden has served delicious Chinese dishes made from beef, pork, chicken and seafood. The shrimp with snowpeas and water chestnut is a house specialty as are the kung pao chicken, General Tso's chicken and tangerine beef. This restaurant's biggest drawing card, however, is its buffet, which carries around 30 items during lunch and 40 items for dinner. The buffet offers all-you-care-to-eat portions of menu favorites like sesame chicken and roast pork as well as soups, egg rolls, desserts and more.

Lotus Garden's atmosphere is subtly Oriental. The two main dining rooms are adequately spacious and reflect a minimalist approach to the Chinese decor. It's open for lunch and dinner, seven days a week.

Virgil's '50s Restaurant
$ • 109 E. Bruce St., Sevierville • (865) 453-2782

When you're sitting in a booth at Virgil's you almost expect Richie, Potsy and The Fonz to walk through the doors at any moment. Everything about this downtown restaurant screams "1950s," from the black and white checkered floor tile to the pastel-colored stools at the counter to the 45 rpm records and other pieces of '50s music memorabilia hanging on the walls and from the ceilings.

While you may be initially drawn to Virgil's

descript as far as ethnic dining establishments go, but the cuisine is authentic and a refreshing break from Mexican fast food. Villa Mexico is open seven days a week for lunch and dinner, and it's located at the end of a strip plaza anchored by Kmart and Kroger supermarket.

The menu offers everything that you'd expect from south of the border—tacos, burritos, enchiladas and various combinations of the three. You'll also find more adventurous entrees like huevos rancheros (ranch eggs), chilis rellenos and chalupas. The house "especialidades" include popular sellers like the chimichanga and the fajitas (beef, shrimp or chicken). If you're not a meat eater, you might select one of the vegetarian platters. Most dinners are served with rice and refried beans. For because of the look, you'll definitely go back for the food. Breakfast and lunch are served Monday through Friday, featuring typical American fare and lots of home country cooking (breakfast is served all day). While most of the meals on the menu are priced around $5 each, there are a few entrees in the $7 to $10 range.

Like any good '50s theme restaurant, burgers and sandwiches are fixtures on the menu, but the real highlights are the homemade foods prepared by the owner's mother. She serves up a number of beef, chicken and fish lunches with her country vegetables on the side. Interestingly, the beef liver and grilled onions is a frequently requested item.

From time to time, "Mom" is also known to prepare several specials that aren't on the menu, such as chicken and dumplings, meat loaf and chicken pot pie, all of which are homemade. That attention to freshness and made-from-scratch philosophy carries through to the desserts too. You'll rave over the coconut, lemon and butterscotch pies. And getting back to the '50s theme, you'll really make the scene when you belly up to the counter and order a banana split or shake from Virgil's soda fountain.

The facility has been a restaurant of one kind or another since 1929, when it was a place you could get a beer and swap a few tall tales. Later, it was known as Newman's Restaurant for about 34 years until Virgil Carr purchased it and reopened it as a '50s restaurant in 1990. As with its predecessors, Virgil's has become a downtown institution and is popular with those who work nearby. They even deliver within the immediate downtown area.

Peyton's Pizza & More
$$ • 115 E. Bruce St., Sevierville • (865) 428-8181

With its high-ceiling architecture—typical of many of the older downtown Sevierville buildings—and its freshly prepared Italian menu, Peyton's is a treat in the heart of the city. Open since early 1998, the eatery prides itself on its traditional Italian cuisine, consisting primarily of pizzas, but also featuring lunch and dinner entrees like chicken Parmigiana, lasagna, fettuccini Alfredo and pasta primavera. They have a variety of Italian sub sandwiches, calzones and bountiful salads, and both lunch and dinner patrons can choose from daily soup, salad and entree specials.

Peyton's pizzas, however, are their stock in trade. You can get either New York style or Chicago style pies with your choice of 18 toppings including Italian sausage, ricotta cheese, spinach and eggplant. We advise not letting your eyes get bigger than your stomach. Even the 14-inch size pie is plenty for two. The slices are massive and, believe it or not, just a couple of slices are enough to satisfy the most voracious of appetites.

Peyton's Pizza is open Monday through Saturday for lunch and dinner. Often throughout the year, they have live entertainment on Friday and Saturday evenings, usually consisting of a solo or duet act performing country or light rock music for dinner accompaniment. Peyton's doesn't serve alcohol, but you are allowed to "brown bag" it, provided you pay their nominal set-up charge. Guests will find plenty of free parking along Bruce Street in downtown Sevierville.

The Old Town Cafe & Deli
$, no credit cards • 152 E. Bruce St., Sevierville • (865) 429-8628

You'll find this little cafe tucked away among the many shops of downtown Sevierville. It has operated as a restaurant under various ownerships for the better part of 50 years, and as The Old Town Cafe & Deli since 1991. Serving lunch only Monday through Friday, it caters especially to Sevierville's downtown work force.

The menu is dominated by sandwiches, subs and pitas. One of the house specialties is the Steak Bomb sub, made of tender steak topped with cheese, onion, mushroom and green peppers. Patrons also rave about the homemade soups and desserts. You can fight off a winter chill with the beef barley or potato soups, or cap off a meal with scrumptious desserts like key lime, strawberry rhubarb and pumpkin pies, cheesecake or several flavors of pudding. Diners will also find daily specials that aren't on the menu, more entree-style offerings such as meat loaf, chicken and pot roast.

The Old Town Cafe & Deli isn't huge. Let's call it cozy and quaint with its bright, clean decor and country accents. If you decide to eat in, you'll have to vie for one of eight small tables or one of the few seats at the counter. Otherwise, they'll be happy to prepare your meal for carry out. If they have enough help on hand, they'll even deliver within the downtown area.

Chef Jock's Roasted Pepper Cafe & Bakery
$$$ • 950 Dolly Parton Pkwy., Sevierville • (865) 908-0033

Owner and chef Giacomo Lijoi (Chef Jock)

has given Smoky Mountain residents and visitors alike some of the finest dining experiences around thanks to his two restaurants. His Tastebuds Cafe has been a popular dining destination in Pigeon Forge for years now (see the "Pigeon Forge" section of this chapter), and he introduced this newer restaurant in 1999. The cuisine at the Roasted Pepper is primarily Mediterranean, and Chef Jock draws on his family's culinary background and his years of experience with each dish he and his staff prepare. Being quite the fitness buff, Chef Jock also strives to serve foods that are high on flavor but low in saturated fats.

Lijoi's dishes are always delicious and sometimes a little out of the ordinary. The dinner menu at Roasted Pepper offers entrees "by land" and "by sea" as well as a variety of pasta dishes. In addition to flavorful preparations of traditional meats such as chicken and steak, you can get entrees like pork tenderloin, veal and even ostrich tenderloin. His seafood repertoire includes scungili-black mussels in herb oil over pasta-and calamari-sauteed squid. All dinners include salad, bread and a side dish. For starters, you might choose stuffed tomatoes, stuffed peppers or congilli-seasoned baby shrimp, spinach, onion and peppers prepared in a cheese sauce and served over angel hair pasta. Desserts vary from day to day but might include Sicilian cheesecake, baklava or rum cake.

Roasted Pepper Cafe has a lunch menu with most dishes costing around $6.50. You'll find personal Boboli-style pizzas as well as quite a few foccacia and pasta dishes. While you're at the restaurant, you might want to check out the fresh breads and desserts at the adjacent bakery. There's also a banquet room that accommodates business meetings, conferences, wedding receptions and the like. Guests will find plenty of free parking on site.

A meal at Roasted Pepper Cafe is a relaxed experience, both during lunch and dinner. The interior motif is simple, yet full of character with its baked tile floors, wooden accents and warm earth tones. At night, the lighting is subdued, and Jock brings in musicians to play dinner music on selected nights. One evening you might hear a guitar-flute duo while another night might bring the sounds of a strolling violinist. The restaurant doesn't serve alcohol, but you can bring your own in with you, and corkscrews and setups are available for a nominal charge. Chef Jock's Roasted Pepper Cafe is open Tuesday through Saturday. Reservations are recommended, especially on weekends.

Walters State Culinary Institute
$ • Pittman Center Rd., Sevierville
• (865) 774-5800

If you've ever wanted to serve as a guinea pig for aspiring young chefs, this is your chance. If not, try it anyway. When you put yourself at the mercy of the students of this community college culinary arts program, you actually get a wonderful four-course meal and great service to boot, all at a remarkably low price. Located at the new Walters State Community College campus in Sevierville, the institute serves lunch to the public Monday through Thursday (dinners are scheduled occasionally, too) throughout the academic year.

The menu changes daily, depending on the whim of the "chef of the day," one of the program's 60-plus students who supervises every aspect of the meal, from menu selection to assignment of cook and wait staff personnel. A typical meal might feature a lineup of potato skins, Caesar salad, chicken breast Parmesan, pork loin, rice pilaf and vegetables. Also, there are the occasional "international weeks" during which cuisine from various ethnic cultures is served buffet style.

All guests are required to make reservations. Since menus are planned weeks in advance and distributed to those on the institute's mailing list, available spots usually fill up quickly, and some meals even sell out weeks ahead. So it's a good idea not to wait until the last minute to reserve your table.

Walters State's culinary program has been in operation since 1998, and the school originally used an old restaurant facility in downtown Sevierville as its "campus." The school, which now takes up an entire wing of the college's

INSIDERS' TIP

Major chain restaurants have made a limited incursion into Gatlinburg at this writing, with more sure to come. The current list in Gatlinburg includes Applebee's, Ruby Tuesday's, Hard Rock Cafe, T.G.I. Friday's and O'Charley's, all with locations on the Parkway. In keeping with another local growth industry, the Hard Rock Cafe is the only restaurant in the Smokies with a wedding chapel on the premises—talk about a way to pass the time waiting for a seat! Fast food chains are heavily represented on or near the Parkway in the downtown area.

new $6.5 million building, boasts three state-of-the-art kitchens where food is prepared for 75 to 100 guests per meal. The cost of each meal is $7 per person (tax included), and any tips left behind help cover the culinary arts program's scholarship fund and operational expenses. Plenty of free parking is available at the Walters State campus.

Chiang House
$$-$$$ • 624 Parkway, Sevierville
• (865) 428-5977

Let's say you're in the mood for an Oriental meal, but you can't make up your mind about what you're hungry for. You could go to a Chinese restaurant or a Japanese steak house or a sushi bar. If you're the indecisive type, just go to Chiang House and make up your mind when you get there! This versatile house of Far East cuisine offers traditional Chinese dishes as well as those prepared Japanese hibachi style; and yes, there's even a separate sushi bar. It's only been in business since 1997, but this place is the only sushi and Hibachi game in town, making it a big draw among locals and tourists both.

We'll start with the Chinese menu. You can select from more than 60 entrees, including poultry, beef, pork, seafood and vegetarian dishes. If you're undecided, the owners recommend General Tso's Seafood, House Scallops and Shrimp or House Two Delicacies (shrimp and chicken). Dinner and lunch entrees are both served with rice.

Add the element of entertainment to your Chiang House experience with their Japanese Teppan-Yaki meals, where the food is prepared at your table hibachi style. Kids and adults both absolutely love watching the highly trained chefs as they juggle, twirl and spin their cutlery like masters. "Oohs," "ahhs" and lots of applause from the diners are almost guaranteed. The cooking of the meal is a true show and as much fun as actually eating it. Teppan-Yaki dinners include a shrimp appetizer, Japanese soup and salad, and the entrees are served with rice and vegetables. The shrimp and scallop dinner is mouth watering, and the filet mignon is one of the more popular dishes.

If you've ever wanted to sample exotic tastes from the sea like squid, octopus or eel, you'll have your chance at Chiang House's sushi bar. If you're not that daring, try the tuna, shrimp or salmon. The bar serves more than 15 types of sushi and sashimi, as well as sushi rolls and larger combination platters that will give you a representative sampling from the sushi menu.

For those who want to try a little bit of everything, you can dive into the lunch or dinner buffet, featuring soups and entrees from the Chinese menu and even sushi rolls. At Chiang House, you can also order a beer with your meal; they carry a good selection of domestic brands in addition to several imported Japanese labels. The restaurant is open seven days a week for lunch and dinner. Reservations aren't required, but they are accepted.

Rocky River Brewery & Grille
$$$ • 1444 Hurley Dr., Sevierville
• (865) 908-3686

This restaurant and microbrewery was one of the premiere tenants of Sevierville's Governor's Crossing development when it opened in 1998. Located just off the Parkway, along the banks of the Little Pigeon River, Rocky River Brewery & Grille serves up hearty American fare along with an award-winning slate of microbrewed lagers and ales. You can dine there for lunch and dinner seven days a week.

Among the restaurant's biggest food sellers are the chicken fingers from the appetizer menu, Black Angus steaks (ribeye and New York strip) and pizzas baked before your eyes in Rocky River's own wood oven. You'll enjoy your meal in one of several dining areas accented by stacked stone walls and lots of warm color. The lofty, wooden ceilings add to the open feel of the restaurant. When weather permits, they also open the ample outdoor terrace for riverside drinking and dining.

The brewery is a large, glass-enclosed room that makes up the hub of the restaurant. Patrons can watch as brewmeisters oversee production of as many as 10 different labels. If their schedule allows, they'll even give you a guided tour of the facility, which is marked by many shiny, silver, 1,420-gallon fermenting vats. At any given time there are at least six different beers being brewed and served, mostly of German and English varieties. Among the more popular labels are the Ten Point (similar to a light beer) and the Golden Eagle, a bare bottom stout that won a gold metal at the Great American Brewing Festival in Denver.

Rocky River Brewery & Grille hosts an annual beer tasting festival of its own each May, and is also home to a sports bar that we discuss in more depth in our Music Theaters and Nightlife chapter.

NASCAR Cafe
$$$ • 1425 Hurley Dr., Sevierville
• (865) 428-7223

While our general rule of thumb is to focus

on non-franchise properties, we're making an exception in this case since the Smokies are a popular vacation destination among the NASCAR faithful. Debuting at Governor's Crossing in 1999, this restaurant is the fourth NASCAR Cafe to spring up in the Southeast. It helps racing fans kill many birds with one stone, offering not only food, but entertainment and shopping, all trimmed with a racing edge. We'll start off with the restaurant itself, which serves lunch and dinner seven days a week.

The entrees encompass something for most tastes. Chicken, steaks, chops, ribs, pasta and seafood appear with thematic names like Collision Chicken and Rockingham Ribeye. Club and barbecue sandwiches and burgers fill out the sandwich section. A familiar lineup of deep-fried appetizers and big salads round out the menu. The desserts are impressive. The Chocolate Fudge Tire is a chocolate bar cake served under vanilla ice cream and chocolate fudge sauce, and the Banana Split The Field is a huge version of this dessert favorite.

If you're into NASCAR, however, the decor alone is worth the trip. Monitors showing racing events are stationed around the room, and championship banners hang from the high ceiling. But the most eye-catching aspect of your time at the cafe is the steeply banked, curved section of race track installed at ceiling level, dominating half the room. On this track are mounted eight life-sized stock car replicas. At 45-minute intervals, the cars' wheels begin to spin, smoke bellows from the track as the tires "burn rubber" and the roar of gunning engines and squealing tires adds to the effect as another "race" gets underway. You might just as well be eating on the infield at Bristol!

Found just off the foyer is the Fuel Center, a bar serving a decent selection of imported and domestic beers on tap and in bottles as well as wine coolers. The lounge has happy hour specials during the week, and, when demand warrants, live entertainment on specified nights.

INSIDERS' TIP

Are you a breakfast person? Does a big stack of buttermilk pancakes smothered in butter and syrup make your mouth water? The Smokies are dripping with restaurants that specialize in pancakes and/or breakfast, beyond the several mentioned here. They're easy to spot—you'll usually find the word "pancake" somewhere in the restaurant's name. You don't have to travel very far to find one, either. Just in Pigeon Forge and Gatlinburg, there are nearly 15 different breakfast houses (that don't belong to national chains) where you can start your day off with pancakes, waffles, omelettes and yes, those famous Southern grits!

The rest of the NASCAR Cafe facility is dripping with pure racing ambience. There's a large, well-stocked gift shop full of NASCAR clothing, souvenirs and collectibles. Throughout different areas of the restaurant you'll find lots of glassed-in NASCAR memorabilia, including photos, helmets, trophies and plenty of other speed demon stuff. Outside the restaurant, stock cars (both real and replicated) are placed strategically throughout the parking lot. And if all this isn't enough, there's a fun center inside featuring 25 racing-oriented video games and a driving simulator.

Berry Ridge Grille
$$ • 1625 Parkway, Sevierville
• (865) 908-2969

From the early 1990s until the summer of 1998, this restaurant was known as Five Oaks Beef and Seafood, and was a dining tradition for locals and vacationers alike. Although the menu has changed substantially since those days, the quality of the food is still way above par, and the prices are even lower than they were before. One thing that hasn't changed, thankfully, is the building itself—a beautiful, antebellum structure that served as a farmhouse until its conversion to a restaurant.

Berry Ridge Grille bills itself as a place for "casual Southern dining." This is true: Shorts and sneakers are never frowned upon, and the menu boasts a number of dishes that could best be described as native to the region. However, the atmosphere and the quality of the food both leave you with the impression that you're having a "fine dining" experience.

The restaurant is open seven days a week, serving lunch and dinner. Both menus include salads, sandwiches, specialty entrees, items "From The Grille" and desserts. The meals are home cooked and are served in large portions. Fresh bread, soups and sides accompany the entrees. Choose from dishes like Southern style country fried steak, baked Virginia ham and center cut pork chops as well as pasta and seafood dishes. The chicken and dumplings and

Breakfast in a bright sunny restaurant is a great way to start your day.

Photo: Courtesy Sevierville Chamber of Commerce

Granny's Pot Roast have become favorites with the clientele. For dessert, be sure to try the homemade ice cream.

If you're not in a big hurry (diners here usually aren't), get up and take a look around the restaurant. The white, two-story building was built in the 1800s and was part of the Ogle family's horse and cattle farm. Black and white pictures from the farm's heyday are mounted on the wall in one of the dining rooms. Today, the house is decorated in elegant shades of burgundy and hunter green. Many of the rooms still have wood floors and warm, wood paneling. Ceiling fans and fireplaces are fixtures in most of the dining areas. Rooms in the back and on the south side have lots of windows for light and cheery dining during the day.

The upstairs part of Berry Ridge Grille is split between dining areas and the restaurant's private club. They sell memberships to area residents and out-of-towners for $25 quarterly. In exchange, members can bring along their own alcohol and have it served in the club's cozy atmosphere. The restaurant itself, however, does not serve alcohol.

Applewood Farmhouse Restaurant
$$$ • 240 Apple Valley Rd., Sevierville • (865) 428-1222

We should probably preface this write up with a short primer on Apple Valley Farms, an operational apple farm in Sevierville that has grown into an immensely popular tourist stop. Besides sporting two full service restaurants, it's also home to the Apple Barn General Store and Cider Mill, the Apple Butter Kitchen, The Candy Apple and Chocolate Factory, The Creamery and the Apple Barn Winery. Read about this "delicious" Sevierville stopover in the Close-up of our Shopping chapter.

There are actually two restaurants that are part of the Apple Valley Farms complex— Applewood Farmhouse Restaurant and the newer Applewood Farmhouse Grill. Since their menus are very similar, we'll focus on the original Farmhouse Restaurant and include a few distinguishing facts about the newer Farmhouse Grill in parting.

As would be expected, the apple reigns supreme at Applewood Farmhouse Restaurant. You can get breakfast, lunch and dinner there along with plenty of apple-licious side dishes. Mornings start out with all the traditional breakfast favorites like omelets, pancakes, eggs and biscuits. Big appetites might be interested in the Farmhouse Special Breakfast, featuring your choice of nine different main items ranging from bacon to country ham hash and even rainbow trout. Each main dish comes with an Applewood Julep, applesauce muffins and apple fritters, homemade apple butter, biscuits, fried apples, grits and sausage gravy, home-fried potatoes and two eggs cooked to order. Don't forget to ask for a doggy bag!

Lunches and dinners are also loaded with extras but include a few different side dishes like homemade vegetable soup, mashed potatoes and a choice of vegetable. As for the entrees, some of the "Farmhouse Favorites" include Farmhouse Southern Fried Chicken, Farmhouse Old Fashioned Chicken & Dumplings, chicken pot pie and Applewood Pork Loin. The last is a tender, boneless pork loin smoked over apple wood and served with homemade apple relish.

The Applewood Farmhouse Restaurant is located in what was once an actual farmhouse, built in 1921. It was refurbished and opened in 1987 as a restaurant. As it exists today, the building has retained much of what was surely its original charm. A friendly, white-washed exterior welcomes you into a world of country simplicity. The floors are wood and the wallpaper is highlighted by strips of apple designs along the ceiling molding. There are few accent pieces, but this maintains consistency with the restaurants overall minimalist look. One of the rear dining rooms is surrounded by windows and offers views of the rest of the Apple Valley complex and the lazy Little Pigeon River just beyond.

The newer restaurant, Applewood Farmhouse Grill, was opened on the Apple Valley Farms sight in 1995. Although the construction is newer, it was designed to resemble its older sister. The breakfast and lunch menus are very similar to those of the original restaurant, but side salads and desserts are not included in the price of the dinners as they are at Applewood Farmhouse Restaurant. Overall, however, the prices on the dinner menu are a little less expensive. Both restaurants have a reasonably priced children's menu with kids' favorites like grilled cheese sandwiches, burgers and fried chicken.

Pigeon Forge

Restaurants in Pigeon Forge are not allowed to sell alcohol of any kind by the drink. There is one exception, Alf's, which you'll read about below.

Alf's

$, no credit cards • 1965 Parkway, Pigeon Forge • no phone

When it opened in 1976, this restaurant was outside Pigeon Forge city limits. As such, it was able to sell beer by the drink. Years later, when it was annexed by the city, it was "grandfathered in" and allowed to continue serving. Until just a few years ago, it was the only place in the county north of Gatlinburg that served any kind of alcohol, so it became a favorite among locals who wanted to go out for a beer but just didn't feel like driving to Gatlinburg or Knoxville. As a result, it's a bit of an institution.

Alf's is easy to find. It's located on the Parkway directly across from the Louise Mandrell Theater. The signboard in front of the restaurant has remained unchanged over the years as far as anyone can recall: "Good Food, Cold Beer." The relatively small dinner menu features steaks, ham, chicken, chops and a few varieties of seafood, and most of what shows up on your plate is fried. Although dinners average around $7 each, the lunches are more reasonably priced at around $3. Burgers and other types of sandwiches are standard for lunch.

Admittedly, Alf's isn't going to win any culinary awards, but sometimes there's more to a restaurant than the food. You can shimmy into a booth and order a domestic beer by the bottle or the pitcher. For entertainment, there's a juke box, and you can look at the collection of license plates from all over the country that adorn Alf's walls. Or, you can listen in on the conversations of some of Pigeon Forge's more colorful locals. Any way you view it, Alf's is proof that sometimes the simple things in life are often the most memorable.

Alabama Grill

$$$ • 2050 Parkway, Pigeon Forge • (865) 908-8777

This celebrity-themed restaurant stands between two popular music theaters on the Parkway—Anita Bryant's Music Mansion Theater and the Louise Mandrell Theater. It's named after the country group, Alabama, and is almost as much a museum of country music as it is a restaurant. Between the music, the videos and the 750-plus pieces of country memorabilia found throughout, Alabama Grill pays tribute to dozens of country music artists, including the restaurant's namesake.

The Alabama Grill experience begins before you even enter the restaurant. Outside, you'll find a limousine formerly used by the band as well as one of their custom tour busses. You can peek into the windows of the limo or take a self-guided tour through the bus.

When you enter the lobby, you'll come face

How 'Bout a Fried Balogna Sandwich?

Surrounding the grandeur of the Smokies and the glitter created by the cities that host their visitors, Sevier County still lives in a kind of time warp that's disappearing fast. While it holds on, the rural atmosphere that exists just outside the Smokies corridor hides a lot of treasures that a lot of people thought was gone from the American scene forever: The Mom & Pop general store.

This is a place few will remember, where locals, mostly farmers and other close-to-the-earth laborers, stop by daily for a loaf of bread or a dozen fresh eggs, and as often as not stick around for a sandwich or a soft drink while they're at it. If you're here for the "whole hog," your meal will probably include:

- A fried balogna sandwich (self explanatory).
- A Moon Pie—a purely Southern concoction made in Nashville for close to a century. A Moon Pie is a chocolate cookie about four inches across, covered with marshmallow cream and dipped in chocolate... yuummmm!
- A big dope—a carbonated beverage, typically a 12-ounce Coke, Pepsi or, if you're really Southern, RC Cola.

These places aren't real long on ambience, and sometimes they don't have a place to sit, but they do have a short menu of honest-to-God food that'll stick to your ribs and drive a nutritionist to the brink of madness. And it won't cost you an arm and a leg to eat. No self-respecting tour guide would be caught dead in these places, and don't look for a four-star rating or a maitre d'. The cook may be an old man, an older woman, or a kid that stands on a milk crate to reach the grill. They may or may not write down your order, and you'll usually pay for whatever you tell the person at the cash register you had to eat. And you'll usually get away with a cholesterol-laden fried sandwich or other simple fare, French fried potatoes or onion rings, and a soft drink you picked out of the cooler, for less than a five-dollar bill.

Most of these establishments are small grocery stores with a grill and a lunch counter, and most serve breakfast and lunch. They usually open around 7 AM and serve through mid-afternoon. With a few noted exceptions, these businesses are on roads that ring the Smokies corridor, and you'll find them on your way to some attraction or accommodation mentioned elsewhere in this book.

The places on this list had to meet three simple criteria to be mentioned: 1. They have to sell some other commodity (usually gas and/or groceries) besides food; 2. Everything they serve must be cooked before your eyes; and 3. Their menu *must* offer either a fried bologna sandwich or home-baked biscuits (most have both).

Throw away your diet for a while and enjoy a sample of what the locals really eat, in the places where they really eat it. This section won't include a price code, but we'll throw in the price of a bologna sandwich ("FBS" before the street address) to give an indication: Like we said earlier, a five-dollar bill will probably return a little change for each person eating. A note on locations: All of the places mentioned are listed as being in Sevierville or Gatlinburg. These places are all on perimeter roads, and are either within the city limits or in unincorporated areas. There are none in Pigeon Forge proper, but a few are in areas of the county very close to that city.

Sevierville

Starting on Dolly Parton Parkway (U.S. 411E), we'll work our way south on Middle Creek and Pittman Center Roads. The first listing is the oldest known business of this type in continuous operation by a single family.

(Continued on next page)

RESTAURANTS

Lunch time at McCarter's Market—East Parkway, Gatlinburg

Photo: Dick McHugh

Stanley Creswell Grocery

FBS: $1.59 • 1366 Dolly Parton Pkwy., Sevierville • (865) 453-2402

The late Stanley Creswell opened his first grocery near this site before World War II. His children continue to operate the grocery and grill today. The current location, built in the early '70s, is less than a mile east of Sevier County High School. Seating for about 30 is distributed throughout the store wherever room is available. The grill is open Monday through Saturday, 5 AM to 2:30 PM.

Middle Creek Market & Deli

FBS: $1.59 • 1319 Middle Creek Rd., Sevierville • (865) 453-6224

One of two markets owned by the Chance family (Ralph is frequently the mayor of Pigeon Forge), Middle Creek Market's grill is open from 5 AM to 7 PM Monday through Saturday and from 7 AM to 4 PM on Sunday. Both of the Chance family's markets (see below) are renowned for two-fisted hamburgers and generous servings. A single order of fries or potato wedges is ample for two adults.

Chance's Market

FBS: $1.59 • 2060 Pittman Center Rd., Sevierville • (865) 453-8817

The other Chance family enterprise; this one seats about 30 at tables and stools, with a menu that's virtually identical to the Middle Creek store. More Chance family members seem to work in this location, and one of them will gladly deliver your order to your table if things aren't too crowded. The grill is open from 6 AM to 7 PM Monday through Saturday, and 7 AM to 6 PM Sunday.

Dunn's Market and Grill

FBS: $1.29 • 2650 Upper Middle Creek Rd., Sevierville • (865) 429-5804

Seven tables are scattered through Dunn's Market, with seating for as many can fit around them. The grill is open Monday through Saturday from 6 AM to 9 PM, and Sunday from 6 AM to 6 PM. Get there early for biscuits; Dunn's are considered by a highly prejudiced clientele to be the best thing on the menu.

Hatcher's Grocery & Hardware
FBS $1.65 • 1386 Wears Valley Rd., Sevierville • (865) 453-4726

When the Hatcher family built this store in 1973, there wasn't another building within a mile in either direction. Since the Parkway in Pigeon Forge is only two miles distant at traffic light #3, things have changed a lot in that direction. Going the other way (toward a little-used entrance to the national park and Townsend), there's still a lot of open land. Hatcher's is kind of at the edge of the two worlds defined by the Smokies corridor. Like its contemporaries around the periphery of the corridor, the Hatchers' business is intended mainly for local usage, but they don't ask anybody where they're from. The menu is typical: Simple, hearty fare that you can enjoy while sitting at the 10-stool counter or one of the 3 booths in front of the picture window. Drinks other than coffee and iced tea are self-serve from the cooler. While you're waiting for your food (nothing's pre-cooked) you can browse through the grocery store or find just about any home-repair item you can think of in the hardware section. Check your gas gauge before leaving—if you're heading away from Pigeon Forge, it's going to be a while before you see another set of pumps.

Gatlinburg

McKinney's Market
FBS: $1.35 • 819 East Parkway, Gatlinburg • (865) 436-2272

There's no seating at Faye and Dale's (local terminology), but there is a drive-up window for your second visit and those that succeed it. Locally favored for its deli sandwich menu, McKinney's is a favorite stop for a cup of coffee and a biscuit sandwich on a chilly morning. Most of the morning clientele are firemen and construction workers on their way to work. McKinney's is a handy place to know— in addition to the deli/grocery and gas pumps, there's a family-owned auto parts and repair shop on the property. They're also open 24 hours during the season.

McCarter's Market
FBS: $1.75 • 103 Mills Park Rd., Gatlinburg • (865) 436-4951

Don't let the address fool you—this place is on East Parkway, about 4½ miles east of downtown Gatlinburg. The mailbox is on Mills Park Road. A local landmark for more years than anyone recalls, McCarter's serves breakfast starting at 7 AM, and if you want biscuits you'd better be there before 9. A full slate of sandwiches for lunch is complemented by a lunch special Monday through Friday, until they run out of it. The house special is "Ron & Giff's Burger," a patty melt on special bread. McCarter's soup beans are locally famous. One of the larger places, McCarter's has seating for about 10 at the counter and several tables. The grill is open until 3 PM daily except Sunday. The market's open from 7 AM to 8 PM every day.

RESTAURANTS

to face with what could best be described as a sort of Alabama shrine. A large painted mural of the band dominates one wall, and below it are glass cases containing personal items donated by each of its members. The far right wall of the lobby is covered with many of the band's gold records. To the left is a newly expanded gift shop where you'll find all sorts of Alabama merchandise like T-shirts, CDs and cassettes.

Inside the main room of the restaurant is a large dining area flanked by several smaller dining alcoves. A giant neon guitar hangs over the center section, and all of the walls are packed to capacity with memorabilia. Most of the pieces are either costumes, gold records, musical instruments or photographs of country stars ranging from Dolly Parton to Clint Black. You'll see one of Elvis Presley's guitars and a red jumpsuit that The King wore on stage. Complementing the artifacts, several television monitors play hits by country stars old and new.

At the far end of the dining room is a small stage backed by another mural of the band, this one made of stained glass. Once each hour, the restaurant's large video screen drops down to the stage and shows the band playing a ten-minute musical tribute to other country artists. During the tribute, the Alabama Grill server staff gets on stage for a line dancing performance. Audience members are welcome to join in and try out some boot scootin' steps.

No, we haven't forgotten that this is a restaurant, so on to the food! Alabama Grill serves lunch and dinner all week long. Many of the menu inclusions like the soups, desserts and bread are all freshly made on site; altogether, there are some 60 different items available. Those interested in a sandwich will find burgers in half-pound portions and a club sandwich that's loaded from top to bottom. From the dessert menu, there's an interesting cheesecake with an Alabama twist— a swirl of sweet potato.

Entree specialties include Alabama's "World Famous" Ribs and The Big Texan, a 16-ounce, country fried steak served with gravy and mashed potatoes. You might also be intrigued by RoadKill 59, a chicken fried chicken breast topped with brown gravy, smoked pit ham, Swiss cheese and bacon smoked over apple wood. There are both fried and grilled dishes from the kitchen, and all entrees are served with freshly baked bread.

Eddie's Heart and Soul Cafe
$$$ • 140 Showplace Blvd., Pigeon Forge
• (865) 453-0833

You'll find this popular Pigeon Forge eatery just off the Parkway, next door to Country Tonite Theatre. What you get when you're there is a dual offering of "music for your heart and food for your soul," as the restaurant's mission statement reads. Owner Eddie Anders is a gifted musician and vocalist who spent about a decade on the contemporary Christian music circuit, performing with groups like Daybreak, Truth and the Bill Gaither Trio. Nowadays, he shares his musical talents with his restaurant patrons, performing regularly throughout the day beginning at 11 AM. For now, we'll focus more on the dining aspects of Eddie's Heart and Soul Cafe. To learn more about Anders' background and the cafe's live performances, see our Music Theaters and Nightlife chapter.

The restaurant is open seven days a week for lunch and dinner. Guests have an eclectic set of menu choices to ponder. Entrees include various steak and chicken dishes as well as baby back ribs, fried seafood and several varieties of fettucine. Lunchtime visitors may want to dig into one of the

menu's many burgers, sandwiches or salads. And be sure to save room for dessert. Most of the sweets are personally made on site by the restaurant's manager and his mother. Incidentally, Anders has given most of the dishes names that are special to him in one way or another. Nancy's Chicken Nachos Supreme are named for his wife, and the Chicago 10-ounce Ribeye Steak is named for the music group, Chicago, one of Anders' early musical influences.

The layout of Eddie's Heart and Soul Cafe is a wide open, two-tiered dining room. At one end is a fireplace and doors that open on to a porch (for warm-weather dining). The other end of the room is dominated by Eddie's stage, complete with its multiple keyboard setups. On the wall above the stage is a bank of 16 video monitors that present a steady stream of music videos when Eddie isn't performing.

What really grabs the visitor's eye, however, is the collection of memorabilia found throughout the restaurant. Most of them are personally autographed gifts from a who's who of celebrity musicians, athletes, politicians and more. Among Anders' favorites are a suit and Bible from Dr. Billy Graham, autographed guitars and drum heads from the group, Chicago, and a Doobie Brothers tour jacket given to him by band member Michael McDonald. While you're browsing, you might also want to check out Heart and Soul's gift shop, which accounts for most of the main lobby.

Alan Jackson's Showcar Cafe
$$ • 2301 Parkway, Pigeon Forge
• (865) 908-9007

If you're a fan of hearty American fare, country music star Alan Jackson, custom automobiles or any combination of the three, you need to visit this, one of the Smokies' newest celebrity-themed restaurants. The food definitely has a flavor that's as country as Jackson's music. But Showcar Cafe is as much a feast for the eyes as it is the palate. Guests and passers by alike are greeted outside the restaurant by anywhere from 15 to 25 custom showcars and trucks, some of which are part of Jackson's personal collection of vehicles. On display are a DeLorean as well as Jackson's own Dodge Viper and his original tour bus.

Foodwise, Showcar Cafe serves three meals daily, beginning with the Gone Country breakfast buffet from 8 to 11 AM.

INSIDERS' TIP
While most Smoky Mountains restaurants don't require reservations, calling ahead is definitely advised for larger parties (15 or more) and tour groups.

Scrambled eggs, country ham, sausage, biscuits and more are available in limitless portions. Lunch and dinner are then served from the menu. Signature entrees include country fried steak, roast beef, meat loaf and oven fried chicken. Also choose from marinated steaks and seafood. All entrees are served with a choice of Alan's Iron Skillet Cornbread or Angel "Drop" Biscuits and a choice of side dishes.

Also on the menu are appetizers, burgers, sandwiches, entree salads and pizzas. Desserts are made from scratch using Jackson's mother's recipes. Be sure to try the fudge brownie sundae and the pecan pie. Showcar Cafe also has a Soda Shoppe that specializes in non-alcoholic beverages, with more than 40 from which to choose.

On entering the restaurant, you'll discover a gift shop (naturally) on one end of the lobby. On the other side is the Soda Shoppe that operates in summer only, serving up not only beverages, but cool desserts as well. This is also a good place to keep the kids occupied with video games or a game of pool.

The large, wide-open dining room is marked by a predominance of ceiling fans and Alan Jackson memorabilia. The upper level provides booth seating while tables are found on the lower level. There are a few cars and motorcycles on display inside the dining room as well. Several video monitors are located throughout the restaurant, although attention is drawn to the giant screen television on the south wall. Music videos by Alan Jackson play regularly throughout the day.

Mel's Diner
$ • 119 Wears Valley Rd., Pigeon Forge • (865) 429-2184

Although it was constructed in 1993, Mel's is a classic diner in the architectural sense with its shiny, silver railroad car appearance. You'll find it just one block off the Parkway on Wears Valley Road in Pigeon Forge. Inside, take a nostalgic journey back to the 1950s in the restaurant's cozy, sleek interior among the retro color scheme and rows of booth seating.

One of the neat things about Mel's is that it's one of the few dining establishments in the Smokies that's open 24 hours a day, seven days

a week. For breakfast, they serve traditional morning fare like eggs and omelets, pancakes and waffles, and biscuits with gravy (don't forget, you're still in the South!). The rest of the menu consists primarily of American staples like burger and sandwich baskets and dinner platters, available between 11 AM and 10 PM. Platter entrees include hefty portions of pork chops, ham, meat loaf, country fried steak and many more. They come with bread and a choice of two side vegetables.

Be sure to allow room for dessert at Mel's. The cakes, pies and sundaes are out of this world, and the shakes come in flavors like butterscotch and pineapple as well as in interesting taste combinations like Chanana (chocolate-banana) and Strawnana (strawberry-banana). And if you don't feel like going out to eat, that's okay. You can call Mel's takeout express line, (865) 429-8562, for delivery within a limited area.

Chef Jock's Tastebuds Cafe
$$$ • 1198 Wears Valley Rd., Pigeon Forge • (865) 428-9781

Tastebuds Cafe is the first of two area restaurants opened by chef Giaccomo Lijoi (Chef Jock, as he's better known). The cuisine here is primarily French and definitely not typical of what you'll find in most area restaurants. For example, as an appetizer you might try the Shitake & Spinach Fromage in French Pastry or the Artichoke & Smoked Jarlesburg Dip. After trying these, potato skins tend to pale in comparison. Pasta, poultry, seafood, beef and pork entrees are prepared with only the freshest ingredients and with a European touch. Among the menu favorites is the Chicken Jean Pierre, a plump breast sauteed in butter, garlic, shallots, mushrooms, parsley, provolone, Chardonnay and cream. The Veal Chef Jock is another house specialty similarly prepared. For the more health conscious, some pasta and chicken dishes are prepared without oil. From time to time, Chef Jock will also present customers with nightly specials such as rack of lamb or ostrich. The desserts are made fresh and change from day to day.

The restaurant is a little off the main drag, two miles off the Parkway on Wears Valley Road in Pigeon Forge. The atmosphere is relaxed and elegant without being ostentatious.

INSIDERS' TIP

Night owls don't have many choices for 'round-the-clock dining in the Smokies. But if you've got a late-night craving, you can visit Mel's Diner on Wears Valley Road in Pigeon Forge or either of two Huddle House locations, one on Dolly Parton Parkway in Sevierville and the other on the Parkway in Pigeon Forge.

RESTAURANTS

The dining room is very intimate—okay, it's small. In fact, the seating capacity is 52, and they're almost always full for lunch and dinner. As a result, reservations are highly recommended here, especially for a Friday or Saturday night. Calling a day or two ahead will usually get you a table. But don't let any of this intimidate you. As at most restaurants in the Smokies, you can "come as you are," and casual attire is entirely welcome. By the way, Chef Jock's doesn't serve alcohol, but you can bring your own with you.

Tastebuds Cafe is open for lunch Tuesday through Friday. Dinner is served Tuesday through Saturday. The restaurant is closed on Sunday and Monday. Chef Jock also personally caters and prepares meals for any size party. See the Sevierville section of this chapter to read about Lijoi's other restaurant, Chef Jock's Roasted Pepper Cafe & Bakery.

Bel Air Grill
$$$ • 2785 Parkway, Pigeon Forge
• (865) 429-0101

Bel Air Grill is a small regional chain of '50s style restaurants that started in Alcoa, Tennessee, in 1990. There are now five of them throughout East Tennessee. At the Pigeon Forge site, lunch and dinner are served all week long, and burgers are the restaurant's claim to fame.

The Bel Air Cheeseburger is an eight-ounce patty grilled to order with your choice of toppings. Like the other burgers and sandwiches on the menu, it's served with fries. In general, the menu is beefy, including entrees like baby back ribs, New York Strip steak and Fonzy's Filet, a nine-ounce tenderloin cut (a house favorite). Shrimp, pork and seafood dishes are served as well, and the mesquite-grilled salmon is another popular item. Most entrees come with soup or salad, rolls and a choice of fries or a Bel Air Spud.

You can start out your meal with Bel Air Grill's own Loaded Baked Potato Soup or the deep fried onion loaf. To cap things off, your '50s dining experience wouldn't be complete without one of their shakes, malts or ice cream floats. That '50s feel is enhanced overall by the interior decor, marked by checkerboard floors and tablecloths, a jukebox and dozens of custom automobile photographs mounted on the walls.

Bennett's Pit Bar-B-Que
$$$ • 2910 Parkway, Pigeon Forge
• (865) 429-2200
$$ • 714 River Road, Gatlinburg
• (865) 436-2400

Just because you're surrounded by Eastern mountains doesn't mean you can't dig in to the hearty, zesty flavors of the Southwest. Both Sevier County Bennett's serve satisfying portions of pork, beef, chicken and ribs prepared just the way barbecue aficionados like them. The lunch and dinner menus present a broad selection of hickory-smoked and mesquite-grilled entrees, a 40-item, all-you-can-eat soup and salad bar, barbecue sandwiches and much more.

Separately, or in various combinations, Bennett's offers five basic meats from its hickory smoker: chopped pork, sliced beef brisket, sliced sausage, chicken and pork spare ribs. Other entrees like steaks, shrimp and chicken breasts are flamed over the mesquite grill. Interestingly, Bennett's serves breakfast as well. That menu contains morning favorites like pancakes, omelets, biscuits and more, but also features a number of breakfast specials like hickory-smoked portions of ham, bacon, pork chops and even a ten-ounce strip.

The cooking methods used at Bennett's are true to good Texas form and result in foods that are moist, tender and packed with flavor. The meats start with a generous basting in Bennett's special recipe barbecue sauce. They're then smoldered over hickory wood and smoked for up to 14 hours. Then it's on to the open-pit hickory fire where selections are grilled to order.

Bennett's is a Denver-based chain with about 20 franchises nationwide. The Pigeon Forge Bennett's opened in 1991, and about a year later, the second one appeared on River Road in Gatlinburg. The Gatlinburg location also has a full service cocktail lounge where you can relax with a game of pool, darts, video games or televised sports. Both restaurants are open year-round.

Apple Tree Inn
$$ • 3215 Parkway, Pigeon Forge
• (865) 453-4961

This site has been a restaurant of some kind since the late 1940s. Having opened for business in 1967, the current Apple Tree Inn is one of the oldest operating restaurants in Pigeon Forge. In case you're wondering, it's not a hotel, nor was it ever a part of one. It was named, however, for a live apple tree that stood in the center of the restaurant's outdoor patio when it first opened.

Apple Tree Inn is open for breakfast, lunch and dinner seven days a week, although it is closed the better part of December through March. The menu presents familiar American offerings like sandwiches as well as beef, seafood and poultry entrees. Morning patrons can order from the breakfast menu or take on the all-you-can-eat breakfast and fresh fruit bar.

The house specialty, however, is what they call "family-style dining." Diners can choose from as many as four meats, four vegetables, soup or salad plus dessert and beverage, which are served on trays at your table. Family dining is often a less expensive prospect than ordering some of the other menu entrees, and the price is even lower for children. Family dining for lunch is also less expensive than it is in the evenings or on Sundays and Thanksgiving day.

Santo's Italian Restaurant
$$$ • 3270 Parkway, Pigeon Forge
• (865) 428-5840

Owner Santo Baiamonte brought his experience as a head chef in some of the area's finer restaurants to his own dining venture, which opened in 1991. His well-rounded Italian menu offers a host of traditional native dishes, including chicken, veal, seafood and pasta creations. It's one of those menus where everything sounds good, making the narrowing-down process a laborious one. The Chicken Parmigiana, Veal Parmigiana and five varieties of spaghetti are all customer favorites. Other items to weigh are fettuccine with snow crab, vegetarian lasagna and the fried calamari appetizer. All entrees come with a choice of salad or minestrone soup in addition to fresh, hot garlic bread. Chefs prepare all sauces, soups, desserts and entrees fresh daily.

Santo's serves dinner only, beginning at 4 PM. If you dine in between 4 and 6 PM, you can take advantage of the "early bird" specials, several moderately priced entrees that change weekly. If you make your visit after dark, however, you'll get the most out of the restaurant's ambience. The subdued lighting and background accompaniment of the house pianist help create a relaxed dining experience. Although the atmosphere comes across as elegant, Santo's is very family-friendly. Children and casual attire are both quite welcome.

The Old Mill Restaurant
$$$ • 2944 Old Mill Ave., Pigeon Forge
• (865) 429-3463

This restaurant stands next door to one of Pigeon Forge's most famous historical sites, The Old Mill. (See our Attractions chapter for more on this working mill.) The Old Mill Restaurant, however, is a veritable newcomer, having opened in 1993. From an architectural standpoint, these two neighbors on the banks of the Little Pigeon River blend together well. The restaurant is a sprawling timber-look building that has gone a long way toward matching the exterior ambience of the mill. Inside the restaurant, wood floors, rafters and simple country furnishings add consistency to the motif. The main dining room is split between two levels, allowing most diners pleasant views through large picture windows overlooking the Little Pigeon River below.

Three meals a day are served, all rife with flavors of the South. The Old Mill Country Breakfast is based around pancakes with grits, eggs, coffee, juice, muffins and biscuits. You can then add morning extras like bacon, ham or sausage. Both the lunch and dinner menus feature quite a few Old Mill Southern-Style Specialties like country fried steak, sugar cured ham and chicken pot pie for lunch or pork loin, chicken and dumplings and pot roast and gravy for dinner. The dinner menu also has a large selection of both fried and grilled entrees, including beef liver, catfish and ribeye steak. Most dinner entrees come with The Old Mill's trademark corn chowder and homemade fritters plus salad, vegetables and dessert. For lighter dining, there are several salad, fruit and vegetable plates from which to choose.

Duff's Famous Smorgasbord
$ • 3985 Parkway, Pigeon Forge
• (865) 453-6443

Many of you may recognize the Duff's name. For years these buffet-style family restaurants were fixtures throughout Middle America. Slowly, the chain dwindled away, and today only one Duff's still stands—this one in

Pigeon Forge. It's open from mid-February through December, serving lunch and dinner only in the off season months and adding a breakfast smorgasbord from May through October.

Actually, don't go to Duff's expecting to order from a menu, period. The restaurant specializes in its huge food bars. For one price, you have your choice of at least six hot entrees (fried chicken is always there), six vegetables, nine salads and ten desserts plus beverages. Carving stations with roast beef and ham are open after 3:30 PM on weekdays and all day on Saturday and Sunday. Duff's signature dessert is the Hurricane Cake, a spice cake topped with a gooey, buttery, brown sugar topping. Repeat visitors ask for it by name.

Gatlinburg

Back in 1981, when Gatlinburg was *the* destination in the Smokies, the city fathers foresaw great economic potential in the upcoming 1982 World's Fair being planned in Knoxville. Among the many changes they brought about to milk that potential was a liberalized alcohol code that permitted the sale of liquor by the drink in restaurants. Surprisingly, the city has maintained its insistence that spirits could only be sold with meals, thus preventing the descent into Hades that a lot of the locals predicted.

Gatlinburg's move into liquor sales has proved a boon to the local schools (taxes on liquor sales must, by state law, be used only for education), and has caused the neighboring cities to examine their own policies toward alcohol. In the following list, mixed drinks, beer, and wine are available with your meals unless otherwise stated. Also, as promised earlier, we'll tell you what the parking situation is on an individual basis.

The age factor also contributes to a phenomenon you probably wouldn't notice unless we brought it up. Atmosphere is not nearly as pronounced a factor in Gatlinburg restaurants as it is in the area to the north, because Gatlinburg's are generally older and don't feel obligated to compete for business by doing much other than offering good food and good service at reasonable prices. Accordingly, our descriptions of Gatlinburg's restaurants will omit all but the most obvious architectural and "ambience oriented" details, and will concentrate on the menus. We're also stretching the envelope slightly to include some regional chains that merit inclusion because they've gone to extra effort to fit into the local picture.

Our usual route prevails; we'll work the

Parkway from end to end, and then go east out East Parkway to pick up a few places outside the downtown business district. One final disclaimer: Each restaurant mentioned here, and it's not a complete list, is a free-standing structure devoted to food service. None of the places are in or associated with hotels, motels or attractions, and only three are in shopping malls.

Down the Parkway

The Old Heidelberg Castle
$$ • 138 Parkway, Gatlinburg
• (865) 430-3094

Originally established in 1975 by the late Bruno Rode, the Heidelberg is now operated by his son Harald. It's just past the "Welcome to Gatlinburg" sign on the Parkway, with ample parking right at the door. Consistent with its Bavarian-flavored motif (lots of snowy mountains and castles adorn the walls, and the staff dresses in Alpine garb), the dinner menu features a lot of German dishes with names only true Teutonics will get right the first time. German is also the language of choice among the staff, who will cheerfully assist you in pronunciation and description of the various "schnitzels und wursts." When things get a little slow (and even sometimes when they don't) Harald Rode dons his famous tuba, and he and his staff wander through the place singing Tyrolean songs nobody's ever heard, but everybody joins in anyway.

The Heidelberg is open year round, serving breakfast from 8 to 11 AM, a luncheon menu that's heavy on sandwiches from 11 AM to 4 PM, and their trademark Bavarian dinner dishes from 4 until closing, usually at 11 PM. A children's menu is available. Seating for 250 means that nobody has to wait too long to be seated.

Smoky Mountain Trout House
$$$ • 410 Parkway, Gatlinburg
• (865) 436-5416

They're a little vague about how long the Trout House has been in business, but Trout Eisenhower, the establishment's signature dinner, was so named during Ike's administration (1952-60). While the usual restaurant fare is available and cooked as well as anyone around can do it, the piece de resistance here is the local king of the game fish, caught fresh daily and offered in a dozen different presentations, some of which you'd never associate with a fish. You've probably heard of trout almondine, but how about trout dipped in sauce, coated with provolone cheese, and cooked in peanut oil? The Trout House is one of those "urban myth" places you hear about from time to time, a place that looks as unpretentious as a "greasy spoon" but leaves you knowing you've encountered culinary greatness. Just outside of the bustle of downtown, the Trout House opens at 5 PM for dinner, and is kind of intimate—reservations are recommended for groups larger than six. Municipal parking facilities are within easy walking distance of the restaurant in both directions, and the green route trolley stops at their door.

Atrium Restaurant
$ • 432 Parkway, Gatlinburg
• (865) 430-3684

One of Gatlinburg's favorite local spots, the Atrium is open from 7 AM to 2:30 PM for a full meal or a quick breakfast or luncheon sandwich. Seating for 100-plus provides outstanding people watching locations (a plate glass window is the only thing between the diner and the street), and the Atrium has its own four-story waterfall as a backdrop. The light and airy setting is enhanced by a profusion of plant life in hanging baskets and wall planters. The Atrium offers 25 varieties of pancakes for breakfast and a wide selection of soups, sandwiches, and entrees for lunch, with free parking at the front door. No alcohol is served.

No Way Jose's
$ • 555 Parkway, Gatlinburg
• (865) 430-5673

The appearance of No Way Jose's may take authenticity to an extreme—the place looks like an urban renewal program somebody forgot about, say 10 years ago. Don't be fooled; when you get past the cluttered exterior and into the dimly lit dining room that really doesn't look like it seats 160, you're in for a treat. Daily deliveries of the best fresh meat and vegetables are cooked in authentic Mexican style and served in generous portions that leave you wishing you had room for more. Margaritas and Mexican beers complement the meals, and the menu includes enough "Gringo" dishes to satisfy the less-adventurous palates in your group. Free parking is available at the front door, and the downtown aquarium parking lot is just across the street. No Way Jose's opens at 11 AM to catch the lunch crowd, and closes around 10 PM.

North China Chinese Restaurant
$ • Parkway, Gatlinburg • (865) 436-6572

Situated at the back of Charlie's Alley shopping mall, North China is also approachable from River Road, where there's a handy commercial parking lot. Opened in 1979, North China is a Gatlinburg mainstay with about 50 seats and a menu that's anything but "one from column A, one from column B." Every dish on the menu (and there's a bunch to choose from) is prepared in the regional style of the area it represents, and it's cooked and served by people who've been there. The large Hsieh family keeps bringing help over when they need it. And be prepared to eat Chinese—all 60 of the main menu selections and the dozen or so soups and appetizers are ethnic. The only concession to Occidental tastes is the drink selection, which includes American soft drinks and beer in addition to the Oolong tea. Family style dinners are available, where each person selects an entree that's served in enough quantity that everybody in the group can sample everything on the table. North China is open daily from 11 AM to 10 PM.

Pancake Pantry
$, no credit cards • 628 Parkway, Gatlinburg • (865) 436-4724

Arguably the favorite visitors' breakfast spot in the downtown area, the Pancake Pantry doesn't really need parking—it's within three blocks of more than a thousand motel rooms in the downtown and Baskins Creek areas. Open for breakfast and lunch, the Pancake Pantry's breakfast menu includes more ways to fix a pancake than you'd ever believe possible, and the soup-and-sandwich luncheon menu fills you up nicely without stuffing you. Opened in the early '70s, the Pancake Pantry's outstanding architecture and quick, friendly service have made it a landmark in downtown Gatlinburg.

Legends by Max
$$ • 650 Parkway, Gatlinburg • (865) 436-7343

In the middle of the Parkway in downtown Gatlinburg (no parking), Legends by Max leans heavily on grilled and barbecued foods in a setting that evokes memories of how it used to be. The stone front and simple floor plan (about 100 seats) invite you to relax, and the selection of a dozen or more smoked and grilled meats and seafood dishes is equally inviting. The Maxwells have been feeding people well in the Smokies for a long time, and this is their third venture—the others are the Berry Ridge Grille in Pigeon Forge (which is rhapsodically described in that section) and Maxwell's Beef and

Couples looking for an intimate dining experience have planty of places to choose from.

Photo: Courtesy Gatlinburg Department of Tourism

RESTAURANTS

Seafood, (see p. 115). The lunch menu at Legends by Max is a local favorite that includes an outstanding variety of specialty sandwiches. Sunday afternoons, locals gather at the bar to watch NFL games and enjoy items from the appetizer menu at both of the Maxwells' Gatlinburg locations.

Lineberger's Seafood Co
**$$ • 903 Parkway, Gatlinburg
• (865) 436-9284**

A refugee from the low country of South Carolina, Lineberger's features one of the most complete lines of fresh Atlantic seafood in the area. The restaurant is strongly reminiscent of the seafood houses that line Murrell's Inlet, just south of Myrtle Beach, which is exactly what the Lineberger family had in mind when they opened in Gatlinburg almost 20 years ago. The window views afforded from most seats make Lineberger's a great place for people-watching as you await and enjoy the extensive variety of seafood dishes and platters cooked to your order. Landlubber offerings like steaks, chicken, and chops will suit the aquatically challenged, but a visit to Lineberger's shouldn't really be for that type of eating.

Lineberger's opens at 4 PM Monday through Friday, and noon on weekends.

Best Italian Cafe and Pizzeria
**$-$$ • 968 Parkway, Gatlinburg
• (865) 430-4090**

The name may seem a little arrogant at first, but nobody who's ever eaten at the Best walks away complaining. Opened in 1975 in half the space it currently occupies at the back of Elk's Plaza, this is as authentic an ethnic restaurant as a native of New York City can make it. Atmosphere? "Fuggedaboudit!" People come here to eat. Again and again. If it's Italian, they make it; if not, see the quote above. "The Best" made its local reputation in the '70s, when it was the only pizza place in town (it's still the overwhelming favorite of locals), and grew from that start to a full-fledged eatery. From antipasto and garlic rolls that defy description as appetizers, through absolutely authentic entrees with those great names that roll so trippingly off the tongue (fettuccine, manicotti, parmigiana) to the sinful desserts you struggle to eat, "The Best" justifies its name. And as you go back to the real world singing softly to yourself, you won't even remember what the place looked like, but you'll remember where it is. The Best Italian Cafe is open seven days a week from 11 AM to 11 PM Sunday through Thursday, and until Midnight on Friday and Saturday. Parking is convenient in the small

Elk's Plaza lot adjacent to the restaurant and the commercial parking deck across the Parkway.

Howard's Restaurant
$$ • 976 Parkway, Gatlinburg
• (865) 436-3600

For more than 50 years, Howard's was that memorable place in the middle of downtown where people sat right out in the open along the parkway. Now closer to the south end, it's still the same people serving the same great food in a bigger setting. As close to an old-fashioned eatery as you'll find anywhere, Howard's features a full line of hearty steaks and gourmet burgers, skillet-cooked trout, and baby back ribs cooked just the way you like 'em, on both the grown-up and children's menus. Long famous for homemade French fries, desserts, and salad dressings, Howard's new location includes a spacious upstairs lounge where you can relax until it's time to get serious about eating. The lounge has live entertainment Wednesday through Saturday evenings. Open year 'round for lunch and dinner, Howard's is convenient to the Elks Plaza parking lot.

The Park Grill
$$$ • 1110 Parkway, Gatlinburg
• (865) 430-7899

One of the city's architectural wonders, the Park Grill is built almost entirely of huge spruce logs. The main beams in the restaurant are two feet in diameter. The bright, airy feeling conveyed by the massive structure is complemented by the extensive use of leaves as a primary decorating motif and the park ranger uniforms on the staff. All of it is a reminder that the Park Grille is one of the area's larger benefactors of Great Smoky Mountains National Park. It wouldn't be a tragedy if the food took a back seat to the surroundings, but that's not the way it is. The menu is eclectic and outstanding, with something to satisfy any taste in grand fashion. The pork tenderloin is a local legend, and so are the homemade desserts made fresh daily by the resident pastry chef. The Park Grill is an adventure in fine dining in amazing surroundings. Parking is available behind the restaurant. Open every day at 4 PM.

Maxwell's Beef & Seafood
$$$ • 1103 Parkway, Gatlinburg
• (865) 436-3738

This is a place where you may get the feeling you're being watched by someone or something other than the wait staff. You're right, but we'll get to that in a minute. The original

Maxwell family location has a long-standing reputation for serving a wide variety of quality food in a most satisfying manner. The original menu, emphasizing fresh seafood and chicken, is now featured as Maxwell's Signature Dinners. The expanded menu now includes seven additional seafood dishes, including the delicious orange roughy that tells you you're in a place that really knows what good seafood is; a selection of beef and chicken dishes to satisfy the heartiest meat-eater; and enough varieties of linguine to make the pasta maven swoon. The cozy dining room is a lot bigger than it looks, and the separate bar makes waiting for your table a lot easier than standing around in some lobby. Plenty of free parking is available right next door. Maxwell's is open Sunday through Thursday at 4:30 PM and Friday and Saturday at 4.

Oh, yeah, that feeling you're being watched? When you enter Maxwell's ask the greeter where Max is. They'll be happy to point out Gatlinburg's oldest and biggest piranha, who spends his time watching the diners—whether they're watching him or not.

Burning Bush Restaurant
$$$ • 1151 Parkway, Gatlinburg
• (865) 436-4669

A long-time favorite, the Burning Bush has a cozy feel to it that's hard to find in most of today's restaurants. The intimate dining rooms and all-wood furniture complement the rustic interior, and the down-home charm of the staff makes you feel welcome all day. And if you happen to hit the Burning Bush at breakfast time, you may need help walking out after the "Breakfast Bountiful," probably the most varied spread you've ever seen to start a day. All meals at the Burning Bush are made special by the attentive staff, who have a knack for anticipating your every need. Limited parking is available at the front door, and there's a good-sized parking lot behind the restaurant.

The Peddler Restaurant
$$$ • 820 River Rd., Gatlinburg
• (865) 436-8735

Just off the Parkway, the Peddler is located in one of Gatlinburg's most historic buildings: The center of the structure is the log cabin that was the homeplace of Hattie Ogle McGiffin, the city's acknowledged matriarch. The Peddler is part of a small regional chain that operates like an independent restaurant. The local management is deeply involved in civic and national park affairs.

Custom-cut steaks (they bring the loin to

your table and you tell them how big a steak you want) and fresh seafood dishes make the Peddler a "special occasion" favorite for families and couples looking for one really sumptuous meal to put an exclamation point on their trip to the Smokies. The Peddler's salad bar is considered one of the best in the area; you have to be careful not to load up on salad items so much that you can't eat the entree. The Peddler has its own parking lot in front of the building—if the lot's full, figure you're going to wait the better part of an hour to get seated. Open daily at 5 PM, The Peddler stays open until everybody's served.

Out East Parkway from Traffic Light #3

Black Bear Restaurant
$ • 478 East Parkway, Gatlinburg
• (865) 436-5401

"The Bear" has been in business since Bill Proffitt built it in 1964 on what was then the edge of town (it's about two blocks up U.S. 321N from the Parkway). He's still active in the business, and usually takes care of the breakfast crowd; the kids handle the rest of the day. The menu is good, solid, wholesome Southern food, from fresh biscuits and gravy every morning to a complete dinner menu that includes everything you'd expect to find in a large southern home. Using mainly local supplies, the Black Bear cooks (no "chefs" here) prepare every meal as if they were cooking for their own families. Servings are generous, including the kids' menu, and the iced tea is the stuff legends are made of. This is a medium-sized, unpretentious *family* restaurant with no dress code and no desire to do anything but feed you as well as anybody around, at prices nobody else even approaches. All menu items are available for carry-out. The Black Bear has its own spacious parking lot.

Greenbrier Restaurant
$$$ • 370 Newman Rd, Gatlinburg
• (865) 436-6318

Convenient but well removed from any other distractions, the Greenbrier is located on a mountaintop just 1½ miles from traffic light #3. Take East Parkway out to the traffic light at Newman Road (Virgil's Motel is on the opposite corner), turn right, and drive up into the parking lot where the road ends. Some member of the Hadden family will probably be waiting to show you to a table, either overlooking the highway you just came off or set in an intimate room where your group has the place to itself.

While beef dishes are the staple here (prime rib lovers will think they've gone to Heaven), the Greenbrier also has an extensive seafood menu, including a catch of the day, and they do more artistic things with chicken than anyone else in the area. To ensure fairness, the Greenbrier refuses to take reservations, but if they know you're on the way they'll try to have your table waiting when you arrive. Because of the size of their several dining rooms, the Greenbrier can accommodate groups of up to 30 people. The barroom is a local favorite when there's football on television. The Greenbrier's advertising says they're open from 5 PM to 9:30 or 10, depending on the day of the week, but nobody's ever been accused of running a guest out because the clock said it was time to close.

Mountain Lodge Restaurant
$ •913 East Parkway, Gatlinburg
• (865) 436-2547

There's seating for about 125 people in the deceptively large Mountain Lodge, which means you probably won't have to wait long to get seated for breakfast or lunch. Open daily from 7:00 AM to 3:00 PM, the Mountain Lodge is a huge local favorite for its extremely Southern breakfast menu and its large selection of lunch goodies. The daily menu special is on a blackboard at the entrance; the way the staff (which usually includes several of the Smith family that owns the place) treats you will make you think you're the most special thing that's happened to them all day. Ample parking is available on both sides of the building.

The Open Hearth Restaurant
$$$ • 1654 East Parkway, Gatlinburg
• (865) 436-5648

Long a standard-bearer for gracious dining, The Open Hearth has moved from its former location as the westernmost restaurant in town to its current new quarters as the city's easternmost eatery. The new location, 4½ miles east of traffic light #3, provides a unique dining experience, with the waters of Dudley Creek running right under you and the National Park as your view. Wildlife sightings are common as you try to choose from the full menu that includes five appetizers and seven soups and salads. The special Saturday and Sunday brunch, served from opening until 3 PM, is a local favorite. With an acre of parking and one of the largest dining rooms in the Smokies, the Open Hearth is pleased to accommodate group reservations and wedding parties.

Music Theaters and Nightlife

No one disputes the fact that the Smoky Mountains are this area's top tourist drawing card. But let's face it, after dark, the national park isn't that fun—unless you're camping out! So what does everyone do in the Smokies after the sun retreats for the day? Plenty. Sure, you can go to a restaurant, but after that you might decide that the night is still young.

We have many nighttime entertainment suggestions for you, separated into two categories. Most Smoky Mountains nightlife comes courtesy of the area's many music and variety theaters, all of which are profiled in the first part of the chapter. These are all family-friendly shows in which the entertainment is wholesome, and alcoholic beverages are not served. But we also know there are those of you who like to dance, make fools of yourselves on a karaoke machine or sit back and relax with a locally brewed beer. The Nightlife section of this chapter will detail some places where you can find that particular sort of live or interactive entertainment.

LOOK FOR:
• Music and
  Variety Theaters
• Nightlife

Music and Variety Theaters

The transformation of the entertainment scene in the Smokies over the past five years or so has been nothing short of phenomenal. Prior to 1994, there were only three or four smaller music halls in Pigeon Forge and one theater in Gatlinburg. That was the extent of the area's music theater "community." What has taken place in the years since has been a strong and steady push by local governments and developers to turn Sevier County into a virtual musical mecca. The hope is that vacationers will make pilgrimages here as much for the entertainment as they do for the mountains and other tourist drawing cards.

Around these parts, comparisons are constantly being drawn between the Smokies and another fertile music theater market, Branson, Missouri. Some hope that Sevier County reaches the levels that Branson has in terms of numbers of theaters, visitors, etc. The majority consensus, however, is that even among city leaders, is that any growth experienced in the music theater industry must be accompanied by cautious and measured doses of attention to the future. Everyone around here enjoys the direct and residual monetary effects of a strong music theater presence. But no one wants miles and miles of congested, bumper-to-bumper traffic like they have in Branson.

The verdict at this point—so far, so good. There are now about 15 music and variety theaters in the county, most of which are still located in Pigeon Forge, but many of which reflect the efforts by Sevierville and Gatlinburg to get a leg up in the market. Most of the shows are music-oriented, with an emphasis on country music. However, if your tastes reside elsewhere, you won't feel left out. Some area shows tip their hats to other musical genres such as rock 'n' roll, Broadway, gospel and bluegrass. Then there are the theaters that have their focus more on comedy and variety. Finally, sprinkle on top of all that the fact that celebrities with a fair amount of name recognition—like Lee Greenwood, Louise Mandrell and Anita Bryant—have their own showplaces in the Smokies where they perform in person. The result is a menu of diverse entertainment choices that growing numbers of tourists are getting hooked on.

All of the area's music and variety theaters are wheelchair accessible, nonsmoking facilities. They also have adequate free parking, except in one case (noted later) where you'll have to pay. Each is equipped with concession stands and, in most cases, souvenir shops full of everything from coffee mugs to T-shirts to tapes and CDs by the theater's artists. The theaters tend to be very audience-friendly. You can take your drinks and snacks into the auditorium with you, and although video taping and audio taping are prohibited, most venues allow flash photography during performances. All theaters sell reserved seats, so it pays to buy early if you know which shows you want to see, so you'll have a better chance at a good seat.

Note that the ticket prices quoted in our write-ups include tax, and that most theaters have discounted prices for groups. While the ticket prices we've quoted are confirmed prices for the 2000 season, be sure to verify any theater's ticket prices when making reservations. And it's always highly advisable to make advance reservations, especially during peak season. If you do so by phone, a credit card number is required. If you purchase your tickets ahead of time at the theater's box office, both cash and credit cards are accepted; personal checks are not. Finally, while you'll find that we've given you a general sketch of each theater's seasonal schedule, we recommend calling each theater to get specific dates for any particular time period.

Sevierville

Lee Greenwood Theater
2450 Winfield Dunn Pkwy., Sevierville
• (865) 933-8080, (800) 686-5471

Since 1996, this music theater has been the anchor of Riverbluff Landing , a shopping/dining/entertainment development located just off Winfield Dunn Parkway (Tenn. 66) near Kodak. The gorgeous 2,000-seat theater is open from April through December, and features Grammy Award winner Lee Greenwood himself performing nightly along with a large supporting cast of singers, dancers and musicians.

Greenwood's show, entitled *Portrait of America,* puts the spotlight on well-known tunes associated with the cities of America. The lineup includes several musical salutes to other artists as well as Greenwood's own string of hits from the country charts. Of course, he can't seem to escape any performance without closing with his enduring anthem, "God Bless the U.S.A."

Throughout each two-hour show, Greenwood displays not only his strong singing voice, but also his instrumental skills on piano and saxophone.

Visually, Greenwood's shows are captivating, with lots of scene changes, elaborate costumes and complex lighting effects. Each November, the theater presents its annual Christmas show, which closes out the year with elements of the regular season show along with holiday-oriented segments.

Generally, Greenwood does one show, four to six evenings per week beginning at 8 PM. From October through December, several 3 PM matinee performances are scheduled as well. Tickets for the Lee Greenwood Theater are $26 each. Children 12 and younger get in free to all shows (two per paying adult, except for the New Year's Eve gala). In addition to the theater box office, tickets can also be purchased at Tanger Five Oaks Mall in Sevierville (see our Outlet Malls chapter). Visit the theater's web site at www.leegreenwood.com.

INSIDERS' TIP

There are a couple of ticket agencies in the county that deal exclusively in tickets to Smoky Mountain theaters. They offer one-stop ticket purchasing convenience, often at a discounted price. Call Discount Show Ticket Outlet at (865) 428-7676 or Smoky Mountain Show Tickets at (865) 429-5070.

Southern Nights Theater
1304 Parkway, Sevierville
• (865) 908-0600, (800) 988-7804

They started out as school teachers, working as part time musicians at Dollywood and area hotels. But since 1997, Sevier County's own Smith family has enjoyed the luxury of performing in its own music theater. The show doesn't have a lot of bells and whistles from a technical standpoint, but what it does have is top-notch performing by Charlie, Jim and Charlie Bob Smith as well as their backup musicians, the Southstar Band.

The talent assembled delivers country, gospel, bluegrass, pop and oldies over the course of a two-hour-plus show. Plus, there's comedian David Moore who tickles the audiences' collective funny bone at different points throughout the evening. There's plenty of laughter to go around, though. The Smiths themselves are pretty funny guys, and their on-stage demeanor is very relaxed and disarming. They have a way of making you feel like you're sitting in their living room while they put on a show. Although the auditorium seats close to 1,000, the layout is intimate. This lends itself well to the fact that Southern Nights shows are fairly audience-interactive.

New to Southern Nights in 2000 is regular guest performer Eddie Miles. Miles did an Elvis Presley tribute as the headliner at Memories Theater for several years before taking his show to Myrtle Beach, South Carolina. Now he's back in the Smokies, performing at Southern Nights Theater two days a week. You'll still hear a few Presley tunes in his set, but his show now reflects a broader range of musical influences.

Southern Nights Theater is open January through December. Eddie Miles performs on Friday and Saturday from January through March and on Saturday and Sunday for the rest of the year. Beginning in April, the Smiths perform Monday through Friday at 8 PM and at 3 PM on Thursday as well. In October, more matinees are on the schedule, and beginning in November, the gang puts on a Christmas show to wind up the year. Tickets cost $23 each, and children 12 and younger are admitted for free (two per paid adult admission). Senior citizen tickets are $19 each.

Governor's Palace Theatre
179 Collier Dr., Sevierville
• (865) 428-5888, (888) 439-1111

One of the latest entries into the Smokies entertainment scene is this 1,750-seat music theater located in the heart of Governor's Cross-ing, a newer shopping/dining/entertainment development located just off the Parkway in Sevierville. Governor's Palace features two different shows each day. At 10 AM, four mornings per week and at 7:30 PM each Sunday night, guests can see the legendary Blackwood Quartet. Then at 8 PM, five or six nights a week (along with occasional matinee performances), the theater's high-tech musical production show, *Boots, Boogie & Blues,* steps into the limelight.

Governor's Palace Theatre became the home of gospel music's Blackwood Quartet in 2000. The quartet's roots go back over six decades, making the Blackwood name very well known in the realm of gospel music. Over the course of its history, the Blackwood Quartet has won eight Grammy Awards, seven of gospel's Dove Awards and sold more than 40 million records.

Today's incarnation of the group is fronted by Ron Blackwood, son of founding quartet member, R.W. Blackwood. In addition to the quartet's soaring and inspiring gospel harmonies, the group delivers traditional country songs, including tributes to artists like Larry Gatlin and The Oak Ridge Boys. You'll even hear some oldies but goodies from the '50s added in to help balance the repertoire. The theater's comedian (and also their musical director), Craig Hodges, keeps audiences chuckling between musical sets.

Each Blackwood Quartet show is a solid, high-energy vocal performance; the enthusiasm shown by the group is infectious, and can't help but sweep audiences away with its from-the-heart sincerity. The music is complemented by the playful sense of camaraderie shared by each of the quartet's members.

Boots, Boogie & Blues is a two-hour, high-energy salute to different genres of Southern-rooted music. The theater's three different stages are all utilized to showcase country, blues, rock 'n' roll, jazz and even the Miami sound. A talented ensemble cast of singers, dancers and musicians is supported by big-budget costumes, scenes and lighting schemes.

Each November, the theater's lineup is altered somewhat when the evening show changes to a Christmas production. Entitled *Christmas At The Palace,* this holiday show fea-

INSIDERS' TIP
If you've had too much to drink and you don't have a designated driver with you, don't even think about trying to drive. Please call a taxi or, if you're in Pigeon Forge or Gatlinburg, take a trolley back to your hotel if it's on a trolley route (see Getting Here, Getting Around).

MUSIC THEATERS AND NIGHTLIFE

tures the same cast and musicians from *Boots, Boogie & Blues,* but presents a healthy dose of traditional and contemporary Christmas tunes in an innovative and heartwarming fashion.

And if all we've mentioned so far isn't enough entertainment for you, you might be interested in the celebrity concert series staged at Governor's Palace. On most Saturday evenings throughout the season, entertainers ranging from rock 'n' roll legends to country giants deliver a single 7:30 performance. Some of the stars appearing during the series' first two seasons were Jim Nabors, Eddy Arnold, Jerry Reed, George Jones, Deana Carter and Fabian.

The Governor's Palace season runs from April through December. Ticket prices for the Blackwood Quartet are $18.50 for ages 12 and older, with a senior ticket price of $16.60. Tickets for both *Boots, Boogie & Blues* and *Christmas At The Palace* are $23.75 for ages 12 and older and $21.75 for seniors. Two-show packages with which you can see both the Blackwoods and the evening show are available for $35. Children 11 and younger are admitted free with a paying adult. The celebrity concerts vary in price, depending on the artist, but in the past have ranged in price from $16 to $30.

Pigeon Forge

Louise Mandrell Theater
2046 Parkway, Pigeon Forge
• **(865) 453-6263, (800) 768-1170**

Join the multi talented star, Louise Mandrell, at her "home" in the Smoky Mountains. Opened in 1997, this 1,400-seat auditorium is part of Pigeon Forge's Music Road development and the place where Mandrell shines approximately 250 dates each year. There are usually four to six shows each week, beginning at 7:30 PM.

Mandrell's showplace is typical of the newer, larger theaters in that it packs in a lot of visitors and gives those visitors their money's worth, boasting a large troupe of backing singers and dancers and an ensemble of gifted live musicians. For two hours each performance, Mandrell and company touch a lot of musical bases, incorporating not just country and bluegrass, but gospel, patriotic and Big Band numbers as well. In November and December, she stages a separate Christmas show, complete with flying snowflakes, dancing snowmen, winter skating and songs of the holidays.

Ms. Mandrell works magic on stage, not just musically, but in a literal sense. Her regu-

lar season show features a large segment devoted to illusions, some of them large-scale, performed by the star herself. Mandrell also shows off her musical skills, quickly switching musical hats as she shows off on the fiddle, upright bass, accordion and drums, just to name a few.

There are several unique high points of the show which make it stand out from a production standpoint. For example, Mandrell flies down to the stage over the audience in a parachute harness. Another time, she dances a musical number on the giant, 16-foot-long keyboard featured in the movie *Big.* For a Latin American number, Mandrell takes the stage sporting an outrageous rainbow sherbet-colored outfit with a 40-foot, ruffled train and balancing a gigantic fruit basket on her head, a la Carmen Miranda.

In addition to the evening performances, there are a few 2:30 PM matinees sprinkled into the schedule during peak season and the holidays. In October, Mandrell does two or three matinees a week. The theater also schedules a few special, limited-engagement concerts by visiting artists throughout the year. Mandrell's guests in 1999 included Ricky Van Shelton and Roy Clark. Tickets to Louise Mandrell's show are $28.75 for adults 18 and older, $16.60 for ages 13 to 17 and $11.05 for ages 4 through 12. Children 3 and younger are admitted free with a paid adult.

Anita Bryant's Music Mansion Theater
100 Music Rd., Pigeon Forge
• **(865) 428-7469**

In 1999, Anita Bryant became the latest in a growing influx of celebrity talent to set up shop in the Great Smoky Mountains. Following the examples set by local performers Lee Greenwood and Louise Mandrell, she purchased Music Mansion Theater from Dollywood in spring and had a brand new show on the boards just in time for the heavy seasonal crowds of autumn. Bryant brings a hefty resume to the Smokies, one that includes such job titles as beauty queen (second runner-up in the 1958 Miss America pageant), singer, actress, host, television spokesperson and author.

After a few years out of the public eye, Bryant got back into the world of entertainment in the early 1990s, performing at various music theaters in Branson, Missouri. In fact, Bryant had actually been on her way to scout out a theater opportunity in Myrtle Beach, South Carolina, when she made what was to be just a brief stopover in the Smokies. That detour, of course, evolved into permanent residency.

Bryant's show, *Anita With Love,* is similar in structure and style to her Branson show, but the Smoky Mountains version is basically a brand-new entity. The two-hour-plus stage presentation has a little bit of everything musically, including classic and contemporary country hits as well as chart-busters made famous by Bryant herself in the '60s and '70s. The show's repertoire is well-rounded with segments featuring pop oldies from the '50s and '60s. Fleshing out things nicely is guest perfomer, Ray Peterson, best known for his classic renditions of "Tell Laura I Love Her," "Fever" and "Corinna, Corinna." In keeping with Bryant's strong senses of patriotism and religious faith, the second act of the show is devoted to songs representative of those two musical genres.

Singer and former beauty queen Anita Bryant brought her music and variety show to the Smokies in 1999.

Photo: Courtesy Anita Bryant's Music Mansion Theater

Backing Bryant up in the massive, 2,000-seat Music Mansion Theater is a wonderful orchestra and a troupe of nine singers and dancers who often shine on their own when Bryant is offstage making costume changes. Eye-catching costumes, massive sets, well-coordinated technical elements and even the use of laser lighting all complement the show's solid musical delivery.

Anita With Love isn't the only stage offering at Music Mansion, however. Beginning in November, Bryant's show changes completely as *Home For Christmas* takes the spotlight. The theme of that show, obviously, is a celebration of the holidays, particularly the birth of Christ. Also, beginning with the 2000 season, Bryant is expected to kick off a third show called *Gospel Gathering* that will go up on Sunday afternoons only.

Anita Bryant's Music Mansion Theater is open April through December, with performances of *Anita With Love* running five to six evenings a week through October. When *Home For Christmas* starts in November, there will be five or six evening shows as well as a few matinee performances weekly. Sunday's *Gospel Gathering* is expcted to take place three Sundays per month. Ticket prices are $25.40 for ages 12 and older, while children 11 and younger are admitted free; Senior citizen tickets cost $23.20.

Glasgow Comedy Dinner & Show
Music Rd., Pigeon Forge
• **(865) 908-0003, (888) 908-5284**

Pigeon Forge's latest addition to Music Road is located next door to Music Mansion on the Parkway. What guests discover inside is a combination comedy/variety show, music show and dinner attraction. What also makes it distinctive is that as many as four shows are presented daily, each accompanied by a meal.

As the name implies, comedy is the thrust of the Glasgow theater. With an emphasis placed on stand-up comedy, the theater's stage is also home to variety acts like magicians, jugglers and ventriloquists performing family-friendly shows. The acts are all seasoned professionals with television, film or concert credits. Balancing the slate of entertainment are singer Tami Pryce along with the Reboppin'

Swing Daddies, a hot 1940s-style Big Band under the direction of Grammy Award nominee Tom Bruner.

The auditorium itself is intimate and well thought out in design, despite the fact that it seats close to 650 people. And, as mentioned, patrons are served a multi-course meal from a preset menu during the performance. Breakfast includes scrambled eggs, smoked sausage, potatoes, a biscuit, fresh fruit, cinnamon rolls and a beverage. Lunches and dinners feature juicy pot roast served with country vegetables, potatoes, bread, dessert and a beverage.

Besides being a showplace of comedy, Glasgow Comedy Dinner & Show is also the site of a comedy college, where students pay tuition to attend full time classes to learn the craft of stand-up comedy. Instructor Martha Bolton, a former writer for Bob Hope, gives students classroom time as well as on-stage time in the afternoons. During the stage sessions, guests can watch the aspiring funnymen hone their skills for the reasonable price of a one-dollar contribution to the college's scholarship fund.

Glasgow Comedy Dinner & Show is open five to six days a week from late March through December, with shows at 9 AM, 12 PM and 5 PM, although some days may have only one or two of those showtimes scheduled. If demand warrants, an extra show can be scheduled at 8:15 PM. Adult prices (13 and older) are $27.18 for breakfast shows and $31.56 for lunch and dinner shows. Children 8 through 12 pay $16.30 for all shows, and those ages 3 through 7 pay $9.76 for all shows. Children ages 2 and younger are admitted free provided that they sit in an adult's lap and share their meal. You can learn more about the theater at www.glasgowcomedytheater.com.

Smoky Mountain Jubilee
2115 Parkway, Pigeon Forge
• (865) 428-1836

Having opened its doors back in 1984, *Smoky Mountain Jubilee* is now the longest-running music show in Pigeon Forge and the second oldest operating theater in the county. It's one of the smaller area auditoriums in size (seats about 900), but owner Elmer Dreyer has been packing in crowds by the busload for quite a stretch now. A longtime favorite with Smoky Mountain visitors, the *Jubilee* gets a lot of repeat business from fans who can't get enough of the theater's unadulterated blend of country, gospel and bluegrass.

Smoky Mountain Jubilee is a family operation, an arrangement that seems to work well with the theater's philosophy of providing a wholesome family-oriented show. Dreyer is the emcee of the show and plays guitar as well. His daughter, Gayla, has been a featured vocalist with the show since day one, and you'll even find Dreyer's wife running the box office and working the phones.

On stage, *Smoky Mountain Jubilee's* cast includes an eight-piece band, a gospel quartet, several featured female vocalists and a resident clogging troupe, the Tennessee Highsteppers. From the show's first downbeat to the closing number, audiences soak in everything from blistering bluegrass fiddle and banjo to crooning country classics to perfectly jelled gospel harmonies. There's even a little bit of oldies rock 'n' roll thrown in for good measure.

Comic relief is provided by resident funnyman Highpockets, a hillbilly character who takes the stage several times during each performance wearing highwater overalls, a sleeveless flannel shirt and a floppy felt hat. He plays an affable and sometimes dimwitted rube to Dreyer's straight man. Highpockets' Elvis send-up is always a show highlight.

The gang at *Smoky Mountain Jubilee* generally performs weekends only January through April, four nights a week in May, six nights a week during peak season and about four nights a week during November and December. Curtain time is 8:30 PM, and tickets are $18.50 each. Children 11 and younger are admitted free, and senior citizens receive a $1 discount off the full price.

Hillbilly Hoedown Theatre
2135 Parkway, Pigeon Forge
• (865) 428-5600

For those craving a show with true Smoky Mountain flavor, *Elwood Smooch's Hillbilly Hoedown* is a good choice. Who is Elwood Smooch, you ask? To put it simply, we'll say that he's just one of the many comical characters presented by Hoedown front man Billy Baker. A more visual thumbnail sketch of Elwood would describe his baggy pants, crossed eyes, missing teeth and sometimes spastic comic demeanor. Smooch is a quintessential lovable rube, and the man that brings him to life is able to contort his body and facial expressions in a manner that would make Jim Carrey envious.

With the help of his other characters like Chlorine (a well-endowed, mumu-clad woman), Uncle Mildew (who claims to be the world's oldest stand-up comedian) and Elwood Presley (self explanatory), Baker brings guaranteed laughter and smiles to his audiences. In a show format that also includes a superb band,

The Smoochers, and an assorted cast of comedians and featured vocalists, Hillbilly Hoedown is two hours of hayseed hilarity interspersed with A-plus country and bluegrass music. Each performance also features Baker as he takes the stage sans his alter egos to sing a number of vocal standards in his richly pleasing baritone voice.

Billy Baker brings a full show business resume to his theater, including a long-time stint as a clown with Ringling Brothers and as a regular on *Hee Haw*, where his Elwood Smooch character gained a national following. Nowadays, he conjures up good ol' mountain humor in the barnlike atmosphere of the 450-seat theater. That hillbilly flavor is accentuated during the show by slide projections depicting scenes of the Smoky Mountains' natural beauty and rich history.

Elwood Smooch's Hillbilly Hoedown is open weekends only in February, three nights a week in March, four to five nights a week in April and May and six to seven nights a week in peak season. The theater presents a special Harvest Show from late September through mid-November, and after a short break, the action resumes in late November when the Christmas Show begins its run on a limited schedule through mid-December. The last week of the year is devoted to a Highlights Show, featuring the best elements of the Hoedown's three different shows. Admission prices are $21 for adults ages 20 and older, $18.50 for ages 55 and older, $13 for ages 13 through 19 and $6 for ages 6 through 12. Children younger than six are admitted free.

Memories Theatre
2141 Parkway, Pigeon Forge
• (865) 428-7852, (800) 325-3078

Next door to Smoky Mountain Jubilee and Hillbilly Hoedown you'll find Memories Theatre, home of another of the longer-running shows in Pigeon Forge. Since 1990, Memories has made its mark with the musical tribute, honoring a host of country, gospel and rock 'n' roll greats through the songs that made them famous. The anchor of each Memories show, however, is the Elvis Presley tribute.

Since 1995, the tribute has been ably performed by Lou Vuto, a talented Bronx,

New York, native who resists being labeled an "Elvis impersonator." The humble Vuto prefers to view his act as a way of helping people remember Elvis rather than serving as a way of becoming an Elvis clone. From his vocals to his flamboyant costumes to his pelvic swivels, Vuto captures the essence of Presley in every sense. In the process, Vuto has become quite the attraction and even has his own fan club. Throngs of screaming women flock to the 900-seat venue to swoon over Vuto as he liberally distributes scarves and kisses.

Helping add authenticity to the Elvis tribute is the presence of Charlie Hodge, Elvis Presley's longtime friend, aide and band member. Hodge makes his first appearance each night in the role of the raconteur, relating his personal experiences with Elvis to the audience in a casual, one-to-one manner. Later, he joins the band on stage, lending guitar and backing vocals to Vuto's tribute.

The Elvis portion of the show is only the second half of each Memories performance. The first half is devoted to other musical tributes to artists that have ranged from Roy Orbison and the Beatles to Garth Brooks and Dolly Parton. The songs are handled by the seven-piece Memories Showband as well as The Three Inspirations, a female vocal trio. Overall, the cast has such a large repertoire to its credit that it frequently changes the show's makeup from night to night.

Memories Theatre is open weekends only in February and March, four days a week in April, November and December, and five to six days a week May through October. Showtime is 8:15 nightly. Tickets are $20 for ages 13 to 55, $18.50 for anyone over 55 and $5 for ages 7 through 12. Children 6 and younger are admitted free.

INSIDERS' TIP

If you want to get an autograph from your favorite performer or even pose for a photograph with them, they're usually very accessible and willing to oblige after a performance (sometimes during intermission). You can bring your own memorabilia for them to sign; otherwise, the theater gift shops will be happy to oblige by selling you a T-shirt or glossy photo if you're empty handed.

Country Tonite Theatre
129 Showplace Blvd.,
Pigeon Forge
• (865) 453-2003,
(800) 792-4308

Since opening in Pigeon Forge in 1997, Country Tonite Theatre has presented its audiences with a fast-paced, high-energy show brimming with a broad spectrum of country music. With a beautiful, 1,500-seat auditorium as the setting, *Country Tonite's*

Pigeon Forge's Dixie Stampede *is full of high-speed thrills ...*

Photo: Courtesy Dixie Stampede

*... and good ol' American
patriotism.*

Photo: Courtesy Dixie Stampede

Guests at Dixie Stampede *can enjoy two different shows throughout the year—during the regular season...*

Photo: Courtesy Dixie Stampede

... and during the holidays.

Photo: Courtesy Dixie Stampede

The Krofft Puppets are a favorite part of the Louise Mandrell show.

Photo: Courtesy Louise Mandrell Theater

At her Pigeon Forge theater, the multi-faceted entertainer stars in about 250 shows each season.

Photo: Courtesy Louise Mandrell Theater

*Louise Mandrell and Friend,
giving it their all.*

Photo: Courtesy Louise Mandrell Show

A big "Howdy!" from the cast at Country Tonite.

Photo: Courtesy Country Tonite Theatre

Madness in the Heart of Gatlinburg

"Unique" hardly begins to describe an evening at Sweet Fanny Adams Theatre. It's totally different from any other type of entertainment you'll see in the Smokies (or most other places, for that matter). In fact, the theater bills itself as the only area alternative to country music shows, presenting a two-hour extravaganza full of musical comedy that literally brings tears to the eyes (happy tears, not sad ones).

Your experience starts even before you enter the theater; the building's facade is reminiscent of a theater from America's Old West or an English music hall. On the inside, that "turn-of-the-century" look still dominates. The auditorium seats fewer than 200 and the stage is small, but once the lights go down, the comedy is dished out in huge portions. The humor is broad, full of slapstick and downright silly, but it's also undeniably hilarious. And one of the great things about the shows at Sweet Fanny Adams Theatre is that they're enjoyable for all ages.

The first half of each evening consists of a short musical comedy. Since opening in 1977, owners Don and Pat MacPherson have written/directed/produced nearly 40 different shows for their theater (each season features two new shows that play on alternating nights of the week). The titles of the shows themselves are usually a big hint as to what you're in for. Productions from previous years have included *Not Quite Snow White, Lucifer McRotten Strikes Again,* and *Everything You Wanted To Know About Davy Crockett, But Were Afraid To Ask.* Are you starting to get the picture?

Bringing these comedy gems to the boards nightly is the Great Victorian Amusement Company, the theater's troupe of performers that includes the MacPhersons and about five other thespians, some of whom have been Fanny Adams mainstays for years. By the way, if you ask the MacPhersons to tell you about the origins of the "Great Victorian Amusement Company" or "Sweet Fanny Adams," you'll undoubtedly hear some sort of colorful and entertaining tale. You

The cast of Sweet Fanny Adams Theatre.

Photo: Courtesy Sweet Fanny Adams Theatre

can be sure that it's probably nothing close to the truth, but you'll have a better time if you accept their answers for what they are!

After the intermission ("knock before entering the restrooms," you'll be reminded), the show forges ahead with an old fashioned singalong and a vaudeville-style revue of music and comedy sketches. During the revue, you may be fortunate enough to catch them on a night when they're doing the "paper dance;" and although we won't give away any secrets here, we will tell you that the singalong is always special for one "lucky" member of the audience. From beginning to end, the audience is very much a part of the show, and don't worry—it's never in a threatening way. The intimate feel of the room plus the fact that the actors have little regard for "the fourth wall" both make for a night of interactive fun that just can't be captured in most area theaters.

Sweet Fanny Adams Theatre is truly a family affair. Pat's parents, Betty and Paddy O'Doherty, are box office manager and technical director, respectively. In past seasons, the MacPhersons' son, Chris, has been a featured performer at the theater (in addition to being a clown with the Ringling Brothers circus). Both Pat and Don have extensive backgrounds in theater, having worked at one time or another as singers, dancers, actors and directors throughout the United States and Europe. They settled in Gatlinburg in the '70s for the dual purpose of raising their children and finding a place where they could develop and produce their original shows. After just one night at Sweet Fanny Adams Theatre, we think you'll agree that what they've developed over the past two decades is, indeed, very original and a Smoky Mountain treasure in its own right.

cast of musicians, dancers and featured vocalists all sizzle throughout the two-hour-plus salute to country music's legendary performers, both past and present.

In a sense, there really are no "stars" at *Country Tonite,* but rather a strong ensemble cast of talent that dishes out musical tributes to country artists ranging from Patsy Cline to Charlie Daniels. As a fresh twist, *Country Tonite's* featured singers include youth vocalists who always seem to win audiences over with their charm, and the crowds especially love *Country Tonite's* funnyman, Bubba, The Redneck Ranger. Bubba comes on frequently during each performance as a slow-witted park ranger who gets big yuks, typically using other cast members as straight men.

The original *Country Tonite* show opened in Las Vegas in 1992, and expanded to Branson, Missouri, in 1994. The Pigeon Forge production runs from late March through December, usually six days per week. Except for a few isolated dates, there are two shows daily, at 3 and 8 PM. Country Tonite's holiday show premiers annually in November, augmenting the regular show with strong influences of Christmas music and decoration.

In addition to the afternoon and evening country music shows, Country Tonite Theatre is home to a morning magic show, Terry Evanswood's *Grand Illusion.* At 10 AM, six days a week, Evanswood brings everything from large-scale illusions to close-up sleight-of-hand to the Country Tonite stage in the area's only show to feature magic exclusively. Consummate skill on the part of Evanswood, along with top-notch assistants, lighting, music and smoke effects (not to mention four-and-a-half tons of props and equipment!), all combine to create a very enjoyable morning for all ages. By incorporating comedy, live animals and even audience participation into his show, Evanswood has crafted a well rounded show.

During the two-hour performance, guests witness Evanswood's variations on a number of classic feats of prestidigitation, such as levitation, sawing a person in half, disappearing in a box and escaping from a trunk. In addition, there are plenty of other illusions that are probably unfamiliar to most audiences. And thanks to the use of a hand-held camera and the theater's large overhead video screens, the audience can even try to follow Evanswood's skilled magician's hands as he astounds everyone with close-up favorites like the "cup and balls" routine as well as a number of card tricks. Speaking of cards, one of the most amazing segments of the show is the one in which Evanswood works with multiple decks of cards, seemingly producing them from thin air, fanning and manipulating them in ways that defy logic.

Evanswood, a Chicago native, has been studying magic since his parents gave him his first magic set at the age of 8. He started out performing at neighborhood birthday parties but has now appeared all over the world, including Las Vegas and the famed Magic Castle in Hollywood. At the age of 21, Evanswood became the youngest person ever to perform at the Magic Castle, which is also the headquarters for the Academy of the Magical Arts.

Tickets to Country Tonite's afternoon and evening music shows are $23.15 for adults and $12 for children ages 13 through 17. Kids ages 12 and under are admitted free. Tickets to Terry Evanswood's morning magic show are $16.50, and children 10 and younger get in free. You can find Country Tonite Theatre on the Internet at www.countrytonite.com.

Comedy Barn Theater
2775 Parkway, Pigeon Forge
• (865) 428-5222, (800) 295-2844

You can't miss this place when you're driving down the Parkway in Pigeon Forge. It literally is a huge, metal, barn-like structure that towers high above most of the buildings around it. And once you've located this 1,000-seat theater, the show is certainly worth stopping in for. Since it opened in 1994, it's become one of the most attended shows in the area. In part, that's probably because it's been one of the few theaters in the area that places an emphasis on comedy. But at The Comedy Barn, you also get magic and some good 'ol country music in addition to clean, family-friendly humor, making it one of the more popular tickets in town.

The theater's rural motif is as prominent on the inside as it is on the exterior; the stage's backdrop is a barn facade, and performers enter and exit through two barn doors. And while there is a bit of a country flavor to the show, that "twang" is more of an accent to the show rather than a traditional lampooning of Southern stereotypes. Each evening's entertainment is staged by an ensemble cast of talent consisting of jugglers, fire eaters, ventriloquists, magicians and, of course, stand-up comedians who have credits ranging from *Hee Haw* to *Evening at the Improv*. It's interesting to note that everyone in the cast (even the owners) get directly involved in running other operations of the theater—everything from selling concessions to parking cars!

The show's lineup is staggered with segments of country and bluegrass music courtesy of The Comedy Barn All-Star Band and its gifted pickers. The host for each performance is Grandpa Duffy, an animatronic hillbilly character perched in the window of his old country cabin. On closer inspection, however, you realize that Duffy is actually playing a real banjo! His mechanical head and body are combined with the real hands and voice of one of The Comedy Barn's cast members to provide an interesting "manimatronic" experience.

Amazingly, The Comedy Barn is open 365 days a year, and even does shows on Thanksgiving and Christmas Day. Shows start at 8:15 PM, and during peak season, there are almost always 3:15 and/or 5 PM matinees on the bill as well. Tickets to The Comedy Barn are $18.50 for adults. Each child 11 and younger (per paid adult) gets in free.

Dixie Stampede
3849 Parkway, Pigeon Forge
• (865) 453-4400, (800) 356-1676

Saddle up, pardners, and get ready for a stampede at this unique Pigeon Forge dinner show that's owned by Dollywood. For over a decade, *Dixie Stampede* has been one of the top theater draws in the Smokies. Each performance is a multi-faceted event that includes trick riding, horseback competitions, music, magic, comedy and a full, multi course meal.

The premise of the *Dixie Stampede* show is a friendly, Civil War-style rivalry; the audience is divided into "North" and "South" sections that "battle" each other during the evening through a series of horse riding contests and other competitions. Most of the contests are staged by *Stampede* cast members who are dressed in appropriate blue and gray uniforms. Down in the arena's large, oval-shaped performance area, they saddle up their steeds and go head-to-head in feats of horse riding speed, skill and dexterity. There are contests involving direct participation by some audience members while others require group efforts from both sides as a whole. Overall, there's a lot of whooping, cheering and foot stomping!

Outside the framework of the competition, there's plenty to see, including high-speed trick riding, large-scale magic illusions and hilarious comedy. There are a few impressive visuals as well. At one point, a large stage is lowered from the ceiling revealing Southern belles and gentlemen decked out in period costumes. There are also state-of-the-art lighting effects plus a massive, shimmering American flag and revolving replica of the Statue of Liberty that are revealed during the show's finale, which joins North and South in a unifying patriotic salute to America.

Dixie Stampede does everything on a large scale, and being a dinner attraction, provides a meal that is no exception to that rule. Dinner consists of a whole rotisserie chicken, a slice of barbecue pork loin, creamy vegetable soup, a biscuit, corn on the cob, potatoes, a hot apple turnover and a beverage. Each course is served en masse during the show by the wait staff, which is actually considered part of the *Stampede* cast and is also decked out in Civil War regalia. By the way, if you're finicky about table manners, you can check your ettiquete at the door. There's no silverware at *Dixie Stampede*—everything's eaten by hand!

Dixie Stampede is open for a few dates immediately after New Year's Day, then runs on a limited schedule from late January through February. They're open four days a week in March, and starting in April, the theater is open seven days a week through October. In November and December, Dixie presents its Christmas show four to five days a week through the end of the year. The regular show time throughout the year is 6 PM, but during peak season and many off-season weekends there are two shows daily, at 6 and 8:30 PM. When there's a demand, they'll even do a third matinee show. Admissions to Dixie Stampede are $32.68 for adults and 16.34 for ages 4 through 11. Children ages 3 and younger are admitted free if they sit in a parent's lap and share their meal. Management does expect a $3 increase in prices sometime in the middle of the 2000 season, however.

Gatlinburg

Sweet Fanny Adams Theatre
461 Parkway, Gatlinburg • (865) 436-4039

The Smokies' oldest music variety theater features shows six nights a week April through September, seven nights is October, and a holiday show or weekends in November and December. Tickets are $16.95 for adults and $5.50 for kids 12 and under. (See this chapter's Close-up for more information

Nightlife

All but two of the establishments included below sell alcohol (the movie theater and Eddie's Heart & Soul Cafe), but you should know that each city has different ordinances

when it comes to selling by the drink. See our Restaurants chapter or Area Overview for the specifics, but we'll run down the basics here as well. In Sevierville and outside any city's limits (in the county), only beer can be sold by the drink, and only in some restaurants. Pigeon Forge prohibits alcohol by the drink altogether while in Gatlinburg, you can purchase wine, liquor and beer in most restaurants and bars.

Reel Theatres Movies on the Parkway
713 Winfield Dunn Pkwy., Sevierville
• (865) 453-9055

If you want to catch a flick while you're in Sevier County, there's only one game in town. Fortunately, it's a pretty good game, offering popular, first-run box office attractions seven days a week on six screens. In 1985, Reel Theatres ran a triplex facility near downtown Sevierville (in the building now occupied by the Sevierville Civic Center). In 1994, the theaters moved into a brand new, state-of-the-art facility on Winfield Dunn Parkway (Tenn. 66).

In addition to comfortable seating, each auditorium is equipped with Dolby Surround Sound and Digital Theater Sound to enhance the audio portion of its movies. There is also a video arcade and, of course, a well-stocked concession stand featuring all the standard movie theater favorites.

Throughout the year, Movies on the Parkway generally presents one matinee and two evening shows on each screen. During summer, there may be as many as three matinees per day, depending on the movie. They also feature special midnight screenings each Friday. Between Memorial Day and Labor Day, there are midnight shows on Saturday nights as well.

Admission to Reel Theatres Movies on the Parkway is $6.25 for ages 13 and older and $4.25 for children ages 4 through 12 as well as anyone age 60 and older. Children younger than 4 are admitted free but may be required to sit in a parent's lap during sell-out situations. During bargain matinees (movies that begin before 6 PM), tickets are $4.25 each for all ages. You can reach the theater's information line at the number above and receive specific show times, information on coming attractions and directions to the theater.

Rocky River Brewery & Grille
1444 Hurley Dr., Sevierville
• (865) 908-3686

Nighttime entertainment is slowly but surely making its way into Sevierville, thanks to places like this. Rocky River Brewery & Grille is a restaurant/microbrewery/sports bar located on the Little Pigeon River at Governor's Crossing. You can learn about its dining and beermaking aspects in the Restaurants chapter.

If you're interested in getting together for brews and appetizers and maybe a televised ball game, check out the sports bar adjacent to the main restaurant. There is a large-screen TV and a number of video monitors strategically placed throughout the bar for game-day viewing. For amusement, the sports bar has several video games as well as pool tables and dart boards; pool tournaments are held on Monday nights. Live entertainment includes a deejay on Wednesdays, karaoke on Thursdays and a band on Tuesdays, Fridays and Saturdays; guest performers are usually from the country and rock 'n' roll genres. Of course, whatever you do at the sports bar, you can enjoy it with any of the distinctive beers created at Rocky River's own microbrewery.

Eddie's Heart and Soul Cafe
140 Showplace Blvd., Pigeon Forge
• (865) 453-0833

Since Pigeon Forge restaurants can't sell alcohol, you don't see much "nightlife" there outside the realm of music theaters. But at Eddie's Heart and Soul Cafe, owner Eddie Anders does serve a good meal along with an inspiring one-man show. Beginning at 11 AM daily, Anders takes the stage and showcases his talents on vocals, keyboards and, from time to time, guitar. His voice is both mellow and strong and very easy on the ears. He performs on and off throughout the day and evening, especially during peak lunch and dinner hours (in between, he's next door, performing live at Country Tonite Theatre), and each set at the cafe usually lasts for the better part of an hour. There is never a cover charge to watch the show, although it's presumed that most guests are there to eat something.

Anders sees his performances, however, as more than just a backdrop to a meal. He considers his show a ministry of his religious faith, a way to creatively communicate the gospel to audiences in an easy-going manner. But this place is nothing like church—the atmosphere is relaxed and upbeat. Anders' repertoire reflects the fact that he spent about a decade on

the road as a vocalist on the contemporary Christian music circuit, working with groups like Daybreak, Truth and the Bill Gaither Trio. While gospel music is well represented, it's also accompanied by healthy doses of country, rock 'n' roll and sprinklings of the hard-to-classify. You'll hear songs ranging from "Butterfly Kisses" to "Stayin' Alive" to the theme from *Bonanza!* During the Christmas holidays, the song list shifts to include mostly seasonal tunes, both secular and religious.

Although Eddie is the feature attraction during peak season, the entertainment lineup varies a bit during winter. In years past, the restaurant has staged different theme nights through the week, including an open talent competition and a Southern Gospel night.

The Old Heidelberg Castle Restaurant
148 Parkway, Gatlinburg
• (865) 430-3094, (800) 726-3094

It's known to area residents simply as "The Heidelberg," but it has a solid reputation among locals and vacation regulars as being a fun place to eat dinner. The restaurant serves up good portions of delicious, authentic German cuisine for lunch and dinner. However it's the live show, beginning at 5:30 nightly, that holds most of the charm for this long-time Gatlinburg night spot. There is no cover charge to see the show, and since it takes place in a restaurant, minors are welcome.

The entertainment is delivered by the Bavarian Funmakers Band. The group's men and women are both decked out in traditional Bavarian attire (including lederhosen for the men). The band's repertoire includes lively polkas and beer-drinking songs, many of which come through with that trademark German "oom-pah-pah" sound. You'll see and hear instruments like the accordion, alp horn (as in the Ricolah commercials), tuba (you're welcome to throw quarters into the tuba's huge bell!) and an entire array of differently pitched cowbells. During the show, diners are welcome to take to the dance floor with some polka footwork or the outrageous "Chicken Dance."

Although The Heidelberg is open all year, autumn is an especially fun time to visit. The restaurant hosts its own Oktoberfest celebration, running from late September into early November. On tap is the Funmakers' usual

MUSIC THEATERS AND NIGHTLIFE

INSIDERS' TIP

In addition to the nightspots included in this chapter, you'll also discover that many area hotels, especially those in Gatlinburg, have in-house lounges where you can order a beer, cocktail or glass of wine.

show in addition to lots of singalongs, contests and dancing. Whether you're dining or just there for the show, the Heidelberg has a full bar which includes several labels of imported German beers. You can find out more about The Heidelberg in our Restaurants chapter.

Club 2000
148 Parkway, Gatlinburg • (865) 430-3094

This nightclub is adjacent to The Heidelberg restaurant (not coincidentally, since both places are owned by the same man). Club 2000 is open from 9 PM to 1 AM, seven days a week, but you must be 21 to enter. The weekly schedule varies throughout the year, but among Club 2000's typical nightly offerings are televised sporting events, darts, karaoke, dancing, live bands and an "open jam" night (usually Wednesday), when local musicians can show up and create their own musical action in an impromptu session.

Edgewater Hotel
402 River Rd., Gatlinburg • (865) 436-4151

You can either enjoy karaoke fun or a live band playing in the hotel lounge on Friday and Saturday nights. Musical styles vary from band to band, but in the past, styles have included country and light rock. There is no cover charge to enter, although you must be 21.

Blaine's Grill & Bar
812 Parkway, Gatlinburg • (865) 430-1978

If you like to dance, this restaurant in downtown Gatlinburg is the place to go. Seven nights a week, the tables are cleared from the main floor, and the DJ cranks out dance music from 9 PM to 1 AM. Many of the tunes are contemporary while some are modernized dance mixes of older rock 'n' roll favorites. The clientele is primarily in the 20-something age range, but those 30- and 40-something fogies who still like to get out on the floor and shake their stuff to a loud, pounding dance beat will love Blaine's too. The big nights to go are Friday and Saturday, although there is a $3 cover charge on those nights. Every now and then, live musical acts will be brought in to perform; a cover charge is in effect then as well.

Blaine's is a full service restaurant and bar (formerly Ronnie Milsaps' Keyboard Cafe) located on the corner of Parkway and Airport Road. From the outside, the three-story building is reminiscent of a Bourbon Street facade with its upper level porches and iron railings. Inside, the main bar, dining areas and dance floor are on the second level. There is a smaller bar area with limited seating on the third level. Although it is a restaurant, Blaine's stops serving food at 9 PM, which is when the dancing starts. As such, you must be 21 to enter after that time.

Smoky Mountain Brewery
1004 Parkway, Gatlinburg • (865) 436-4200

This restaurant and microbrewery are located at Calhoun's Village near the south end of Gatlinburg's Parkway. The village itself is unique in that it offers visitors plenty of free parking. The brewery is easily found just a few buildings back from the Parkway.

Smoky Mountain Brewery provides entertainment six nights a week. Typically, you'll find karaoke Saturday through Tuesday (Tuesday's one of the big nights) and live bands Wednesday through Friday. The bands present varied styles ranging from light rock to bluegrass. The shows run from around 9 PM to 12:30 AM, and except for one or two weeks out of the year, there is no cover charge. You don't have to be 21 to enter, but naturally, you must be to consume alcohol.

The main dining room, full service bar and entertainment section are upstairs. The heavily raftered room provides a simple and casual tavern-style atmosphere. There is a large-screen television, which is the center of attention during televised sporting events (especially Tennessee Volunteer football games). Those ordering from the menu will find a hearty selection of subs, sandwiches and calzones as well as the restaurant's specialty—pizza. You can enjoy your meal in the main dining area or on the glassed-in porch.

Downstairs is where you'll find the microbrewery. The menu features as many as 13 different beers, although at any given time, anywhere from six to nine of the labels are being served. Four of the house brands are always on tap: Cherokee Red Ale, Mountain Light, Black Bear Ale and Old Thunder Road. In addition to these there are several brewmaster's specials and seasonal selections to complement the overall selection.

INSIDERS' TIP

Be sure to check area hotels and restaurants for money-saving coupons to area shows. You'll typically receive a $1 or $2 discount. Also, don't forget to pick up those free tourist-oriented magazines that are usually rife with coupons as well (see Media).

Attractions

Let's start with a hypothetical question. How many go-cart tracks does one town need? What would you think—four, five... seven? In Pigeon Forge alone there are more than 15 individual go-cart track operations, many of which have two or three tracks apiece. The majority of them are located within two miles of each other along the Parkway. Add Sevierville's and Gatlinburg's go-cart establishments to the mix and you've created heaven on earth for the speedster wannabe.

When it comes to Smoky Mountain attractions, however, go-carts are just one slice of a very large pie. In fact, just about any business you encounter along the Smokies corridor that's not a hotel, a restaurant or a shop is likely to be an attraction of some sort. From the Sevierville fringes all the way to the national park entrance, you'll come across a little of everything—from museums and historical sites to a lot of things that are just out-and-out fun, like white water rafting, haunted houses, professional baseball and even indoor skydiving.

One of the main things to keep in mind is that these attractions rely heavily on marketing themselves as "family" activities—those that can be enjoyed by all ages. For the most part, this is the case. Anyone who's ever drawn back the blade at a miniature golf course knows that the challenge of knocking a little colored ball into a dragon's mouth has universal appeal. Other attractions like museums and water parks also attract a wide age range.

But there are dividing lines when it comes to classifying activities according to their age appropriateness, which is why we've shared coverage of "what to do" between this chapter and Kidstuff. Between the two, you'll learn about most everything even loosely labeled as an attraction in the Smokies.

What to expect at
Amusement Centers

Along the way, we've given many places write ups in both Attractions and Kidstuff, and we've done a lot of cross referencing, especially when it comes to what we call "amusement centers." These are the places that usually have some combination of go-cart racing, miniature golf, bumper boats, video arcades, and other pay-to-play games and amusements. It's not unusual to find things just for younger children side-by-side with activities just for the big people. In such cases, we've split our coverage. In this chapter, we focus more on activities like the amusement centers' faster go-cart tracks and more "daredevilish" rides. In Kidstuff, we emphasize the things in which younger children can participate, like miniature golf, bumper cars and junior go-cart tracks. But Kidstuff has information for grown-up fun as well. After all, why should the kids have all the fun?

There are many universals you'll encounter from one amusement center to the next. First, think "safety." You play at your own risk on things like bungee towers and go-cart tracks; management prohibits deliberately bumping go-carts into each other and against track guardrails. Needless to say, pregnant women and people with heart and back conditions shouldn't participate in these activities.

Second, you can count on most go-cart rides lasting anywhere from three to six minutes. We've avoided comparing the speeds of the go-carts from one business to the next. If you were to ask each track manager who has the fastest carts in town, you'd hear an unqualified "We do!" from every one. Also, you'll notice that several go-cart tracks are referred to as "slick tracks." This means that the driving surface is smoother than normal surfaces. Speeds are a little slower, but drivers have fun spinning their wheels on the turns!

Finally, most amusement centers are open year round. In season, you can count on businesses being open seven days a week from around 9 or 10 AM to as late as midnight or 1 AM in some cases; at night, facilities are appropriately lit. As for the off-season, you'll find that several establishments cut back to weekends only or some other limited schedule. However, most of the managers with whom we spoke weren't willing to commit to definite autumn and winter schedules. Often, they choose to improvise and let factors such as the weather and holiday-related visitation determine when they're open. Your best bet for weekly and daily schedules in the off-season is to call ahead.

General Notes About Attractions

Most Smoky Mountain attractions provide adequate free parking, especially those in Sevierville and Pigeon Forge. In Gatlinburg, there are places that don't have parking. Not to worry: In such cases, you can pay to park in a city lot or garage, or you can access your destination on foot or by trolley.

Except for a few spots that are off the main drag, we're presenting our attractions in the order they're found traveling south from I-40's Exit 407 to the national park entrance. Unless otherwise indicated, all prices include sales tax.

Whether you're young or young at heart, you'll surely find something to see, hear, drive, paddle or jump off that will make your visit to the Smokies a little more memorable. Now it's time to go out and play!

Sevierville

Tennessee Smokies baseball
Interstate 40 Exit 407, Sevierville
• (865) 774-0033, (865) 637-9494

Professional baseball has found a new home in East Tennessee! The Smokies, AA minor league affiliates of the Toronto Blue Jays, are ushering in the millennium at their brand new stadium in Sevierville.

Beginning in April 2000, the Smokies are playing more than half of their 140-game schedule at the new ballpark located just off I-40 at Exit 407. The facility features 6,000 fixed seats, grass berm seating for an additional 2,000 spectators on the hillside beyond the outfield, 18 private suites and two patio areas. There is a restaurant inside the stadium (overlooking the field) that's open year round, and visitors can also stop by the new county welcome center located on the 25-acre site. The Southern League season runs from April through early September.

In 1999, the Smokies announced they would no longer play at Knoxville's Bill Meyer Stadium, the city's home of minor league baseball since the mid-1950s. Multiple project bids were made on a new stadium for the team; propos-

als included renovations to the existing stadium as well as alternate sites for a new facility. After a strong show of support from Sevier County in terms of season ticket sales as well as an attractive bid on a new facility, the franchise made the decision to make the 18-mile move closer to the mountains.

Ticket prices for the 2000 season range from $4 to $12; there is also an additional charge for on-site parking. Season tickets are also available in different packages. For more information on the Smokies, you can visit their website at www.smokiesbaseball.com.

Scenic Helicopter Tours
1949 Winfield Dunn Pkwy., Sevierville
• (865) 453-6342

One of the most memorable ways to experience Smoky Mountain views is from high up in the air. This tour operator with over 25 years experience will take you on local helicopter flights that cover different areas between Douglas Lake and Pigeon Forge. These flights range from three-minute introductory flights for $10 per person to 12-minute flights over Dollywood and the Pigeon Forge foothills for $42 per per-

ATTRACTIONS

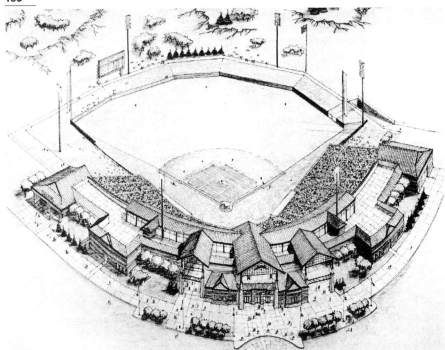

The Tennessee Smokies play in a brand new ballpark just off the interstate.

Photo: Courtesy Tennessee Smokies

son. There are longer scenic mountain flights going as far as Gatlinburg and Wears Valley, lasting anywhere from 18 to 40 minutes and costing upward of $100. With both the local and the scenic flights, the exact flight times are flexible.

Scenic Helicopter Tours is open year-round, but flights only run when weather permits. Children younger than 2 fly free, and the company accepts Mastercard and Visa as payment.

Great Smoky Mountain Helicopters
1101 Winfield Dunn Pkwy., Sevierville
• (865) 429-2426

This helicopter tour company flies a number of local routes, starting with a very short introductory flight for $5.50 per person (a quick up-and-down trip). There are a number of longer tours that range as far as flights over Dollywood that cover 24 miles and cost $48 per person. Except for their eight-mile and 12-mile tours, all flights must have a minimum of four paid seats. That means that if there are two of you, you'll need to wait for two more people to fly with you—or you can pay for all four seats. Smoky Mountain Helicopters also offers custom flights that provide more scenic mountain viewing. These flights can cost up-

wards of $100 per person and must be at least 30 minutes in duration. Mastercard and Visa are accepted.

Great Smoky Mountain Helicopters is open seven days a week year round, weather permitting. Tours begin at 9 AM in season and at 10 AM between Labor Day and Easter; tours end at sunset throughout the year.

Blazing Wheels Raceway
925 Winfield Dunn Pkwy., Sevierville
• (865) 429-1029

Blazing Wheels offers three go-cart tracks for Older "drivers." The Super 8 Track's double figure-eight course is open to those ages 12 and older who are at least 4 feet 10 inches tall. The cost is $6 per person. The Nas-Track is a fast, tri-oval circuit available only to those ages 16 and older who have a valid I.D. The cost is $7 per person. The Pro Track is a slick, cloverleaf track on which three different carts are run. For $6, children at least 12 years old and 4 feet 10 inches tall can drive the Pro Track racer. The Indy racer, which also costs $6, can be driven by children at least 8 years old and 4 feet 3 inches tall. For $7, you can take out the two-seat racers, although you must be an adult to drive a passenger. Blazing Wheels offers a discounted package price of $50 for ten tickets.

Floyd Garrett's Muscle Car Museum
320 Winfield Dunn Pkwy., Sevierville • (865) 908-0882

If you're a "gear head," you'll feel like a kid in a candy store at this showplace of American custom and vintage performance cars. Open since the spring of 1996, the museum houses a collection of 90-plus "muscle cars" and occupies a massive 35,750 square feet of floor space. Most of the vehicles on display are owned by Floyd Garrett, and each has been reconditioned to virtual perfection. Automotive fans can enjoy up-close inspections of cars like NASCAR star Richard Petty's 1977 STP Monte Carlo as well as speedsters driven by racers Bobby Allison and Dale Earnhardt. Visitors can also view walls lined with racing memorabilia, check out a display of rare racing engines and browse the gift shop, which is stocked full of souvenirs for the NASCAR junkie. Floyd Garrett's Muscle Car Museum is open seven days a week throughout the year, except for Thanksgiving and Christmas. Admission is $8.95 for adults and $3.26 for children 8 through 12; children younger than 8 are admitted free. Normal operating hours are 9 AM to 7 PM daily.

The cast bronze statue of Dolly Parton in front of the Sevier County courthouse is a favorite photo subject of Smoky Mountain vacationers.

Photo: Courtesy Sevierville Chamber of Commerce

Sevier County Courthouse
Court Ave., Sevierville • no general phone

After the Great Smoky Mountains, the towering 75-foot spire of this century-old structure is usually the second thing that grabs your attention when driving into the city of Sevierville. One of the most recognized and photographed courthouses in Tennessee, the building maintains a stately presence in an otherwise rapidly developing tourist market. In 1976, it became the first Tennessee courthouse to be placed on the National Register of Historic Places. The exterior is predominantly red brick with a foundation of large, locally quarried limestone blocks. The architecture is Victorian and features an imposing clock tower surrounded by a number of smaller domed structures on the rooftop. The clock is the same one that was installed 100 years ago and to this day still faithfully chimes the hour and half-hour.

The present structure is the fifth to serve as county courthouse and was completed in 1896 at a total cost of just over $21,000. In 1971, plans to do away with the aging building were scrapped in favor of a complete renovation, which included gutting virtually all of the wood used in its interior. This was done to minimize the occurrence of fires that had devastated an earlier Sevier County courthouse. In the years

ATTRACTIONS

that followed, two annexes were added to the original building—fortunately, these additions were made with considerations for both modern practicality as well as architectural compatibility.

Another popular subject for sightseers' cameras is the statue of Dolly Parton located on the east lawn of the courthouse. Sculpted by noted local artist Jim Gray, the life-sized, cast bronze figure rests on a large rock base and depicts Sevier County's most famous offspring in her younger years, sitting with a guitar in her arms and a smile on her face. Because most of the courthouse's noteworthy attributes can be seen from the outside, a worthwhile visit there can be made any time of day, even if all you do is pull your car up to the curb and put your camera into action.

Sevier County Heritage Museum
167 E. Bruce St., Sevierville
• (865) 453-4058

Take a trip back through time and see cherished relics and artifacts that tell the story of Sevier County's rich history. Inside, visitors can take a chronological tour that offers glimpses into the lives and times of the people who settled and developed the area. From the tools and arrowheads of early Indian inhabitants to an authentic telephone operator's switchboard of the mid-1900s, the museum's multiple displays and tributes bring treasured legends and memories to life.

All aspects of the lives of area pioneers and settlers are explored. Looking over preserved treasures like spinning wheels, butter churns, pantaloons and corn shellers allow the visitor to conjure up images of a vanished era. See materials used in the construction of 18th and 19th century homes and marvel at the hand craftsmanship of muzzle-loading flintlock rifles. Other displays pay homage to Sevier Countians who served their country on the battlefield in the Civil War and World War II. Many of the items on hand, including photographs and newspapers, were donated by residents whose families had helped shape the events of their day. Those who wish to delve deeper into the past can peruse an extensive catalog of newsletters published by the Smoky Mountain Historical Society or purchase one of many different books on various facets of local history.

Located in downtown Sevierville, the building in which the museum is housed is historically significant itself. It was erected in 1940 and for years served as the city's post office. The museum originally opened in the summer of 1995 in correlation with Tennessee's bicentennial celebration. Although admission is free, the museum also welcomes private donations. Its hours of operation are Monday, Tuesday, Thursday and Friday from noon to 5 PM and Saturday from noon to 3 PM. You can park for free anywhere along Bruce Street.

Smoky Mountain Deer Farm and Exotic Petting Zoo
478 Happy Hollow Ln., Sevierville
• (865) 428-3337

Visitors have been flocking to the Deer Farm and Petting Zoo for over a decade to feed and get face-to-face (and often hand-to-mouth) with a live menagerie that includes camels and zebras, kangaroos and llamas, ferrets and reindeer. Although more than 70 percent of its visitors are adults, we've still included our detailed profile of the Deer Farm and Petting Zoo as a Close-up in the Kidstuff chapter. We felt that where children were concerned, this Smoky Mountain attraction is a great alternative to arcades and miniature golf courses. But as we mentioned, adults certainly love it too!

Admissions to the Deer Farm and Petting Zoo are $6 for ages 13 and older and $3 for ages 3 to 12. Children ages 2 and younger are admitted free. Prices do not include sales tax. Discounted rates are available for groups of 15 or more. To feed the animals, use only the special feed provided, which comes in cups ranging from 12 ounces ($1.50) to 32 ounces ($3.50).

The facility is open year-round, seven days a week except for Thanksgiving and Christmas. Daily hours are from 10 AM to 5:30 PM. Throughout the year, ticket sales stop one hour before closing. It's best to call ahead to verify hours during periods of bad weather. Owners Greg and Lynn Hoisington also operate Deer Farm Riding Stables, which is located on the same property. See our chapter on Parks and Recreation for more information on horseback riding opportunities.

Forbidden Caverns
455 Blowing Cave Rd., Sevierville
• (865) 453-5972

While you won't exactly journey all the way to the center of the earth, you'll get a good feel for what it might be like in this large underground cave located approximately 20 miles east of downtown Sevierville. Stalactites, stalagmites, towering chimneys and grottoes are among the many natural formations to be seen on your adventure. Interestingly, the natural temperature inside the caverns remains at a steady 58 degrees year-round. Enhanced by special lighting effects and a stereophonic sound presentation, your guided, 55-minute tour is chock full of memorable sights and will take you a half-mile into the heart of English Mountain. The trails are well lighted, and handrails have been provided where necessary. In addition to the rock structures, you'll also see a running stream that's believed to flow from a lake deep within the mountain. While you're there, you'll also learn about the people who carved out the cavern's colorful history, from the Eastern Woodland Indians who used the cave as shelter to the moonshiners of the 1920s and 1930s.

Forbidden Caverns' season starts April 1 and continues seven days a week through November 30. It is also open December 26 through January 1. Normal business hours are 10 AM to 6 PM. Admission prices are $8 for adults and $4 for children ages 5 through 12. Souvenirs and refreshments are available, and there is free parking for cars and buses.

The Mine
1430 Hurley Dr., Sevierville
• (865) 453-7712

Have you ever wanted to prospect for gems the way the old timers did? Now you've got your chance! At The Mine, you can sift through bags of gem-rich North Carolina soil in search of naturally occurring precious stones. Located at Governor's Crossing, this new 13,000-square-foot attraction is the sister site of the original Pigeon Forge Mine, a long time fixture on that city's Parkway. See The Mine's listing in the Pigeon Forge section below for details on how to become a real life "miner 49er."

NASCAR Speed Park
1545 Parkway, Sevierville
• (865) 908-5500

Ladies and gentlemen—start your engines! With eight tracks spread out over 25 acres, NASCAR Speed Park packs a lot of go-cart fun for speedsters young and old. The $15 million theme park opened in 1999, making it the county's third largest attraction (after Dollywood and Ober Gatlinburg).

The tracks are all different and offer something for every driving preference and skill level. At one end

of the spectrum is the Baby Bristol track for drivers who are at least 3 feet 4 inches tall. The small, single-loop circuit is just right for youngsters. At the other extreme is the quarter-mile Smoky Mountain Speedway track, which features 5/8-scale cars that go quite a bit faster than your average go-cart. You must be at least 5 feet 4 inches tall to drive on this track.

In between are other courses—The Qualifier, Young Champions, Slidewayz, The Intimidator and The Competitor—that range from basic oval shapes to multiple-turn surfaces. Minimum height requirements for these tracks range from 4 feet 8 inches tall for The Qualifier to 5 feet 2 inches for The Competitor. The Family 500 track has double-seat carts so that adults and children can burn rubber together. Drivers must be at least 5 feet 4 inches tall, and passengers must be at least 3 feet 6 inches tall.

If you're the competitive type, you'll probably enjoy NASCAR Speed Park's timing and scoring system that measures lap times of each car down to thousandths of a second. The system is similar to the one used by NASCAR in its Winston Cup, Busch Grand National and Craftsman Truck series.

There is an admission price, of sorts, to enter NASCAR Speed Park. Those more than 4 feet tall pay $5 to get in, but receive seven tickets which can be used for go-cart racing or concessions. Those shorter than 4 feet pay $3 to enter and are given five tickets. The number of tickets required to drive on the tracks ranges from four tickets for the Baby Bristol track to seven tickets for most of the bigger tracks. The quarter-mile Smoky Mountain Speedway takes 20 tickets plus an additional, one-time, $5 fee for a required Speed Park license.

Once you're in the park, you'll likely need more tickets if you plan on taking more than one cart ride. These can be purchased at several locations throughout the park. Individual tickets sell for $1 each, or you can purchase one of several packages that offer larger numbers of tickets at discounted prices. Booklets come in denominations of up to 150 tickets. In addition to track admissions, tickets can also be used at Speed Park's concessions areas.

As a licensed activity of NASCAR, this attraction has a lot in store for fans of one of the fastest growing spectator sports in the country. All 240 of the park's

INSIDERS' TIP
A number of area rides and attractions have minimum height, weight and age requirements. We've included most of that information in this chapter, but it's a good idea to call ahead before visiting these places, especially if you plan on taking children.

ATTRACTIONS

The original clock in the century-old Sevier County courthouse still faithfully rings on the hour and half-hour.

Photo: Courtesy Sevierville Chamber of Commerce

Stop Grill and souvenir shops full of Speed Park memorabilia and apparel.

NASCAR Speed park is open year-round. In spring and summer, daily hours are from 10 AM until at least 10 PM; they may stay open until midnight if the masses allow. Once tourist visitation starts to slow down in Sevier County after Labor Day, the park is open from 4 to 10 PM on weekdays and from 11 AM to 10 PM on weekends.

Pigeon Forge

Mountain Valley Vineyards
2174 Parkway, Pigeon Forge
• (865) 453-6334

This Pigeon Forge wine maker provides free guided and self-guided tours of its operation. From the grape crushing machine to the massive steel fermenting tanks to the automated bottler, visitors can get a first-hand glimpse at a process that has produced national award-winning vintages. Those interested in tasting the finished product can sample, at no charge, any of Mountain Valley's 14 labels at their tasting bar.

downsized race cars are custom designed and built. Five actual NASCAR show vehicles are on display throughout the property as are more than 100 items of NASCAR memorabilia and hundreds of photos of NASCAR events and stars. For Speed Park's opening ceremonies, racing stars Dale Earnhardt, Jeff Gordon, Dale Jarrett and Rusty Wallace were on hand to help get things off to a fast start. More visits from NASCAR drivers are planned to coincide with future special events.

There's plenty to be found inside the main building, including the 28,000-square-foot Speed Dome arcade, featuring 60 racing games and driving simulators. You'll also find the Pit

Mountain Valley Vineyards is one of only 17 wineries in the state of Tennessee, and primarily uses grapes from regional vineyards. Seven of the vineyards utilized are located within a 60-mile radius of the winery itself. Because 85 percent of the grapes used are grown in-state, Tennessee agricultural laws allow Mountain Valley Vineyards to market its product in a city that otherwise is not permitted to sell wine. Forty different types of grapes and a variety of other fruits such as raspberries, blackberries and strawberries are put through a fermenting process that can take anywhere from one to five years. The result: a menu of dry, semisweet and dessert wines that has stood head to head with some of America's best. Mountain Valley Vineyards is open 365 days a year.

Ogle's Water Park
2530 Parkway, Pigeon Forge
• (865) 453-8741

The whole family can easily spend an entire day or more at this water park devoted to wet, warm-weather fun. Water slides (ten, to be exact) are the mainstay of Ogle's sprawling outdoor complex, most of which require several flights of stairs to reach the top. On the Hydro Chute, you have your choice of several different tubular slides that carry you to the bottom at a comfortable speed with a number of moderate turns along the way. For a more frenzied ride, the Twin Twister will send you on a somewhat disorienting journey, propelling you at a slightly steeper rate along tubes that twist and spiral their way to a shallow pool below. If pure speed is what you're looking for, check out the Rip Tide Slide, two open, parallel chutes which drop steeply from the apex, level off slightly, then send you plummeting sharply again to the water below.

If your idea of water fun is of a more relaxed nature, you can rent inner tubes and float on Ogle's Lazy River ride, where 250,000 gallons of water gently carry you down a long, winding, circular course. For a more realistic ocean feel, grab your tube and jump into the wave pool, where you can float and bob among large swells of water or let the breakers wash you up on to shore. Younger children will find more suitable activities at Tadpole Island, a scaled-down kiddie haven featuring tot-size slides and tunnels, all surrounded by a large, shallow wading area.

Ogle's Water Park provides an ample amount of both shaded and unshaded deck seating. Other amenities include dressing rooms with lockers and showers, several food and snack bars located throughout the park, an arcade area and a gift shop where beach wear and other souvenirs are sold. Admission prices are $17.95 for anyone 12 and older and $16.95 for ages 4 through 11; children 3 and younger are admitted free. Season passes, two-day passes and group rates are available, as are 50 percent discounts offered in conjunction with a number of area motels. The park is open weekends only in May from 10 AM to 6 PM and daily, June through August, 10 AM to 7 PM.

The Track
2575 Parkway, Pigeon Forge
• (865) 453-4777

Before you get behind the wheel or do any-thing else at this sprawling family amusement center you'll need to buy tickets. Individual tickets are $2.50 each, or you can purchase six for $12, 24 for $40 or 48 for $74. Also, before you head out to play you might grab one of The Track's brochures. It has a map that will help you navigate the many different areas, including the concessions facility, restrooms and the arcade.

Although there's a lot to take on at The Track, the focus is on go-cart racing. There are two twisty, curvy, outdoor tracks on site. The first, simply called The Track, utilizes one and two-seat carts. One-seaters cost two tickets, and solo drivers must be at least 4 feet 6 inches tall. For two-seaters, drivers with passengers pay four tickets, and the driver must be at least 16 years old. Passengers in two-seaters must be at least 3 feet tall. Those between 3 feet and 4 feet 2 inches tall ride for free while passengers between 4 feet 2 inches and 4 feet 6 inches must pay one ticket extra.

The other outdoor track, the Wild Woody, is a multi-tiered wooden track that goes through several humps and corkscrew twists. You must be at least 4 feet 10 inches tall to drive a single go-cart on the Wild Woody, which costs three tickets. Drivers with passengers pay five tickets, and the driver must be at least 16 years old. Two-seater passengers on the Wild Woody must be at least 3 feet tall. If you're between 3 feet and 4 feet 6 inches tall, you ride along for free. If you're between 4 feet 6 inches and 4 feet 10 inches tall, you pay an extra ticket.

If you're in search of an even bigger adrenaline rush, fork over the eight tickets required to bungee jump from The Track's 60-foot tower. No experience is necessary. See Kidstuff for more information about other amusements The Track has to offer.

Elvis Museum
2638 Parkway, Pigeon Forge
• (865) 428-2001

Elvis may have left the building, but he sure left a lot of stuff behind! Get an up-close peek at the largest privately owned collection of Elvis Presley memorabilia found outside the walls of Graceland—everything from clothes to cars, guns to guitars. The sounds of Elvis' music fills the air as you approach the front doors. Inside, you'll see plenty of authentic personal effects that belonged to The King, including stage costumes, backstage notes, sports gear, gifts from fans, jewelry and sunglasses. There are several larger items in the collection as well, like the last limousine owned by Presley and living room

Whitewater rafting is a great way to seek adventure while cooling off on a summer day.

Photo: Courtesy Pigeon River Outdoors

furniture from his Hollywood home. For those interested in adding to their own collection of Elvis trinkets, there is a souvenir shop on site, carrying a healthy selection of music, videos, books and other assorted knick-knacks. In operation since 1982, Elvis Museum is open all year except for Thanksgiving and Christmas. In-season business hours (May through August and October) are 9 AM to 10 PM; off-season hours are 10 AM to 7 PM. Admission prices are $7.99 for adults, $5.99 for any student older than 12, $3.99 for ages 6 to 12, and children younger than 6 are admitted free. Prices do not include sales tax.

Winston Cup Race World
250 Island Dr., Pigeon Forge
• (865) 429-2030

At this NASCAR-themed amusement center, you have to buy tickets beforehand to participate in the various activities. When purchasing your tickets, bear in mind that even though they only cost $1 each, most activities will cost you anywhere from three to seven tickets apiece. There is a discounted price of $20 for 25 tickets.

The Indoor Speedway is a multi-curve track that costs five tickets to drive. Operators of one-seat carts must be at least 4 feet 6 inches tall. Two-seater carts cost seven tickets each, and the driver must have a valid license and be at least 5 feet 2 inches tall; passengers must be at least 3 feet tall. The Outdoor Speedway features realistic looking, scale miniatures of Winston Cup stock cars. It costs seven tickets to drive the high-bank, single-circuit course. Drivers must be at least 5 feet 2 inches tall and have a valid driver's license.

Back inside the Race World building you'll enjoy an 18-hole miniature golf course, bumper cars and the 2002 Cyber Coaster, a roller coaster simulation ride. You'll also find a snack bar and a 4,000-square-foot gift shop stocked to the brim with NASCAR apparel and souvenirs. For a real touch of NASCAR authenticity, you can check out the several bona fide Winston Cup stock cars parked inside. Each is displayed with information about its race history.

In spring of 2000, Winston Cup Race World debuts The Intimidator, a brand new, full size, wooden roller coaster named in honor of NASCAR legend Dale Earnhardt.

Star Tracks
2757 Parkway, Pigeon Forge
• (865) 429-5580

Star Tracks features three outdoor, single-loop go-cart tracks, two of which are for older kids and adults. The Family Slick Track is a covered track open to ages 7 and older. Admission is $5 per ride. The Pro Track is for ages 12 and older. The cost is also $5 per ride with a discounted price of five rides for $20. Any double seat carts cost $7. The driver must be at least 12 years old and the passenger must be at least 4 years old.

Laserport
2782 Parkway, Pigeon Forge
• **(865) 453-0400**

See our Kidstuff chapter for details on all the indoor laser tag fun that awaits you here. If you're in search of go-cart action, Laserport has an outdoor, single-loop track that costs $4.75 per ride or $12 for three rides. Drivers must be at least 4 feet 6 inches tall. Drivers of two-seat carts ($5.75 per ride) must be at least 16 years old.

Rockin' Raceway
2839 Parkway, Pigeon Forge
• **(865) 428-3392**

There are three go-cart tracks at this amusement center, two of which are for ages 10 and older. The Pro Track costs $6, and drivers must be at least 14 years old and 4 feet 6 inches tall. No passengers are allowed on the Pro Track. On the Grand Prix Track, which costs $5 per ride, solo drivers must be at least 10 years old. In the two-seat carts, drivers must be at least 18, and passengers must be 3 to 9 years old. The cost for passengers is $2.

Rockin' Raceway offers more than just racing, however. Ripline is a unique amusement for those who aren't afraid of heights. After taking stairs to the top of a 70-foot tower (formerly a bungee tower), you're strapped into a harness, hooked on to a taut cable and sent zooming down the 100-yard-long wire at about a 30-degree angle to the ground (not too steep). Ripline costs $10 per ride or three rides for $25. Next to Ripline is a rock-climbing wall on which climbers can harness up and scale the 30-foot vertical wall using only projecting rocks and a safety cable for support. The cost to climb is $5.

On The Hawk, up to 24 passengers at a time take a potentially nauseating pendulum ride that sends them in complete, multiple loops. The Hawk costs $5 and requires that riders be at least 4 feet tall. The Orbitron is one of those three-dimensional contraptions (like the astronauts used to train with) that spins you in three directions at once. You must also be 4 feet tall and fork over $5 for the privilege. Inside the main building, you'll find the SR2V simulator, in which "passengers" take a virtual high-speed trip around a race course for only $3 per person.

The Mine
2865 Parkway, Pigeon Forge
• **(865) 453-7712**

An old-style water tower and animatronic prospector welcome you to this attraction, which has been open since 1986. The activity is unique—you actually buy a bag of dirt, dump it into a prospectors' sluice box and sift the dirt away in a flume full of running water. Any precious stones that happen to remain are yours to keep. The dirt sold at The Mine comes from the the gem-rich soil of Franklin, North Carolina, and costs $5 for one bag or $9 for two bags. They guarantee that you'll find at least one stone in each bag; if not, you get another bag for free. Among the precious and semi-precious stones that can be discovered are rubies, sapphires, emeralds, topaz, amethyst and garnet.

Once you've mined your gem(s), your options vary. First, they'll give you a free appraisal in their "assay office." From there, you can either simply pocket the uncut gem and go home, or you can get quotes on cutting and mounting your stone, which does cost extra—sometimes substantially extra. You can even watch as the folks at The Mine cut the gems and manufacture gold and silver jewelry settings on the premises. In most cases, you'll receive same-day service.

If you really want to be "hands-on," you can join The Mine's Gem Cutters Club. For a one-time fee of $75, you get approximately four hours of one-on-one instruction from a professional gem cutter who will show you how to cut your own stone. Members also receive 10 percent discounts on merchandise on subsequent visits. For those who aren't interested in prospecting at all, The Mine has cases full of finished jewelry pieces for sale as well as novelty and gift items made from various gems and stones.

In 2000, The Mine debuts its second location at Governor's Crossing in Sevierville (see listing in Sevierville section above). Although the new Mine is much larger in size and offers pricier lines of finished jewelry pieces, the basic attraction of sifting through dirt in search of natural treasures is still the main focus.

Fast Tracks
2879 Parkway, Pigeon Forge
• **(865) 428-1988**

There are three outdoor go-cart tracks (two for ages 10 and older) at this multi-faceted family entertainment center. On the multi-curved Pro Car Track, you must be at least 10 years old and 4 feet 6 inches tall to drive alone. To take a passenger, you must be at least 16, and your passenger must be at least 3 feet tall and 3 to 9 years old. The Pro Cars cost $5 per ride or five rides for $20, passengers cost $2 extra. The Naskarts, which are somewhat faster, take drivers 16 and older on a single loop for $6 per ride or five rides for $25.

For the more adventurous, there's the Ejection Seat, a "reverse bungee" ride that hurls riders rapidly skyward to a height of approximately 100 feet, followed by several up and down bounces on the springy cords. The Ejection Seat costs $20 for one person or $25 for two people. Other Fast Tracks offerings include The Orbitron, a stationary, multi-axis device that spins you in three directions at once, and a trampoline where you can go nuts jumping with the added security of safety cords to keep you from flying away.

Adventure Raceway
2945 Parkway, Pigeon Forge
• (865) 428-2971

Adventure Raceway features one outdoor track—another of the many wooden go-cart tracks that sprang up on the Parkway in 1999. The curvy, multi-level wooden section was added to the existing figure-8, ground-level track. The cost is $7 per ride, and drivers must be at least 4 feet 6 inches tall. See Kidstuff for more information about Adventure Raceway and its sister attraction, Adventure Golf.

Smoky Mountain Car Museum
2970 Parkway, Pigeon Forge
• (865) 453-3433

Since 1956, this showplace of rare and vintage cars has offered self-guided tours through the history of the automobile. The collection of more than 30 cars and trucks features such notable vehicles as the silver Aston-Martin driven by James Bond in the films *Goldfinger* and *Thunderball,* Al Capone's bulletproof Cadillac, Elvis Presley's 1971 Mercedes Benz and the "Silver Dollar" car owned by Hank Williams, Jr. A number of classic antiques are on display as well: a 1930 Duesenberg, a 1909 Hupmobile and a 1915 Ford Model T, just to mention a few. All of the cars on display have been reconditioned and are in running order.

What makes this museum truly unique is that it's much more than just a "car museum." Most of the wall space and virtually every spare nook and cranny are packed with hoards of interesting antiques and memorabilia. Many of the relics are, of course, automobile-related: newspaper clippings, photographs, model cars, antique gas pumps and mechanic's tools. You'll also see items that would seem equally at home in any antique mall: old manual typewriters, nickelodeons, gumball machines and even a display of different types of barbed wire! For the souvenir hunter, there is a gift shop on the premises, and auto enthusiasts are sure to find something to their liking in the museum's assortment of collectible books and magazines.

Admission to Smoky Mountain Car Museum is a reasonable $5 for adults and $2 for children ages 3 through 10. Children younger than 3 are admitted for free. The owners prefer to remain noncommittal about their annual opening and closing dates, describing their season as running from "early spring through late fall." They also recommend calling ahead for specific hours of operation, although the museum generally is open from mid morning to early evening.

Parkway Slick Track
3068 Parkway, Pigeon Forge
• (865) 428-7750

This covered, open-air slick track is a short, single-loop course that keeps carts fairly close to each other and makes for exciting driving action. Solo drivers must be at least 13 years old, and drivers of two-seater carts must be at least 16 years old. Passengers in two-seaters must be old enough to sit upright and remain safely buckled into the cart. The cost for single-seat carts is $5; two-seat carts cost $10. Parkway Slick Track has a discounted price of $10 for three tickets, Monday through Thursday only.

Flyaway
3106 Parkway, Pigeon Forge
• (865) 453-7777

Have you ever wanted to go skydiving, but chickened out because of your fears of heights and unopened parachutes? Now, you have no more excuses. Flyaway is one of only two indoor skydiving simulation facilities in the United States (the other is in Las Vegas). It provides novices and seasoned skydivers alike the opportunity to experience the sensation of high-speed freefall in a safe, indoor environment. First-timers start off with a half-hour training session in which safety and body positioning techniques are discussed. After approximately 20 minutes of equipment preparation (flight suit and protective gear are provided), you're ready to soar in Flyaway's 21-foot-tall wind tunnel. A large airplane propeller, located under the mesh wire floor, generates wind speeds of up to 120 miles per hour and creates a column of air on which participants can learn the fundamentals and intricacies of freefall flight. Five "divers" enter the padded tunnel simultaneously and divide 15 minutes of flight time between them.

Flyaway is open all year, but has limited hours during the off season. They recommend calling in advance for a current schedule. The cost of the training and first flight (three minutes of personal air time) is $22.58, but you can tack on an additional three minutes for just under 10 bucks more. Group rates (11 or more), coaching packages and five-ticket books are available. There is an additional cost if you would like a video of your adventure. Participants at Flyaway are required to be in good physical condition and weigh at least 40 pounds. Maximum weight allowances are 220 pounds for those under 6 feet tall and 230 pounds for those over 6 feet. Children younger than 18 must be accompanied by a parent or guardian. Casual clothing with socks and sneakers is suggested.

Pigeon Forge Super Speedway
3275 Parkway, Pigeon Forge
• (865) 429-4639 (track), (865) 429-8600 (Sky Coaster and Sky Scraper)

Super Speedway has a single-loop go-cart track for drivers age 12 and older (no height restrictions). One-seat carts cost $5 per ride, and two-seaters cost $10. For those of you who get your kicks in the air, look for the Sky Coaster and Sky Scraper. On the Sky Coaster, up to three people sit in harnesses that are pulled back by a cable and released, sending riders swinging back and forth like a giant pendulum. If you haven't just eaten a big meal, consider the Sky Scraper. Riders are strapped into a cage that is swung over and over like a pendulum in 360-degree loops by a large mechanical arm. You must be at least 3 feet 6 inches tall (and slightly insane) to ride both the Sky Coaster and the Sky Scraper. Both cost $20 per person per ride, but be sure to ask about ad-

justed rates if you're in a group or visiting when business is slow.

Carbo's Police Museum
3311 Parkway, Pigeon Forge
• (865) 453-1358

Calling all cars! Calling all cars! Be on the lookout for one of the most impressive private collections of police memorabilia in the nation. This Pigeon Forge attraction, which opened in 1976, is home to a 5,000-plus piece showcase of authentic police items, including guns, badges, uniforms and handcuffs (just to name a few) from police departments all over the United States and around the world. Most of the items are displayed in glass cases and line the walls from floor to ceiling throughout Carbo's self-guided tour.

Among some of the more notable exhibits are gangster-related items, collections of illegal weapons and drug paraphernalia confiscated in arrests as well as the prominently featured Buford Pusser display. The life of the McNairy County, Tennessee, sheriff of *Walking Tall* fame is told through newspaper clippings, videos and even Pusser's own clothing and police equipment. The centerpiece of the Pusser exhibit is the 1974 Corvette in which Pusser was killed in a controversial and fiery crash in Adamsville, Tennessee, in 1974.

Carbo's Smoky Mountain Police Museum is open from 10 AM to 5 PM on a varying schedule throughout the year. The museum is closed November through March, open Friday through Sunday in April, open every day but Thursday in May, September and October, and open seven days a week from June through August . Admission is a reasonable $6.50 for ages 11 and older and $3.25 for ages 10 and younger.

Smoky Mountain Slick Track
3322 Parkway, Pigeon Forge
• (865) 428-4955

This outdoor slick track runs along a bent, single-loop course and offers close-knit, competitive driving action. Solo drivers must be at least 4 feet 9 inches tall. Drivers with passengers must be at least 16 years old, and passengers must be at least 3 feet 4 inches tall. All single-seat go-carts cost $5 per ride, and two-seaters cost $10 per ride. Smoky Mountain Slick Track offers a discounted price of four rides for $16.

Riverside Raceway
3315 S. River Road, Pigeon Forge
• (432) 908-7255

There are two outdoor go-cart tracks at the

ATTRACTIONS

Feel the need for speed? Choose from nearly 20 go-cart operators in the Smokies

Photo: Courtesy Blazing Wheels

25-minute tours are conducted every half hour for the general public, and special tours are available for large groups. The cost of the tour is $3 for adults, $1.50 for children seven through 12, and children six and under are admitted free.

Movie Rider
3370 Parkway, Pigeon Forge
• (865) 428-8511

At this movie attraction, you won't just be a passive spectator—you'll feel like you're part of the action. Viewers are strapped into chairs mounted on moving platforms that tilt, dip and shift in synchronicity with the 70-millimeter film, which is displayed on a giant 40-foot by 30-foot screen. The 17-minute features are two-part presentations that put you safely in the seats of such thrilling settings as roller coaster rides or high-speed race cars. Films change throughout the season.

Movie Rider is open daily year round between 5 PM and midnight. There is also a limited daytime schedule that varies throughout the year, so it's advisable to call ahead to verify matinee showings. Admission prices are $9.25 for adults and $7.25 for children 10 and under. Group rates are available. Most major credit cards are accepted. Participation by pregnant women, claustrophobic people or anyone with back, head or neck problems is discouraged. You must be 42 inches tall to participate.

Rebel Yell Raceway
3643 Parkway, Pigeon Forge
• (865) 453-9461

Another "racing plus" conglomerate, Rebel Yell has a pro track and junior turbo track where $5.00 buys a single ride. The 4-foot height rule is in effect. The venue is also the home of a simulated gem mine, a vertical accelerator, and a dinosaur-infested miniature golf course. At Rebel Yell Gem Mining, "prospectors" can cull through specially prepared bags of gem-laden earth looking for precious and semi-precious stones. On-site experts will help to find and identify stones. Bags are priced at $4, $5, or $6,

Raceway's location just off the Parkway near the Old Mill neighborhood. The single-loop wedge track is for drivers who are at least 4 feet 8 inches tall. Single carts cost $6, and two-seaters cost $10. The Tennessee Twister is a brand-new wooden go-cart track with multiple levels and corkscrew turns. You must be at least 5 feet tall to drive. The Tennessee Twister costs $7 for one-seaters and $10 for two-seaters. Drivers of all two-seat cars must be 16 years old, and passengers must be at least 3 years old. If you want to drive both tracks, you can do so for a discounted price of $11.

Riverside Raceway also has the Sling Swing, a multi towered setup that uses bungee cords to fling passengers either up and down, side to side or both! It costs $15 to ride vertically or horizontally and $25 to ride both ways.

The Old Mill
2944 Middle Creek Road, Pigeon Forge
• (865) 453-4628

Just a block off the Parkway at traffic light #7 and across the river stands the Old Mill, a still-working grist mill built in 1830. It was the center of all activities in the old days, and is still in the middle of the shopping area most long-term visitors remember. The mill is on the National Register of Historic buildings, and still grinds corn into flour for sale in the general store. Guided tours of the mill are available in the summer and fall months. The scheduled

The Smoky Mountain Car Museum has been a Pigeon Forge attraction for more than 40 years.

Photo: Courtesy Smoky Mountain Car Museum

or two bags of any size may be purchased for $7, $9, or $11. The vertical accelerator ride (they call it the "Ejection Seat") will rocket one or two riders into space for $20 apiece; a second shot, if you can handle it, is $5. Jurassic Golf features huge prehistoric creatures on a very fast concrete links layout. An 18-hole round costs $5; an additional dollar buys 36 holes.

Wild Wheels & Waterbugs
3735 Parkway, Pigeon Forge
• (865) 453-7942

The southernmost of Pigeon Forge's myriad amusements on the Parkway, Wild Wheels is a sparkling clean layout featuring two go-cart tracks, a bumper boat pool, a big arcade and a four-station bungee jump tower (no waiting!). Bungee jumping from the quad tower is priced at $20 for the first jump and $10 for another if one isn't enough. If you need proof that you really did take "the plunge," they'll shoot a video of your attempted suicide for $10. The bumper boats have an age limit of 7 years for solo riders at $5 a head, which is also the going rate for a 12-minute trip on either of the two go-cart tracks. The junior track (7 years, minimum height 4 feet) has two cart configurations, as does the big track (age 10, height 54 inches). A special rate schedule permits a mix-and-match package of 10 rides on the go-carts and/or

bumper boats for $35. The large arcade features a broad selection of electronic and interactive games.

Gatlinburg

Everything in Gatlinburg is convenient, and attractions are no exception. With the exception of five (three of which are on River Road a block off the Parkway), every attraction in Gatlinburg is contained in a four-block section of town. As previously mentioned, some attractions that are geared specifically to the younger set are also included in the "Kidstuff" chapter, and most of those are also in or very near the center of town.

Dinosaur Golf
160 Parkway, Gatlinburg • (865) 436-4449

Two 18-hole courses wander through a real forest of simulated prehistoric creatures. Among the oldest amusements in the area, Dinosaur Golf is a throwback to the miniature golf courses of the 1950s and '60s, with strategically placed rocks and water to challenge the best of putters. Their biggest regret is that they can't figure out a way to tie in a few windmills. Greens fees are $5 for one course or $6 for both. Additional plays are another dollar.

Hillbilly Golf
340 Parkway, Gatlinburg • (865) 436-7470

Another oldie, with a really spectacular twist: You can't walk to the course. Hillbilly Golf's two 18-hole courses are on a mountaintop 300 feet above the Parkway, and the only way to get to them is to ride an incline railway. The ride is part of the admission, of course, and while you're waiting for the rail car you can visit the arcade or get in a few strokes on the practice green. Once you get to the top you'll play on your choice of courses (or both) set in the wilderness, with mountaineer hazards like stills and rock walls to make your shot selections a little more difficult. Adults 13 to 60 pay $5, children 4 through 12 and seniors 60 and older pay $4 and children 3 and under are free.

Riverwalk
River Road, Gatlinburg

One of the most pleasant results of a massive ongoing urban beautification program begun in 1997, Riverwalk is an island of serenity on the northern edge of the downtown business district. The renewal project actually begins before traffic light #3, where the utilities have been buried to leave an uncluttered skyline, but our concern at the moment is the stretch that joins the river itself where River Road runs diagonally off the Parkway at traffic light #5. From that point to Maples Lane, about half a mile distant, Riverwalk is a pleasant stroll along the west prong of the Little Pigeon River at a reasonable enough remove from the downtown activity to make the noise and lights seem a million miles away.

The variegated sidewalk, sometimes brick and cobblestone, sometimes faux boardwalk, sometimes just plain cement, is flanked by old-fashioned globe streetlights, reminiscent of gaslights at the curb, and a wrought iron fence along the river bank. The fence is festooned with thousands of planters filled with home-grown flowers, courtesy of the Parks & Recreation Department's full-time horticultural staff. Early on, a footbridge across the river provides the main access to the new Ripley's Aquarium. That bridge and the sidewalk leading to Gatlinburg's Mysterious Mansion a few blocks down are the only two points where businesses are accessed directly from the Riverwalk; for the rest of the way it's just you and the water and those millions of fresh flowers.

If you want to get a closer look at the river, or go fishing in it (regulations are in our Parks and Recreation chapter), several stairways along the way lead to the river's edge, where the local duck population nests. And if strollin' and sittin' are more your style, several benches and gazebos have been provided. In a way, the Riverwalk is a reminder of what Gatlinburg used to be: A sleepy, friendly little town where you could just forget about your troubles for a while in nature's beauty. And you thought nobody listened when you asked what ever happened to that nice little town.

Ripley's Aquarium
88 River Rd., Gatlinburg
• (865) 430-8808

A major attraction in the southeast United States will open its doors in Sevier County early in the summer of 2000. Ripley's Aquarium, which is nearing completion in the heart of downtown Gatlinburg, is a 100,000-plus square foot marine attraction

The Guiness Museum highlights world records of all kinds.

ATTRACTIONS

which will be home to thousands of fish and other types of aquatic life from around the world. More than 1.3 million gallons of man-made seawater will be utilized to house the various exhibits throughout the $42 million facility.

The centerpiece of the aquarium will be an underwater acrylic tunnel in which visitors will ride through 700,000 gallons of water on a 320-foot moving glide path. The journey will bring viewers just inches away from large sharks, poisonous ocean predators and numerous varieties of tropical fish. The aquarium will also feature other sea oddities such as the giant octopus and its eight-foot-long tentacles, the sea dragon and the giant spider crab, the largest crustacean in the world.

Ripley's Aquarium will also house classrooms and a theater where on-staff educators will use lectures and films to expand visitors' knowledge of the sea and its residents. Intern study programs will eventually be developed for those seriously interested in careers in marine science. Rounded out with a gift shop and a deli-style restaurant with outdoor veranda, Ripley's Aquarium becomes major drawing card for the Smokies as the area enters the new millennium.

The Guinness World Records Museum
631 Parkway, Gatlinburg • (865) 436-9100

Take just about any adjective you can think of, add "est" to the end, and you'll find it at the Guinness Museum. From the moment you walk through the unusual whale's mouth and belly that forms the museum's opening, the Guinness folks will show you the biggest, smallest, baddest, longest, shortest, best, worst, and richest of everything they've been able to uncover in more than 40 years of research. Since it's entertaining as well as educational, there's a little bit of the silliest thrown in as well.

Two jam-packed floors of superlatives in the worlds of art, sport, music, movies, television, and human nature will entertain you for as long as you want to stay, and probably teach some things you didn't know about people you thought you knew pretty well. For instance, what has Oprah Winfrey got the world's biggest of at the moment? And how high do you come on the world's tallest man? Admission to the Guinness Museum is $7.95 for adults, $5.95 for senior citizens and teenagers, and

$3.95 for children under 12. Children under six are admitted free Special group rates are available on request. The Guinness World Records Museum is open seven days a week from 9 AM to 11 PM, except Christmas. (And Oprah's got the world's biggest salary, by the way.)

World of Illusions
716 Parkway, Gatlinburg • (865) 436-9701

Just about nothing is real at World of Illusions—we think. These people do more with smoke, mirrors, and lighting than anyone around. Consider this: You can stand there and see an Imperial Warrior beam down from his star ship, but you can't touch him, and you can turn the tables on Superman by spotting him with X-ray vision. Your friend can disappear while holding your hand, and a laser illusion will convince you that Elvis is alive. You can walk away from your shadow and watch Count Dracula turn into a flying bat, and Merlin, the world's best-known wizard, will appear before you and levitate. Watch carefully—you never know what will happen next—or seem to. World of Illusions is open from 10 AM to 10 PM daily. Admission is $5.99 for adults, $3.99 for kids 7 to 17, and children under 6 are admitted free with a paid admission.

> **INSIDERS' TIP**
> Many of the prices you'll find quoted for area attractions don't include sales tax. For your information, Tennessee sales tax is 8.5 percent.

The Gatlinburg Fun Center
716 Parkway, Gatlinburg • (865) 430-8985

Six different amusement venues (including on-site arcades with the latest in high-tech competition) stretch across the back of Reagan Square Mall in the heart of downtown Gatlinburg. Hours of enjoyment are available for the whole family in a close enough environment that nobody gets lost or separated by much distance. We'll present the attractions as they appear from left to right as you enter the complex. Prices vary depending on combinations of activities and group size. Groups of 10 to 15 who play together will save $1 a head for each venue; 15 or more in a group can expect a $2 discount . The Gatlinburg Fun Center is open every day but Christmas from 10 AM until the last customer is served and goes away happy.

Old Gatlinburg Golf & Games
(865) 430-4653

Here are two unusual miniature golf courses laid out on the hillside that integrate old buildings into the play. Gatlinburg's Old Town

Take a close-up look at the Clampett's car from **The Beverly Hillbillies.**

Photo: Courtesy Zwing Advertising

Square Course delivers a local history lesson at every hole, including how the city got its name. The Smokies Old Mountain Trail Course describes the development of the Great Smoky Mountains National Park in a peaceful setting reminiscent of the park itself. One hole plays through a replica of the old Elkmont post office. A single round of golf on one course is $5.95 for anybody over 5 years old, while toddlers can play for $3. One of the best bargains in the area is the $8.95 golf pass that allows unlimited play for five consecutive days.

The Trampoline Thing
(865) 430-8985

This special trampoline has attached bungee cords that let you soar to heights you never dreamed possible while protecting you from any injury. $5.95 buys a three-minute turn, which is plenty of time to get in all the bouncing you can enjoy.

Fort Adventure
(865) 436-2326

Completed just as we go to press, Fort Adventure offers three family entertainment features under one roof. Prices hadn't been announced when we went to press, but look for something between five and 10 dollars per venue, with special package prices for different combinations. This big building at the back of the Family Fun Center used to house a huge laser tag center, and now it's been divided to provide a smaller laser tag with the same sound and light effects. New in the building are a 3-D movie theater using special glasses and special effects that place you in the scene (you'll love the part with the spiders), and a bumper car track where the entire family can express their innermost feelings at the wheel of a bumper car.

Venturer Motion Ride Movie Theater
(865) 430-8985

This is more than moving seats. The Venturer is a full simulation ride that places you in the middle of the action. Four different movies are available, from the popular roller coaster to an interplanetary excursion in sight and sound. The Glacier Run is a race through an arctic ice quarry that's so gripping you'll be too busy to shiver, and the Smash Factory is a trip through one horrifying crash after another. After a preview of all four, a single ride is $6.45 and any two can be seen at one sitting for $8.95.

Bankshot Basketball
(865) 430-8985

This attraction is a fun-filled combination

of miniature golf and basketball, where angled backboards put a special slant on every shot. Accuracy counts big in this contest of skill, and a little knowledge of plane geometry can't hurt. A trip through the Bankshot course is $4.95 with no time limit.

Terror on the Parkway
716 Parkway, Gatlinburg
• (865) 436-4636, (865) 436-9701

A new slant in haunted houses: At Terror on the Parkway, the house comes to you as you sit frozen in fascination in a room filled with things that go bump. And wiggle. And giggle. And scream their heads off. It's truly a terrifying collection of sights and sounds, complete with spooky lighting and other-worldly sounds (in stereo, yet) from the dark side. If it doesn't remind you of your worst-ever nightmare, it'll probably provide you with a new one. A full serving of fright is available daily from 10 AM to 10 PM at $3.99 for adults and $2.99 for children 12 and under. Group rates are available for those who hate to shriek alone.

Gatlinburg Sky Lift
765 Parkway, Gatlinburg • (865) 436-4307

When it opened in 1954, the Sky Lift started from a point almost as sparsely settled at the bottom as it was at the top. Now leaving the Parkway in the center of downtown, it travels across River Road and 700 feet up the south face of Crockett Mountain. At the summit, the panoramic view of Gatlinburg and the surrounding Smokies is breathtaking. Safe, two-person lift chairs stay comfortably close to the ground during the ascent, and the automatic camera takes pictures as each chair approaches the top, providing a delightful souvenir. Other souvenirs and snacks are also available at the summit's rustic gift shop. The Sky Lift is most popular in autumn, as the fall colors take on whole new dimensions when viewed from the top of Crockett Mountain. Cameras are welcome on the Sky Lift, giving all riders the chance to take one-of-a-kind shots of downtown Gatlinburg and Mt. LeConte together. Adult admission is $8, and children 11 and under ride for $5. The Sky Lift is open daily from 9 AM to 9 PM in April, May, September, and October; from 9 AM to 11 PM in June through August; and during posted hours November through March.

Ripley's Believe it or Not! Museum
800 Parkway, Gatlinburg • (865) 436-5096

Robert Ripley (1893-1949) was a cartoonist by trade and an adventurer and world traveler by choice. Supported by his syndicated radio show, which was the first program ever broadcast simultaneously to a world wide audience, and his world-famous comic strip, begun in 1918 and still running, Ripley traveled to 198 countries collecting unusual (some may say bizarre) facts, legends, and artifacts from places most people hadn't even heard of before Ripley went there. It's not stretching a point to call Ripley the father of trivia.

Believing it or Not(!) starts with a leap of faith at the entrance: Don't be concerned that the museum is going to collapse around you—the "interesting" architecture is just a warm-up for what you'll see during your self-guiding tour through three stories of exhibits in various forms, from the actual stuffed remains of a two-headed calf born in Gatlinburg to rare film footage shot in the early part of the 20th century. A lot of the exhibits are "hands on," allowing the visitor to experience such delights as actually touching a real shrunken head or playing a giant keyboard by dancing on it (remember the Tom Hanks movie *Big*?). The one-way layout erases concerns about families or groups getting separated, and everybody can go at their own pace until the end of the tour. The friendly attendants will tell you it's about a 45 minute tour, but plan on spending more time—this place, with more than 500 exhibits, is a real schedule-trasher. Ripley's Believe it or Not! Museum is open from 10 AM to 9 PM Sunday through Thursday, and 9 AM to midnight Friday and Saturday, every day but Christmas. Admission is $8.99 for adults, $5.99 for children aged seven to 17, and children under six are admitted free when accompanied by a paying customer.

Gatlinburg's Space Needle
115 Airport Road, Gatlinburg
• (865) 436-4629

Set in the middle of a family entertainment complex that will be covered in depth in our "Kidstuff" chapter, the Space Needle is a vantage point from which a full 360-degree view is possible. Two elevators whisk you up to a 65-foot diameter deck, 342 feet above the ground. All of the principal peaks of the southern range of the Smokies are in view, and an unparalleled look at the city will give you a better feel of how it's laid out. The Space Needle becomes the focal point of the city every New Year's Eve, when Gatlinburg's own lighted ball drops to welcome the new year just like its slightly larger cousin a bit east of here. Admission to the Space Needle is $5 for adults, $4 for teen-

Ripley's Haunted Adventure will give you a scare.

Photo: Courtesy Zwing Advertising

movies a day (the Great Smoky Mountains will join the parade in 2001), the MEGA Theatre offers a variety of wilderness experiences that's as informative as any travelogue you'll ever see, and the immensity of the screen is used to full effectiveness at all times. Each movie runs from 35 to 45 minutes, and all performances start on the hour. Schedules are posted daily, and the friendly ticket sellers can tell you what changes are coming. Admission is $8.50 for a single adult ticket, $6.50 for seniors and students, and $5.50 for children. Double feature tickets are $13.50, $11.50, and $8.50, respectively. In keeping with its portrayal of nature subjects in its singular fashion, the Great Smokies MEGA Theatre is an active supporter of the Great Smoky Mountains National Park. The adjoining Walk in the Park gift shop features Park-oriented merchandise, and is also supports the Park with direct contributions based on sales.

Ripley's Moving Theater
904 Parkway, Gatlinburg
• (865) 436-9763

Two separate features assault your senses in this specially designed experience. Once you're strapped into your custom chair (minimum height requirement 43 inches), the 70mm screen comes alive and the six-channel digital sound system enters through every pore in your body. For the next five minutes you will be buffeted in eight different directions (sometimes all at once) as your seat moves with the action on the screen. The first feature starts with a roller coaster that elicits so much screaming that you can't hear your own, and then things get exciting. In rapid succession, the roller coaster becomes a desert dune buggy in a very crowded desert, and then a roaring snowmobile in a forest full of narrow trails and other snowmobiles.

The second feature is a little more sedate but equally frightening. It's a scenic ride through some lovely mountains that turns into a runaway logging truck ride down a frightening mountain road. One way or another, they're going to make you scream. Ripley's Moving Theater is open from 10 AM to 9 PM Sunday through Thursday, and 9 AM to Midnight Friday and Saturday. Admission is $6 for a single showing, $9 if you think you can handle both shows in one sitting.

agers and senior citizens, $2 for children 6 to 12, and free to children under 5 in the company of an adult. The Space Needle is open from 10 AM to at least 9 PM (later if business demands) year-round, except Christmas.

Great Smokies MEGA Theatre
322 Airport Road, Gatlinburg
• (865) 430-9999

For jaw-dropping awe, the MEGA Theatre's where it's at. The giant IMAX screen, more than 60 feet tall and about 45 feet wide, portrays vistas like nothing else. Using such natural wonders as the Amazon River, Mount Everest, the undersea world of dolphins and other aquatic life, and the majestic American gray wolf, the IMAX camera seems to crawl inside its subject as well as lay out a bigger panoramic scene than the unaided eye can see. And the sound goes right through you.

With a schedule of at least four different

ATTRACTIONS

Mountain Magic

You don't hear the words "skiing" and "Tennessee" used in the same sentence very often, and there's a reason for that. In the local vernacular, "They ain't but one ski resort in all of Tennessee, and we've got it!" And what started in 1962 as a sometimes (when there was snow) run down a mountain to a cinder block building has grown into a year-round resort that's a mainstay of Gatlinburg's tourist economy.

Ober Gatlinburg today is a sprawling year-round ski resort/amusement park tucked into a five-acre niche in Mt. Harrison, 1,400 feet above downtown Gatlinburg.

It's a two-mile ride from the tram terminal on the Parkway (highly recommended) or seven miles of two-lane mountain road (not recommended at all). In fact, Ski Mountain Road is frequently closed to all but local traffic (Ski Mountain is a large residential area) during the ski season. If you happen to be caught "topside" with your car when the road gets closed, you can always ride the tram down and then go back up some time later (maybe days later) to retrieve your vehicle. *Please, please ride the tram.* Round trip fare is $7 for adults and $4 children seven to 11. If you're going skiing, show your tram ticket to the lift ticket seller; the price of the tram ride will be deducted from the lift ticket.

The aerial tramway is wonder all by itself. Two counter-balanced tram cars run continuously, transporting up to 120 people and their equipment on each trip. At 10 minutes per trip at peak operating times, that's about 1,400 people an hour, and it's not an exaggeration to say the tram runs at peak capacity most of the time in the winter. It would take 60 cars with four people per car, running non-stop, two hours to do what the tram does in one, and they'd use about 125 gallons of gasoline in the process. The tram has had exactly zero accidents since it opened in 1973, a tribute

(Continued on next page)

The Alpine Slide is an exciting way to get down the mountain.

Photo: Courtesy Ober Gatlinburg

ATTRACTIONS

to the original construction excellence and the skills of its maintenance crew. (By contrast, Ski Mountain Road averages two cars a day off the road in the summer—we don't even want to talk about when there's snow on the ground).

The tram was designed, engineered, and built by Von Roll, Ltd, a Swiss firm founded in 1810. The tram cars are suspended on a complicated cable system designed to support more than 500,000 pounds per car. That's more than 10 times the weight of a car loaded to capacity. Leaving the docking stations at each end of the 10-minute journey, the tram glides two miles to its opposite terminal. The views alone are worth the cost of the ride ticket, and more photographs are taken from the Ober Gatlinburg tram cars than any other single known spot in the area.

Departing from the tram at the resort, you find yourself in an enormous indoor mall, and where you go from there depends a lot on the time of year. From this point we'll describe Ober Gatlinburg from the perspective of the calendar.

Day by Day

The indoor section doesn't change a lot between seasons. As you leave the tram dock, the concession coupon booth is dead ahead. If you plan to do anything at all while you're on the mountain, buy a book of coupons. $22.50 will buy a book of 20 coupons with a value of $1.25 each (you do the math), and the coupons are legal tender at most of the activities and ride-type attractions. The Municipal Black Bear Habitat is to your immediate left. Beyond the bear habitat, a line of souvenir shops and snack bars forms a ring around the skating rink, two floors below ground level. People-watchers sit at tables along the side, or lean on the rail at the end of the rink. Across the rink from your vantage point, the indoor midway usually teems with kids of various sizes and ages engaged in all manner of physical activity. Completing the circle at your right, the arcade is alive with the strange mix of sounds and lights that can't be found anywhere else. Lets look at each of these areas in a little more detail.

The Municipal Black Bear Habitat is a privately funded zoo dedicated to behavioral research on the American black bear (Ursus Americanus), the living symbol of the Great Smoky Mountains. A small population of non-releasable bears is maintained at the habitat in as close to a natural state as possible, and yearling bears born as the result of the natural mating process are released in bear sanctuaries managed by the Tennessee Wildlife Resources Agency. Medical care of the resident bears is provided by the University of Tennessee's College of Veterinary Medicine. The bears are observed by graduate students for digestive efficiency and sibling interaction. A nominal admission fee (one coupon or a posted cash equivalent) helps support the bear habitat A museum exhibit outside the habitat provides interesting background information on black bears, including graphic displays of what happens when people make the mistake of treating wild bears like house pets.

Several gift and specialty shops line the wall along the side of the ice rink, offering a variety of local handcrafts and souvenirs. A couple of snack bars provide a chance to grab a drink or a meal and sit rinkside watching the skaters while resting your feet.

The indoor ice rink is a spacious sheet of ice, more than 10,000 square feet in area. With over 400 pairs of rental skates available in almost every size, the rink gives interested spectators a chance to experience the joys of an activity seldom seen this far south. The $6.25 (or five coupons) fee includes skate rental and up to three hours of continuous ice time.

Spread throughout the rest of the mall are a variety of midway-type attractions, most of which run no more than three coupons. A special kiddie section has several rides for the toddler set. Games of skill and chance are usually good for a laugh, especially the spider web, a giant velcro-covered air cushion that into which kids in padded suits hurl themselves, and the bungee run, where two participants test their strength against each other and a bungee cord. The cord always wins, but so does the person who can run farthest down a 35 foot alley before being snapped back into the air cushion by the cord around their waist. A batting cage provides virtual pitchers from little league to major league ability that release pitches up to 60 mph.

Out of sight of the tram terminal, the restaurant and lounge are on the mountain side of the building on the second floor, offering a great view of the ski slopes.

Outside the mall, a bunch of outdoor activities operate year-round, weather permitting. Dominating the scene is every mother's nightmare: The Air Boingo double bungee tower. 60 feet high, the bungee tower provides a platform for otherwise perfectly sensible people to wrap a high-strength elastic cord around themselves and jump into space. Coupons are not usable for the bungee jump, which costs $15 per leap. Beside the tower is the Trampoline Thing, where a bungee setup allows jumpers to attain ridiculous heights without having to jump off anything. Three coupons will buy three minutes on the trampoline.

Over to the left, a figure-8 road course awaits the budding Indy driver. 700 feet long, the race course features NASKART go-carts and high banks to keep you on the track. Height and weight restrictions apply in certain weather conditions, and the track closes in extreme weather.

At the other end of the outside area, convenient to the customer service and first aid stations, the longest scenic chair lift in the South goes to the summit of Mt. Harrison. It's a relaxing 15-minute ride with lots of photo quality scenery, and a bluegrass band at the top will entertain you while you enjoy the view. About halfway down on the return trip, you may choose to get off the sedately-paced chairlift and finish the trip down in true white-knuckle fashion at the control of the Alpine Slide, a dry track simulated bobsled run. The manually-controlled sled lets you set your own speed through the woods and curves as you drop 200 feet in an 1800-foot ride. Speeds range from scary to horrifying. Round trip fare for the chair lift is three coupons, and three more will buy a ride on the Alpine Slide. A special multiple-ride discount is available for those wishing to dare the Alpine Slide three times.

The Good Ol' Summer Time

When snow is out of the question, the foot of the ski slopes is taken over by three interesting water raft rides. The Blue Cyclone Rapids features an inflated bobsled with handles that carries up to two people twisting, turning, and usually screaming at the top of their lungs, more than 600 feet through a closed tube on a cushion of water. The Lightnin' Raft Ride and the Shoot-the-Chute are basically identical, each sending a raft down a 240-foot course with a vertical drop of 40 feet. the Lightnin' River Raft is open all the way, and the Shoot-the-Chute is covered for most of its distance. The Blue Cyclone is a three-coupon ride, and the other two go for two coupons each.

Kiddie Land moves outside in the summer with additional playground equipment. Kids 3 to 11 years old can enjoy the down-sized slides, ladders, crawling nets, and swinging bridges, or ride on the carousel, cars, sno-mobiles, or the Rio Grande train. Kiddie Land admission is one coupon, and each ride costs one more.

Baby It's Cold Outside

When the weather turns cold (usually around December 1 at 2700 feet) and Gatlinburg goes into Winterfest mode, Ober rocks. It's skiing time in Tennessee, and this is the only game around. With eight slopes, three full lifts, the most efficient snow-making equipment available, and a kaleidoscope of plans to fit any budget, Ober Gatlinburg is at its absolute best. With all the different programs available for age groups, family or larger groups, and special sessions, the best thing to do here is contact the lodge when you arrive. They'll tailor the best plan for your circumstances. However, here's an idea of what a family of four could expect to spend if they appeared at the tramway terminal in street clothes:

Tram tickets—$22. Lift tickets (All day Saturday—the highest rate—$96.00, including tram rebate). Complete equipment rental—$52. Ski school—$32. The

(Continued on next page)

ATTRACTIONS

Ober Gatlinburg is Tennessee's only ski resort.

Photo: Courtesy Ober Gatlinburg

total is $202 for a full day of activity for a family of four. Compared to what you'd pay for the same family to see a college football game, it's pretty reasonable—compared to a professional football game, it's dirt cheap.

First, let's talk about snow. A lot of it falls on the resort during the winter months, but you can't take chances with an operation this big. Ober Gatlinburg's snow-making system is capable of laying down enough snow overnight to provide ample powder when Mother Nature doesn't cooperate. It's a little different from natural snow, in that manmade snow is more like a ball, or a "puff," where the natural stuff is a mostly flat flake. Manmade snow is softer, fluffier, and longer-lasting than natural, and provides an excellent foundation when a natural snowfall occurs. Snow is made by the placement of snow guns at strategic points on the slopes and turning 'em on. Mogul Ridge, one of the favorite advanced runs, has permanently placed guns. The point here is that Ober doesn't need snow to provide skiing; they need cold weather, and that's usually not a problem.

All of the indoor activities and a few of the hardier outdoor ones previously mentioned go on as usual during the ski season, but the emphasis is on getting you on the slopes, and it starts the minute you debark from the tram. Skiers who don't already have their lift tickets are guided to the booths to get them (remember, they'll deduct the cost of your tram ticket, but you have to show it to them). Next, for those who need it, is the equipment rental area. You name it, they got it. You can get off the tram in street clothes and be totally outfitted to ski in about 10 minutes, at a cost that will range from $12 to $35, depending on the type of stuff you rent. Breakage insurance is included in the rental fee. In addition to regular and shaped skis, snowboards are also available for rent at about $25, with a deposit required.

First time skiers and snowboarders are required to attend ski school before

ATTRACTIONS

going on the slopes. The instructors are professionally trained to get rookies on the hill as quickly and confidently as possible, and classes are usually broken down into ability and age levels. Group classes run about an hour. A nominal fee (under $10) is charged for beginner group lessons, and private lessons are available for individuals ($25 per hour) or groups of no more than three ($15 per additional pupil). Snowboarding lessons are taught by group only, and run $15 for a 1½ hour session.

On to the slopes! Under full operational conditions, Ober Gatlinburg's two quad and one double lift can move 6,000 people up the slopes per hour, so there's seldom any waiting. Skiers at every level of expertise will be challenged by the eight slopes. Ober Chute, an intermediate run of 4,400 feet with a vertical drop of 556 feet, is a favorite because of its length; Mogul Ridge, a 300-foot washboard with a near-vertical 235-foot drop, will test the best. Cub Way, the beginner run, is a gentle slope with enough length to build confidence to tackle the tougher slopes.

Ski sessions are scheduled according to projections for attendance. The best time for avid skiers to hit the slopes is Monday through Thursday, when the resort is open from Noon to 10 PM, with two scheduled sessions, the combo (all hours) and the night session (6 to 10 PM). All trails except Grizzly, the appropriately named run through the woods, are lighted for night skiing. Non-holiday Fridays have three scheduled sessions: Day (8:30 AM to 4:00 PM), twilight (3 PM to 10 PM) and night (6 to 10 PM). On Fridays and Saturdays in the holiday period (just before Christmas through New Year's), day (8:30 AM to 4 PM) and twilight (3 to 10 PM) sessions operate. All Sundays have a single day session from 8:30 AM to 5 PM. Some twilight sessions are scheduled on Sundays by local option; ask if you're interested.

If you weren't aware of Ober Gatlinburg's existence before, you should check it out the next time you're in the Smokies. With enough variety to please just about any visitor, Ober Gatlinburg is a pretty good destination for the family that's looking for some close-in fun that will appeal to everybody.

Ripley's Haunted Adventure
908 Parkway, Gatlinburg • (865) 430-9991

This is an interesting premise for those who truly enjoy getting scared stiff by real people offering to commit various unpleasant acts during a trip through an abandoned casket factory. From the time you enter the funicular rail car that takes you up to the second floor until you scramble out of the elevator that delivers you back to the safety of the Parkway, the Haunted Adventure is an intense journey through a netherworld that wouldn't be nearly as creepy if some of the exhibits didn't keep joining your group. And we don't even want to talk about the spiders. Or the rats. In fact, they're not nearly as scary as the escaped prisoner who only wants to "play" with you, or the butler who shows up at some of the least opportune times. And when you finally get in the elevator to return to sanity, don't be too quick to breathe a sigh of relief; like the man says, "It ain't over 'til it's over."

Ripley's Haunted Adventure is open from 10 AM to 9 PM Sunday through Thursday, and 9 AM to midnight Friday and Saturday, every day except Christmas. Admission is $8.99 for adults and $5.99 for children 8 to 18. Because of the intense nature of this attraction, Ripley's asks that children under age 8 not be taken along.

Star Cars
914 Parkway, Gatlinburg • (865) 430-7900

When it comes to way-out designs for special cars, nobody does it better than George Barris. Starting back in the 1960s with the customized Pontiac GTO used by the Monkees and the first Batmobile, George Barris has been in constant demand to design cars that not only set the live characters that used them apart from the crowd, but that also became stars themselves. The self-guiding three-story tour of specialty cars only begins with George Barris designs—also on display are cars actually owned by such luminaries as Elvis Presley and Frank Sinatra, and a special NASCAR exhibit features video highlights of the careers of several drivers. Each car is in its own setting with scenes from its movie or television show and accompanying sound track. TV and movie buffs will get their memories jogged thoroughly as they pass by the cars that became stars. Admission is $7.95 for adults, $5.95 for teens and seniors, and $3.95 for children.

ATTRACTIONS

Christus Gardens
510 River Road, Gatlinburg
• (865) 436-5155

A mainstay in Gatlinburg for almost 40 years, Christus Gardens is a Christ-centered attraction of exceptional beauty. The beautifully planted and manicured exterior sets Christus Gardens apart from the moment you enter the parking lot alongside the Little Pigeon River. The mood throughout is one of reverence. Entering the building, a circular exhibit of early American and European bibles and artifacts provide a diversion while waiting to start the 20-minute tour of dioramas. A short slide presentation describes the inspiration and construction of the facility, followed by a walking tour through 10 separate dioramas depicting significant events in the life of Jesus Christ. From the Nativity to his ascension into heaven, Jesus is shown surrounded by people whose life he affected, and who affected his. The figures are life-size and extremely lifelike, all dressed in authentic period costumes.

The tour concludes in the atrium featuring the six-ton block of marble with the face of Jesus carved in bas-relief. The face, which never lets you out of its sight, seems to actually turn as you pass by it. It's reputed to be the single most frequently photographed item in Gatlinburg. Beside the atrium is the Place of Parables, a circular exhibit of life-size paintings in Old Masters style depicting the Parables of Jesus. Also in the Place of Parables is a display of coinage used in Biblical times, including the Shekel of Tyre, reputedly the type of coin paid to Judas.

The grounds of Christus Gardens are an attraction by themselves. Planted and maintained with seasonal flowers, the grounds come alive during the Christmas season with special lighting effects that routinely stop traffic. Christus Gardens is completely wheelchair accessible, and has plenty of parking for both cars and buses. Christus Gardens is open from 8 AM to 9 PM April through October, and 9 AM to 5 PM November through March. Admission is $8.50 for adults, $3.50 for children 7 through 12, and children 6 and under are admitted free. Special rates and tours are available to groups with advance reservations.

Ober Gatlinburg
1001 Parkway, Gatlinburg
• (865) 436-5423, (800) 251-9202 ski line

What started as Gatlinburg Ski Resort in 1969 and consisted of a single slope running down to a cinder block building (when there was enough snow to open it) has grown over the years into one of the largest ski resorts in the southeast. It's also a year-round attraction that's challenging that Parton girl's theme park in Pigeon Forge for overall entertainment supremacy in the Smokies. Ober Gatlinburg is happening! Seven miles from downtown at the top end of Ski Mountain Road, Ober is a five-acre amusement park in the non-ski season, and a several hundred-acre amusement park/ski resort with eight slopes in the winter.

Access to the resort is best attained by riding the aerial tramway out of the middle of downtown to the resort mall. The tram ride is an attraction in its own right, covering two miles on its 1,400-foot ascent. It's faster, much safer, and more environmentally sensible to ride the tram than to negotiate the seven twisting miles of Ski Mountain Road. A huge variety of year-round amusement venues in the covered mall is enough to make a family trip worthwhile at any time of year. There's no admission charge to the mall itself, and the cost of most of the amusements is payable in coupons purchased from a central ticket office adjacent to the tram dock. The amusements themselves and the cost breakdown are covered in depth in the Close-up in this chapter. Ober Gatlinburg is open year-round from 9 AM to 10 PM.

Rafting in the Smokies
2470 East Parkway, Gatlinburg
• (865) 436-5008, (800) 776-7238

Whitewater rafting has come into its own as a Smokies trip experience, and that's as it should be. There's no better way to enjoy the unmatched scenery of the Smokies than from the middle of a river, and there's no better way to gain an appreciation for the awesome power of Nature than to plunk down in the middle of it for some hair-raising, white-knuckle excitement in a totally safe environment. No experience is necessary (they've got professional guides with remarkable credentials), and children aged eight and up and weighing at least 70 pounds can join in the fun. Rafting in The Smokies provides three different ways to enjoy rafting in the mountains, and they all start the headquarters on East Parkway, about six miles east of traffic light #3 in downtown Gatlinburg, or the Pigeon Forge office at 3249 River Road. The Gatlinburg headquarters is actually in the mountain town of Pittman Center, a well-kept secret that would like to stay that way The headquarters staff will provide tickets and directions to the appropriate outpost for the planned trip. (Note: This can get a little confusing. If you've made telephone reservations and already have received your tickets and directions in the mail, you can just go directly to the outpost). All rafting trips go as planned, regardless of weather conditions—if there's any question about what you're facing, pack a bathing suit, a complete change of clothes, and a towel. That'll do in warm weather; if it's cool or worse, wool socks and sweaters are recommended. And be sure of this: You *are* going to get wet, probably to your. Showers and changing rooms at the outpost will let you depart as warm and dry as when you arrived.

So now we're headed for the outpost. If the trip planned is on the Big Pigeon River, it's about an hour drive along the western edge of the Great Smoky Mountains National Park to the outpost—the directions given are excellent. If Nantahala is your destination, the drive is a bit longer, and will take you into North Carolina through the Park and Cherokee.the outpost, here's what to expect:

Big Pigeon River: Two trips are available on the Big Pigeon, and they're as different as night and day. The Big Pigeon run is rated as the most exciting whitewater raft ride in Tennessee. Starting just below the Waterville Electric Plant, the Big Pigeon River is a maelstrom of roaring water, and your raft is right in the middle of it. Flanked by the National Park on one side and Pisgah National Forest on the other, the Big Pigeon run drops sharply through five miles of almost continuous rapids in a fast-moving hour and a half. Listen to your guide, and enjoy the trip. The power company has guaranteed that they'll release water from the dam on Tuesdays, Thursdays, and Saturdays through the rafting season keep those days in mind for the hottest rafting. For those not quite into fear and loathing on the water but like getting wet, the lower Pigeon float trip is just the ticket. Leaving from the outpost, the float trip rides the swift, gentle current for 3½ miles through one of the most beautiful stretches of forest in North America. Rafters are allowed at some points to get in the river and swim along. The float trip takes about an hour and a half, and the shuttle is waiting to return everybody to the outpost. The Big Pigeon whitewater raft run costs $39 per boater; the float trip $15 a head.

Nantahala is your choice, you're in store for an eight-mile plunge through the gorge of the same name. The spectacular beauty of the Nantahala National Forest surrounds you for the entirety of the trip, which takes less than two hours. It's a tiny bit tamer than the Big Pigeon, but you've got a little better chance to enjoy the breathtaking scenery. The Nantahala rafting adventure costs $27 per adventurer.

Rafting is still regarded to be a coming sport, and its popularity is growing . Most first-time rafters plan their next vacations around the times when the water is best. Rafting in the Smokies is open every day, March through October.

ATTRACTIONS

Dollywood

Dollywood's address is 1020 Dollywood Lane, Pigeon Forge.

For information on the park and its programs, call (865) 428-9488 or (800) 365-5996.

Or you can check out the park online at www.Dollywood.com.

One hundred and eighteen acres of rides, attractions, music shows and mountain crafts make Dollywood the cornerstone of all-around fun in the Smoky Mountains. Open since 1986, Dollywood is the namesake of Dolly Parton, renowned country music star and Sevier County's most notable native. She is also a part owner who remains very active in the continued development of the park.

The operational theme is one of a mountain community ripped from the pages of history.

Abundant greenery and beautiful flower gardens enhance the ambience of the park's numerous rustic wooden structures. The park was built around a previously existing amusement park that had been in place for many years, operating most recently as Silver Dollar City theme park in the late '70s and early '80s. Since taking over, however, Dolly and company have continually added on to the complex—new features are introduced to the public every year. Since the closing of Opryland in Nashville, Dollywood is now the largest and most visited theme park in the state and hosts upwards of two million visitors each year. It has also been quite beneficial to the local economy, as evidenced by the fact that the various businesses that make up Dollywood Entertainment have become Sevier County's largest single seasonal employer.

There are two ways to get to Dollywood. One is to take Dollywood Lane from traffic light #8 on the Parkway in Pigeon Forge to the main park entrance, which is clearly marked by signs. The other is to follow Middle Creek Road south out of Sevierville. This "back entrance" isn't indicated by signs, but you can easily see the wide expanses of Dollywood's many parking lots that let you know you've arrived. An attendant is stationed at both entrances to take your parking fee.

Dollywood is open from mid-April through December. The park is open daily throughout the summer and runs on a more limited schedule during the other months. Hours of operation vary, depending on the time of year. Generally the park's open from 9 AM to 9 PM during the summer and 10 AM to 6 PM during the spring and fall. Dollywood also hosts a celebrity concert series featuring many of the nation's top country music artists. These concerts are presented more or less once a week in season.

The following prices are the most current available, but are of course subject to change in the future. From mid-April through October, admission prices to the park are $29.99 for ages 12 and older, $20.99 for ages 4 through 11 and $24.99 for seniors ages 60 and older.

Tickets to the celebrity concert series vary, but average around $17. You have to pay for admission to the park as well if you're attending a 2 PM concert, but not for a 7 PM show. None of the above prices includes sales tax. For more detailed information on Dollywood's schedule and the most current admission prices, call their information office and/or request a current brochure.

A number of discounts and price breaks are offered to enhance the value of your visit. Children 3 and younger are admitted free, and discounted prices are offered during Dollywood's Christmasfest in November and December. Group rates and season passes are available as well. In fact, if you purchase a one-day ticket and like what you see, you can apply the full value of your ticket toward a season pass that same day. And you're more than halfway there: A season pass actually costs less than the price of two one-day tickets.

Another way to stretch your dollar at Dollywood is to arrive after 3 PM, in which case your admission on the next operating day is free. This works especially well on hot summer days when you can take advantage of the cooler evening temperatures and the park's 9 PM closing time.

Admission prices include unlimited access to all shows, rides, attractions, craft showcases and special events. As such, you can squeeze a lot of activity into one day (or two) without parting with too much more cash. But to park, eat, shop and play games, you'll need to bring a good reserve of spending money. It costs $5 to park, and trams will take you from your parking area to the main entrance (or you can take either of the Dollywood trolleys operated by the cities of Pigeon Forge and Gatlinburg; see our Getting Here, Getting Around chapter for details). Generally, expect to pay inflated prices at the theme park's restaurants and other food concessions. The best way to approach this is to realize that this is simply a standard practice of theme parks and tourist destinations as a whole. The point is, be prepared and just have fun.

Around the Park

Now that we've given you an overview of the park, it's time for some detail on many of the interesting aspects that makes Dollywood special.

One of the best things about Dollywood is that it embodies in one (albeit expansive) location much of what people want out of a trip to the Great Smoky Mountains. Yes, it's a theme park with plenty of fun rides and attractions, but those thrills represent just one facet of your experience there. In contrast to places like Six Flags, where rides are the staple, Dollywood also offers its visitors a broad canvas of options, all presented professionally and in a first-class manner. The setting represents an old mountain community of yesteryear. It serves a slice of Appalachian life, telling many a homespun tale via mountain music, crafts and awesome wonders of nature. Although we can only scratch the surface of what's to be found there, we will point out some of the highlights and hopefully give you a good feel for what's in store.

Take Me For a Ride

Inside the park, you'll discover rides that go both fast and slow, many rides that get you wet and some that are designed just for the little ones.

Two different roller coasters can be found on the property—a relatively tame indoor coaster and the outdoor Tennessee Tornado, which debuted in 1999. Complete with twists, turns and multiple upside down loops, the $8 million thrill ride replaces the old Thunder Express roller coaster that was a Dollywood fixture for years. After its initial climb of 137 feet, the Tennessee Tornado plummets 128 feet through a carved out mountain tunnel at over 60 miles per hour. From there, passengers continue on a curvy, loopy ride that lasts almost two full minutes.

Of course, there are rides of a more sedate nature. Amusement park mainstays like The Wonder Wheel (a classic Ferris wheel) and The Dollywood Express (an authentic steam-driven train) provide a pleasant means of taking a load off your feet. Watch out, though—The Dollywood Express inevitably gets "robbed" by outlaws!

Another of Dollywood's newer additions is a contender in the ongoing game of theme park one-upmanship. Daredevil Falls, which premiered in 1998, is currently the highest and fastest log flume ride in the country. What starts out as a tranquil drift with the currents culminates in a drop off that sends you and your fellow riders plummeting at 50 miles per hour to a splashy welcome below. Another of our personal favorite water rides is The Mountain Slidewinder. This minimally wet ride is akin to a water slide, but its multiple riders occupy large foam rafts during their winding, rocking, speedy journey to the bottom.

INSIDERS' TIP

For the 2001 season, Dollywood plans to open its own 35-acre water park. Scheduled to debut Memorial Day weekend, the $20 million park will feature attractions such as tube slides, speed slides, a family raft ride, a children's play area, a 25,000-square-foot wave pool and a Lazy River water ride. Guests can also take advantage of snack areas, an arcade and plenty of shaded seating.

DOLLYWOOD

Whether it's colorful wildflowers, the grandeur of the Smokies, or Dolly Parton's radiant smile, Dollywood visitors are surrounded by beauty.

Photo: Courtesy Dollywood

Enjoy the scenery of the Smokies aboard the Dollywood Express train.

Photo: Courtesy Dollywood

Special times include Dollywood's Harvest Festival ...

Photo: Courtesy Dollywood

... and Smoky Mountain Christmas Festival.

Photo: Courtesy Dollywood

DOLLYWOOD

Sample the classic tastes of the mountains at Dollywood's Grist Mill.

Photo: Courtesy Dollywood

The Robert F. Thomas Church in Craftsman's Valley allows visitors a special place to give thanks for the beauty of the Great Smoky Mountains.

Photo: Courtesy Dollywood

DOLLYWOOD

Dollywood features nearly 40 live musical performances a day, with something for every taste.

Photo: Courtesy Dollywood

The Smoky Mountain Rampage is a twisting adventure through the rapids and waterfalls of a whitewater river.

Photo: Courtesy Dollywood

DOLLYWOOD

Daredevil Falls: the country's highest, fastest waterfall ride.

Photo: Courtesy Dollywood

Master blacksmith Mike Rose hand-forges works of art in his daily demonstrations of this ancient craft.

Photo: Courtesy Dollywood

Visitors to Jukebox Junction can "Let the Good Times Roll" at a show that brings alive the music of the '50s.

Photo: Courtesy Dollywood

An Interactive Experience

Dollywood's attractions offer something for all ages. One that's unique is Eagle Mountain Sanctuary, the nation's largest preserve of non-releasable bald eagles. Presented in cooperation with the National Foundation to Protect America's Eagles, this 1.5-million-cubic-foot aviary recreates the natural habitat of our national symbol and is used for the purposes of education, rehabilitation and breeding. This safe haven is also the site of the Wings of America-Birds of Prey demonstration. Viewers can get up close and personal with some of nature's most interesting flying specimens, such as bald eagles that swoop down gracefully over the heads of the audience. Of course, this is all done under the supervision of specially trained handlers.

Dreamland Forest is anchored by what Dollywood bills as "America's largest interactive treehouse"—two large three-story structures that contain dozens of fun activities for kids ranging in age from toddlers to teens. Treetop games and gadgets include a birdhouse village, "grapevine gossip phones" and a magic looking glass. Further into the attraction, children will discover a three-level Beehive area where they can shoot foam balls at targets (and each other) from air guns. Don't worry, the kids won't shoot their eyes out, and even parents can get in on the fun helping gather balls on the lower level with their special collection devices. The Bullfrog Creek section of Dreamland Forest is where the younger ones can get wet with squirt guns, water blasters, fountains and more. Non-participating parents will find plenty of benches nearby for safe and relaxed viewing.

Another must-stop attraction if you're visiting Dollywood with children is Imagination Station. Kids can dig in to dozens of hands-on educational exhibits as well as crafts, games and puzzles. There's even a Lego Construction Zone with thousands of bricks available for creative building. The best part is that the Legos won't wind up under your sofa cushions when the kids are finished.

Music, Music, Music

Music is a given at Dollywood, and that's to be expected considering that music is Dolly's original claim to fame. There is a definite emphasis placed on country and gospel music, although one of the shows journeys back in time with the songs and dances of the 1950s. Much of what you'll see on the stages of Dollywood are straight-ahead, live music performances: one features legends of the Grand Ole Opry stage while two others showcase members of Dolly's family, including her brother, Randy.

Other stage shows add further visual elements to the mix. In *Paradise Road,* which premiered in 1998, Dolly's life is showcased in a Broadway-style production show that spotlights many of her most beloved songs. *Heartsong* takes viewers on a musically enhanced journey through the Great Smoky Mountains with a large-screen motion picture presentation. *Showcase of Stars* is Dollywood's celebrity concert series that brings some of country music's biggest acts to Pigeon Forge.

Country stars like Pam Tillis, Marty Stuart, Loretta Lynn and Ronnie Milsap are just some of the entertainers that have appeared on the stage of Dollywood Celebrity Theatre. In previous years, Dolly herself also performed in benefit concerts in support of The Dollywood Foundation, an organization devoted to improving education in Sevier County (see the Close-up in our Education and Childcare chapter for more).

Another new Dollywood attraction for 1999 was the Southern Gospel Music Hall of Fame and Museum. Located near the park's entrance, next to Showstreet Palace Theatre, this facility utilizes a variety of memorabilia and artifacts that pay tribute to the Southern Gospel artists who have shaped and influenced their genre of music. The attraction also features a "living museum" which uses numerous exhibits to examine the past, present and future of Southern Gospel music.

Craftwork

One of the factors in the Dollywood equation that lends itself so well to the park's mountain home theme is the abundance of craftspeople that populate the complex.

INSIDERS' TIP

If you or one of your group gets accidentally jostled and loses a soft drink, an ice cream cone, or any other food product, go back to the booth where you bought it and tell them what happened. Dollywood's work force is trained to replace the lost goodies at no charge.

Craftwork has long been a staple of the mountain lifestyle in the Smokies, so it's only natural that those skills would be on display here. Masters of time-honored art forms like glass blowing, pottery throwing, candle making and blacksmithing can be found conducting impressive demonstrations of their skills. There are plenty of craftspeople working here year-round, but during Dollywood's annual Harvest Celebration in October and November, visiting craftsmen and women from across the country join in to help create the Smokies' only outdoor crafts festival. Complete with music and festive fall decorations, Harvest Celebration is an excellent complement to the changing of the foliage colors in the mountains (see our Annual Events chapter for more).

A Smoky Mountain Christmas

The arrival of winter doesn't necessarily put a chill on the fun at Dollywood. During its Smoky Mountain Christmas festival, which usually runs from mid-November until the end of the year, the park takes on a whole new identity. It's really one of the single best seasonal celebrations in the county.

In terms of appearance alone, Dollywod is a spectacle as more than two million holiday lights twinkle throughout the park. You'll also want to look for Carol of the Trees, a new attraction that incorporates music and special lighting effects. Elsewhere at Dollywood, the many music shows adapt Christmas themes, and there are other attractions on hand just for winter, including a giant Santa's workshop. Holiday foods and special concerts help round out the festival, and if that weren't enough, you can still ride the Tennessee Tornado in the middle of winter—a December roller coaster ride will certainly add new meaning to "chills and thrills."

Getting Around

Dollywood is divided into several major sections that revolve around different themes and reflect various aspects of the Smokies and Americana. Within the boundaries of each area are a variety of rides, attractions, shows, restaurants and shops related to that zone's theme.

Showstreet Palace, found just inside the main gates, is the site of Dollywood Celebrity Theatre. Dollywood Boulevard is an area that recreates a small, hometown main street. Jukebox Junction takes you through a time warp back to the good ol' 1950s, complete with a neato diner. Rivertown Junction features several shops as well as Smoky Mountain Rampage, a whitewater rafting ride. You'll have trouble dragging your children away from the Country Fair area. With carnival midway rides and games, Imagination Station and a log flume ride all in one compact location, the young ones could linger in this section alone for hours and hours. In The Village, you'll discover the depot for The Dollywood Express and an antique carousel. Dreamland Forest is where you'll find the Mountain Slidewinder ride in addition to all the children's activities we mentioned earlier. The arts and crafts hound will feel right at home in Craftsmen's Valley, the place where you'll find demonstrations of most of the old-time mountain arts. This is also where Dollywood's two roller coasters and its bald eagle preserve are found.

We'll close with a few "strategies" for making your visit to Dollywood a little smoother. First, carry your cash and smaller electronics in plastic zipper bags. This will help ensure that they stay dry when you're riding any of the park's numerous "wet" rides. To best maximize your time at Dollywood, try visiting during the off-season, if possible. The crowds are smaller and you'll spend a lot less time waiting in lines for rides. We also suggest getting there when the gates open, starting your tour of the park in either Craftsman's Valley or Country Fair and working your way back toward the front. This will help you avoid a lot of traffic early on.

Kidstuff

LOOK FOR:
- Sevierville
- Pigeon Forge
- Gatlinburg

While *you* might be coming to the Smokies for hikes or craft shopping or music shows, you can't always count on your children enjoying those same activities. What's a parent to do? Plenty, if you keep your eyes open. If you just take a cruise down the Parkway in Sevierville, Pigeon Forge or Gatlinburg, there's a good chance your kids will constantly point out the window, begging "Can we stop here?" Welcome to The Midway.

In this chapter, you'll find all kinds of ways for kids to have fun, including traditional amusements like miniature golf, bumper boats, go-carts and arcades. But purveyors of fun in the Smokies haven't limited themselves to these. There's laser tag, public library programs, museums and a water park, not to mention Dollywood, the most visited theme park in Tennessee!

A Few Words About Amusement Centers

We've done a lot of cross-referencing between Kidstuff and our Attractions chapter. Quite a few of the businesses you'll read about in this chapter are what we refer to as "amusement centers" (featuring go-carts, miniature golf, arcades, bumper boats and other activities where you pay-as-you-go). Bear in mind that some of these activities aren't suitable for all youngsters, especially those younger than 10. Most go-cart tracks, for example, have specific age and height minimums when it comes to operating the carts.

What we've done in such cases is split our coverage of many amusement centers between Kidstuff and Attractions. Since it's a safe bet that most children will be accompanied by adults, this chapter gives comprehensive descriptions of what the centers have to offer all ages. That way, the grown-ups can play right along with the kids. Information about things like the faster go-cart tracks, bungee towers and other "grown-up" stuff are also covered in Attractions.

There are a few universals you'll encounter from one amusement center to the next. First, think "safety." Go-cart track managers prohibit deliberately bumping carts into each other and against track guardrails. Needless to say, pregnant women and people with heart and back conditions shouldn't participate in these activities. Second, you can count on most go-cart and bumper boat rides lasting anywhere from three to six minutes.

We also won't be going in to any details on the arcades. For those of you who, for some strange reason, have never been in one, we'll be considerate and tell you to look for some combination of the following: video games, video simulators, pinball machines, air hockey tables, pool tables and coin-operated kiddie rides. In some places you'll also see carnival-type games like ski ball and basketball shooting. Many of the arcades have games that award tickets, which can then be redeemed for prizes (those worthless trinkets that kids find fascinating!) Naturally, change machines are always on hand to convert your bills into quarters or tokens.

Finally, assume that most go-cart tracks, miniature golf courses and arcades provide adequate free parking. In Gatlinburg, there are places that don't have parking. You can pay to park in a city lot or garage or you can access your destination on foot or by trolley. Most amusements are also open year-round. During the in-season (May through August), you can count on them being open seven days a week from around 9 or 10 AM to as late as midnight or 1 AM in some cases.

As for the off-season, you'll find that several establishments cut back to weekends only during winter months. However, most of the managers with whom we spoke weren't willing to commit to definite autumn and winter schedules. Often they choose to improvise and let factors such as the weather and holiday-related visitation determine when they open. Your best bet for weekly and daily schedules in the off-season is to call ahead.

Assume that the prices we've quoted in our write-ups include sales tax, unless we note otherwise.

Child's Play

What all the listings in this chapter have in common are ways for the young ones to enjoy themselves. As in Attractions, well start in Sevierville, then putt, bungee and go-cart ourselves all the way down through Gatlinburg. And hey! If you old fogies aren't careful, you might just find yourself having a pretty good time as well.

Sevierville

Blazing Wheels Raceway
925 Winfield Dunn Pkwy., Sevierville
• (865) 429-1029

Take your pick from four different outdoor tracks that offer racing fun for children as young as 4 years old. The Super 8 Track is a double figure-eight course open to children 12 and older who are at least 4 feet 10 inches tall. The cost is $6 per person. The Nas-Track is a fast, tri-oval circuit available only to those ages 16 and older who have a valid ID. The cost is $7 per person. For younger drivers, the Kiddie Track is available for ages 4 through 9 with a minimum height requirement of 3 feet 6 inches. The cost is $4.

The Pro Track is a slick, cloverleaf track on which three different carts are run. For $6, children at least 12 years old and 4 feet 10 inches tall can drive the Pro Track racer. The Indy racer, which also costs $6, can be driven by children at least 8 years old and 4 feet 3 inches tall. For $7, you can take out the two-seat racers, although you must be an adult to drive a passenger.

In addition to racing action, Blazing Wheels Raceway offers a small, midway-style dinosaur ride for $3, open to all ages. At Bankshot Basketball, hoopsters can work their way through a challenging free throw competition in a miniature golf type of course. The cost is $5. There is also a small indoor arcade for video fun as well as several coin operated kiddie rides outside. Blazing Wheels offers a discounted package price of $50 for 10 tickets.

Wilson's North American Wildlife Museum
870 Winfield Dunn Pkwy., Sevierville
• (865) 429-5626

Want to see what a moose looks like up close? How about a mountain lion, a bison or a grizzly bear? You can get very close to these beasts and more at this 15,000-square-foot wildlife exhibit. But that's because none of the animals is exactly, well, alive. The owner is a professional taxidermist, and he's obviously put a great deal of time into the collection, preservation and mounting of the many species on display.

The self-guided tour takes you through a meandering course constructed to resemble a cave tunnel. Along the way, more than 50 glassed-in dioramas depict North American animals in their natural habitat. In addition to land dwelling animals, various species of birds and fish are also shown in lifelike settings. The overall effect is enhanced by the recorded sounds of nature playing in the background.

Admission to the North American Wildlife Museum is $5.95 for adults and $3.95 for children 12 and younger. Group rates are available, which works out well for the many school groups that come to walk among the animals. Prices do not include sales tax. The museum is open from 9 AM to 6 PM Monday through Saturday and from 1 to 5 PM on Sunday.

Sevier County Public Library
321 Court Ave., Sevierville
• (865) 453-3532

Every Thursday is story day at the library! From September through May, story hour starts at 10:30 AM and provides a free and entertaining experience for pre-school children and their parents. During the session, volunteers read aloud to the children from age-appropriate books. Participation by pre-school and day care groups is especially high during these school year months.

From June through August the library uses Thursdays for its Summer Reading Program. In addition to the normal morning story, the children can also listen to guest speakers from the community, such as firemen, veterinarians and even clowns! These folks will use their time to tell the children about their occupations. The kids especially enjoy going outside to check out the real squad cars when a local policeman is part of the program.

The library itself has a separate section for children's books and has approximately 2,000 children's videos on its shelves. Sevier County residents can easily obtain a library card, of course, but out-of-county residents can also check out materials with either proof of local property ownership or a $10 deposit.

Smoky Mountain Deer Farm and Exotic Petting Zoo
478 Happy Hollow Ln., Sevierville
• (865) 428-3337

You won't find lions and tigers and bears (oh my!) at this unique animal exhibit, but you will encounter quite a few species of animals that can be just as interesting. Children and grown ups alike have been flocking to the Deer Farm and Petting Zoo for over a decade to feed and get face-to-face (and sometimes hand-to-mouth) with a menagerie that boasts quite a unique bunch of residents, including camels and zebras, kangaroos and llamas, ferrets and reindeer. They even have pony rides for the little ones. Intrigued? See the Close-up in this chapter for more information on how to "talk to the animals."

Admissions to the Deer Farm and Petting Zoo are $6 for ages 13 and older and $3 for ages 3 to 12. Children ages 2 and younger are admitted free. Prices do not include sales tax. Discounted rates are available for groups of 15 or more. Understandably, area school and day care groups are frequent visitors to this place. To feed the animals, use only the special feed provided, which comes in cups ranging from 12 ounces ($1.50) to 32 ounces ($3.50). Pony rides cost $3.75 each.

The facility is open year round, seven days a week except for Thanksgiving and Christmas. Daily hours are from 10 AM to 5:30 PM.

Throughout the year, ticket sales stop one hour before closing. Pony rides are available from 10:30 AM through 5 PM April through November only, and the availability of pony rides depends on the weather. The owners also advise calling ahead to verify hours during periods of bad weather.

The same folks also operate Deer Farm Riding Stables, located on adjacent property. See our chapter on Parks and Recreation for more information on horseback riding opportunities.

NASCAR Speed Park
1545 Parkway, Sevierville
• (865) 908-5500

For a complete run-down of what this mega-sized go-cart park has to offer, see our write up in Attractions. Here, however, we'll tell you what's in store for kids.

The Baby Bristol track is for drivers who are at least 3 feet 4 inches tall. The small, single-loop circuit is just right for younger speed demons. The Qualifier track has a couple of extra bends in it, but is still fairly short. You must be 3 feet 8 inches to drive on The Qualifier. The Young Champions track is longer and has a lot of twists and turns along the way. Those who are at least 4 feet tall will be busy with their steering wheel on this track.

Speed Park also has the Family 500 track, where double-seat carts allow adults and children to tear up the track side by side. Drivers must be at least 5 feet 4 inches tall, and passengers must be at least 3 feet 6 inches tall.

You do have to pay just to enter NASCAR Speed Park. Those more than 4 feet tall pay $5 to get in, but receive seven tickets that can be used for go-cart racing or concessions. Those shorter than 4 feet pay $3 to enter and get five tickets. The number of tickets required to drive on the tracks varies. Baby Bristol costs four tickets, The Qualifier costs five tickets and both Young Champions and Family 500 cost six tickets apiece.

In addition to the tickets you receive on entering the park, you can purchase more tickets once you're through the doors. Individual tickets sell for $1 each, or you can purchase one of several packages that offer larger numbers of tickets at discounted prices. Booklets come in denominations of up to 150 tickets. In addition to track admissions, tickets can also be used at Speed Park's concessions areas.

Besides the go-carts, kids will also love the huge Speed Dome arcade, featuring 60 racing video games and driving simulators.

NASCAR Speed park is open year-round.

In spring and summer, daily hours are from 10 AM until at least 10 PM, although they may stay open until midnight if the masses allow. Once tourist visitation starts to slow down in Sevier County after Labor Day, the park is open from 4 to 10 PM on weekdays and from 11 AM to 10 PM on weekends.

Pigeon Forge

Ogle's Water Park
2530 Parkway, Pigeon Forge
• (865) 453-8741

Here's a really fun place to keep the kids (and yourselves) wet and cool on those hot summer days. Water slides reign supreme at this outdoor water park: The Twin Twister, the Rip Tide Slide and the Hydro Chute are among the slides that will send you twisting, turning and dipping all the way to the bottom. Some of the slides are faster than others, but they're all a blast!

In addition to the slides, you can rent inner tubes and float on Ogle's Lazy River ride, or you can grab your tube and hop into the large wave pool. While most of the offerings at Ogle's Water Park are more suitable for school-age children, the younger ones can have their own fun and feel like part of the action at Tadpole Island, a sizable kiddie area featuring tot-size slides and tunnels, all surrounded by a large, shallow wading area.

Admission prices are $17.95 for ages 12 and older, $16.95 for ages 4 through 11, and children 3 and younger are admitted free. Season passes, two-day passes and group rates are available, as are 50 percent discounts which are offered in conjunction with a number of area motels. The park is open weekends only in May from 10 AM to 6 PM; from June through August it's open daily from 10 AM to 7 PM. For a more comprehensive look at Ogle's Water Park, see the Attractions chapter.

The Track
2575 Parkway, Pigeon Forge
• (865) 453-4777

We're not really sure how to classify this place. Is it a small amusement park or a huge amusement center? Considering that miniature golf and go-cart racing are the anchor activities here, we'll go with the latter. Before you turn

the kids loose, you'll want to purchase tickets. Individual tickets are $2.50 each; you can purchase six for $12, 24 for $40 or 48 for $74. To help you navigate The Track's layout, a handy, colorful brochure is provided which maps out all of the different areas, including the concessions facility, restrooms and the arcade.

There are two twisty, curvy, outdoor tracks on site. The first, simply called The Track, utilizes one- and two-seat carts. One-seaters cost two tickets, and solo drivers must be at least 4 feet 6 inches tall. For two-seaters, drivers with passengers pay four tickets, and the driver must be at least 16 years old. Passengers in two-seaters must be at least 3 feet tall. Those between 3 feet and 4 feet 2 inches tall ride for free while passengers between 4 feet 2 inches and 4 feet 6 inches must pay one ticket extra.

The other outdoor track, the Wild Woody, was a new feature in 1999 and helped usher in the advent of wooden go-cart tracks in the Smoky Mountains. The driving surface is actually a hybrid combination of the original, ground-level, concrete track and a newer, add-on section-a multi-tiered wooden track that goes through several humps and corkscrew twists. The driving is a little slower than on the run-of-the-mill go-cart track, but, like wooden roller coasters, the wooden tracks give cartsters a ride you can really feel.

You must be at least 4 feet 10 inches tall to drive a single go-cart on the Wild Woody; the cost is three tickets. Drivers with passengers pay five tickets, and the driver must be at least 16 years old. Two-seater passengers on the Wild Woody must be at least 3 feet tall. If you're between 3 feet and 4 feet 6 inches tall, you ride along for free; if you're between 4 feet 6 inches and 4 feet 10 inches tall, you pay an extra ticket.

For golfing action, you can try out the two 18-hole putt-putt courses of Gator Golf. Both courses have various animal and wildlife figures adorning the landscape. The cost is two tickets per person per 18-hole round for ages 11 and older. Ages 4 to 10 can golf for one ticket, and kids 3 and younger can tag along for free.

Daredevils might want to fork over the eight tickets required to bungee jump from The Track's 60-foot tower. For those who want to remain closer to the ground, Bumper Cars are available to anyone taller than 4 feet 2 inches. You can drive them for two tickets per trip. If you want to get wet on a hot sum-

INSIDERS' TIP

Some of the prices you'll find quoted for area attractions do not include sales tax. For your information, Tennessee's sales tax is 8.5 percent.

mer day, you might be interested in the bumper boats. You must be 4 feet 2 inches tall and pay two tickets to operate the bumper boats, but those who are shorter can ride with an adult operating.

The younger children in tow might particularly enjoy The Track's Kid's Country. This area features a number of carnival style rides on a pint-sized scale. Rides include miniature versions of a train ride, swings and a Ferris Wheel; there's even a Kiddie Kart Raceway where the smaller ones can burn rubber on their own track. Drivers of the Kiddie Karts and the Rookie Karts must be at least 4 feet 2 inches tall and pay two tickets. Kid's Country is closed during most of January and February, even when the rest of The Track is open.

Winston Cup Race World
250 Island Dr., Pigeon Forge
• (865) 429-2030

Just one block off the Parkway, between traffic lights 3 and 4, lies Race World's mammoth, indoor-outdoor facility with multiple amusements geared especially to the NASCAR fan. You'll find go-carts, miniature golf and even a full-size wooden roller coaster, all on the premises. At Race World, you need to buy tickets beforehand to participate in the various amusements. When purchasing your tickets, bear in mind that even though they only cost $1 each, most activities will cost you anywhere from three to seven tickets. There is a discounted price of $20 for 25 tickets.

The Indoor Speedway is a multiple curve track that costs five tickets to drive. Operators of one-seat carts must be at least 4 feet 6 inches tall. Two-seater carts cost seven tickets each, and the driver must have a valid license and be at least 5 feet 2 inches tall; passengers must be at least 3 feet tall. The Outdoor Speedway, is a high-bank, single-circuit course that costs seven tickets. Drivers must be at least 5 feet 2 inches tall and have a valid driver's license. The Outdoor Speedway features realistic looking scale miniatures of Winston Cup stock cars.

Back inside the Race World building there is an 18-hole miniature golf course with a NASCAR theme (5 tickets for ages 11 and older, 3 tickets for ages 10 and younger), bumper cars (5 tickets) and the 2002 Cyber

Coaster, a roller coaster simulation ride (5 tickets). You'll also find a large arcade, a snack bar and a 4,000-square-foot gift shop stocked to the brim with NASCAR and racing apparel and souvenirs.

In recent years, Winston Cup Race World has made substantial modifications to its exterior acreage with the addition of a couple of roller coasters. The Little D is a short kiddie coaster for those under age 13. Before 5 PM on weekdays, it costs two tickets to ride. After 5 PM and on weekends, it costs three tickets. Premiering in spring of 2000 is The Intimidator, a brand-new, wooden roller coaster named in honor of NASCAR great Dale Earnhardt.

Star Tracks
2757 Parkway, Pigeon Forge
• (865) 429-5580

In addition to a fairly large indoor arcade, this amusement center features three outdoor, single-loop go-cart tracks. The Family Slick Track is a covered track open to ages 7 and older. Admission is $5 per ride. The Pro Track is for ages 12 and older. The cost is also $5 per ride with a discounted price of five rides for $20. The Junior Track is available only to ages 4 through 6, and the cost is $4. Any double seat carts cost $7. The driver must be at least 12 years old and the passenger must be at least 4 years old. This is another establishment that sticks to age minimums rather than height restrictions. Drivers who meet age requirements but are still on the small side can take advantage of booster seats that are provided.

Laserport
2782 Parkway, Pigeon Forge
• (865) 453-0400

Welcome to high-tech laser tag fun! The laser games take place inside a large labyrinth interior with ultraviolet lighting. Combatants are divided into two teams, red and green, with up to 20 players per team. After a few minutes of briefing on how to play the game and use the equipment, players are suited up and let loose to blast away the opponent. Games last for ten minutes; the team with the most points at the end wins. Afterwards, players are given a computer printout of their shooting efficiency, including data on the numbers of successful shots

INSIDERS' TIP

A number of area rides and attractions have minimum height, weight and age requirements. We've included most of that information in this chapter, but it's a good idea to call ahead before visiting these places, especially if you plan on taking children.

made and hits taken. At Laserport, players are given infinite lives and shots, eliminating the need to reload laser guns.

Players as young as 5 or 6 years old can participate, depending on their size. The cost is $7.75 per game or $18 for three games. During summer months, you can buy one game and get one free between 9 and 10:30 AM. In the off-season, the same deal applies between 10 and 11:30 AM. Laserport also offers annual memberships where you pay a one-time $20 fee, receive your first game free and then pay $3 per game afterwards. Each membership can only be used by the person in whose name it is purchased.

In addition to laser tag, Laserport has an outdoor, single-loop go-cart track that costs $4.75 per ride or $12 for three rides. Drivers must be at least 4 feet 6 inches tall. Drivers of two-seat carts must be at least 16 years old, and passengers must be able to sit upright and remain buckled into the safety harness. Two-seaters cost $5.75 per ride. You'll also find a massive indoor arcade at Laserport that is open year round.

Rockin' Raceway
2839 Parkway, Pigeon Forge
• **(865) 428-3392**

This diverse amusement center has three go-cart tracks for racing fun. The Pro Track costs $6, and drivers must be at least 14 years old and 4 feet 6 inches tall. No passengers are allowed on Pro Track. On the Grand Prix Track, which costs $5 per ride, solo drivers must be at least 10 years old (no height restrictions). In the two-seat carts, drivers must be at least 18, and passengers must be 3 to 9 years old. The cost for passengers is $2. There is also a junior go-cart track for ages 4 to 10 that costs $4 per ride.

Rockin' Raceway offers more than just racing, however. Ripline is a unique amusement for those who aren't afraid of heights. After taking stairs to the top of a 70-foot tower (formerly a bungee tower), you're strapped into a harness, hooked on to a taut cable and sent zooming down the 100-yard-long wire to the ground at about a 30-degree angle (not too steep). Ripline costs $10 per ride or three rides for $25. On the rock climbing wall next to Ripline, climbers can harness up and scale the 30-foot vertical surface using only projecting rocks and a safety cable for support. The cost is $5.

On The Hawk, up to 24 passengers at a time take a potentially nauseating pendulum ride which sends them in complete multiple loops. The Hawk costs $5 and requires that riders be at least 4 feet tall. The Orbitron is one of those three-dimensional contraptions (like the astronauts used to train with) that spins you in three directions at once. You must also be 4 feet tall and fork over $5 for the privilege. For the younger ones, Rockin' Raceway also has several carnival type kiddie rides (miniature Ferris Wheel, etc.) which only cost $2 each. There is also a kiddie roller coaster for ages 2 and older that costs $3 to ride.

Inside the main building, you'll find the SR2V simulator, in which "passengers" take a virtual high-speed trip around a race course for only $3 per person. There is also, of course, a very large, well-equipped video arcade.

Fast Tracks
2879 Parkway, Pigeon Forge
• **(865) 428-1988**

Here's another multi-faceted entertainment center with fun for kids of all ages. The centerpieces of the facility, naturally, are the three outdoor go-cart tracks. On the multi curved Pro Car Track, you must be at least 10 years old and 4 feet 6 inches tall to drive alone. To take a passenger, you must be at least 16, and your passenger must be at least 3 feet tall and 3 to 9 years old. The Pro Cars cost $5 per ride and $2 for a passenger. The Naskarts, which are somewhat faster, take drivers 16 and older on a single loop for $6 per ride or five rides for $20. On the Junior Track, drivers ages 4 through 9 can zip around a small, single-loop track for $4 each.

You'll also find bumper boats at Fast Tracks. Ages 6 and older can drive themselves for $5 per voyage. You must be at least 12 to drive a passenger; passengers pay $2, and they must be 3 to 6 years old. By the way, you can purchase five tickets for $20, but they can only be used on the bumper boats, the Pro Car Track and the Junior Track.

The strong of heart may want to try out the Ejection Seat, a "reverse bungee" ride on which one or two people are strapped into a seating cage at ground level as bungee cords are pulled tight from high above. The cage is then released and riders are hurled rapidly skyward to a height of approximately 100 feet; from there they enjoy several up and down bounces on the springy cords. The Ejection Seat costs $20 for one person or $25 for two people.

Other Fast Tracks offerings include The Orbitron, a stationary, multi axis device that spins you in three directions at once and a trampoline where you can go nuts jumping with the added security of safety cords to keep you from flying away. Younger children will probably prefer the many kiddie rides that cost $2 each or seven for $10. All the kids will have a blast in Fast Tracks' indoor arcade.

Adventure Golf and Adventure Raceway
2925 Parkway, Pigeon Forge
• (865) 453-9233
2945 Parkway, Pigeon Forge
• (865) 428-2971

Let's start with the go-carts! Adventure Raceway features one outdoor track-another of the several wooden go-cart tracks that sprang up on the Parkway in 1999. The curvy, multi level wooden section was added to the existing figure-eight, ground-level track. The cost is $7 per ride, and drivers must be at least 4 feet 6 inches tall. Adventure Raceway also has bumper boats that cost $5 per ride. You must be 3 feet 6 inches tall to operate the boats.

At Adventure Golf, you'll find one of the more attractive and interesting miniature golf courses in the area. In fact, own-ers claim that it's the oldest commercial minia-ture golf course in Pigeon Forge. The figures and statues found on the site are mammoth versions of a dinosaur, a shark, an octopus and more; large shipwreck and castle scenes add to the landscaping. Adventure Golf has two 18-hole courses that cost $6 each, and there's also an indoor arcade for gaming fun.

Professor Hacker's Lost Treasure Golf
3010 Parkway, Pigeon Forge
• (865) 453-0307

Although this newer attraction is devoted ex-

You're never too young to learn how to ski.

Photo: Courtesy Ober Gatlinburg

clusively to miniature golf, there's not very much that's "miniature" about it. Its features easily grab your eye as you motor down the Parkway. An Aztec pyramid, a volcano and a twin prop plane reminiscent of the Indiana Jones films are among the life-sized props that tower above street level and enhance your putting experience.

The twin 18-hole courses are built around a theme of exploration and adventure. According to course "legend," Professor Ephraim A. Hacker discovered an abandoned mining train that had been built by the Germans during World War I for the purpose of helping finance their war effort. Once you've selected your putter and ball, there is an actual train waiting to take you and your fellow golfers up an inclined railway to the top of the park. From there, you can choose either the Gold course, which takes you under a large waterfall, or the Diamond course, which takes you through the pyramid.

Lost Treasure Golf costs $7 per course for ages 13 and older and $5 for ages 5 through 12. Children 4 and younger play for free. It costs $3.50 for any age to play a second course.

Ultrazone
3053 Parkway, Pigeon Forge
• (865) 428-2444

At Ultrazone, laser tag gamers can hunt each other down in a 3,800-square-foot play area designed to resemble a destroyed city. The layout also features three sniper areas from which shooters can pick off their opponents from aerial vantage points.

After a ten-minute period of equipment briefing and suiting up, players enter the game area and compete in a three-team system with up to ten players on each team. After each 15-minute game, players get computer readouts detailing how many hits they made and how many times they were hit. At Ultrazone, anyone age 7 and older can play for $8.75 per person. With groups of 10 or more, the price goes down to $6.75 per person.

Parkway Slick Track
3068 Parkway, Pigeon Forge
• (865) 428-7750

This covered, open-air slick track is a short, single-loop course that keeps carts fairly close to each other and makes for exciting driving action. Solo drivers must be at least 13 years old, and drivers of two-seater carts must be at least 16 years old. Passengers in two-seaters must be old enough to sit upright and remain safely buckled into the cart. The cost for single-seat carts is $5; two-seat carts cost $10. Parkway Slick Track has a discounted price of $10 for three tickets, Monday through Thursday only. In addition to the track, they also have a small open-air arcade area and an indoor gift shop.

Fantasy Golf
3263 Parkway, Pigeon Forge
• (865) 453-4183

This is actually the address and phone number for Ogle's Gift Outlet, located next door to the golf course. That's where you must purchase your tickets to Fantasy Golf's two 18-hole courses, which, from a purely financial perspective is one of the better miniature golf values in town. You'll find some pretty interesting residents at this facility, such as a giant praying mantis, unicorn and dragon. Ages 6 and older can play all 36 holes for only $6. Children 5 and younger play for free.

Pigeon Forge Super Speedway
3275 Parkway, Pigeon Forge
• (865) 429-4639 (track), (865) 429-8600
(Sky Coaster and Sky Scraper)

Super Speedway has a single-loop go-cart track for drivers ages 12 and older (no height restrictions). One-seat carts cost $5 per ride, and two-seaters cost $10. For those of you who get your kicks in the air, look for the Sky Coaster and Sky Scraper. On the Sky Coaster, up to three people sit in harnesses that are pulled back by a cable and released, sending riders swinging back and forth like a giant pendulum. If you haven't just eaten a big meal, consider the Sky Scraper. Riders are strapped into a cage that is swung over and over like a pendulum in vertical 360-degree loops by a large mechanical arm. You must be at least 3 feet 6 inches tall to ride both the Sky Coaster and the Sky Scraper. Both cost $20 per person per ride, but be sure to ask about adjusted rates if you're in a group or visiting when business is slow.

While you're at Pigeon Forge Super Speedway, also look for coin-operated kiddie rides, the Gyro ride (a stationary, multi axis ride), the Trampoline Thing and Family Arcade, a large, indoor video game center.

Smoky Mountain Slick Track
3322 Parkway, Pigeon Forge
• (865) 428-4955

This outdoor slick track runs along a bent, single-loop course and offers close-knit, competitive driving action. Solo drivers must be at least 4 feet 9 inches tall. Drivers of passengers must be at least 16 years old, and passengers must be at least 3 feet 4 inches tall. For the younger speedsters, there is also a Kiddie Track for children who are at least 3 feet 4 inches tall. All single-seat go-carts cost $5 per ride, and two-seaters cost $10 per ride. Smoky Mountain Slick Track has a discounted price of four rides for $16. If you're not on the track, you can still keep yourself entertained in their indoor arcade.

Riverside Raceway
3315 S. River Rd., Pigeon Forge
• (432) 908-7255

This amusement center is less than one

block off the Parkway near the Old Mill area of Pigeon Forge. There are two outdoor go-cart tracks. The single-loop wedge track is for drivers who are at least 4 feet 8 inches tall. Single carts cost $6, and two-seaters cost $10. The Tennessee Twister is a brand-new wooden go-cart track with multiple levels and corkscrew turns. You must be at least 5 feet tall to drive. The Tennessee Twister costs $7 for one-seaters and $10 for two-seaters. Drivers of all two-seat cars must be 16 years old, and passengers must be at least 3 years old. If you want to drive both tracks, you can do so for a discounted price of $11.

Riverside Raceway also has the Sling Swing, a multi towered setup that uses bungee cords to fling passengers either up and down, side to side or both! It costs $15 to ride vertically or horizontally and $25 to ride both ways. If you don't care to be hurled through the air, you may just want to take it easy in the raceway's small indoor arcade.

Treehouse Golf & Games
3535 Parkway, Pigeon Forge
• (865) 429-8008

It's like suddenly walking into a forest right in the middle of town. Treehouse is actually two 18-hole miniature courses side by side, but it's tough to tell one from the other until you get into them. With tall trees, thick bushes, and running water all around, Treehouse offers an island of serenity in the bustle that exemplifies Pigeon Forge. A single round is $6.60, and an additional game is $3. Considering the prices and the peaceful environment, the $10 all-day ticket seems like a bargain. A good-sized arcade beside the course has a wide variety of games for those not into sylvan golf.

Rebel Yell Raceway
3643 Parkway, Pigeon Forge
• (865) 453-9461

Another "racing plus" conglomerate, Rebel Yell has a pro track and junior turbo track where $5 buys a single ride. The 4-foot height rule is in effect. The venue is also the home of a simulated gem mine, a vertical accelerator, and a dinosaur-infested miniature golf course. At Rebel Yell Gem Mining, "prospectors" can cull through specially prepared bags of gem-laden earth

looking for precious and semi-precious stones. On-site experts will help to find and identify stones. Bags are priced at $4, $5, or $6, or two bags of any size may be purchased for $7, $9, or $11. The vertical accelerator ride (they call it the "Ejection Seat") will rocket one or two riders into space for $20 apiece; a second shot, if you can handle it, is $5. Jurassic Golf features huge prehistoric creatures on a very fast concrete links layout. An 18-hole round costs $5; an additional dollar buys 36 holes.

Wild Wheels & Waterbugs
3735 Parkway,
Pigeon Forge
• (865) 453-7942

The southernmost of Pigeon Forge's myriad amusements on the Parkway, Wild Wheels is a sparkling clean layout featuring two go-cart tracks, a bumper boat pool, a big arcade and a four-station bungee jump tower (no waiting!). Bungee jumping from the quad tower is priced at $20 for the first jump and $10 more if one isn't enough. If you need proof that you really did take "the plunge," they'll shoot a video of your attempted suicide for $10. The bumper boats have an age limit of 7 years for solo riders at $5 a head, which is also the going rate for a 12-minute trip on either of the two go-cart tracks. The junior track (7 years, minimum height 4 feet) has two cart configurations, as does the big track (age 10, height 54 inches). A special rate schedule permits a mix-and-match package of 10 rides on the go-carts and/or bumper boats for $35. The large arcade features a broad selection of electronic and interactive games.

Dollywood Entertainment Park
1020 Dollywood Ln., Pigeon Forge
• (865) 428-9488, (800) 365-5996

If you'd like a comprehensive look at everything Dollywood has to offer, check out the Dollywood chapter of this book. For Kidstuff purposes, we'll focus mainly on the areas of the park that are of more interest to the young ones. After all, we know good and well that children have better things to do than to sit through some boring music show or watch a bunch of dumb old craftsmen!

It's a foregone conclusion that most kids love

rides. Dollywood has wet rides like Smoky Mountain Rampage, the Mountain Slidewinder and the recently added Daredevil Falls, the country's tallest log flume ride. You'll also find a couple of roller coasters, the indoor Blazing Fury and the new, outdoor Tennessee Tornado, an $8 million thrill ride that takes passengers on 360-degree loops and corkscrew twists!

Along your way, you'll find an exciting "movie ride" that takes viewers on a high-speed car chase. And don't forget that you're still in Pigeon Forge; there's also the requisite go-cart track for real driving action. For slower fun, the kids will love an old-fashioned train ride on the Dollywood Express or a whirl on the Dentzel Carousel, an antique, hand-carved merry-go-round.

There are a couple of specific areas of Dollywood that seem to be the most "kid-friendly". Brand new at Dollywood is Dreamland Forest, a $5 million, 15,000 square-foot interactive playground for children. Almost totally replacing what was formerly known as the Daydream Ridge area of the park, Dreamland Forest strives to re-create many of the imaginative adventures of Dolly's childhood. The attraction soars as high as 50 feet in places, and accommodates up to 1,000 kids at one time.

Also popular with kids (especially the younger ones), is the Country Fair section of the park. There are plenty of rides for children of all ages here, including another log flume ride, a circular swing ride and a Ferris Wheel (by the way, even a short line for the Ferris Wheel can mean a deceptively long wait!). There are also small kiddie rides such as trucks, cars and airplanes. You'll even find carnival favorites such as bumper cars, a Scrambler ride and a Tilt-A-Whirl ride.

You can't take your kids to Dollywood without stopping by Imagination Station, also located in the Country Fair area. Kids can dig in to dozens of hands-on educational exhibits as well as crafts, games and puzzles. At one of the more popular displays, you get to make giant soap bubbles using Hula Hoops! Or, try whispering to a friend from across the room using only a couple of parabolic dishes.

There's even a Lego Construction Zone with literally thousands of bricks available for creative building. One area is set up for younger kids to build with the larger Duplo blocks. Another section of the Lego Zone has all kinds of parts with which kids can build race cars. When the cars are completed, the kids (and often, the dads!) get to race their speedsters in head-to-head competition down an inclined race track.

If you look overhead, you'll see several large and impressive works of art made from Legos, including a five-foot-long tube of paint and a life-size motorcycle!

Dollywood is open from mid-April through December. The park is open daily throughout the summer and runs on a more limited schedule during the other months. Hours of operation vary, depending on the time of year; generally they're open from 9 AM to 9 PM during the summer and 10 AM to 6 PM in spring and fall.

The following price schedule is the most current available, but is subject to change. From mid-April through October, admission prices to the park are $29.99 for ages 12 and older, $20.99 for ages 4 through 11 and $24.99 for Seniors ages 60 and older. None of the above prices includes sales tax. It costs $5 to park, but trams will take you from your parking area to the main entrance (or you can ride either of the special Dollywood trolleys operated by the cities of Pigeon Forge and Gatlinburg).

For more detailed information on Dollywood's schedule and the most current admission prices, call their information office and/or request a current brochure. Our Dollywood chapter has more on discounts and season tickets.

Gatlinburg

The scene here isn't as frantic as it is in Pigeon Forge because amusement-type activities had to shoehorn themselves in among the shops that gave Gatlinburg its original reputation as a tourism center. Some of the older attractions hark back to the days when Mom and Dad first came to the Smokies, and the newer ones are striving to achieve the state-of-the-art condition found in the two cities to the north.

Dinosaur Golf
160 Parkway, Gatlinburg
• (865) 436-4449

Two 18-hole courses wander through a real forest of simulated prehistoric creatures. Among the oldest amusements in the area, Dinosaur Golf is a throwback to the miniature golf courses of the 1950s and '60s, with strategically placed rocks and water to challenge the best of putters. Their biggest regret is that they can't figure out a way to tie in a few windmills. Greens fees are $5 for one course or $6 for both. Additional plays are another dollar.

Hillbilly Golf
340 Parkway, Gatlinburg • (865) 436-7470

Another oldie, with a really spectacular twist: You can't walk to the course. Hillbilly Golf's two 18-hole courses are on a mountaintop 300 feet above the Parkway, and the only way to get to them is to ride an incline railway. The ride is part of the admission, of course, and while you're waiting for the rail car you can visit the arcade or get in a few strokes on the practice green. Once you get to the top you'll play on your choice of courses (or both) set in the wilderness, with mountaineer hazards like stills and rock walls to make your shot selections a little more difficult. Adults 13 to 60 pay $5; children 4 through 12 and seniors 60 and older pay $4; and children 3 and under are free.

Fun Mountain
**130 East Parkway, Gatlinburg
• (865) 436-4132**

Fun Mountain is arguably the easiest place in Gatlinburg to find; having the only Ferris wheel in town will do that for you. And that's just the beginning. Set into the mountainside at the city's busiest intersection, Fun Mountain is 23 acres of non-stop enjoyment for any size group from a family to a busload, and all ages are accommodated. From the parking lot at the foot of the mountain (or the adjacent parking deck), the tower elevator goes up three stories from street level to the huge covered pavilion that shelters the kiddie rides, games of skill and chance, snack area, and century-old carousel (originally steam powered). There's also a short animated musical production to give you a laugh while relaxing in the snack/picnic area. At the far end from the entrance, a good-sized (150 games) arcade shares space with a Little Caesar's pizza restaurant. Outside the covered pavilion, Rickey's Rocket, the obligatory mother's nightmare, waits to propel its brave riders skyward with 3G force. The rest of the outdoor midway is standard "county fair" stuff, with the aforementioned Ferris wheel, tilt-a-whirl, bumper cars and boats, high-speed mini-coaster (at Fun Mountain it's the "Himalaya," complete with mountain backdrop). Taking advantage of its setting, Fun Mountain has added a chairlift that takes its riders to the top of the mountain across the street for a spectacular view of the mountains to the south. It's also a good chance to relax for a while. Admission to the park is free, and tickets are available in a variety of packages for most of the rides—special all-day wristbands are usually the best way to go. Tickets don't include admission to the go-carts, Rickey's Rocket, or the miniature golf course that winds down the mountainside. Special rates are available for any group numbering 10 or more, and special event planning (birthdays, anniversaries, etc.) can be done on a call-ahead basis.

Camp Thunder
514 Parkway, Gatlinburg • (865) 430-7223

Weather is not a factor when you're burning it up at Camp Thunder—it's indoors. Driving indoors feels a little strange at first, but once you get used to the slick track it's just like driving outdoors but not as cold, hot, windy, or wet. It's air conditioned and comfortable, and everybody in the family that's over 10 years old and over 54 inches tall (that's four feet and six inches) can give it a ride. A full speed ride runs 35 to 40 laps, depending on skill, and double cars are available for those who need a little help navigating. After a race, go upstairs to the 18-hole Great Smoky Mountains miniature golf course for a round of putt-putt golf on holes laid out to simulate the mountain trails in the national park. Camp Thunder is open seven days a week year-round (except Christmas). A single racer costs $5.95 per run, and a double is $8.95. A round of golf is $5.95 per person, and a racing and golf package is $9.95 for singles and $13.95 for doubles.

> **INSIDERS' TIP**
> A good time to go to a go-cart track or miniature golf course during the summer months is at night. You'll probably pay full price, but the temperatures are cooler and most amusement centers stay open until around midnight.

Anna Porter Public Library
**207 Cherokee Orchard Road, Gatlinburg
• (865) 436-5588**

Historically dedicated to children's education through reading and practical application, Anna Porter has operated programs at the preschool and in-school level for as long as anyone in Gatlinburg can remember. The summer reading program for school-age children every Wednesday is so popular that groups are broken up by age, and volunteer help is necessary to keep order. The volunteers are usually mothers who were in the program when they were

Star Cars has plenty to keep kids entertained.

Photo: Courtesy Zwing Advertising

stuffer, to the desired amount of firmness. After hand-stitching is completed to hold the stuffing in place, the bear is sent down a slide through the gold mine that gives it life. The new bear is then clothed in whatever garb the owner finds appealing (not required), and named. A birth certificate is provided to prove that the bear was indeed made by its new parent. Bears run from $16.99 to $26.99, clothing is optional, and a Polaroid picture of the final product, complete with birth certificate, is

younger. During the school year, the Wednesday program shifts to pre-schoolers, with age-appropriate stories and games. Another popular feature is the Dial-A-Story program, which permits callers to hear a three-to-five-minute story by dialing (865) 430-5026. The cost of this program is underwritten by the Gatlinburg Kiwanis Club. With all this encouragement to go into the library at such an early age, it's no surprise that Gatlinburg's splendid little library is a popular gathering place for the elementary school crowd when classes end every day.

Great Smoky Mountain Teddy Bear Factory
611 Parkway, Gatlinburg • (865) 436-6400

This is a purely commercial enterprise, but it's done in such an engaging fashion that we decided it belongs in this chapter. The idea here is that kids (of all ages) get personally involved in the making, outfitting, and even naming of their own personal version of an all-time American favorite toy/companion, the teddy bear. Starting with a bearskin selected from two sizes (medium and large) and four colors (black, brown, tan, or white) , the new owner stuffs the skin by hand or blows it in with the magic

available for $2 more. This is a fun way to get personally involved in creating a lasting souvenir that will probably become a lifelong friend.

Treasure Quest Golf
653 Parkway, Gatlinburg • (865) 436-3972

Here's a great rainy-day activity: It's indoors! Treasure Quest is a unique take on a theme that's everywhere you look in the Smokies: A miniature golf course that's under cover, and that's clean enough to eat off the floor. 18 holes of fun miniature golf are set in a motif that features pirates and other treasure-hunters, with rock-and-roll background music. Admission is $6.50 for adults (age 12 and up), $4.33 for children 6 to 11, and children 5 and under are free with a paid adult admission.

Earthquake—The Ride
653 Parkway, Gatlinburg • (865) 436-9765

Shake-and-bake on the Parkway. A simulated subway car gets caught in the middle of an earthquake, and you're right in the middle. Motion and electronic wizardry combine to provide a gut-wrenching eight-minute ride that'll leave you gasping for air and wondering if you want to do it again right now, or maybe

All the Deer That's Fit to Feed

You're fairly warned when you enter! The camels and llamas will spit if you invade their space! Even when they do, you can't help but laugh. It's all part of the one-to-one experience at this hands-on petting zoo, located on a 140-acre Smoky Mountain farm. Once you've paid your admission (which is very reasonable when you consider that six bucks won't buy much more than a couple of soft drinks in some parts of the county), you're free to roam the grounds at your own pace and spend as much time as you like looking at and reading about different species of animals. Some of them, like the kangaroos and wallabies, are a long way from home.

There are two pens where you can actually go inside to pet and feed the animals. When you enter the pens of the pygmy goats and the fallow deer, make sure to quickly close the gate behind you! Once inside, feel free to pet these friendly beasts. Be aware, however, that if you're carrying feed (only use feed provided by the petting zoo!), you'll soon become very popular with the animals. If you have smaller children in tow, keep a hand on them or else they may be a little overwhelmed. If you prefer, you can have the little ones feed the goats and deer from outside the fence. Just watch hands to make sure they don't get smashed by the horned males.

You can also feed the various breeds of donkeys, zebras and miniature horses that you'll see. When feeding any of the "horse-like" animals, make sure you feed them with a flat, open palm. There's even a stand where you can purchase apples to feed the live reindeer that live on the premises. There are animals, however, that

Dinner time at the deer farm.

Photo: Courtesy Smoky Mountain Deer Farm and Petting Zoo

you definitely must not feed—kangaroos and wallabies. They must consume a special diet provided by the owners.

As the name implies, there are many varieties of deer that you can visit, including the Sika Deer, Mule Deer and the Reindeer. Along the way you'll see many more types of animals like ferrets, pot bellied pigs, prairie dogs, exotic cattle, emu, doves and sheep! You can be sure that the animals are always well treated and well cared for by owners Greg and Lynn Hoisington. The facility is USDA inspected and approved. Once you've been to Smoky Mountain Deer Farm and Petting Zoo, you'll probably give it your own seal of approval as well.

wait a little while 'til all the body parts get back where they belong. Earthquake admission is $6.50 if you're 12 and over, $4.33 for younger riders.

Fannie Farkle's Amusement Emporium
656 Parkway, Gatlinburg • (865) 436-4057

One of Gatlinburg's original arcades, Fannie Farkle's is distinguished by the fact that the premiums offered by game winners include high-quality collectibles like porcelain figurines and crystal accessories. A couple of games also pay off in Beanie Babies. In business since 1980, Fannie Farkle's is the only stand-alone arcade we're including in this section; you shouldn't be afraid to send your children in alone. The "Ogle Dog," available at the snack bar, is a local favorite for a quick lunch.

The Gatlinburg Fun Center
716 Parkway, Gatlinburg
• (865) 430-8985

Six different amusement venues (including on-site arcades with the latest in high-tech competition) stretch across the back of Reagan Square Mall in the heart of downtown Gatlinburg. Hours of enjoyment are available for the whole family in a close enough environment that nobody gets lost or separated by much distance. We'll present the attractions as they appear from left to right as you enter the complex. Prices vary depending on combinations of activities and group size. Groups of 10 to 15 who play together will save $1 a head for each venue; 15 or more in a group can expect a $2 discount. The Gatlinburg Fun Center is open every day but Christmas from 10 AM until the last customer is served and goes away happy.

Old Gatlinburg Golf & Games
• (865) 430-4653

Here are two unusual miniature golf courses laid out on the hillside that integrate old buildings into the play. Gatlinburg's Old Town Square Course delivers a local history lesson at

every hole, including how the city got its name. The Smokies Old Mountain Trail Course describes the development of the Great Smoky Mountains National Park in a peaceful setting reminiscent of the park itself. One hole plays through a replica of the old Elkmont post office. A single round of golf on one course is $5.95 for anybody over 5 years old; toddlers can play for $3. One of the best bargains in the area is the $8.95 golf pass that allows unlimited play for five consecutive days.

The Trampoline Thing
• (865) 430-8985

This special trampoline has attached bungee cords that let you soar to heights you never dreamed possible while protecting you from any injury. $5.95 buys a three-minute turn, which is plenty of time to get in all the bouncing you can enjoy.

Q-Zar
• (865) 436-2326

A futuristic, laser tag maze filled with fog, lights, and music places you in your very own living video game. Enjoy competing with your own family members in a 20-minute experience with unlimited lives and 150 shots. The sensory experience is a gas: The laser beam is visible when the background is right, and the buzz that tingles your upper body is ample notice that you've been zapped without taking you out of the action. You'll get your own personal scorecard at the end of the game. The Q-zar experience is $8.50 a head, with a special offer of $15.95 for three consecutive games.

Venturer Motion Ride Movie Theater
• (865) 430-8985

This is more than moving seats. The Venturer is a full simulation ride that places you in the middle of the action. Four different movies are available, from the popular roller coaster to an interplanetary excursion in sight and sound. The Glacier Run is a race through an arctic ice quarry that's so gripping you'll be too busy to shiver, and the Smash Factory is a trip through one horrifying crash after another. After a preview of all four, a single ride is $6.45 and any two can be seen at one sitting for $8.95.

Bankshot Basketball
• (865) 430-8985

A fun-filled combination of miniature golf and basketball, where angled backboards put a special slant on every shot. Accuracy counts big in this contest of skill, and a little knowledge of plane geometry can't hurt. A trip through the Bankshot course is $4.95 with no time limit.

Mysterious Mansion
425 River Road, Gatlinburg
• (865) 436-7007

Things go bump in the Mysterious Mansion at all hours of the day and night. It's easy to find the Mansion: Just go over to River Road and look for the only place with a big black hearse parked at the front door. Things get a little creepier when you get inside. Creepy things want to make you their "best friend," there's all kinds of awful noise going on, and the floor keeps acting like it's going to give way. And then there's the rooms with no way in or out, but somehow you got in, and. . . But we could go on like this all night—you really should be there. Getting in costs $5 for adults 13 and older, $4 for kids 7 to 12, and children 6 and under are free. Getting out may cost you a piece of your soul if the residents take a liking to you.

Festivals and Annual Events

As if you didn't already have a million and one reasons to come to the Smoky Mountains, here we present you with 50 more. In our cities you'll find commemorations of seasons and holidays as well as festivals for arts and crafts, nature and mountain ways of life. We celebrate automobiles, romance and the performing arts. And along the way, look out for plenty of great music, delicious food and festive decorations.

While the events included here are by no means a complete representation of all the events that take place in the Smokies each year, we have tried to steer you toward the more popular ones and those with the most longevity. We've sidestepped many events sponsored by retailers that are basically nothing more than gimmicks to enhance business.

In some cases, you'll find that we've outlined larger festivals as well as many of the specific events that take place within them. For example, Winterfest is a countywide celebration that lasts from mid-November through February. Obviously, quite a few Winterfest-related happenings are going on during this period, and we've included many of the more notable ones.

We've departed from our usual north-to-south presentation in this chapter, choosing to instead list the events chronologically. Since most Smoky Mountains events take place on different dates each year, we've stated the general time of each month that they occur. Phone numbers that appear with listings sometimes correspond with the event sites, but in other cases we've given you the number of the event coordinators when we felt that would be more helpful. We have also given you specific prices, but these are also subject to change from year to year.

Many of our inclusions are sponsored by the different cities of the county, so if you would like more information contact:

Sevierville Chamber of Commerce
Office of Special Events
- (865) 908-4103, (800) 255-6411
www.seviervilletn.org/tourism

Pigeon Forge Department of Tourism
Office of Special Events
- (865) 429-7350, (800) 251-9100
www.pigeon-forge.tn.us

Gatlinburg Department of Tourism & Convention Center
- (865) 436-2392, (800) 267-7088
www.gatlinburg-tennessee.com

Gatlinburg Chamber of Commerce
- (865) 436-4178, (800) 568-4748
www.gatlinburg.com

January

Many of the events in January and February are part of Winterfest, which begins in November and runs through February. (Refer to the November section of this chapter for a general overview of the Winterfest celebration.) Also in January, the cities of Pigeon Forge and Gatlinburg are continuing the trolley tours of their respective city's Winterfest lights displays. You'll find all the specifics about those trolley tours in the November section as well.

Wilderness Wildlife Week
Heartlander Country Resort,
2385 Parkway, Pigeon Forge
- (865) 453-4106

Although the events that take place throughout the week occur in different parts of the county, the

Heartlander Resort in Pigeon Forge is headquarters for what has become one of the area's most popular annual events. Wilderness Wildlife Week is nine days of nature hikes and walks as well as seminars, displays and workshops dealing with the study of Smoky Mountain flora and fauna. And you can't beat the fact that the whole thing costs absolutely nothing. The hikes and other programs are led by approximately 90 scientists and other experts in the fields of wildlife, nature and conservation. This all-volunteer staff converges from around the region to lend its expertise on subjects ranging from native black bears to wildflowers.

Generally, the different Wildlife Week events each have a limited number of spots available for participants. Registration takes place at the Heartlander, and is done on a first-come, first-served basis. Registration for any of the week's 40 to 50 hikes takes place the day before the hike. As for the hikes themselves, transportation is provided to various points in the national park for the expeditions that range from short, casual nature strolls to overnight stays on top of mighty Mt. LeConte. Most of the week's lecture-oriented programs take place at the Heartlander. The week typically closes out with a slide presentation at the Heartlander, narrated by guest speaker Bill Landry, host of WBIR TV'S Heartland Series (refer to the Close-up in our Media chapter).

When Wilderness Wildlife Week was in its infancy, the turnout was pretty low, and the number of programs was limited. These days, thousands of people from all over the country journey to the Smokies specifically for this event, which usually takes place during the second full week of the month.

Smoky Mountain Romance
Gatlinburg • (865) 436-2392

With the Christmas holidays behind, the city of Gatlinburg shifts the focus of its Winterfest celebration to the season of love, and more specifically, Valentine's Day. Many of the city's Winterfest light displays are replaced with new glowing scenes such as a luminous wedding party, clouds, hearts and a "Gatlinburg Is For Lovers" display. Smoky Mountain Romance is observed from mid-January through February.

February

Special Olympics Winter Games
Ober Gatlinburg Ski Resort,
1339 Ski Mountain Rd., Gatlinburg
• (865) 436-5423

Each year, physically and mentally challenged youth go for the gold in the snow-covered mountains of Gatlinburg. Athletes ages 11 through 21 compete in alpine skiing and ice skating events during the first weekend in February. The first day of the Olympics is usually reserved for coaching and training. During the next two days, specific competitions take place between 8:30 AM and 4 PM. Gold, silver and bronze medals are given to the top three finishers in each event, and ribbons are awarded to all remaining participants. Closing ceremonies take place during the afternoon of the final day of competition.

There is no admission charge for spectators, but if you opt to take the aerial tramway up to the resort, the trip will cost $7 for ages 12 and older and $4 for ages 7 through 11. Children 6 and younger ride free with an accompanying adult. While you're at Ober Gatlinburg, all the usual attractions and activities are available at their regular prices (see our Attractions chapter). Note that while these Special Olympics normally take place in February, there have been years in the past (including 1999) when the dates were moved up to late January.

Mountains of Chocolate
Gatlinburg Convention Center,
234 Airport Rd., Gatlinburg
• (865) 436-2392

Restaurants and candy shops from all over Sevier County help celebrate Smoky Mountain Romance by displaying their sweetest fare at the convention center over a two-day period in the early part of the month. While Friday's activities are by invitation only, Saturday's chocolate tasting is open to the public from 1 to 4 PM. The admission is $8, and proceeds benefit Friends of Great Smoky Mountains National Park (see our chapter on the national park). Once you're through the doors, however, feel free to sample the confections to your heart's content (or your stomach's discontent!).

Winterfest Fine Art and Photography Show
Smoky Mountain Convention Center,
4010 Parkway, Pigeon Forge
• (865) 429-7350

Winterfest is still going strong in February with this three-day, mid-week art showing during the early part of the month. On exhibit are hundreds of works by more than 40 of the Smokies' best professional artists in a variety of media, including photography. Just in case you're interested in taking something home with you, displayed works are for sale. In previous years, professional area artists like Jim Gray, G. Webb and Robert Tino have participated, as well as the popular photographer Ken Jenkins. There is no charge to attend. Show hours are noon until 7 PM on the first day, 10 AM to 7 PM on the second day and 10 AM to 5 PM on the third day.

Miss Great Smoky Mountains Winterfest USA Pageant
Ramada Inn Four Seasons Convention Center, 756 Parkway, Gatlinburg
• (865) 428-5843

Have you ever wondered where the Miss USA contestants get their start? It all begins with local, preliminary competitions like this one. The pageant is open to young ladies ages 3 to 26. In the teen and miss categories, participants compete for the right to move on to the Miss Teen Tennessee USA and Miss Tennessee USA pageants, respectively. Traditional categories such as talent and interview competitions are part of the evening's lineup. The pageant begins at 7:30 PM, and admission is $8 for adults and $6 for children.

Smoky Mountains Storytelling Festival
Hillbilly Hoedown Theatre, 2135 Parkway, Pigeon Forge • (865) 428-5600
• Patriot Park, Pigeon Forge

Toward the end of the month, the mountain art of storytelling gets into high gear with a weekend of fun at two different Pigeon Forge locations—one indoor, one outdoor. Regardless of where you choose to attend, get ready to be mesmerized by noted local storytellers from the Smoky Mountains as well as surrounding areas of East Tennessee. Admission to the festival is free.

On Friday, the storytelling begins at the Hillbilly Hoedown Theater in Pigeon Forge with a 6:30 PM presentation. The next day, the action moves to Patriot Park where tellers weave their tales beginning at 4 PM. There is no admission charge for either of these two performances.

New to this storytelling festival for 2000 are the "Haunts And Haints" trolley rides. For $3 per person, audience members can board trolleys taking them from Patriot Park to different locations around Pi-

geon Forge, where professional storytellers are waiting to spin their yarns. "Scary Stories for the Family" (suitable for all ages) begins at 9:30 PM, and "Scary Stories for Grownups" gets underway at 10:45 PM.

Shindig & Show Revue
Alternating Pigeon Forge music theaters
• (865) 429-7350

During this annual event, entertainers from music theaters throughout the county are invited to Pigeon Forge to put on a musical extravaganza that takes place over a weekend at the end of the month. Acts participating in previous years have included Lee Greenwood and Louise Mandrell.

Each year, the location of Shindig & Show Revue shifts to a different Pigeon Forge music theater. Over the course of the two days, three different shows are staged. The Friday show starts at 7:30 PM, and the Saturday shows are at 1 and 7:30 PM. Performances usually feature around five different acts. Admission to Shindig and Show Revue is $20 per person or $15 each if you're with a group. All monies taken in go to various local charities that are selected by the performers. Groups receiving proceeds in previous years have included area primary schools, the Shriners and the Boys and Girls Club of the Smoky Mountains.

March

A Mountain Quiltfest
Smoky Mountain Convention Center, 4010 Parkway, Pigeon Forge
• (865) 429-7350

At this free show you'll find exhibits of another time-honored form of mountain arts and crafts. Aficionados will recognize patterns like Double Wedding Ring, Log Cabin and Dresden Plate. Quilters from all across the region will have between 150 and 200 quilts on display and for sale, and there are instructors on hand with classes and lectures to help quilters develop their skills. A Mountain Quiltfest takes place over a five-day period in mid March. Daily hours are 9 AM to 7 PM.

INSIDERS' TIP
Once you know the specific dates you'll be visiting the Smokies, you might want to check with area departments of tourism beforehand to see if any parades or road races (5k or 10k runs) are scheduled for that time. During events such as these, sections of the Parkway and other side roads are often closed to automobile traffic. Knowing about them ahead of time will allow you to adjust your travel plans for the day of a particular event.

April

Great Smoky Arts and Crafts Show
Gatlinburg Convention Center, 234 Airport Rd., Gatlinburg
- **(865) 436-2392**

Each Easter weekend, approximately 10,000 visitors flock to the convention center to see artists from Gatlinburg's renowned Great Smoky Arts and Crafts Community (see our Mountain Crafts chapter) exhibit their talents and offer hand-crafted treasures for sale. Craft products include baskets, candles, dolls, jewelry, pottery, quilts, toys and much more. Representatives from nearly all of the community's 80-plus studios, galleries and shops are present for the four-day event (which takes place in March when Easter falls in that month).

Admission to this arts and crafts show is free. The doors open at 10 AM daily, and closing times vary, depending on the day of the week. This is just the first of several shows that the Arts and Crafts Community sponsors throughout the year; others take place during the Thanksgiving and Christmas holidays (see the November and December sections of this chapter).

Scottish heritage is celebrated at the annual Gatlinburg Scottish Festival and Games.

Photo: Courtesy Gatlinburg Department of Tourism

Smoky Mountain Trout Tournament
Little Pigeon River in Gatlinburg, Pigeon Forge and Sevierville
- **(865) 429-3474**

After a long winter without restocking, more than 5,000 trout are released into the Little Pigeon River running from the national park boundary in Gatlinburg all the way to Sevierville. Participants are allowed to keep what they catch, plus more than $10,000 in prizes is up for grabs as well. Prizes include $500 cash awards for the largest (and smallest) trout, gift certificates, trophies, fishing gear and more.

The two-day event takes place the first weekend of April, and fishing hours are from 6 AM to 4 PM on Saturday and 6 AM to 2 PM on Sunday. The competition is open to anglers of all ages, although entrants are separated into "tourist" and "local" divisions and then subdivided into "adult" and "juvenile" groups. And rodeo organizers say that no matter how they fare with the fishing, all kids who enter walk away with a prize.

The $28 entry fee covers both days of the event, but a Tennessee fishing license and a trout permit in Gatlinburg are also required to participate (see the Parks and Recreation chapter for information on obtaining a license). In addition to the spring event, there is also a fall tournament that takes place the last week of September.

Dolly's Parade
Parkway, Pigeon Forge • (865) 429-7350

Everyone knows it's time for a new season at Dollywood when Sevier County's most famous offspring comes home to kick things off with her annual parade in Pigeon Forge. In mid-April, the bands strike up and the floats start rolling down the Parkway as crowds line the streets, waiting to catch a glimpse of Dolly Parton. In past parades, Ms. Parton has brought some of her friends along to help celebrate—stars like Burt Reynolds and Lilly Tomlin. Around 5:30 PM, the caravan starts on River Road, makes its way north along the Parkway and winds up at the Wears Valley Road intersection.

Smoky Mountain Music Festival
Gatlinburg Convention Center, 234 Airport Rd., Gatlinburg
• (865) 436-2392

This competition features a variety of school bands, orchestras and choirs from around the country performing in almost every conceivable style of music. On Friday, the groups compete in the convention center throughout the day, and on Saturday morning, the outdoor portion of the event is held at Gatlinburg-Pittman High School's football field on U.S. 321 from 9 AM to noon. Smoky Mountain Music Festival starts in the mid to latter part of the month and runs for four consecutive weekends into May. There is no charge to attend.

Spring Wildflower Pilgrimage
Gatlinburg Convention Center, 234 Airport Rd., Gatlinburg
• (865) 436-2392

Each April, near the end of the month, nature enthusiasts from near and far gather in Gatlinburg and the national park to experience the annual arrival of Mother Nature's blossoming beauty. Although most of the actual wildlife viewing takes place in Great Smoky Mountains National Park, the event is headquartered at W.L. Mills Auditorium in the Gatlinburg Convention Center.

From Thursday through Saturday, some 90 different programs are conducted by more than 80 professional tour leaders selected from universities and colleges across the United States. Included in this staff are botanists, photographers and hikers who are eager to share their expertise and experiences with their groups. Programs include half-day and daylong field trips, excursions that range from moderate scenic strolls to overnight trips to Mt. LeConte. Meanwhile, at Mills Auditorium, visitors can view a collection of more than 200 flower and plant species native to the area.

The Wildflower Pilgrimage has deep roots that date back more than 50 years, when the University of Tennessee Botany Department conducted annual field trips in the Smoky Mountains. In 1951, the pilgrimage was officially established in cooperation with the Gatlinburg Chamber of Commerce, the national park and the Gatlinburg Garden Club. That first year, around 400 "posie pilgrims" took part in 11 tours over the course of two days.

Today, per-day registration fees are $10 for adults and $5 for high school and college students. Children ages 12 and younger are admitted free. Mills Auditorium is open for exhibition on Wednesday from 6 to 9 PM, Thursday and Friday from 9 AM to 9 PM and Saturday from 9 AM to 1 PM. To learn more about the Wildflower Pilgrimage, visit its web site at www.goldsword.com/wildflower/pilgrimage.html

May

Ramp Festival
U.S. Hwy. 321, Cosby, Tennessee

We're going to send you a few miles out of your way for this one, but we think you'll agree, it's in a category by itself. First, you're probably wondering what a "ramp festival" is. No, it's not a day to celebrate motorcycle stunt paraphernalia or interstate access points. Ramps are a cross between onions and garlic, and believe it or not, thousands of people travel from all over the country to sample and celebrate this pungent plant. Taking place the first Sunday in May, the festival's activities include country, folk and bluegrass music and the always popular Maid

INSIDERS' TIP

Many of Gatlinburg's annual events take place at the city's convention center at the corner of Parkway and Airport Road. The 188,000 square-foot facility, completed in 1988, includes W.L. Mills Auditorium, an older convention hall that had been in service since 1955. Mills Auditorium and the newer convention center space combined accommodate approximately 200 events in Gatlinburg each year.

of Ramps pageant, a beauty competition for young ladies ages 16 through 21.

Naturally, with a gathering devoted to an edible plant, there's bound to be food involved. Indeed, in addition to barbecue chicken and pig, a variety of ramp dishes are served up. A couple of the more popular ones are ramps with scrambled eggs and ramps served with hoe cake, a type of skillet-fried cornbread. You might want to know that ramps are five times stronger than onions when uncooked. In fact, it's rumored that enough ramp consumption will cause an odor to be released through the pores of the body. We can't validate that, but we do guarantee that if you show up to the Ramp Festival, you will hear plenty of home remedies for getting rid of "ramp breath."

INSIDERS' TIP

While the area's many arts and crafts shows are an effective means of putting the work of local artisans in the public eye, don't forget that the crafts people of the Smokies are still hard at work in their shops during these festival periods.

The history behind the festival dates back almost 50 years to when a visiting *Knoxville News-Sentinel* columnist suggested to some of the Cosby locals that they start a festival in honor of the ramp. Several of the local men proceeded to form a club for just such a purpose, and the rest is history. Today, the event is sponsored by the Cosby Ruritan Club, whose members dig up 50 to 60 bushels of ramps in preparation for the festival. Festival hours are 9:30 AM to 4:30 PM, and it takes place at Kineauvista Hill, a scenic area just off U.S. 321 in Cosby. The admission is $5 for adults and $3 for children ages 11 through 18. Children ages 10 and younger get in free.

Music & Arts Festival
Downtown Sevierville • (865) 908-4103

Sevierville's historic downtown area is the site for a Saturday filled with music, arts and crafts, food and all-around fun in early May. From 10 AM to 5 PM, the festival's music includes local bands, soloists and dulcimer players performing on the veranda of the city's 100-year-old courthouse. The courthouse lawn is transformed into an old-fashioned crafts fair as both novice and established area artists display and sell their work. The north parking lot of the courthouse is where you'll find all the kids—playing games for prizes, getting their faces painted and riding ponies. If you get hungry, food concessions are available. Admission to the festival is free, and there's plenty of free parking around the downtown area.

Gatlinburg Scottish Festival and Games
Downtown and Mills Park, Gatlinburg
• (865) 436-2392

When the Smoky Mountains were settled about 200 years ago, many of the newcomers who settled were Scottish. Today, quite a few descendants of those pioneers still reside in our mountains (Gatlinburg's high school sports teams are even nicknamed the Highlanders). Since the early 1980s, Scots from all across the country (and even Scot wannabes) have gathered in Gatlinburg to celebrate that country's heritage. During the third weekend of each May, members of more than 60 clans drink deep from the well of their culture.

Things get kicked off on Friday with a parade through downtown Gatlinburg featuring kilted men and bagpipe bands. On Saturday and Sunday, the events move to Mills Park off U.S. 321. Admission is $10 on Saturday and $8 on Sunday. The festivities include band competitions, dance contests and sheepdog demonstrations. The different clans have tents set up where visitors can learn about each clan's history and colors. Authentic Scottish cuisine is available for the tasting—hot dishes like meat pies and baked goods like scones.

The Scottish athletic events are always popular with the spectators. Women especially enjoy the men showing their legs in the Bonniest Knees competition, and the caber throw (a telephone pole-like log) is a test of raw strength and skill. Then there's the haggis hurl! In case you're not familiar with haggis, it's a traditional Scottish dish prepared by taking the organs of a sheep or calf, mincing them with a few more palatable ingredients and boiling them in the animal's stomach. It's not hard to imagine why people want to hurl them!

June

American Eagle Weekend
Eagles Landing Golf Course and
Governor's Crossing, Sevierville
• (865) 429-0157, (888) 439-1111

Enjoy three days of music, food, art and more at this fund-raising event benefiting the National Foundation to Protect America's

Rod Runs

What's a rod run? Simply put, it's the catch-all name given to any of the plethora of antique and/or custom automobile shows that invade the Smokies throughout the year. Almost without exception, these shows take place in various venues around Pigeon Forge, usually convention centers and larger hotels. But even along the fringes of the county, you can tell when the rod runs are coming — you can see the convoys and the motorcades of unique vehicles as they parade down Tenn. 66 and through Sevierville on their way to Pigeon Forge.

CLOSE-UP

The types of vehicles that participate in these car shows run the gamut. A few of the names of these events hint as to what you'll see: Chevrolet GMC Pickup Show, VW Bug-In, Original Southern Street Machine Mini-Truckin' Nationals, Pre-49 Street Rod Show, Silver Dollar Rod Run Car Show. And the list goes on and on. It's interesting that these cars and trucks represent no small investment to their owners. Some "gearheads" invest tens of thousands of dollars in refurbishing, customizing and generally babying their vehicles. During the shows themselves, the cars are judged and prizes are awarded. Beyond these immediate circumstances, there's also a lot of shop talk, a respectful admiring of the competition, and a few big-ticket transactions along the way.

When the Smokies first began to attract these events in the 1980s, most of them were staged in Gatlinburg, before Pigeon Forge had really come into its own as a tourist destination. Eventually, the rod runs migrated from Gatlinburg to Pigeon Forge, which welcomed their patronage with open arms. Today, the car shows and the government and businesses of Pigeon Forge coexist together in a mutually beneficial arrangement. The rod runs have a good choice of venues out of which to operate, and the local hotels, restaurants and attractions do a lot of extra business while the auto enthusiasts are in town.

However, many Sevier Countians represent the other side of the coin. To them, the car shows are a nuisance, causing major traffic delays in getting through Pigeon

Taking a look under the hood at one of the many Smoky Mountain custom auto shows.

Photo: Mitch Moore

Forge, even though the Parkway is three lanes wide in each direction. The truth be told, it is slow going. Hundreds of spectators line the sidewalks along the main drag just to watch the cars cruise slowly up and down the street. You'll actually see people who basically set up camp along the roadside throughout the day with their lawn chairs and drink coolers!

So what you think of rod runs depends greatly on who you are. If you're a gearhead or a Pigeon Forge business owner, you're probably glad to see all those cars pull into town. If you're an otherwise disinterested tourist or a local resident trying to get back and forth between Sevierville and Gatlinburg, you might want to take an aspirin and a shortcut (see Getting Here, Getting Around)!

Eagles. Things get kicked off (teed off, actually) on Friday with the American Eagle Classic Golf Tournament at Eagles Landing Golf Course. The tournament hours are 8 PM to 1 PM, and the entry fee is $150 per player.

On Saturday, the action moves to Governor's Crossing, where guests can view a fine art and photography exhibit featuring wildlife and nature studies by some of the area's best-known artists and photographers. View the works in the Governor's Palace Theatre lobby and in the big-top tent next door. Hours for the art exhibit are 11 AM to 8 PM on Saturday and 11 AM to 5 PM on Sunday. Admission is free. On Saturday from 4:30 to 6:30 PM, the art works go up on the auction block for the Friends Of Eagles Art & Photography Auction. The event takes place under the outdoor tent, and the admission is $3.

On Saturday at 3 PM, the music kicks in with the Concert For America's Eagles, running from noon to 3 PM at Governor's Palace Theatre. The two-and-a-half-hour show features live segments by performers and casts from area music theaters. Those showing in previous years have included Louise Mandrell, The Blackwood Quartet and the casts of Country Tonite, Memories Theatre, The Comedy Barn and, of course, the Boots, Boogie & Blues show from Governor's Palace. Tickets cost $25 each.

After the concert, you can go next door to the big top tent for Taste Of The Smokies, a sampling of foods from more than 20 Smoky Mountain area restaurants. The tasting lasts from 3:30 to 5 PM, and costs $25 per person. Participating restaurants in previous outings have included L.G.'s On The River, Alan Jackson's Showcar Cafe, NASCAR Cafe, Chef Jock's Tastebuds Cafe, The Park Grill and The Old Mill Restaurant.

The weekend wraps up on Sunday with the Sunday Worship Service For Creation Care and the Wings Of Eagles Christian Music Concert. The first is a Christian worship service and sing-along held under the tent from noon to 1 PM. The concert is a two-hour-plus showcase of contemporary Christian and gospel music artists as well as Christian comedians. The concert is held at Governor's Palace Theatre from 1 to 4 PM, and the admission is $10.

The National Foundation to Protect America's Eagles is an organization devoted to recovery and protection programs for the American Bald Eagle.

Cosby Dulcimer and Harp Convention
U.S. Hwy. 321, Cosby, Tennessee
• (423) 487-5543

Around the middle of the month, celebrate the music of the mountains at this festival devoted to a variety of folk instruments. Look for beginning and advanced level workshops conducted daily as well as demonstrations in instrument building. There are also special activities for children and a watermelon seed spitting contest. The festivities are highlighted by afternoon mini-concerts and staged concerts in the evening. Limited on-site camping space is available on a first-come, first-served basis.

Admission for both days of the convention is $25. This includes primitive camping privileges. The one-day fee, which includes evening activities and camping privileges, is $15. It costs $5 to attend one evening only (no camping). Children younger than 12 are admitted for half price and senior citizens receive a 10 percent discount. The event, which is well into its third decade, takes place in Cosby, Tennessee, about 20 miles northeast of Gatlinburg on U.S. 321. For specific directions, call Mountain MusiCrafts in Cosby at the number listed above.

July

4th of July Midnight Parade
Parkway, Gatlinburg • (865) 436-2392

This event has the distinction of being the

nation's first Independence Day parade each year. Just after the stroke of midnight on the 4th, the long procession of floats and marching bands winds its way down the Parkway. Naturally, there's no charge for watching.

Patriot Festival
Patriot Park, Old Mill Ave., Pigeon Forge
• **(865) 429-7350**

Join nearly 30,000 revelers to observe Independence Day. Entertainment, games, face painters, clowns and an arts and crafts show last from noon until 10 PM. Then, get ready for a spectacle of fireworks that lights up the night sky in explosive color. The event is free, but due to the limited amount of on-site parking, spectators are asked to park elsewhere and take a trolley to Patriot Park (see Getting Here, Getting Around).

Smoky Mountain Heritage Days
Sevier County Fairgrounds, 754 Old Knoxville Hwy., Sevierville
• **(865) 453-0770, (865) 908-4103**

In mid July, Sevier County Fairgrounds is the site of this two-day festival celebrating the history of mountain life. Hundreds of working historical exhibits can be viewed as well as live steam-powered threshing, old fashioned kids' games, "Hillbilly Olympics," an antique and collectibles auction, the South's largest tractor pull and much more. The gates to the fairgrounds open at 4 PM on Friday and 8 AM on Saturday. In the past, the admission has been $5 for adults, but festival officials advise calling the fairgrounds at the first number listed above for an accurate price quote. Children ages 12 and younger are admitted free.

Gatlinburg Craftsmen's Fair
Gatlinburg Convention Center, 234 Airport Rd., Gatlinburg
• **(865) 436-7479**

This 10-day event in late July is the first of two Gatlinburg Craftsmen's Fairs held between July and October. Visitors can see time-honored mountain crafts and other traditional art forms created before their eyes. More than 150 artisans from across the country are on hand,

Sevierville's Music and Arts Festival.

Photo: Courtesy Sevierville Chamber of Commerce

demonstrating their skills in areas such as folk art, wood turning and ceramic making. Finished products include works in all kinds of media, from leather to oil painting to sculpture.

The Gatlinburg Craftsmen's Fair was created in 1975 when the Southern Highlands Craft Guild left Gatlinburg. In the nearly quarter-century since, the event has grown into one of the most notable crafts happenings, not just in the Smokies, but in the entire southeast United States. The show's quality is maintained through a jury system, which is used to evaluate potential entries. While there are new participants each year, roughly 80 percent of fair exhibitors are regulars. Some have been displaying their skills and wares since the fair originated.

In addition to arts and crafts, live bluegrass, gospel and country music performances keep things hopping. The July fair is open from 10

AM to 7 PM Monday through Saturday and 10 AM to 5 PM on Sunday. Admission to the event is $4 for adults and free for children ages 12 and younger. For additional information, you can visit the fair's web site at www.craftsmenfair.com. Also, see our October listings for the particulars of the second fair.

August

Drums Across America
Sevier County High School,
1200 Dolly Parton Pkwy., Sevierville
• (865) 453-4026, (800) 495-7469

First coming to Sevierville in 1975, Drums Across America is a drum and bugle corps competition that draws competing corps (don't *ever* call them bands) together for an evening of music and precision choreography that leaves most of the spectators slack-jawed and breathless for the better part of three hours. The competition is arranged and conducted by Drum Corps International, and is the oldest continuing competition in the south. The number of competing corps varies, but a minimum of six is a pretty good bet each year. The 1999 competition included teams from Colorado, Delaware, and Canada, and featured performances by several national and world champion groups. In addition to the stirring music and precision routines, Drums Across America demonstrates graphically that there's still a significant

amount of "Heartland America" spirit in a lot of today's youth. Admission is $24, tickets are available in advance by calling the toll-free number listed above.

Food City Family Race Night
Governor's Crossing, Sevierville
• (865) 428-4551, (865) 908-4103

Governor's Palace Theatre and NASCAR Cafe, both located at the Governor's Crossing development in Sevierville, are the sites of this extremely popular event where NASCAR fans get a chance to meet their favorite drivers and see their favorite cars up close. The Sevierville edition of Race Night is one of four such events held annually in different cities throughout the region. Race Nights traditionally take place prior to the different NASCAR Winston Cup and Busch Series races held at Bristol Motor Speedway in Bristol, Tennessee, about 100 miles northeast of here. The Family Race Night in Sevierville takes place prior to the Food City 250 and the Goody's Headache Powders 500 races.

Beginning at 3 PM on this one-day event in late August, fans can meet, greet and get autographs from a who's who of NASCAR Winston Cup and Busch Series drivers. In 1999, the first year the event was held in Sevierville, Rusty Wallace, Kyle Petty and Jimmy Spencer were among the NASCAR drivers making appearances. In addition, cars driven by Ricky Rudd, Rusty Wallace and others were on display.

Visitors at American Eagle Weekend get acquainted with our national symbol.

Photo: Courtesy Pigeon Forge Department of Tourism

Besides the cars and drivers, those turning out for this NASCAR feeding frenzy can climb behind the wheel of a driving simulator, take part in an actual pit stop exercise, dig into free food and enjoy live entertainment going on throughout the event, including a special show at Governor's Palace Theatre. The festivities close with the Rock 'N' Roll Racin' Concert at NASCAR Cafe beginning at 8:30 PM.

Advance tickets to Food City's Family Race Night can be purchased for $4 each at any area Food City supermarket location, the Governor's Palace Theatre box office or any Sevierville welcome center. Tickets cost $5 on the day of the event, and children younger than 12 are admitted free. Proceeds from the event benefit the United Way of Sevier County.

September

Sevier County Fair
Sevier County Fairgrounds,
754 Old Knoxville Hwy., Sevierville
• (865) 453-0770, (865) 908-4103

There's nothing like a good old-fashioned country fair. This week of food, rides, games and exhibits gets started each Labor Day and continues through Saturday night. The fairgrounds, which flank the Little Pigeon River in Sevierville, are the site for the festivities, which include midway rides and games, home-baked pies and preserves and exhibits of prize winning livestock, fruits and vegetables.

Several events are annual favorites, like the tractor pull and the watermelon seed spitting contest. Another highlight of the week is the beauty competition in which young ladies from across the county vie for the title of Fairest of the Fair and the right to wear the crown. Admission to the Sevier County Fair is $3 for adults, and children ages 12 and younger get in free. Daily hours are from 5 to 10 PM.

Smoky Mountain Harvest Festival
Sevierville, Gatlinburg, Pigeon Forge

This is a relatively new countywide festival that more or less evolved from events already taking place among the three main cities. While late September and October have traditionally

---

INSIDERS' TIP

How many individual lights shine in Sevier County during Winterfest? Would you believe there are nearly 10 million lights in city-operated displays alone? Area departments of tourism estimate the following totals by city: Sevierville — more than 500,000; Pigeon Forge—4 million; Dollywood—2.25 million; Gatlinburg—2.5 million. And these figures don't even take into account lights that are displayed by businesses and residences.

---

been a period of heavy tourism (primarily because of the turning of the leaves in the mountains), local governments found that most activity was taking place on weekends, and they wanted to find a way to increase mid-week visitation. Thus, Harvest Festival was created as a sort of umbrella under which existing special events could be gathered. The festival has also spawned new events in keeping with the theme.

Smoky Mountain Harvest Festival begins in mid-September and runs into early November. During this period, you'll see a number of craft fairs and music festivals throughout the county. The centerpiece that ties all the cities together during Harvest Festival is the countywide decorating contest in which area businesses, governments and civic organizations adorn their buildings and grounds with traditional harvest decorations like hay, pumpkins, corn stalks and gourds. Awards are given to winners in a number of different categories.

All of the events included in this chapter for the remainder of September and October are considered to be official Harvest Festival Events by their respective host cities.

Bite of Sevier County
Boys & Girls Club Of The Smoky Mountains, 209 McMahan Ave., Sevierville
• (865) 908-4103

Sample the best cuisine of local eateries at this event that takes place toward the end of the month. Participating restaurants in years past have included Damon's Ribs and The Park Grill. Because of limited seating, tickets must be purchased in advance at a cost of $20. All proceeds benefit the Boys & Girls Club of the Smoky Mountains. There is also a charity auction benefiting Sevierville Primary School. For tickets, contact the Sevierville Chamber of Commerce Office of Special Events at the number above.

"I Love Sevierville" Luncheon
Sevier County Courthouse, Court Ave., Sevierville • (865) 908-4103

On the Friday following Bite of Sevier

Craft fairs are a staple of Smoky Mountain special events.

Photo: Courtesy Pigeon Forge Department of Tourism

County (see the above listing), everyone is invited downtown to find a comfortable spot on the east grounds of Sevier County Courthouse for this casual lunch gathering. A box lunch can be purchased for $6, and while you're eating, you can enjoy live music performances from the courthouse veranda.

Old Fashioned Hayrides
Downtown Gatlinburg • (865) 436-2392

From late September through October, you can climb on board a hay-filled flatbed and take an old fashioned ride through the streets of Gatlinburg. The departure point is the Riverwalk loading zone on River Road. The rides run Sunday through Thursday from 6 PM to 10 PM, and the cost is only $2 per ride.

A Taste of Autumn
**Gatlinburg Convention Center,
234 Airport Rd., Gatlinburg
• (865) 436-2392**

Late in the month, you can get your fill of great food prepared by local eateries. At this one-day event, you can sample items from the menus of participating restaurants beginning at 5:30 PM for a cost of $20. Tickets can be purchased in advance from Gatlinburg City Hall or either Gatlinburg welcome center. Along with the food tasting, the event features a char-

ity auction benefiting United Way of Sevier County.

October

Dollywood's Harvest Celebration
**Dollywood Entertainment Park,
1020 Dollywood Ln., Pigeon Forge
• (865) 428-9488, (800) 365-5996**

Colorful autumn decorations abound throughout the park during Dollywood's Harvest Celebration, combining music, crafts, fall food and fun throughout the month of October. Featured is the Smokies' only outdoor crafts festival with scores of visiting crafts people from across the nation, showcasing and demonstrating their talents. Also, witness the country's largest Southern Gospel music event, the Southern Gospel Jubilee.

One-day tickets to Dollywood range from $20.99 plus tax for ages 4 through 11 to $29.99 plus tax for ages 12 and older. Park hours during Harvest Celebration are 10 AM to 6 PM daily and 9 AM to 7 PM on Saturday; Dollywood is closed on Thursdays in October. See our Dollywood chapter for a complete profile, including more detailed admission and schedule information.

Fall is a busy time in the smokies.

Photo: Courtesy Sevierville Chamber of Commerce

Rotary Club Crafts Festival
Patriot Park, Old Mill Ave., Pigeon Forge
• **(865) 429-7350**

For more than two decades, this arts and crafts event in Pigeon Forge has featured dozens of local crafters as well as those from the Midwest and Southeast, displaying such skills as glass blowing, wood carving and basket making. The festival takes place under a 200-foot tent at Patriot Park, and runs for most of the month. Admission is free, but donations made throughout the festival benefit the many community projects sponsored by the Pigeon Forge Rotary Club throughout the year. Daily hours are 10 AM to 6 PM.

Grand Tennessee Craft Fair
Grand Resort Hotel and Convention Center, 3171 Parkway, Pigeon Forge
• **(865) 453-1000**

The crafts continue in Pigeon Forge during Harvest Festival with this fair that runs through most of October. On display are traditional and contemporary fine arts and crafts, live craft demonstrations and colorful fall decor. With more than a decade of shows in its wake, the Grand Tennessee Craft Fair has grown into one of the largest such shows in the region. Admission to the fair is $2.50, 50 cents of which goes to Ronald McDonald House. Show hours are 9 AM to 6 PM every day. There are outdoor exhibit spaces as well, but the hours there are restricted to 9 AM to 6 PM on Fridays, Saturdays and Sundays only.

Gatlinburg Craftsmen's Fair
Gatlinburg Convention Center, 234 Airport Rd., Gatlinburg
• **(865) 436-7479**

For nearly three full weeks beginning in early October, the Gatlinburg Convention Center hosts tens of thousands of people who come to see live craft demonstrations by artisans from all over the country. See the listing for the summer fair in late July for information on what can be found at both Gatlinburg Craftsmen's Fairs. Admission to the October fair is $4 for adults and free for children ages 12 and younger.

Pig Roast
St. Joseph the Carpenter Episcopal Church, 345 Hardin Ln., Sevierville
• **(865) 453-0943**

Everyone's invited to this annual one-day barbecue bonanza in the middle of the month. From noon until 6 PM, enjoy live music, kids' activities and games, a craft bazaar, silent auc-

tion and a whole lot of great barbecue. The $6 admission covers the cost of the meal, although there is also a child's hot dog plate available for $3. It's a great way to spend a Saturday afternoon and get to know some really nice people.

November

Great Smoky Mountain One-Act PlayFest
Sevierville Civic Center, 200 Gary Wade Blvd., Sevierville
• **(865) 453-5441**

In early to mid-November each year, Sevier County Theatre Guild showcases three new short plays by East Tennessee writers. The plays are chosen by a panel of judges and presented back-to-back during each performance. The festival is not only a good forum for aspiring playwrights but also for local actors and novice directors. The plays run for two consecutive weekends. Show times are 7:30 PM for the Friday and Saturday shows and 2:00 PM for the Sunday matinees. The door admission is $7.

This festival is the only annual event in the region that consistently introduces new plays by area authors. Works produced in previous years have gone on to be published, and the event was nominated for Best Special Work by the Knoxville Area Theatre Coalition for two consecutive years before winning the award in 1998. See our Arts chapter to learn more about Sevier County Theatre Guild.

Winterfest
Sevierville, Pigeon Forge and Gatlinburg

Originally developed as a means of drawing more tourists to the Smokies during the winter, this nearly four-month-long festival has taken its place as the "Big Kahuna" of annual area festivals. Beginning on a Wednesday in mid-November, the county's three main cities each host their own respective kickoff celebrations to launch an entire season's worth of music, parades, decorations, shopping bargains, and millions of holiday lights.

In Sevierville, you can enjoy live music performances, a lighting festival and decorations from 5 to 7 PM at the Community Center on Gary Wade Boulevard. Pigeon Forge's kickoff ceremonies take place at Patriot Park from 5:30 to 8 PM and include the turning on of the city's light displays, a street dance, live entertainment, food vendors and free trolley tours. In Gatlinburg, the kickoff takes place at Ripley's Aquarium of the Smokies. There, you can taste

The lights of Winterfest draw visitors to Pigeon Forge.

Photo: Courtesy Pigeon Forge Department of Tourism

the different entries in the chili cookoff and watch city officials "flip the switch" on millions of spectacular lights. Also on hand are live musicians, clowns and magicians.

Most of the events we have listed for the months of November and December are part of the official Winterfest celebration. For more, refer back to the January and February sections of this chapter.

Dollywood's Smoky Mountain Christmas
Dollywood Entertainment Park, 1020 Dollywood Ln., Pigeon Forge • (865) 428-9488, (800) 365-5996

Dolly's theme park is once again the setting for a large-scale seasonal celebration, beginning just after Winterfest kick-off and running through the end of the year. During this time, Dollywood takes on a whole new character. The first thing you notice is all the lights—2.25 million to be more precise—arranged on buildings, trees, shrubberies and attractions.

As during the rest of its season, music is a staple of Dollywood's Christmasfest. Besides its usual stock of holiday-oriented shows-productions such as Hometown Holidays, Christmas in the Smokies and O Holy Night, the park also stages special musical events. In 1999, for example, the world-famous Vienna Boys' Choir performed at Dollywood's Celebrity Theatre in its first East Tennessee appearance.

Although many of Dollywood's regular-season attractions are closed for winter (water rides don't sound so fun in 40-degree temperatures, do they?), others appear only for the holiday season. Kids will love Peppermint Valley, a Christmas village filled with rides that also serves as home to Santa Claus, Mrs. Claus and merry elves. Plus, all ages will love Carol of the Trees, an impressive new synchronized lighting and music display. And if you still want your thrill rides, you won't be disappointed on that score. The park's new Tennessee Tornado roller coaster keeps zipping along right through the end of the year, adding new meaning to the term "chills and thrills." On top

INSIDERS' TIP

Major special events in Gatlinburg, such as the Fourth of July Midnight Parade or the Christmas Parade can have equally major effects on traffic. It's not unusual to see traffic into the north end of the city backed up for miles on U.S. 441 (The Spur). Entering Gatlinburg via U.S. 321 may be a quicker alternative during these celebrations.

Intricate designs mark the lights of holiday season.

Photo: Courtesy Pigeon Forge Department of Tourism

of all the lights, shows and attractions, Smoky Mountain Christmas still offers plenty of shopping opportunities and holiday foods as well (see our Dollywood chapter).

Dollywood is open Thursday through Sunday only from mid-November until mid-December (except for Thanksgiving day). The park is then open daily until the end of the year, except for Christmas Eve and Christmas day. Call first to verify specific operating hours. Admission to Dollywood's Christmasfest is $21.99 for adults and $9.99 for children ages 4 through 11. Children 3 and younger get in free. Prices do not include sales tax.

Winterfest Trolley Tours
Pigeon Forge • (865) 453-6444, (865) 429-7350

Starting on the Friday after Winterfest gets underway, you can see the lights of Pigeon Forge without the hassle of the driving. Tours run through February, and are offered to all who want to enjoy the city's three million lights. Heated busses and informed hosts will guide you through the history of the displays. The cost of each trolley ride is $3 per person. The tours run Monday, Wednesday and Friday evenings until New Year's Day and then Monday and Friday only through February. Tours depart the trolley office at 6:30 PM. For more specifics about the Pigeon Forge trolley system, see Getting Here, Getting Around.

Smoky Mountain Lights Trolley Tours
Gatlinburg • (865) 436-2392

From mid-November until the end of January, these sightseeing trolleys offer spectacular views of Gatlinburg's Smoky Mountain Lights displays. Tours depart from downtown and cost $4 per person. In November and December, they run Sunday through Saturday at 6:30

and 8 PM. In January, they run Saturday only at 6:30 and 8 PM. However, since tours don't run on Thanksgiving, Christmas and a few other selected days, the city advises calling to verify specific times and dates. See our Getting Here, Getting Around chapter for more information about Gatlinburg trolleys.

Tellabration
Holiday Inn, 3230 Parkway, Pigeon Forge
• (865) 428-2700

On a Saturday in mid- to late November, some of the country's top storytellers take part in this international event along with those in more than 370 other locations worldwide. The show starts at 7:30 PM and features are all kinds of tales and folklore. The $5 admission price benefits the Smoky Mountains Storytellers Association.

Community Chorus Holiday Concert
Smoky Mountain Jubilee,
2115 Parkway, Pigeon Forge
• (865) 428-1836, (865) 429-7350

Join the Pigeon Forge Community Chorus for this annual concert on a Sunday in the middle to latter part of the month. Singers use their voices to help usher in the holidays with a program of Christmas music and other seasonal favorites. The event starts at 2 PM and is free of charge, although guests are asked to make a charitable donation of a non-perishable food item.

Great Smoky Arts and Crafts Show
Gatlinburg Convention Center,
234 Airport Rd., Gatlinburg
• (865) 436-2392

For more than a week surrounding Thanksgiving, this crafts event features the work of artisans from Gatlinburg's Great Smoky Arts and Crafts Community. It's a great way to get a start on holiday shopping. The doors open at 10 AM daily, and closing times vary, depending on the day of the week. Admission is free. See the write-up in the April section of this chapter for more details on what's to be found at all three of the Arts and

Crafts Community's annual shows. Also see the listing below for scheduling information on their Christmas show.

December

Great Smoky Arts and Crafts Show
Gatlinburg Convention Center,
234 Airport Rd., Gatlinburg
• (865) 436-2392

This is the final crafts event of the year for the Great Smoky Arts and Crafts Community. The show gets underway early in the month and runs for approximately 10 days. The doors usually open around 10 AM, and closing times vary, depending on the day of the week. Admission to the show is free. See the write-ups in the April and November sections of this chapter to learn about the Easter and Thanksgiving Great Smoky Arts and Crafts Shows.

Gatlinburg's Fantasy of Lights
Christmas Parade
Downtown Gatlinburg • (865) 436-2392

Lighted floats, marching bands and giant helium balloons trek along the Parkway, basked in the glow of the city's numerous Smoky Mountain Lights displays. The parade, which is usually televised regionally on WBIR Channel 10, takes place the first Friday of the month and starts rolling at 7:30 PM.

Christmas Parade of Toys
Downtown Sevierville • (865) 908-4103

For more than 35 years, this Christmas parade has made its way along the Parkway and surrounding streets located in and around downtown Sevierville. You'll see marching bands, twirlers, decorative floats and, of course, ol' Saint Nick himself. Parade spectators are invited to bring new, unwrapped toys that are taken up by Santa and his helpers as they make their way along the parade route. The procession begins at 4 PM.

Classic "Sleighrides"
Downtown Gatlinburg •
(865) 436-2392

Throughout most of the month, you can experi-

INSIDERS' TIP

The term "Smoky Mountain Lights" refers only to the light displays put up by the city of Gatlinburg during Winterfest. The more general term "Winterfest Lights" is used in reference to displays erected by all cities countywide during that period. This is merely a matter of semantics, but frequently a source of confusion, nevertheless.

ence the next best thing to an old-fashioned sleigh ride on this flatbed truck decorated to look like the real thing. These excursions are similar to the city's Old-Fashioned Hayrides held in September and October. The trips begin at the River Terrace Resort loading zone on River Road and take guests on scenic tours through downtown Gatlinburg. Rides depart every 30 minutes, and the cost is $2 per person.

Live Nativity
**Evergreen Presbyterian Church,
661 Parkway, Sevierville • (865) 428-3001**
This depiction of the events surrounding the birth of Christ has become one of the most unique and moving holiday events to be found in the area. Taking place over a three-day, mid-month weekend, the large-scale, outdoor exhibit depicts seven different live scenes, beginning with Mary being told by an angel that she will give birth, and ending with the mother and Christ child in a peaceful manger scene.

What gives the Live Nativity its authenticity is the fact that real people, along with authentic sets and costumes, are used to tell the story of Jesus' birth. Visitors view these reverent tableaus by walking along a lighted trail that leads from one scene to the next. All the while, spiritual songs of the season fill the air, and if you're lucky, the weather will be cooperative and provide a brilliant star-filled sky. At the end, hot chocolate and cookies await. There is no charge to view the nativity, which is open from 7 to 9 PM on each of the three nights.

Living Christmas Tree
**Gatlinburg Convention Center,
234 Airport Rd., Gatlinburg
• (865) 436-4990**
The Gatlinburg Community Chorale closes out the year with this mid-month performance event. The chorale's members are positioned in a large, vertical Christmas tree. Appropriately colored costumes, bows and garland complete the effect. The music presented is an all-encompassing selection of Christmas music, ranging from spiritual classics like "Joy to the World" to more contemporary holiday favorites like "Winter Wonderland." Admission to the concert is free, and show times are Thursday, Saturday and Monday at 8 PM.

Children's Hayride With Santa And Downtown Open House
**Sevierville Community Center,
200 Gary R. Wade Blvd., Sevierville
• (865) 908-4103**
Let the kids hitch a ride with Saint Nick on a horse-drawn hay wagon while you enjoy live music and refreshments at the Community Center. Or, you may be interested in hopping on board for the trip that travels the length of Bruce Street and tours the downtown area before returning to the loading zone. The hayrides are free and last for about 20 minutes, running continuously between 7 and 9 PM. This event lasts for one evening only, and takes place on a Thursday in the middle of the month.

INSIDERS' TIP

Pigeon Forge has won a number of awards for its festivals and events. While Winterfest is a countywide celebration, the Southeast Tourism Society has twice named Pigeon Forge's celebration of Winterfest as "Festival of the Year." The society also has cited Wilderness Wildlife Week, a Winterfest event held in Pigeon Forge each year, as one of the top 20 events for the month of January in the Southeast.

Shopping

Suffice it to say that this is an immense chapter—but it's not nearly as big as it could have been. Our aim is to introduce you to the kaleidoscope of shopping opportunities available in the Smokies. It would take a much larger space than we've allocated to just list all the businesses in the corridor (do you really *need* to know the details of more than a hundred T-shirt shops, and maybe double that number selling genuine "Made in Wherever" souvenirs?), so we're going to stick to the businesses that survived several cuts. We will break the shops and malls into workable categories by city, so you can narrow your search for specific items down a bit. Because of the rich heritage they represent and their importance to the region, mountain crafts are given their own chapter in this book. Likewise, the factory outlet stores that have helped make the Smokies an even more popular shopping destination earn their own chapter. And we encourage you to look through our chapter on Annual Events, as a number of these offer distinct Smokies items to the discerning shopper.

All of the shops, malls, and galleries listed in this chapter are interspersed with the attractions, restaurants, motels and outlet malls throughout the Smokies corridor. Understanding that they're here because they feel there's a buck or two to be made by accommodating the visitor population, it's logical to conclude that these businesses will operate primarily on the same schedule as their commercial neighbors. From Easter through Thanksgiving weekend, the vast majority of businesses that made the cut in this chapter will be open every single day from about 9 AM to at least 9 PM (any many are open later).

Since the term "off season" is rapidly becoming an anachronism in the Smokies, you can expect enough shops to be open year-round that you can shop any time you're here, although a lot of businesses are closed after 6 PM from January through March. The only day when a majority of businesses are closed is Christmas, and even then you can find open stores in most shopping malls. Note that our area includes a number of the popular chain department and discount stores, including a Kmart, a Big Lots and a Wal-Mart Supercenter at which you could do almost all of your day-to-day shopping. Since we assume most of you have been in a Wal-Mart, we haven't written these places up, choosing instead to devote our limited space to the unique shopping opportunities found here.

LOOK FOR:
* **Shopping Malls**
* **Bookstores**
* **Clothing**
* **Antiques and Collectibles**

Once again, we work from north to south, traveling from Exit 407 on I-40 to the national park entrance at the south end of Gatlinburg. We'll close with a separate section on shopping for food, for those of you relocating to the area, or if you're staying in a condo or cabin and need to stock the kitchen for the week.

So, knowing full well you're going to drop several times, let's go shopping.

INSIDERS' TIP

Several of the merchants' associations in the Smokies publish coupon books that provide discounts and premiums. Check the local welcome centers, lodging places, and brochure racks everywhere for some hidden bonuses.

Sevierville

Shopping Malls and Villages

Maplewood Country Stores
2510 Winfield Dunn Pkwy., Kodak
• **(865) 932-7637**

If you're beginning your venture into the Smokies corridor at Exit 407 of I-40, it won't be long until you reach this unique collective of shops in the Riverbluff Landing development next to Lee Greenwood's music theater. A visit to Maplewood Country Stores is a trip down Memory Lane—the relics and memorabilia placed throughout this indoor shopping village are reminiscent of simpler times. You'll be intrigued by the 19th century post office setup, the street clock and the many authentic vehicles from yesteryear, such as a 1930s delivery truck, a Conestoga wagon and an old horse-drawn taxi.

The individual shops found within also play into the intended nostalgia theme. At the Farmer's Market, you can buy fresh produce actually grown on the Maplewood property. They have a generous stock of pantry items as well that will make cooking and eating a pleasure.

The Country Peddler and Country Elegance shops are both fashioned after old-time general stores and sport a wide selection of gift and collectible merchandise, from the everyday to the exquisite. At Country Elegance Quilts (a separate store from the Country Elegance gift shop), you can choose from a large selection of hand made quilts in a variety of styles and colors. Kady's Korner Ladies' Boutique houses stylish accessories for women, as well as Belle Pointe Sweaters and several lines of crystal.

If you're in the mood for Santas and sleighs, visit Tennessee Christmas, a year round shopping extravaganza where the season of magic can be experienced among countless varieties of Yuletide ornaments and other decorations. The kids will especially enjoy the working model train that snakes its way through the store and continues its journey on an elevated track outside the building.

You surely won't go hungry at Maplewood Country Stores. There's an on-site bakery that makes fresh breads and pastries each morning. For meals, you can order from the full menu, which features a selection of steaks, chops and omelettes made to order. For dessert, they have hand-dipped ice cream and fresh baked goods like pies, cookies and brownies. For even more

sugary goodies, visit Hanna's Sweet Tooth, which bakes homemade fudge daily and carries different varieties of hard candies. Tucked away in one corner of Hanna's is their Kid's Korner, stocked with all kinds of toys and games.

The showpiece of Maplewood Country Stores is McIntosh Mill, an authentic grist mill that was operational over 100 years ago. The mill was disassembled at its original site in West Virginia, moved to the Smokies and put back together by a restoration team. Today, the refurbished mill works once again with most of its original parts. With the help of an on-staff miller, McIntosh Mill grinds locally grown corn into a variety of products, including meals, flours and even popping corn. In fact, many products from the grist mill are used in the Maplewood bakery to make delicious cornbread and other baked goods.

Art lovers might be interested in visiting the mill building's main floor, which is now used as gallery space for the noted area wildlife photographer, Ken Jenkins.

Bookstores

The Master's Touch
147 Forks of the River Pkwy., Sevierville
• **(865) 428-0231**

In addition to shelves full of Christian-oriented reading, this bookstore carries many different versions and translations of the Holy Bible. You'll also find other merchandise like music CDs and cassettes, video tapes, gifts, greeting cards, jewelry and T-shirts. One corner of the store is devoted to children, complete with all kinds of books, games and activities.

Books-A-Million
190 Collier Ln., Sevierville
• **(865) 908-8994**

At the end of Governor's Crossing outlet mall closest to the Parkway, Books-A-Million is probably the largest bookstore in the Smokies. More than 10,000 square feet of space are filled by books, from best-sellers to a variety of volumes on just about any subject you'd want to name. There's a whole wall of magazines and out-of-town newspapers, and a childrens' section (Kids-A-Million) as big as a lot of entire stores. Subjects are well-laid out and clearly labeled (the Travel section contains a great selection of Insiders' Guides). There's a good-sized display of Hallmark greeting cards, and another section contains a lot of local literature and photography. If you want to take a long look at something, you're welcome to take it into the Joe Muggs Coffee Shop in the corner and browse before buying.

Bible Factory Outlet
1645 Parkway, Sevierville
• (865) 774-9005

Located in Tanger Five Oaks mall, the Bible Factory Outlet features a selection of books that deal with most aspects of everyday life (fiction, lifestyles, philosophy, and religion) from a Christian perspective. Greeting cards, calendars, and toys along the same lines are available, along with audio and video tapes. This company has another store in Belz Factory Outlet World in Pigeon Forge.

Clothing

Goody's Family Clothing
1408 Parkway, Sevierville
• (865) 453-0552

This chain of stores started out in Knoxville and has developed over the years into one of the region's best sources for name-brand clothing for men, women and children. Everything from casual sports wear to suits and dresses can be found on the racks at Goody's. The clothing tends to be of a more conservative nature, but it is of good quality and still offers a broad range of style.

The men's half of the store has clothing for adults and a boy's department for the "younger men." The women's half of the store is subdivided into ladies, misses, junior and girls departments. There are also sections for plus sizes and petites. The ladies' shoe department carries brand names like Brook Hollow, Adidas, Keds and Amanda Scott. Both sides have denim sections that feature a tremendous selection of Lee and Levi's jeans and shorts. Teens may be glad to know that Goody's isn't just for their parents. The store does a pretty good job of keeping up with the latest in adolescent fashion trends.

Antiques and Collectibles

(Note: See the Close-up in this chapter for a detailed rundown of antique opportunities in Sevierville.)

S & G Comics & Collectibles
464 Forks of the River Pkwy., Sevierville
• (865) 908-8346

Kids and adults alike will have no trouble losing themselves in any number of fantasy worlds after stepping inside this place. Comic books, both new and used, are the staple product, but sports card collectors will find a fair amount of merchandise as well. Many of S & G'S display cases are filled with baseball, football and basketball cards ranging from the common to the rare and valuable. Sports collectors will also take interest in the poseable action figures and other athletic memorabilia for sale, some of which is autographed.

Sci-fi collectors will want to check out all the different Star Trek and Star Wars collectibles, including trading cards, figures and models. Many of the shop's collectible figures are current hot items from the worlds of film, television and music.

"Surely," you're thinking, "that must be all." Wrong, laser breath! S & G Comics & Collectibles has books, figurines, dice, cards and other supplies for all kinds of role playing games like Dungeons and Dragons. It's time to beam down!

Miscellaneous

Smoky Mountain Knife Works
2320 Winfield Dunn Pkwy., Sevierville
• (865) 453-5871, (800) 251-9306

It bills itself as "The World's Largest Knife Showplace." Once you've strolled through its three levels and 40,000 square feet of sales and display floor space, you probably won't dispute the claim. On the main level, you'll find display case after display case filled with just about anything that cuts—pocket knives, hunting and fishing knives and hatchets. Look for brand names like Case, Buck, Gerber and Remington. Another area is devoted to out-of-the-ordinary weaponry like machetes, swords, Ninja gear, blow guns and even paintball equipment.

On the lower level you'll find sections containing kitchen cutlery, jewelry, toys, T-shirts, gift items and a knife sharpening service. There are also several displays that will make your visit even more visually interesting. Look for the life-size diorama scenes depicting an African watering hole, an Ameri-

INSIDERS' TIP
Blazing hot summer sun notwithstanding, Tennessee law requires that shirts and shoes be worn in all places where the public congregates.

Smoky Mountain Knife Works has over 40,000 square feet of sales and display area filled with knives, collectibles, kitchen cutlery and more. The whole family will enjoy Bubba Bear & the Backwoods Band!

Photo: Courtesy Smoky Mountain Knife Works

can Indian with his canoe and a Civil War soldier with cannon. The kids will be entertained by the Bubba Bear Band, a singing animatronic attraction.

The centerpiece of the lower level is the working grist mill apparatus. Complete with original gears and pulleys, this water-powered wheel works just like it did in the olden days.

The upper level is practically a museum, with many display cases filled with collections of rare and antique knives and related memorabilia. Many of the collections are arranged thematically, including those devoted to film and TV Westerns, weapons of Native American tribes, and Civil War weaponry (there are similar such displays on the main level near the front entrance as well). While most of these collections are for display purposes only, Smoky Mountain Knife Works does have other cases filled with antique and collectible knives that are for sale.

While you're upstairs, you'll also want to check out Trophy Mountain, a display that the store claims is the Smokies' largest indoor mountain and waterfall. Like other parts of the

store, Trophy Mountain is home to a veritable zoo made up of stuffed game and mounted game trophies. Before you leave Smoky Mountain Knife Works, be sure to visit the gift and collectibles area and the sweet shop. They also publish several catalogues annually through which you can place orders over the phone by calling the toll-free number.

Music Outlet
1050 Winfield Dunn Pkwy., Sevierville • (865) 453-1031

Yeah, we know. Everything in the Smokies claims to be an "outlet." But we think you'll find that this one's a little different, and if you're into music, this place is a must-see. Since the mid '70s, the Williams brothers have maintained a large and varied stock of quality, name-brand musical instruments in rather cramped quarters at their ramshackle store on the Parkway in Sevierville. The place was literally so crammed with merchandise and unopened boxes that you could scarcely manage to shimmy around sideways once you were inside!

Business as Unusual in Gatlinburg

If you spend enough time in Gatlinburg and dig in the right corners, you'll learn that a lot of the property in the downtown commercial district is owned by two families, the Ogles (surprise!) and the Reagans (surprise again). That situation probably won't change in the near future because the leaderships of the two families share a pretty hard-nosed attitude about selling land: Don't. What's different between the two families is how they came by their holdings, and how they manage them.

The Ogle family is large and robust, and given to long lives. They're also one of the oldest English-speaking families on the planet, with an unbroken line of succession that goes back 30 generations to 11th-century England, when people didn't have last names. The matriarch of the local Ogle clan is the estimable Hattie Maples Ogle McGiffin, born February 24, 1898, and still

active in family affairs. That's not a misprint: "Granny Hattie" is more than 100 years old. And as impressive as that fact is, throw this one on top of it: Of Hattie's many descendants (40-plus and counting) from her marriage to Charles Austin Ogle (1893-1945), only two have died—her eldest son, Charles Earl, 80, and daughter, Lib Whaley, 78, both of whom died in the last week of December, 1998. Most of the others are active in the family businesses in varying degrees.

Charlie Ogle died remarkably young considering his family's track record. Remembered fondly as "Uncle Charlie," he was one of the most beloved people in Gatlinburg's history. He inherited from his father the family grocery store started by his grandfather Noah (1833-1897), on the present site of the Mountain Mall, which is now managed by Charlie's grandson, Charles Earl Ogle, Jr., a stripling of less than 60 years. In the tradition of their forebears (William and Martha Jane Ogle, the original white settlers, had seven children who produced the astonishing total of 82(!) children among them), the Ogle family has kept the management of their empire in the family. Counting children and three generations of grandchildren, HMO, Inc., the Ogle's land management corporation, has more than 20 family members involved in various aspects of property management.

The property ownership philosophy is simple: A family as big as theirs needed

Hattie Ogle McGiffin, Born 1898. Still active in family arrairs.

Photo: Dick McHugh

a lot of land just to grow enough food to feed them. As their fields became more valuable for development than for agriculture, the Ogles either developed it themselves or leased it to developers. That's how Granny Hattie established herself as one of the finest business minds anywhere in the United States. Finding herself in possession of large tracts of downtown property, some of which she had inherited from her own Maples family, Hattie made or influenced every decision on how the land could best serve her growing family.

The result is an impressive array of family-operated and leased businesses in the downtown area that includes the outright ownership of three shopping malls, several motels, a couple of office/retail build-

(Continued on next page)

SHOPPING

ings, two downtown markets, and long-term land leases on the sites of several large motels. HMO is currently in the hands of the aforementioned Charles Earl Ogle, Jr., who still likes to go down to one of the markets at 5 AM to unload produce (once a grocer, always a grocer). With four generations currently involved in running the businesses estab-

Brownlee Reagan (left) and Charles Earl Ogle Jr.: Two industrious men who help keep Sevier County running.

Photo: Courtesy Dick McHugh

lished by Granny Hattie, and the acquisitive nature and inherent business acumen continuing in her great- and great-great-grandchildren, the Ogle family's benevolent stewardship of the Gatlinburg business community appears to be firmly settled in the right set of hands.

The Reagan story has the same result with a completely different approach. Brownlee Reagan was born in Gatlinburg on August 30, 1926. His great-great-grandfather, Daniel Wesley Reagan (1802-1892) a native of Sevier County before the establishment of White Oak Flats, married Nancy Ogle, one of the 14 children of Thomas, and one of the 82 grandchildren of Billy and Martha Jane Huskey Ogle. Daniel and Nancy Ogle Reagan were the great-grandparents of both of Brownlee's parents.

The Reagans are an industrious lot, known for their hard work and community service. Their land holdings were modest compared to those of the Ogles, but their needs were also not quite as great. Brownlee Reagan appeared to be headed down the family's established path as a police officer and eventually police chief, but he combined his public service with an unusual perception of Gatlinburg's future. He began accumulating land before the tourist boom of the '70s by buying whatever land he could afford that came on the market, and building motels. The current figure is "somewhere between 7 and 10" downtown motels, and an indeterminate number of lodging places in other parts of the nation. He also kept an eye open to the availability of other commercial properties, and in the process has acquired a couple of shopping malls, a restaurant or two, and the Fun Mountain amusement park (see our Kidstuff chapter). Not blessed with a large family, Brownlee Reagan has pretty much handled it all by himself, with some of the load being picked up by son John, who seems to be unfazed at the size of the company he's gradually learning to control.

The Ogle and Reagan families have controlled their holdings and their destinies by maintaining active interests in the community: Hattie Ogle McGiffin lends her name and considerable talents to a variety of civic and charitable causes. Both families are deeply involved in local politics—Charles Earl Ogle, Jr., and Brownlee Reagan have both served the city as commissioners, mayors, Chamber of Commerce presidents, and civic philanthropists.

In the cosmic scheme of things, Gatlinburg is still a young and growing city. Less than 200 years old, it has considerable growth potential in the undeveloped land to the east. When that potential is tapped, the local feeling that it's an Ogle/Reagan empire will probably dissipate. What won't go away for a while is the wondering what would happen if the control had stayed in these capable hands.

Early in 2000, however, they opened a brand-new, 20,000-square-foot complex on Tenn. 66. The brothers have plenty of room to spread out now, but have still made sure that their new store has an even greater quantity and selection of musical merchandise.

Guitarists will find acoustic and electric models by Gibson, Fender and Taylor. Banjos made by Stelling, Deering and Gibson are there too. They can even get top-of-the-line classical guitars and special limited edition acoustic models. Other stringed instruments for sale include dulcimers and violins (or "fiddles," depending on your style of music). There are Yamaha and Slingerland drums and keyboards by Yamaha as well. They have amplifiers by Peavey and sound equipment by Electro Voice. And these guys know what they're talking about when it comes to sound; they've personally installed the sound systems into several of the Smokies' music theaters.

Besides instruments, you'll find drum sticks, picks, strings and other accessories. They have books, sheet music and instructional audio and video tapes. Speaking of instruction, they offer music lessons on how to play the different stringed instruments that they carry; or, they can help you find a good teacher for the other instruments. If your instrument needs a little work, they have a qualified, experienced repairman who will get it back into shape. And if you're interested in hooking up with other area players, you can scan the musician's billboard, which is plastered with notices, flyers and business cards. For the budding virtuoso, Music Outlet has school band instruments for sale.

Wynn's Sports World
540 Winfield Dunn Pkwy., Sevierville
• (865) 453-4877

Welcome to Sevier County's own wide world of sports-and more. With a total of 35,000 square feet of floor space, Wynn's is ably equipped to meet almost any imaginable sporting and gaming need. For general sports like football, baseball and soccer, they carry name brands in balls, related equipment and clothing, including cleats and other athletic footwear.

Large sections of the store are devoted to hunting and fishing gear, including guns, fishing rods and tackle and a huge selection of camouflage clothing. Hikers and campers will also find wide selections in hiking shoes, tents, sleeping bags, backpacks and the like. Golfers—welcome to paradise! Roughly one-fourth of Wynn's store space is devoted to a separate golf shop, full of everything from balls and clubs to shoes and bags. Wynn's diverse inventory includes general sportswear for men, women and children, a full line of boots and shoes and even Boy Scout supplies.

Everything Natural
209 Forks of the River Pkwy., Sevierville
• (865) 453-6112

Although there are quite a few health food stores to be found in Sevier County, this Sevierville store has been around just about longer than any, since 1985, and has an experienced, knowledgeable staff on hand to help you with your shopping.

Naturally (no pun intended), they carry several lines of vitamin, mineral and herbal supplements. In the back room, they also have a selection of loosely ground herbs which can be purchased in non-pill form, helpful for use in food or drink preparation. You'll also find sections of the store devoted to homeopathy, aroma therapy and healthy pet food products.

Those who are into healthful cooking can pick from fresh, organically grown foods as well as prepackaged and frozen items. There is also a good selection of healthy snacks and hiking foods. Not just limited to food consumption, the store offers natural cosmetic items like shampoos and soaps, as well as informative books and magazines.

Pigeon Forge

Shopping Malls and Villages

Bell Tower Square
2470 Parkway, Pigeon Forge

Since 1986, this 30,000 square foot Bavarian-style shopping village has grown into one

INSIDERS' TIP
We can't stress this enough: The summer afternoons around here can get fiercely hot. Dress comfortably, rest frequently, and carry liquids with you. The number of heat exhaustion cases in the area on a daily basis is staggering, and there are just not enough emergency personnel to handle it.

SHOPPING

Lovers of country crafts won't be disappointed in the Smokies.

Photo: Courtesy Maplewood Country Stores

of the top 10 Christmas and collectible destinations in the United States. It's located on the west side of Parkway, just north of the Wears Valley Road intersection. The anchor of Bell Tower Square is Christmas Place, where the trees and stockings are never taken down. When you walk through the doors, you enter a year-round Christmas fantasyland filled with thousands of Yuletide decorations. While an all-Christmas store could easily be presented in a tacky or junky fashion, Christmas Place is first-class all the way.

Dozens of lighted and decorated tree displays fill the main showroom, along with plenty of figurines, decorations and gift items. In the North Pole Village area, you'll find a wide selection of artificial trees, ornaments and lights. Look for collectible names like Department 56, Heritage Village, Snow Village and more. Other areas of Christmas Place contain miniature village scenes, and they even have an in-house floral department. At the east end of the store, keep an eye out for the large stained glass window that looks down on a peaceful nativity scene.

Adjacent to Christmas Place is the Gift Gallery. From the outside, the store resembles the exterior of a giant cuckoo clock, complete with life-size, wooden Bavarian figures and a clock face. Inside is a diverse offering of gift items including candles, clocks and enchanting figurines. Also at Bell Tower Square you'll find the Collectible Gallery, featuring high-quality merchandise by respected names in the collectibles field. You'll see numerous displays containing Armani porcelain, Swarovski crystal, Fenton glass, Tom Clark Gnomes, Thomas Kinkade lithographs and plates from the Bradford Exchange.

Another shop that girls of all ages will enjoy is the Doll Shoppe. Inside, dolls and accessories by Madame Alexander, Lee Middleton, Ashton-Drake and more are waiting for both novice and experienced collector. Next on your visit to Bell Tower Square you might step into Second Nature, featuring collectibles, jewelry, clothing accessories and wall art, all centered around a "nature" theme.

If you've got kids with you, you will have no choice but to stop by Toys and Trains. They have all sorts of model train kits in addition to toys and games that will really help spark the imagination and creativity of your child (that's right, creativity—they don't sell video games). Bell Tower Square also provides a respite for the empty stomach. At Mrs. Claus' Candy Kitchen and Sweet Shop, you can order from a deli-style menu of hot and cold sandwiches, and for dessert, you can try their selection of fresh baked goods like fudges and brownies. Or, you can try a dish of one of their many flavors of ice cream.

Any visit to Bell Tower Square is enhanced by the Bavarian village setting in which the shops are set. The buildings themselves are of Old World architecture and are surrounded by cobbled brick walkways, wildflowers and greenery. If you wish, you can sit on one of the park benches or at the shaded tables to enjoy your lunch from Mrs. Claus' Candy Kitchen and Sweet Shop or just take a load off. In the center of the courtyard area you'll find a couple of points of interest—a large, screened bird cage is home to a parrot, and a large model train setup features cars winding their way through a village scene and running waterfall.

Pine Mountain Village
3152 Parkway, Pigeon Forge

You'll find this strip mall on the west side of the Parkway, just north of the Pine Mountain Road intersection. At Winner's Circle, NASCAR fans will find collectibles and sportswear galore, all with a stock car racing theme. Snuffy's Discount Tobacco has a full line of tobacco products, including cigars and different blends of pipe tobaccos. Good Shepherd Christian Bookstore carries Bibles, books, music and other Christian-based merchandise.

At The Dugout, sports fans will find trading cards and collectibles in their favorite sports. You can pamper your hands and nails at T Nails or shop for mother and baby at Maternity and More. At The Small's World, parents of younger children will find a nice selection of boys' and girls' clothing in addition to toys that can be collected or played with.

While it doesn't necessarily fall under our "shopping" umbrella, there is also a Mail Boxes, Etc. at Pine Mountain Village that would be handy for packaging and mailing home some of your Smoky Mountain loot. This might especially be useful for those who travel to the Smokies by plane or bus. Also at Pine Mountain Village there are places to eat including Papa John's Pizza, Sugar Shack and Peso Peso's Fine Mexican Food.

Old Mill Village

Occupying several blocks east of the Parkway (on or near Old Mill Avenue), this collective of more than 25 specialty shops includes gift stores, art galleries, craft studios and more. The neighborhood is generally clustered around the historic Old Mill, an active grist mill which was built in 1830 on the banks of the Little Pigeon River (see our Attractions chapter).

Old Mill Village doesn't occupy so large an area that you can't see it all on foot. Most of the shops offer free parking, and there's plenty of free parking at nearby Patriot Park. Or, you can take the trolley to the Pigeon Forge Fun Time Trolley office, which is smack in the middle of the village. From there, you can find most of what's available within a block or two. There are also public restrooms at the trolley station.

The atmosphere in Old Mill Village is laid-back and leisurely, and the shopkeepers are always happy to visit with you. The shops listed here are all members of the Old Mill Village Merchants Association. While these businesses represent the vast majority of shops found in the neighborhood, you'll find a few others as well that we haven't included here. Because of the many merchants located in Old Mill Village, we'll simply be listing them by name along with a brief elaboration on their merchandise where needed. In some cases (and we'll indicate so), you'll find individual write-ups on some of these shops in our Mountain Crafts chapter.

Starting with the Old Mill as a reference point, we'll take east you in a counterclockwise direction: The Old Mill Restaurant, Pigeon Forge Craft Center, The Pine Cone Gift Shoppe, American Collection (local handcrafts), Angels Among Us (angels and dolls), Miss Dee's Old Fashioned Photos, The Finishing Touch (unique ladies boutique) and Cornerstone Flowers & Gifts.

On the other side of Old Mill Avenue on the corner of Teaster Lane is Off The Beaten Path (local hand crafts). Traveling one block west on Old Mill Avenue to Butler Street will deliver you to Dixie Darlin (needle art and decorative painting) and Helix Pewter & Copper. Back on Old Mill Avenue are Woolgatherers Needlework (cross stitch and needlepoint supplies), By Design (personalized gifts and custom embroidery), Highlands British Shoppe (gifts from the British Isles), Pigeon Forge Pottery (see our Mountain Crafts chapter), and Waynehouse Artcrafts.

Along Old Mill Street you'll find The Twisted Vessel Gallery, Pigeon River String In-

SHOPPING

struments (see our Mountain Crafts chapter), Enchanted Forest (enchanting sounds, scents and mystical creatures), Smoky Mountain Cat House (everything for the cat lover), The Diamond House, Randall Ogle Gallery, Next Step Heaven Christian Bookstore, Barger's Glass Blowers Gift Shop, Amanda Jayne's (unique gifts and collectibles), Gourmet Coffee Shop, Something Special By Sue (folk art, crafts, clothing and more in a country flavor) and Jim Gray Gallery (see our Mountain Crafts chapter).

Log Cabin Shops
3509 Parkway, Pigeon Forge
• (865) 453-6485

Very similar in appearance to the "hodge-podge" collections of merchants that used to dot the landscape, Log Cabin Shops is a fluid mix of commercial and hand-crafted items in nine shops that offer current fad-type collectibles and made-to-order leather goods. Visiting craftspeople and musical groups keep the place interesting most of the time. Vending machines and an ice cream shop provide refreshments which can be enjoyed at picnic benches while enjoying another favorite pastime, people-watching.

Bookstores

Foozle's
2655 Teaster Ln., Pigeon Forge
• (865) 429-1682

At the extreme northwest corner of Belz Factory Outlet World, Foozle's is chock-full of discounted and reduced-price books in a bright, airy setting. The selection is excellent, and the prices on titles that may be a little out of date approach 80 percent off retail. Foozle's appears to be operated by a bunch of teachers; they lean very heavily on educational material, particularly for the beginning reader. They also encourage their customers to be especially nice to teachers, which can't be an all bad thought. The selection of humorous material is outstanding.

Bible Factory Outlet
2725 Teaster Ln.,
Pigeon Forge
• (865) 429-8170

This shop is almost identical to the one at Tanger Five Oaks mall described earlier, right down to the tile on the floor. It's near the eastern end of Annex #1 in Belz Factory Outlet World.

Book Warehouse
3127 Parkway, Pigeon Forge
• (865) 428-5708

Here, you'll find over 200,000 new books at discounted prices. While the deals are usually pretty good, we will tell you that the titles aren't necessarily hot off the presses. Nevertheless, depending on your needs, this is still a great place to go book shopping. There are fiction and nonfiction books in almost every genre, just as there are in other bookstores. Categories include *New York Times* best sellers and a large selection of inspirational books.

Besides books, you'll also find audio and video tapes, teachers' aids and materials as well as locally made crafts. Book Warehouse has two other Smoky Mountain locations: A smaller version in the Pigeon Forge Factory Outlet Mall across the Parkway, and Mountain Mall in Gatlinburg (see Gatlinburg section of this chapter).

Clothing

Stages West
2765 Parkway, Pigeon Forge
• (865) 453-8086

Saddle on up, pardners and head to Stages West, the Smokies' largest Western store, with over 100,000 items in stock at discount prices. There are over 5,000 pairs of boots in stock by manufacturers like Durango, Tony Lama and Acme-Dingo. For kids, there are more than 1,000 pairs of boots from which to choose. The selection of leather continues with handcrafted purses, wallets, belts and moccasins. If you like to do-si-do, you'll definitely want to visit Stages West; they specialize in Western wear and square dance apparel.

Lid'l Dolly's Children's Dresses
2828 Parkway, Pigeon Forge
• (865) 428-2365, (800) 468-2365

Whether the "dolly" in question happens to be a toy or your own child, you'll find beautiful ways to get her gussied up at this dress manufacturer and retailer. Colorful and frilly is the best way to describe these hand-crafted dresses made primarily for younger children. Made of a polyester-cotton blend, the dresses are machine washable and are appropriate for weddings, beauty pageants or any situation where the little lady needs to look her most adorable. Lid'l Dolly's Dresses has a limited selection of dress-up apparel for the young lad as well.

The shop got its start at Dollywood (naturally) and has since expanded to its present facility on the Parkway in Pigeon Forge. While most of the inventory is made up of dresses for "real" girls, there is a section of the store devoted to collectible dolls and doll dresses. You'll also find a large selection of quilts, and in the front section of the store you can browse through their displays of homemade fudge, jellies and preserves. Even if you're not in the area, you can still make purchases from Lid'l Dolly's Dresses by calling their toll free number. They'll send you current dress and price information, and you can place your order over the phone.

Circle E Factory Boot Outlet
2746 Parkway, Pigeon Forge
• (865) 453-1749

When Circle E opened its doors in the '60s, it was about the only building at the south end of Pigeon Forge. Now it's surrounded by motels and restaurants. Circle E is also reputed to be the first business in Pigeon Forge that used the word "outlet" in its title. Circle E features an impressive selection of boots from utility (Dan Post and Dingo) to full-dress (Tony Lama and Justin) at competitive prices, along with work shoes, Stetson hats, and one of the most complete lines of square dance apparel in the Southeast.

Antiques and Collectibles

China and Gift Mart
2680 Parkway, Pigeon Forge
• (865) 453-5679

More than 300 different patterns of china are available at discounts of up to 70 percent at this Pigeon Forge shop that's been in business since the mid-'80s. They stock over a dozen name brands, including Noritake, Royal Worcester, Wedgewood, Nikko, Lenox, Royal Doulton and Muirfield. The selection is all first quality, and includes complete place settings and accessories.

In addition to china, China and Gift Mart carries flatware by Oneida, Retroneu and Towle Silversmith as well as collectibles by Precious Mo-

ments, Cherished Teddies and Emmett Kelly, Jr. Another section of the store, called Christmas and Collectibles, offers 15,000 square feet of gorgeous Christmas decorations, fine collectibles, dolls and more.

The Barn Owl
3629 Parkway, Pigeon Forge
• (865) 428-0846

A collector's must-see, The Barn Owl carries Hallmark and Precious Moments items (some that go back a few years) and high-class figurines and sculpture. They also carry an excellent selection of expert level jigsaw puzzles from Milton Bradley, Springbok, and Ravensberger.

Miscellaneous

Cat's Compact Discs and Cassettes
1977 Parkway, Pigeon Forge
• (865) 429-4600

In 1998, this regional chain of music shops brought its wide selection and low prices to the Smokies. The store carries CDs (mostly) and cassettes in all genres of music, but most of the store's inventory is centered around rock/pop and country. For more eclectic tastes, however, there's also rap, reggae, jazz, classical, comedy and movie sound tracks.

Besides a generous inventory of new CDs, Cat's also has racks full of used compact discs at discounted prices in its Dog Pound. You can also trade in your own CDs for store credit. One neat, customer-friendly service that the store offers is access to the Cat's Listening Posts (instead of scratching posts-get it?). At three different stations, you can put on headphones and listen to selected new releases before you purchase a disc (and face it, we've all bought clunker albums based on one great song!).

Rocky Top Outfitters
2721 Parkway, Pigeon Forge
• (865) 429-3474

You'll not only find supplies for fishing and camping at Rocky Top, but you can receive instruction and guide services from this licensed outfitter. As for equipment, most of their

INSIDERS' TIP
We haven't mentioned tattooing and body-piercing parlors because the local business communities would rather such establishments weren't here. The city of Gatlinburg is trying to enact legislation strong enough to prohibit these businesses. Be all of that as it may, it's your right to know that there are three tattoo parlors in Sevierville and three on the Parkway in Gatlinburg between traffic lights #1 and #3.

SHOPPING

stock is for fishermen. They have fly rods, spin rods, reels and all kinds of flies, baits and lures. Look for rod and reel brand names like Redington, Shimano and Hoffman. They also carry a large selection of Ultimate Poppers and single-hook rooster tail spinners. Although the emphasis is on fishing gear, there is limited selection of camping equipment as well.

Rocky Top Outfitters brings more than 17 years of guiding experience to its customers, having conducted trips on 11 lakes and on more than 3,000 miles of rivers and streams. They do lead some hunting trips, but most of their guide business is fishing related. They conduct about 200 guided trips annually.

In addition to guiding, the Rocky Top staff offers fly fishing instruction, handmade jigs and flies and award-winning taxidermy services.

Smoky Mountain Candy Makers
2880 Parkway, Pigeon Forge
• (865) 453-9213

There weren't too many businesses on the Parkway in Pigeon Forge 25 years ago, but this candy shop was one of them. Since 1973, this family-owned confectioner has been turning out delectable treats like taffy, fudge, candy apples, suckers and hand-dipped chocolate and nut clusters. About 90 percent of the goodies in stock are made on the premises. In fact, if you visit at the right time, you'll be able to see the staff of candy makers turning out their products before your eyes. If you're lucky, you might even get to see the taffy machines pull, roll and wrap!

Pigeon Forge Toy and Hobby Shop
2884 Parkway, Pigeon Forge
• (865) 428-0918

If you're looking for a child's toy that offers more than the mindless distraction of a video game, then you've come to the right place. For 15 years, owner C.P. Brackett has offered a unique line of toys, games and hobby supplies for children of all ages, many of which are educational and inspiring to the imagination. Among the shop's wide assortment of goodies are dress-up costumes, stuffed animals, challenging games and puzzles and Playmobil play sets for younger children. There are also plenty of supplies and materials on hand for doll houses, model railroaders, builders of plastic models and collectors of die-cast figures and military miniatures.

The shop is also the site of Adventures in Toyland, a doll and toy museum featuring more than 5,000 items. Most of what you'll see are dolls, including Barbies, Star Trek figures, Campbell's Soup kids and a whole lot more. Some of the dolls date back to the 1700s. There are also board games and other toys from years past in the museum's display cases. While there is no charge to browse the toy shop, there is a nominal fee to tour the museum.

Lace Outlet
579 Dollywood Ln., Pigeon Forge
• (865) 428-6705

This is one of those places where you really don't know what to expect, and you're usually right. The Lace Outlet holds an amazing collection of miscellany for such a small building. Besides the advertised selection of ribbon, bolt lace, bolt fabric, and quilting supplies, which is outstanding, the Lace Outlet carries one of the biggest collections of hokey souvenirs in the area. It's an interesting gamut, going from fine handmade quilts to outrageous oversized (like tent-size) panties with messages in varying degrees of taste.

Gatlinburg

When you go shopping in Gatlinburg you're in one of the most retail-intensive areas in the eastern United States. Gatlinburg has crammed 14 shopping malls and more than 100 free-standing retail shops of dizzying variety into less than a half-mile of non-stop browsing space, and that only tells about half the story. You can walk the full length of the Parkway from traffic light #3 to #10 in about 15 minutes—if you're wearing blinders. A knowledgeable shopper will take an evening (anywhere from three to six hours) to do one side, and save the other side for another time.

A popular alternative is to use the half-and-half approach. Starting at about the Village shopping plaza

There's something for every sweet tooth in the Smoky Mountain shopping experience.

Photo: Courtesy Sevierville Chamber of Commerce

(Reagan Terrace is also a popular starting point), walk east (toward the Ferris wheel at Fun Mountain); stay on the Parkway by crossing Highway 321 at traffic light #3, and browse the shops at Carousel Mall and along the Parkway to the Atrium restaurant. At this point, cross the Parkway (use the crosswalk—you have the right-of-way, but be careful) and walk back to the Mountain Mall; if you still have time and strength on your side, go on to Baskins Square or Market Place. For the second half, head west (toward the park entrance) to traffic light #8 (the Space Needle). Cross the Parkway and return to the previous finishing point. Each of these routes will use up a few hours without losing sight of the start/finish point.

There are additional shops and malls at both ends of this route, but they're more spread out. The best way to get to them is to drive to a parking lot near the end and work the same way as before: Hit one side of the street, cross, and return on the other. It's just not feasible to list every shop in town, but we'll give an overview of all the malls and shopping villages on the Parkway, and some detail on a representative sampling of the more established businesses. We'll also give some space to those shops that struck us as more interesting or fun than the norm. Remember, we always go from north to south, running in the same order as the traffic lights. Wear comfortable shoes.

Shopping Malls and Villages

Carousel Mall
458 Parkway, Gatlinburg • (865) 436-7625

Standing at the intersection of the Parkway and East Parkway, Carousel Mall is built into a hillside so steep that ground level on the East Parkway is three stories above ground level on the Parkway, less than 100 feet away. Either way you enter, short stairways and a central elevator take you through several levels devoted mostly to art and collectible galleries. Local artist Jim Gray has a ground-floor (Parkway side) gallery here (see our Mountain Crafts chapter for more information), and the Neumann Gallery on the top level specializes in Civil War art and artifacts. The Rampant Lion offers gifts with a southwestern flavor, and Earth's Treasures features unusual geodes and sculptures of stone and metal.

Riverbend Mall
511 Parkway, Gatlinburg • (865) 436-3063

Two levels of convenient shopping include

fine giftware at Barbara's Elegants, a long-time Gatlinburg mainstay, along with Miss Kitty's old-time photos, camping and fishing supplies at Old Smoky Outfitters, and Thomas Kinkade artworks at Things Unique. Novelty machines line one wall of the ground floor for the amusement of family members who'd prefer not to shop.

Mountain Mall
611 Parkway, Gatlinburg • (865) 436-5935

The largest retail concentration in town, Mountain Mall is a six-level structure containing 40 shops of various description. The split-level design makes stair-climbing more negotiable, and the elevator stops at all levels. There's also an interesting little escalator that only goes up. From fast-food at three different locations to top-of the-line collectibles and the world's hottest sauces, the Mountain Mall is worth an extended stay indoors. A three-story wooden fountain at the west end sends water plummeting through a fascinating series of weight-activated ducts. Among the original tenants when the Mall opened in 1978 are Wicked Wanda's, Gatlinburg's longest-operating T-shirt shop; The Rhythm Section, the city's first record business; The Gatlinburlier, the only shop in town that's dedicated entirely to the smoker; and Aunt Mahalia's Candy, the first local sweet shop to open a satellite location. The newer shops include the Tennessee Teddy Bear Factory described in our "Kidstuff" chapter, and the Book Warehouse, covered in its specific section of this chapter.

Baskins Square Mall
631 Parkway, Gatlinburg • (865) 430-2104

Running away from the Parkway toward River Road, Baskins Square has eight shops and three restaurants stuffed into a deceptively small area surrounding a brick courtyard. The Mountain Woodcarvers is a local mainstay of more than 20 years, as are Duffy's Tavern and the Funnel Cake Shop. The Terri Waters Gallery is covered in the craft section of this chapter. Cory's Dolls has a variety of collectible merchandise. The Little Sparrow shop and the White Wolf Gallery specialize in Native American products.

The Village—A Shopping Place
634 Parkway, Gatlinburg • (865) 436-3995

In the heart of downtown Gatlinburg, a group of shops is truly a slice of the Old World. The Village, which has pedestrian entrances on the Parkway and Baskins Creek Road, is a collective of 27 shops and eateries that offer something a little beyond the everyday.

Apples To The Core

What do Adam and Eve, Johnny Appleseed, Sir Isaac Newton and William Tell all have in common? Well, each might have at least had a passing interest in spending a day at Applewood Farms in Sevierville.

If you're a lover of apples, you will truly be in your element. If you don't particularly care for apples, you'll probably enjoy yourself anyway. And like most interesting places in the Smokies, you can easily spend a lot of time there and wonder where the day went.

The place is easy to find, about a half-mile off the Parkway at the Sevierville-Pigeon Forge border on Apple Valley Road. The complex, which is open year-round, is nestled along the banks of the Little Pigeon River. The hillside apple orchards and whitewashed buildings are the giveaway that you've reached your destination.

The complex is made up of different shops and eateries all set against the backdrop of a working apple farm. You can stroll the property and see where 14 different varieties of apples are harvested from more than 4,000 trees. (By the way, want to know why the trunks of the apple trees are painted white? The paint reflects heat during the spring and fall to keep the trunks cooler. It also has a repellent to discourage nibbling by rabbits and field mice.)

What happens to all those apples once they're harvested is where your options begin at Applewood Farms. The Apple Barn General Store was one of the first commercial ventures to appear on the property, in 1981. It was constructed inside the old barn that had stood on the property when the current owners purchased the farm in 1977. The General Store was first created as a place to market the apples from the orchard.

The General Store still carries bushel baskets full of fresh apples to be sure, but

(Continued on next page)

The Apple Barn General Store in Sevierville.

Photo: Mitch Moore

SHOPPING

also much, much more. You can buy apple butter and apple jellies made next door in the Apple Butter Kitchen. Other sections of the store display cheeses, smoked hams, bacon, dried fruits and popcorns. There are areas featuring gift items and an upstairs craft and basket loft.

Around the same time the General Store opened, the owners also cranked up the Cider Mill, so customers could see the apples being processed into apple cider. Nowadays, you can still see the mill at work, and in the Cider Bar, visitors can purchase fresh apple cider along with fried pies made in the neighboring Apple Pie Kitchen. (Another tidbit: Apple cider is a perishable product that will ferment if not refrigerated. Apple juice, on the other hand, is pasteurized and can be stored at room temperature.)

Since the early 1980s, the Applewood Farms complex has been fruitful and multiplied. At The Candy Apple and Chocolate Factory, you can watch workers make candied and caramel apples as well as homemade fudge, taffy, stick candy and lots more. Experienced candy makers use all natural ingredients in their old fashioned recipes. If you visit The Creamery next door, you'll find home made ice cream sundaes, sodas and shakes and even fresh baked apple breads (you were expecting bananas?).

Wine connoisseurs will definitely want to stop by the Apple Barn Winery. Since it opened in 1995, many of the winery's labels have won numerous awards at national and international wine competitions. You can stop by the winery's tasting bar and sample from their menu of 10 different wines, most of which are made from apples. Their most popular vintage is the Apple Blush, a semi-sweet wine made from an apple-grape blend.

There are two different dining establishments found at Applewood Farms. The first, the Applewood Farmhouse Restaurant was converted from the actual farmhouse that had originally stood on the farm since 1921. Just a few years ago, the Applewood Farmhouse Grill opened for business. We go into more depth on both of those places in our Restaurants chapter.

The Village's true charm, however, lies in its architecture and surroundings. Its idyllic backdrop includes rock gardens, wildflowers, water fountains and interesting relics like a British phone booth. Local wildlife are no strangers to The Village—squirrels, hummingbirds and even the occasional bear have been known to pay visits to the court yards.

The shops themselves generally convey an Old World look through an eclectic mix of architectural styles and designs, with moss and vine thriving on their facades. A great many of the furnishings and fixtures that go into the makeup of each shop are either unusual, antique, rare or some combination of the three. For example, the front porch of one particular shop was obtained from the old parsonage of Knoxville's Second Baptist Church.

Other shops use pieces like beveled glass, wormy chestnut wood and antique staircases to flesh out the Old World effect. Even the archway that forms the main entrance to The Village is historically significant. The bricks are believed to have been made by area slaves around 1843. Supposedly, they were used to construct the first brick building in Sevier County around that same time.

The 27 tenants occupying The Village offer shoppers merchandise ranging from unique and hard-to-find gifts to fine art to gourmet coffees and desserts. We've listed all of them below, along with brief parenthetical descriptions for those whose names aren't necessarily self-explanatory.

The Golf Gallery, Scandinavia Shop, Southern Crafts Shop, The Taylor Girls (ladies' boutique), The Silver Tree (for the silver lover), Desserts & More Cafe, The Christmas Tree, Sweethearts Ice Cream Parlor & Eatery, Turn of the Century Portraits & Weddings/Chapel in the Village (photography and wedding chapel), Candle Cottage, Alice Moore Gallery, Cartoons & Toys, Coffee & Company, Hofbrauhaus Restaurant & Cheese Cupboard, The Donut Friar, The Jelly Jar (jellies, jams, preserves, etc.), Whiff -N-Pouff (ladies' fashions and accessories), Garden Gate (wind socks, bird feeders, chimes, etc.), The Hayloft (fine leathers and western wear), The Art of Glynda Turley & More, Another Me Clothier (missy and plus fashions), Holidays (merchandise for your favorite holiday), Hills Creek Collection (Mark Hopkins bronze works), Thomas Kinkade At The Village (the art of Thomas Kinkade), Alpine Shop & More (traditional European merchandise), God's Corner (Christian music, books, Bibles, etc.) and Celtic Heritage (Scotch-Irish merchandise).

The Market Place
651 Parkway, Gatlinburg • (865) 436-3251

Built in 1980, the Market Place features imposing Georgian-style architecture and beautiful landscaping, with a waterfall and fountain at the River Road end. A full line of Christmas merchandise is available year-round at Lindz's, and the Civil War memorabilia at Armour House is impressive. The Candle Carvers and Good News (wood) Carvers are usually demonstrating their crafts. Fast food is available at the Yogurt Shop.

Riverside Mini-Mall
715 Parkway, Gatlinburg • (865) 436-4460

It doesn't look like an honest-to-goodness shopping mall, but the 14 Riverside shops and booths stretched along the Parkway in front of the Riverside Motor Lodge comprise the oldest collection of retail shops under one roof in the downtown area. Rustic Redwood Signs has been at the same location since 1971, and the Silver Express opened in 1975. The Funnel Cake booth, opened in 1987, is a relative newcomer to this interesting array of merchants.

Reagan Terrace Mall
716 Parkway, Gatlinburg • (865) 436-7781

Built around a courtyard on the Parkway, Reagan Terrace's 12 shops include Barbara's Elegants, an upscale gift shop with other locations in town; Southern Touch Crafters, an eclectic collection of handcrafts and custom embroidery; Fantasy Fotos Emporium; a NASCAR theme shop; and several food shops. Reagan Terrace sits in front of the Gatlinburg Fun Center, described in our Attractions chapter.

Downtown Traders
805 Parkway, Gatlinburg
• (865) 436-4692

This one is different in that it's entirely below the sidewalk. A pretty little brick walk leads to a courtyard with a rock garden grotto that's a nice photo opportunity. The Buckboard is the anchor shop here, taking up about half of

the mall with its collection of Tom Clark gnomes, local crafts and Western-themed goods. Cactus Jack's restaurant features a marvelous choice of sandwiches. Smoky Mountain Collectibles has a broad line of NASCAR merchandise, and Lynn Anderson's Sweet Hut offers sugary sustenance.

Elks Plaza
968 Parkway, Gatlinburg • (865) 436-7550

As you might guess from the name, this is the home of Gatlinburg's BPOE Lodge 1925, which takes up the second story. Included in the mall below are The Best Italian Restaurant; the Hillbilly Gift Shop; Aromatherapy; and long-time merchants Carolyn's Crafts and The Paintin' Place. Carolyn's is one of the larger craft supply houses around, and the Mathis family has been hand-painting ceramic pieces at the Paintin' Place for two generations.

Tramway Mall
1001 Parkway, Gatlinburg
• (865) 436-5423

The jumping-off point for the aerial tramway to Ober Gatlinburg (see our Attractions chapter), the Tramway Mall has goodies at the Kandy Kitchen, gifts at the Silver Galleon and Shelley's Baskets (sometimes Shelley's out in front painting), and the Ober souvenir and clothing shop. If you're on your way up the mountain, film and camera supplies are available at the Camera Shop.

Calhoun's Village
1004 Parkway, Gatlinburg
• (865) 436-6004

A recent entry, Calhoun's Village is anchored by Smoky Mountain Brewery and Pizza, Gatlinburg's only mini-brewery. A small collection of shops and galleries ranges from fine art at PAWS (Porter Art Work Studio) and the Native American oriented Bampton-Greene Gallery to the fantasy world of electric trains at Whistle Stop Junction. Local crafts are featured at Appalachian Attitude, described in the Mountains Crafts chapter.

River Oaks Mall
825 River Road, Gatlinburg
• (865) 436-9551

River Oaks is primarily a "local service" location. It's notable for the fact that it contains the only downtown liquor store and walk-in medical clinic, along with a full-service florist. A large chalet rental office and a hair salon fill out the slate at River Oaks.

Sevierville's "Antique Alley"

It would practically require another entire book to give you a comprehensive list of what you can find in the antique and collectible stores along the first few miles of the Smokies corridor. If you like antique stores, collectible shops and flea markets, you might just have met your match. And if you really like these kinds of places, you may actually find yourself spending a day or more along just one stretch of highway—Tenn. 66 between I-40 and downtown Sevierville (Winfield Dunn Parkway).

What you'll see runs the gamut between the quintessential antique store, with its finer furnishings and pieces, to the contemporary flea market, where you'll find a mixed bag of collectibles and general merchandise. In between, there are many establishments that do business under the moniker "antique store," whose vendors deal in everything from true rarities to, well, junk. But in this game, one man's junk really is another man's treasure.

Just about every business leading into Sevierville that calls itself an antique store or flea market operates on a consignment basis. Stall or booth space is rented to vendors (for varying time periods), and when a sale is made, the store gets a certain percentage of the price (this also varies from store to store). Some of the larger "antique malls" have hundreds of vendors displaying their wares under one roof.

We'll take you on a brief journey down Tenn. 66, highlighting many of the antiques and collectible shops found along the way, but we'll also point out a few antique stores in downtown Sevierville that are also definitely worth browsing.

Along Tenn. 66, you'll find a couple of large flea markets—Great Smokies Craft Fair and Flea Market (actually just off Tenn. 66 on Dumplin Valley Road) and Flea Traders Paradise. While it may be possible to find some legitimate antiques at these places, much of what's for sale is newer merchandise, including collectibles, craft items, clothing and much more. Both markets boast sizable square footage and seemingly countless vendors.

A wide range of antiques and collectibles awaits the Smoky Mountain visitor.

Photo: Mitch Moore

Most of the establishments along Tenn. 66, however, are good places to find older items like collectible figurines and toys, old books, tools, antique glassware and housewares that are sure to induce nostalgia. You might stop at Action Antiques & Collectibles, which is housed in a large, weather-worn barn that oozes character. Some items here would be better off at someone's yard sale, but overall, this is an interesting layover. At Ole Smoky's Rivershack, you'll find a similar mix of goods as well as more contemporary collectibles and souvenirs.

If you're looking for smaller items or larger antique furnishings, consider stopping by The Tudor House or Heartland Antiques & Collectibles. Both carry an eclectic mix of goodies, but the latter has a slightly better selection of furniture pieces. One of the better shops found along Tenn. 66 is Memory Lane Antique mall, where there is a good balance between furniture and higher-quality antiquities.

If a large selection is a priority to you, try visiting Riverside Antique & Collectors Mall. This sprawling, two-level complex houses an impressive array of merchandise, old and new. You could spend hours at this one place alone.

If you're an aficionado of legitimate antiques, you need to visit downtown Sevierville where you'll find antique beds, tables, chairs, dressers and more at Wagon Wheel Antiques on Bruce Street. Just a couple of blocks away on Main Street, you'll discover Antique Outfitters, a shop with plenty of interesting furniture finds as well.

Bookstores

Beneath the Smoke
467 Parkway, Gatlinburg • (865) 436-3460

This shop is dedicated to Mother Nature in all her splendor, and could be included in any category in this chapter. We chose to list it as a bookstore because the variety of literature is so great. Art, sculpture, and camping products all exalt the great outdoors, and the selection of handbooks and guidebooks to the flora and fauna of the Southeast is outstanding. The variety of bird guides is the best we found in the area.

Book Warehouse
611 Parkway, Gatlinburg • (865) 430-5972

Constituting practically the entire "E" level of the Mountain Mall, this Book Warehouse location has 1,200 square feet of space laid out to accommodate a full spectrum of fiction and non-fiction, with an outstanding selection of local guide books for birdwatchers and hikers.

A Little Bit of Heaven
734 Parkway, Gatlinburg • 436-5433

Specializing in Christian publications and recordings, A Little Bit of Heaven is Gatlinburg's oldest bookstore. Small gifts and souvenirs with a Christian theme are complemented by an exceptional selection of religious and secular greeting cards for all occasions.

Clothing

The Hemp Store
411 Parkway, Gatlinburg • (865) 436-8300

Here's a kicky little shop featuring clothing and accessories from natural fibers. Tie-dyed clothing and new-age jewelry items are also available, along with a selection of in-your-face environmental bumper stickers, pins, and posters. And if you have any need for hemp rope, this is one of the few places where you'll find it sold in bulk.

Jonathan's
733 Parkway, Gatlinburg • (865) 436-7148

A downtown mainstay since the late '70s, Jonathan's features an extensive line of upscale name brand sportswear and accessories, and a broad line of camping supplies and literature. In the Gatlinburg tradition, Jonathan's clings to the belief that service and attention to detail are still important to its customers.

King's Designer Name Brand Outlet
978 Parkway, Gatlinburg • (865) 436-7805

One of the larger shops in the downtown area, King's offers designer labels at competitive prices. The spacious display area is arranged by clothing type to allow each family member to compare clothing by several designers without searching through a bunch of displays.

Antiques and Collectibles

Morton's Antiques & Baseball Cards
409 Parkway, Gatlinburg • (865) 436-5504

Doing business at the same location since 1949, Morton's is noted for its art glass and porcelain antiques, and for its spectacular line of Italian inlaid wood furniture. A small selection of very rare (and very pricey) baseball cards and old coins is available for serious collectors. At our last look, Morton's had vintage Babe Ruth, Honus Wagner, Willie Mays and Mickey Mantle trading cards, some of which bore five-digit price tags.

Something Special
525 Parkway, Gatlinburg • (865)

Enter an enchanted world of dragons, wizards, castles, and other mythical things in pewter and porcelain. Unusual hand-painted porcelain and metal thimbles make this shop a collector's paradise.

Gazebo Gifts
529 Parkway, Gatlinburg
• (865) 436-4064

Pre-dating the 1975 tourism boomlet, the Gazebo features specialty bottles and a gorgeous array of glass vases and bowls. Their collection of ANRI woodcarvings (Hummel-like carved wood figures) is one of the largest in the eastern United States. Your children are welcome, but hang on to them.

Miscellaneous

Victorian Reflections
454 Parkway, Gatlinburg • (865) 430-5057

This shop offers a *very* Victorian selection of hand-painted porcelain and glass merchandise, including Tiffany lamps and chandeliers. Special orders are available, and can usually be produced in a few days

Lloyd's of Gatlinburg
465 Parkway, Gatlinburg • (865) 436-7997

A popular gift shop since 1972, Lloyd's carries a mixed bag of big and little goods. Pine furniture and stained glass share space with an eclectic array of knick-knacks. Lloyd's selection

INSIDERS' TIP
It only shows if you're really looking for it, but the Parkway in Gatlinburg runs steadily uphill toward the national park entrance. Consider that when planning your assault on the downtown shopping district.

of small brass bells is one of the best around. The gallery of Southwestern furniture and sculpture adjoins the original shop. And don't worry about getting your big furniture items home—Lloyd's has its own delivery service.

Lorelei Candles
600 Parkway, Gatlinburg • (865) 436-7833

Probably the biggest supplier of novelty candles in the eastern United States, Lorelei Candles is a local company that will show up again in the Mountain Crafts chapter. The downtown store carries an exhaustive sampling of the more than 500 different novelty and art candles designed and manufactured at Lorelei's factory/showroom in the Great Smoky Arts and Crafts Community.

Clock Peddler of Gatlinburg
608 Parkway, Gatlinburg • (865) 436-5605

It's all about time at the Clock Peddler. If it tells time, they've got it or can get it. From bedside and kitchen novelty clocks to grandfather models with everything short of a symphony orchestra, and movements from wind-up and pull chain to the latest quartz model, the Clock Peddler has it all. And don't worry about getting your grandparent clock home in the family sedan—the Clock Peddler will arrange shipping for any large purchase.

The Lemon Tree
636 Parkway, Gatlinburg • (865) 436-4602

Another of the older downtown emporia, The Lemon Tree has offered a combination of local quilts and crafts and fine collectibles for more than 20 years. Their collection of lighthouse reproductions is outstanding, and the Precious Moments selection is big enough to include a lot of older and retired issues.

Ola Kate's Candy Kitchen
645 Parkway, Gatlinburg • (865) 436-3720

Homemade candy is one of the oldest businesses in Gatlinburg, and Ola Kate's is one of the oldest candy makers. For a take-home souvenir to give you a sweet memory of your trip, or something to munch while walking the Parkway, Ola Kate's candy is always fresh, because the small staff never seems to be able to get ahead of the demand.

The Karmelkorn Shop
647 Parkway, Gatlinburg
• (865) 436-4373

Rick Berrier is as established a Parkway fixture as the weekend traffic. He's been up to his elbows in the wonderful things he does with popcorn for as long as anyone can remember, and he still looks like a kid. Get to the Karmelkorn Shop early in your stay—Rick's deals on refillable boxes will keep your fingers sticky for your whole trip at remarkably low cost.

The Acorn Shop
648 Parkway, Gatlinburg
• (865) 436-5073

The original tenant in the Ogle Building since 1964, the Acorn Shop carries a line of quality souvenirs and the largest selection of knives in Gatlinburg. Every knife maker you can think of, and a few you'll discover, are represented in the Acorn's selections. The Acorn is also a favorite of local seamstresses and quilters looking for that special pair of scissors they can't function without.

Old Tyme Portraits by Treadway/ The Tobacco Emporium
702 Parkway, Gatlinburg
• (865) 436-0458

Gatlinburg's oldest "dress-up" photo shop has a new twist: In addition to the interesting and amusing get-ups that allow you to express your personality in graphic new ways, the Treadway brothers have added a tobacco products outlet where the prices for brand-name and generic products are well below the market. The upstairs cigar bar is a smoker's paradise.

Aunt Mahalia's Candies
708 Parkway/952 Parkway/Mountain Mall, Gatlinburg • (865) 436-7792

The first candy shop in town to open multiple locations, Aunt Mahalia's has been threatening the dental health of three generations of visitors to the Smokies. It's hard to imagine the Parkway without the distinctive red-and-white striped Aunt Mahalia's stores beckoning to your sweet tooth from just about anywhere on the Parkway.

Glassblowers of Gatlinburg
729 Parkway/Mountain Mall, Gatlinburg
• (865) 436-9114

Bob Myrick and his family started out in the early '70s with a small storefront operation on the present site of their three-story shop. With the addition of their Mountain Mall location in 1979 the Myricks solidified their reputation as one of Gatlinburg's leading merchant and philanthropic families. The Glassblower shops carry an impressive array of high-class glass and ceramic sculpture, and a huge selection of souvenir jewelry. Personalizing of glass items is available while you wait.

Magnet-O-World
738 Parkway, Gatlinburg
• (865) 430-9022

If it sticks to metal, it's here. More than 100,000 magnets are displayed in this fun-house that passes for a retail store. There's enough variety of amusing, amazing, and appealing magnetic note holders in this place to make you go home and buy a bigger refrigerator.

Ole Smoky Candy Kitchen
744 Parkway, Gatlinburg
• (865) 436-4886

Back when Gatlinburg was a lot smaller, the Candy Kitchen provided some of the most popular entertainment. Tourists came by the score to sit on the benches out front and watch the candy makers work their magic in the big picture window. Then they went inside and bought everything they saw being made, and usually more. The news is all good: Despite the fact that new forms of entertainment have thinned the crowd a bit, the benches are still there, and so are the candy makers in the window. Shops like this one are the reason Gatlinburg still enchants a large number of visitors looking for a simpler, gentler way of life.

One Hour Photo
754 Parkway, Gatlinburg
• (865) 436-7556

The typical visitor to the Smokies takes a lot of pictures. One Hour Photo gives that visitor a chance to see the pictures they took while there's still time to do it over if something went wrong. They'll also tell you what (if anything) went wrong, how to fix it, and where to go to find more photo opportunities. And they've got whatever supplies you need to insure that you get all the pictures you want to take.

Nature's Kingdom
916 Parkway, Gatlinburg
• (865) 436-5510

Wildlife forms are represented here in every fashion imaginable. Rugs, wall hangings, soft and cast toys, sculpture, and fine art all honor the beauty and dignity of wild animals in their natural habitats.

The Rock Shop
958 Parkway, Gatlinburg
• **(865) 436-5106**

Established in the '60s, the Rock Shop carries anything that started out as a piece of some kind of stone. Arrowheads, custom jewelry, sculpture, and geodes all have their place in this quiet haven devoted to the beauty that only Nature can provide.

The Gatlinburg Shop
963 Parkway, Gatlinburg
• **(865) 436-3454**

Local headquarters for Department 56 collectibles, the Gatlinburg Shop also carries a fabulous line of hand-painted blown glass Christmas ornaments from world-famous artists. The selection of lifelike cast resin animals is among the best around.

Shopping for Food

If you're vacationing in the Smokies, you'll probably do your fair share of eating out in restaurants. Bon appétit! However, for those who may be watching their pocketbooks a little more closely, those who are staying in a cabin or condo and need to stock the pantry for the week or for those who might be relocating to the area, we thought we'd point you in the direction of some area supermarkets.

All but one belong to regional or national chains, and in most cases, you'll find the usual variety of grocery departments (bakery, deli, etc.). In Sevierville, there is a Food Lion on Main Street, just one block west of the Parkway. On the Parkway itself, near downtown Sevierville, is a Kroger supermarket. As you continue on the Parkway toward Pigeon Forge, you'll come across a Food City and later, a Wal-Mart Supercenter that features a complete selection of groceries.

As much of Sevierville's residential growth has taken place on the east end of town, there has been a similarly growing demand for a major supermarket in that area. Traditionally, city residents have always had to drive into the thick of tourist traffic to shop for food. It has long been rumored that Food City will build a new store on Dolly Parton Parkway, and it is expected that construction will indeed begin within the next year or two.

In Pigeon Forge, there's a Kroger store, just off the Parkway on Wears Valley Road. Further along the Parkway, toward the southern end of the strip, there's another Food City. In Gatlinburg, the Village Market on the north Parkway just off the Spur, is the second biggest market in town. The only business in Gatlinburg large enough to legitimately call itself a supermarket is Battle's Food Center, located on East Parkway (U.S. 321), a little over two miles from downtown. Like Sevierville, Gatlinburg has a rumored Food City under construction on East Parkway. As a general rule, you should know that the closer you get to Gatlinburg, the higher supermarket prices tend to be.

INSIDERS' TIP
Don't ask us to explain it, but Gatlinburg has an ordinance that prohibits the wearing of masks or face coverings in the downtown shopping area. They make an exception for Halloween, but only for kids.

Outlet Shopping

Shopping has replaced crafts as the second biggest reason families come to the Smokies on vacation (Great Smoky Mountains National Park is still number one). Most of the reason for that fact is that a couple of Pigeon Forge entrepreneurs made a decision in 1983 that changed that city's fortunes dramatically and quite permanently.

When Pigeon Forge was awakening after the Knoxville World's Fair, somebody took notice of a new national shopping trend where clothing manufacturers were opening their own stores in malls commonly referred to as "factory outlets." Since Pigeon Forge was suddenly attracting scores of thousands of new people who weren't just passing through any more, why not see how this latest craze would fare? And so the Factory Merchants Mall (now the Pigeon Forge Factory Outlet Mall) was built at the northwest end of the Parkway, next to (then) the only music theater in town, which is now an independent outlet store. Now it's in the middle of town, and what was a strip mall with about 10 shops is actually two separate malls in a multi-level complex of several buildings with over 80 outlet shops and concessions.

The success of Pigeon Forge Factory Outlet and the adjoining Z Buda Outlet Mall was significant enough that ears pricked up all over the place, and suddenly Pigeon Forge was a mecca for bargain-minded shoppers everywhere east of the Mississippi. It's frankly kind of appalling for an old-timer here to find out how many of these people have never even heard of the Great Smoky Mountains National Park and have no intention of going there.

A word or two about outlet shopping: *Caveat Emptor* (Let the buyer beware). The idea of manufacturers franchising outlet stores to sell more merchandise is a good one, and a huge majority of the outlets in all of the malls have honest-to-goodness bargains available in every product line you can think of. Most of this merchandise is first-quality or clearly marked (particularly in the case of electronic devices and power tools) as "reconditioned," which usually means that the case is not in its first generation, but the components are new. Our experience while "shopping" most of the outlet stores indicates that it's a good idea to do a little homework before venturing onto the outlet scene. If you know what you're looking for, you should also have a pretty good idea of what you'd consider a bargain price. The good news is that the worst you'll do is pay retail for some things in stores that call themselves "outlets" but are not actually franchised by a company. To be sure you're getting the real thing, the best thing to do is restrict your shopping to names you know.

It appears that outlet malls are not a fad. The speed with which they've sprung up, and the names hanging out their shingles at the outlets, indicate that this is the coming thing in shopping. Pigeon Forge is at the forefront of the whole movement, with Sevierville coming up fast. To illustrate this point, Pigeon Forge's outlet malls were the city's

LOOK FOR:
- Sevierville
- Pigeon Forge
- Teaster Lane
- RiverView and RiverVista

leading revenue producer from 1997 through 1999; the total reported revenue from outlet shopping from those three years averaged nearly 30 percent of the city's total, and was almost twice the total of lodging revenues, the next highest source. With eight major outlet malls already operating, a ninth under construction in a choice Pigeon Forge location, and land available for as many more as want to come in, it looks like Sevierville and the Forge have struck another iron at just the right temperature. (Because of a lack of buildable land, Gatlinburg passed on this particular enterprise.)

Here's a list of the outlet malls currently operating in Sevierville and Pigeon Forge, along with their locations, and a rundown of each mall's shops. Store listings are arranged by category wherever possible. Significant characteristics are noted in the listings wherever clarity dictates, as well as brief descriptions where the names of shops are not widely known or don't obviously indicate the nature of the business. Just about every outlet mall has at least one bookstore; we'll name the bookstores in each mall in this section, and describe them in detail in their own section in the Shopping chapter. As usual, we'll move from north to south. To get all of the information available in one place, there's a separate section of outlet mall literature at the Pigeon Forge welcome center on the Parkway, just south of traffic light #2.

Sevierville

Governor's Crossing Outlet Center
212 Collier Dr., Sevierville
• **(865) 429-2320**

You'll be seeing this name a lot. Governor's Crossing is a full-fledged resort complex that opened in the spring of 1998 with plans for several restaurants, motels and theaters that'll all be covered in their own chapters. The 25 outlet shops at Governor's Crossing take up a small corner of the total development, which only proves how big the development is. The mall's posted business hours are from 9 AM to 9 PM Monday through Saturday, and 9 AM to 6 PM on Sunday, but some stores stay open later..

Governor's Crossing currently includes **Angel's Touch Dolls, Bon Worth** (clothing), **Books-A-Million, Bugle Boy, Capacity** (clothing), **Claire's Accessories, Cost Cutters** (gifts), **Country Clutter** (crafts & souvenirs), **Earth Bound Trading Company** (clothing), **GNC General Nutrition Center, Ham 'n Goodys** (delicatessen), **Hound Dogs** (clothing), **Linen Barn, Myrick's Jewelry, Oneida, Perfumania, Rocky Boot Outlet, Rue 21** (clothing), **Shoe Carnival, Speed Zone, The Sunglass Superstore, The Sweatshirt Co., Tools & More** and the **VF Factory Outlet** (clothing).

Tanger Five Oaks Mall
1645 Parkway, Sevierville
• **(865) 453-1053, (800) 408-8377**

The entrance to Five Oaks is on the Parkway about a half-mile south of Governor's Crossing. At he rate they're building, you'll soon be able to walk from one to the other in less time than it takes to drive. With nearly 90 shops

currently operating and more being built, Five Oaks is now the largest outlet mall in the area. How big is it? Well, it's big enough to have its own free trolley shuttling passengers around the acreage, and they're trying to figure out how to add to the 12 existing buildings without going underground.

Five Oaks is toward the upscale side, featuring labels associated with some of the more exclusive clothiers, and also has as strong a mix of merchandise as you'll find. The mall's posted business hours are seasonal. In January and February, the posted hours are 10 AM to 6 PM Sunday through Thursday, and 10 AM to 6 PM Friday and Saturday. The hours for the rest of the year are 9 AM to 9 PM Monday through Saturday, and 9 AM to 6 PM Sunday. Please note that these are minimum operating hours; businesses wishing to open earlier and close later are permitted to do so.

Clothes horses at Tanger can shop at **American Outpost, Anne Klein, Baby Guess/Guess Kids, Banana Republic, Big Dog Sportswear, Brooks Brothers, The Children's Place, DKNY, Duck Head, Elisabeth, GAP Outlet, Guess? Factory Store, Haggar Clothing Co., Johnston & Murphy, Kasper A.S.L., Koret, Liz Claiborne Outlet Store, Nautica, Peaches 'N Cream, Polo/Ralph Lauren Factory Store, Reebok Factory Direct, Rockport Factory Direct, Tommy Hilfiger, Westport Premier** and the **Woolrich Company Store**.

For shoes and hosiery, check out the **Dexter Shoe Factory Outlet, Johnston & Murphy, L'eggs Hanes Bali Playtex, Liz Shoes, Nine West, Olga Warner, Socks Galore & More, SAS Shoes** and **www.FOOTGEAR**.

The mall features home furnishings at

Croscill Home Fashions, Dan River Outlet, Lenox Factory Outlet, Reed & Barton, Stiffel Company Store and Villeroy & Boch. For housewares, stop by **Corning-Revere, Le Gourmet Chef** or **Sunbeam-Oster.**

Five Oaks features prepared foods as well, from stores like **Country Ritz, Fudgery, Harry & David, Mountain Edge Grill** and **Pepperidge Farms.** When you get tired of shopping and need some nourishment, you can stop at the **Chop House** or **Hickory Hams Cafe & Deli.**

Finally, the mall includes several specialty retailers, like the **Bible Factory Outlet, Cosmetics Company Store, Disney, Kirkland's, Lee Greenwood Ticket Outlet, Music for a Song, Paper Factory, Perfumania, Tool Warehouse, Totes** and **We're Entertainment.**

Pigeon Forge

As we continue into Pigeon Forge, we'll look first at a brand-new development on the Parkway, then at the two Parkway malls in the center of town, then double back to the Teaster Lane malls. The best way to get into the Pigeon Forge Factory Outlet and Z Buda malls is to turn right at the driveway at traffic light #4 and follow it to the upper level. If parking is available to your right at the top, take it—it's your best chance to see both malls without getting too far from your vehicle.

The Shops at Eagle's Nest
Parkway, Pigeon Forge

Ground for this new mall had just barely been broken when we went to press. The developer tells us this new entry in the outlet sweepstakes will include 50 to 60 shops, most of which are satellites or branches of shops already existing in the other area malls. We'll follow the progress of this development, scheduled to open in late spring or early summer, and include details in our next update.

Pigeon Forge Factory Outlet Mall
2850 Parkway, Pigeon Forge
• (865) 428-2828

The original outlet mall, located on the west side of the Parkway, identified by sloping orange metal roofs. It includes about 50 shops

in eight buildings on two levels. Most parking is on the upper level, with access and egress available on Florence Street at the back. The Factory Outlet Mall abuts on two sides with the Z Buda mall. Hours for both malls are seasonal: Off-season (January through mid-March) hours are 10 AM to 6 PM Sunday through Thursday, and 10 AM to 9 PM Friday and Saturday. In-season hours are 9 AM to 9 PM Monday through Saturday, and 10 AM to 7 PM Sunday. Individual store hours may vary, but all stores in Pigeon Forge Factory Outlet and Z Buda Outlet malls are expected to be open during posted hours.

For clothing stores, the Factory Outlet features **Arrow/Gold Toe, Bon Worth, Bugle Boy, Capacity, Carter's Childrenswear, Claire's, London Fog, Oshkosh B'Gosh, Rue 21, Shadowline** and **Van Heusen.**

Shoe and hoisery stores include a **Banister/Easy Spirit Shoe Outlet, Bass Factory Outlet, Boot Factory, Dexter Shoe Factory Outlet, General Shoe Warehouse, L'eggs/Hanes/Bali/Playtex** and **Rack Room Shoes.**

For housewares, check out the **Black & Decker Outlet, Chicago Cutlery, Corning/Revere, Fieldcrest Cannon, Kitchen Collection, Mikasa Factory Store, Oneida Factory Store, Pfaltzgraff Factory Store, Tools & More** and **Welcome Home** (home accessories and giftware).

You can eat or buy prepared foods at the **Great Southern Fudge Factory** and **Sporty's Deli.**

Finally, amongst its specialty shops, the Factory Outlet offers **Aunt Mary's Yarns, Bath & Body Boutique, Book Warehouse, Buxton** (leather), **Christmas & Afghans, Jewelry & Handbag, K-B Toy Outlet, Perfumania, Samsonite Company Store, Sunglass World, Tote's,** and **Wallet Works.**

Z Buda Mall

Directly behind and beside Pigeon Forge Factory Outlet (you'll think you're in the same mall), Z Buda shares the upper level parking lot. Built shortly after Pigeon Forge Factory Outlet, the Z Buda Mall has about 25 shops, half a dozen or so restaurant/fast food properties, and an arcade. Unlike most of the other outlet malls, Z Buda is not loaded with national brands. This mall is as close as you'll come to the "flea

Attractive landscaping makes outlet shopping a pleasant experience.

Photo: Courtesy Sevierville Chamber of Commerce

Cream Shop, Jewelry Sample Shop, Leather & More, Maggie's Deli, Moon Craft (women's clothing), **Mountain Man** (military surplus, camping gear), **Owens Leather, Peddler Gift Shop, Pen & Ink Calligraphy, Prestige Fragrance & Cosmetics, Redwood Signs & Airbrush, Robears Excellent Yogurt, Shades of Mexico** (house fixtures), **Silver & Shades** (jewelry & sunglasses), **Slots-O-Fun Speedway** (slot track auto racing), **Smoky Mountain Gold & Diamonds, Snack Shack, Sock World, Sunglass Shack, Team Sports** (licensed clothing), **Tees 'N Togs** (tee shirts) and **Yosemite's Sandwiches.**

The Teaster Lane Outlets

This is a concentration of outlet malls in a single area that's currently about 20 percent as long as the Parkway, with the potential to be longer and more densely developed. While the casual observer would probably guess the number of malls to be anywhere from three to seven, the actual number is four, with the biggest taking up space on both sides of Teaster Lane. Coming from the north, turn left at traffic light #2 (Teaster Lane) or #3 (East Wear's Valley Road). From the south, turn right at traffic light #5 (Jake Thomas Drive), then left at Teaster Lane.

Tanger Outlet Center
175 East Wear's Valley Rd., Pigeon Forge • (865) 428-7002, (800) 408-5775

This is a medium-sized strip mall, kitty-corner from Belz Mall. It offers about 30 shops (and growing) in a compact two-level setting with convenient parking. Posted hours are 10

market" (no offense intended) appearance of the very early outlet malls. It's a fun place to prowl because unexpected bargains pop up in the least likely places. Because of the unusual nature of this mall, we'll list all of the properties in a single list, with brief descriptions where the name of the business doesn't tell you what it sells.

At the Z Buda Mall, you'll find **Booneway Farms** (jellies), **Bumbershoot Books, Christmas & Dolls** (unusual glass Christmas ornaments & porcelain dolls), **Country Cabin Crafts** (mostly wood handcrafts), **Game Room** (arcade), **Gift Gallery** (jewelry & souvenirs), **Gordon Garments** (swimwear), **Handbag Heaven, Handbags & Belts, Ice**

AM to 6 PM Monday through Thursday, and 10 AM to 9 PM Friday and Saturday in January and February, and 9 AM to 9 PM Monday through Saturday, 10 AM to 7 PM Sunday, March through December.

The wide array of clothing stores at Tanger includes an **Anne Klein Factory Store, Eagle's Eye, Eagle's Eye Kids, Eddie Bauer Outlet Store, Gant, J. Crew, Jones New York, Liz Claiborne Outlet Store, London Fog, Oshkosh B'Gosh** and **Reebok Factory Direct.**

Shoes and hosiery can be found at **Easy Spirit, Florsheim** and **L'eggs/Hanes/Bali Express.** For housewares and home furnishings, check out **Far-berware Inc.** or the **Springmaid-Wamsutta Factory Store.** You can stop for a bite to eat at the **Deli Factory/ TCBY.** Specialty shops here include **American Outdoor Recreation** and **Jordana's.**

Belz Factory Outlet World
2655 Teaster Ln., Pigeon Forge
• (865) 453-3503, (865) 453-7316

Boasting the biggest parking lot of the bunch, the Belz mall consists of two large malls, a free-standing anchor outlet on the east side of Teaster Lane (building #1 is the only truly enclosed mall in the area), and a strip annex with its own parking lot on the west side. The current numbers are about 65 shops in the west side malls and another 15 in the strip annex. One of the kiosks in the closed mall (Building #1) is the only known place where you can buy discounted tickets to most of the music theaters in Pigeon Forge. On days when the parking lots aren't jammed, the usual practice is to drive from the main mall to the strip annex—it saves a lot of walking.

Quickest access to Belz from the Parkway is to turn at East Wear's Valley Road (traffic light #3, directly across from Wears Valley Road) and go up to the traffic light at Teaster Lane. If you're coming from Sevierville, turn left on Teaster Lane (traffic light #2) and follow it around. Mall hours during January and February are 10 AM to 6 PM Sunday through Thursday and 10 AM to 9 PM Friday and Saturday. For the balance of the year, the mall hours are 9 AM to 9 PM Monday through Saturday and 9 AM to 7 PM on Sunday. Old Time Pottery, the 90,000

square foot specialty store that anchors the main structure, observes the latter hours year-round.

Building #1 boasts a number of clothing stores, including **American Outpost, Bass Company Store, Bon Worth, Burlington Brands, Capers, Casual Male Big & Tall, Dress Barn, Full Size Fashions, Geoffrey Beene, Izod, Jaymar/Sansabelt, Jockey Factory Store, Koret, Maidenform, Petite Sophisticates, SBX, The Sweatshirt Company** and **Van Heusen.**

The rundown of shoe stores is no less impressive—**Bass Company Store, Converse, Famous Footwear, General Shoe Warehouse, Hush Puppies Factory Direct, Naturalizer, Sock World #1** and **Vans Shoes.** Housewares are covered at **Famous Brands House-wares Outlet** and **Royal Doulton.**

There's as much food to choose from at Belz as at any mall in the area: **Chick'n Lick'n Broasted Chicken, Geno's Italian Eatery, Great American Cookie Company, New Deli, Pigeon Forge Fudge Company, Scoops, Smoky Mountain Express** (soups, sandwiches, etc.), **Smoky Mountain Fruit & Nut, Subway, Sweet Shoppe** and **TCBY Yogurt.**

For specialty shops, Building #1 offers **American Tourister** (luggage and accessories), **Camp Coleman** (camping supplies), **Diamond & Eelskin Factory Outlet, Discount Show Tickets, Foozle's Books, Fossil, Fuller Brush Factory Outlet, Jewelry Outlet, Leather Loft, Mad Hatter, Music 4 Less, The Paper Factory, Perfumania, Prestige Fragrance & cosmetics, Sunglass Hut, Toy Liquidators** and **Vitamin World.**

For clothing at Building #2, check out the **Bugle Boy Outlet Store, Capacity, Duck Head** or **Levi's Outlet by Design.** Shoes are available at **The Boot Factory,** and the **WestPoint Pepperell Mill Store** offers fine housewares. Building #2's specialty shops include the **Bible Factory Outlet** and **Old Time Pottery** (general merchandise).

There's more of everything in Annex Two (across Teaster Lane), including clothing at **Alan Stuart Menswear, Big Dogs Sportswear, Casual Corner, Members Only, $9.99 Stockroom, Westport, Ltd.** and **Westport Woman.** Annex Two shoe options are **Banister/Easy Spirit Shoe Studio, Bike Ath-**

OUTLET SHOPPING

INSIDERS' TIP

Most of the Pigeon Forge outlet malls are served by the Pigeon Forge trolley system. This is a convenient way to see the outlets, but could be a problem if you have to ride the trolley back to your lodging place with a good-size load of packages.

letic, **Etienne Aigner, Nike Factory Outlet** and **Rack Room Shoes.** For specialty shops and accessories, Annex Two offers **Booneway Farms, Caribbean Traders, Fragrance Outlet** and **Jewelry & Leather Outlet.**

RiverView and RiverVista

The newest entries for now, RiverView and RiverVista are adjacent strip malls in distinctive pink brick buildings that appear to be extensions of the Belz annex on Teaster Lane. They are locally owned, and expansion plans exist in a form still not solid enough that the developers will make any firm statements beyond the fact that there's a half-mile of empty land between RiverVista and the next road, and they own or have options on all of it. RiverView and RiverVista are operated by one management company and keep the same hours as Belz Factory Outlet World, which has them surrounded on two sides; the Little Pigeon River is at their back. Since neither mall has more than 12 stores, we'll list them in alphabetical order without classification.

RiverView Factory Stores
2684 Teaster Ln., Pigeon Forge
• **(865) 429-2781**
Shopping options at RiverView include **Deep Discount Art & Framing, Home &**

Garden Factory Outlets (gardening tools & supplies), **Hoover Company** (housewares), **Jewelry & Handbags, Parton's Candle Works, Quilts International, Riverview Grill, Sunglass Superstore, Tool Factory Outlet, Unique Peddler** (gifts & souvenirs) and **Warehouse Golf.**

RiverVista Factory Stores
RiverVista offers another handful of stores, including Angel's Dolls, Toys, & Gifts, Brass Crafters, Corning/Revere, Dalton Rugs, The Pro Shoppe (golf equipment), The RCA Store (electronics) and Smoky Mountain Gourmet.

You could cram several days absolutely full of mall-crawling and see nowhere near half of the outlet stores in the Smokies corridor, and it'd probably take another two or three days to recover. The seasoned outlet shopper who is determined to see *all* of the shops in *all* of the malls will probably require some form of residence in the Smokies area. Outlet malls are apparently here to stay, and the jump-start Pigeon Forge got 10 years ago appears to have positioned the Smokies area at the forefront of the industry. For as long as this particular type of shopping remains popular, look for this area to maintain and probably increase its international leadership in the field.

Mountain Crafts

Before the outlet malls, water slides, amusement parks, and myriad other attractions brought tourists to this valley, even before the Great Smoky Mountains National Park was anything more than a gleam in the eye of a group of conservationists around the region, Gatlinburg was nationally known for the variety and enduring quality of the handcrafted merchandise being produced in practically every home and marketed nationally by the Pi Beta Phi women's fraternity. The term "Gatlinburg" is used advisedly here—it was the center of the industry, which flourished in the mountainous areas where farming wasn't practical, and craftspeople from Pigeon Forge and eastern areas of the county brought their crafts into Gatlinburg to sell.

This chapter is dedicated to the small number of native and immigrant craftspeople who are trying to keep the heritage of handcraft alive in the Smokies. It will also expose one of the area's best-kept secrets, one that has been known to extend some trips to the Smokies for a few days. To keep things on a fairly level plane here, a few ground rules will have to be observed: First, the term "handcraft" is narrowly defined. To qualify, any goods offered for sale must be produced either by guiding material through a stationary tool (like cutting on a band saw or weaving on a loom), or by guiding the hands or a hand-held tool over moving or stationary material (like throwing on a potter's wheel or whittling a piece of wood). Additionally, the artisan must begin working with unfinished raw material, like wooden or composition boards, bolt cloth, hides, or tubes of paint.

The development of the handcraft industry was the result of a great deal of bush-beating by the Pi Beta Phi teachers when they arrived in 1912. They provided a market for the local artisans without requiring the locals to do anything more than they'd been doing all along, and everybody was happy with the arrangement. The trailblazers who subsequently opened businesses to increase their merchandising possibilities gave the large cottage industry a more localized group of outlets without significantly reducing Pi Phi's slice of the pie. The local businesses gave the home-based craftspeople a chance to produce more merchandise without really straining themselves, and encouraged the idea of crafts as a family trade. The craftspeople who migrated to the area brought new crafts with them, which had no adverse effect on the existing home-based producers.

While the number of craft businesses has increased steadily, Gatlinburg still has a lot of people who work at home. These are the "invisible craftsmen," and we're not going to expose them beyond noting the fact that they're still out there. These artisans are content to work in privacy and to sell their production to area shops, which then sell them to the public. The number of cottage businesses is probably larger than ever before, for a couple of reasons: First, there are more sales outlets available

LOOK FOR:
- Sevierville
- Pigeon Forge
- Gatlinburg
- Great Smoky Mountains Arts & Crafts Community

to the artisans; second, the life cycle of craftspeople usually finds them retiring from the public view into the cottage end. The financial rewards are smaller because they're selling at wholesale prices instead of retail, but the general feeling is that the freedom to work at their own pace is adequate compensation.

Today's invisible craftsperson is most likely a woodworker, a basketmaker, a weaver or a quilter. In addition to being native crafts, the time required for most of them to be done properly almost dictates that the work be done without distraction. The number of cottage woodworkers is very large (it's well over half the total of active craftspeople) because woodworking, as one of the oldest and more popular crafts, is in more demand than the public artisans can hope to supply. The common bond of the invisible craftspeople seems to be the desire to work in solitude. Whatever their reasons, these invisible craftspeople have chosen the reclusive lifestyle that is frequently accredited to all artisans, and their counterpart shops respect that choice. As it was in the beginning, the cottage craft industry of the Smokies remains an integral part of the heritage and attractiveness of the mountains, perpetuating the deep-seated conviction of the Appalachian people that they alone will choose the terms that define their lives.

Now that we understand what we're talking about here, we'll start with a few Sevierville and Pigeon Forge institutions. Then we'll move down the road to Gatlinburg, where Pi Beta Phi's large footprint is still clearly visible. Special pains will be taken to point out the shops where you can expect to watch craftspeople actually plying their trades. One final disclaimer: These businesses are for the most part small, family operated enterprises, with no more than a few employees. Expect hours of operation to be limited to daylight hours, with at least one day a week off, usually Sunday. A lot of the craftspeople don't post their hours because they live basically from day to day, so we haven't even bothered trying to list when these places are open. Our best advice would be to call ahead on the day you want to visit to make sure the shop's open.

There's just one other little consideration before we start this tour, and that is what you can expect to pay for handcrafted goods and art. Pricing, like most everything else the craftspeople and artists do, is a very personal matter, and it leads to some interesting variations. As a rule (to the extent that rules apply to craftspeople), you can expect to find prices that are surprisingly low when you consider what you're getting. The best way to put it into perspective is to think what you pay for a skilled tradesman like a plumber, an electrician, or an auto mechanic for an hour's work, and compare it to the price of a broom that takes a few hours to make, or a fine carving that may have taken several days. The best way to approach craft shopping is to consider that, in most cases, your purchase is worth what you pay for it. And the current craze in collectibles notwithstanding, handmade craft items have great potential for being upgraded to heirlooms in the histories of most families.

Sevierville

Pickings in Sevierville are pretty slim, because the city has always been the center of government and local commerce. The on-going entry into the tourism market has brought Sevierville into the overall picture in a big way, but handcrafts and art were never a part of the city's picture. The two artisans listed here, however, are among the most important artists in the area.

The Robert A. Tino Gallery
812 Old Douglas Dam Rd., Sevierville • (865) 453-6315

The Robert Tino Gallery is located in a family-owned farmhouse clearly visible and accessible from Winfield Dunn Parkway (Tenn. 66), about a mile north of Dolly Parton Parkway. Robert Tino, one of the younger artists in the

area, has built an admirable reputation within the local artists' community. His sensitivity to the natural beauty of the world around him is translated to canvas in whatever medium Tino chooses. A Sevier County native, Robert Tino has benefited from the tutelage of several artists in the area, and has returned the favor by assisting several promising young artists in starting their own careers. Tino's work, and that of his proteges, is displayed in a century-old farmhouse that's been in his family since it was built.

Ottolini Studios
116 Parkway, Sevierville • (865) 453-1563

Chuck Ottolini is the area's most accomplished stained glass artist, with several commissioned works in local churches and civic centers. His imaginative approach to the use of glass and natural materials for decorative stained glass work and distinctive signage have made Ottolini a local favorite of individuals and organizations looking for a truly distinctive way to express their personalities and beliefs in a monumental way.

Pigeon Forge

The move by Pigeon Forge toward a family-centered commercial base took a toll on that city's craftspeople by covering them up with a lot of noise and neon lights. A few stubborn souls have survived the onslaught, and they've pretty much concentrated themselves in the Old Mill area, clustered around the oldest continuing craft business in the city. To get to the area, turn east off the Parkway at traffic light #7 (Old Mill Ave.), cross the river, and look for a place to park. Every shop listed here, and many of others that will be described in the Shopping chapter, is within walking distance.

Jim Gray Gallery
3331 S. River Rd., Pigeon Forge
• **(865) 428-2202**

Jim Gray is one of the better-known of the Smokies' large group of superb artists. In addition to his flair with paint and canvas, Jim Gray is a sculptor of considerable talent. His most visible local work is the Dolly Parton statue on the courthouse lawn in Sevierville (see "Attractions"). This Pigeon Forge gallery, set on the west bank of the Little Pigeon River, is a sampling of Jim Gray's talents in various artists' media. Established in the area since the early 1970s, Jim Gray is a prime benefactor of the Great Smoky Mountains National Park; he's created several original paintings for the Park's benefit. He was also an early resident of the Great Smoky Arts & Crafts Community, and has three galleries in the area. The other two are in Gatlinburg, one on the Parkway and one in a converted church in the arts & crafts community.

Pigeon Forge Pottery
2919 Middle Creek Rd., Pigeon Forge
• **(865) 453-3704, (865) 453-3883**

Founded by the late Douglas Ferguson in 1946, Pigeon Forge Pottery is still owned and operated by the Ferguson family. The pottery, which stood alone for years across the street from the Old Mill, is now the centerpiece around which Pigeon Forge's craftspeople have located their shops. From simple and functional pottery items to abstract representations of the surrounding animals and mountains, Pigeon Forge Pottery is world-famous for its high technical and artistic standards. The classic black bear and raccoon figures produced in several sizes by the Ferguson family are among the world's most recognized souvenirs of the Smokies.

The Leathercrafter
2919 Middle Creek Rd., Pigeon Forge
• **(865) 453-2069**

A working leather shop featuring the works of more than a dozen regional craftspeople, The Leathercrafter has a full line of handbags, belts, and accessories, and an impressive array of gun belts and holsters for Old West fans. The Leathercrafters is one of the few places in the area where saddlery and tack repairs are available.

Twisted Vessel Gallery
3335 Old Mill St., Pigeon Forge
• **(865) 453-4945**

Just down the street form the Pigeon Forge Pottery, a new generation of the Ferguson family is using pottery and other natural materials as functional contemporary art forms. A modern gallery setting displays new approaches using time-honored materials to bring craftsmanship into harmony with progressive thinking.

INSIDERS' TIP
Don't be afraid to ask pointed questions in craft shops. A working craftsman has very few secrets as far as what he does and how.

Randall Ogle Gallery
3300 Old Mill St., Pigeon Forge
• **(865) 428-2839**

A self-taught native artist, Randall Ogle is well known for his portrayals of Cades Cove historic buildings and pastoral scenes. New interest in old times is being generated by Ogle's nostalgic collection of Sevier County farm scenes and old community landmarks, especially the wonderfully detailed reproduction of vintage cars that give Ogle's scenes a traceable time frame.

Pigeon River String Instruments
3337 Old Mill St., Pigeon Forge
• **(865) 453-3789**

Bob Lazenby is one of the very few practicing luthiers (makers of stringed instruments)

MOUNTAIN CRAFTS

Entrance sign at the intersection of East Parkway and Glades Road.

Photo: Dick McHugh

left in the nation. His Appalachian plucked and hammer dulcimers are becoming collectors' items because of the rarity of handmade stringed instruments, but he's still producing them so people can enjoy making music on the most popular truly American instrument. The shop also features a wide collection of banjoes, guitars, and other music makers, any of which Bob will be glad to step out from behind his workbench and demonstrate.

Gatlinburg

Still the area leader, Gatlinburg's craft heritage is going through the same growing pains as the rest of the city. It's not easy to find actual craftspeople downtown, but locally made handcrafts and art are available if you know where to look. We'll start with the downtown area, then move out East Parkway to point out some real treasures on our way to the biggest concentration of independent artisans in North America.

Downtown

Vern Hippensteal Gallery
452 Parkway, Gatlinburg • (865) 436-4328
Yes, Virginia, this is the same Vern Hippensteal we featured in the Bed & Breakfast chapter as a leading innkeeper. Vern Hippensteal is a highly educated, self-taught artist whose watercolor scenes of mountain flora and fauna are established as among the best in the area. More Hippensteal art is available at the large gallery and framery he operates in the Great Smoky Arts & Crafts Community (see separate listing below).

Jim Gray Gallery
458 Parkway, Gatlinburg • (865) 436-5262
Jim Gray's talents are described above in the Pigeon Forge listings. This gallery is in the Carousel Mall. Another Jim Gray property is located in the Great Smoky Arts & Crafts Community.

Arrowcraft
576 Parkway, Gatlinburg • (865) 436-4604
Built in 1926 by Pi Beta Phi as a local outlet for Gatlinburg's artisans, Arrowcraft was purchased in 1993 by the Southern Highlands Craft Guild. As a regional outlet for one of the nation's largest craft associations, Arrowcraft is an outstanding gallery of traditional Appalachian crafts of all kinds, produced by the best of several hundred regional artisans. The nicest part of visiting Arrowcraft is the knowledge that everything displayed in the museum-like

setting is a handmade item you can take home with you. Arrowcraft is located adjacent to the Arrowmont School campus (see our Arts and Education chapters.) Also on the grounds of the shop is the re-constructed cabin originally built from the logs William Ogle cut for the home he never saw, but which housed his widow Martha Jane and those of her family who were the first white settlers of the area that became Gatlinburg.

Terri Waters Gallery
631 Parkway, Gatlinburg • (865) 436-5647

Terri Waters is a Gatlinburg native and one of a family of distinguished artists—she'll tell you which family. Her stunning triptych "Mt. LeConte Dawn" would be a crowning achievement for any artist, but Terri's best known for her Smokies Wildflowers watercolor series. The Terri Waters gallery is located in Baskins Square shopping mall.

The Appalachian Attitude
1004 Parkway, Gatlinburg
• (865) 430-3327

Located in the middle of Calhoun's Village, the Attitude features the works of several local and regional artisans, including a broad selection from members of the Great Smoky Arts & Crafts Community. Owner Buie Hancock is an accomplished potter; we'll visit her shop shortly.

East Parkway

Heading out of downtown Gatlinburg on East Parkway (U.S. 321N) toward the Great Smoky Arts & Crafts Community, a few notable shops and two of Gatlinburg's oldest craft businesses make worthwhile stops.

E. L. Reagan Furniture Shop
149 Poplar Ln., Gatlinburg
• (865) 436-5289

Established in 1922, Reagan's Furniture Shop is Gatlinburg's oldest business under continuous management by the same family. In this case, it's Harlan Reagan, E. L.'s son, and Harlan's son-in-law Lester Flynn. Originally powered by a water wheel and belt-driven tools, Reagan's was the primary provider of furniture to the fledgling hotel industry in the '20s and '30s, and continues to build custom furniture and other fine woodwork at their original location. Poplar Lane is three blocks east of the Parkway; turn left at the sign, and follow the road across the river.

Kear's Broom Shop
659 Cartertown Rd., Gatlinburg
• (865) 436-4343

Kear's Broom Shop is well worth the side trip required to get there. Turn left at the light at Ridge Road, then take the first right (Cartertown Road) about a mile to the broom shop on the left—it's easy to spot. Elmer Kear started tying brooms for Pi Beta Phi in 1928. His great-grandsons David Kear and Monie Parton are operating the business today, supplying durable and attractive brooms to several shops as well as their own. Several testimonies to the durability of Kear's brooms are found in the shop, including one that was used daily for more than 25 years. The shop also produces a wide selection of canes and walking sticks from wood they collect themselves in the mountains.

The Great Smoky Arts & Crafts Community

The Great Smoky Arts & Crafts Community has altered the lifestyles of several tourists over the years by turning them into residents. Three miles east on East Parkway (U.S. 321) from traffic light #3 in downtown Gatlinburg, the Great Smoky Arts & Crafts Community begins at the intersection with Glades Road. If you don't already have a brochure, get one at the first stop, which is the parking lot to the right as you approach the intersection.

The term "The Great Smoky Arts & Crafts Community" can be taken in two contexts: First, it's a recognized geographic area bounded by the loop formed by Glades Road, Buckhorn/Bird's Creek Road, and East Parkway. With the exception of the Bird's Creek corridor, the area is totally contained within the city limits of Gatlinburg. Second, it's an organization of artists and craftspeople who own and operate businesses within the loop. The organization prints and distributes the excellent brochure that describes the area and lists member businesses, and is the best guide through the neighborhood. Whether or not an individual shop belongs to the organization is of very little consequence to the visitor, but without their efforts (and ours) you'd be flying blind on a country road.

A quick geography lesson: We're using traffic light #3 in Gatlinburg as a jumping-off point in keeping with our earlier promise, and Glades Road is the starting point if you come east out of Gatlinburg. There are two other approaches to the Community:

1. If you're coming in from Sevierville or Pigeon Forge on Bird's Creek Road, you'll see a sign that says "Now Entering the Great Smoky Arts & Crafts Community" on your right about four miles from Caton's Chapel school. If you don't have a brochure, stop at John Cowden Woodcarvers, just beyond the sign on the right. They'll give you a brochure and tell you how to make the complete loop and leave the way you came in (or any other way you choose);

2. If you're coming from the east on U.S. 321, turn right at Buckhorn Road a mile after you cross the Little Pigeon River on the Conley Huskey bridge—look for the sign on the left as you approach Buckhorn. Stop at the first complex of shops on the right for information. It's less than a half-mile in.

The Great Smoky Arts & Crafts Community got started in 1937, when Carl Huskey opened the Village Craft Shop in Whippoorwill Hollow. Carl's son Charles Ray keeps the family business alive as a cottage industry provider to several shops in the area. The area was pretty sedentary until the late '70s, when it zoomed from a dozen or so shops in 1970 to 25 in 1975. The organization was formally chartered in 1978 with 28 charter member businesses, of which almost half are still operated by their founders or a succeeding generation. By the end of the '80s the secret was out among artisans, and the area has bloomed into a major commercial district (albeit a sprawling one, covering an 8½ mile loop) with over 100 businesses of various types.

The Community is laid out along the corridor described earlier, with a few side trips to shops a little more remote, but all the roads are hard-surfaced. The area is laced with signage that keeps you from getting terribly lost, and there is ample parking at every shop in the Community. Soft drinks and food are readily available from vending machines and several small eateries, which will be pointed out.

Once you're safely into the bosom of the Community, you're in a mostly rural area populated by the shops and galleries of the local artisans. These people are preserving Gatlinburg's original industry by keeping alive

the local heritage of handwork and fine art. Some of the shops are operated by second and third generations of local families who've been engaged in their crafts for nearly a century. Others are professional artisans who came here to practice their crafts because the area is one of the few in this country where craftspeople can still make a living on their own terms. The combination of native and immigrant craftspeople and artists makes this the largest concentration of independent artisans in North America, and no other area is even close. The operative word here is "independent": For the most part these people depend on their own talents for their income, with no known subsidies.

Because of its size, it's difficult to see the entire Great Smoky Arts & Crafts Community in a single day. You can either accept this notion and plan your trip by studying the brochure and deciding what shops appeal to your particular interests, or you can slice the trip into a couple of days. One other suggestion: The city operates a trolley route through the Glades that's designed for tourism. You can board the Yellow route trolley at the Gatlinburg City Hall parking lot on East Parkway (parking is free). For a dollar, you can ride the yellow trolley through the Great Smoky Arts & Crafts Community, get on and off as often as you like, and see most of the Community. The trolley stops at most of the shop complexes along the way, and takes about thirty minutes to make a complete loop. It's a great way to map a trip if you're a detail freak; you can ride around without getting off, decide where you want to go once you get back to your car, and then drive through at your leisure with a more informed perspective.

The listings that follow include names and descriptions of shops within the Great Smoky Arts & Crafts Community's geographic boundaries that are known to produce a significant percentage of the merchandise they sell, and where you may expect to see craftspeople working, without regard to whether these shops are members of the organization. We'll begin at the Wood Whittlers complex at the intersection of East Parkway and Glades Road. For

INSIDERS' TIP

The local craftspeople are merchants who take a lot of pride in what they do, and what they do is usually their principal source of income. One of the things that bugs them more than anything else is being treated like a flea market exhibitor. You may try to bargain with these people if you feel like it, but don't be surprised if their normally cheerful attitude chills quickly.

consistency's sake, our travels through the Community will follow the clockwise route of the organization's brochure.

Village Candles
1400 East Parkway, Gatlinburg
• **(865) 436-4299**

This is Gatlinburg's original candle maker. Richard and Stephanie Lang cast more than 1,000 different designs from their own molds and finish them in a fashion so attractive that you wonder if anyone would actually burn them.

Lucite by Louise
1400 East Parkway, Gatlinburg
• **(865) 436-8849**

Harry Maloney uses new technology to create his handcrafted masterpieces. Using tools designed primarily for woodworking, Harry cuts intricate designs into clear plexiglass. Keychains, desk accessories, and one-of-a-kind lamps and plaques can be personalized while you wait. And get Harry to talk to you while you're there; you'll figure out quickly that he's not from around here.

The Leather Works
1400 East Parkway, Gatlinburg
• **(865) 436-4014**

Founded by Al Shirley in the early '80s, The Leather Works produces a variety of custom articles and represents the works of several area craftspeople. Their selection of leather handbags is the biggest in Gatlinburg.

Don Ringstrom Gallery
1400 East Parkway, Gatlinburg
• **(865) 436-9226**

Don and Sylvia Ringstrom don't look like they've been in business 25 years. They don't look like they've been out of high school for 25 years, but they have. An accomplished artist in several media, Don Ringstrom has been painting scenes of the Smokies for as long as anyone in the area, and is recognized as one of the best. Custom framing is available for your choice of prints.

The Betty Jane Posey Gallery
1402 East Parkway, Gatlinburg • 430-7874

Betty Posey is a rarity among artists—she sells many originals without ever making prints of them. Working across media lines and capturing everything she sees in her mind's eye as well as her own, Betty Posey's imaginative approach to painting is the envy of her peers.

Cecil's custom matting and framing set off Betty's originals. Prints of some of Betty's works are available as note cards and stationery.

Buie Pottery
1402 East Parkway, Gatlinburg
• **(865) 436-3504**

A fine arts graduate of the University of Tennessee, Buie Hancock creates a colorful variety of useful and decorative pottery from start to finish. From bathroom items to oil lamps, every product at Buie Pottery is one-of-a-kind.

Scrimshaw, Knives, Silversmithing
1402 East Parkway , Gatlinburg
• **(865) 430-3496**

The influence of the southwestern Indians is clearly visible in the silver work of Paul Stewart. Sterling silver and semi-precious gemstones dominate Stewart's handiwork in this shop that also features knives and scrimshaw by Newman and Peggy Smith. Jewelry repairs are available.

The Wood Whittlers
1402 East Parkway, Gatlinburg
• **(865) 436-7187**

Owned and operated by the Compton family since 1944, the Wood Whittlers is a leading producer of fine woodwork and carvings using both local and exotic woods. The workshop alone at the Wood Whittlers is bigger than most of the shops in the community, and the showroom is a woodworker's heaven. Anything having to do with wood is available, from rough wood to finished masterpieces, including a complete selection of how-to books and woodworking tools. Every woodworker in the Gatlinburg area is emotionally or directly attached to the Wood Whittlers. Shirl Compton, the company's founder, was a principal employer and teacher in the industry from the end of World War II until his death in 1977, and the company still finds ways to help struggling new craftspeople. The idea for organizing the craftspeople came to life at the Wood Whittlers in 1978.

Lorelei Candles
335 Glades Rd., Gatlinburg
• **(865) 436-9214**

When Lori Tierney was a college student in 1979 (she still looks like one), her father's candle factory in Sevierville was destroyed by a fire. Lori dropped out of school, bought a building on Glades Road, and sifted the ashes of her father's business until she had reclaimed enough molds to start her own factory. Some of those

Borne of necessity, mountain crafts are now big business.

Photo: Courtesy Gatlinburg Department of Tourism

resurrected molds are probably still in use among the several thousand novelty candles produced daily at Lorelei, along with a line of original art candles that's constantly being updated and expanded. One of the largest employers in the Great Smoky Arts & Crafts Community, Lorelei Candles operates a second retail outlet in downtown Gatlinburg that's described in detail in the Shopping chapter.

Gemstone Custom Jewelry
337 Glades Rd., Gatlinburg
• (865) 436-4448

Malcolm (Mac) and Susie Macdonell stopped off in Gatlinburg in 1976 on their way to their planned retirement home in Costa Rica. The visit was extended when Mac rented a shop to store his jewelry-making equipment and set it up to give himself something to do. Gemstone Custom Jewelry was an instant hit with the locals who know a good thing when they see it, and became a landmark business in the Great Smoky Arts & Crafts Community because of the excellent work and outgoing personalities of its owners. Costa Rica will have to wait: Gemstone Custom Jewelry, a charter member of the Great Smoky Arts & Crafts Community, will probably go on producing fine jewelry from precious metals and stones for a long, long time.

Gary McCoy-Craftsman in Leather
513 Glades Rd., Gatlinburg
• (865) 436-6890

You'll know Gary's in his shop if you see his motorcycle parked outside. "Free spirit" is an appropriate description of this long-time resident, but the quality and beauty of his belts and leather accessories are solid testimony to his ability. His work ethic is really outstanding, for good reason: He has to work long hours year-round to keep his inventory presentable.

House of Douglas Scottish Bakery
517 Glades Rd., Gatlinburg
• (865) 430-7568

While it's a little bit outside the context of "craft" as generally defined in the Great Smoky

Arts & Crafts Community, you'll love what the Douglas family does with food. Authentic Scottish scones, bridies (meat-filled turnovers), meat pies, and sausage rolls are great finger food for your trip through the Community, and specially made gourmet picnic lunches and dinners will give you another reason to remember the area fondly.

Morning Mist Galleries
601 Glades Rd., Gatlinburg

Morning Mist is a large shopping mall—in excess of 20 shops with a high turnover. Among the regulars are a couple of food service facilities, several gift shops that come and go on a regular basis, and the following five shops where craftspeople produce and sell their wares.

The Woodware Co.
(865) 430-1565

Darrell and Jean Moore came off the craft show trail several years ago to establish this unusual shop where you can watch your name cut out of wood or cut into a variety of interesting shapes to use as key chains. Their scroll saw mastery is complemented with a line of larger wood items that can also be personalized while you wait.

A Touch of Tiffany
(865) 436-9456

What Dorothy and Herb Jones do with stained and beveled glass is a sight to behold. From simple (and simply beautiful) night lights and suncatchers to stained glass lamps and windows, the Jones' artistry with glass is so pretty you'll have trouble deciding what to take home.

Glades Homemade Candies
(865) 436-3238

Here's another Gatlinburg tradition practiced by another native family. Connie and Ronnie Bohanan whip up daily batches of fudge, brittle, taffy, and hand-dipped chocolates to satisfy the most demanding sweet tooth. Helped when necessary by Connie's parents Billy Ray and Helen Moore, Glades also produces a full line of sugar-free dietetic candies.

INSIDERS' TIP

There are a lot of craft shows going on in the area throughout the year, particularly in October and November. This is a good way for the visitor to see a bigger selection of crafts, but if your interest is in *local* crafts, be careful. The visiting artisans who come here to do shows are pretty good or they wouldn't be here, but they leave when you do. If you have a problem with an item you bought at a craft show, it's sometimes hard to find the craftsperson; you don't have that problem if you bought it from a local establishment.

MOUNTAIN CRAFTS

Smoky Mountain Gold
(865) 436-6805

The DeSanto family has a lot of fun with gold in this shop that makes the proprietor look like a mad scientist. John produces a line of natural items dipped in gold while Carolyn's specialty is rose petal jewelry. John Jr. creates his own brand of custom jewelry nature art. There's always something interesting going on at Smoky Mountain Gold.

Cardwell's Bird House
(865) 430-9192

Charles Cardwell is a Gatlinburg native who was apparently born with a carving knife in his right hand and a camera where most people have eyes. Cardwell's carvings of birds and other mountain creatures (his raccoons are a personal favorite) are so distinctive that the veteran carving aficionado doesn't even have to look for the signature on the bottom. A fixture in the Great Smoky Arts & Crafts Community since the early '70s, Charles Cardwell's local following is the envy of a lot of his peers.

First Impressions Pottery and More
612 Glades Rd., Gatlinburg
• (865) 436-3642

The first impression you get in this shop is that a lot of real talented people are contributing some real nice handcrafts to it. The reality is that it's all being done by Jim Coffelt, a multi-talented Sevier County native who can work magic with whatever tool he picks up. Coffelt started out as a wood carver in high school, worked as a potter's apprentice for awhile, and dabbled in art and serious woodworking during a few winters. Now he spends his winter as a guest instructor in woodworking at the Arrowmont School of Crafts (See our Education chapter).

Alewine Pottery
623 Glades Rd., Gatlinburg • (865) 430-7828

Function and form come together in Robert Alewine's beautiful and useful pottery items. From kitchen utensils to bathroom accessories to oil lamps, Robert Alewine's attention to detail and special painting and glazing techniques set his work apart from any other. Alewine is the only potter in the area who is know to "foot" every piece he produces, to ensure that all his pieces sit evenly without rocking.

Spencer Williams Wildlife Art
623 Glades Rd., Gatlinburg •
(865) 430-4291

The breadth of Spencer Williams' ability to capture the essence of wild animals on canvas is almost breathtaking. Williams' portrayals of native and exotic wildlife create just the right impression, from the sheer joy of raccoons and otters at play to the majesty of the white tiger. If you're into animal paintings, Spencer Williams' shop should be a must-see on your vacation.

Adoughable Things/Shucks Y'All
623 Glades Rd., Gatlinburg
• (865) 436-7616

An interesting pair of alternative uses for bread dough (which you usually eat) and corn shucks (which you usually throw away). The Hopfs have been doing their bread dough ornaments and cornshuck floral creations in the Great Smoky Arts & Crafts Community for more than 15 years.

Spinning Wheel Crafts
711 Valley Rd., Gatlinburg
• (865) 436-7793

Bea Bakley is a third-generation native weaver who's been doing her rag rugs, place mats, and table runners forever. Husband Elmer keeps just enough space cleared on his work bench to produce a complete line of traditional folk toys and intricate wind-driven whirligigs that will dress up any yard or patio that needs a truly unusual decoration.

Future Relics
664 Glades Rd., Gatlinburg
• (865) 436-4423

Pottery that's as aesthetic as it is useful is Jeff Hale's specialty. Decorative Raku and shattered and reconstructed one-of-a-kind clocks, tiles, and vases make this pottery feel as much like an art gallery as a working studio.

Cliff Dwellers
668 Glades Rd., Gatlinburg
• (865) 436-6921

This historic building was previously the oldest craft shop in downtown Gatlinburg, and was moved into the Glades and reconstructed. It's now a fine art and craft gallery featuring the works of several contemporary and tradiional artisans, one or more of whom demonstrate their craft on-site regularly.

Church Mouse Gallery
670 Glades Rd., Gatlinburg
• (865) 436-8988

The largest of Jim Gray's three locations in the Smokies, this one's in a restored church building that's more than 100 years old (the new church is a few blocks up the road). A complete collection of Jim Gray prints and sculpture is available, along with the works of several regional artisans. A special feature, available only in the Church Mouse Gallery, is the amazing stone sculpture and bronze castings of noted Canadian Mohawk artist Thomas Maracle.

Cosby Hill People Crafts
676 Glades Rd., Gatlinburg
• **(865) 430-4675**

From useful to whimsical to just nice to look at, the products of Carl and Libby Fogliani remind us of the way the hill people used to live. Simple hand toys of wood and cloth, bird feeders, pine cone wreaths, and quilts and quilting supplies (including hard-to-find quilt frames) all flow from the hands of these versatile craftspeople.

The Smiths
676 Glades Rd., Gatlinburg
• **(865) 436-3322**

Scrimshaw by Cherokee artisan Peggy Smith and custom knives and silver work by her husband Newman stand out in this shop featuring local and regional Native American artifacts and handcrafts. Newman Smith's custom knives are nationally known for their originality and durability.

Ownby's Woodcrafts
684 Glades Rd., Gatlinburg
• **(865) 436-5254**

One of the area's oldest working craftspeople, James "Lum" Ownby and wife Jan produce a broad line of wood products from native materials, assisted by daughter and son-in-law David and Jody Penny. Lum Ownby is one of the few craftsmen still active who started out whittling at a card table in downtown Gatlinburg. Ownby's Woodcrafts is located in the former home of the late Lee M. Ogle, one of the progenitors of Gatlinburg's craft industry.

Ogle's Broom Shop
688 Glades Rd., Gatlinburg
• **(865) 430-4402, (800) 443-4575**

Located in a log cabin that was moved out of the National Park around 1940, Ogle's Broom Shop is a name that's been around almost a century. David Ogle, the current proprietor with his wife Tammie, is a fourth-generation broommaking Ogle; his father Wayne was a nephew of the aforementioned Lee M. "Pop" Ogle, credited by many as the father of the broom industry in Gatlinburg. (Lee Ogle was also related to Elmer Kear, the founder of Kear's Broom Shop in the Cartertown settlement.) David and Tammie employ the same techniques that the Ogles have used since the beginning—advances in technology are helpful to the cosmetic appearance, but a broom tied by Tammie Ogle in 1999 is in no way different from one tied by Lee Ogle or Elmer Kear in 1925.

Concrete Statuary Designs
701 Glades Rd., Gatlinburg
• **(865) 436-3524**

If Dale Teague hadn't already been a world-class weightlifter when he went into this business a decade back, he would have become one just by showing up for work. Dale & Kathi (also an accomplished weightlifter) pour mixed concrete in molds all day, making bird baths, flower pots, fountains, and indoor and outdoor ornaments. Don't worry about the weight of your purchase; there's always someone on hand to load it for you, or to arrange shipping.

Wholesale terms are available for volume buyers.

Smoky Mountain Pottery
744 Powdermill Rd., Gatlinburg
• **(865) 436-4575**

A true production pottery, Smoky Mountain is a constant beehive of activity. Dennis and Gay Ann McEvoy seem to be everywhere at once, throwing pottery on their own wheels or supervising the pouring of clay into molds for the hundreds of wall plaques and other accents and ornaments, small to large. Smoky Mountain Pottery will be happy to pack and ship your purchase, and they always welcome wholesale inquiries.

Whaley Handcrafts
804 Glades Rd., Gatlinburg
• **(865) 436-9708**

Opened in 1954 by Frank and Augusta Whaley as a weaving business, the shop is now operated by son Randy, a woodcarver of the highest order. Randy Whaley has earned a reputation as a master carver with his large renditions of animals, birds, and fish. Lathe turnings and carvings by other members of the large Whaley family find their way into the shop, and Frank shows up now and then with some of his exquisite woven place mats. Whaley Handcrafts is a charter member of the Great Smoky Arts & Crafts Community.

MOUNTAIN CRAFTS

Gatlinburg Ceramics
805 Glades Rd., Gatlinburg
• **(865) 436-4315**

The ceramicists' profession is proud to have Judy Bailey as a member since 1973. A nationally recognized producer and teacher, Judy does the job from start to finish. She pours her own molds (several of which she makes herself), and hand-paints and fires a dazzling selection of useful pitchers and bowls and decorative holiday items. Reproductions of antique oil and electric lamps are also a crowd favorite. Judy Bailey is a charter member of the Great Smoky Arts & Crafts Community, and has been a board member and president of the organization almost continuously since the organization was formed in 1978.

Mullikin Antique Clock Restorations
944 Glades Rd., Gatlinburg
• **(865) 436-6717**

Old-world craftsmanship is the standard at Mullikin's. Carl and Judy Mullikin depend on a lot of their friends all over the country to find antique clocks for them to restore to complete working order. This craft requires an encyclopedic knowledge of clockworks dating back to the 18th century, and the ability to make parts that are needed for their restoration. After that, a cabinetmaker's skills are required to make the clock case (usually wooden) look like brand-new. The Mullikins have all of this knowledge, and their efforts make it possible for the visitor to own an authentic antique clock in perfect working order. Complete use and care instructions are included with every clock.

Baxter's Stained Glass
1069 Ogle Hills Rd., Gatlinburg
• **(865) 436-5998**

Visitors are always welcome at Baxter's, and they'll find themselves right in the middle of whatever John and Donna have going on—there's really no point where the workshop ends and the showroom begins. The Baxters have been making their suncatchers, candle holders, night lights, and windows since 1984 in the shop that adjoins their home, a short drive back into the woods off Glades Road.

John Cowden Woodcarvers
4242 Bird's Creek Rd., Gatlinburg
• **(865) 436-3629**

John Cowden is a third-generation whittler who learned cabinet making from Shirl Compton after World War II. Following in his father's and grandfather's footsteps, John Cowden carved animals on the front porch of Hattie Ogle's Bearskin Shop in the '40s, until he opened his own shop in the Glades in 1954. A charter member and original director of the Great Smoky Arts & Crafts Community, John Cowden is arguably the oldest remaining active woodcarver in the Smokies today.

G. Webb Gallery
795 Buckhorn Rd., Gatlinburg
• **(865) 436-3935**

Located in a 1910 homestead at the corner of Glades and Buckhorn Roads, the G. Webb Gallery has a garden so rich in wildflowers and other natural wonders that the artist need only to walk out the front door for a lot of his inspiration. Custom matting and framing to provide the perfect complement to your selection are available while you wait.

Highlands Craft Shop
725 Buckhorn Rd., Gatlinburg
• **(865) 430-7560**

Here's a smorgasbord of local crafts from the best of the cottage industry. This is the only shop in the Great Smoky Arts & Crafts Community where fine lathe turnings and small furniture items from the Village Craft Shop are available. The Village Craft Shop, founded on John's Branch Road in 1937, is the oldest continuous business in the Great Smoky Arts & Crafts Community, and one of the oldest in the Smokies.

Smokies' Edge
540 Buckhorn Rd., Gatlinburg
• **(865) 436-3988**

Don Getty was one of the first tenants of the Mountain Arts complex when it was built in 1985. His distinctive style in original leather handbags, wallets, and decorative accessories has been expanded to include a line of beautiful lathe turnings he started producing after attending winter classes at the Arrowmont School a few years back. Maybe it's something in leather, but Don's another free-spirited type who uses a motorcycle as basic transportation. It's not unusual for him to load up his equipment and head west in the dead of winter to indulge his passion for skiing in the mountains of Colorado.

Otto Preske - Artist in Wood
535 Buckhorn Rd., Gatlinburg
• **(865) 436-5339**

When Otto Preske built his two-story log cabin home and showroom in 1976, it was the only shop on his side of the road for two miles. He has persevered to the point where he's now in the middle of several buildings. Otto's skill as a wood sculptor is unmatched in the area, and his large commissioned sculptures of sacred objects are in churches throughout the midwestern and southern United States. How good is Otto Preske? Give him your picture and enough time to do the job, and Otto will carve your likeness.

Folkart by Betsy
522 Buckhorn Rd., Gatlinburg
• **(865) 430-5925**

You have to see this one—Betsy Mansell bakes bears. Not real bears, of course; Betsy molds her distinctive Teddy-type animals and bakes them to provide a realistic finish to a truly unusual craft item. Bears are baked daily and placed in original settings. You can't eat 'em, but you'll have a lot of fun explaining to the folks at home how you came to own a Smoky Mountain Baked Bear.

Cobblestone Creations
522 Buckhorn Rd., Gatlinburg
• **(865) 430-5021**

You have to see this shop to believe it. Ron and Myriam Nolcken create a variety of art products by painting rocks. From small animals painted with impeccable detail to art dolls and doorstops, the Nolckens have no competition for what they do. Their trademarked Rock-a-Bye Baby dolls, wrapped in swaddling made from old quilts, are amazing.

Vern Hippensteal Gallery
480 Buckhorn Rd., Gatlinburg
• **(865) 436-4372, (800) 537-8110**

Possibly Gatlinburg's most successful native artist, Vern Hippensteal came to prominence when he built this imposing gallery in 1982. His reputation has grown steadily since as his watercolor depictions of the mountains he's always called home have increased in popularity. His work is also available at his downtown gallery described earlier, and at Hippensteal's Mountain Inn (see the chapter on Bed & Breakfast Inns).

Pewter by HeDKo
250 Buckhorn Rd., Gatlinburg
• **(865) 436-7671**

Founded in 1969 as the only shop of its kind in Tennessee, HeDKo spins and casts pewter into fine dinnerware and accessories. John Thomas uses a woodworker's lathe to turn discs of copper and aluminum into items ranging from dinner plates to thimbles. It's a fascinating blend of artistry and brute strength, and every piece is signed by the artist.

Turtle Hollow Gallery
248 Buckhorn Rd., Gatlinburg
• **(865) 436-6188**

Wood turnings and original basketry are the hallmarks of this gallery that features the work of several regional artisans. Proprietor Ross Markley is also a guest lecturer and instructor at the Arrowmont School of Arts & Crafts, described in our Education chapter.

Great Smoky Mountains National Park

The Great Smoky Mountains National Park is an international treasure. One of the most ancient undeveloped pieces of real estate on Earth, the park has been molded and softened by eons of natural forces into a user-friendly visitor's paradise, with just enough manual development to provide limited access to most of its wonders.

Now recognized as an international biosphere, Great Smoky Mountains National Park has an excellent chance of surviving man's attempts to screw it up by "limited" development and "strategic" deforestation by the real estate and lumber industries. One of the biggest concerns of local management is that America's most-visited national park will be "loved to death" by the upwards of 10 million well-intentioned visitors who pass through each year.

The park is the prime reason this area is a principal tourism destination. Everything else is locally regarded as eyewash that owes its existence to the park. Every survey taken in the area—and there are enough that survey-taking is an industry by itself—reveals that an overwhelming percentage (currently about 37 percent) of the area's visitors are here to see the park first. The other attractions get their fair share of attention, but less than 10 percent of all survey respondents rate other attractions as the primary reason they're here. Number two? Shopping—and that subject takes up more pages in this book than any other.

Great Smoky Mountains National Park is unique among federally operated American facilities because it wasn't originally owned by the government. Largely a wilderness area in the early part of the 20th century, and largely owned by various lumber companies and individuals, the area along the Tennessee-North Carolina border was purchased through an organized effort by people in both states and donated to the government to be preserved as a national park. Most of the work of actually creating the park (roads, bridges, etc.) was done by the Civilian Conservation Corps (CCC), one of the myriad federal programs designed to help end the Great Depression of the '30s. Because it was privately owned, certain strings were attached to the donation to the government, one being that the park must never charge an admission fee. The government has thus far held up its end of the agreement.

The other side of the coin is that funding for improvements in Great Smoky Mountains National Park is hard to come by in times when the Department of the Interior's budget isn't real flush. To that end, two non-profit organizations provide fund-raising projects and volunteer support. The Smoky Mountains Natural History Association, established in

1953, produces most of the printed material offered in the park, and finds private funding sources for projects that don't fit into the normal budget process, like wildlife management programs and educational exhibits.

Friends of the Great Smoky Mountains National Park, organized in 1995, helps provide funding for larger-scale projects and facilities, and assists in lobbying state and federal agencies for additional funding. One of the Friends' most visible activities is the creation of vanity license plates in Tennessee and North Carolina to provide a continuing revenue stream. As status symbols go, this one is very big in the counties surrounding the park in both states. Friends of the GSMNP has also placed collection boxes at strategic points to raise funds that stay in the park to provide upkeep services. All help is appreciated.

These two organizations have put their considerable influence and talents behind the most ambitious project ever undertaken by the National Park Service, or any other research organization on the planet: A complete inventory of plant and animal life in the park that's under way as you read this page. The All Taxa Biodiversity Inventory (ATBI) is the biggest long-term scientific program ever undertaken in the history of the world, and is expected to take a team of several hundred (perhaps thousands) knowledgeable scientists and support staff 10 to 15 years to complete. That's what those people you might see with clipboards, laptop computers and calculators are doing. They're even using global positioning satellite technology to document the exact location of everything they find. Construction of a forensic laboratory began in 1999 to provide on-site space to study the results of the program.

When the ATBI is completed sometime in the second decade of the 21st century, it's anticipated that the number of known species within the park will increase tenfold. For example, when a small group of scientists came into the park for a three-day weekend to study algae and diatoms (this is deep scientific stuff—diatoms are single-cell algae), 85 percent of what they found was previously undiscovered. This estimated surge in knowledge, where the currently documented number of 9,800 species of flora and fauna is expected to exceed 100,000, will change the way our children and generations to follow them learn the natural sciences. The increase in knowledge is expected to engender a re-classification of a lot of known species of plants.

While the great majority of new discoveries will probably remain obscure or unnoticed outside of the scientific community, new species of butterflies and fish could attract public attention. The discovery of two new flies and one turtle never before seen on the planet occurred in the *planning* stages of the inventory, while the whole idea was still being considered, and two new salamanders and a toad that have never been seen before popped up in Cades Cove! Discover Life in America, a national non-profit research agency, is coordinating the project. Because the researchers will study areas most people bypass, this inventory may also be the greatest thing going on in the park that you never saw.

Great Smoky Mountains National Park has the fortunate characteristic of being situated in one of the world's few mountain ranges that runs predominantly east and west. During the most recent ice age (about 10,000 years ago—you probably missed it), the Smokies caught a lot of debris from glaciers moving down North America from Canada, trapping various plant life forms at various altitudes. As a result, the Smokies now contain more tree species (130 known) than all of Europe, and more flowering plants, ferns, fungi, mosses, and lichens than any other spot on Earth. All totaled, there are more than 3,000 different vegetative plant species (not including trees) in the park's 800 square miles.

The park is one of the best preserved temperate deciduous (leaf-bearing) woodlands in the world, and the 100,000 acres of virgin timber within its boundaries make up the largest pristine forestland east of the Mississippi. A three-hour hike from 1,500 feet to the range crest above 5,000 feet contains as much diverse forest growth as you could see in a three-day drive-and-hike marathon from Georgia to Newfoundland. With the proper timing, you can see enough different flowering plants bloom over a 90-day stretch to make you wonder if the Smokies have a perpetual spring season.

The story on animal diversity is equally impressive: Great Smoky Mountains National Park is home to more than 50 mammals, 200 birds, 70 fish and 80 reptiles and amphibians. The latter group includes 25 species of salamander alone, the largest collection in the United States. The red-cheeked salamander is a local phenomenon found nowhere else on the planet. This is all great information to take home with you, and it may come in handy when conversations turn in the direction of things natural, but the learning experience is enhanced by actually visiting some of the places where these facts can be seen and felt. And when the All Taxa Biodiversity Inventory reaches its conclusion, you can come back and learn again what treasures this wilderness contains.

What follows is a description of the wonders available to visitors who enter this paradise on a short-term basis. For those planning to stay longer and really get back to nature, contact the park headquarters at (865) 436-1200 for detailed information. Better yet, stop in at the Sugarlands Visitor Center to inform them of your intentions.

WARNING:

Your first close-up encounter with some of the resident wildlife could very well occur at Sugarlands, where deer and a variety of smaller furry creatures graze on the lawn and occasionally try to mooch a treat from the visitors roaming the grounds.

Which brings us to the park's most important rule: *Don't approach any wild animal — anywhere!* The animals appear to be friendly, which will probably cost them their lives someday, but they're just hungry, which could cost you or someone close to you a body part you probably had other plans for. First, none of the forest animals know where the food ends and your fingers, hands, or even your arm begins. Further, the preservation of the wildlife in the park depends on their being required to find their own food. If they depend on humans to feed them, they will either starve to death when there aren't any humans around, or they'll be put to death because they become dangerous and aggressive beggars when they lose their self-reliance, or they'll be slaughtered by poachers who will take advantage of an adult black bear's dependence and will kill it for its claws alone.

You're going to hear this a lot in the park, and everybody here knows it's tough to resist the temptation to feed an animal that will come to you for a handout, but you *must* resist. If it's a truly hungry animal, it may take your hand as part of its handout.

Into the Woods!

We'll start by recommending a visit to the Sugarlands Visitor Center, a few minutes into the park from the Gatlinburg/Park By-pass end. From anywhere in Gatlinburg, just head for traffic light #10 and don't turn; from Pigeon Forge, come down the Parkway Spur about four miles to the park by-pass on the right (just past the visitor's information center) and take it around Gatlinburg. Remember the great photo opportunities at the two turn-offs. When either route brings you to the intersection of U.S. 441 and Little River Road, turn right on Little River and immediately right into the Visitor Center parking lot.

If the Park Service had its way, every visitor would be required to spend some time at one of the visitor centers before going into the park proper. Sugarlands is an attraction all by itself, with museum-type exhibits of flora and fauna, an outstanding 20-minute film in its own ultra-modern theater, an excellent bookstore featuring many local authors, and a host group of highly-trained, friendly personnel to tell you anything you want to know about the park. Schedules are prominently posted showing the times and locations of "Ranger Walks and Talks," an informal program where park rangers meet with visitors in the park. Guided walks on some of the shorter trails, evening campground talks, and hayrides in Cades Cove help bring the park staff and the public closer together to improve the public's appreciation of the value of this natural resource.

Sugarlands is the best single place to pick up reams of literature on every developed attraction within the park. You can also become acquainted with the rules of conduct in the park. The rules may seem a bit restrictive, but think about what your back yard would look like if 10 million people came into it over the course of a year, and each one of them picked one blade of grass and left one plastic soft drink bottle. A visit to the Sugarlands Visitor Center is a great way to temporarily restore your faith in government; it's an uplifting demonstration of your tax dollars at work.

Once you've decided what your day in the park will involve, it's time to move on. When you

Park visitors can see how things used to be done at Heritage Days.

Photo: Courtesy Great Smoky Mountains National Park

leave the Sugarlands Center, you'll come out on Little River Road, and it's time to make your first big choice: Turn *right* if you're headed for Elkmont, Metcalf Bottoms, the Sinks, Tremont, or Cades Cove. (We'll deal with each of these individually below in the order you'll encounter them.)

If your goal is the chimneys, alum cave, Morton overlook, Newfound Gap, or anything in North Carolina, turn *left* on Little River Road, go back to U.S. 441 (about a hundred yards), and hang a right.

Now, a few specifics depending on which way you turned:

If You Turned Right Leaving the Visitor Center

You're on Little River Road, and it'll be more than 20 miles before you see another building or neon sign. Little River Road is flat and serpentine, , and was almost totally destroyed by the devastating flood of 1994. Rebuilding took two years to complete, so you're on one of the better roads in the park. Little River Road is closed to commercial vehicles except tour buses. Along with some spectacular scenery, here's what Little River Road has to offer:

About five miles from Sugarlands, the Laurel Falls trail goes off to the right. It's paved, and for the one-mile stroll back through the pine-oak forest to Laurel Falls it's as level as you're going to find in the park. The falls themselves are quite lovely, and the trail passes directly under them.

Another two miles up the road, the Elkmont campground road goes off to the left. The campground was the site of the original Wonderland Hotel and several cabins belonging to a select few influential citizens. Both are now deserted and receiving minimal maintenance while the park service and local preservation groups decide their fate. Because they're old and falling down, public entry is discouraged. Elkmont campground is a favorite jumping-off place for some of the more challenging hiking trails in the western sector of the Park.

Continuing west, the next point of interest is Metcalf Bottoms picnic area, about four miles up. The picnic area stretches for about a half mile along the Little River, with plenty of tables, charcoal grills and fire pits. The river is shallow (and very cold), excellent for swimming, and one of the most popular places in the park to begin a tubing adventure.

A short drive across the river, the entrance road goes onto an unpaved trail. Turn right on the trail and a short distance up is the parking area for the Little Greenbrier School, an original one-room schoolhouse. Little Greenbrier was an actual school, and a "teacher" is in attendance during the summer to conduct lessons the old-fashioned way. It's a fun little half-hour diversion. Warning: If you miss the trail, or turn right instead of left coming back out, you're headed for Wears Valley and you're on your own. If you wind up at Wears Valley Road, turn right; you'll be in Pigeon Forge presently.

Little River runs right alongside the road from Metcalf Bottoms for a couple miles to the Sinks, so tubers can be escorted without losing sight of them. *Tubers: Get out of the river before you get to the Sinks.* There's room along the river as soon as the bridge comes into view.

One of the truly awesome works of nature in the park, the Sinks is a sinkhole of undetermined depth that causes the Little River to roar and swirl madly in a maelstrom that's every kid's dream and every mother's nightmare. The sight of young people diving into the river from the tops of limestone cliffs at heights that should be illegal is enough to make most parents shriek with horror. The Sinks is fascinating and beautiful. And dangerous. No kidding—a couple of young people die here every year trying to do something stupid. Enjoy it from your car, or stand a respectful distance back along the edge, and move on.

A mile or so further, the road crosses Meigs Creek. If you look up the creek to the left, you'll see Meigs Falls, one of the prettiest waterfalls in the park. Meigs Creek is one of the places where river otters were re-introduced to the park a few years ago in a highly successful program that's become very popular with the visitor population. There is no more delightful creature anywhere than the otter at play, which is how he spends most of his life, and if you really get lucky, you'll see one here.

The next several miles of Little River Road follow the river on the right with sheer limestone crags coming down the left side. At the intersection of Tenn. 73, you can go off to the right for gas, food, snacks, or a meal in Townsend, if you're so inclined. If you keep going on Little River Road, the entrance road to the Great Smoky Mountains Institute at Tremont is about a mile up on the left (see below for more on Tremont) and you'll be in Cades Cove in about five more miles of wilderness driving. If you go into the cove, do yourself a favor: Spring for the quarter, or

Mt. LeConte as seen from Newfound Gap Road.

Photo: Courtesy Great Smoky Mountains National Park

LeConte Lodge

In the late 1960s, astronaut Wally Schirra once joked from his orbiting spacecraft, "We're coming to you live from the Apollo Room, high atop everything." Such a greeting could be appropriately revised and used by the folks who run LeConte Lodge, a mountain retreat perched atop the third highest peak in the entire Smokies range. At 6,500 feet above sea level and one vertical mile above Gatlinburg, LeConte Lodge is an overnight haven for the ambitious hiker in search of a satisfying meal, rustic accommodations, good company and unparalleled views.

For those wary of long, strenuous hikes, this journey may not be your cup of tea. There's only one means of getting to the top of Mt. LeConte and that's by foot.

Several hiking trails lead to the lodge from different starting points in the national park. On Newfound Gap Road you'll find trail heads for Alum Cave Trail (4.9 miles) and the Boulevard Trail (8 miles, the first 2.7 of which are actually the Appalachian Trail). From Roaring Fork Motor Nature Trail, which is accessible by car from downtown Gatlinburg, you'll find the origins of three LeConte-bound routes. Trillium Gap Trail is 8 miles long, Bulls Head Trail is 6.4 miles long (the first half-mile of which is the Old Sugarlands Trail) and Rainbow Falls Trail, which runs for 6 miles before intersecting with Bulls Head Trail for the last half-mile to the lodge.

LeConte Lodge, the highest elevated guest lodge in the eastern United States, was built in 1924 and today serves up to 50 guests nightly between late March and mid-November. Advance reservations are required and should be made about a year prior to visiting. The cost is $80 per person per night, and what you get for your money is pure simplicity. There is no electricity, telephone service or running water. Light is provided by kerosene lamp; heat, by stove. Since there is no road to the top of the mountain, supplies are airlifted up to the retreat each spring. The rest of the season, llamas are utilized to bring up fresh supplies like food and clean linens

LeConte Lodge offers a top-of-the-world view.

three times a week. The native South American beasts ferry dirty linens and garbage on their trips down.

The outpost is laid out like a compact little village, a collective of primitive cabins anchored by an office, a dining hall and common bathrooms. The cabins vary in size, sleeping anywhere from two to six people. The larger ones are older, of log and mortar construction, with bunk beds and wood stoves inside. The smaller ones have outer shells of wooden boards. Scattered about the grounds are picnic tables and old-fashioned water pumps for drinking, hand washing or tooth brushing.

Guests of the lodge get two meals during their stay. Dinner is usually a traditional "meat and potatoes" affair with roast beef, mashed potatoes, green beans and cornbread. Wine is served with dinner. Breakfast consists of eggs, Canadian bacon, hot cakes, grits, biscuits and coffee. Between meals, overnighters are on their own as far as keeping themselves entertained. In colder weather, many huddle in the warmth of their cabins, passing the time by reading, making music, playing games or engaging in pleasant conversation with new friends. On temperate days, you're more likely to find guests outside enjoying the views of surrounding mountain peaks or Gatlinburg in the valley far below.

The lodge itself doesn't really provide the best views from LeConte, however. You can hike a half-mile to Myrtle Point, which is an excellent spot to view sunrises, or you can climb two-tenths of a mile to Cliff Top, which has 180-degree western exposure for remarkable sunsets.

whatever it costs nowadays, for the self-guiding brochure. It's a great little guide, and the Park can use the money.

To do the trip justice, figure on a minimum of two hours in Cades Cove—an hour or so of driving around the full eight-mile loop, and at least an hour's combined time spent at the several home sites and churches. If you brought a picnic with you, you're welcome to pull over and enjoy it anywhere along the loop road that there's space to pull completely off the road. Animal sightings along the road usually bring traffic to a stop, but it tends to clear quickly. And watch the meadow closely when you see clusters of animals; they're usually not all cattle. Cades Cove is your best chance to see wild turkeys and the reclusive red fox. Various Rodentia—raccoons, rabbits and relatively harmless (if left alone) skunks—hang around the parking lot at Cable Mill and the Oliver homestead. The campground (see our Campgrounds and RV Parks chapter) and picnic area are near the end of the loop road. Refreshments and a small line of sundries are available at the campground store.

Tremont—Connecting People and Nature

Great Smoky Mountains Institute at Tremont
9275 Tremont Rd., Townsend, TN 37882
• (865) 448-6709, fax (865) 448-9250

About 20 miles west of the Sugarlands Visitor Center, Great Smoky Mountains Institute at Tremont conducts a series of educational programs designed to provide hands-on training to nature lovers of all ages. Institute programs are conducted by the Great Smoky Mountains Natural History Association, in cooperation with the National Park Service. Using the national park as a classroom, the Institute's educational programs for all ages are internationally renowned for their leadership in the field of residential environmental education.

A wide variety of three- and five-day courses bring natural and cultural education to groups of elementary and high school students, with specific lessons selected by their teachers. Students are housed in a dormitory that holds up to 125 people, fed family-style in a dining hall, and taught in an environment that has several indoor classrooms and one outdoor laboratory about 20,000 acres in size. Course fees are remarkably low considering what's involved—they range from

INSIDERS' TIP

Leave as small a footprint as you can. This area will remain virginal as long as everybody does what they can to see that no trace is left of the fact that mankind is aware of the existence of Great Smoky Mountains National Park.

about $90 to $120, depending on course content, with discounts available for early registration.

The summer months are loaded with age-sensitive adventure camps. Week-long camps in June, July, and August give kids a wilderness adventure they'll never forget as they actually hike the trails, swim in the cold rivers, sing around the campfire and choose their own schedules from a fascinating menu, all under the watchful care of professional rangers. The Discovery Camp (ages 9-12) and Wilderness Adventure Camp (ages 13-17) sessions run Monday through Saturday each week, and cost between $225 and $275. For the truly adventurous child, the National Wildlife Federation Partnership offers three intensive 12-day camping programs that will give kids in the same age groups enough fun and training that they'll be able to live on a diet of tree bark, nuts and water for the rest of their lives. The NWFP camps start on Monday morning and end on the second Thursday following. All-inclusive

costs are $650 for the 9-12 and 13-14 age groups, and $680 for those 13 through 17.

It's not like the adults are being ignored here, either. Several adult courses are offered throughout the year, ranging from hiking adventures to wilderness first aid to photography workshops to elderhostels. Week-long and weekend courses are available on a schedule that's not quite as structured as the academic courses. For up-to-date adult scheduling and any other information, contact the Institute or visit their website at smokiesnha.org.

Whatever your destination when you left Sugarlands, bear in mind that on your return you're going back over the same road you traveled. If it's late afternoon, the traffic sharing Little River Road with you is going to increase a bunch when you get to U.S. 441. Be prepared to move slowly toward Gatlinburg, and consider taking the by-pass toward Pigeon Forge. Even if you're heading for Gatlinburg, taking the by-pass and doubling back on the Parkway is an option.

If You Went Back to U.S. 441 (Newfound Gap Road) and Turned Right

You'll be going south and uphill for the next 16 miles, after which you'll be going down for another 17. There are a lot of curves that some might call dangerous, so be careful. It's a good road, it's just not straight or level. As a matter of information, Newfound Gap Road is the highest thoroughfare in the eastern United States. It's also usually self-governing, because the volume of traffic makes it hard to drive too fast.

There are several short nature trails, also referred to as quiet walkways, on Newfound Gap Road. They're usually no more than a quarter-mile into the woods, and they're a nice opportunity to stretch your legs and learn a little about the natural history of the park. The cutting of paths to create quiet walkways is an ongoing project in the park. Some walkways are closed from time to time to let them recover from human incursions, and new paths are cleared in the immediate area. Since they are in a state of flux, it's tough to tell you exactly where to look for quiet walkways; keep your eyes open. One clue to keep in mind is that there's usually a "turnout" cleared where you can pull off the road and park.

The first landmark on the right is the Chimneys picnic area about five miles from the Sugarlands Visitor Center. Situated along a particularly noisy and rocky stretch of the west prong of the Little Pigeon River about two miles below its source, Chimneys is a big local favorite. It cleanses the soul to grab a bucket of chicken or some other fast food and run up there at the end of a busy day and sit on a rock. Or to take along the fixings for a cookout on one of the many grills the Park Service has provided. Daylong parties are commonplace at Chimneys, and your chance of seeing wildlife is excellent. At dusk, a few bears will appear looking for supper, and they've been known to invite themselves right onto a particularly appealing picnic table. If it happens to you, don't argue; stand back a respectful distance until the bear is finished. And don't expect a thank-you. Remember, it's his home you're visiting.

INSIDERS' TIP

Hunting is absolutely forbidden in the Park. Fishing is OK with state licenses (see our Parks and Recreation chapter for details — no federal stamps are necessary), but the taking of brook trout is also illegal. The brookie is a protected species. Live bait is prohibited — you may fish only with a single hook and artificial flies or lures. If you're not sure of what's on your hook, let it go.

Continuing up (literally) Newfound Gap Road, the over-and-under loop is a creative approach to road-building in an area not designed for such things. To avoid tunneling through the mountain, the CCC road builders constructed a 360-degree loop where the road travels up the mountainside in a constant spiral and passes over itself, all in less than half a mile.

A few miles further on, the popular Alum Cave trailhead is on the left (along with its large parking lot). The Alum Cave trail crosses the Appalachian Trail, which is a wonderful way to travel from Maine to Georgia if you *really* enjoy hiking. Many dedicated hikers walk the Appalachian Trail in several stages over a period of time, and hundreds will take it on as a summer-long project. Pigeon Forge resident Morgan Briggs, a locally-renowned "ridge runner," walked the entire 2,150-plus miles in the summer of 1998.

INSIDERS' TIP

Thunderstorms can gather very quickly and dump a lot of precipitation on the park in very short order. If you get caught in a thunderstorm, stay low to avoid lightning strikes and seek shelter immediately. The storms don't last long, and they're the reason everything around you is that lovely shade of green.

Alum Cave is one of the popular trails in the park in its own right, and leads to caves where the Confederate army mined alum to make gunpowder during the Civil War. It's a five-mile round trip with a 1400-foot elevation gain, rated as moderately strenuous by the National Park Service. If you're headed for LeConte Lodge, you can leave your vehicle at the Alum Cave lot—it's patrolled by the Park Service. (We've got a special section on LeConte Lodge later on.) The "Medium" rating assumes that you're properly attired for hiking (good, strong hiking-style shoes are highly recommended), and have minimum survival equipment (water, maybe a first-aid kit) with you.

A few more miles will bring you to Morton Overlook on the right. This is one of the more popular scenic stops, providing a panoramic view of totally unspoiled wilderness. It's worth a few minutes. Panhandling bears frequent this area in the late afternoon.

The Newfound Gap parking area is the next stop, after a couple of miles of extreme turns on a fairly steep grade. Remember this part going up; it's even more fun coming down. Just stay cool.

Newfound Gap, elevation about 4,600 feet, is the natural top of the park. There's a large parking lot for scenic viewing of 360 degrees of splendor, and a tablet marks the spot where President Franklin Roosevelt dedicated the park to the American people in 1940. The parking area has been enlarged and improved in the half-century since FDR was there, but the view you're seeing is exactly what he saw in 1940.

Proceeding south, the Tennessee/North Carolina border and Clingman's Dome Road come up almost simultaneously. Clingman's Dome Road goes off to the right and leads to the Clingman's Dome observation tower seven miles away. The tower, about a half-mile up a strenuous trail from the parking lot, is reputed, at just over 6,000 feet, to be the highest point in Tennessee. There are some people around who will present a persuasive argument (like any accurate map) that Clingman's Dome is in North Carolina, but the Park Service and the two states say otherwise.

Clingman's Dome Road is "trailhead central," with five locations along the road and at the overlook parking lot. The trails along Clingman's Dome Road are rated from medium to strenuous, and all are long and mostly downhill from the road, which means you'll be coming uphill to get back. The Spruce-Fir trail, about midway between Newfound Gap and the Dome, is a short, nearly level walk through a high-elevation forest of virgin timber. It's the only one of the five on Clingman's Dome Road that's recommended for non-serious hikers.

Back to Newfound Gap: The road you've followed up out of Gatlinburg for what seems to be a lot longer than 16 miles is now over the top, and you're going to descend steadily for about 17 miles to the Oconaluftee Visitor Center at the south end of the park. Along the way you'll have several opportunities to pull over and enjoy the scenery, which is little different than north of the gap. The Smokemont Campground on the left as you descend is a few miles short of Oconaluftee, and Mingus Mill is just ahead on the right. At the end of a short walking trail, Mingus Mill is a working grist mill, grinding corn into flour with an overshot wheel (the water flows over the wheel). Products from the mill are available for sale. It's an interesting place, completely devoid of any commercial gimmickry, and the only place in the park other than the visitors' centers and the campground stores where you'll find merchandise for sale. It would be a shame to come this far and not spend a few minutes there. And your brakes could use some cooling-off time.

One more mile takes you into the pioneer farmstead at the Oconaluftee Visitor Center. This is a real-life exhibit of how the settlers of Appalachia lived in times past, and it's worth your time to check it out. Dead ahead is Cherokee, North Carolina. It's covered in detail in our Daytrips chapter.

It probably would be a good idea to head back toward Gatlinburg in time to be off Newfound Gap Road in daylight. In the summer this would mean leaving Cherokee by 6 and leaving Newfound Gap no later than 7. If those curves just short of Newfound Gap impressed you going up, they're even more impressive coming down in daylight. Coming down after dark? Make up your own adjectives.

This section has covered the two most popular excursions in Great Smoky Mountains National Park, and each of them will pretty well use up a day because of the distances they cover. Also, because you know where they are, you might choose to devote some more time to picnicking at Metcalf Bottoms or Chimneys, or to a tubing excursion with an extended visit to contemplate the wonder of the dreaded Sinks.

The next section covers a couple of lesser-known but wonderfully satisfying side trips that don't require entering the park proper, but afford a wilderness experience without ever getting more than a few miles from civilization. It is commonly held among the locals that any visit to the Smokies isn't complete without spending some time in Great Smoky Mountains National Park. Even if your only real purpose in coming here is to shop the outlets (an honorable pursuit), you should at least get a look at the beauty of the park. You wouldn't go to Myrtle Beach and not look at the ocean, would you? Of course not.

The Cherokee Orchard-Roaring Fork Motor Nature Trail

The trip we're describing here is tailor-made for those who feel obligated to see the park since they're here anyway, and it just happens to be one of the most beautiful ways you'll ever spend a couple of carefree hours. What we're talking about is another local favorite, the Cherokee Orchard-Roaring Fork Motor Nature Trail. It's a one-way drive on the northern slope of Mt. LeConte, and you leave downtown Gatlinburg to start it. The Motor Nature Ttrail (local parlance) is about 10 miles long from start to finish, and you can make it in an hour or spend a day. Most people (non-hikers) spend up three to four hours on the Motor Nature Trail, including a stop somewhere along the way for a picnic lunch, if you happen to have one with you.

For starters, you want to be on Airport Road heading out of downtown Gatlinburg. You can get there by going through town to traffic light #8, or by taking Cherokee Orchard Road at traffic light #6. Just stay on Airport Road past Mynatt Park (another nice picnic site with charcoal grills—see our Parks and Recreation chapter) and into the woods. About a mile up is the Noah Ogle Homestead at Junglebrook, the first of several homesites the park service has preserved along the trail. Take a few minutes and tour this farm and mill settled by the son of Martha Jane Huskey Ogle, Gatlinburg's first white settler. There's a pamphlet available that explains it.

Continuing away from town, you'll see a turnout or two if you're interested (they're trailheads for the Rainbow Falls and Mt. LeConte trails—serious stuff), and maybe some wildlife. You might notice that the trees on the left are in more orderly rows than usual; that's the remnant of Cherokee Orchard, one of the last settled areas of the park.

Approaching the Motor Nature Trail, you'll see that the road you're on continues. It loops around the orchard and returns to Gatlinburg. You want to turn right onto the Motor Nature Trail (it's clearly marked), and it's highly recommended that you buy the self-guiding brochure at the entrance. If you're not already sold on the value of these little pamphlets, this one should do the trick. It's 50 cents on the honor system. We'll let the pamphlet be your guide around the Motor Nature Trail, and we'll supplement it slightly with a little advice based on a lot of personal experience.

Pine Tops, an early landmark, offers an interesting view of Gatlinburg and a nice picnic site. It's also known as a hangout for hungry bears, so be vigilant. If a bear joins your

INSIDERS' TIP
There are a lot of snakes in the Park — about 25 species, of which only two are poisonous: The timber rattler and the copperhead. Snakes like warm spots and sunlight. Be careful when climbing on rocks.

There's something for everyone in the national park, from rushing waterfalls ...

Photo: Courtesy Great Smoky Mountains National Park

... to historic buildings ...

Photo: Courtesy Great Smoky Mountains National Park

GREAT SMOKY
MOUNTAINS
NATIONAL PARK

... to wildlife ...

Photo: Courtesy Great Smoky Mountains National Park

... and bucolic mountain scenery.

Photo: Courtesy Great Smoky Mountains National Park

GREAT SMOKY
MOUNTAINS
NATIONAL PARK

Ranger talks help interpret the history of the park.

Photo: Courtesy Great Smoky Mountains National Park

Rule No. 1: Don't ever feed or approach the animals.

Photo: Courtesy Great Smoky Mountains National Park

The Motor Nature Trail is one of the park's most popular drives.

Photo: Courtesy Gatlinburg Department of Tourism

GREAT SMOKY
MOUNTAINS
NATIONAL PARK

picnic, excuse yourself and go sit in your car until the bear finishes. You're on his turf, and the bear is neither a gracious host nor a grateful guest. Because they're so used to having people around, bears in the Smokies don't fear people the way they should. *Don't, under any circumstances, try to pet or feed a bear.* Regardless of how cute you find them, these are wild animals, and should be treated with respect and given a wide berth whenever you encounter them. Be especially cautious if you see a mother bear and a cub; the mothers are terribly protective and won't think twice about attacking if they feel their youngsters are threatened.

Heavy traffic could slow you down at the Trillium Gap Trail parking lot. Unless you want to hike to Trillium Gap (moderate to difficult, 2½ miles), get through this area as quickly as possible. This is the point where you stop going up and start going down.

You'll find a couple of neat things at the turnoff by the old cemetery, a short distance from the Trillium Gap Trail parking lot. First, across the road is a good-sized confluence of three streams. A short scramble down the bank (stay on the path for better traction) will give you a view of some real busy water at a decibel level you won't believe. Back across the road, if you take the path past the cemetery (very short), take your camera; there's a meadow where the sight of young animals playing is fairly common. This isn't well known or documented—if you're treated to a Bambi moment, enjoy it and kind of keep it to yourself. And you're welcome.

Shortly after the cemetery, the Baskins Creek Bridle Trail crosses the road. Be alert for riders on horseback—they have the right of way.

INSIDERS' TIP

To help you plan your day a little better, here's a mileage chart of distances from the Sugarlands Visitor Center to some of the more popular destinations: Chimneys Picnic Area: 5 miles; Newfound Gap: 16 miles; Clingman's Dome: 23 miles; Cherokee, N.C.: 34 miles; Elkmont picnic area: 7 miles; Metcalf Bottoms picnic area: 12 miles; Cades Cove: 27 miles; Greenbrier Cove: 5 miles; Cosby Campground: 22 miles.

The Ephraim Bales place is very popular among picnickers. It's the largest open space on the trail and has a great stream with large rocks you can relax on. The Bales place is also a fascinating look at how the original settlers lived. The living quarters will make you wonder how the high birth rate in the mountains was possible. You should stop here for a few minutes to let your brakes cool.

Now you're really going downhill. You're also going to encounter a few fairly sharp turns and a narrow bridge or two. Stay alert. Stop and look at the Thousand Drips. It's not often you'll see a waterfall coming right down on the road. The Reagan tub mill and farmhouse are the last stop on the trail. The farmhouse is an interesting departure from the rest of the architecture in the Park—it was ordered precut from a Sears catalog.

When you exit the Motor Nature Trail you'll be on Roaring Fork Road. A short drive through a residential/condo neighborhood will bring you to the traffic light at East Parkway (U.S. 321), less than a mile from the Parkway at traffic light #3. Turn left to go back to downtown Gatlinburg. You've just completed a journey of about 15 miles through an enchanting area packed with local history and marvelous scenery, and you never really left Gatlinburg.

Greenbrier

There's one more picnic/wildlife area that's nice to visit because of its isolation, and that's the Greenbrier picnic area about five miles east of Gatlinburg on East Parkway (U.S. 321). The road goes off U.S. 321 to the right and runs along the middle prong of the Little Pigeon River, another usually busy stretch of water. After you've passed Buckhorn Road at the bottom of the long, steep grade on U.S. 321, look for the sign about a mile further on that says "Greenbrier." If you miss it you'll cross the river immediately. Just turn around and go back.

The Greenbrier road is about five miles long, quite narrow, and mostly unpaved. Since it runs alongside the river, the number of parked cars can make it practically a one-way road at some points. As a matter of local custom, the cars coming out have the right of way. Be alert for pedestrians and bicyclists.

There are several points along the road where small parking areas have been carved out of the woods for people to get out and walk down to the river. The Middle Prong is moderately deep and fairly wide, with a strong current, and it's a favorite swimming site because of the large rocks that serve as diving, jumping, and sunbathing platforms. Tubing is also popular here. The river turns away from the road about five miles in from the highway, providing a beautiful picnic area with tables, charcoal pits, and rest rooms. Another great local favorite because of its accessibility and privacy, the Greenbrier picnic ground is also visited frequently by deer who will roam through without paying much attention to the human population, as long as said population returns the favor.

About a mile past the picnic grounds, a bridge across the river leads to the Ramsey Cascades Trail (not for novices). The remnants of several residence fence lines are visible in the area around the parking lot. Greenbrier Cove was once a bustling community, populated mostly by Whaleys, and a few of them are still around.

Beyond the bridge, the main road terminates in a loop about a mile further on, and there's a picnic pavilion there with tables and a concrete floor. And outhouses. This is a real nice spot for family or small-group gatherings, and the pavilion is very handy if a sudden summer rain should come along. The road ends at the Porter's Creek Trail, an easy two-mile walk beside a stream with a lot of pretty cascades. The National Park Service built a cantilever barn at the end of the Porter's Creek trail a few years back. Nobody knows exactly why they built it, but the cantilever barn is an architectural style unique to East Tennessee and disappearing quickly. This barn, and one in Cades Cove that's more than a century old, may soon be the only ones left in the area.

INSIDERS' TIP

There's nowhere in the park to buy food or any kind of supplies. If your plans involve staying in the park all day, you might consider a picnic. Most of the places designed for visitors have some sort of facility where you can eat; you just have bring it with you.

Greenbrier is an area that has the Park Service a little concerned. It's there because the Greenbrier Cove settlers created the road before the Park was established, and it made sense to keep it open without a lot of preservation or construction necessary. It's a leading candidate for what the Park refers to as "over-use," where the number of people tramping through an area will destroy its natural ecology. Public incursion into the Greenbrier area hasn't threatened it yet, and probably won't as long as the public continues to obey the Park maxim, "Take nothing but pictures; leave nothing but footprints."

A-Camping We Will Go

Here's another amazing statistic: According to figures developed by the park's public affairs office, less than 10 percent of the 10 million people who visit Great Smoky Mountains National Park every year ever get off the pavement. That means there's more than 795 square miles of backcountry out there that are seldom seen and never felt. This is good news to the Park Service folks who are trying to keep the wilderness serene, and it's even better news to those visitors who come here seeking solitude and oneness with nature.

It's out there if you want to go enjoy it close-up and personal. There are two ways to approach "roughing it" in Great Smoky Mountains National Park. You can stay in a developed campground in your RV, trailer, or tent, like civilized campers. Or you can go out into the wild and live like Tarzan. Both choices are easy on the pocketbook, especially the Tarzan route—it's free. We'll deal with each choice, starting with the developed campgrounds.

Our Campgrounds and RV Parks chapter describes four developed campgrounds in the park that are close enough to the Smokies corridor to be considered part of it, and explains the rules for usage. Listed here are the remaining six, four of which are in North Carolina. We'll list the two Tennessee sites first, followed by the North Carolina campgrounds listed from east to west. Remember, we're listing these campgrounds only because they're in the national park—the closest one is more than 50 miles from Gatlinburg. To reserve spaces in national park campgrounds, call (865) 436-1266 for Tennessee and (704) 497-1930 for North Carolina.

Tennessee

Look Rock Campground
Foothills Parkway

The Foothills Parkway defines the western border of Great Smoky Mountains National Park, and the section Look Rock Campground is on is on accessible only off Tenn. 73, about 10 miles west of Townsend. At an elevation of 2,600 feet, the Look Rock campground is the highest in the Tennessee portion of the park. Look Rock is open late May to November 1, with 92 sites. Site rental is $12, and RV length is restricted to 35 feet.

Abrams Creek Campground
Happy Valley Road, somewhere in East Tennessee

Remember the old line, "You can't get there from here?" Well, here it is. Abrams Creek campground is on the extreme western edge of Great Smoky Mountains National Park, convenient to nowhere, and accessible only by taking Happy Valley Road off U. S. 129, some 30 miles south of Maryville, which is about 15 miles west of Townsend. The campground is open from mid-March to November 1 with 16 campsites. Site rental is $10 per night, and RV length is restricted to 12 feet.

North Carolina

Big Creek Campground
Waterville

The Big Creek area is about six miles south of Exit 451 on I-40, right at the Tennessee-North Carolina border. The campground is in a valley surrounded by woods. No RVs are allowed in this 12-site enclave, open from mid-March to November. Campsite rental is $10 a night.

Cataloochee Campground

Way deep in the woods and way up in the mountains, Cataloochee Campground really requires a map to find. Really. The Great Smoky Mountains Trail Map ($1 at any visitor center) will show the unnamed roads that lead to the Cataloochee Campground at location D-11. Cataloochee is 2,610 feet up in the mountains, with 27 available campsites. Open from mid-March to November 1, campsites at Cataloochee are $12.

Balsam Mountain Campground

If you like the idea of going to Cataloochee, you'll love Balsam Mountain. There are two ways to get to Balsam Mountain—we're only going to show you one, because the other one could require pack animals. Balsam Mountain campground is at 5,310 feet elevation, and is easily the highest campground accessible to vehicles in the park. The 46 campsites are open from late May to late September, and RV length is restricted to 30 feet. Campsite rental is $12 a night. To get there, take the Blue Ridge Parkway north from Newfound Gap Road (U.S. 441) about 12 miles to Heintooga Ridge Road on the left. Don't worry about missing Heintooga Ridge Road—it's the first one you'll come to. Turn left and follow the road into Balsam Mountain, about eight miles.

Camping Au Naturel

It would be nice to say you're welcome to just go lose yourself in the forest for whatever time you'd like, but you can't. The Park Service is a branch of government after all, and while they have no problem with your wandering in the wilderness for an indefinite period, they want to know you're out there. They'd also like to know approximately where you are during your stay, so they're quite insistent that you register for a backcountry permit at any ranger station, campground, or visitor center. Registration is totally free, and requires only that you fill out a simple form and drop it in a mail box.

You will have to contact the Park Service if you plan to stay at a site where campsites are rationed because of space limitations. Since only 15 of the 98 backcountry sites in the park are rationed, it's a simple task to plan your camping to avoid rationed sites. First, spend a buck for the Great Smoky Mountains Trail Map. Unless you can identify all 98 of the backcountry campsites and all 16 of the trail shelters in the park. The map and any park personnel will answer all of your questions, but we'll list a few of the more important points here just to give you an idea of what you're getting into.

1. It's very strongly recommended that you stay on the trails at all times (not unreasonable-there's more than 850 miles of trails in the park).

2. Maximum party size is eight.

3. You can spend no more than three consecutive nights at a campsite, and no more than one night in the same trail shelter.

INSIDERS' TIP

In cold-weather seasons, be particularly careful to avoid hypothermia, the lowering of the body's core temperature. Hypothermia kills one or two people a year in the park, even in the summer, because they didn't have warm clothing handy after they went wading in a cold stream and came out into a sudden rainstorm.

4. You must stay each night in a designated site and follow your identified itinerary.

5. Horses are permitted in the park on marked trails, and horse parties may only stay at campsites designated for horse use on the map—50 such campsites are so designated, of which nine are rationed.

6. All food for horses must be packed in—grazing is prohibited.

7. Horses are not permitted within 100 feet of trail shelters or in cooking areas of campsites.

8. When not being consumed or transported, all food and trash must be suspended at least 10 feet off the ground and at least four feet from any tree branch to keep it out of the reach of bears (there's an illustration on the map to show how this is done).

Strapping a pack on your back and getting off the main roads is a great way to experience the park's solitude.

Photo: Courtesy Gatlinburg Department of Tourism

9. All plants, wildlife, and historic features are protected by law. Do not cut, carve or deface any trees or shrubs.

10. Polluting park waters is prohibited—do not wash dishes or bathe with soap in any stream.

11. Firearms and hunting are prohibited.

Anyone arrested by park rangers for violation of any rule is subject to trial in a federal court. The maximum fine for any conviction is $500 and/or 6 months in jail for each violation.

INSIDERS' TIP

Don't be surprised if you feel a little short-winded while you're in the park. You're probably not used to the higher elevations. If you're going to be in the woods for an extended time, take plenty of water with you and *drink it.* Dehydration is a by-product of oxygen deprivation at high altitudes.

Take a Hike!

We've outlined several of the more convenient hiking trails in the park at the points where they begin and given brief descriptions concerning length and degree of difficulty. We recommend you stick to these trails and the quiet walkways the Park Service has provided. Most of the 850 miles that cross the park like a giant spider web are intended to connect primitive campgrounds and trail shelters so any hiker can see the park without having to strike into uncharted forest. It's difficult to argue with the folks who believe the park should be a deeply tactile experience, and can only be truly appreciated if you go out and get semi-lost in it, but the fact is that the park is there for what you want it to be. If that involves walking around in it, wonderful. If not, that's OK, too. But if you do plan to hike anywhere in the park beyond a short stroll, talk to the Park Service people at the Sugarlands, Cades Cove, or Oconaluftee visitor centers, and get whatever literature you can to make your hiking experience safe and memorable. In addition to the invaluable Great Smoky Mountains Trail Map, there's a huge selection of books on the subject by Park Service and civilian experts.

GREAT SMOKY MOUNTAINS NATIONAL PARK

Parks and Recreation

When you distill any Smoky Mountains experience down to its essence, you're left with one irrefutable fact—people come here to have fun. Whether you're an adult or a kid, play is an essential part of life—especially when you're on vacation, but just as much so once you're comfortably settled into a community's lifestyle. Those that live and visit here find that the area's trademark backdrop of mountains, woodlands and waters make the Smokies a natural when it comes to outdoor recreation. And, various city governments and businesses have also done their part to see to it that ample indoor recreational activities are available as well for all who choose to take advantage.

What you'll find among the following pages are plenty of ways to enjoy the beauty of the Smokies and, at the same time, have a little fun and maybe even get some exercise. There's really no better combination of activities we can think of. We do have a few specific notes about what you will and will not find in this chapter. For example, Great Smoky Mountains National Park is such an exhaustive subject in its own right that we've given it its own chapter. There you'll find plenty of information on the park's more popular outdoor endeavors like camping, hiking and fishing.

Even on its own, camping in the Smoky Mountains is such a broad subject that we've covered it in several other areas of the book as well. In this chapter, you can refer to the section on Douglas Dam Park, or you can check the Campgrounds and RV Parks chapter for more comprehensive opportunities for roughing it. Fishing is another subject that gets multiple coverage. Again, we've addressed it in the National Park chapter, but in this chapter, refer to our write up on Douglas Dam Park as well as the section on Gatlinburg.

Then there are several popular forms of recreation that you won't find in this chapter at all—rather, we've felt it more appropriate to place them elsewhere. Information on ice skating, snow skiing and white water rafting, canoeing and inner tubing are all found in Attractions. And don't worry—we haven't forgotten about golf! It has its own chapter as well.

Finally, a few remarks about the structure of this chapter. We start out with a profile of Douglas Dam Park in northern Sevier County. That's followed by listings for places you can rent canoes or inner tubes to enjoy a self-guided float down some of our most scenic rivers. Next are sections on the facilities and recreational programs offered by each of Sevier County's three primary cities. Following that are a host of non-civic recreational activities that we've grouped by category. We then close with a separate section on youth sports opportunities, which include both civic and independently organized programs.

INSIDERS' TIP

The Sevierville Parks and Recreation Department also operates Eagles Landing Golf Course in Sevierville. Refer to ou Golf chapter for the details.

Douglas Dam Park
Tennessee Highway 338 or
Tennessee Highway 139

In 1942, the Tennessee Valley Authority (TVA) constructed Douglas Dam on the French Broad River, primarily to help provide the surrounding area with much needed electricity. The man-made reservoir that resulted was appropriately named Douglas Lake. One of the more pleasant outcomes of the TVA's actions was the development of a recreational area surrounding the dam itself. Today, visitors can access both the waters above and below the dam at little to no cost. What they get in return are gorgeous summertime views and a variety of warm weather activities like fishing, boating, swimming and camping.

From Tenn. 66 (Winfield Dunn Parkway) you can access the area via Tenn. 139, although the more logical and direct approach is to go east on Tenn. 338 (both routes are known as Douglas Dam Road—see our Getting Here, Getting Around chapter for clarification). No matter which route you choose, you'll encounter small markets along the way that sell food and fishing and camping supplies. If you haven't already stocked up before leaving on your outing, these convenience stores might be your last best chance for provisions. Once you get into the TVA area, the pickings are slim (more on that below).

On arriving at the park, signs will give you a choice of heading toward the "headwaters" or the "tailwaters." Headwaters are the lake waters above the dam, and tailwaters refer to the continuing French Broad River below the dam. We'll start with the headwaters. To help you avoid any confusion, we'll point out a couple of commercial ventures that you'll find as you near the headwaters area, neither of which is affiliated with TVA. Douglas Lake Marina offers gasoline and permanent boat docking, and nearby is Sevier County Campground, located right on the lake. The campground is described fully in the Campgrounds & RV Parks chapter.

The TVA headwater facilities include a free boat launch ramp, restrooms and picnic areas. There is also a designated swimming area, complete with sand. The best time to swim there is during the peak summer months, when lake levels are at their highest. Regardless of the time of year, however, you swim at your own risk—there are no lifeguards on duty.

Most of the headwaters area is devoted to camping spots, some of which include RV hookups. Primitive camping is allowed as well. Most

sites include a parking spot, picnic table and a barbecue grill. Rates are $11 per night for sites without hookups and $15 per night for sites with hookups. Payments are deposited on the premises on the honor system. For more information on amenities and payment procedures at Douglas Dam Park, see our chapter on Campgrounds and RV Parks.

Once you get out onto the lake itself, you've got 30,600 acres of waters before you, not to mention 550 miles of shoreline. The waters are ideal for boating, water skiing or use of a personal watercraft. For the safety of yourself and your fellow boaters, please be sure to observe all TVA water regulations, which are posted at the boat launch.

If you choose to go to the tailwaters area on the other side of the dam, you'll be faced with a few more forks in the road and more destination choices as you approach. Don't worry—there is plenty of adequate signage to point you toward the location you're seeking. Just above the tailwaters you'll find two overlook areas, both of which provide stunning views of Douglas Dam itself (in case you're curious, it's 705 feet long and 202 feet high). The upper overlook has restrooms, free picnic sites and a covered picnic pavilion which can be reserved for $50 a day by calling (865) 587-5604 or (865) 632-3791.

A campground and a boat launch are located further below, right on the French Broad River. As with the headwaters area, use of the ramp is free, and the same rules and regulations apply to the campground (see our Campgrounds and RV Parks chapter). As you near the ramp and the camping area you'll see Douglas Lake Canteen, a small store where you can purchase a fishing license, bait and snacks. As we hinted earlier, the store's selection is fairly narrow, but it will do in a pinch. For more details on requirements for purchasing a Tennessee fishing license, refer to the Gatlinburg section of this chapter.

Canoeing and Tubing

Outdoor Adventure Center
2228 Winfield Dunn Parkway, Sevierville
• (865) 428-6112

For as little as $15 per person, you can get right out onto the scenic rivers of East Tennessee. Outdoor Adventure Center rents canoes for excursions on the French Broad River and

There's nothing like a calm float down a lazy river.

Photo: Courtesy Mountain View Canoe and Kayak Trips

inner tubes for relaxing floats down the Little Pigeon River. Both guided and unguided trips are available.

The canoes accommodate up to two adults and two children. The cost is $19.95 per person, but children 11 and younger are only $5 each with paid adults on board. Canoe trips run along a seven-mile stretch of the French Broad River beginning at Douglas Dam and ending at Ellis Bend. The outings usually last about three hours. Inner tube rentals are $15 per person, and trips down the Little Pigeon last from two to three hours. Once you're out on the river, you're free to spend the time any way you please—fishing, swimming, sightseeing or just going with the flow.

The Outdoor Adventure Center staff delivers you to the put-in points and is waiting for you at the end of your trip to transport you back to your car. If you want, you can rent a canoe and haul it yourself to your own favorite river spot, provided you have the proper equipment to transport it. No experience is necessary to take the canoes out, but life jackets are required and provided by the operators.

Outdoor Adventure Center is open for business from May through October, although daily operating schedules depend primarily on the number of reservations they have as well as the water level of the French Broad River. Usually, most of the staff is out on the water, so if

you just drop by, there may be no one in the office. They advise calling ahead to schedule your trip and to arrange your departure time.

It's also a good idea to ask if water is being released from Douglas Dam on the day you're planning to canoe. Why? On many days, water is released in the afternoon, which results in a swifter current, not to mention a swifter canoeing trip. If you're interested in a slower, more leisurely pace, morning trips are your best bet.

RiverQuest Scenic Family Adventures
925 Winfield Dunn Pkwy., Sevierville
• (865) 774-1029

Canoes, kayaks and even inflatable rafts are all available to take out for unguided, scenic floats down the French Broad River. Participants are shuttled to the put-in point near Douglas Dam and returned to the office from the take-out spot. While on the river, there's plenty to do, from just taking in the scenery to fishing, swimming and observing native wildlife.

Rates for kayaks range from $21 to $40 for short trips (one to two hours) and from $31 to $60 for long trips (three to five hours). In between, rates vary depending on the sizes and weight limits of the kayaks. Canoe rentals range from $36 to $40 for short trips and from $48 to $60 for long trips. Inflatable rafts cost $21 and $34 for short and long trips respectively. Fishing packages are available from $44 to $60, depending on the number of participants. The time limit on the fishing trips is five hours, and there's a charge of $10 per boat for each additional hour. Finally, inner tubes can be rented for $15 each. Tube trips take place on either the Little Pigeon River or the French Broad River, depending on their respective water levels. Prices do not include sales tax.

In addition to shuttle service, RiverQuest provides instruction, life jackets and, of course, paddles. Children must be at least 4 years old. Guests are asked to wear shorts or a bathing suit and tennis or water shoes. A towel and a change of clothes might not hurt either in case you get soaked! Reservations aren't necessary, but there are no refunds; trips go rain or shine.

RiverQuest is open seven days a week in season, and on a limited schedule in the off season, depending on weather conditions.

Smoky Mountain Paddle Company
2130 Winfield Dunn Parkway, Sevierville
• (865) 774-5005, (877) 226-6386

Canoe fun is the name of the game at this outdoor outfitter that began operations in 1999 at the corner of Boyd's Creek Highway and Winfield Dunn Parkway (Tenn. 66). One of its strategic advantages is its location right on the Little Pigeon River, allowing customers to put in on site. Staff members are waiting at trip's end to deliver you back to your vehicle courtesy of an air-conditioned van.

After starting off with a short three-quarter-mile length of the Little Pigeon River, canoers enter the French Broad River at the two rivers' confluence. From there, it's another 4.75 miles to the take-out point at Ellis Bend. Along the way, the current is steady and relatively slow, speeding up only slightly through one brief stretch of rapids. The owners say that the current is tamer in the mornings and faster later in the day when waters are released through Douglas Dam upstream. Overall, however, the ride is quiet and offers views of the mountains, neighboring farmland and overhead bluffs. It usually takes from two to three hours to complete the 5.5-mile journey.

Owner Geof Hanisek, a graduate forester, likes to point out the many opportunities for wildlife watching that are available on the trip. If you keep your eyes peeled, you might spot animals such as deer, muskrat, turtles, osprey and great blue herons. You may even get lucky and see a bald eagle flying free in the wild. Paddlers are encouraged to bring binoculars and cameras to enhance and preserve the sights. If nature watching isn't your thing, feel free to bring your fishing gear or a picnic spread for any of the trip's resting points.

Smoky Mountain Paddle Company's rates are $34 per canoe for one or two people for a half-day, with additional passengers costing $3 each; total canoe occupancy is limited to two adults and two children. All-day rentals are available for $59. Group and discount packages are offered as well. They're open daily in season, and run a more limited schedule in the off season, depending mainly on weather conditions.

No experience is necessary to take the canoes out; children as young as 2 can ride along, provided that there is a properly fitting life jacket available and that the parents feel comfortable with the situation. There is a short introduction for guests before the trip, and life jackets for all occupants are issued by the company. Paddlers are encouraged to call ahead for reservations and to wear casual clothing (sneakers, shorts, etc.) on the day of the trip. Alcoholic beverages are prohibited. To learn more about Smoky Mountain Paddle Company, visit them on the Internet at www.canoefun.com.

Shirley's Texaco Service
1141 Parkway, Gatlinburg
• (865) 436-4109

Located at traffic light #10, right at the Park entrance Shirley's maintains a large stock of truck tubes for sale only, at about $10 apiece.

McKinney's Market
819 East Parkway, Gatlinburg
• (865) 436-2272

About a mile east of traffic light #3, McKinney's rents tubes for $5 a day, with a $10 deposit. You'll get your $5 back when you return the tube in good condition.

Maples Brothers Gas & Grocery
1674 E. Parkway, Gatlinburg
• (865) 430-3766

East of town and near the popular middle prong of the Little Pigeon river in the Greenbrier area of the Park, Maples Brothers tube rentals run about $6 a day, with a cash deposit required.

Proffitt's Crafts
2169 East Parkway, Gatlinburg
• (865) 436-8701

Almost within sight of the Greenbrier entrance to the National Park, Proffitt's has a selection of tubes available for rent at $5, with a refundable $10 security deposit.

Enjoy a picnic in Sevierville City Park.

Parks

Sevierville

One of the best things about living in or even visiting Sevierville is the number of programs offered through the city's department of parks and recreation. What's even better is that much of what's available is either free or very reasonably priced, and it's accessible to anyone, even vacationers. On top of all that, you'll find that most of these activities around two centralized locations, the Sevierville Community Center, which opened in 1982, and Sevierville City Park, established in 1974. To reach either by phone, call (865) 453-5441. Or, you can explore their web site at www.seviervilletn.org/leisure.htm.

Sevierville Community Center
200 Gary R. Wade Blvd., Sevierville

Conveniently located near downtown, just one block off Dolly Parton Parkway, the community center provides many diverse forms of recreation, mostly in a climate-controlled, indoor environment (outside, there's a walking/jogging trail and a playground for the kids).

The center is open seven days a week year round except for the months of June, July and August, when it's closed on Sundays. Normal hours of operation are 8 AM to 9 PM Monday through Friday, 9 AM to 4 PM on Saturday and 1 to 6 PM on Sunday (September through May). While it wouldn't be practical to completely cover all of the center's specific schedules and fees here, we will provide you with a good starting point from which you can explore on your own.

One of the center's more popular offerings is the 25-meter, six-lane swimming pool. Open year-round, the pool's daily schedule is generally divided between lap swimming, exercise classes and open swimming (just for fun). There is a diving board in the deep end, and a certified lifeguard is always on duty. Several instructional programs are available, including swimming lessons and water exercise classes. They'll also teach you how to be a water safety instructor or a lifeguard.

The base fees for pool access are $2.20 for adults, $1.50 for children and 85 cents for spectators. Booklets of 25 tickets as well as four-month and yearly passes are available at discounted prices. Group rates are available for birthday parties and other private groups, but reservations must be made in advance. At all times, children 7 and younger must be accompanied by someone age 18 or older, and normal pool schedules are subject to change due to swim meets.

Of course, what would a rec center be without a gymnasium? The space can be used as a full-size basketball court or divided into two volleyball courts. If you want to just show up and shoot hoops with whoever else happens to be there, there's no charge, but the cost to rent part or all of the space costs $11 per hour or more. If a game of volleyball is what you're interested in, the same rental fees apply. There are two racquetball/walleyball courts on the premises that cost $2.75 per person per hour before 4 PM. After 4 PM and on weekends, the rates are $3.95 for adults and $2.75 for children and seniors. With all of the above sports, you can bring your own stuff or rent balls and other equipment from the office.

The gymnasium is also a great place to get an aerobic workout. Instructors utilize step aerobics, interval aerobics, cardio kickboxing and body design programs (using hand weights) to work with anyone with beginner to advanced level skills at both low and high impact levels. In the Hatha yoga classes, breathing, stretching and toning techniques are taught. Classes are offered Monday through Saturday, generally in the early morning and/or late afternoon. Daily fees are $2.80 for adults and $2.45 for seniors. Twelve-class passes are available at a discounted price.

At the Sevierville Community Center, they'll also (clap) pump you up! The fitness center includes multi-station weight machines, free weights, rowing machines, stair climbers and stationary bikes to help you in your strength and/or cardiovascular training. If you're interested in combining both types of exercise, the center offers aerobic weight training classes Monday through Thursday in the early morning and/or middle evening.

Fees for regular use of the fitness center are $1.95 daily for adults and $1.35 daily for Senior Citizens. Discounted rates are offered for four-month and yearly passes. Note that the center requires you to attend a one-time orientation program before allowing you to use the fitness center. Aerobic weight training classes cost $2.80 per individual class session or $44.10 for morning classes (twice weekly for three months) and $66.15 for evening classes (three times weekly for three months).

Bowling offers a good way to have fun, socialize and maybe even work a few muscles along the way. The community center's bowling center has 10 air conditioned lanes.

Operating hours are Monday through Saturday from 10 AM to 11 PM and Sunday from 1 PM to 6 PM (closed Sundays, June through August). Fees range from as low as $1.25 per game for Senior Citizens to as high as $1.95 per game for adults after 6 PM. League rates and children's rates fall somewhere in the middle, and group rates are slightly higher. The shoe rental fee is $1.10. In addition to open play, the center is the site of an annual New Year's Eve party as well as several monthly tournaments and bowling leagues; the latter generally run from September through May.

Speaking of league play, the Sevierville Community Center has organized adult leagues in other sports besides bowling. Three-on-three basketball leagues usually run October through December and cost around $45 per team to join. Racquetball players have the choice of joining a fall league, which starts up in September, or a winter league in February. Both leagues cost $42 per person. A winter coed volleyball league plays from January through March and costs about $100 per team.

If you have children, the whole family will appreciate the many kid-oriented recreational programs made available at the Community Center. These programs are fun-filled, educational and affordable and allow the kids to participate in activities like swimming, arts and crafts, games and bowling. There is an ongoing after-school program as well as Christmas, spring break and summer camps (see our Education and Child Care chapter). You'll also find youth athletic programs like a 7th and 8th grade basketball league and the Youth American Bowling League (see the Youth Sports section of this chapter). Annual events include a kid's dog show and a track and field meet.

Sevierville City Park
**1005 Park Rd.,
Sevierville**

Especially during the summer months, Sevierville City Park becomes a beehive of activity. The sense of community belonging is strong as you see softball teams going head-to-head out on the diamond, family reunions taking place in the covered pavilions and friends enjoying strolls around the walking trail at sunset.

INSIDERS' TIP

Sevierville's Department of Parks and Recreation also oversees operations of the Sevierville Civic Center, which is located next door to the Sevierville Community Center on Gary Wade Boulevard. Formerly a triplex movie theater, the building was renovated and reopened in 1998 as a multi use facility for the community. The center's large LeConte Auditorium seats up to 400, and is used for civic meetings, trade shows, theater presentations, etc. Also in the building is Sevierville's City Council chamber, which seats 110. Both rooms, as well as smaller conference rooms, are available to the public for rental.

Quiet country roads are a great place for exercise.

Photo: Courtesy Gatlinburg Department of Tourism

The favorite park hangout from late May through Labor Day weekend is the outdoor pool and food concession area. Pool hours are Monday through Friday from 11 AM to 6 PM, Saturdays from 10 AM to 6 PM and Sundays from 1 to 6 PM. The main pool is quite large, with shallow and deep waters as well as a diving area. Smaller wading pools accommodate younger children, and two certified lifeguards are on duty at all times. The main building houses showers and restrooms. Fees for swimming at the park are the same as those for the community center pool. As with the community center pool, this pool can also be reserved at group rates for private functions, but these events must be held after regular pool hours and by reservation only.

Outdoor playing surfaces include a four-goal basketball court, a regulation soccer field, two junior size soccer fields and eight tennis courts, four of which are lighted for night play. There are also four lighted baseball/softball fields that are used for Little League programs as well as adult league play. Men's and women's softball leagues play during the spring and summer, and a coed league goes into action in the fall.

One section of the park is located along the banks of the West Prong of the Little Pigeon River. This area is dominated by large shade trees, and features a number of picnic tables and barbecue grills. Several covered picnic pavilions are on site as well. These can be used at no cost, but since demand for them is high (especially in summer), it's best to make reservations in advance through the parks department. Oh, and while you're there, keep an eye out for one of the park's permanent residents, a rare albino squirrel!

Circling the majority of the City Park complex is a half-mile-long walking/jogging trail. Near the west side of the park you'll find an entrance to another trail, the Memorial River Trail Greenway. This eight-foot-wide path runs for two miles, starting at City Park and running alongside the West Prong of the Little Pigeon River. The trail crosses the Parkway and continues north to Main Street. The trail is well-landscaped and has plenty of lighting and park benches.

Pigeon Forge

As in Sevierville, many of the recreational activities to be found in Pigeon Forge are administered through the city government. Currently, there are two city parks that serve the folks of Pigeon Forge well with free, easily accessible facilities. For more information on both parks as well as any of the city's recreation and athletic programs, you can contact Pigeon Forge's Department of Parks and Recreation at (865) 428-3113.

While Pigeon Forge doesn't currently boast a community center like those in Sevierville and Gatlinburg, construction is now under way on just such a facility. Work is expected to be completed by late 2000 or early 2001. The $10 million to $12 million center is taking shape on a 16-acre site on McGill Street, within walking distance of two Pigeon Forge schools. Current plans project that the center will include a bowling center, a library, a gymnasium with basketball courts and an elevated jogging track, racquetball courts, a weight room, indoor and outdoor pools and an on-site day care center. Plenty of parking is allowed for in the blueprints.

Pigeon Forge City Park
McGill St., Pigeon Forge

This park is handily located just off Wears Valley Road, only a couple of blocks from the Parkway. The site centers around three baseball/softball fields, an outdoor basketball court, six tennis courts (four of which are lighted) and a playground. A 1.25-mile walking/jogging trail surrounds most of the area, and there is also a covered picnic pavilion. While there is no cost to use the pavilion, city officials do recommend making reservations since it is frequently in use.

Patriot Park
Old Mill Ave., Pigeon Forge

Patriot Park is located just one block off the Parkway in the heart of Pigeon Forge's Old Mill Community. And, as the site of the city's main

trolley office (see our Getting Here, Getting Around chapter) as well as many of its special events (see our Annual Events chapter), the park is frequented by locals and vacationers alike.

Three soccer fields (two regulation, one smaller) dominate most of Patriot Park's acreage. At the southwest corner of the park, a charming gazebo has even been used for private wedding ceremonies. At the northwest corner is a covered picnic pavilion which, like the one at the city park, can be used at no cost (again, reservations are encouraged). Surrounding the soccer fields is a half-mile walking/jogging trail.

Before the city educational/recreation complex on Wear's Valley Road was completed, this was Pegeon Forge's only public park, and it didn't have an official name. When the new city park opened in 1990, during the Persian Gulf War, Patriot Park was christened. On display in a glass enclosure near the park entrance is a Patriot missile (we presume it's unarmed), identical to the ones used by U.S. forces during the Persian Gulf War. The missile battery was donated by the Raytheon Corporation, the manufacturer of Patriot missiles. It's one of only four on display in the United States. Also on the premises, at the far east end of the grounds, is a 32-foot-high and 28-foot-wide replica of the Liberty Bell, which is constructed of an aluminum frame with a shell made of woven metal lace. Both displays help play up the park's patriotic theme.

Patriot Park is the site of a number of city-sponsored special events held each year in Pigeon Forge. Among them are traditional holiday events like the annual Patriot Festival on the 4th of July and the city's official Winterfest Kickoff celebrations.

Gatlinburg

The gateway city's matriarchal attitude is heavily indicated in the way it treats its residents. Long a leader in entertaining visitors, Gatlinburg takes excellent care of her own as well, with a wide variety of recreation programs designed to provide cradle-to-grave diversion for whatever interests may develop. While these programs are designed primarily for local use, the need of visitors to the Smokies to get involved with local activities is accommodated by special considerations in most activities.

One of the more interesting and fun diversions for fishermen in Gatlinburg is the trout fishing program, which allows game fishing right in the middle of town. We'll deal with the downtown fishing details once we dispose of the obligatory info: The types of licenses required.

You need three items to fish in town: a federal stamp, a state license, and a municipal permit. A special federal stamp is required for trout fishing in Tennessee. It costs $12 a year and can be purchased with a Tennessee fishing license. The state fishing license availability chart looks like a train schedule, but the essence is this: Any child under 13 can fish in Tennessee without a license. Adult licenses are based on resident and non-resident status—an annual fishing license

PARKS AND RECREATION

costs $21 for a resident and includes hunting privileges, while a non-resident annual fishing license (no hunting allowed) is $26. A one-day fishing license is available to residents only, for $2.50. Non-residents may buy a three-day fishing license for $10.50 or a 10-day license for $15.50. Tennessee or North Carolina fishing licenses are required to fish in the Great Smoky Mountains National Park, and each is honored at all locations inside the park, regardless of which state you might be in the time. Other licenses (handicapped, veterans, senior citizens, can be purchased at Tennessee Wildlife Resources Agency field offices—call the East Tennessee Regional Office at (800) 332-0900 for details.

The Gatlinburg Recreation Department raises trout from fingerling to adult size in feeding pens at Herbert Holt Park and releases them into the city's streams on a weekly schedule through the tourist season. The local trout program has a creel limit of five fish per day during the April through November catch-and-keep season, and possession of more than 10 fish at any one time is prohibited. From December through March, all fish caught must be released unharmed, and possession of trout during that season is prohibited. Fishing is permitted daily except Thursday (the day the streams are stocked) from a half-hour before sunrise until 30 minutes after sunset.

A single rod and single hook are required year-round. There are no bait restrictions or minimum length requirements during the catch-and-keep season, but artificial lures are required during the catch-and-release season. Two areas are designated as "children's streams," where only children 12 and under can fish, with a daily creel limit of two fish. The designated children's streams are Dudley Creek and the Little Pigeon River at Herbert Holt Park, and LeConte Creek in the Mynatt Park area. Local police are authorized to act as game wardens within the city limits.

A regular state fishing license and a federal trout stamp are required before the special municipal permit can be purchased for $2.50 per day. This is a great way to teach a kid how to fish without ever leaving civilization, and the stocking program almost guarantees a good-sized trophy sometime during the season. The two most popular adult fishing spots in the city are both on the west prong of the Little Pigeon River, right in the middle of town. The area along River Road between Christus Gardens and the bridge at Greystone Heights Road is easily accessible from the Riverwak (see our Attractions chapter) and is usually well stocked. The

Floating down a river: a great family activity.

Photo: Courtesy River Quest

stretch that runs parallel to the Parkway heading north from behind Ruby Tuesday's restaurant to the bridge at traffic light #2 is a little more private, with motels and a few businesses hiding the river from the street traffic. Details of the program are available at City Hall, the Gatlinburg welcome centers, Ace Hardware on East Parkway (U.S. 321N) between downtown and City Hall, and Proffitt's Woodcrafts on East Parkway, about five miles east of town.

Gatlinburg operates three beautiful municipal parks, each with its own special attraction. All three have covered pavilions with picnic tables and cooking facilities, which are available for group use at no cost. Reservations may be made by calling the Gatlinburg Recreation Department at (865) 436-4990.

Herbert Holt Park

This award-winning facility is on the site of the old sewer plant at the north end of the city, and is only visible from the spur. The road into the park is north of traffic light #1 (turn right coming toward town, left going out). Herbert Holt Park's picnic pavilion has a huge barbecue grill for sheltered cooking. Picnic tables with individual cooking grills along the stream are convenient to the playground and horseshoe pits. A short hiking trail above the rest rooms provides a nice way to walk off a meal or build a pre-feast appetite. The city's trout-rearing facility, lies beside the pavilion at Herbert Holt Park in what used to be the sewage plant settling beds. Trout of various sizes are visible to the public, along with special provisions made to foil the flock of blue herons that moved into the park the day after the first trout fingerlings were brought in.

Mynatt Park
Airport Rd.

The biggest, oldest and most complete municipal recreational site in the city, Mynatt Park is about six blocks from traffic light #8. An absolute jewel, Mynatt Park pretty much has it all, including picnic tables and charcoal grills in a shaded section alongside a busy stream, a large pavilion for group use (same number as above), a lighted basketball court, six tennis courts, horseshoe pits, playground equipment at two sites, a baseball diamond, and plenty of open land for free-form play. There's even a gazebo convenient to the pavilion that's become a popular spot for al fresco weddings. Mynatt Park is a great favorite with the local population, who turn out in force to walk their pets and watch Little League baseball. A word to the wise: The Mynatt Park pavilion is the most-requested facility in the

city. If you're planning anything that includes this particular site, call as far in advance as possible.

Mills Park
Mills Park Rd.

Adjacent to the Community Center and Gatlinburg-Pittman High School, Mills Park is primarily an athletic venue. Lighted softball and football fields are in almost constant use by high school and youth organizations, and the high school uses the quarter-mile track as its home oval. The only concession stand in the municipal park system is convenient to the football and softball fields, and sits right in front of the two lighted tennis courts (also a home site for the high school team). At the other end of the park, a pavilion with picnic tables is close to the playground and jogging trail. Mills Park Road runs off East Parkway (U.S. 321N) about five miles from downtown. Two parking lots are convenient to whatever type of activity you've planned, and the high school and community center parking lots handle the overflow for large events like the Scottish Games each spring (see our Annual Events chapter).

Gatlinburg Community Center
Mills Park Rd., Gatlinburg
• (865) 436-4990

The Gatlinburg Community Center is a wonderful fall-back solution if your plans have been disrupted. The community center is a 50,000-plus square-foot indoor facility that's jam-packed with things to do. To get there, take East Parkway (U.S. 321N) about five miles out from traffic light #3 in Gatlinburg to Mills Park Road. Turn left and go about a half-mile

> **INSIDERS' TIP**
>
> The Sevierville Community Center offers a self-directed fitness program in which participants earn points for activities like working out in the fitness center and jogging. Points can then be redeemed for free swimming, bowling, aerobics and racquetball passes. See? No pain, no gain!

until you see the big sign, and turn left. The parking lot is at the top of the hill. Usage fees are moderate to dirt-cheap, and the center is open seven days a week. Our tour begins with the swimming pool, goes up progressively for two levels to the multi-purpose area and gymnasia, then returns to the ground floor to visit the racquetball courts and bowling center/game room complex.

The 25-meter swimming pool is available for open swimming any time there's not a swim meet or a group activity (adult lap swimming is OK during afternoon and evening water exercise classes). Pool admission is $1.50 a session for adults 13 to 65, 75 cents for children 4 to 12 and adults 65 and over, and free to children under 4. Frequent swimmers can buy extended-use passes to the pool—a pass good for 25 visits is $22.50 for adults and $11.25 for children and senior citizens. For the truly addicted aquaphile, an unlimited use 6-month pass is available at $54 and $27, respectively, by age group. Water exercise classes are conducted Monday, Wednesday, and Friday from 11 AM to Noon, and Tuesday and Thursday evenings from 7 to 8 PM. The cost is 25 cents *plus* the pool admission fee. Certified lifeguards are on duty at all times the pool is open.

On the second floor, a patio area with tables and chairs provides a bird's-eye view of the pool. Snacks and soft drinks are available at vending machines nearby. The multi-purpose room next to the upstairs patio is big enough to accommodate a meeting of 300 people, or can be divided for two smaller events. The hourly rental rate includes use of the fully equipped kitchen. The multi-purpose room is the meeting place for the Gatlinburg Garden Club, the Gatlinburg Retired Citizens Club and the Gatlinburg Community Chorale. It's also used for specialty classes that occur through the year in subjects as varied as line dancing and CPR-first aid.

The central hallway that runs the length of the building looks down into the racquetball courts. The double gymnasium has several basketball goals, including junior-height models. Equipment usage is free during open play, but some form of collateral is required (car keys and driver's licenses are the usual adult fare; kids can leave textbooks, wallets, etc.). During fall and winter, the gym is booked pretty solid on weekday evenings for adult basketball and volleyball leagues. Aerobex classes are conducted in the gym on Monday, Wednesday and Friday mornings from 9 to 10 AM, and in the exercise area above the gym on Tuesday and Thursday evenings from 5:30 to 6:30 PM. Daily admission to Aerobex is $3, a 12-ticket booklet is available for $25, or a yearly membership is $270.

The Tone Zone, an exercise area with weight machines and other torture devices, provides a complete fitness center with qualified supervision available for counseling. A one-hour orientation session is required on your first visit. Pick your price: Admission to the Tone Zone costs $2 a day, $5 a month, $24 for a six-month pass, or $36 a year. For a price comparison, check out any health club in the world.

Back downstairs, the four racquetball courts that line the central hallway are very popular with the locals, and have spawned several champions at the local and regional level. Racquetball courts are rented on an hourly basis. $2 per person gets you an hour's use Monday through Friday before 5 PM, and on evenings and weekends the rate is $3 per player. Racquets are available for rental at $1 per hour, and racquetballs are sold for $3 a can. A 15-hour racquetball card can be used in either prime or non-prime time for $27. Wallyball, a singular twist on volleyball, is a popular game for groups. Rental of a racquetball court for wallyball is $6 an hour, including the net and ball.

Large locker and shower rooms are convenient to all perspiration-inducing activities, with direct entry to the swimming pool. If you want a locker for storage while using the facilities, that'll set you back anywhere from a dime to 40 cents, plus tax, per day, depending on locker size. Long-term locker rental rates are available.

The bowling center and game room are on the first floor, with separate entrances that also open to the rest of the building. The bowling center has eight synthetic lanes. Local leagues take up most of the lanes through the week from October through March, but open bowling is available every day and most weekend nights. Open bowling before 6 PM is $1.25 per game. After 6, the price jumps to $1.50 for adults 19 to 65, while junior and senior citizen rates don't change. Shoe rental (you must use bowling shoes—either yours or theirs) costs $1 a pair. To prevent gutter balls, channel bumpers can be installed in the lanes for 50 cents a game extra. Open bowling discount cards provide 25 games at a 40 percent savings: The adult card is $22.50, and juniors and senior citizens can buy a discount card for $18.75. Specialty tournaments (moonlight bowling, no-tap, Scotch doubles, etc.) are conducted most Saturday nights during the bowling season.

Adjacent to the bowling center and its refreshment area is the game room, containing two professional billiard tables, two world-class ping-pong tables, and an air hockey table. An hour of billiards costs $1. Ping-pong is free, but you need your own ball. They're available at the bowling counter for a quarter if you don't have one with you. Air hockey costs 50 cents a game—first player to seven goals, or the leader after seven minutes of play, wins.

Horseback Riding

A cautionary note: Horseback stables will invariably require you to sign a release form before you ride in which you agree not to hold the business responsible if you happen to take a nasty spill. In other words, you ride at your own risk.

Sevierville

Douglas Lake View Stables
1650 Providence Rd., Sevierville
• **(865) 428-3587**

These riding stables are located among scenic rolling hills near Douglas Lake, just a few miles off Tenn. 66. They've been providing guided horseback tours for about 10 years, and offer approximately 20 different horses for riders of all levels of experience. The stables are open year–round, opening at 8 AM in the summer and during the off season at 9 AM. Closing hours vary, depending on the weather, the time the sun sets and how many riders are around at the end of the day.

It costs $25 per hour to ride. They do offer an "early bird" special, which is a one-hour ride at half price if you arrive at opening. Typically, tours last anywhere from a half-hour to three hours, though some can last all day. Among the different rides available are lakeshore rides, mountain rides, trips to an old Indian burial ground and moonlight rides. For those who are even more romantically inclined, owner Jim Chambers, a chaplain, will perform wedding ceremonies and vow renewals for couples on horseback. Weddings range from $60 to $195.

Cedar Ridge Stables
1816 Chapman Hwy., Sevierville
• **(865) 428-5802**

At Cedar Ridge, scenic trails lead riders among wooded, rolling foothills. Both guided and unguided tours are offered for novice and experienced riders alike. Approximately 18

horses are available from which to choose. While you're there, ask if "Dan" is on the premises. Dan has been with the company for years, and is at least worth a quick look-see. Although he's an absolutely immense horse, he's as gentle as a lamb (a very, very large lamb).

Cedar Ridge offers half-hour rides for $15 and one-hour rides for $20. The stables are open year–round. In season, business hours are usually 9 AM to 6 PM. Hours vary in the off season, so it's usually best to call ahead.

Deer Farm Riding Stables
478 Happy Hollow Ln., Sevierville
• **(865) 429-2276**

You'll find these stables in the scenic hills east of Sevierville off U.S. 411. They're owned by the same family that operates the Smoky Mountain Deer Farm and Exotic Petting Zoo, which is located on the same property (see the Close-up in our Kidstuff chapter). Gentle horses are available for anyone age 5 or older, with the maximum weight for riders at 230 pounds. It costs $11 to ride for half an hour and $16 for a full hour. Group rates are available for 15 or more people.

The well-maintained trails are a comfortable eight feet wide and are shaded by trees for approximately 80 percent of the route. Deer Farm also provides riding instruction, mounting stands, padded equipment and guides who will tow your younger riders if you wish. Speaking of young riders, pony rides are also available near the stables for $3.75 each. Deer Farm Riding Stables are open from mid March through November, and their daily hours are 10 AM to 4:30 PM.

Five Oaks Stables
1650 Parkway, Pigeon Forge
• **(865) 428-9764**

These stables are owned by the same people who run Cedar Ridge Riding Stables. Although their address technically places them in Pigeon Forge, you'll actually find the entrance to the stables on the Parkway in Sevierville, just shy of the Pigeon Forge border. As such, it's one of the more conveniently located riding establishments in the area. Like at Cedar Ridge, you can ride for a half-hour for $15 or one hour for $20. There are no age or weight limits.

The stables have over 60 gentle horses from which to choose for your scenic trip through nearby rolling and wooded hills. At Five Oaks, only guided tours are provided, and guides are experienced. They're open year-round, and run tours from 9 AM to 6 PM.

Horseback riders have their choice of several stables in the Smokies.

Photo: Courtesy Gatlinburg Department of Tourism

Middle Creek Riding Stables
2909 Millers Way, Sevierville
• (865) 428-8363

Okay, here's another address that requires explanation. For all intents and purposes, the stables are located in Pigeon Forge, just past Dollywood off Upper Middle Creek Road. But because they are outside city limits, they are in "the county" and are given a Sevierville address (just remember that the stables are near Dollywood).

Middle Creek Riding Stables are part of the same company that owns the Cedar Ridge and Five Oaks stables, so you'll see the same pricing structure here—$15 for half-hour rides and $20 for one-hour rides. Kids ages 5 and younger ride for only $5 if they share a horse with an adult (using a provided custom saddle). About 20 horses are on hand to take riders on guided and unguided tours along hilly, wooded trails. The stables are open year round, from 9 AM to 6 PM in the summer and 10 AM to 5 PM in the off season.

Gatlinburg

There are two riding stables convenient to Gatlinburg, and both are operated as concessions within the boundaries of the Great Smoky Mountains National Park. For the sake of consistency, we'll describe them here.

McCarter's Riding Stables
U.S. 441S, Gatlinburg • (865) 436-5354

Founded in 1931 in downtown Gatlinburg, McCarter's Riding Stables are now inside the Park boundary south of town, near land once owned by Peter McCarter. Peter's son Marvin and Marvin's son Pete are the current proprietors. This business is one of Gatlinburg's five oldest, and is the oldest riding stable operation under continuous family ownership in the eastern United States. Experienced trail guides lead groups of any size over a variety of wilderness trails through the Great Smoky Mountains National Park. Individual rates are $15 an hour per rider, and the rule of thumb is the longer the ride, the higher you'll go into the mountains. Children age 5 and older are welcome, and a weight limit of 200 pounds is enforced. While certainly not forbidding, this is demanding terrain, and inexperienced riders are cautioned to consider that before riding out. McCarter's is open from early March through November.

Smoky Mountain Stables
East Parkway, Gatlinburg • (865) 436-5634

About four miles east of downtown Gatlinburg on U.S. 321N, Smoky Mountain Stables is owned and operated by Kenny Kear, a Gatlinburg native with an impressive string of credentials as a trainer of champion show horses. Open from early March through November, Smoky Mountain Stables has the same age and weight restrictions as McCarter's (above), and several mountain-savvy guides are on hand to ensure that the ride through the mountains will be as safe and pleasant as possible. It's important to consider that you're riding in an untamed wilderness, both at this stable and at its previously mentioned counterpart. The experience and local knowledge of the guides at both stables is best proven by the fact that neither stable has ever had a customer seriously enough injured that medical assistance was required to remove the rider from the Park.

Fitness Centers

National Fitness Center
950 Dolly Parton Pkwy., Sevierville
• **(865) 429-2400**
This 42,000-square-foot fitness center (which debuted in 1999) is one of the largest in East Tennessee. Facilities and programs are available for men and women of all ages. The upstairs half of the building contains an aerobics studio, a massive area of free weight and circuit training equipment, an indoor track and more than 60 pieces of cardiovascular equipment such as stair steppers, treadmills and stationary bikes. While you're working out on the cardio equipment, you can plug into one of 14 overhead television monitors. Downstairs areas include a junior Olympic size pool, juice and snack bar, sauna, hot tub, locker rooms, ladies' workout room and day car center.

National Fitness Center also offers an incredible variety of fun and healthy classes with certified instructors. Among the subjects available are karate, yoga, dance and aerobics. While the center provides a free child care facility, there are also special programs just for kids, including swim lessons, dance, karate and even summer camps with an emphasis, naturally, on fitness.

Health education and disease prevention are stressed. You can attend workshops on nutrition, blood pressure, cholesterol, back pain, smoking cessation and more. The center's staff also includes certified trainers to help you design your own personalized workout program based on the results of your initial fitness test.

The club offers a wide range of payment plans, ranging from daily rates to monthly and yearly membership packages. The center is open Monday through Friday from 5 AM to midnight. Saturday hours are 8 AM to 8 PM, and on Sunday it's open from 12 to 6 PM.

Martial Arts

Smoky Mountain Ishinryu Karate
1203 Cardonna Dr., Sevierville
• **(865) 453-1472**
This school has been teaching Ishinryu karate for more than six years under owner and Chief Instructor, Sonny Newman. Newman brings his 5th degree black belt status and 17 years of experience to his school, which averages about 15 students throughout the year. He continues his own personal training by working out with some of the highest ranking black belts in region.

Students of all ages are welcome—Newman has worked with children as young as 4 years old. It costs $40 per month to join, although the fee is a little less for younger students, and family and group discounts are available as well. Group classes meet Tuesday and Thursday evenings from 6 PM to 8 PM, but private lessons can be scheduled for other hours. In addition to classroom workouts, students are also encouraged to participate in tournaments and attend seminars.

Sevierville Ishinryu Karate Club
(865) 428-1894
Chief instructor Bill Marshall operates this karate school at Sevierville Intermediate School located on High Street. Classes meet every Monday and Wednesday from 6:30 to 8:30 PM. The club is open to males and females ages 7 and older. It costs $25 a month to participate.

Sessions usually start out with warm ups and exercises by all students then break up into individual instruction groups that are divided by levels of experience. Marshall himself is a 6th degree black belt with over 25 years of experience. Assisting him are any of his group's black belt students. While Marshall encourages his students to take part in area karate tournaments, he doesn't put too much emphasis on them in terms of advancement. Rather, his approach is to stress the fundamentals of karate in order to move up to the next belt.

Youth Sports

Baseball and Softball

Greater Sevierville Little League
(865) 429-6998
Since 1996, this league has given area boys

and girls ages 5 through 18 the opportunity to participate in America's Pastime. As with Little League baseball nationwide, Sevierville's teams are built on the principles of having fun while learning the skill of the sport. Each child is guaranteed to play at least two innings of each six-inning game. Sevierville Little League is open to any child regardless of physical or mental disability.

Teams are grouped by age. Five- and 6-year-olds play T–ball, while 7- and 8-year-olds play coach-pitch ball. Ages 9 through 18 are divided into two-year age groupings. Registration for the regular season takes place in February, and the games are played from April through June. There is also a fall league in play during August and September. In the fall, the emphasis is on training and development, and actual games are played in the older divisions only.

The cost to play in the Greater Sevierville Little League starts at $25 per season. However, fees are dependent on the parents' ability to pay. If a particular family isn't able to afford the fee, they are not required to pay for their child to participate. The league furnishes all equipment except for baseball cleats and gloves.

Sevier County Baseball Association
(865) 428-0171

The key distinction between the Sevier County Baseball Association and the Sevierville organization is that the former primarily draws its players from Pigeon Forge, Gatlinburg and Sevier County at large. The league is open to boys and girls ages 5 through 15, and the players are grouped in two-year spans. Five- and 6-year-olds play T–ball, and 7- and 8-year- olds are in the coach-pitch division. The older teams are subdivided by age groupings and have their own pitchers.

The season begins in April and consists of 60 to 70 games, culminating in tournament play in mid-July. Players are guaranteed a minimum playing time per game of six defensive outs and one turn at bat.

All games are played at Pigeon Forge City Park. Registration begins prior to the start of the season and costs $11 per player. Team sponsors and parents are responsible for providing uniforms and equipment.

Football

Sevierville Little League
(865) 429-5366

In this organized football league, kids have been strapping on the pads and tearing up the gridiron for nearly 40 years. The league is open to both boys and girls, although the girls are somewhat of a rarity. Children must be between 5 years old (and in kindergarten) and 11 years old to play. There are four divisions altogether, with several teams in each division. Two divisions of "grasscutters" are for ages 5 through 8 and two divisions of "pee wees," are for kids between 9 and 11. Each year, registration begins the third Saturday in July and runs for several days. The cost is $40 per child, but the league provides all playing equipment except for cleats. The season begins in early August, and after a nine-game schedule, wraps up with a "Super Bowl" game in late October.

Basketball

7th and 8th Grade Basketball League
200 Gary R. Wade Blvd., Sevierville
• (865) 453-5441

Sponsored by the Sevierville Department of Parks and Recreation, this youth basketball program plays at the Sevierville Community Center. It is designed for 7th- and 8th-grade youngsters who are not playing on school-sponsored teams. The league helps the kids develop their hoop skills in a fun and competitive manner. The league plays from mid-October through late January and the fee is only $3.15. Registration takes place at the start of the season.

INSIDERS' TIP

Fishermen who venture out to Douglas Lake will find it to be a bountiful source of many different types of fish. The best time to drop lines in the headwaters is in the spring, when you're likely to be more successful catching crappie or large mouth bass. In the summer, try trolling for bass, but keep your bait in the top 25 feet of water where there's more oxygen. In late summer and autumn, you might try for both large mouth and white bass, and in the winter, try using minnows as bait for crappie. Fishing in the tailwaters is also best in the spring. Depending on your bait, you're likely to catch more different kinds of fish in the river than in the lake. The main thing you'll need to watch out for is the surge in waters that occurs when the dam's generators are running.

Soccer

American Youth Soccer Organization (AYSO)
P.O. Box 5588, Sevierville • (865) 429-2976

Soccer has really caught on with youngsters in the United States over the last 10 years or so. Local Sevier County children are fortunate to be able to participate in AYSO, a program that stresses positive coaching, balanced teams and good sportsmanship. Best of all, each child is guaranteed to play at least half of every game.

All of these factors add up to a truly fun league that manages to avoid the cutthroat spirit of heated competition so prevalent in many youth sports leagues these days. At AYSO games, you never hear venomous parents yelling at referees as they try to live vicariously through their children. The kids are taught that having fun is more important than winning. As a result, a lot of children that would ordinarily slip through the cracks of organized sports get a fair chance to participate and develop their skills.

Sevier County is included in AYSO Region 440, with teams located in Sevierville, Pigeon Forge and Gatlinburg in addition to Caton's Chapel, New Center, Kodak and Pittman Center. The smaller communities usually just have one or two teams per age division. Cities like Sevierville that have larger permanent populations may have as many as ten teams per division, especially among the younger ages.

AYSO is open to any boy or girl from age 5 to 18. In this range are seven different divisions of two-year age groupings. Among the younger kids (Divisions 7 and 6), the teams are coed. When the kids get up to Division 5, the boys and girls are usually split into separate leagues. AYSO offers both fall and spring seasons. In the spring, the teams in Divisions 5 and higher go head-to-head at the end of the regular season and compete in a countywide tournament. All children who participate get some sort of trophy or medal for their efforts.

Registration takes place several times annually. The best time to sign up is during the spring tournament, but if you miss that, there's another big push in the fall when school starts. It costs $23 per child to play in either the spring or fall seasons and $28 to play in both, and there are discounts for registering more than one child per family. The costs of equipment and uniforms are extra.

Bowling

Young American Bowling Association (YABA)
200 Gary R. Wade Blvd., Sevierville • (865) 453-5441

This kids' bowling league is sponsored by Sevierville's Department of Parks and Recreation and plays at the Community Center's bowling lanes. The program is open to kids ages 6 through 18, and the fun takes place each Saturday morning at 9:30 AM beginning in mid September. The cost is a one-time fee of $7 plus a weekly fee of $6.

Golf

LOOK FOR:
• Area Golf Courses

Compared to other vacation spots in the South like Myrtle Beach, South Carolina, or the Pinehurst area of North Carolina, the Smokies aren't huge as a golf destination. The landscape doesn't lend itself to multiple course layouts, and the mountain lifestyle that been in place here since, well, forever, isn't one that leads to a lot of golf.

That doesn't mean, however, that if you're coming here you should leave your clubs at home. There are four beautiful golf courses spread about Sevier County, and all but one is within five miles of the Smokies corridor. Two are less than 10 years old, and one closed down recently for a year to undergo a complete renovation. Two are municipally owned, and top-flight course architects designed all four. Greens fees vary slightly from course to course, and most have in-season and off-season rate schedules—all quoted rates are in-season. Because the local temperatures remain moderate through December, it's not unusual to see golfers out on most of the area courses year-round, but the idea of coming to the Smokies to play golf in January and February isn't really a good one.

Reserved tee times are recommended from spring through fall, and some form of golf/lodging packages are available at most courses. They're described here from north to south, starting with the newest.

Eagles Landing Golf Club
1556 Old Knoxville Highway, Sevierville • (865) 429-4223

Laid out along Tenn. 66 between I-40 and Dolly Parton Parkway, Eagle's Landing opened in 1994. The course is owned by the City of Sevierville. From downtown Sevierville, go west on Dolly Parton Parkway (U.S. 411/441) less than a mile from the Tenn. 66 intersection to the next traffic light at Old Knoxville Highway. Turn right and go about 2.5 miles. You'll see the course on the right before you see the driveway. If you're somewhere on 66, take Boyd's Creek Road (Tenn. 338—there's a traffic light) west about 1.2 miles to Old Knoxville Highway and turn left. The course entrance is a little over a mile on the left.

The course is essentially flat, wide open for now (that'll change as the trees planted along the fairways mature), and very forgiving. The par 72 layout runs from 6900 yards at the championship tees to an almost pitch-and-putt 4600 from the ladies tees. Wide Bermuda grass fairways are bordered by rough that isn't a real hazard. The Little Pigeon river wanders through the course, providing more scenery than anything else, but it can jump up and bite you if you're not paying attention.

Information on course layout approaches the overload stage, with five tee levels to shoot from. Pin placements are changed daily according to a zone diagram, and all pins are placed in the same zone every day. The scorecard shows the zoning for each green, and they'll tell you before you tee off which zones to shoot for.

Eagles Landing breaks the day into three parts, with fees sliding to match the time of day. Regular fees (Opening until 2 PM) are $39.50 weekdays and $46 weekends. From 2 to 4 PM, fees are $34 and $39 respectively, and the twilight rate of $24 kicks in at 4 PM every day. Carts are required, and all fees include carts. Eagles Landing is a member course of the Na-

Beautiful scenery might make you forget you're in the bunker.

Photo: Courtesy Sevierville Chamber of Commerce

tional Audubon Co-operative Sanctuary Program, a national organization dedicated to preserving wildlife on golf courses. Non-play areas of the course are maintained as wildlife refuges, and sightings of deer, otters, beavers, several duck species, Canada geese, and even wild turkeys lend a grace note to playing the course. American bald eagles have been seen over the course as well. Eagle's Landing has golf package tie-ins with several area lodging facilities, and has detailed information available on the Internet—their web site is at www.smokymtnmall.com. Advance tee times are recommended during the summer to avoid long waits once you arrive.

River Islands Golf Club
9610 Kodak Road, Mascot
• (865) 933-0100, (800) 347-4737

Let's just get this out of the way and be done with it: River Islands is a spectacular golf course. Laid out alongside and in the middle of the French Broad River, River Islands is visually as pleasing as any course you'll play anywhere. Getting there requires a little more attention to the road than the other three area courses, but it's worth it.

Coming out of Sevierville on Winfield Dunn Parkway (Tenn. 66), turn left at the traffic light at Tenn. 139 (Kodak Road). It's the first traffic light after you cross the river on 66. Look for the blue and white signs. About three miles in on Tenn. 139, look for the Northview fire hall on the right, and take the next left (it's a four-way stop). Less than a mile later, turn right at Kodak Road, and follow it about three miles to the course entrance on the left. You'll see most of the course before you get to the driveway.

River Islands is an Arthur Hill design, and is the only course in the area rated by *Golf* magazine (four stars). It's a classic links-style layout, with five holes distributed among three natural islands in the French Broad River. Being laid out entirely along a river bottom, it's pretty level; it's also heavily forested. This course also has the interesting distinction of being located in two counties; from the tee at

the par-3 third hole in Knox County, your drive crosses the river and the county line, coming down 175 yards later on the green in Sevier County. Tee layouts make River Islands whatever you want it to be: The forward tees neutralize the ever-present river, and the back tees will test your club selection skills. The fairways are a particularly lush Zoysia grass that feels almost spongy but sets a ball up nicely. Of the four courses, this is the one that can bring you to your knees the quickest and for the longest time. Played from the championship tees, River Islands is a test of every shot-making skill in the game. From the two intermediate tees it's a constant challenge, and from the ladies tees it's not really a pussycat but it's a lot drier.

Greens fees are $40 Monday through Friday and $49 Saturday and Sunday until 11 AM. Fees drop to $32 and $42 respectively from 11 AM until 3 PM when the twilight fee becomes effective. After 3, it's $20 Monday through Friday and $25 Saturday and Sunday. This is an arduous course despite its relative flatness, and carts are required. Due to its extreme popularity, River Islands requires reserved tee times during the tourist season.

Gatlinburg Country Club
520 Dollywood Lane, Pigeon Forge
• (865) 453-3912, (800) 568-4748

The Gatlinburg Golf Course is the oldest and most mountainous of the bunch. Established in Pigeon Forge in 1955—because that's where the land was available—the club was closed for an entire year in 1993 and completely renovated. To get there, turn off the Parkway at traffic light #8 (the Dollywood light) in Pigeon Forge. You'll see the course on the right long before you get to the clubhouse driveway.

Gatlinburg is the only course of the four in the area that's landlocked, and the only water at all is two artificial lakes that play with your head on the 18th hole. The layout stretches about 6300 yards and par 71 from the longest tees, 4710 yards and par 72 from the ladies' tees, and it's like playing two completely different

INSIDERS' TIP

Bent Creek Golf Village has combination golf/lodging packages available at several levels, depending on size of party and length of stay. Details are available at (865) 436-3947 or (800) 251-9336. As municipally-owned facilities, Gatlinburg and Eagles Landing are constrained from arranging packages with commercial lodging places, but package information is available from the Sevierville Chamber of Commerce [(865) 453-6411, (800) 255-6411] or the Gatlinburg Visitor's and Convention Bureau [(865) 436-2392, (800) 267-7088].

The city of Sevierville owns Eagles Landing.

Photo: Courtesy Sevierville Chamber of Commerce

courses. The front nine is reasonably level and sandy, with three long par fives. Fairways are broad and most of them run downhill to the greens. Indian guides are no longer required on the back 9, but you may feel the urge to yodel from time to time. The 12th hole, aptly named "Sky Hi," is internationally known for its 200 foot drop from tee to green, making the 195-yard length look like a greenside chip shot. Play it long—there's nothing between the tee and the green but deep wilderness and the occasional cloud. There are very few sidehill lies on the back nine; most of the fairways look like canyons. Gatlinburg is a lot of fun to play if you really enjoy variety. Approaching 50 years old, the course lets its natural growth provide most of the challenge and scenery. Carts are required on this course, and you'll appreciate that fact after a round. Regular greens fees are $41 Sunday through Thursday and $51 on Friday and Saturday. Twilight fees of $36 and $46, respectively, start at 2 PM. A hun-

dred memberships are available at $750 a year, but don't reach for your checkbook just yet. The waiting list for memberships is just slightly shorter than the one for annual tickets to the Masters tournament.

Bent Creek Golf Village
3919 East Parkway, Gatlinburg • (865) 436-3947, (800) 251-9336

The farthest course from the Smokies corridor, Bent Creek lays along the foot of Webb's Mountain about 10 miles east of Gatlinburg on U.S. 321. A word of warning: Bent Creek is situated on a large resort property named Sunterra Resort. Don't be confused by the presence of signs bearing both names as you approach the course.

The course is a Gary Player design, running from a fairly flat front nine to a couple of mountain goat specials on the back. At 6200 yards from the championship tees to 5100 for the ladies, the course is medium length par 73,

INSIDERS' TIP

We know we've said it before, but it's worth saying again: Three of these courses (Eagles Landing is the exception) have extreme elevation changes. Since you've come to play golf and not climb mountains, don't quibble with the mandatory cart rule; you'll thank them at the end of the day.

with generous fairways and forgiving rough. Most of the greens are moderately sloped with practically no bunkers in front. There's a lot of water on the course, but it only comes into serious play on a couple of holes. Bent Creek is a very playable course for the intermediate golfer. For the fanatic who's only coming here to play golf, the resort has several combination golf/lodging packages available. Regular greens fees are $49 Sunday through Thursday and $54 on Friday and Saturday. Twilight fees are $27 every day, starting at 4 PM. Carts are required. Bent Creek's easy accessibility and long-term reputation make it a local favorite, and tee times are at a premium during the season.

Hit it straight—many of our fairways are tree-lined.

Photo: Courtesy Gatlinburg Department of Tourism

Weddings

How serious is the wedding business in the Smokies? More than 21,000 couples tie the knot here each year—exponentially more than the entire population of Sevier County. As a possible spin-off of the area's reputation as a premier honeymoon and romantic getaway destination, the Smokies have become a favorite spot for both weddings and marriage renewals.

LOOK FOR:
• Sevierville
• Pigeon Forge
• Gatlinburg

Tennessee's liberal marriage laws probably have a lot to do with it too—if you can see over the counter and your partner is of like mind and the opposite gender, the county court clerk will issue you a marriage license for $36 (cash only, please). And you don't even have to live in Tennessee to get a license here.

Seriously, if you can provide proof of age with a valid ID, you can get a marriage license at age 18 without parental consent, or at 16 with on-site parental consent. (That means all parents involved—if there's a single parent, the other parent's absence must be documented by death certificate, custody agreement, etc., and be presented with the license application.) In extreme circumstances, a court order can be requested for people as young as 14, with the same parental stipulations. There's no blood test required, no waiting period, and a duly-empowered official is as near as the telephone.

Arrangements are easily made for anything you want in a service, from a quiet ceremony in the woods to a full-blown society event in any one of some 40 chapels of varying sizes and degrees of circumstance (see section below).

The county court clerk's office is in the courthouse in Sevierville, (865) 453-5502. Office hours are Monday through Friday, 8 AM to 4:30 PM and Saturday from 8 to 11 AM. There are two branch offices as well. In Gatlinburg, go to the Shilling Center office building, about two blocks off the Parkway on Reagan Drive. The phone number is (865) 430-3404, and office hours are Monday and Friday from 8:30 AM to 3 PM, Wednesday from 8:30 AM to 12 PM and Saturday from 9 AM to 3 PM. In Pigeon Forge, visit City Hall on Pine Mountain Road, (865) 908-6613. This branch is open Saturdays only from 9 AM to 5 PM.

Goin' to the Chapel

Not too many years ago, you could count the number of wedding chapels in the county on one hand; these days you need both hands—about four times. As the scenic backdrop of the Great Smoky Mountains became a natural honeymoon destination, the wedding chapel industry slowly took root. Some may say that the chapels were meeting an already existing need. Others may contend that the Smokies became the "Wedding Capital of the South" because of the proliferation of chapels. In actuality, there's probably a little bit of truth to both schools of thought.

The option of a chapel wedding can be attractive to prospective married couples for a number of reasons. For one, they are often less expensive than large church weddings, and they can be planned more easily, in a shorter period of time. Wedding chapels can offer unique alternatives to the traditional wedding, including multi-denominational services and out-of-the-ordinary locations. One of the most appealing aspects of the chapel wedding is the fact that all of the elements of the event can be coordinated centrally, in a cooperative effort between the couple and the chapel's staff.

Admittedly, when one hears the term "wedding chapel," images of the cheesy glitz of Las Vegas may come to mind. We definitely don't want to leave you with the impression that any of our chapels are the quickie-marriage type of operation where you'll be hitched in less than ten minutes by an Elvis clone who hands out casino chips as a gift. Yes, you can get married in a relatively short period of time, but the chapels we've included are established, reputable businesses with tasteful, attractive facilities.

And you won't have to worry about someday finding out that your marriage wasn't legal. Each of the chapels we've listed (and most likely those we haven't) use ordained ministers to perform the ceremonies, most of whom have backgrounds in various Protestant denominations. Although all chapels offer nondenominational, Protestant-based ceremonies, there are those (which we'll mention) that are also able to provide marriage rites in other religious faiths. Just to be on the safe side, however, always ask about your minister's credentials, no matter where you choose to wed.

What to Expect from a Chapel

The chapels we've chosen will present you with a fairly wide range in terms of price and available services. Just about every chapel offers its own preset wedding packages, and you'll also find those that are willing to work with you to put together the kinds of services and amenities that you'd like.

What you get boils down to how much you're willing to spend. You can get a basic, straightforward ceremony for as little as $60 in some places. On the other hand, you can still spend thousands of dollars, just like you would in a larger church wedding. In between the extremes is where you have to decide what you want out of your wedding—a simple exchange of vows in a chapel or a more elaborate ceremony in a unique setting like a gazebo, waterfall or scenic garden. Some chapels can even arrange for you to be married on horseback or in a helicopter!

The chapels we've profiled provide most of the traditional tokens that are associated with wedding ceremonies themselves. Depending on the specific package, your wedding can include music (live or recorded), flowers, a garter, a cake, candles, mints and nuts, a wedding album, and more. All of the wedding providers with whom we spoke can either directly supply or make arrangements with other businesses for related services like photography, videography, limo transportation, and honeymoon lodgings, as well as receptions and catering. In some instances, a chapel might offer wedding packages that include honeymoon vacation activities like horseback riding, snow skiing, whitewater rafting or music theater shows.

For payment, you'll find that most major credit cards and cash are accepted. If you are reserving a chapel for a specific date, you will likely have to post a deposit of some sort; the deposit may vary depending on the total price of the wedding and the length of time between reservation and wedding. In most cases, deposits can be paid with either credit card or cash.

Most chapels will take walk-ins, but whether you will be accommodated or not depends on if the chapel has already been booked and if a minister is available. If you drop by on a Saturday in the summer or in February (Valentine's Day fever!), you're not likely to have much success. You'll probably have better luck with a walk-in wedding on a weekday morning in the off season. Your safest option: Call ahead of time and schedule your wedding.

Finally, bear in mind that the addresses we've included with the chapels below are primarily for the companies' business offices. In some cases, the chapel itself is not located at that address, and you'll need to start your inquiry by either calling or stopping by the business office first. You can make the assumption that our wedding chapels are open year-round, although some are closed on major holidays.

For this chapter, we've divided our listings up by city, then listed the chapels alphabetically within each.

INSIDERS' TIP

If you've already obtained your marriage license in another Tennessee county, you can bring it with you for your Smoky Mountain wedding as long as your ceremony takes place within 30 days of the issue of the license.

Sevierville

A Precious Moment Wedding Chapel
110 Echota Way, Sevierville
• (865) 428-6312, (888) 741-5683

Although it's only been joining couples in matrimony since 1997, this chapel offers a variety of wedding packages in a scenic resort setting. Located just off Winfield Dunn Parkway (Tenn. 66) at Echota Resort in Sevierville (see our Vacation Rentals chapter), the chapel itself is a spacious log structure with a "woodsy" interior look. With its cathedral ceilings and stacked stone fireplace, the room conveys a mountain lodge atmosphere. The chapel accommodates up to 90 people, and reception facilities are available on premises.

A Precious Moment Wedding Chapel offers several wedding ceremony options. With one of their more popular packages, couples can get married in their Echota Resort cabin. This wedding services provider has a staff of four, in addition to having three ministers on call. The chapel can be reached by e-mail at MomentWed@aol.com.

Smoky Mountain Wedding Chapel
158 Court Ave., Sevierville
• (865) 428-4741, (800) 922-2052

Couples have been saying "I do" at this downtown Sevierville chapel for more than a decade. Since it's located across from the Sevier County Courthouse, there is short ground to cover between getting your marriage license and walking across the street to the chapel. Reverend Robert Parsons, a retired Methodist minister, conducts the ceremonies in the chapel, which features an altar surrounded by white lattice, colorful flowers and greenery. The facility accommodates up to 25 people.

Smoky Mountain Wedding Chapel can make arrangements for weddings in other locations. Previous ceremonies have taken place at sites like the Cades Cove area of the national park and The Old Mill in Pigeon Forge. In addition to the Sevierville chapel, Reverend Parsons also has wedding chapels in Pigeon Forge that operate under the same business name.

Pigeon Forge

Back Home Wedding Chapel
3435 Teaster Ln., Pigeon Forge
• (865) 428-7998, (888) 835-7673

A variety of unique ceremonial settings is available through this wedding chapel, which has been in operation since 1996. Couples-to-be can choose from packages that range from traditional candlelight ceremonies in the chapel itself to outdoor weddings by a gazebo, bridge or waterfall. Other packages include horse and carriage weddings and even helicopter ceremonies!

The chapel, which is separate from the business office, is located on Chapel Ridge Road in Pigeon Forge. Its cedar structure conveys what the owners call a "rustic elegance." Inside, candelabra, cedar pews, a golden chandelier and burgundy carpet highlight the interior, which will seat as many as 35. Back Home Wedding Chapel has two ministers available and a regular staff of six to assist you with your options.

Golden Valley Chapel
4201 Dellinger Hollow Rd., Pigeon Forge
• (865) 436-3700, (800) 783-3737

Since 1996, Golden Valley Chapel has offered new couples a picturesque, country setting in which to say their vows. Located approximately three miles from the Parkway in Pigeon Forge, the chapel is an attractive wood structure that overlooks a peaceful mountain lake.

The spacious chapel seats up to 75 guests and offers an eclectic look that includes a prominence of wood with accents of burgundy and green. Candles, flower arrangements and antiques help adorn the interior. In addition to the chapel, wedding services can also be held at the outdoor gazebo where up to 15 guests can be seated. You can find out more about Golden Valley Chapel on the Internet at www.thesmokies.com/golden_valley.

In The Smokies Wedding Chapel
2225 Parkway, Pigeon Forge
• (865) 429-7274, (800) 893-7274

This wedding business actually runs two chapels, both of which are separate from the Parkway business office. The Smokey Ridge Chapel, located on a panoramic mountaintop, seats up to 40 guests within its cedar walls. The Mountain Mist Chapel seats as many as 80 and also is located in a secluded country setting.

In The Smokies has been conducting weddings since the early 1990s. They have access to five church-ordained ministers, and employ a staff of 12 wedding coordinators. They provide a number of different wedding packages, some of which include gazebo weddings, on-site receptions and honeymoon accommoda-

Another couple ties the knot.

Photo: Courtesy Gatlinburg Department of Tourism

tions. You can learn more about In The Smokies Wedding Chapels on the Internet at www.smokymtnmall.com/mall/smkwed.html

Gatlinburg

Chalet Mountain Wedding Chapel
890 Holly Branch Dr., Gatlinburg
• (865) 430-5568, (888) 686-5683

This place is truly in the mountains. On Mt. Harrison, near Chalet Village, you'll find this sparkling white Victorian-style chapel which seats 25 to 30 and was opened in 1997. You'll find a predominance of white on the inside as well, along with wooden pews, burgundy carpeting and a six-foot-tall stained glass angel. Other Chalet Mountain wedding settings include a gazebo and a 25-foot waterfall.

The chapel offers a full slate of wedding package amenities, including fully catered wedding receptions in the on-site ban-

quet facility that accommodates 60 people. The company also has a rental and realty office that offers approximately 60 chalets for honeymoon lodging. Discover more information on Chalet Mountain Wedding Chapel at its Website: www.chaletmountain.com.

Chapel in the Glen
412 Glades Rd., Gatlinburg
• (865) 436-5356, (800) 537-1505

A beautiful hilltop in the Great Smoky Arts and Crafts Community is the setting for this wedding chapel, in operation since 1995. The white pine chapel (complete with bell tower) and award-winning landscaping welcome couples into an interior decor replete with "woodsiness." A teal runner down the main aisle leads toward the altar, which is highlighted by a stacked stone wall and candelabra. The chapel seats 40 comfortably.

There are outdoor ceremonial settings as well, including a gazebo, a reflecting pond and a water-

INSIDERS' TIP

Typically, wedding chapels are busiest from May through October. Also, because of Valentine's Day, February is a hot month for tying the knot. Your chances of having a spontaneous walk-in ceremony are better during the other months of the year.

fall. Chapel in the Glen provides a full-time staff of six to help couples with wedding preparations. They do perform walk-in ceremonies, but caution that they will not join couples who have just met and are looking for a speedy wedding. To learn more about Chapel in the Glen, you can find them on the web at www.chapelwedding.com.

Cupid's Chapel of Love
706 E. Parkway, Gatlinburg
• (865) 430-3851, (800) 642-8743

Owner Rose Fisher opened her chapel in 1995, and in the years since has built up her business to the point that at times, she has bookings as far as two years ahead. That doesn't mean she's booked solid for the next two years, but it does mean that her availabilities for walk-ins are few and far between.

The quaint chapel is built of white-washed hand-hewn logs. Inside, the pew cushions and carpeting are shades of burgundy, and the walls are lined with colorful stained glass windows. Seating is available for up to 65 guests. Near the altar is a trellis with a climbing vine and magnolias. Outdoor settings include a bridge over a stone waterfall and a gazebo.

Cupid's Chapel has several wedding packages available, including the '50s Nostalgia package complete with oldies music. They can also arrange weddings on horseback for "outdoor" types. Some packages include lodging at Cupid's Love Nest, their own honeymoon accommodations.

The chapel uses four ministers and a regular staff of 16, most of whom have been with Fisher since day one. In addition to traditional, nondenominational ceremonies, Cupid's can also make arrangements to perform weddings of other religious faiths. They are open 365 days a year. Find out more on the Internet at www.tennweb.com/cupid.

Evergreen Wedding Chapel
109 W. Ogle Dr., Gatlinburg
• (865) 436-3400, (800) 464-3401

When you pull into this downtown Gatlinburg chapel, you're greeted by a quaint, traditional white facade. The interior is adorned with fixtures and trappings like candelabra, stained glass windows and hunter green carpeting.

Near the altar, a large brass arch is surrounded by ivy and magnolias. The pews can accommodate 25 comfortably.

Open since 1994, Evergreen Wedding Chapel and its staff of four perform traditional, nondenominational wedding services. They have several wedding packages from which to choose, and they can coordinate honeymoon accommodations as well. Visit them on the Internet at www.evergreenchapel.com.

Gatlinburg's Little Log Wedding Chapel
1350 E. Parkway, Gatlinburg
• (865) 436-8979, (800) 554-1451

This chapel is located near the entrance to the Great Smoky Arts and Crafts Community on U.S. 321. As the name states, the building itself is of log construction and offers a combined decor of rustic log and refined elements like stained glass windows, flowers and candelabra. It seats 30 people. Outside the chapel, a gazebo that's used for ceremonies can seat four to six guests.

Little Log Wedding Chapel has been in business since 1992. Their staff of ministers and coordinators will provide wedding services seven days a week. Visit their web site at www.tennweb.com/logchapel.

Mountain Laurel Weddings
1901 E. Parkway, Gatlinburg
• (865) 430-8986, (800) 408-8577

The decor of this Gatlinburg chapel looks like "a garden wedding brought inside," in the words of owner Jayne Wallis. The building's native stone and French windows are accented on the inside by flowing, ivory lace curtains. In addition to holding ceremonies in the chapel, which seats 50, they also perform outdoor weddings in garden or gazebo settings. Conducting the nondenominational ceremonies is the Reverend Wilson Lonas, an ordained Baptist minister who has been performing weddings for over 60 years.

In the wedding business since 1996, Mountain Laurel Weddings offers preset wedding packages, or their staff of five will happily work with you to create your own. They can also make arrangements for off-site receptions, and they can provide post-wedding lodging through their Victorian

---

WEDDINGS

INSIDERS' TIP

If you're definitely planning on a chapel wedding in the Smokies, consider making your wedding arrangements before making your honeymoon lodging reservations. You may get a better accommodations deal as part of your wedding package than if it had been purchased separately.

Gettin' Hitched at Jimmie Temple's

Amidst the growing competitiveness of the Smoky Mountain wedding chapel scene, there's one place that's managed to turn a deaf ear to the furor and quietly carry on the task of bringing man and woman together in matrimony for over 30 years.

Would you believe it's a feed store?

We kid you not. At Temple's Feed and Seed Store in downtown Sevierville, proprietor Jimmie Temple will perform your wedding ceremony (perfectly legal) as long as you've got a valid Tennessee marriage license. Couples have been going to Temple's to "pledge their troth" since Jimmie first became a Sevier County Commissioner in 1966.

Once you've presented your license, Temple, now in his 70s, takes you back into his office and leads you to "the marryin' corner" (a spot in front of the closet doors). If you haven't brought your own witnesses, Temple will scrounge some up for you, even if they're unwitting feed store customers. His civil ceremonies last about 20 minutes, which include the vows and even a little bit of pre-wedding
counseling. At the end, Temple reads "A Prayer For The Bride And Groom," an anonymously written piece of verse that he's been sharing with couples for years.

As busy as the man is presiding over marriages, it's a wonder that the family feed and seed business gets properly tended to. But there's plenty of family around to keep store customers happy, and Temple still manages to perform around 600 weddings each year. Overall, he estimates having joined between 12,000 and 15,000 couples since he began. So how do so many people find out about this place? "Word of mouth," is the simple explanation offered by Temple, who also served as Sevierville mayor in the early 1960s. "People that get married here tell their family, friends and coworkers about this place." Oh, and did we mention that he's also been profiled on CNN and written up in several regional newspapers?

The marriage man—Jimmy Temple logs in another newlywed couple.

Photo: Mitch Moore

WEDDINGS

One might assume that most of the couples who make the pilgrimage to Temple's are locals. Not true. As verification, Temple randomly picks out a date from one of his many marriage log books. On one particular day, couples from nine different states in the eastern U.S. stopped in to say "We do." Most probably discover that besides the unique aspect of getting married in a feed store, there are practical reasons as well. For one, Temple's is right across the street from the Sevier County Courthouse, where most couples get their marriage licenses. Also, Temple doesn't charge for his services. All he asks is that you make a donation to his church. By the way, he never handles the money personally; his son, James, takes it straight from the donation box to the church every Monday morning.

Over the past three decades, Jimmie Temple has seen it all, from the humorous to the touching. "Every one of the weddings is different—but some are more different than others," Temple muses. He told us one tale of a man who wanted to marry his common law wife of many years without it being announced in the newspapers. The couple needed to be legally married so that their grandson could receive some needed public assistance, but they were too proud to admit to the rest of their family that they had never officially tied the knot in the eyes of the law. With his typical compassion, Temple obliged the couple.

Temple frequently receives cards, letters and personal drop-in visits from folks he's married in the past. "Seldom a day goes by that someone doesn't drop by to visit for a minute." After that, it's back to work—milling grain, hauling fertilizer and occasionally marrying a couple of strangers. It's all part of a typical day down at the ol' feed and seed store.

WEDDINGS

Honeymoon Suites. The web address is www.smokymountainweddings.com.

Smoky Mountain Memories Wedding Chapel
122 Parkway, Gatlinburg
• **(865) 430-3834, (800) 258-6797**

Just as you enter Gatlinburg at the north side of town, you'll see this wedding chapel which has been in business since 1992. The quaint, traditional chapel, which seats 40 people, is located on a mountain stream and has an interior featuring candelabra, ivy and flower arrangements. For those looking to say their vows in an outdoor setting, patio and gazebo weddings are available as well.

The chapel utilizes three ordained ministers with Southern Baptist backgrounds, all of whom will perform nondenominational, Christian weddings. Smoky Mountain Memories Wedding Chapel has different packages of services from which to choose, some of which include honeymoon lodging in their Victorian Honeymoon Suites. Find them on the Internet at www.smokymountainmemories.com.

Victorian Gardens Wedding Chapel
571 E. Parkway, Gatlinburg
• **(865) 430-5683, (800) 597-1371**

As you're driving away from downtown Gatlinburg on East Parkway (U.S. 321), you can't help but notice this large white, Victorian-style chapel—with a seating capacity of 80, it's one of the largest ones in the area. The interior's colors are white with burgundies and mauves as accents. Two-story stained glass windows and large chandeliers add to the elegance found inside.

Although most of their ceremonies are nondenominational ones performed by an ordained Southern Baptist minister, Victorian Gardens has arranged for non-Christian weddings in the past. Since 1997, they have offered a broad range of options in their wedding packages, and have featured on-site receptions in their solarium. Victorian Gardens maintains a staff of eight to ten people to assist couples-to-be. Learn more about this chapel at its web site: wedding-chapels.com.

INSIDERS' TIP
We're just going to throw this one out there so you'll know. The Hard Rock Café in Gatlinburg is the only member of that national chain that has a wedding chapel on the premises.

The Arts

There's just something about a snow-capped mountain peak, a misty waterfall or a still country meadow that can't help but inspire artistic expression. Whether that inspiration ultimately translates into a painting of wispy watercolor, a multi-textured wood carving or a classic mountain tale, there's no denying that the Smoky Mountains have long been fertile ground for those who transform thoughts and feelings into what we loosely call "art."

If you ask those who live around here to name specific examples of "art," you're likely to get different answers. Some will quickly point to the hand-produced wares of mountain crafts people. Others might name their favorite music theater show. Others still might cite the work of their favorite local painter. Of course, all would be correct. However, in discussing the artistic and cultural landscape of the Smokies, we've divided this vast territory into two general camps. We've labeled one category as art that caters largely to the tourist and vacation markets. This includes the wide world of Smoky Mountain arts and crafts studios, including individual painters and their galleries. You'll find an in-depth discussion of these types of creative art in our Mountain Crafts chapter.

Similarly, we are also lumping the many music theaters of the Smokies under a more commercial umbrella. These shows feature talented musicians, singers, comedians and dancers who hail from all across the country (not to mention our own back yard). Refer to our Music Theaters & Nightlife chapter for a more detailed look at Sevier County's ever-growing community of performance venues.

In this chapter, however, we'll be looking at a different brand of the creative and performing arts—the less financially motivated offerings that, for the most part, promote participation as much as they do patronage. Several of our inclusions are nonprofit organizations with volunteer members who simply enjoy "art for art's sake." But in these cases, being "amateur" from a financial standpoint doesn't necessarily translate to "amateurish" work. On the contrary, Sevier County boasts theater and choral groups whose work rivals that of some of their professional counterparts.

The bad news is that because Sevier County has long been a haven for professional craftsmen and performers (who generate revenue), the other types of arts haven't always enjoyed that same favored status within local communities. The good news is that as resident populations have increased in recent years, the demand has likewise grown for accessible creative outlets. Hopefully, as interest in the arts flourishes at the grass roots level, support, recognition and respect will follow in kind from the local governments and the citizens in general.

The best news of all is that for a county with a relatively small permanent population, there is no shortage of means by which one can leap headlong into artistic endeavors. So let that serve as a cattle call of sorts for all you actors, painters, writers, dancers, singers, musicians and crafts

INSIDERS' TIP

The Sevierville Community Center and the Sevier County Public Library (also in Sevierville) both have exhibition rooms that are often used to display the work of amateur artists.

people. And if you're the non-participatory type who simply wants to sit back and enjoy the fruits of someone else's artistic labors—we're here to tell you that the fruit is ripe for the picking.

East Tennessee Writers Guild
P.O. Box 504, Kodak 37764
• (865) 436-2078

Devoted to the enjoyment and promotion of the art of writing, this group meets monthly to read and critique the works of its members. Both fiction and nonfiction writing are explored. The writers also hold workshops that explore various aspects of the writing and publishing industries, covering such topics as how to obtain copyrights and watching out for unscrupulous publishers. The guild is open to anyone interested in improving their knowledge of writing and getting published; annual dues of $20 are required of regular members. East Tennessee Writers Guild meets the third Thursday of each month from 6:30 to 8:30 PM at the Sevierville Community Center on Gary Wade Boulevard.

INSIDERS' TIP

Many of the area's nonprofit guilds and associations publish periodic newsletters that keep members and other interested parties up-to-date on group activities. Most will be happy to put you on their mailing list.

Elizabeth Williams School of Dance
636 Dolly Parton Pkwy., Sevierville
• (865) 453-9702

Since 1985, this dance academy has taught classical ballet, pointe, jazz dancing and tumbling to aspiring dancers ages 3 to adult. Instruction is available for dancers at all levels of experience. Although the length of any student's overall participation is open-ended, the school's regular sessions run concurrent with the school year. Summer sessions and a summer dance camp are available to students as well. Each spring, Williams' school presents its annual recital, where all students get the chance to show off their steps. The school also holds annual tryouts for three different performing companies that participate in numerous local, regional and national events throughout the year. In past years, students have appeared in venues at Disney World and Six Flags Over Georgia.

Gatlinburg Community Chorale
P.O. Box 5, Gatlinburg 37738
• (865) 436-4398

Offered as a non-athletic activity by the Gatlinburg Department of Recreation, this choral group is open to anyone age 16 or older. Founded in 1981, the Gatlinburg Community Chorale averages about 50 members throughout the year, and except for the director and the accompanist, all members are volunteers and no auditions or interviews are required to join.

Each year, the chorale puts on two major shows (three performances each) at the Gatlinburg Convention Center. The Living Flag, which is usually presented on Memorial Day weekend, is a showcase of patriotic music and show tunes along with some religious songs. The Living Christmas Tree, naturally, is a presentation of religious and secular music that celebrates the holiday season.

The "Living" moniker attached to both shows comes from the fact that the chorale's members are actually arranged on stage in the form of an American flag or a vertical Christmas tree, complete with red, white and blue colors or greenery and tree ornaments, depending on the event. No admission is charged for either of the annual concerts, and the City of Gatlinburg provides free parking for attendees. Being an entity of the Department of Recreation, the group has represented the city at various municipal functions over the years, including Gatlinburg's 4th of July Midnight Parade (See our Annual Events chapter).

Knoxville Museum of Art
1050 World's Fair Park Drive, Knoxville
• (865) 525-6101

Located in downtown Knoxville, overlooking World's Fair Park, this art museum has in recent years featured exhibits by such noted artists as Rodin, Ansel Adams, Red Grooms and M.C. Escher. Other exhibits throughout the year explore all types of art media, including painting, sculpture and photography. Even the art works of ancient civilizations have made their way into KMA's galleries. Although it's located well outside the bounds of our familiar Smokies corridor, we felt it's good enough to be included in this chapter. The Knoxville Museum of Art is explored in more detail in the Knoxville section of the Daytrips chapter. If you happen to make a Knoxville excursion part of your East Tennessee experience, this museum's worth a look-see.

THE ARTS

Sevier County Theatre Guild

Until 1995, Sevier County's only community theater company suffered from bouts of temporary enthusiasm. The group was known for showing intermittent signs of organization and producing a show, only to fade into the shadows until its next revival months or even years later. Despite this sporadic pattern, the guild did manage to put bring a number of shows to "the boards" that enjoyed local success, including traditional community theater offerings like *Bye Bye Birdie* and *Our Town.*

The year 1995 seemed to begin a watershed period for Sevier County Theatre Guild. Its first production in several years, the nostalgic musical *Bells Are Ringing,* brought together a cast made up of people who were relatively new to the area as well as those who had been with the guild since its earlier days. Since then, SCTG has gained momentum and popularity with each show it has produced. It has also gone from being

an unorganized gathering of actors into a chartered, not-for-profit corporation that continues to embrace a philosophy of "by the people and for the people."

In recent years, the guild has brought a number of well-known shows to the stage. Productions of *The Crucible, The Odd Couple, Godspell, Bus Stop* and *Twelve Angry Men* have impressed audiences with both the quality of acting and technical elements involved.

The only factor that's been a hindrance to the guild has been its lack of a permanent home. Leading a nomadic existence reminiscent of theater's infancy, SCTG has migrated from venue to venue, utilizing everything from school auditoriums to civic centers. Currently, the group is in the process of raising the funds and the community support necessary to secure a full-time residence.

Despite being in the midst of an organizational adolescence of sorts, Sevier County Theatre Guild has been an innovative force among its peers. In 1996, the guild inaugurated the Great Smoky Mountain One-Act PlayFest, an annual presentation of short plays by East Tennessee writers, making it the only such event of its kind in the area. The festival, which is usually stages each November at the Sevierville Civic Center, has been an excellent showcase for the writing, directing and acting abilities of local and regional talent. For two consecutive years, PlayFest was nominated for "Best Special Work" by the Knoxville Area Theater Coalition; the festival won the award in 1999. (See our Festivals and Annual Events chapter for more information.)

The Theatre Guild gives local actors a chance to shine.

Photo: Courtesy Sevier County Theatre Guild

Pigeon Forge Community Chorus
P. O. Box 1390, Pigeon Forge 37868
• (865) 453-8574

This chorus has been an entity of the City of Pigeon Forge since its formation in the early 1990s. Its steady average membership of 50 encompasses vocalists of all ages and backgrounds. The group has no requirements for membership other than a desire to sing and to have a good time. That philosophy is revealed in the chorus' motto, "We don't sing because we're happy—we're happy because we sing." Pigeon Forge Community Chorus puts together two annual presentations, an outdoor 4th of July show at Patriot Park and an indoor WinterFest program held at the Smoky Mountain Jubilee music theater (see our Festivals and Annuals Events chapter). The musical styles performed attempt to appeal to a wide audience and include patriotic tunes, music from the '50s and '60s, show tunes and Christmas music.

Sandra J. Blaine Gallery
556 Parkway, Gatlinburg • (865) 436-5860

This 1,800-square-foot facility is located on the second floor of the main educational building of Arrowmont School of Arts and Crafts (see our Mountain Crafts chapter). Since its construction in 1970, the gallery has regularly featured works of fine art in all imaginable media; on the average, exhibits are displayed for six to eight weeks at a time.

Throughout the year, the gallery provides numerous opportunities for amateur and professional artists alike to show their work. During its annual faculty invitationals, Arrow-mont's resident instructors are able to display their creations, while smaller sections of the facility are devoted to the finished work of students. The school also hosts a number of juried shows throughout the year which spotlight the talents of locally, regionally and nationally known artists. Several times each year, Arrowmont sponsors conferences devoted to a particular artistic medium. During these conferences, the main gallery's exhibition space becomes a showplace for works done in that medium.

Sandra J. Blaine Gallery is open Monday through Friday from 8:30 AM to 4:30 PM. Saturday's schedule is from 8:30 to 11:30 AM and 1:30 to 4:30 PM. Tours are self-guided. Admission to the gallery is free; many of the pieces you'll see on display, however, are for sale.

Sevier County Choral Society
P.O. Box 5997, Sevierville 37864
• (865) 654-7227

This new group, sponsored by the Tuesday Evening Music Club, was founded in 1998 for the purpose of advancing the appreciation of of choral music in Sevier County and East Tennessee. According to its mission statement, the society's focus is "presenting musical masterworks in an excellent, enjoyable, and enthusiastic manner for the purpose of enhancing musical expertise in both performing and listening." The Sevier County Choral Society is an independent, secular, not-for-profit organization open to anyone who loves music and is willing to seriously commit to group projects.

Through the work of classical composers like Bach, Mozart, Schubert and Handel, the group brings that genre of music to its audiences during three performance seasons—Fall/Christmas (two concerts), Winter/Spring (two concerts) and Summer (one recital). Concerts take place at Sevierville Civic Center, and you can learn about specific performance dates by calling the society at its phone number above.

Sevier County Heritage Museum
167 E. Bruce St., Sevierville
• (865) 453-4058

A free, self-guided tour of this museum brings the history of Sevier County to life with exhibits that date from ancient Indian civilizations to the 20th century. Housed in the building that once served as Sevierville's post office, the museum utilizes artifacts like Indian pottery and tools, relics from the homesteads of early pioneer settlers and everyday items like butter churns, spinning wheels, farm implements and guns. In addition to the actual physical evidence of the past, the museum makes good use out of newspapers and photographs to flesh out accounts of the people, places and events that shaped local history.

Although admission to Sevier County Heritage Museum is free, donations are welcome. Its hours of operation are Monday, Tuesday, Thursday and Friday from noon to 5 PM and Saturday from noon to 3 PM. You can park free anywhere along Bruce Street in historic downtown Sevierville. See the Attractions chapter for more specific information about what the museum has in store for its visitors.

Sevier County Theatre Guild
P.O. Box 5461, Sevierville 37864
•(865) 687-7068

Until 1995, the Sevier County Theatre Guild (SCTG) was little more than a group of stage enthusiasts who occasionally got together to put on a show. Since then, they've found their legs and have become players (literally and figuratively) on the regional theater scene. Find out more about Sevier County's only community theater group in this chapter's Close-up.

Smoky Mountains Storytellers Association

P.O. Box 9426, Knoxville 37940
• (865) 428-6701

Storytelling in the Smoky Mountains is a big deal, and you'll find plenty of people who not only consider it a passion, but are able to supplement their income with it as well. Whether it's a humorous story, a mountain fable passed down through generations or one of many "Jack Tales" (Jack, of beanstalk fame), storytelling in these parts is pretty much an art form in itself and helps to preserve and perpetuate the culture of the Smokies.

The Smoky Mountains Storytellers Association evolved from a group of people who had periodically gathered to tell stories in the Cades Cove area of the national park, beginning in the late 1980s. Realizing that they could function better as an organized collective, they became a chartered, not-for-profit group in 1994. Since then, they have maintained a steady membership of about 30 people, most of whom are storytellers. Some members function primarily as listeners (otherwise, why tell a story?) and some are involved in the more promotional and administrative aspects of the organization.

Each year, the group participates in a number of local and regional storytelling events and festivals including Tellabration as well the Smoky Mountain Storytelling Festival in Pigeon Forge and the Townsend Heritage Festival. Smoky Mountains Storytellers Association meets once a month at Lawson-McGhee Library in Knoxville. The group requires annual membership dues of $15.

Tuesday Evening Music Club

P. O. Box 126, Gatlinburg 37738
• (865) 436-7017

This musical society was first organized in 1920; today, its members remain devoted to the purposes of performing and learning about music. With a roster of approximately 25 active members, the Tuesday Evening Music Club is comprised mainly of vocalists and pianists, although there are no specific membership requirements to join. From September through November and January through April, the group presents a different themed program each month. Genres of music include classical, show tunes, sacred and patriotic. Performances usually take place at either Markhill Village, a retirement community in Sevierville (see our Retirement chapter), or at the First Presbyterian Church in Sevierville.

Each year, the club also participates in a choral group consisting of choir members from several Sevierville area churches. For roughly three decades, these combined choirs have presented an annual concert on the first Sunday night in May. Several members of the Tuesday Evening Music Club participate in other area music groups, including the Sevier County Choral Society.

Cherokee, North Carolina

A journey from the Tennessee side of the Smokies to North Carolina's side is a little like traveling to a parallel dimension. Both places are similar, but at the same time, a little different in important ways. Both are growing tourist centers that border opposite sides of Great Smoky Mountains National Park. However, the character of each destination is distinct from that of its counterpart. The area we've chosen for this chapter, the Cherokee Indian Reservation, has its fair share of shopping, attractions and entertainment opportunities, but most of them are very much flavored by the character and the culture of the people that inhabit the region. There's a lot to do, see and learn about while you're in Cherokee. In fact, there's much more than you could possibly take on in one day.

The 56,000-acre Cherokee Indian Reservation, known by the people who live there as the Qualla Boundary, borders Great Smoky Mountains National Park on the south and also includes the southern terminus of the Blue Ridge Parkway. At one time the Cherokee culture was prevalent throughout the Carolinas. Its influence can still be seen today, in the names of many towns and other geographic features in this area (Nantahala National Forest, Tuckasegee River), as well as in the foods that are staples in Western North Carolina. The 11,000 members of the Eastern Band of Cherokee (as opposed to the Western Band, similarly relegated to Oklahoma) have done their part to keep the culture alive. For much more on the history and background of the Cherokee, we encourage you to pick up a copy of *The Insiders' Guide to North Carolina's Mountains.*

Like Sevierville, Pigeon Forge and Gatlinburg, Cherokee's tourism season generally runs from May through October. From November through April, some area businesses are closed, although lately, many are finding it easier to stay open all year as larger numbers of tourists discover everything Cherokee has to offer. When planning a visit to Cherokee during the off-season, be sure to check ahead of time to make sure that your intended lodgings, attractions, restaurants and other places to visit will be open when you're there. We've included seasonal schedules for many of the attractions outlined below.

Speaking of lodging, the Cherokee Indian Reservation contains nearly 50 motels, over 100 rental cabins and almost 30 campgrounds from which to choose, many of which are easily accessible from the heart of the reservation. Other locations offer scenic riverside and mountainside settings. Most of the hotels and motels are independent "mom and pop" establishments, but there are several nationally known franchises to be found. We've detailed a few overnight options below under "Accommodations."

Understandably, craft and gift shops abound on the reservation, dealing in everything from tourist souvenirs to art, jewelry and clothing. If

LOOK FOR:
• **Getting There**
• **Attractions**

you're interested in narrowing your search for shopping finds to authentic products made by Native American craftsmen, you might want to start with this list endorsed by the reservation (look for more information on some of these below): Bear Meat's Indian Den, Bigmeat Pottery & Museum, Cherokee Heritage Museum & Gallery, Eagle's Nest Gift Shop, Happy Hunting Ground Crafts, Keener Craft Shop, Medicine Man Crafts, Museum of the Cherokee Indian, Native American Craft Shop, Qualla Arts and Crafts, Talking Leaves Bookstore, Trail of Tears Gallery and Traditional Hands Gallery.

Getting There

The simplest way (although not always the quickest) to get to Cherokee from Sevier County is to take U.S. 441 from Gatlinburg into the national park and simply follow it all the way into Cherokee. As the crow flies, it's about 35 miles from Gatlinburg, but the road is curvy and often steep. Especially during peak season periods, traffic consists of large numbers of sightseers, so you'll be lucky to ever do more than 40 miles per hour. Count on a good one-hour drive from Gatlinburg. During the winter, U.S. 441 is sometimes closed because of snow, ice or landslides. Always be sure to contact the national park's information line if you're in doubt about road conditions.

The drive along U.S. 441 is worth it, however. You'll see vast, towering mountainsides and deep valleys that stretch toward the horizon. In October, when the leaves are changing, the foliage becomes a patchwork quilt of fiery color blanketing the landscape. Along the way, there are a good number of pull-offs and parking areas where you can stop and relax while you take in the views or put your camera to work. See our national park chapter for more information about what you'll encounter along the way.

Once you get to Cherokee, you'll find that things are laid out pretty simply. U.S. 441 merges with U.S. Highway 19 (which runs perpendicular to U.S. 441), forming a "T." Most of what you'll be interested in lies on or just off these two roads within a radius of only a few miles. There are a lot of signs, and with the aid of a map, you shouldn't have much trouble finding what you're looking for.

Cherokee Attractions

An exploration of Cherokee Indian Reservation reveals a wealth of Native American cultural activities that are both educational and entertaining. We've outlined a few.

Oconaluftee Indian Village
Drama Rd., off U.S. 441, Cherokee
• **(828) 497-2315**

Oconaluftee Indian Village is a re-creation of a Cherokee village circa the mid- to late 1700s. Cherokee guides lead visitors on tours depicting history through craft exhibits, replicas of early homes and a seven-sided Council House as well as demonstrations of beadwork, canoe and pottery making, blow guns and more. The presentation is done in a forested outdoor setting and gives visitors an authentic glimpse into traditional Cherokee ways of life.

While you're there, you'll also see indigenous plant life in the Cherokee Botanical Garden located along the village's nature trail. Oconaluftee Indian Village is open 9 AM to 5:30 PM from mid May through late October. Prices are $10 for adults and $6 for ages 6 through 12; group rates are available.

The Museum of the Cherokee Indian
U.S. 441 at Drama Rd., Cherokee
• **(828) 497-3481**

The Museum of the Cherokee Indian has undergone a $3.5 million renovation in recent years, and now utilizes state-of-the-art technology to tell the story of the tribe's history. The museum is an interactive attraction in which visitors are able to learn about the Cherokee past by walking through "time zones" representing specific periods and events, from prehistory through modern times, including the infamous Trail of Tears. Along the way, computer-generated images, lasers, lights and sound effects enhance the rituals and history that have long been kept alive by Cherokee "myth keepers." There's also a terrific gift shop. The museum is open year-round except for Thanksgiving Day, Christmas Day and New Year's Day. From mid-June through August, operating hours are 9 AM to 8 PM. From September through mid-June, hours are from 9 AM to 5 PM. Admission is $6 for adults and $4 for children ages 6 through 12; group rates are available.

Unto These Hills Outdoor Drama
Drama Rd. and U.S. 441, Cherokee
• (828) 497-2111

You can absorb more Cherokee history at this acclaimed outdoor drama, *Unto These Hills*. The show is presented evenings at Mountainside Theatre, a 2,800-seat, outdoor amphitheater. The show was created in 1950, and has since been viewed by more than six million people. The story begins with the arrival of Hernando de Soto and closes with the Cherokee migration along the Trail of Tears. The cast and technical crew of more than 130 people, many of which are descendants of the characters depicted, bring the Cherokee story to life through drama, traditional dances, costumes and a strong musical score. *Unto These Hills* is performed nightly (except Sundays) between mid-June and late August. Reserved tickets are $16 for all ages, and general admissions are $41 for ages 13 and older and $6 for ages 6 through 12.

Cherokee Heritage Museum and Gallery
Saunooke Village, U.S. 441, Cherokee
• (828) 497-3211

In addition to showing a new exhibit each month, this museum is a great place to shop for authentic Cherokee items like masks and crystals. There's also a selection of educational taped tours, books and craft demonstrations. The museum is open year-round, and admission is $2.50 for ages 11 and older, $1.50 for ages 6 through 10 and free for ages 5 and younger.

Qualla Arts and Crafts Mutual
U.S. 441 and Drama Rd., Cherokee
• (828) 497-3103

This craft cooperative displays the works of some 350 Cherokee artisans, in addition to offering crafts from other American Indian craftspeople from across the country. The store has a fine selection of

historical baskets, masks, pottery, finger-weaving and woodcarving. It's open year-round at 8 AM daily; there is no admission charge.

Other Attractions

Harrah's Cherokee Casino
777 Casino Dr., Cherokee
• (828) 497-7777, (800) HARRAHS

This legal gambling establishment, operated by the Eastern Band of Cherokee Indians, did for Cherokee what Dollywood did for Tennessee's Smokies—that is, helped it start the transition from a seasonal destination to a year-round one. Since 1997, Harrah's has provided gaming action and live entertainment 24 hours a day, seven days a week. It's very much like what you'd find in Las Vegas or Atlantic City, with a few exceptions that we'll address shortly.

If you arrive at Harrah's in your car, you can either park free in one of the many parking areas or pull up to the main building and have your car valet parked for $2 on weekdays and $4 on weekends. If you park in the lots, you can either walk to the casino or take Harrah's free shuttle to the front doors. A few rules before entering: you must be 18 or older to play the games, and although alcohol is not permitted on the premises, smoking is. Video taping is not allowed, but flash photography is welcome.

Inside, you'll find more than 1,800 video gaming machines spread out over 50,000 square feet of casino floor space. And yes, all of the gambling at this Harrah's is done on video machines. However, you'll still find video versions of all the typical casino games like blackjack, poker, keno, craps and Lock 'n' Roll, Harrah's own version of the basic slot machine. The games have minimum costs ranging from 25 cents to $1. In addition to quarters, machines also take small and large denomination bills.

Near the main entrance is the Games Master area, where staff members will help you learn how to play the different games. Although the games are all played on machines,

CHEROKEE, NORTH CAROLINA

One of many displays in the renovated Museum of the Cherokee Indian shows life-size figures of Ostenance, Cunne Shote and Woyi in London, England during the 1760s.

Photo: Courtesy Cherokee Tribal Travel & Promotion Office

CHEROKEE,
NORTH CAROLINA

Pottery making and several other ancient crafts are demonstrated at the Oconaluftee Indian Village, a re-created village of the 1750s open from mid-May through the latter part of October.

Photo: Courtesy Cherokee Tribal Travel & Promotion Office

The colorful Eagle Dance is performed during the summertime outdoor drama Unto These Hills *in Cherokee, North Carolina.*

Photo: Courtesy Cherokee Tribal Travel & Promotion Office

One of Cherokee, North Carolina's favorite photo attractions, a 20-foot redwood statue of Sequoyah, the inventor of the syllabary. The statue is located in front of the Museum of Cherokee Indians.

Photo: Courtesy Cherokee Tribal Travel & Promotion Office

CHEROKEE, NORTH CAROLINA

At shops such as Qualla Arts and Crafts, in Cherokee, visitors will find a wide selection of Cherokee hand-crafted products such as: "booger" masks, pipes, baskets, beadwork, jewelry, and much more.

Photo: Courtesy Cherokee Tribal Travel & Promotion Office

Cherokee craftspeople are known worldwide for woodcarvings, pottery, baskets, beadwork, stone carvings and much more.

Photo: Courtesy Cherokee Tribal Travel & Promotion Office

Cherokee basket weavers demonstrate their craft at the Oconaluftee Indian Village.

Photo: Courtesy Cherokee Tribal Travel & Promotion Office

they're very user-friendly once you figure out what you're doing. There are no buttons to push or levers to pull. All actions are conducted by simply touching a finger to the appropriate spot on the video screen. When you're ready to start pumping quarters, you'll find three cashier areas along the perimeter of the main floor. After that, you're on your own. If you need assistance with a particular game, you can call for an attendant by pushing a button on your machine. You'll also find plenty of servers on the floor, distributing free non-alcoholic beverages.

There is more to Harrah's than just gaming, however. Harrah's Cherokee Pavilion is a large auditorium adjacent to the casino that accommodates up to 1,500 people for concert performances, show revues and even boxing matches. Performers that have appeared on the pavilion stage include B.B. King, Roberta Flack and The Temptations. Tickets to these shows range anywhere from $20 to $100, depending on the performer, and can be purchased at the box office in the casino. During peak season, there are shows nightly at 8 PM, with occasional 2 PM matinees. Performances are scheduled sporadically during the off season.

Harrah's Cherokee Casino has three restaurants on the premises. At the Fresh Market Square, you can get lunch and dinner in an all-you-care-to-eat, buffet format for one single price. The menu boasts a wide selection of international and traditional dishes. For a casual lunch, dinner or late-night snack, you might try the Winning Streaks Deli, and for a more upscale dining experience, there's also The Range Steakhouse, featuring entrees like steak and lobster.

If you have children with you on your trip to Cherokee, don't let that necessarily discourage you from visiting Harrah's. The casino has a special area called Planet 4 Kidz, an arcade and snack bar where younger "players" can have

fun putting their own quarters to good use. Harrah's offers a child care service that charges $5 per hour for ages 6 weeks through 3 years old and $3.50 per hour for ages 4 through 12. Children ages 13 through 17 do not require adult supervision in the arcade. It's open from 10 AM to 10 PM Sunday through Thursday and from 10 AM to 2 AM on Friday and Saturday. In addition to the arcade, Planet 4 Kidz provides fun and entertaining programs to keep the younger set interested while the old folks try to double the college fund in the casino.

Other amenities found at Harrah's include a coat check facility, a passenger lounge area for those awaiting bus transportation, plenty of restrooms and the Jackpot Gift Shop.

Tribal Bingo
U.S. 19, Cherokee • (828) 497-4320, (800) 410-1254

At Tribal Bingo, which is also operated by the Eastern Band of Cherokee Indians, you can play one of the South's favorite games of chance for $1,500 as well as progressive jackpots, and all prizes are awarded in cash. The facility accommodates up to 1,200 players and is open seven days a week year-round.

Santa's Land Family Fun Park and Zoo
U.S. 19, Cherokee • (828) 497-9191

From late May through the end of autumn, the entire family can have vacation fun with a Christmas theme at Santa's Land Family Fun Park and Zoo. You can ride the Rudi-Coaster or the Ferris Wheel, take a train ride, cruise on the paddleboats or enjoy many other activities. The kids will get a kick out of visiting with Santa and his elves while the adults visit the park's many shops. There are also live shows, restaurants and the Santa's Land Zoo where you can pet and feed a variety of domestic and exotic animals. The park is open daily from 9 AM to 5 PM, and the single admission price of $13.95 (children 2 and younger get in free) allows visitors access to all activities.

INSIDERS' TIP
If you're traveling from Sevier County to Cherokee specifically to visit Harrah's and you're not up to the drive, consider contacting The Casino Shuttle Company at (423) 428-0270. This is a private shuttle service that's not owned by Harrah's, but does provide transportation exclusively to that destination using 25-passenger busses. They'll pick up from most hotels, motels and overnight rental accommodations in Sevierville, Pigeon Forge and Gatlinburg. There are also designated pick up points in each city for local residents. In season, they run four to five trips daily, and at least one per day during the rest of the year. The round trip cost is $20 per person, and there are group discounts for eight or more people.

CHEROKEE, NORTH CAROLINA

Cherokee Fun Park
U.S. 441, Cherokee • (828) 497-5877

At Cherokee Fun Park you'll find two miniature golf courses, a go-cart track, a game room, bumper boats and kiddie rides for the little ones. This attraction is open from April through October from 10 AM to 10 PM, with more limited daily hours during the off season months. Prices vary according to the ride.

Oconaluftee Islands Park

Naturally, being in such a beautiful, mountainous setting, you'll also find yourself face to face with a host of outdoor activities that allow you to capture the essence of any Smoky Mountain experience. Oconaluftee Islands Park is a recreational facility located on a patch of acreage in the middle of the Oconaluftee River. Wheelchair-accessible by footbridge, the park has picnic tables, grills, a covered pavilion and a walking trail. Along the trail, you'll encounter nine different audio stations that are part of the park's Talking Trees project. At the stations, visitors learn about the use of the different trees present at the site as well as their value to the Cherokee culture. There is no charge for use of park facilities.

Oconaluftee River Trail
U.S. 441 at national park entrance, Cherokee

Oconaluftee River Trail is a 11/2-mile trail (one way) that runs from the national park entrance sign on U.S. 441 to the Oconaluftee Park visitor center. The trail is flat and well-maintained and takes visitors on a peaceful trek through a wooded setting accented by the sounds of the Oconaluftee River.

If you'd like to take a more active role in Cherokee's great outdoors, there are many other activities for the partaking, including mountain biking, tubing, white water rafting, trout fishing and horseback riding.

Daytrips

LOOK FOR:
• Knoxville
• The Backbone of Tennessee
• Ashville, North Carolina

Frankly, it's hard for us to imagine anyone finding themselves at a loss for something to do in the Smokies. There are enough activities here to fill up weeks and weeks of hard-earned vacation time. However, if you're still itching to get out and explore the surrounding region during your stay, we aim to oblige.

Remember that the Smoky Mountains are centrally located within a one-day drive of two-thirds of the country's population. When it comes to searching for a brief excursion away from the mountains, that same centrality works in your favor. A host of great daytrips lie within only an hour's drive or so from the Smokies, and these short hops are the ones we've included.

Since Knoxville is only a half-hour's drive from Sevier County, we've given it more extensive coverage than our other selections. Beyond that, get ready for road trips to Oak Ridge, Tennessee; Asheville, North Carolina; and maybe some places you might not have even heard of. We'll show you attractions, shopping and a lot of rich Southern history. When you're done, just don't forget that our Smoky Mountains are waiting for your return.

Knoxville

Getting to Knoxville from the Smokies is a simple proposition. You have two choices, both of which require starting near downtown Sevierville, where U. S. 441, U.S. 411 and Tenn. 66 all converge. From there, one option is to head north on Tenn. 66 until you get to I-40. Then follow I-40 west for about 20 miles, at which point you start encountering Knoxville exits.

The other choice is shorter as the crow flies, but because of numerous stoplights near Knoxville, the driving time is roughly the same as if you take the interstate. That route involves heading west from Sevierville on Main Street (a.k.a. U.S. 411, a.k.a. Chapman Hwy.). Follow this road all the way through Seymour and you'll find yourself angling north toward the southern fringes of Knox County. Eventually, the road takes you into the heart of downtown Knoxville itself.

And since were downtown already, why not start our Knoxville daytrip here?

World's Fair Park and Surrounding Areas

Sometimes, a physical structure becomes so closely associated with a city that it becomes an icon of sorts. New York City has the Statue of Liberty, St. Louis has its Gateway Arch and Knoxville has the Sunsphere. You've surely seen pictures of it. It looks like a giant, reflective copper-colored golf ball perched high atop a steel gardened "tee."

Once the proud centerpiece of the 1982 World's Fair, the 266-foot Sunsphere now stands unused in an area that is still officially called World's Fair Park. The space inside the golden orb has been used for everything from meeting rooms to a restaurant, but nothing ever really caught on with the public. Currently the Sunsphere is closed for renovation, and it won't reopen to the public until 2002 (more on that below).

Regardless, visit the World's Fair Park neighborhood, wedged between Henley Street and Cumberland Avenue on the west side of downtown. The Sunsphere is still an impressive object to view, and there are plenty of places to shop as well as things to do and see in the surrounding area, much of the latter at little to no cost.

A good place to start is the historic Candy Factory building on World's Fair Park Drive. It was constructed in 1919 by Littlefield and Steere Candy Company, a confectioner whose candies were prominent in the South during the early decades of the 20th century. The building was renovated for the World's Fair, and today is the operational site of the South's Finest Chocolate Factory, (865) 522-2049, one of the only full-line chocolatiers in Tennessee. In fact, members of the families who owned Littlefield and Steere help manage the existing chocolate factory. In case you're wondering —yes, there's a candy shop full of goodies on site.

The other floors of the Candy Factory building are occupied by art galleries, gift shops and craft centers. The Arts Council of Greater Knoxville, (865) 523-7543, has its offices there, and the Knoxville Museum of Art, (865) 525-6101, operates a gift gallery on the main floor. Also on the main floor is an information center that provides a wealth of free literature on Knoxville area hotels, restaurants and attractions.

Speaking of the Knoxville Museum of Art, the gallery facility itself is located next door to the Candy Factory building on World's Fair Park Drive. Constructed in 1990, KMA houses multiple galleries that have held a diverse range of traveling exhibits over the years. Featured have been works by classic artists like the sculptor, Rodin, as well as more contemporary artists like Ansel Adams and Red Grooms. KMA has displayed everything from the treasures of ancient Peru to modern art made from trash. The museum also has an eclectic and admirable permanent collection of more than 1,000 objects in all media.

In addition to the exhibits, visitors can browse the gift shop or attend hands-on workshops, lectures and theatrical performances. Throughout the year, KMA's award-winning jazz concert series, Alive After Five, draws big crowds each Friday evening in the museum's Great Hall. Alive After Five costs $5 for non-members and $2.50 for UT students. A buffet is available for around $6 plus tax, but the exact cost depends on the caterer being used.

Museum admission is free for KMA members and children younger than 12, $4 for adults, $3 for seniors ages 65 and older and $2 for ages 12 through 17. For groups of 15 or more the cost is $3 for adults; for school tours, it's $2 per person. The museum is open Tuesday, Wednesday, Thursday and Saturday from 10 AM to 5 PM, Friday from 10 AM to 9 PM and Sunday from 12 to 5 PM. It's closed on Mondays and some major holidays.

Directly across the street from the Knoxville Museum of Art is Fort Kid, a free playground for ages 2 through 12. There are all kinds of things to climb over, slide down, crawl under, shimmy through and hang from. Just about all of the equipment is made of wood or tires, and it's designed to help spark the kids' imaginations as they play. Nearby are restrooms and a snack shop. Standing tall with historic grace, overlooking Fort Kid, is a short row of Victorian houses that were also renovated for the World's Fair. These days, the pastel-colored buildings are home to galleries, shops and the Knoxville Performing Arts Institute.

INSIDERS' TIP

George Vanderbilt's family wealth was first amassed by his grandfather, Cornelius Vanderbilt, a shipping magnate. George decided to settle in the mountains of western North Carolina after visiting there in 1888, concluding that the climate would be beneficial to his mother's health. After six years of construction, the Biltmore home was completed in 1895.

Everything we've described in this neighborhood is located on the west side of the waterway at World's Fair Park. You can cross to the other side on foot by bridge. There, you'll find the Sunsphere, the existing Knoxville Convention Center (which has more shops and restaurants) and the Tennessee Amphitheatre, (865) 523-4227. This outdoor concert venue is visually distinctive with its triple canopies made of white, Teflon-coated nylon. In warm-weather months, the outdoor amphitheater is the sight of musical performances by big-name acts from the worlds of rock 'n' roll, country and other genres.

The city is in the process of building a new 460,000-square-foot convention center that will occupy a site just south of the current facility. Construction is expected to be completed in the summer of 2002. Beginning in mid-2001, the World's Fair Park itself will begin a total makeover, including renovation of the Sunsphere, all of which will be finished in 2002.

DAYTRIPS

The World's Fair Park was the site of the 1982 World's Fair and remains home to some of Knoxville's most popular attractions, including the Knoxville Museum of Art, the Tennessee Ampitheatre, the Candy Factory and the Sunsphere.

Photo: Courtesy Knoxville Convention and Visitors Bureau

The University of Tennessee, Knoxville

Immediately south of World's Fair Park, the campus of one of the nation's leading universities stretches for more than a mile along Fort Loudoun Lake. Justly famous for its nationally ranked athletic programs and facilities, UTK is consistently cited as one of the nation's top 25 educational values among all colleges and universities. An average student population of 26,000 includes students from every state and more than 100 countries, pursuing studies in 15 colleges and schools. The main campus is isolated enough to provide an intimacy not usually found in a "downtown" school, but convenient to downtown Knoxville and several shopping malls. Cumberland Avenue, the northern boundary of 90 percent of the campus, is a main Knoxville traffic artery. The campus proper is laid out so that resident students live in easy walking distance to their classrooms and athletic facilities, and "Fraternity Row" is almost exactly centered in the campus. A drive (or even a stroll) through the campus is an interesting diversion if you're downtown and looking for a way to kill some time in pleasant surroundings. For general campus information, call (865) 974-1000.

Knoxville Zoological Gardens

Welcome to an amazing world of wildlife, displaying animals both familiar and exotic. More commonly known as the Knoxville Zoo, this 54-acre park was opened in 1948, and today it hosts more than 400,000 visitors annually. The simplest way to get to the zoo from any direction is to take Exit 392 off I-40 at Rutledge Pike. From there, just follow the signs to the zoo, which is adjacent to the Knox County Fairgrounds. Plenty of parking is available for zoo visitors at a cost of $2.

The Knoxville Zoo, (865) 637-5331, is laid out in a more or less linear pattern. The tour is self-directed, and the walkways and signs keep you pointed in the right direction. Along the route, you'll see a lot of animals you've heard of, and quite a few that may be totally new to you. Look for native black bears, baboons and an extensive collection of reptiles in the early going of your walk. Following is a stretch of large outdoor habitats that are home to elephants and white rhinos. Also nearby is the unique red panda, which actually resembles a large fox.

At Penguin Rock, you'll enjoy watching those lovable, waddling creatures as they play in their splashy habitat. At the Kid's Zoo, the children will really enjoy crawling through Prairie Dog Pass, a series of tunnels that let the kids pop up into special plexiglass domes, allowing them to go nose-to-nose with the zoo's prairie dog population. Nearby are a children's petting zoo and camel rides.

Birds are prominently displayed at the Knoxville Zoo. One exhibit takes you on an authentic outdoor tour through a Central American rain forest that puts you in the same enclosed area as several exotic species of flying creatures. There is also an amphitheater where demonstrations of free-flying birds are staged three times daily (except Mondays). Featured are birds of prey, along with talking parrots, penguins and other winged wonders.

The animals of Africa are well represented at the Knoxville Zoo. One of the largest outdoor animal habitats you'll encounter there is the African Plains, where you'll see zebras, giraffes and Marabou storks living in harmony. In the African Forest, look for the simian inhabitants of Chimp Ridge and Gorilla Valley. At the African Pridelands, you'll see adult lions roaming their territory. If you're lucky, you'll get some close up views of the baby lions playing near one of the glass walls separating man from beast. Along the way, you'll find other ferocious felines like tigers, leopards and cheetahs as well as a few unsavory characters such as the vulture, the hyena and the African wild dog.

Many of the exhibits throughout the zoo are equipped with Story Boxes. These boxes provide informative audio narration that give visitors a little more background on the animals

INSIDERS' TIP

Over the years, the Knoxville Sunsphere has certainly endured its share of abuse in the form of good-natured humor. The television show *The Simpsons* even aired an entire episode that revolved around Bart and his young friends road tripping to Knoxville (without an Insiders' Guide?!) to see the World's Fair. They arrive to find that not only are they 14 years too late but that the Sunsphere is now a wig outlet! In a sad, satirical poke at Knoxville's most famous structure, Bart and his rowdy companions throw rocks at the Sunsphere until it topples to the ground. Talk about no respect!

DAYTRIPS

than is provided on the exhibits' placards. However, to activate the boxes, you must use a special "key" given only to zoo members. Also throughout the park there are ample numbers of restrooms, refreshment vendors and gift shops. During the summer, there are even hoses that spray mists of water to help keep you cool in the heat.

At the main entrance you'll find the Zoo Shop, the main gift store where you can pick up a map of the zoo and rent strollers ($5 for a single, and $7 for a double) and wheelchairs ($5). By the way, all of the zoo's exhibits are wheelchair accessible. The Knoxville Zoo is open from 10 AM to 4:30 PM every day except for Christmas. Later closing times are in effect during warmer weather. Admissions are $6.95 for adults and $3.95 for seniors ages 62 and older and children ages 3 through 12. Discounted rates are available for groups of 20 or more, and the zoo accepts major credit cards as payment.

Ijam's Nature Center

The Knoxville Zoo isn't the city's only haven for nature lovers. Ijam's (pronounced EYE-ums) Nature Center, (865) 577-4717, is a nonprofit, environmental and education center on the Tennessee River, where visitors can get close to dozens of species of native animals, plants, trees and flowers. From downtown Knoxville, cross the Tennessee River via the Henley Street Bridge, take a left on Blount Avenue and follow the signs. Ijam's is located on Island Home Avenue, about 2½ miles from your starting point.

The 80-acre nature reserve offers different and interesting areas to explore —a forest, meadows, sinkholes, a spring-fed pond and gardens. Living among these environs are animals like opossum, muskrats, rabbits, snakes, turtles and frogs as well as breeds of birds like ducks, owls and herons. Among the native vegetation are native grasses, trees and wildflower species like toothwort, trillium, trout lily and bloodroot.

Visitors can view the park by taking any of the 3½ miles of mulched and paved trails (some are wheelchair-accessible) that meander about the acreage. A map is provided to help you navigate your way around the refuge and show you what types of wildlife to look out for in its different sections. One of the more scenic routes is the River Trail, which actually runs out over the Tennessee River via a boardwalk.

At the heart of Ijam's Nature Center is the education center surrounded by a paved plaza, waterfall pond, pavilion and gardens. Inside the center, visitors can browse the gift shop or view the center's many educational exhibits. Of particular interest is the giant cross-section of a 353-year-old tree that was cut down in the 1940s.

In keeping with its mission statement to "increase knowledge, understanding and appreciation of the natural world," Ijam's offers multiple environmental and scientific education opportunities in addition to the self-guided nature trail tours. The center features entertaining programs like Owl Prowls and Bat Walks as well as canoe trips, summer day camps and group tours. Visitors can even take part in the many special events, like the Fall Festival and Plant Sale and Symphony in the Dark, that are held at Ijam's annually.

Kids especially love exploring the natural world around them. Needless to say, Ijam's is a popular school field trip destination, and they'll even host kids' birthday parties with themes like Reptiles and Amphibians or Insects and Spiders! Older kids can take advantage of Ijam's Junior Naturalist program, and younger children can participate in the Wee Ones Series, where they learn about animals and plants through activities, songs, crafts and live animal presentations.

The trails at Ijam's Nature Center are free and open daily from 8 AM until dusk. The Nature Center and the Museum Store are open Monday through Friday from 9 AM to 4 PM, Saturday from 12 to 4 PM and Sunday from 1 to 5 PM.

The Backbone of Tennessee

The Great Smokies area of Tennessee is a programmed tourist destination where myriad activities can keep a family busy for untold periods of time. But you already know that. What escapes the notice of a huge number of visitors

INSIDERS' TIP

Metropolitan areas like Atlanta and Nashville are also within an easy half-day's drive of the Great Smokies. If you're interested in visiting either of those markets, check out the two Insiders' Guide books devoted to those cities.

The Knoxville Zoo is home to numberous natural exhibits, a variety of animal species and is known globally as one of the world's best breeding zoos.

Photo: Courtesy Knoxville Convention and Visitors Bureau

DAYTRIPS

seeking a true "wilderness" experience is that that experience is also in the neighborhood. But, because what we're talking about here is wild and woolly country, it's not immediately accessible on four-lane highways or visible from your hot tub. What we're talking about is the northern half of Tennessee's central spine, the Cumberland Mountains, and the river gorges that provide scenic views from 500-foot cliffs, all within two hours of the Smokies corridor. A day trip to any of these places can be experienced entirely in daylight hours during the summer and early fall, and the scenery is well worth the time and effort.

Big South Fork National River and Recreational Area

The Big South Fork of the Cumberland River and its tributaries wind through 90 miles of scenic gorges and valleys in the Big South Fork National River and Recreational Area, an unimproved wilderness that straddles the Kentucky-Tennessee border. Call (865) 569-9778 for information. The southern end begins at the Bandy Creek Visitor Center, about 15 miles west of Oneida, Tenn., on Tennessee Highway 297. From I-40 westbound, Exit 347 (Harriman/Rockwood) is U.S. Highway 27; go north about 60 miles to Oneida, and take Tennessee Highway 297 west into the park (about 15 miles). From I-75 northbound, use Exit 144 and follow Tenn. 63 west about 20 miles to Tenn. 297, and then through Oneida into the park. If your plans include riding the Big South Fork Scenic Railway (highly recommended, and dealt with separately later on), your target is Stearns, Ky., about 20 miles north of Oneida on U.S. 27 and Kentucky Highway 92.

You can get your bearings and a lot of local information at both visitor centers. The Bandy Creek (TN) center, (931) 879-3625, is open year-round except Christmas. Hours are from 8 AM to 6 PM June through October, and 8 AM to 4:30 PM November through May. The Kentucky Visitor Center, (606) 376-5073, is open daily May through October from 9 AM to 5:30 PM. Hours may vary November through April. The park is open year-round, and there are no entrance fees. Once you park your car at either visitor center, you're in a wilderness area dominated by the rivers. There are very few amenities, even in the camping areas. As a "deep" wilderness, Big South Fork is a bird-watchers paradise, with sightings recorded of more than 160 resident and migratory species. Commercial licensees provide whitewater rafting, canoe rentals, and horseback riding excursions. Five campgrounds within the park provide facilities ranging from primitive to pre-historic for nominal fees, and backcountry camping is permissible anywhere you want to throw down a bedroll. Keep the term "wilderness" uppermost in your mind at all times; while you're not totally isolated from civilization, this is not a trip for people unaccustomed to a fairly uncompromising lifestyle.

Big South Fork Scenic Railway

The thing that attracted humans to this area in the first place was coal. It was the world's chief source of fuel for industry, railroads, and shipping, and mining that coal was southeastern Kentucky's very lifeblood. Time and technology have all but eliminated the coal industry in Kentucky and Tennessee, but the memory of how it was in the heyday of coal mining in "company towns" is preserved at the Blue Heron Mining Community in the Big South Fork National River and Recreation Area. The best way to see this historic town is on the Big South Fork Scenic Railway, (606) 376-5330. Leaving Stearns, the covered, open-air train travels several miles through mountains and meadows (think of it as a continual photo-op) to the Blue Heron Mine, once an actual mining town that's been preserved by the National Park Service as a historical site. The self-guiding tour through the community shows how coal was mined and how the people who mined it lived, loved, worshiped, and died. The round trip is about three hours in total length. Trains depart the Stearns depot at 10 AM every day, with additional trips at 2 PM on weekend days during the summer. A third departure at 11:30 is scheduled during the busy weekends in October, when the autumn colors are their most unbelievable. Fares are $5 for children aged 4-12, $10 for adults to age 60, and $9.50 for senior citizens. Children under 3 ride free, and group rates are available on request.

Historic Rugby

In 1880, the noted British author and social reformer Thomas Hughes founded the community of Rugby as a classless, co-operative society where Britain's younger gentry, who weren't going to inherit the family wealth, could build a "new community through agriculture, temperance, and high Christian principles." How he even found this lovely location, much less decided to take his stand here, is lost in antiquity, but Thomas Hughes found it nonetheless, and he brought a lot of his rich friends with him.

The experiment, like every socialist attempt before or since, flopped. Thomas Hughes' legacy, however, is a living museum of more than 20 decorative, gabled buildings, that gives the visitor an understanding of how Victorian culture and Tennessee mountains were not exactly a match made in heaven. Recommended for serious students of history, Rugby is listed on the National Register of Historic Places. Daily guided tours and frequent festivals throughout the year provide an interesting view of a Utopian idea that's about the last thing you'd expect to find in the wilderness of Tennessee's Cumberland plateau. Call (865) 628-2441 for information.

Rugby is 35 miles west of I-75 Exit 141 (Tenn. 63 west to U.S. 27, then west on Tennessee Highway 52), and 35 miles north of I-40 Exit 347 (U.S. 27 north to Tenn. 52, then west to Rugby). Historic Rugby is laid out along a half-mile stretch of Tenn. 52, and is open year-round. General admission for the guided tours is $4 for adults and $2 for students. Admission fees are used to maintain the village.

Asheville, North Carolina

Asheville has always played a prominent role in the development of western North Carolina, especially gaining vibrancy around the turn of the century. At that time, Asheville built its reputation as a place where those of poor health could retreat and recuperate in a cool, mountain climate. When the city became connected to surrounding regions by the railroad, it began to truly stake its claim as a tourist destination. For much more information on Asheville and the surrounding mountain counties of North Carolina, pick up a copy of *The Insiders' Guide to North Carolina's Mountains*.

Getting There

From downtown Sevierville, take U.S. 411N. and follow it for approximately 25 miles east (yes, U.S. 411N. heads east) to Newport, Tenn. At Newport, take I-40 eastbound and follow the signs to Asheville. Once you near Asheville, you can either stay on I-40 (more convenient to Biltmore Estate) or take Interstate 240, which routes you more through the heart of Asheville and is more accessible to downtown.

If your point of origin is downtown Gatlinburg, take U.S. 321N. to Foothills Parkway, which will take you directly to I-40. From there, you'll take the interstate the rest of the way to Asheville as in the directions from Sevierville.

From Pigeon Forge, there is no direct route to I-40 without having to follow one of the above routes. If you want to keep it simple, make your way to downtown Sevierville or Gatlinburg and follow the directions above. In either case, there's a little bit of backtracking involved. Base your decision on which city you're closer to as well as other factors like the heaviness of incoming and outgoing traffic.

If you're starting from Pigeon Forge and you're a shortcut-taking kind of person, consider following Dollywood Lane out of town until it dead ends about ten miles to the east. Take a left on Bird's Creek Road, and within a mile you'll see a sign for a right turnoff onto Pittman Center Road. Follow Pittman Center Road all the way to U.S. 321N. and take a left. From there, continue to Foothills Parkway as in the directions from Gatlinburg.

Once you're on I-40, however, you're in for a wondrous, scenic drive that winds you to the crest of the Smokies range at the North Carolina border and then back down through beautiful vistas until you reach Asheville. Since the roads are hilly and curvy and the speed limits generally don't top 60, count on anywhere from an hour-and-a-half to two hours to make the drive.

Speaking of scenic drives, consider going into North Carolina through Cherokee and then taking the Blue Ridge Parkway to Asheville. Overall, the parkway is a 469-mile stretch of road running from Tennessee to Virginia that offers the motorist some of the most spectacular views of the Appalachian range. The drive combines nature's beauty with historical sites, mountain wildlife and numerous camping and picnic sites. At its extreme ends are Great Smoky Mountains National Park and Shenandoah National Park.

Biltmore Estate

This 250-room, French Renaissance chateau on 8,000 forested acres was the private residence of the millionaire, George Vanderbilt, and his wife, Edith, at the turn of the 20th century. In

Enjoy a glass of Biltmore wine with your dinner after you've toured the estate's grounds and gardens.

Photo: Courtesy The Biltmore Company

The University of Tennessee, Knoxville, the state's oldest and largest campus, is home to more than 25,000 students. Known throughout the country for its nationally ranked men's and women's athletic program, UT-Knoxville also ranks among the nation's premier research universities.

Photo: Courtesy Knoxville Convention and Visitors Bureau

1930, the Vanderbilts' daughter and son-in-law opened up the estate to the public, charging an admission to help add a boost to the local economy during the Great Depression. Today, Biltmore Estate hosts more than 800,000 visitors annually. It stands as a monument to the opulent heights reached by one successful American family.

It was as much a showplace 100 years ago as it is today, featuring then state-of-the-art luxuries that were only afforded by the wealthiest of people. Over the course of the two- to three-hour, self-guided tour, visitors can marvel at technology that was ahead of its day — amenities like central heat, electric lights and appliances and indoor plumbing. Overall, allow yourself the better part of a day to take in everything the whole estate has to offer.

Biltmore Estate is most easily reached by taking Exit 50 off I-40. From there, signs will guide you to the main entrance, which is flanked by a gift shop and a group sales office. The main driveway takes you to the Reception and Ticket Center where you can purchase your tickets. You'll be given a free guidebook to assist you in your tour, but more in-depth literature is available for purchase as well. There's also a scaled down replica of the entire estate on display inside, which will help you get your bearings as you plan your visit.

From the Ticket Center, it's a 3-mile drive to the main house. Along the way, you'll pass through some gorgeous countryside. The trees and shrubberies are all carefully orchestrated plantings, originally designed by the Vanderbilts' landscape architect, Frederick Law Olmsted. As you approach the house, you will be guided into one of several free parking lots. You're then left with only a short walk to the house. From the outside, the Biltmore home is truly palatial in appearance. Designed by architect Richard Morris Hunt, it's limestone facade and four acres of ground area lend to its stately presence among the immaculately maintained lawns and gardens surrounding.

Once you enter, the tour starts on the main floor, and allows partial to full entry of many of the rooms that the Vanderbilts used for entertaining and dining. Typical of almost all of the mansion's rooms, the salon, billiard room, banquet hall, music room, tapestry gallery and library are liberally and ornately adorned with fine furnishings, fix-

INSIDERS' TIP

Knoxville may mave lost its minor league baseball team, but the city still has a pro sports team in the Knoxville Speed, a minor league hockey outfit that plays its home games at Municipal Auditorium.

DAYTRIPS

tures and artwork. Featured are many of the treasures collected by George Vanderbilt in his travels, such as 16th-century tapestries and a chess set once owned by Napoleon Bonaparte.

The grand staircase spirals its way between all levels of the home, and guides visitors to the upstairs levels. There, guests get an inside glimpse at some of the private living areas of the Vanderbilt family, including Mr. and Mrs. Vanderbilt's separate bedrooms as well as a host of guest rooms and sitting rooms.

Perhaps the most interesting area of the home, the basement is not only where the Vanderbilts' guests enjoyed several indoor recreations, but where the servants lived and performed many of their daily tasks. The indoor bowling alley is one of the oldest in existence, and the indoor pool still boasts its original underwater lighting. Family and guests stayed fit in the gymnasium with its once cutting-edge exercise equipment. Visitors can also view the many kitchens, pantries and laundry facilities utilized by the Vanderbilt's house staff of 80-plus. Staff members lived in small individual rooms in the basement and had their own common dining room and sitting room for relaxation.

The tour concludes back on the main floor with a pass through the Bachelor's Wing of the house and quick peeks into the smoking room and gun room. On exiting, guests are pointed to an adjacent courtyard and set of buildings once used as stables. Today, the structures house several gift shops and eateries, including a bakery, ice cream parlor, confectionery and the Stable Cafe, a full service restaurant. For convenience, restrooms and an ATM machine are available in the Stable Courtyard area.

No visit to the Biltmore Estate is complete without a walking tour of the massive and colorful gardens. Your guide book indicates the different walking trails that criss cross the grounds, leading past tour highlights such as the Italian Garden and its three formal pools, the four-acre Walled Garden (half of which is planted with just roses) and the Bass Pond. The latter is located one-half mile from the house and features a boat house and waterfall.

Among the many beautiful and fragrant flowers that bloom throughout the year are tulips, dogwoods, azaleas, roses and chrysanthemums. Flowering shrubs and many varieties of wild-flowers also color the landscape, and in autumn, the estate's thousands of acres go through their annual kaleidoscopic metamorphosis.

Of course, what we've described only scratches the surface of the Biltmore experience. A casual drive along the estate's many miles of paved roads reveals acres and acres of farmland, all part of George Vanderbilt's vision of a self-sufficient estate. Situated in the middle of the acreage, about three miles from the house, you'll find the Deerpark Restaurant, one of three full service restaurants located on the property.

Five miles from the house is the Biltmore winery, open since 1985. The 96,500-square-foot facility is located in one of the buildings originally used in the estate's dairy operations. Tours of the winery take visitors through the entire wine making process. A tasting room, wine shop and The Bistro restaurant complement the experience.

Currently, construction is underway on a 213-room deluxe inn located on the Biltmore property. Inn on Biltmore Estate (as it's officially known) is a $31 million lodging scheduled to open in spring of 2001. It will be located on a hill above the Biltmore Estate Winery and will afford terrific mountain vistas from porches, balconies and guest areas.

Biltmore Estate is open year-round except for Thanksgiving and Christmas (incidentally, the home achieves new levels of visual splendor during the holidays with all its candles, poinsettias, wreaths, 35-plus Christmas trees and thousands of feet of garland!). The house is open from 9 AM to 5:30 PM, seven days a week. The rest of the estate and the Reception and Ticket Center are also open throughout the week, from 9 AM to 5 PM between January through March and 8:30 AM to 5 PM the rest of the year.

The winery is open seven days a week, from 11 AM to 6 PM, January through March and from 11 AM to 7 PM, April

The Blue Ridge Mountains showcase Asheville's distinctive skyline.

Photo: Courtesy Ashville Convention and Visitors Bureau

through December. Throughout the year, the winery opens at noon on Sundays. All of the Biltmore's restaurants and eateries are open year-round, except for Deerpark Restaurant, which is closed January through March. Biltmore shops are open year round, opening between 9 and 10 AM (depending on the shop) and closing at 6 PM.

Smoking is not permitted in any of the restaurants or in the Biltmore house itself. Also forbidden in the house are pets, photography, videotaping, sketching and any food or drink. Except for some sections of the house and gardens, most areas are handicapped-accessible. Hosts are stationed throughout the house to help answer your questions, and optional Behind-the-Scenes and Rooftop Tours are available for an additional charge.

Regular admission to Biltmore Estate is $29.95 for adults and $22.50 for ages 10 through 15. In November and December, the prices are $32.95 for adults and $24.50 for ages 10 through 15. Children ages 9 and younger are admitted free year round with a paying adult. To learn more about Biltmore or find out about specific annual events taking place there, call (800) 543-2961 or visit the estate on the Internet at www.biltmore.com.

Other Attractions and Points of Interest

If you're looking for more to do in Asheville, you won't be disappointed. A visit to the city's historic downtown district could, in and of itself, take up the better part of a day. Many of the buildings you'll find there managed to escape the urban renewal process that has compromised the downtowns of so many other American cities. With a prominence of art deco architecture, much of Asheville's historical charms are still intact. Thanks to the efforts of various preservation-minded groups in the 1970s and a more recent renaissance of sorts in the 1990s, this section of town still has quite a strong pulse.

Today, visitors will discover an abundance of shops, boutiques, galleries and restaurants as well as a strong antique district and even condominiums. Whether you're looking for a unique eatery or special gift to remember your visit, there's something to be found for every budget among the businesses of downtown Asheville. One structured way of

INSIDERS' TIP

When visiting the Biltmore home, you can rent audio cassette players that enhance the self-guided tour with useful information.

Knoxville's Old City

East of World's Fair Park, on the other side of downtown Knoxville, is a little neighborhood known as The Old City. Bordered by Central Avenue, Jackson Avenue, Gay Street and Summit Hill Drive, it is now regarded as one of the more colorful sections of Knoxville. However, its present character is nothing compared to that of its lively and often notorious past. So, before we tell you what you can find in The Old City today, let us take you back about one hundred years, to the days when gunslingers, gangsters, prostitutes and bootleggers made this section of downtown Knoxville their stomping grounds.

From the late 1800s through the early 1900s, there were quite a few characters, famous and infamous, who found themselves woven into Old City history. One night, Buffalo Bill and some Native Americans from his Wild West Show got drunk and decided to shoot holes into the walls and ceilings of one of the saloons. On that same street in 1901, Kid Curry, a member of Butch Cassidy's Hole-in-the-Wall Gang, shot two local deputies and escaped on horse across the Gay Street Bridge. During Prohibition, Knoxville was known as a clearinghouse for alcohol, and gangster Al Capone was often rumored to be in town.

In general, the area was considered to be less than savory. A newspaper article from 1900 regarded Central Avenue as being where "nine tenths of the criminal element congregate." The article went on to describe all-night saloons, cheap lodging houses and prostitutes in abundance. Over the years, the neighborhood was the site of a race riot, a hanging, a train wreck and a hiding place for runaway slaves on the Underground Railroad.

The Old City shows the way Knoxville used to be.

Photo: Courtesy Knoxville Convention and Visitors Bureau

DAYTRIPS

Today, things are decidedly different. The structures are still there, their turn-of-the-century architecture reminiscent of the Old City of yesteryear. However, the buildings are now filled with new and vibrant businesses that appeal to all demographics. The streets are lined with restaurants, nightclubs and coffee houses where aspiring musicians and poets often get the chance to present their fledgling works. There are unique shops, boutiques and antique galleries, many of which house treasures straight out of The Old City's past.

On the cultural front, local artists display their works in the various restaurants and shops, and theater goers attend shows at a performance space shared by many of the region's acting companies. Once a year, the Knoxville Area Theatre Coalition holds its Spotlight Festival in The Old City. During this two-day event, the Coalition's member theater companies stage plays at different venues around the neighborhood. Attendees get to see as many as six plays over the course of a day.

Throughout the year, there are other special events and happenings in The Old City, such as the Folk Music Festival and many others that are tied into holiday celebrations on Halloween, New Year's Eve, Mardi Gras and St. Patrick's Day.

About five years or so ago, The Old City was enjoying the height of its modern popularity. Unfortunately, a few isolated incidents of crime have tarnished the neighborhood's strengthening reputation. Despite the setbacks, Old City promoters and business owners are working as hard as ever to rehabilitate the area's image. In the meantime, we recommend that you check it out and hopefully do your part to make the Old City, once again, a neat place to be.

---

seeing the area is to follow Asheville's Urban Trail, a self-guided walking tour that highlights significant architectural and historical points. Maps can be obtained from the visitor's center at Asheville's Chamber of Commerce on Haywood Street.

The life and times of one of the century's most influential writers can be relived at the Thomas Wolfe Memorial on Market Street. At the visitor center, you'll find exhibits and audio visual programs that highlight the life of the Asheville native. Also displayed are works of art based on quotes from Wolfe's works. Normally, the memorial includes a tour of the Victorian-style boarding house run by Wolfe's mother, where the author spent a good part of his boyhood. Although much of the structure was destroyed by fire, and is in the process of being refurbished, the visitor center alone is well worth the stop. This attraction is open year-round but runs on a slightly more limited schedule from November through March. Admission prices are only $1 for adults and 50 cents for students.

Asheville, like the rest of western North Carolina and Tennessee's Smokies as well, is a haven for mountain crafts people. You'll see the work of some of its best representatives at the Folk Art Center, located on Blue Ridge Parkway at Milepost 382. The center is also the corporate headquarters for the Southern Highland Craft Guild. The guild has an active juried membership of more than 700 craftsmen, and only their works are displayed in the various guild-owned shops found across the region, including the Arrowcraft Shop in Gatlinburg (see our Mountain Crafts chapter for details).

The main gallery of the Folk Art Center hosts a wide range of exhibitions throughout the year, including the annual Members' Exhibition, which showcases works in all craft media, from the traditional to the contemporary. The center is also home to a permanent collection of craft objects dating back to the turn of the century. Adjacent to the main gallery is the Robert W. Gray Library Collection, one of the region's most notable resources of craft publications and books on Southern Appalachian history.

Visitors to the Folk Art Center are likely to show up on any of its special event days that take place throughout the year, such as Fiber Day, Clay Day and Wood Day; these events often provide hands-on opportunities for

DAYTRIPS

guests. Craft demonstrations can also be seen from April through December, showcasing the talents of artists working with brooms, corn shucks, wood and more. The Folk Art Center is open year round except for Thanksgiving, Christmas and New Year's days. The doors open at 9 AM, and admission is free (although donations are welcome).

One of the Southern Highland Guild's craft shops can be found on site at the Folk Art Center. The Allanstand Craft Shop is generally regarded as the nation's first craft shop, having been founded in 1895. It was in downtown Asheville until 1980, when it moved to its current home. Currently, it houses works of pottery, wood, glass, fiber, metal and jewelry made by members of the Southern Highland Guild. Another guild shop, Guild Crafts, is also located in the Asheville area, at 930 Tunnel Road (U.S. Highway 70).

Pack Place Education, Arts & Science Center is multi faceted complex located in downtown Asheville consisting of five different museums and cultural attractions. The Asheville Museum of Art, Western North Carolina's only art museum, displays 20th-century American art in a variety of media. The museum's permanent collection and special exhibits showcase the work of artists from around region and the nation.

At The Health Adventure, kids of all ages can learn about the human body, challenge their minds and stimulate their imaginations in the attraction's 11 different galleries. Kids 8 years old and younger can also enjoy their own world of fun in The Health Adventure's Creative Play-Space. Pack Place is also home to the Diana Wortham Theatre, a 500-seat multi-use facility that is the setting for a diverse range of performing arts, including music concerts and theatrical performances.

Pack Place's Colburn Gem And Mineral Museum has been dubbed "a mini Smithsonian of gems" by *The Washington Post*. An appropriate attraction, given the abundance of gems and minerals found in North Carolina's soil, this museum has numerous displays and hands-on exhibits devoted to stones from around the world. Finally, don't forget about the YMI Cultural Center. Commissioned as the Young Men's Institute by George Vanderbilt in 1893, this refurbished cultural center contains various galleries that host exhibitions, classes and performances presenting African American art, culture and history.

Neighborhoods and Real Estate

If you browse through Smoky Mountain area real estate listings, you'll frequently come across the headline "Views, Views, Views!" It's no wonder. Though abundant, views of the majestic Great Smoky Mountains are a treasured commodity around here. You could argue that views are what it's all about when it comes to the local real estate market. Those mountains are what brought tourism here in the first place, and time has proven that many who find the Smokies "a nice place to visit" do, indeed, want to settle among them as well. Then, consider all the people who have migrated to Sevier County to work in the businesses and industries that service the vacationer. The result has been long-term growth in all areas of real estate—not just in the sheer numbers of properties being developed, bought and sold, but in the very nature of the industry itself.

Trying to put a finger on the short-term pulse of the market, it might be hard to get consistent feedback. One area real estate broker hypothesized that in some cases, a strong economy can actually cause sellers to raise their asking prices since buyers can still benefit from the lower payments afforded by favorable interest rates. Subsequently, these higher prices result in fewer buyers. If, in fact, that has been the case, the good news is that the Smoky Mountain real estate scene has become more of a buyer's market as owners have dropped their asking prices in recent years. According to statistics from the local Multiple Listing System (MLS), the number of overall real estate transactions increased by 18 percent between 1997 and 1998. More good news for home owners and buyers is that thanks to the large amount of revenue generated by tourism, property tax rates in Sevier County are among the lowest in Tennessee.

Those who are seriously considering relocating to the area should be given a few general notes up front about what to expect when it comes to the housing situation. If your idea of a "dream house" is a historically significant structure on a quaint, tree-lined street, you're going to find slim pickings. With certain exceptions, the communities of the county are characterized by neighborhoods and subdivisions that have generally been around fewer than 30 years, much of that being developed just within the last ten years. There are pockets of homes in the central areas of Gatlinburg and Sevierville that have longer histories, but basically, you're looking at a fairly new market. In the more isolated, rural areas outside the main communities, you'll find mixes of both newer and older homes; it's not uncommon to find an old, fixer-upper farmhouse situated within a mile of a new, sprawling cedar and stone home perched atop multiple grassy acres.

You'll also find that Sevier County is an architectural patchwork quilt in which the styles and types of homes vary from community to community, depending on the prevalence of tourist activity in that area.

LOOK FOR:
- **Neighborhoods**
- **Apartments**
- **Real Estate Listings**
- **Real Estate Companies**
- **Auctions**
- **To Build or Not to Build**

VISIT US TODAY!
www.insiders.com

Part of one town might have a generous supply of ranch style homes. Another section of another town might be saturated with chalets built into steep hillsides. Yet another area might provide a steady landscape of newly constructed log cabins. Condos are becoming increasingly popular county-wide, and in both the cities and the rural areas there are numerous sites to place mobile homes. In the northern half of the county, variations on the standard ranch style house are typical, while southern Sevier County has more cottages, cabins, condos and chalets. What you ultimately choose depends on your aesthetic preferences, your price range and, to some degree, your motives for moving here in the first place.

To shed further light on the gradations in the Smokies' real estate marketplace, we'll take you through the area's primary population centers and give you some of the basic information about what you'll find and how much it will cost. We've divided this section according to Sevier County's three primary towns, but throughout each, we'll cut a wide swath of territory, incorporating several smaller, outlying communities. Because it's the primary residential center of the county with a year-round population of about 8,000, Sevierville and its outlying areas will receive a little more attention than the smaller cities of Pigeon Forge and Gatlinburg.

Sevierville

One of the more rapidly expanding areas, both commercially and residentially, is the Tenn. 66 corridor that runs for about eight miles from I-40 to Sevierville and also encompasses the small, unincorporated community of Kodak. This whole area, residentially speaking, is an especially popular location among couples in which one partner might work in Sevier County and the other may commute to a neighboring market like Knoxville or Jefferson County. Kodak's proximity to a number of surrounding job markets and its relatively light traffic make it a favorite site to put down roots. Northview Elementary School is also located there. Overall, home resale values are generally considered to be good.

Anyone who's home shopping in this territory can use some advance information about the utility services available. First, note that the city of Sevierville has annexed the narrow strip of land bordering both sides of Tenn. 66, from I-40 all the way in to the main part of the city. The homes and businesses that are so annexed receive all city utilities, except for sewer service, which stops a little north of the French Broad River. Most of the residential locations along Tenn. 66, however, lie outside the annexation boundaries. Some of those still receive city services, but at higher rates. In the other cases, utilities are either provided by companies that service surrounding areas, or septic and well water systems are utilized. When looking at a home that borders Tenn. 66, be sure to ask your real estate agent about its sources of electricity, water and sewer.

There are a number of subdivisions in the Kodak/Tenn. 66 area, some of which are worthy of mention here. Bentwood, which started development in 1990 had several of its speculative homes featured in the local Parade of Homes showcase during its first year of existence. With approximately 30 houses now completed there, prices in Bentwood start around $180,000 and go up. Another subdivision in this region is Grandview, across Tenn. 66 from the Lee Greenwood Theater. It was first developed as an exclusively upscale neighborhood, but after years of subsequent phases, many of its initial restrictions have been relaxed. As a result, less expensive homes are more prevalent further back into Grandview's newer additions. You'll find homes ranging from around $100,000 up to $300,000. The Royal Heights neighborhood lies within Sevierville city boundaries. Consisting of more upscale homes, you'll find prices generally starting at about $150,000 and peaking in the $500,000 range. Swanns Ferry, which started development in the mid-1990s, features lots bordering Eagles Landing Golf Course; home sites start at $55,000.

On our next stop, we're going to take a slight detour and briefly leave Sevierville altogether. The Seymour/Boyds Creek area is similar to Kodak in that it offers a convenient location for the couple that has careers split between Sevier and Knox counties. Seymour is a small community about 12 miles from Sevierville that lies in the extreme northwest end of the county, right along the Knox County border. Although it is regarded a "hot" area in terms of commercial development, Seymour is primarily a residential suburb of Knoxville with three public schools, one private school and handy access to the rest of Sevier County via Chapman Highway. Boyds Creek Highway connects Seymour to Tenn. 66 with a 12-mile stretch of road. On this scenic drive, you'll find a mixture of older, historical homes and newer construction of subdivisions like Valley View Farms. This area serves its residents well with distant but unobstructed views of the Great Smoky Mountains.

The real estate agents with whom we spoke quoted price ranges of about $125,000 to $150,000 for newer homes in the Seymour area. Taking into account homes of all ages, the average selling price of a house was a little over $100,000, according to 1998 MLS statistics. Although there was agreement that buyers can usually get more bang for their real estate buck compared to other communities in the market, the downside is that these properties don't appreciate as quickly as in places like Pigeon Forge or Gatlinburg. For that reason, Seymour is a better buy for someone who plans on staying put for a while. Again, many new residents are choosing to buy in newer subdivisions. Some of the popular developments are Van Gilder, Van Haven, Double D, Sharps Vista and Clydesdale.

Back in Sevierville, you'll find several major pockets of residential concentration that offer homes with a more diverse range of prices and ages. If you're driving in to Sevierville on Chapman Highway from Seymour, you'll come across the Hardin Lane neighborhood just as you near downtown. As you turn off onto Hardin Lane, you'll encounter several apartment complexes (see apartment section below), but further back, you'll enter a nice, established neighborhood where the homes date back to the 1970s. The streets are quiet and the yards are green and wooded—this could explain, in part, why these homes appear on the market infrequently. Prices here hover in the $100,000 to $125,000 range, although there are several homes in the neighborhood that are more upscale and more expensive. In the past several years, there has also been a lot of new construction activity in nearby developments like Paine Lake, Steeplechase and Saddleback Ridge. There, you'll find homes in an assortment of scenic settings including the banks of the Little Pigeon River and a nearby hillside. Prices are in the $110,000 to $200,000 range.

Downtown Sevierville is home to many of the older, two-story homes with wooden exteriors. Some of these date back to the early 1900s and have historical value. This section of town is noteworthy for its proximity to retail businesses and schools as well as county and city government offices. However, the same families have occupied a lot of these homes for years, and they don't appear very frequently on the market.

One of the fastest growing regions of Sevierville is the area east of Middle Creek Road. Commercially, land bordering Dolly Parton Parkway has been very active of late with frequent construction of offices, retail space and restaurants. Much of this came in response to the rapid residential growth in that part of town. The area in general has thrived because of a migration of local residents away from the more central, tourist-trafficked areas of Sevierville. As for housing, there are quite a few neighborhoods, both new and old, that border key streets and roads like Dolly Parton Parkway, Earnest McMahan Road and Pullen Road. Broadly speaking, this area features rolling countryside with awesome Smoky Mountain views. As with the Kodak area, be sure to check with your real estate agent about utility services for these homes; some lie within city limits and some do not.

Among the more well established areas are upscale neighborhoods like Birchwood and Blalock Woods. These both date back to the 1970s and are marked by large, handsome homes that are fairly well separated from each other and sit on wooded tracts. Birchwood homes start around $110,000. In Blalock Woods, values are higher, with homes starting around $150,000. Rivergate is a popular new area that offers housing in the $80,000 to $100,000 range with the benefit of city utilities. Since lots were first auctioned off there in 1996, homes have sprung up like dandelions. Somerset Downs falls somewhere in between the old and new classifications. It also has large, attractive homes in a more sprawling setting, but utilizes water wells and septic tanks. Prices there start around $150,000.

INSIDERS' TIP

In 1998, the average selling price of a three-bedroom home in Sevier County was $120,769, according to MLS statistics. Two-bedroom homes averaged $111,498 and condominium units averaged $78, 680.

Near Somerset Downs are the newer Sunrise Estates and Snappwood, where nice, modern homes started going up in the early 1990s. Houses in Sunrise Estates top out in the $160,000 neighborhood while Snappwood homes cover a wider price territory. They start as low as $120,000 with a few going in to the $300,000 and $400,000 range. Other names to look for include Shaconage, which is located off Pittman Center Road, and Victoria Landing, a hilltop condominium development with units starting at around $125,000. One of the best known subdivisions in this neck of the woods is Belle Meadows. The homes there are relatively new, large and attractive, but because it does receive city utilities, the lots are somewhat small and the houses are situated pretty close to each other. Nevertheless, it's a very popular neighborhood for families with children. Prices start around $130,000.

If you travel even further east on Dolly Parton Parkway (U.S. 411, which eventually becomes Newport Highway) and turn south onto Long Springs Road, you'll be on your way to two towns that are favorites among those who desire scenic, remote settings. New Center and Jones Cove, both of which are unincorporated, are 10- and 20-minute drives from downtown Sevierville, respectively. While these communities offer little commercially, each has its own elementary school. In addition to the more idyllic atmospheres found there, the property values of these two hamlets are very competitive compared to their neighboring markets. The average selling price of a home in New Center was $97,000 in 1998; for Jones Cove the corresponding figure was only $83,000. These figures are in line with a general assumption to be made about real estate prices in Sevier County: You'll usually find better prices on houses and land located in the more rural undeveloped areas.

Another section of Sevierville that offers nice homes in varying price ranges is the residential area that lies just west of the Parkway and runs from Forks of the River Parkway south to Lynn Road near the Governor's Crossing development. A conglomeration of different subdivisions, this area is sometimes generally referred to as Marshall Woods, which is actually the name of just one of its more popular neighborhoods. Within its streets, you'll find a little bit of everything, from large, split-level homes on quiet, shaded streets to houses that are more of the cookie-cutter variety, but still make for good values in this popular family setting. This area hasn't seen a lot of recent construction. Most of the building activity there took place from the 1960s through the 1980s.

Pigeon Forge

Pigeon Forge has probably experienced more commercial growth than any city in the county within the past 10 years, but it accounts for the smallest population among Sevier County's three main towns.

Upon seeing nothing but tourist-oriented businesses along the Parkway, vacationers to Pigeon Forge have often asked, "Where do people around here live?" One only needs to travel a block or two in either direction off the Parkway. While the main strip consists of one commercial venture after another, there are bands of residential areas that run parallel to the Parkway on both sides, from one end to the other. When you drive into these neighborhoods, it's like entering a whole new world. The often chaotic atmosphere of amusement rides, attractions and traffic is immediately supplanted by tranquil environs consisting of ranch-style homes and cabins on quiet streets. At the same time, however, you're never far away from all the shopping and recreation.

There are also residential areas along the arteries that feed into Pigeon Forge's city limits from the county. Side roads like Henderson Chapel Road, Wears Valley Road, Mill Creek Road, Dollywood Lane and Middle Creek Road all contain quite a mix of homes in terms of age, style and price. Speaking in general terms, the residential construction in Pigeon Forge has gradually evolved over the decades. The real estate picture is one of old frame farm houses, brick ranchers and cabins often mixed together in a random fashion, with few clearly defined "neighborhoods." In 1998, the average home in Pigeon Forge sold for about $108,000.

Much of Pigeon Forge's more recent construction is geared to the vacation and overnight rental markets and usually consists of cabins, cottages and condos (see our Vacation Rentals chapter). These types of properties can be found on or near the secondary roads mentioned above.

A heavy concentration of cabins and log homes can also be found in the community of Wears Valley. About eight miles southwest of Pigeon Forge, this unincorporated town has become a heavy contender in its own right in the second home market. A popular location with retired people as well as vacation/investment homebuyers, Wears Valley is very much of the same nature as Gatlinburg when it comes to real estate. For one, property values are a little higher than those in other parts of the county. Undeveloped house lots can go for as much $40,000, and the average sale price of a home in 1998 was more than $140,000. But on the plus side, property values seem to appreciate well. What makes this area so popular is its setting. Nestled in a peaceful valley at the foot of Cove Mountain, Wears Valley provides its residents with tremendous views in a laid back, country setting. The community also has its own back entrance to Great Smoky Mountains National Park via Lyon Springs Road.

Another community that's easily accessible from Pigeon Forge is Caton's Chapel. Traveling approximately 10 miles out Dollywood Lane will take you to this unincorporated town, the location of which makes for handy back road access to Pigeon Forge, Sevierville and Gatlinburg. In addition to convenience, Caton's Chapel also retains a tranquil, country setting. Outside of a few small stores and an elementary school, there's not a lot of activity. The growth that has taken place out there has been a blend of permanent residency and investment in second homes and rental property.

Gatlinburg

Like Pigeon Forge, its neighbor to the north, Gatlinburg has a daily population of more than 30,000 people during the peak season, most of whom are tourists. Only about 3,500 people call Gatlinburg "home" on a year-round basis. Since the city is surrounded by the national park on three sides, it is somewhat limited when it comes to finding new areas into which this permanent population base can expand. Gatlinburg is also topographically confined by its location, tucked in the narrow valleys among the Smoky Mountain foothills. There are a lot of businesses and homes packed and wedged into the compact dimensions of central Gatlinburg. The surrounding hills and mountainsides are also liberally dotted with chalets, cabins and condos. The only release valve that has been able to allow for physical expansion has been the area surrounding U.S. 321 (East Parkway), heading north and east away from downtown Gatlinburg.

Also, as with Pigeon Forge, the makeup of Gatlinburg's residential communities is a jigsaw puzzle of development that has evolved over the years. Locals live in a hodgepodge of commingled house styles, including cabins, chalets, cottages, condominium developments and even some traditional ranch style homes. Many of these homes are found along the numerous side roads that feed into U.S. 321. Near that highway, you'll find Quail Run, where homes can be found in the $150,000 range. One of the more recent subdivisions on the scene is Brent Hills, also located off U.S. 321 in the neighborhood of Mills Park and Gatlinburg-Pittman High School. There are also several established residential pockets found fairly close to central Gatlinburg. These include the Roaring Fork area, the Baskins Creek neighborhood, the McClain addition off River Road and the neighborhood near Gatlinburg's Mynatt Park. Outside Gatlinburg city limits, there seems to be an endless network of intertwining, country back roads, along which you'll find random scatterings of homes which can include cabins and older farm houses.

Because of its proximity to the national park, Gatlinburg real estate prices tend to be higher than those in other markets in the county. Although the selling prices of homes there averaged more than $133,000 in 1998, there are more affordable permanent homes to be had. You can find prices in the $90,000 ballpark, and of course, the diligent home shopper should always keep his or her eyes open for the occasional "steals" that pop up from time to time. Lot prices can fall within a wide range. In Brent Hills, for example, lots start at around $24,000 and go up into the $30,000 to $40,000 range.

Another section of Gatlinburg deserves to be treated as an entirely different animal when it comes to real estate—the area generally referred to as "Ski Mountain." This unique section of town, that began developing in 1968, is spread along the east face of Mt. Harrison and occupies more than 1,000 gorgeous, wooded acres. Driving just a couple of miles up Ski Mountain Road from downtown Gatlinburg, you'll reach Chalet Village, a realm where the chalet indeed reigns supreme. There are also quite a few condominium developments further up the mountain as you near the top (by the way, the ski resort of Ober Gatlinburg is located at the summit of this

Auctions are a viable alternative to traditional real estate buying and selling.

Photo: Courtesy McCarter Real Estate and Auction

mountain; see our Attractions chapter for more). Overall, chalets and condos account for approximately 75 percent of the homes found in this region. Although we deal with condos in more detail in the Vacation Rentals chapter, there are several names worth mentioning here, including The Summit, Edelweiss, High Alpine and High Chalet.

In the Ski Mountain area, the terrain is hilly and sometimes downright steep, but the setting is unsurpassed with its abundant woodland growth, rugged complexion and the always present native black bear. Those fortunate enough to live there year-round never grow tired of viewing the nearby mountains that dominate their picture windows.

The tradeoff is that this is some of the most expensive property in the entire county. In 1997, the average selling price of a three-bedroom chalet was close to $160,000. Properties in the $200,000 and $300,000 range are common. Condominiums can be found in a wide range of prices, starting as low as $35,000 for a one-bedroom unit to as high as $150,000 for a two- or three-bedroom unit. Prices often depend on the condo's location as well as its amenities. As for the demographics of Chalet Village homeowners, most are permanent residents, many of those being retirees. Understandably, however, there are a lot of homes that were purchased as vacation homes or investment properties; commonly, in these cases, the owners are absent and the properties are put on rental programs.

Another part of the county that's attracted both permanent residents and investment is the corridor of land along U.S. 321 between Gatlinburg and the community of Cosby in neighboring Cocke County. Along this stretch of real estate you'll find resort communities like Cobbly Nob, Acadia and Deer Ridge where houses and condos can be purchased for both permanent or vacation residence. All of the properties mentioned offer outstanding mountain views in a remote country setting as well as numerous amenities and convenient access to Bent Creek Golf Course. Homes in this area run, on average, from $150,000 to $200,000. Condos cost as little as $40,000 and as much as $160,000.

Apartments

Just 10 years ago, apartments were in woefully short supply in the Smokies. Back then, the modern, sprawling mega complexes typical of suburban America were virtually nonexistent here. The few developments that did exist contained only a handful of units and had few on-site amenities. As the tourism industry began to snowball in the late 1980s and early 1990s, more and more people heeded the siren song of the Smokies and ventured here in search of business and employment opportunities. Accordingly, the demand for apartments and other long-term rentals grew. In response, developers began meeting those needs. Today, the situation has improved markedly, although there is still a somewhat narrow selection available when it comes to sizes and styles of apartment. Even today, one- and three-bedroom units are overwhelmingly outnumbered by two-bedroom setups.

Fortunately, finding vacant apartments in general is much easier than it used to be. Only a few years ago, when apartments were scarce, your best bet was to grab the local newspaper first thing in the morning and start making calls. The good ones were rarely available and when they were, they were snatched up quickly. Now that more complexes have been built, there is a little more competition, and you see more advertisements for apartments in area newspapers and magazines. Renters should also be pleased to know that monthly rates in Sevier County are reasonable compared to surrounding markets. In 1998, the average rent for a two-bedroom apartment was $395, according to East Tennessee Development District statistics.

The vast majority of apartment complexes are in Sevierville. Gatlinburg and Pigeon Forge are better known for scatterings of long-term rentals (more often in the form of single-family homes and duplexes) rather than centralized apartment developments. As such, the complexes mentioned below are all in Sevierville, and even though it's not a totally comprehensive review of what's available in that city, it does represent most of the larger developments with the greatest number of units.

Off Dolly Parton Parkway, places like The Meadows, River Country Apartments and River Walk Apartments all offer attractive, modern two-bedroom units in good neighborhoods, close to schools. All three of these developments have swimming pools on the premises. Rents among these properties range from $425 to $650 per month, and year-long leases are required. Another area of Sevierville that offers a high number of units is the Hardin Lane neighborhood, just off Chapman Highway near the Little Pigeon River. There, you'll find three complexes within a short distance of each other, all requiring one-year leases. One and two-bedroom units are available at Mountain View Apartments in the $200 to $500 range, but the rate is dependent on your income. At Raeco Apartments, all units are two-bedroom and range from $375 to $400 per month. Nearby Woodland Park Apartments offers one-bedroom units exclusively and limits its clientele to senior citizens age 62 and older (see our Retirement chapter). Just off the Parkway in Sevierville is Cross Creek Village Apartments, with two-bedroom layouts in single level units and townhouses ranging from $415 to $550 per month.

Finding Real Estate Listings

A useful resource for the Smoky Mountains property seeker is *Homes & Land of the Smokies*. This publication is part of the largest real estate publishing network in the country, which, as a whole, distributes millions of magazines annually throughout thousands of real estate markets nationwide.

The Smoky Mountains edition of *Homes & Land* has been in print for over 15 years and is generally regarded to be the area's primary printed source for real estate listings. *Homes & Land* of the Smokies turns out 12 slick, full-color issues per year distributed in typical high-traffic areas throughout Sevier County. The magazine is also accessible via the Internet at www.homes.com. In 1998, this site was recognized by *The Wall Street Journal* as being one of the best real estate web pages in the nation. Those wishing to subscribe to *Homes & Land* by mail can do so at a cost of $36 for 12 issues or $18 for six issues.

Another resource for locating Smoky Mountain real estate listings is *The Mountain Press,* the county's daily newspaper (see our Media chapter). Properties for sale and lease are found in the paper's classified section each day, and on Sunday, *The Mountain Press* features a separate real estate section with both classified ads and display ads for local real estate companies. Of course, accessing a real estate company's web site is often another excellent means of viewing its most current inventory. We've included Internet addresses, where available, in our company profiles below.

Real Estate Companies

The growth of real estate as a service industry spread like kudzu through this area in the 1990s. In Sevier County alone, there are approximately 135 real estate firms with affiliated agents totaling well over 1,000 (including resort and time share agents). By comparison, only a little more than 100 real estate companies and a few hundred agents served the Smokies in 1993. Succumbing to the corny temptation to call the local real estate business a "cottage" industry, we can say with certainty that its lifeblood has been a direct transfusion from the popularity of the Smokies as a tourist destination.

In this section, we've included a representative sampling of real estate companies found in Tennessee's Great Smoky Mountains. Although each firm we've mentioned is found within Sevier County borders, we have included a geographic mix with offices found in some of the county's outlying areas in addition to the primary cities of Sevierville, Pigeon Forge and Gatlinburg. These companies represent diverse shares of the local market and generally offer a wide variety of real estate services. Some have in-house or affiliated property management companies, and some do not. Those that do typically operate some sort of short-term rental program through which a client's investment properties or second homes are leased out when not being occupied by the owner. Since this section of the chapter focuses on the buying and selling of real estate, we've made only passing references to overnight rentals here. For more details on that subject, refer to the Vacation Rentals chapter in this book. There, you will find listings for many other companies that will manage your own investment property or through which you can lease someone else's on a short-term basis.

Those who might be looking to buy real estate in the Smokies should be aware of the practice of "buyer's agency." Following a growing trend in real estate nationwide, Tennessee passed legislation that allows real estate agents to break away from the traditional practice of representing only property sellers and instead enter into similar fiduciary relationships with buyers. Such compacts ensure that the real estate agent works in the buyer's best interests when trying to purchase a home, business or piece of land. The terms of such relationships are spelled out in contracts, and of course, a real estate agent cannot act as a buyer's agent and a seller's agent within the same transaction.

Finally, a bit of semantics. The name "Realtor" is a trademark name signifying a member of the National Association of Realtors (NAR). Although not all real estate businesses are members of that association, each of the companies we've listed below is a member of NAR through either the Great Smoky Mountains Association of Realtors or the Knoxville Association of Realtors. One reason we've done so is that more than half of the real estate companies and agents in the area are Realtor members anyway, and since these associations require continuing education and adherence to a strict Code of Ethics by their members, we feel that steering you in that direction is a wise course of action. Realtors also serve their clients and customers through exclusive access to the area's Multiple Listing System, a direct-access line of information on all Realtor listings currently on the market.

Barbara's Real Estate Company
815 E. Parkway, Suite 1, Gatlinburg
• (865) 436-9303, (800) 233-9088

In business since 1973, Barbara's Real Estate is the oldest realty company in Gatlinburg still being operated by its original owner. Barbara Stevens runs a full-service company with a crew of five affiliate brokers who specialize in residential properties, many of which are found in the Gatlinburg area. Barbara's Real Estate handles referrals through a variety of relocation companies, and Barbara is always ready to use her lifetime of residency in Gatlinburg to add a quality of expertise to your real estate transaction. You can find out more about this agency by visiting www.barbarasrealestate.com on the Internet.

Century 21 Four Seasons Realty
1441 Wiley Oakley Dr., Gatlinburg
• (865) 436-2121
239 E. Parkway, Gatlinburg
• (865) 436-2100, (877) 436-2100
Factory Outlet Mall, Pigeon Forge
• (865) 428-2121, (877) 908-2121
729 Parkway, Sevierville • (865) 429-2121

This Century 21 franchise has served the real estate needs of the Smoky Mountains since the early 1980s. The main office (the Wiley Oakley Drive address) sits in the mountainous, view-laden Chalet Village section of Gatlinburg, one of the county's main focal points of investment and overnight rental property. The majority of the business done out of this particular office is geared toward that market. However, in the years since it started, three other branch offices have opened throughout the county. Each of these four offices varies in terms of the market it reaches and the types of property that it represents. The two Gatlinburg offices work more frequently with condos and chalets used by retirees or as investment properties. The Sevierville branch sees more action in the primary residential market. In the Pigeon Forge office, you'll find a diverse mix of all types of properties. More than 50 agents and administrative members collectively make up the staff of these four Century 21 offices.

In addition to advertising in area publications, Century 21 Four Seasons Realty distributes, at no charge, its own four-color quarterly publication that showcases many of the properties available among the four offices. You can also find them on the web at C21-4Seasons.com or www.c21fourseasonsrealty.com.

Colonial Real Estate
953 Dolly Parton Pkwy., Sevierville
• (865) 453-3333, (800) 336-1899

One of this company's greatest strengths is its lineup of 14 agents, a solid, experienced core who have been on board since owner/broker Steve Lane opened for business in 1985. Many of Colonial's affiliate brokers are consistent million-dollar producers and rank among the top selling agents in the area. Colonial Real Estate is a full-service agency, listing and selling all types of property from residential to commercial to lots and acreage. A good percentage of their inventory is made up of primary residence homes located throughout the county. The company was voted "Best Real Estate Company in Sevier County" by readers of The Mountain Press in 1998. Their Internet address is www.gsmar.com/colonialproperties.

ERA Full Service Realty
720 Parkway, Sevierville
• (865) 908-4111

It started out small in 1996, but their ERA franchise has since exploded on the Smoky Mountain real

estate scene, now boasting 11 friendly, knowledgeable agents. In addition, the company has tripled its figures in terms of customers, number of properties sold and sales volume. In 1997, ERA Full Service Realty was voted the "Best Real Estate Company in Sevier County" in The Mountain Press' annual Reader's Choice Awards.

Greenbrier Valley Resorts and Real Estate
3629 East Parkway., Gatlinburg
• (865) 436-2015, (888) 546-1144

Although this agency has been in existence since 1986, broker Laurie Contois and agents have taken their business to new levels since taking over the company's operations several years ago. The majority of this company's listings are located along the corridor from Gatlinburg to the resort community of Cobbly Nob, about 15 miles away. Most of the properties represented are residential, but one of Greenbrier's agents is a commercial specialist. The company is also involved in long-term management, with 42 properties currently in its rental program. You can learn more about Greenbrier Valley Resorts and Real Estate at www.cobblynob.com.

Hagood-McCarter Real Estate
10718 Chapman Hwy., Suite 6, Seymour
• (865) 577-0604

Located in the Seymour community, approximately 12 miles west of Sevierville, Hagood-McCarter Real Estate can easily serve both Sevier County and neighboring Knox County. Since 1995, broker Hubert McCarter and his agents have worked with residential property, commercial property and acreage, most of which is in the Seymour area. They are members of the Knoxville Association of Realtors and are MLS participants with both the Knoxville association and Great Smoky Mountains Association of Realtors. Check out their Website at www.usit.com/property.

McCarter Real Estate & Auction Company
3140 Newport Hwy., Sevierville
• (865) 453-1600, (877) 282-8467

Over the years, this company has slowly evolved from a full service real estate company to one that is exclusively an auction house. Owner and auctioneer Scott McCarter started the business in 1983, successfully tapping into the demand for auction sales, a property selling method that has become increasingly popular in the area. The company almost exclusively utilizes "absolute" auctions, by which properties are sold on the day of the auction, regardless of the final high bid. Including McCarter, there are a total of three auctioneers on staff, all of whom are members of the National Auctioneer's Association. Conducting approximately 25 auctions annually, McCarter Real Estate works primarily in home sales, but also with vacant lots, farms, estates and commercial properties. Find out more about them at www.mccarterauction.com.

Prudential Wise Associates
3230 Parkway, Suite A-2, Pigeon Forge
• (865) 453-1044, (800) 944-5586

Broker Sydney Whittaker opened for business in January 1995 and has been quite successful in the residential market since then. Much of the agency's residential business is in second homes and vacation homes in both the Gatlinburg and Pigeon Forge areas. Also involved in managing commercial property, Prudential Wise Associates is just one division of a full service Prudential company that also deals in insurance and securities.

Realty World Barnes Real Estate
2264 Parkway, Pigeon Forge
• (865) 453-5181, (800) 222-0589

This Realty World franchise is the oldest real estate company in Pigeon Forge and one of the oldest in the entire county, having first opened its doors in 1969. Owner/broker Don Clayton's staff of nine agents has decades of collective experience and makes up a company that can handle all types of properties and real estate transactions. Realty World Barnes Real Estate also operates a property management division that features over 50 different properties on its rental program. Learn more about this company on its web site: www.realtyworld-barnes.com

RE/MAX First Choice Realtors
1338 Parkway, Suite 9, Sevierville
• (865) 453-8006, (800) 736-2903

This RE/MAX franchise has undergone massive growth over the past several years and now boasts 8 agents who handle a wide range of real estate properties. In addition to the usual mix of primary residential, commercial and acreage, RE/MAX First Choice Realtors specializes in chalet sales in both Gatlinburg and Pigeon Forge and is also involved in developing a number of new area subdivisions. Owner/broker Roy Helton, who opened First Choice in 1986, also does consulting work with several companies that do high-volume investment in area rental properties. RE/MAX' own rental program has nearly 100 properties that are managed through the company. Learn more on the Internet at www.homes-in-the-smokies.com.

Select Real Estate
605 Wall St., Sevierville
• (865) 908-0301, (800) 858-2464

Since starting her own company in 1996, owner/broker Kathy Leedy has taken her years of expertise in Smoky Mountains real estate and built up a business that serves the entire county. Many of Leedy's affiliate brokers bring different areas of expertise to the fore, helping make Select Real Estate a well-rounded company in terms of the types of services it can provide. Among the areas in which her agents specialize are corporate relocation, commercial property, overnight rentals and business brokerage. To learn more about this company, you can find them on the Internet at www.selectre.com.

Shular Realty
2851 Winfield Dunn Pkwy., Kodak
• (865) 428-2600, (800) 628-9073

This full service company, founded in 1972, has seven agents on board and offers the advantage of being the first real estate company you'll encounter after exiting I-40. Approximately 60 percent of the properties that Shular lists and sells are in the Kodak, Sevierville or south Jefferson County area, according to broker Joyce Scott. In addition to the usual mix of residential and commercial real estate, this company also develops and sells entire subdivisions in areas like Kodak and nearby Dandridge. Visit their web site at www.shular.com.

Sunset Cottage Rentals and Realty
3630 S. River Rd., Pigeon Forge
• (865) 429-8478, (800) 211-4599

With more than 10 years of experience in the real estate field, owner/broker Dayna Day started her own company in Pigeon Forge in 1995. Having initially focused on the overnight rental aspect of her business, Day has developed the listing side of her enterprise to a point of equal footing with her rentals. She currently has over 50 properties on that overnight rental program and, along with her staff of affiliate brokers, deals in homes, commercial properties and acreage all over the county. They're on the Internet at www.sunsetcottage.com.

Virginia Graves Realtors
446 E. Parkway, Suite 6, Gatlinburg
• (865) 436-3200, (888) 699-5263

Although her office has only been open since January of 1997, Virginia Graves brings about two decades worth of real estate experience to her customers and clients. With six agents in house, this company provides a full spectrum of real estate services, focused primarily in the investment property market of the south end of the county. Virginia's company has experienced tremendous growth in its first few years, and in 1998, Virginia was given national recognition by being named to the "Who's Who in Executives and Businesses" registry for 1998-1999.

Wears Valley Real Estate
2750 Wears Valley Rd., Sevierville
• (865) 428-3896, (800) 553-1425

On the far west side of Sevier County in the scenic Wears Valley community, this company does a lot of business in the second home market. While most of their activity is in the Wears Valley area, Wears Valley Real Estate represents properties from buyers and sellers all over the county. The business has been in operation since 1989, and owner/broker Craig Reed has four agents on staff. They also have more than 20 properties on their rental program, most of which are cabins. Their web address is www.wearsvalley.com.

The Auction Alternative

Over the years, one alternative to listing and buying property through traditional real estate methods has emerged with an enthusiastic following—buying and selling property through auctions. The practice is especially strong in Sevier County, where auctions initially flourished and grew more popular through heavy regional advertising in newspapers, radio and television. Auction companies themselves have traditionally thrived on strong word-of-mouth recommendations. Currently, approximately seven area real estate companies utilize auctions to a significant extent. The types of property that go up on the block are varied and include subdivision home sites, houses, farms, estates and commercial properties.

INSIDERS' TIP

Property taxes in Sevier County are among the lowest in the state of Tennessee at $1.40 per $100 of assessed value. City rates are 38 cents in Sevierville, 12 cents in Pigeon Forge, 21 cents in Gatlinburg and 32 cents in Pittman Center.

Two of the more frequently used auction methods are absolute auctions and confirmation sales. In absolute auctions, the property is sold on the day of the auction to the highest bidder, regardless of the price. This obviously has advantages for the buyer, who may wind up getting a great deal. In a confirmation sale, the owner can exercise the option of accepting or rejecting the final high bid. While this does provide a measure of protection to the seller in terms of guaranteeing a good sale price, this method tends to attract fewer bidders, which can actually reduce the chances of a higher sale price being offered.

Regardless of the method used, auctions in general have many benefits. The seller knows that his property will be moved on a specific date, on his terms and conditions. Buyers know, of course, that they can possibly get a good price. In the case of developed subdivision lots, prospective buyers have the convenience of inspecting the site before the sale and often selecting the "pick of the litter."

Those interested in using an auction service should learn as much as they can about the company and its reputation. Much of this can be done by checking references through the company's previous clients. Property owners might also check any professional affiliations that the firm might have, such as membership in the National Association of Auctioneers. When it comes to paying the auction company, sellers can often negotiate the terms, which usually involve some sort of commission. As for buyers, they are required to pay a deposit on the day of the auction and also sign a demand note that backs up the financial obligation. The buyer can then arrange financing through the institution of his choice; sometimes the auction company has its own financing program established through a local lender.

To Build or Not to Build?

Compared to other areas of the state and even the nation, the new home construction business in the Smokies is in pretty good shape. One 1998 study, commissioned by the City of Gatlinburg, compared new construction growth in rural areas that adjoin national parks and other wilderness areas to rural areas that do not border such regions. The latter communities historically experienced only about a four percent growth rate in new construction while construction in the rural communities near national parks typically grew at a rate of 25 percent. The towns of Tennessee's Great Smoky Mountains are right in line with this trend, with the inherent beauty and grandeur of the area continuing to be influential factors in the expansion of that new homes market. A booming economy and its accompanying low interest rates have also encouraged housing starts. While there are typical "off" times during periods of interest rate increases or higher materials costs, the construction business has grown steadily and is expected to remain strong for many years to come.

The builders with whom we spoke agreed on a number of trends when it came to construction in Sevier County. Many of the new homes built are used for retirement purposes. As the nation's ever-growing number of retirees seek more active lifestyles, the Smoky Mountains region is becoming a popular nesting ground for seniors who want to spend their leisure years near a variety of activities set in a healthy and scenic environment. Many of these people had vacationed here in earlier years and saw the Smokies as a natural choice for a retirement destination. A significant percentage of new homes is also going up as second homes and investment properties for both local and out-of-town owners who are playing into the vacation rental market.

As for the types of homes under construction, there are no cut and dried answers when it comes to size and style. The typical three-bedroom ranch home is still popular in the more primary residential areas of the county like Sevierville. In areas with hilly terrain, split level homes are in great abundance. Investment properties and vacation homes frequently tend to be log cabins or chalets, and can be found, not only in the mountainous regions of Gatlinburg, but also in other scenic settings like Wears Valley and the Douglas Lake area in the northern part of the county. Recently, the log home industry has become an entity in itself, with its own selection of area companies that specialize in the sale and construction of those rustic dwellings. Condominium developments and planned communities are becoming more prevalent in all regions of Sevier County, and are especially popular among retirees because of their on-site amenities and maintenance programs.

Construction prices also vary greatly, depending on location. Building in more mountainous terrain is usually more expensive because of the added costs of hillside excavation and extra foundation and basement materials. Beyond that, land costs are another crucial factor. While actual construction costs are pretty much in line with those of neighboring Tennessee counties, land prices in Sevier County are higher (as we've mentioned), adding to the overall cost of building a home. While you can get better land prices in the rural, undeveloped parts of the county where there are no city services, there is a tradeoff in the form of additional costs for septic and well water systems.

Media

Whether you're talking about television, radio or newspapers, the communities of Tennessee's Great Smoky Mountains are somewhat dependent on their proximity to Knoxville when it comes to major media influence. Sevier County does lay claim to a radio station, two locally published newspapers and, naturally, a passel of magazines geared to serve the tourist. But as one surfs the television and radio dials or scans area newspaper and magazine racks, it becomes clear that these mountains' primary sources of information lie elsewhere.

This is a situation that gives readers a more proactive choice when it comes to the nature of information they desire and the means by which they choose to receive it. On one hand, there are those who must have their daily doses of *USA Today, The New York Times* or CNN; those are all available here. On the other hand, there are still some around these parts who are content to sit back, put their feet up and enjoy the more insular offerings of the local paper. As far as they're concerned, most of the nation may know what the Smokies have to offer, but they aren't necessarily interested in what the rest of the world has to offer them. So take your pick. No matter how involved or detached you care to be, you'll be well accommodated.

LOOK FOR:
• Newspapers
• Tourism Publications
• Television
• Radio

Newspapers

Sevier County is served by one daily newspaper and one weekly, both published in-county. Several papers from peripheral areas have also made their way into area newsstands, including *The Knoxville News-Sentinel, The Knoxville Journal, Tri-County News* and the *Seymour Times*. We'll give you thumbnail sketches of the two local publications as well as *The Knoxville News-Sentinel,* since these are the biggest players in the Smokies' newsprint medium.

The Mountain Press
119 Riverbend Dr., Sevierville
• (865) 428-0746

The Mountain Press is a study in contrasts. While it has remained very much a small town newspaper with a conservative, local focus, it has managed to grow into a daily publication that currently operates out of a modern, 22,000-square-foot facility that opened in 1995. The paper's full-time staff of more than 60 people generates a circulation of approximately 10,000 issues per day, reaching Sevier and surrounding counties. Subscriptions account for approximately 70 percent of this circulation; the remainder is available in racks and news stands.

The Mountain Press has a long history of producing award-winning editorial and has been honored with numerous accolades from the Tennessee Press Association. In 1998, it garnered eight awards in such categories as Features, News and Makeup & Appearance. Inside its pages, readers will find the typical array of hometown news, including everything from 4-H livestock contests, local politics and high school sports to coverage of area crime and new commercial development. There are a number of regular departments, some of which have a distinct rural bent, focusing on such topics as agriculture or veterans' affairs. There is even a daily feature called Personality, in which one local resident has his or her photo along with a short bio plastered on the front page of *The Mountain Press,* in full color. It's surprising how often readers actually know the person being profiled! Suffice it to say that such a vehicle could only work in a small town environment.

Beyond the reporting of community happenings, there is also limited coverage of events from around the region, the nation and the world. While the daily version of *The Mountain Press* can vary from one to two sections, the Sunday edition is fairly thick for an operation of its size. In addition to the standard fare, readers will also find expanded real estate coverage, an entertainment and TV listings section, Sunday comics and the *USA Weekend* magazine insert. *The Mountain Press* also publishes a monthly insert, Experienced Living, that's especially geared toward senior citizens as well as an annual newcomer's edition that's chock full of useful information for anyone relocating to the Smokies.

The Mountain Press can trace its history back to 1897, when it was originally known as the *Record-Republican.* Through the years, the paper went through various mergers and changes of ownership and name. For many years operating as *Montgomery's Vindicator.* In 1964, the publication was split into two versions, *The Gatlinburg Press* and *The Sevier County News-Record.* In 1984, the two were combined into *The Mountain Press* that area residents know today. In June 1995, ownership of the paper was taken over by Paxton Media, based in Paducah, Kentucky.

The cost of *The Mountain Press* is 50 cents daily and $1 on Sunday. Terms for in-county home delivery range from one month ($9.50) to one year ($113.30). There is also a discounted senior citizen rate of $99.90 for a year.

Tennessee Star Journal
2713 Parkway, Pigeon Forge
• (865) 453-0626
The tagline under this weekly publication's nameplate says it all: "A Hometown Southern Newspa-

per." Serving Sevier County and neighboring Jefferson County, its focus is decidedly local in scope, presenting features and departments that capture the flavor of life in a small town. Being a weekly newspaper, there is less emphasis on time-critical events that could be considered "old news" six or seven days after the fact.

Generally, there is a positive slant on much of the reporting, and overall, the *Tennessee Star Journal* reflects the conservative nature and values of the communities it serves. This fact reveals itself through the regular features that appear in its pages. "Looking Back" offers in-depth examinations of area history and "Viewpoints and Faith" addresses religious issues; you'll also find columns with names like "The Farm Gal" and "Down Memory Lane," which play into the *Tennessee Star Journal's* quaint portrayal of the rural South.

The newspaper is owned by local businessman Kenneth Seaton, who also owns a local chain of hotels and motels. The *Tennessee Star Journal's* full-time staff of nine produces ten thousand copies that circulate each Friday. In addition to rack distribution and subscriptions, a copy of the paper is placed in each of the rooms in Seaton's accommodations chain.

The *Star Journal* has taken its share of awards of late. Recent honors include a second place finish in the Tennessee Press Association's Best Special Issue category for its coverage of Dolly Parton's annual parade in Pigeon Forge. It has also received a certificate of merit from the state of Tennessee for its "Looking Back" column.

The paper costs 50 cents per issue; two-year subscription rates are $20 per year for Tennessee residents and $24 for those living outside the state.

The Knoxville News-Sentinel
208 W. Church Ave., Knoxville
• (865) 523-3131
This daily has served Knoxville and surrounding areas since 1926 when *The Knoxville Sentinel* (founded 1886) merged with *The Knoxville News* (founded 1921). Today, the paper occupies a wide berth on the ideological spectrum. It can reflect the more liberal viewpoints of a medium-sized university city while

never straying too far from the Bible Belt population it serves. On a daily basis, *The News-Sentinel* provides a good dose of world and national news coverage in addition to that of regional and local happenings. The multiple sections of the Sunday edition offer a full range of news, features and other information including editorial, arts and entertainment, lifestyles and automotive.

The News-Sentinel is owned by the E.W. Scripps chain and employs a staff of over 500 people. Operating out of its current facility for over 60 years, it circulates anywhere from 120,000 to 180,000 copies daily, depending on the day of the week. The paper has a strong presence in Sevier County through both rack distribution and home delivery. The Wednesday edition features a special section called Community News that is distributed in Sevier County and southern Knox County. This section has news of a more local flavor for residents of those areas.

The daily cost of *The Knoxville News-Sentinel* is 50 cents, and the Sunday edition costs $2. Monthly subscription rates are $17.95 for the daily and Sunday editions, $11.50 for weekends (Friday through Sunday) and $9.50 for the daily editions only.

Tourism Publications

Along with brochures and rack cards, tourist-oriented publications are on the front lines when it comes to providing vacationers with information on what the Great Smokies have to offer. They're found everywhere — welcome centers, chambers of commerce, shopping centers, convenience stores, supermarkets — anywhere that publishers suspect that large numbers of travelers may gather. While sporadic perusal of magazine racks and displays always reveals new contenders in this stiff competition for visitor readership, we will be profiling seven publications which have effectively proven themselves over the years to be the con-

sistent leaders in both tourist readership and local advertising.

First, some generalizations about what most of these magazines have in common. They are all primarily advertising-centered, with varying degrees of editorial content (we'll go into more detail in the write-ups). Much of the editorial you do find is more "advertorial" in nature; although the stories are usually positive promotions of that magazine's advertisers, they can be entertaining and informative, nonetheless. For the most part, advertisers consist of music theaters, arts and crafts shops, restaurants, attractions, hotels and motels, as well as retail shops and outlet centers (see related chapters for our favorite picks).

These publications almost always contain money-saving coupons in addition to area maps and handy charts that organize theater, restaurant and hotel information into user-friendly formats. Many of the magazines also include calendars of events and useful information related to Great Smoky Mountains National Park (see our chapters on those subjects). Any of these publications would serve as a useful companion to your *Insiders' Guide,* and let's not forget the best part — they're all free in area racks (though in most cases you'll pay a few bucks for a subscription or to get a single copy sent in the mail).

Best Read Guide of the Smoky Mountains
429 Forks of the River Parkway, Sevierville • (865) 908-9845

This compact, digest-size magazine is presented monthly in a slick, full color format. With nearly 1 million copies distributed each year, *Best Read Guide* contains a healthy balance of advertising and editorial. In addition to the Smokies, *Best Read Guide* is also published in 17 other vacation markets, most of which are located along the east coast. Subscription rates are $20 per year in the United States, $30 per year in Canada and $50 per year in other

> **INSIDERS' TIP**
>
> As you travel the Winfield Dunn Parkway between I- 40 and Sevierville, you'll notice a couple of establishments that claim to be tourist information centers. While you can, indeed, access an ample supply of brochures, rack cards and tourist publications at these places, be aware that they are operated by vacation rental developers who may also hit you up with some form of sales pitch. Visitors are certainly under no obligation to participate, but sticking with the city operated and sanctioned information centers will ensure that you're not hit with the hard sell when all you're really interested in is learning about what there is to do in the Smokies.

countries. Single copies cost $3 in the United States and Canada and $5 elsewhere. You can find *Best Read Guide* on the Internet at www.bestreadguide.com/smokymtns.

Guide to the Smokies
628 Wall Street, Sevierville
• (865) 428-4654

Locally published, *Guide to the Smokies* is a slick, full color, standard size magazine that appears seasonally, four times per year. Heavy on advertising, it does contain a smattering of articles in addition to maps, charts and a calendar of events. *Guide to the Smokies* has an annual distribution of 650,000. If you can't pick up a free copy in the area, individual copies can be ordered by phone for $5 each, or a one-year subscription can be purchased for $14.95.

Tennessee Smokies Visitors Guide
2638 Parkway, Pigeon Forge
• (800) 422-0742

This slick, full color magazine packs a lot into each of its two annual issues. There is plenty of advertising, but the editorial content within is also abundant. Stories cover a diverse range of topics including entertainment, shopping, golf, the national park and profiles of outlying communities like Cosby and Townsend. *Visitors Guide* is published by Vista Graphics in Virginia Beach, Virginia. This company has *Visitors Guides* in 12 other markets, primarily throughout North Carolina and Virginia. The Tennessee Smokies edition of *Visitors Guide* has an annual distribution of 700,000. Individual copies can be ordered by phone and shipped at a cost of $5. Visit them on the Internet at www.vgnet.com.

The Vacationer
1109 Oak Cluster Dr., Sevierville
• (865) 428-8009

Although the percentage of advertising in this standard, slick magazine is fairly close to that of editorial offerings, much of the latter is in the form of short write ups pertaining to advertisers. There are, however, several features

in each issue that make for worthwhile reading. *The Vacationer* is Published by Mellon Communications, which puts out eight issues per year. You can find *The Vacationer* on line at www.mellonmarketing.com.

The What-to-Do Magazine of the Great Smoky Mountains
P.O. Box 764, Pigeon Forge, 37868-0764
• (800) SUNNY DA

In publication since 1993, this digest-sized magazine has been one of the consistent area leaders in advertiser coupon redemption, making it popular with tourists and advertisers alike. There is a good balance between advertising and editorial, although most of the information contained in *What-to-Do* is related to Great Smoky Mountains National Park, including hiking charts, a park map, seasonal forecasts and useful profiles of different sections of the park.

What-to-Do is printed twice per year with a total circulation of 400,000. It is one of the few publications of its kind with exclusive distribution in area hotel rooms. While the in-room magazine contains no hotel or motel advertising, an expanded edition of 200,000 copies is also printed, which is made available in the typical high-traffic distribution points and contains a special section of lodging advertisers. Publication of *The What-to-Do Magazine* was taken over by Sunny Day Guides of Virginia Beach, Virginia, in 1998. Sunny Day publishes similar magazines in 14 other travel markets stretching from the east coast to Lake Tahoe. Visit their web site at www.what-to-do.com.

What's Showing in the Smokies
P.O. Box 764, Pigeon Forge
• (800) SUNNY DA

As the sister publication of *The What-to-Do Magazine,* this arts and entertainment journal provides readers with a companion piece that places its emphasis on music theaters, attractions and the arts, in addition to shopping and dining. Also a part of the Sunny Day publishing family, *What's Showing* is printed in tabloid format on high-quality paper with an abun-

INSIDERS' TIP

WATE Channel 6, Knoxville's ABC affiliate, was that city's first television station, signing on in 1953. Since 1965, WATE has operated from The Greystone, a stone mansion that was constructed in 1885. Having originally served as the home of Union Army officer, Major Eldad Cicero Camp, The Greystone was utilized as an apartment complex during World War II before being purchased and restored by WATE. The building is on the National Register of Historic Places.

The Heartland Series

Since 1984, viewers of this series of abbreviated documentaries have been regularly introduced to what its producers call "a celebration of a people and their land." Produced and aired by WBIR Channel 10, each of the Heartland Series' five-minute segments explores some aspect of East Tennessee life, usually from an historical or environmental perspective. The series is part time capsule, part history lesson and part cautionary tale, all presented in a delightful and easily digestible format. Each weekday morning, noon and evening, host and narrator Bill Landry takes audiences on captivating explorations of the people, places and events that were and still are responsible for shaping the region into what it is today.

Some of the segments are character studies, such as the reflective conversation with Herb Clabo, a gentleman who had grown up in the Roaring Fork community before it was absorbed by the national park in the 1930s. Through the course of a casual stroll with Mr. Clabo, viewers get an inside glimpse into what it was like to live in the mountain communities of old.

Other episodes reveal facets of antiquated mountain lifestyles. One in particular deals with the rituals of doing laundry in the days before washing machines, dryers and detergent. A woman who once lived in the Sugarlands area of the Smokies (before the creation of the national park) relates the laborious routines of wash day, from the boiling of water and adding of homemade lye soap to the drying of the clothes on lines and the inevitable chore of ironing.

Another popular Heartland Series format is the reenactment, where true events and fables from the pages of regional history are recreated through visual portrayal by actors as well as narration. A viewer favorite from the first season was "The Cow Barn," a charming account from the life of Wiley Oakley, a Gatlinburg legend who was best known as a pioneering mountain guide of the early 1900s. Host Landry himself frequently winds up with principal roles in these tales, many of which are quite humorous.

Sometimes, you'll see things on The Heartland Series which make you wonder if they're not pulling your leg. One segment details the honest-to-God practice of making wintergreen candy from birch trees by adding sugar to the strippings of a birch's sap layer. At other times, series producers are most definitely pulling your leg. Each April 1st, they present what appears from the outset to be a typical Heartland installment. By the end, viewers realize they've been royally suckered into a hilarious April Fools' Day prank. An example is the episode where university scientists demonstrate how they have learned to generate electricity from trees. It all seems on the up-and-up until the researchers begin running wires from household appliances to tree trunks. As you watch them switch on a food mixer that's electrically connected to a tree, you slowly realize that you've been had.

All joking aside, much of the focus of The Heartland Series is on the preservation of the environment, particularly that of the Smoky Mountains. Going beyond its usual five-minute snapshot, the series has produced several half-hour-long documentaries on such topics as the health of Little River, the region's foresting industry and the reintroduction of the red wolf into the national park. For its efforts, The Heartland Series has received numerous awards in the area of environmental awareness and protection.

The Heartland Series was started by WBIR in 1984 as a six-month project to commemorate the 50th anniversary of the creation of Great Smoky Mountains National Park. After its initial half-year run, public opinion was so overwhelmingly in favor of extending the series that producers decided to continue the project for another six months. That six months turned into another six months, and 15 years later, The Heartland Series is still going like the Energizer Bunny.

(Continued on next page)

MEDIA

MEDIA

Over the course of its run, close to 1,000 episodes have been produced. The best of the series have been compiled into more than 20 video volumes, with each tape containing approximately 30 of what producers consider to be the best episodes from a particular year. In addition, special videos that focus on Reelfoot Lake, Cades Cove and Big South Fork have been put together that present in-depth studies of each of these areas of Tennessee. Heartland Series videos can be purchased at select locations, including Heartland Antiques in Pigeon Forge, Wears Valley Antique Gallery in Wears Valley and Davis Kidd Booksellers in Knoxville. They are also available on loan through Anna Porter Public Library in Gatlinburg and Sevier County Public Library in Sevierville.

Bill Landry hosts WBIR's The Heartland Series.

Photo: Courtesy WBIR TV

dance of full color. Advertising and editorial are in equal proportion; stories include celebrity interviews, show and restaurant reviews as well as features on hiking and Smoky Mountain history. *What's Showing* is printed six times per year, with an annual circulation of 330,000. Find them on the Internet at www.what-to-do.com.

Television

Nowadays, anyone still receiving television channels via the good old rooftop antenna is part of a rapidly vanishing breed. This is especially true in Sevier County, where the hilly terrain and the 25-mile distance from Knoxville, the nearest source of network affiliates,

don't always make for good broadcast reception. While the area's two cable companies are responsible for bringing most viewers their programming, there are limits to the geographic range that they service, thus leaving some rural dwellers out in the cold. Those who live outside the reach of the giant spools of coaxial cable either rough it with antennae or purchase satellite systems. It's not uncommon to see a mobile home on a secluded mountain lot with a satellite dish dominating the front yard!

Broadcast Stations

Tennessee's Smokies pick up affiliates of the three major networks as well as a Fox affiliate and a public television station. All of these broadcast stations are located in the Knoxville area, the 64th-largest television market in the country.

The three network affiliates have been on the air since the early- to mid-1950s. Each remains active in community involvement through participation in and sponsorship of various public service projects and charitable causes. Of particular interest to the Smokies is the annual Friends Across The Mountains telethon, produced each year by WBIR Channel 10, the local NBC affiliate. Proceeds from this charity event go to Friends of Great Smoky Mountains National Park, or "Friends of the Smokies," as they're more commonly known. Friends of the Smokies is a nonprofit organization which assists national park administration in preserving and improving the condition of the park (see our chapter on Great Smoky Mountains National Park). In 1999, the 3rd annual Friends Across The Mountains event raised over $140,000.

WATE Channel 6 (ABC)
WVLT- Channel 8 (CBS)
WBIR Channel 10 (NBC)
WTNZ Channel 43 (FOX)
WKOP/WSJK Channel 15/Channel 2
(Public Television)

Cable Television Companies

Intermedia
(865) 544-0099

This company provides service to homes and businesses within the city limits of Sevierville, Pigeon Forge and Gatlinburg. Viewers can choose from a list of more than 50 channels, including several premium movie channels. Tourists might be interested in tuning in to any of the three visitor-oriented channels carried by Intermedia. Channel 5 and Channel 35 are advertising showcases for area retail shops, outlet centers, restaurants and attractions. Channel 35 also airs a lot of programming on the shops of the Great Smoky Arts and Crafts Community. Many of these craft shops are profiled in detail with up-close interviews and on-site demonstrations. Debuting in 1998, the Visitors' Information Channel appears on Channel 54, providing similar profiles of area music and variety theaters as well as some crafts and attractions coverage. The show's hosts take viewers inside theater doors for interviews with local stars like Lee Greenwood and Louise Mandrell.

Comcast Communications
(865) 637-5411

Formerly known as Greenbrier Cablevision, this company serves areas outside the city limits of Sevierville, Pigeon Forge and Gatlinburg. Their services extend to outlying areas like Townsend, Walden's Creek, the resort community of Cobbly Nob and parts of neighboring Cocke County. Comcast carries more than 40 channels on its menu, including five premium channels. This company also has its own visitor-oriented programming on Channel 8, the "What's Up" Channel, which introduces viewers to area shops, restaurants and attractions.

Radio

Mix 105.5 (105.5 FM) and WSEV (930 AM), located in Sevierville, are the only radio stations bradcasting from the Smokies. Until February 2000, Mix 105.5 was owned by Dollywood and had the call letters WDLY. Referred to as "Dolly's Station," it played country music, while the sister AM station, WSEV, had more of a gospel emphasis. When Dollywood sold the two stations to East Tennessee Radio Group in early 2000, the new owners changed the name of the FM station to Mix 105.5 and replaced the country music with an adult contemporary format. WSEV is still primarily a gospel station.

The remainder of the stations we've included are located in the Knoxville area. While we haven't listed all the Knoxville stations pertinent to the different categories, we have attempted to base selections on how strong a particular station's signal is received in Sevier County.

Christian and Gospel
WRJZ 620 AM
WSEV 930 AM
WYLV 89.1 FM
WJBZ 96.3 FM

MEDIA

INSIDERS' TIP

When visiting Great Smoky Mountains National Park, tune your radio into 1610 AM to receive information park activities, events and schedules.

Classical

National Public Radio 91.9 FM

Country

WQBB 104.5 FM
WIVK 107.7 FM

Top 40 and Popular

Mix 105.5 (adult contemporary)
WWST 93.1 FM ('80s and '90s pop)
WJXB 97.5 FM (soft rock)
WMYU 102 FM ('60s and '70s pop)

Rock

WNFZ 94.3 FM (alternative)
WOKI 100.3 FM ('80s, '90s and '70s)
WIMZ 103.5 FM (classic)
WXVO 106.7 FM (alternative)

Talk and News

WNOX 990 AM
WNOX 99.1 FM

MEDIA

Education and Childcare

We East Tennesseans are familiar with the jokes and stereotypes. We're well aware that there are those (especially our northern friends) who imagine that we run around all day in overalls and straw hats, without shoes, a stalk of wheat dangling from one corner of the mouth. Surely, we send our children off each morning to the ol' one-room schoolhouse where the teacher gives the little tykes a rudimentary dose of the Three Rs (that is, if they even attend school at all!).

Despite any preconceived ideas you may have about the state of education in these Tennessee hills, we're happy say that Sevier County children and adults alike have access to a full slate of progressive educational programs on all levels, both public and private. To be sure, there are school systems throughout the region, especially those in more rural areas, that aren't so fortunate. But Sevier Countians have built an educational infrastructure that makes their children a treasured priority.

Fact is, the tourism industry isn't the only thing that's endured sweet growing pains. Thanks to a constantly expanding base of permanent residents, our local public school system has found itself in a perpetual state of development and metamorphosis. Although the very nature of our existence in the Smokies intertwines us with tourism, no one has lost sight of the fact that this is still a terrific place to raise children. Since education is an integral part of that upbringing process, great emphasis has been placed on the importance of having quality teachers and up-to-date facilities to prepare our children for their futures.

To use computer jargon as an analogy, the Sevier County school system has done quite a bit of upgrading in recent years, including both "hardware" and "software." As for the hardware, construction of new schools and additional classrooms has just barely managed to keep up with swelling enrollment. When it comes to the software, local schools have benefited from broad-minded approaches to curriculum and solid accreditation standards. Even the subject of year-round school was deliberated in recent years—it fell short of implementation, but there was still substantial interest in giving it a whirl, and the issue may rear its head again someday.

Regardless of whether a child attends public or private school, the state of Tennessee requires that he or she attend kindergarten. To register, the child must be 5 years old on or before October 1 of the year he or she plans to attend. The registration procedure requires parents to provide a certified copy of the child's birth certificate along with an up-to-date immunization record and medical examination forms signed by the child's physician or the Sevier County Department of Health. Such health records are considered valid if they are dated any time between the start of school and the previous January 1. The public school system has a pre kindergarten screening process as well, and most private schools, of course, have their own individual application and interview processes.

LOOK FOR:
- **Public Schools**
- **Private Schools**
- **Home Schooling**
- **Adult Education**
- **Full-time Childcare**
- **After-School and Summer Programs**

This chapter begins with an overview of the Sevier County public school system, followed by a look at area private schools as well as the new frontier in local education—home schooling. You'll also find profiles on the many adult education programs found in the county, including our local community college annex. The second half of the chapter focuses on child-care and preschool opportunities as well as after-school programs and other services that benefit the concerned parent.

Public Schools

Sevier County School District
226 Cedar St., Sevierville • (865) 453-4671

Unlike many districts, Sevier County allows parents to send their children to any school within the system, regardless of residence. A family in Sevierville may enroll their teenager at Gatlinburg-Pittman High School, for example, or a younger child who lives in Seymour might attend Sevierville Primary.

As mentioned previously, one of the primary challenges the local school board has faced is how to accommodate the growing number of children who enter the school system each year. That number is currently over the 12,000 mark and rising.

The county's incorporated and unincorporated communities include 11 elementary or primary schools, six intermediate and middle schools and four high schools. Also included in the public system are a vocational center (at Sevier County High School) as well as institutions that serve adults and special needs children.

To stave off overcrowding, the school system recently completed a three-year, $30 million construction and renovation program that touches most of the communities in the county in one way or another. Many are benefiting from badly needed new schools, classroom additions and remodeling projects. Pigeon Forge recently underwent an interesting shuffling process. In 1999, they launched the county's fourth high school, which now occupies the former Pigeon Forge Middle School. In turn, the middle school moved to the existing primary school, and the primary school moved into a brand new facility. Financial expenditures are another sure indicator of growth. Between the 1997-98 school year and the 1998-99 year, the county's total budget rose from $52.5 million to $62 million.

Approximately 1,600 employees (roughly half teachers, half support personnel like custodians and cafeteria workers) are currently employed by Sevier County schools, although this number is sure to increase as enrollment rises. Teacher salaries here are generally on an

equal footing with those in other Tennessee districts. Beginning salaries range from the mid to upper $20,000s, depending on whether the teacher has a bachelor's or master's degree. As of 1999, the average salary was a little over $30,000 per year. Teacher-student ratios are favorable; by 2001, Tennessee is required to have maximum ratios of 1-to-20 for kindergarten through 3rd grade, 1-to-25 for 4th through 6th grades and 1-to-30 for 7th and 8th grades.

Of course, modern buildings and an adequate teaching staff don't necessarily add up to a quality education. Sevier County schools pride themselves on their accreditation standards. Since 1991, every school in the system has been accredited by the Southern Association of Colleges and Schools. Its requirements for educational standards and student-teacher ratios are tougher than the minimums set forth by the state.

Administrators have implemented a number of programs to help local students keep pace with their peers nationwide, with particular recent emphasis on development in math and technology. The 21st Century program, for example, put computers into every 5th, 6th and 7th grade classroom; current efforts are going into equipping 8th grade classrooms as well. Other programs focus on developing accelerated math skills for 7th and 8th graders and language and math skills at the primary level. Incidentally, the county does not operate on a "track system" that separates classrooms according to student ability. Rather, classes contain children with a mix of ability levels.

On the secondary level, students have a fair amount of flexibility in selecting their educational path. In 8th grade, each student is asked to choose between a college preparatory or a vocational curriculum for his or her upcoming high school years, and approximately 60 percent of the county's high school students are on track for a college education. Despite the path chosen, all students must complete a basic core of credits, in addition to seven or eight electives dependent on the student's area of emphasis. High school students can also earn college credit through advance placement courses and the Dual Enrollment Program, the latter being in conjunction with Walters State Community College (see the section on "Adult Education" in this chapter).

When it comes to standardized test scores, the report card is mixed. Between the 1991-92 school year and the 1997-98 year, area ACT scores rose in English, held steady in math and science reasoning and declined just slightly in reading. Compared to schools statewide, scores in Sevier County high schools were an average of one point higher in all subject areas. SAT results have not been as favorable. Between the 1995-96 academic year and the 1997-98 year, verbal scores in Sevier County declined five points, math scores dipped one point and combined scores dropped six points. Compared to other school systems in the state, average Sevier County SAT scores were more than 60 points lower. It should be noted, however, that most college-bound students in Sevier County take the ACT test instead of the SAT.

On average, between 60 and 70 percent of graduates from high schools in Sevier County go on to college. Remember, though, that this number reflects the fact that roughly 60 percent of all high school students are on a college prep curriculum compared to the 40 percent who are on a vocational track. Overall, around 80 percent of Sevier County's high school graduates go on to some form of post-secondary education, including college and vocational schools.

In the area of special education, the Sevier County school system is well equipped to serve the educational needs of learning disabled and handicapped students ages 3 to 22. Every school in the district has some sort of special education program. In some cases, special needs children are integrated into regular classrooms; there are also self-contained classes for students with significant disabilities that can't be served in regular classrooms. Students that are more severely impaired can be enrolled in Parkway Academy, a facility adjacent to Sevierville Middle School that utilizes specially trained instructors and individualized curricula. The school system also offers outlets for exceptionally gifted students with its Children with Special Abilities program.

Private Schools

The small number of private schools in Sevier

County might be evaluated from different perspectives. An argument could be made for the fact that the broad base of laborers in the tourist industry (who make between $5 and $7 per hour) simply can't afford private schools. While there is some validity to that, it's also true that many residents are simply happy with the public school system.

On the flip side of the coin, some parents enroll their children in private schools because of dissatisfaction with the public system. One of the primary complaints received about public schools is that they lack the Christian emphasis that a growing number of parents desire for their children (the same rationale applies to home-schoolers). Two of the three private schools we've included are church-affiliated institutions.

Covenant Christian School and Preschool
1625 Old Newport Hwy., Sevierville
• (865) 429-4324

This private school, a program of Christ Covenant Reformed Episcopal Church, started out with only 10 students in 1988. More than a decade later, the school boasts an overall enrollment of around 280 (including home-schoolers). Their current facility was constructed just a few years ago to accommodate recent growth. The student body ranges from 3-year-olds to 12th graders. The majority of students are found in the lower grades, although there are about 24 kids at the high school level.

The curriculum is a nondenominational Christian-based one, with all subjects being taught from a Christian perspective. Daily activities include a chapel service and prayer. Covenant Christian is a day school that runs on typical school day hours. Enrolled students can be picked up as late as 5:30 PM. In summer, the school operates its Staying Sharp program that helps students keep their skills up to speed during the vacation months. It is available for grades 1 through 6 only.

Covenant Christian School also serves as a satellite facility for its home school program (see section on home schooling in this chapter). Of the school's total enrollment of 280, nearly 140 are educated at home by their parents. Parents who wish to

EDUCATION AND CHILD CARE

INSIDERS' TIP

Reflective of the demographic makeup of the county's general population, the students in Sevier County schools are overwhelmingly white. Minorities make up less than five percent of the student population; one percent is African-American, one percent is Asian and one-and-a-half percent is Hispanic.

participate in the program must submit an application (and fee), and on approval pay an annual tuition as well as the cost of the curriculum. The curriculum can be purchased through the school, but if it is obtained elsewhere, it must be approved by the school.

The Day School
435 Parkway, Sevierville • (865) 428-2620

Since 1990, this not-for-profit private school has utilized the Montessori philosophy to educate children age 2 through 6th grade. The school uses hands-on programs that center around the individual development of each child. Students' needs are met according to their different levels of development and paces of learning. Although only the kindergarten is accredited, Day School students consistently test in the top one-fifth percentile on national achievement tests, and as a result, have not encountered difficulty in transferring educational credits to other schools.

The school's enrollment averages around 50 students per year in three main age groups. The toddler classroom is for ages 2 and 3 and has a student-teacher ratio of 8-to-1. The preschool is for ages 3 to 6 and includes the kindergarten level; the student-teacher ratio there is 11-to-1. The school age levels include grades 1 through 6, and the student-teacher ratio is 8-to-1. The entry process is nondiscriminatory. The primary concern of administrators is that a child's parents are supportive of the Montessori philosophy.

Although the school maintains typical school day hours, the building is open from 7:30 AM to 5:30 PM, Monday through Friday. The tuition price includes after-school care up until closing time. The Day School also has a summer education program that includes a Montessori curriculum in addition to fun warm-weather activities. Currently, the summer program is only available to the preschool levels, but plans are underway to extend it to the school-age levels and include activities like a computer camp.

In 1999, The Day School broke ground on a new school building to be located in the Two Rivers Business Center, Just off Tenn. 66 near Kodak. The 5,000-square-foot facility will allow the school to accommodate an enrollment of up to 100 students. Construction plans include a spacious playground and plenty of parking.

King's Academy
202 Smothers Rd., Seymour
• (865) 573-8321

Founded in 1880, King's Academy is the oldest continuously run school in Sevier County. It provides a high quality, college preparatory education, not only for local children, but for those from across the nation and as many as 50 different countries. Originally known as Harrison Chilhowee Baptist Academy, the school is run by a president and board of trustees appointed and approved by the Tennessee Baptist Convention. Accordingly, students study a well-rounded curriculum presented with a Christian-centered worldview.

The school, for kindergarten through 12th graders, operates as both a day and boarding facility; the boarding program is only available to 7th through 12th grades. To be accepted, children cannot have been expelled from another school, nor have had severe behavioral problems, and administrators look for previous exemplary behavior in the application process.

The school's recent enrollment was 260 students, the highest number since the community of Seymour built its own public high school in 1961. Contributing to that growth has been the school's elementary program, implemented in 1995. In the years since, enrollment in the younger grade levels has grown at a rate of 40 percent annually. Of the students who graduate from King's Academy, approximately 95 percent go on to college, the highest such percentage among area secondary schools. With an average class size of 16, student-teacher ratios are well below the maximums allowed by the state.

The school boasts a state-of-the-art computer lab and offers special programs like the Experiential Curriculum for the Outdoors classroom (ECO). A required course in the upper level grades, ECO takes students into the Smoky Mountains twice a year. The intent is to teach them skills like hiking, camping, repelling and canoeing while at the same time developing an appreciation of God's glory through the wonders of nature.

Extracurricular activi-

INSIDERS' TIP

Tennessee is currently one of only three states in the country to implement educational and training programs into the state's welfare system. Adults may receive benefits for up to 18 months while developing their educational and job skills. Parents can receive child-care benefits for up to two years while they attend school.

ties are well supported at King's Academy. It maintains a full sports program, fielding secondary level teams in sports like football, basketball and baseball. The campus also has an Olympic size pool and gymnasium. Overall, the school is spread out over a 67-acre campus and exudes the feel of a small college. During the summer months, its retreat and conference center hosts activities like band clinics, athletic camps and church retreats. Also in the summer, the school offers an English as Second Language program that is primarily designed to assist its Latin American and Asian students.

Home Schooling

For more and more families nationwide, the option of home schooling has become a viable alternative to public schools. Nationwide, the number of home school families is estimated to be between 1.0 and 1.5 million while regionally, it's estimated that around 3,000 families in Knox County and surrounding counties teach their children at home. The reasons for such a choice vary and can range from dissatisfaction with public schools to assisting a learning disabled child. Since the Smokies are locked firmly in the heart of the Bible Belt, one of the more common reasons cited is that home schooling gives parents the freedom to incorporate their religious values into their children's education.

Generally, parents who educate their children at home operate through and are accountable to a "satellite" school. In some cases these schools can be part of a public school system, but in the vast majority of instances, satellite schools are private religious schools. Parents can create and administer their own curriculum, and working under the umbrella of a religious school usually allows for fewer snarls with governmental regulation or interference.

Nevertheless, Tennessee has several laws to which home schoolers must adhere. Children must attend class for at least four hours per day, 180 days out of the year. They must also take periodic standardized achievement tests. Although there are no particular curricular requirements at younger grade levels, children at the high school level must complete a certain number of credits in subjects like English, math, science, etc. If the child plans on attending college, parents will generally choose an educational plan geared toward helping him or her score well on college entrance exams.

Within the prescribed limits, parents may tailor the curriculum to suit the child's needs and abilities. Materials can be purchased through the various satellite schools or through any number of companies that specialize in home school curricula. Locally, parents interested in getting started in home schooling may want to contact the Smoky Mountain Home Education Association. Their e-mail address is coryb@esper.com. They'll help you take those first steps and also refer you to one of several local support groups for home education families.

Adult Education

Who says you can't teach an old dog new tricks? In Sevier County, educational opportunities for adults include classes within the public school system as well as on the private level. Whether you're going for your high school equivalency, interested in taking a computer class or starting on a college degree, there are several options waiting for you here in the Smokies.

Adult Education Program
226 Cedar St., Sevierville • (865) 453-4671

Funded and administered through the county's public school system, the Adult Education Program offers free classes on a variety of levels, serving about 600 adults each year. Basic skills classes help adults improve in the areas of reading, writing and math. Those pursuing a high school diploma can choose from two routes. They can attend classes at White's Adult High School in Sevierville or they can take any of the GED equivalency classes offered at various times and different locations throughout the county. Annually, the Adult Education Program gives out approximately 125 diplomas.

Tennessee Technology Center
109 Industry Dr., Sevierville
• (865) 453-5644

This vocational school operates through 28 sites statewide, including the one in Sevierville. Accredited by the Council of Occupational Education, the Sevierville branch teaches courses in industrial electricity and computer electronics. Each course is worth 27 college credit hours, and upon completion, students may then seek certification in their field, if they wish. Graduates are qualified to work in such occupational fields as residential and industrial wiring or computer, TV, VCR and stereo repair.

The center maintains an average of 14 full-

The Dollywood Foundation

In 1988, hometown girl Dolly Parton and the Dollywood Corporation jointly established the Dollywood Foundation to develop and support educational programs in Sevier County. In its 10-plus years of existence, the foundation has raised more than $3 million dollars; funds have come from individual and corporate donors as well as through celebrity benefit concerts staged by Ms. Parton herself.

Thus far, the proceeds have gone toward numerous programs within the local public school system, such as first-grade teaching assistants, guidance counselors, computer labs and college scholarships. Outside the schools, an after-school tutoring program has been implemented at the Boys & Girls Club of the Smoky Mountains (see the write-up in this chapter).

One of the foundation's hallmark achievements has been the Imagination Library, which began development in 1995. The Imagination Library is designed to foster an interest in reading among preschool children and to help kindle their imaginations. Any child 5 or younger may register to receive a free, hardcover book in the mail once a month until he or she begins attending school. Children born at Fort Sanders Sevier Medical Center in Sevierville automatically receive their first book and registration form at birth. If a child begins collecting the library at birth, he or she will amass a total of 60 books by the time kindergarten rolls around. To date, close to 90,000 free books have been distributed to more than 5,200 preschoolers in Sevier County.

Interest in the program is sparked by the Imagination Library's "Imagineer," who regularly drives her specially-made "train" to day-care centers, Head Start programs and libraries throughout the county, reading to children and encouraging them to join the program. In 1998 alone, the Imagineer made well over 150 different visits to area children.

The Imagination Library program has received glowing praise and recognition at local, state and national levels. In May 1998, U.S. Department of Education Secretary, Richard Riley, cited the library as being a model reading program. In November 1998, the National Council of Teachers of English recognized the program with its annual Literacy Award. In 2000, the Imagination Library program is expanding to communities nationwide. Schools in states including Georgia, South Carolina, Missouri and Alabama are expected to participate.

All aboard the Dollywood Foundation's Imagination Express.

Photo: Courtesy Dollywood

time students who attend class five days a week for six hours per day. There are usually about 28 part time students attending either two or four nights per week. All students must have a high school or GED diploma to enroll. Registration takes place at the beginning and middle of each quarterly term.

Walters State Community College
1720 Old Newport Hwy., Sevierville
• **(865) 774-5800**

Calling itself "The Great Smoky Mountains Community College," Walters State is a two-year, non residential college serving more than 6,000 students among its different campuses. Sevierville's annex is one of three branches of the main campus, which is based in Morristown, Tennessee (about a one-hour drive from Sevierville). Individual courses are taught in various facilities in more than 10 East Tennessee counties. The Sevierville site has an enrollment of around 800 students per semester. About 60 percent of day students are recent high school graduates while 60 percent of those who attend evening classes are older students seeking continuing education.

Accredited by the Southern Association of Colleges and Schools, Walters State offers Associate of Arts, Associate of Science and Associate of Applied Science degrees. The first two degrees are university parallel programs easily transferable to most four-year colleges; the majority of Walters State students pursue one of these degrees. The Associate of Applied Science degree is a non-transferable, technical education path. In recent years the Sevierville campus has not been equipped to teach science classes, so those requirements have been met at the Morristown campus in order to complete a degree. In 2000, however, a new $6.5

million, 68-acre campus is in operation in Sevierville, offering science courses and allowing for full satisfaction of most areas of study.

Dozens of courses are offered in Sevierville, including those in computer science, math, English and history. Two of this campus's flagship programs are studies in culinary arts and in hospitality management. The first gives students students real world experience in food preparation by cooking and serving lunches and dinners that are available to the public (see our Restaurants chapter). Hospitality Management prepares students for careers in hotel and motel management, an appropriate field for such a tourist-oriented area.

To enroll, new students must provide proof of two doses of measles, mumps and rubella immunization since their first birthday. They must also submit an application and corresponding fee, provide a high school transcript, have ACT or SAT scores sent to the admissions office and, of course, follow the appropriate class registration and fee payment procedures.

In addition to degree-related studies, Walters State offers a number of other programs designed to reach out to all segments of the population. Each semester, about 25 non-credit "community-oriented" classes are taught in subjects ranging from art to business education; the majority are in the field of computer studies. For prospective college students, college credit courses are available to high school juniors and seniors with a B average. Students who have difficulty attending classes at the main campus might want to take advantage of the college's distance learning opportunities such as Interactive Television courses (which utilize closed-circuit TVs) and Internet courses, through which some or all of a course's work can be completed on line.

Childcare

We'll start by looking at the state of full time day care for children younger than school age; later in this section is a subsection on after-school and summer programs for older kids.

Full-Time Programs

While the local public school system has made admirable efforts to keep up with the county's swelling school-age population, the same hasn't always applied to the area's child care industry. That isn't a commentary on the quality of existing child care, necessarily, but on the amount of it. Many day care

INSIDERS' TIP

For parents in search of part time care for younger children (pre kindergarten), one option is a "Mother's Day Out" program. Usually sponsored by churches, these programs provide several hours of fun for the kids a few days during the week. They can be accommodating to the parent who works part time or simply needs a break for some self-nurturing.

facilities and preschools consistently find themselves at maximum capacity with a waiting list of names. It's not a hopeless situation, however. Sevier County's 30 licensed child-care centers (excluding in-home facilities) are allowed a combined, maximum enrollment of 1,918 kids. Statistics for 1998 indicated that slightly more than 1,600 children were enrolled in this type of facility, so childcare can be found if you do some digging. And it's never to early to begin the search process.

In your quest for childcare, we'll help you do some sorting by first making a distinction in classification. You basically have a choice of going with an unlicensed care giver or one that's licensed by the Tennessee Department of Human Services. The state requires anyone caring for more than four non-related children to be licensed, regardless of whether the setting is in the home or at a center. Maximum student-teacher ratios should range from 5-to-1 for infants between 6 weeks and 15 months of age to 25-to-1 for children age 6 and older. In 1999 there were slightly more than 50 licensed childcare operations in Sevier County. Of that number, 20 were in-home facilities.

We would definitely advise steering clear of any unlicensed day care that cares for more than four non-related kids. But it's otherwise difficult and sometimes foolhardy to make generalizations when comparing unlicensed, in-home care (for four or fewer non-related children) to licensed child-care centers. Some licensed day care facilities might be bad choices; by the same token, some small, unlicensed, in-home providers might provide a wonderful and safe environment. The latter type of care can usually be found by scanning classified ads in local papers or by watching supermarket and other types of community bulletin boards. Also note that while the state doesn't require an in-home day care with four or fewer children to be licensed, there are those that voluntarily register with the Department of Human Services and are subject to monitoring procedures.

The bottom line in any case is to do research. This involves more than just comparing rates. Parents should take their children to the facility in question and see how the kids react to the environment, the teachers and the other children. Ask the director about things like teachers' qualifications, student-teacher ratios and discipline policies. Most importantly, get several references and follow up by actually checking on them. As an added peace-of-mind measure, you might contact the Department of Human Services to see if the caregiver in question has received any negative reports. Finally, trust your parental instincts; even if everything seems great on the surface, don't hesitate to continue your search if any particular childcare leaves you with that "unsettling" feeling that parents sometimes get.

Another distinction you might want to consider is the difference between a day care and a preschool. You'll find that many area childcare centers include the word "preschool" in their name. A childcare provider isn't supposed to call itself a "preschool" unless it teaches a specific curriculum that helps prepare children for kindergarten and school. Since these teaching materials are an added expense for preschools, rates are usually a little higher. Your choice ultimately depends on what you want your child to get out of the experience.

Statistics from the Tennessee Department of Human Service indicate that the average weekly cost of day care for one child in Sevier County is $61.50. Broken down by type of facility, the prices don't vary much from group to group. On the high end, childcare centers average $64 per child per week while at the lower end of the spectrum, in-home providers caring for eight to 12 children charge $59 per child per week. If you look at average costs per age group, there still is not a lot of variance. On the high end, the costs of care for infants (up to 12 months old) and toddlers (12 months to 2 years old) average $69 and $67 per week, respectively. For 2 to 5-year-olds, weekly costs average from $65 to $60.

What you get for your money will vary from center to center, so always ask specific questions when doing your research. As we mentioned, some day care providers teach a preschool curriculum while others simply offer structured play. Some places include meals in the price, while others provide snacks only. Other cost-related considerations include discounts for enrolling more than one child and fees for late pick-ups.

After-School and Summer Programs

Just because the kids are big enough to go to school doesn't mean that the issue of quality childcare ends. Many families with working parents and little extended family still must provide the children with a place to go after school and during the summer months. And as with any child-care situation, it's important to find a safe, fun and educational environment in which the youngsters can thrive.

An obvious place to start is with some of the area's licensed day-care centers and preschools. Several have after-school and summer camp programs in addition to full time care for preschoolers. In some cases, the center will even pick the kids up at school and transport them to the day care. Specific after-school activities may include play time, craft projects or homework periods. In summer, field trips to movie theaters, amusement centers and swimming pools are popular with the kids. Naturally, rates will vary depending on the individual facility and the scope of its programs.

Outside the day-care environment, there are a few other resources that have proven themselves to be popular with local families when it comes to after-school and summer care.

Boys & Girls Clubs of the Smoky Mountains
209 McMahon Ave., Sevierville
• (865) 428-5437

This nationally known "Positive Place For Kids" opened in the Smokies in 1991. According to the club's mission statement, its purpose is to "Serve the community by helping our youth build character, develop social skills, inspire dreams and instill leadership qualities necessary to become successful, contributing citizens of Sevier County and beyond." The Boys & Girls Club is open to all children ages 6 through 18, regardless of race, religion, culture or income.

After many years of hard work and a $1.5 million fundraising campaign, the club moved into a brand new facility in the summer of 1998. There is a well-equipped game room (no video games), a large, multi-purpose gym and an arts and crafts center where kids receive instruction in drawing, painting, clay work and more. The Boys & Girls Club also provides several opportunities throughout the year to take part in outdoor activities like camping, hiking and fishing. Its services and activities include homework assistance and tutoring, computer education classes, drug and alcohol prevention programs and nutrition programs.

One of the club's most attractive aspects is its affordability. An annual enrollment fee of $20 per child covers all of his or her expenses during after-school care. There is also an eleven-week day camp that runs during the summer. Registration for the summer camp begins in the spring, and there is an additional cost to attend.

The club is almost always at full enrollment

(540 children), and the recent waiting list had more than 300 names. At the end of each year, current members get the first opportunity to sign up for the following year; after that, names are taken from the waiting list. Anyone new to the area who is interested in joining is advised to get on the waiting list as soon as possible. Boys & Girls Club of the Smoky Mountains is open from 3 to 7 PM, Monday through Friday during the school year. In summer, the hours are 7 AM to 6 PM. The center is open from 8 AM to 5 PM on school holidays but is closed on major holidays.

Sevierville Community Center
200 Gary R. Wade Blvd., Sevierville
• (865) 453-5441

To learn about everything this community center has to offer, refer to our Parks and Recreation chapter. Fortunately, much of what's available is incorporated into the center's after-school and summer programs.

During the school year, children ages 6 through 11 can unwind after a hard day of hitting the books with educational and fitness-oriented activities like swimming, bowling, games, outdoor play and crafts; an afternoon snack is also included. Both the community center and Sevierville City Park are used for educational and fitness-oriented fun. The after-school program runs throughout the academic year, ending daily at 6 PM. The program is usually full, with even more kids on a waiting list, so early sign-ups are highly recommended.

The community center has other programs to serve children year-round. The center sponsors short camps during the Christ-

INSIDERS' TIP

If you're interested in receiving information about child-care resources for low income families, or if you'd like to check out the background of a particular child-care center, you can contact the Sevier County office of the Tennessee Department of Human Services at (865) 429-7005.

mas and spring break vacation periods. There is also an after-school bowling league that meets at the bowling center daily from 3 to 5 PM. When school's out for the year, the community center runs a summer camp that takes up to 100 children ages 6 to 11; registration begins in March. In addition to taking advantage of the community center facilities, the kids go on numerous field trips to places like the city park pool, local amusement centers and movies. Summer hours are 7:45 AM to 3:30 PM weekdays; extended after-camp hours are 3:30 to 5:30 PM.

Gatlinburg Community Center
Mills Park Rd., Gatlinburg
• **(865) 436-4990**

Although it doesn't operate an after-school program, this community center runs a series of six week-long day camps through the summer for ages 5 through 12. Each week is tailored to a different age group and features a specific theme. Activities range from arts and crafts projects to rock climbing, white water rafting and trips to the Knoxville Zoo. A maximum of 15 children get into each session, and sign-ups begin the first Monday in May. Weekly costs range from $40 to $60 except for the camp for 9- to 12-year-olds. That program is a multi-night excursion which, in previous years, has cost around $120 per child. Daily hours for the community center's day camps are from 8:30 AM to 3:30 PM, except for the 5- to 7-year-old group, which attends from 10 AM to 3 PM.

Options for Low-Income Families

Head Start
(865) 453-8959

This federally funded program serves 157 3- and 4-year-olds in eight different centers throughout Sevier County. Head Start was de-

signed as a cognitive preschool program that works in the areas of education, health and social services, parent involvement and literacy, to help families and children become more self sufficient and to prepare children for school. It primarily serves children from low-income families, but approximately 10 percent of enrollment is reserved for special needs children, regardless of income. Special needs children are integrated into the regular Head Start classrooms.

Countywide, Head Start has facilities in Wears Valley, Pigeon Forge, Sevierville and two in the northern section of the county near Kodak. Six of the eight centers are half-day programs that run from either 8 AM to 12 PM or 12 to 4 PM, and are for 4-year-olds only. The two full-day centers are open from 6:30 AM to 6 PM and admit both 3- and 4-year-olds. These are more geared toward working parents and parents involved in school or other vocational training.

There is no charge for the partial-day programs. The full-day centers charge $50 per week, but families that can't afford the cost can apply for financial assistance through the Tennessee Department of Human Services and the state's Child Care Brokers program.

On a daily basis, children at Head Start centers are exposed to a comprehensive preschool program and more. Typical activities include working on letter and number skills, learning about health and nutrition, taking field trips and developing social skills. Beyond the basics, all children are given speech and hearing tests, dental checkups and psychological evaluation in the classroom within the first 45 days of the term, all of which are paid for by Head Start.

The Head Start program in Sevier County has traditionally worked closely with the public school system, and it's been successful in preparing young children for school. It's not an uncommon occurrence for kindergarten teachers in the local public schools to be able to pick out a Head Start kid from the rest of the class, based on that child's preparedness.

Healthcare and Wellness

In what is probably a rare turn of events, the medical care field has actually stayed ahead of the curve during the explosion of tourism and population in Sevier County over the past decade. Rescue services and medical care have stayed abreast of the increasing demand by training practically every city and county employee in first aid and CPR, and the combination of a constantly growing population and the still-rural charm of the area continues to attract medical professionals to the mountains.

The county's only hospital has also committed itself to medical excellence by attracting generous donations for building and service expansions. By joining a large regional medical system, Fort Sanders Sevier Medical Center has made available to its patients facilities and services far beyond the reach of a "rural" hospital. Mental health has also become a significant concern as the nation's attention has shifted from restorative to preventive care, and several area churches conduct on-going family-centered "wellness" programs. The single public mental care facility and the oldest retreat center in the city are listed.

The list of medical services and facilities that follows has been compiled to provide the visitor with a service provider convenient to wherever they might be when such service becomes necessary. The hospital and walk-in clinics are fully cognizant of the population make-up of the Smokies corridor, and tend to lean toward the idea of treating their patients as guests who've had a bad turn of luck. All of the facilities listed accept most insurance programs and national credit cards. If payment is a problem, they'll work something out. The clinics usually operate Monday through Friday from 8 or 9 AM to 4:30 or 5 PM, but calls at all hours are answered.

LOOK FOR:
- **Hospitals and Convalescent Centers**
- **Walk-In Clinics**
- **Chiropractic Clinics**
- **Mental Care**
- **Self-Help Groups**
- **Veterinary Services**

Local Emergency Numbers

Any emergency	911
Medical Emergency Hotline	(865) 453-7111
Tennessee Highway Patrol	(865) 693-7311
Sevier County Ambulance Authority	(865) 453-3200
Sevier County Sheriff's Department	(865) 453-4668
Sevierville Police Department	(865) 453-5507
Sevierville/Sevier County Fire Department	(865) 453-9276
Pigeon Forge Police Department	(865) 453-9063
Pigeon Forge Fire Department	(865) 453-4044
Gatlinburg Police Department	(865) 436-5181
Gatlinburg Fire Department	(865) 436-5112
Pittman Center Police/Fire Department	(865) 436-9684

Hospitals and Convalescent Care Centers

Sevierville

Fort Sanders Sevier Medical Center
709 Middle Creek Rd., Sevierville
• (865) 429-6100

What was a small, well-run but very limited rural hospital as recently as 1990 has grown into one of Tennessee's recognized leaders in overall health care. Fort Sanders Sevier Medical Center, still locally referred to as "Sevier County," has expanded in every direction (including straight up and down) until the original building is no longer visible. The current emergency room is larger and has a bigger staff than the original hospital had, and the addition of special-care facilities like the state-of-the-art intensive care unit and the six-bed Dolly Parton Birthing Center have raised its level of available service to that of most metropolitan hospitals.

The current configuration includes a 79-bed acute care facility and an on-site 54-bed nursing home providing intermediate and skilled long-term care. Complete in- and outpatient surgical services are provided in more than a dozen specialties. Therapeutic services are available in long and short-term programs, and support group contacts are usually on hand. As the hospital has continued to grow in a largely unsettled area of the county, it has had the added benefit of becoming the geographic center for the construction of several professional centers offering medical service in every conceivable fashion, with most of the specialists having hospital certification.

Fort Sanders Sevier Nursing Home
709 Middle Creek Rd., Sevierville
• (865) 453-7111

Adjacent to and operated as a satellite service of the Fort Sanders Sevier Medical Center, the Fort Sanders nursing home provides 24-hour nursing care and service to residents at ICF Level I and skilled Level II. Various activities (exercise classes, craft classes, special holiday programs) are available for ambulatory residents.

Sevier County Health Care Center
Beal Rd., Sevierville • (865) 453-4747

Dedicated to more serious care of the aging and terminally ill, the Sevier County Health Care Center has 149 beds and is certified in all phases of treatment, rehabilitation, and hospice services.

Pigeon Forge

Royal Care of Pigeon Forge
415 Cole Dr., Pigeon Forge
• (865) 428-5454

Royal Care specializes in rehabilitation services intended to return injured and incapacitated patients to mainstream living through inpatient and outpatient programs designed to meet the individual needs of the patient. Physician involvement is one of Royal Care's keys to developing and implementing individual programs to suit the needs of the individual patient.

Walk-In Clinics

Sevierville

Healthstar Physicians, PC
1105 Oak Cluster Dr., Sevierville
• (865) 908-3636

One of the newer entries on the local healthcare scene, Healthstar is a regional organization of walk-in clinics. The only one in the Smokies corridor is staffed by an MD and two PA-Cs (Certified Physician's Assistants), with a sizable administrative staff. Healthstar provides a full range of services, including diagnostic and urgent care, with the latest technology available. The clinic is open Monday through Friday from 8 AM to 5 PM, and Saturday from 9 AM to 1 PM. Most insurance plans are accommodated, and the clinic accepts MasterCard, Visa, and Discover cards

Pigeon Forge

Valley Medical Center
330 Wears Valley Rd., Pigeon Forge
• (865) 908-1302

Valley is an independent clinic that includes medical and chiropractic service under one roof (the chiropractic clinic is described later). A single doctor handles medical services with the aid of a nurse/receptionist. Diagnostic services and treatment are handled with the latest technology, and walk-in traffic is welcome. Valley is open Monday through Thursday from 9 AM to 5:30 PM, and Friday from 9 AM to Noon. Most insurance programs are accommodated, and Valley accepts MasterCard, Visa, and Discover cards.

Medicenter of Pigeon Forge
3342 Parkway, Pigeon Forge
• (865) 453-1122

Right in the center of Pigeon Forge, Medicenter is at traffic light #7. One MD is assisted by five administrative employees in providing care up to the urgent level, including simple fractures. Medicenter is an independent clinic, open Monday through Friday from 8:30 AM to 5:30 PM and Saturday from 9 AM to Noon. Most insurance programs are accepted, as are MasterCard, Visa, and Discover cards.

Gatlinburg

Gatlinburg Family and Urgent Care
611 Oak, Gatlinburg • (865) 430-7369

Staffed by a PA-C and a Medical Assistant under the supervision of an MD, this clinic is convenient to downtown Gatlinburg. It's in the River Oaks shopping center on River Road, a block off the Parkway. Basically a family practice center, the clinic is equipped to handle minor surgical procedures and simple fractures, and does its own lab work. The clinic is open Monday through Friday from 8 AM to 5 PM. Insurance agreements are pending at this time. Out of state checks are accepted, as are MasterCard, Visa, and Discover cards.

First Med Family Medical Clinic
1015 East Parkway, Gatlinburg
• (865) 436-7267

Gatlinburg's original walk-in clinic, First Med is operated by an MD during the week and a PA-C on Saturday. This independent clinic is equipped for urgent care and diagnostic services, but doesn't apply casts. First Med is open Monday through Friday from 9 AM to 3 PM, and Saturday from 9 AM to Noon. Some insurance plans are accepted, along with MasterCard, Visa, and Discover cards.

Chiropractic Clinics

Sevierville

Ratcliff Chiropractic Clinic
826 Middle Creek Rd., Sevierville
• (865) 453-1390

The Doctors Ratcliff (there are two of them)

apply the techniques of spinal manipulation to promote healing and better general health through non-surgical means. Specializing in personal and sports injuries, the Ratcliff Clinic is one of the area's oldest practices in continuous operation. The clinic is open Monday, Wednesday, and Friday from 8 AM to 6 PM, and Tuesday and Thursday from 8 AM to 4 PM. Most insurance programs that cover chiropractic care are accommodated. MasterCard, Visa, and Discover cards are also accepted.

Pigeon Forge

Chiropractic Wellness Center PC
330 Wear's Valley Rd., Pigeon Forge
• (865) 908-1302

Within the confines of the Valley Medical Center described in Walk-in Clinics, the Chiropractic Wellness Center is operated by a DC and three physical therapy assistants. Full chiropractic services are available, and the MD at Valley Medical Center is virtually in the next room if chiropractic techniques aren't suitable to any situation. The center is open Monday through Thursday from 9 AM to 5:30 PM, and accepts most insurance programs and MasterCard, Visa, and Discover cards.

Mental Care

Overlook Center, Inc.
124 N. Henderson Ave., Sevierville
• (865) 453-3446

Overlook provides crisis intervention services and long and short term counseling. For emergency services, call the hot line at (865) 588-2936.

Self-Help and Advocacy Groups

Nicotine Anonymous Support Group
709 Middle Creek Road, Sevierville
• (865) 429-9052

Available to all comers who are trying to kick any form of nicotine habit, Nicotine Anonymous meets on the first Monday of every month at 6:30 P.M. in the Fort Sanders

INSIDERS' TIP
If your situation requires ongoing attention, like a chronic disease or respiratory care, the person who handles check-in at your lodging place can usually provide you with a telephone number for specialized care; if not, call the emergency services number at Fort Sanders Sevier Medical Center: (865) 453-7111.

HEALTHCARE AND WELLNESS

Sevier Medical Center conference room.

Overeaters Anonymous
709 Middle Creek Road, Sevierville
• (865) 428-6109
For those with problems pushing away from the table, Overeaters Anonymous meets at 1:30 every Thursday in the Fort Sanders Sevier Medical Center conference room.

SafeSpace
Sevierville • (800) 244-5968
A quick-response service for battered wives, SafeSpace provides shelter and support services for women in Sevier County regardless of residency status. Legal and court assistance are available when needed, along with round-the-clock counseling, referrals, and emotional support. A support group is available weekly for residents, and child care can be arranged.

Note: In addition to the help groups listed above, *The Mountain Press* runs a listing called HelpLine once a week that includes information on other groups. The HelpLine column appears every Thursday on the comics page, and includes listings of several self-help and support organizations, complete with meeting times and places.

Retreat Center

Steiner-Bell Mountain Haven
3610 East Parkway, Gatlinburg
• (865) 436-5575

Veterinary Services

It's not unusual for visitors to the Smokies to bring pets with them, and why not? We're dealing with families here, and a lot of American families have furry, finny, and feathered members. If your animal friend gets a case of the punies during your vacation, here's a list of veterinary clinics that provide complete services, including boarding and overnight hospital care.

Sevierville
Mountain Home Veterinary Hospital
302 Middle Creek Rd., Sevierville
• (865) 453-9346

Parkway Animal Hospital
104 S. Boulevard Way, Sevierville
• (865) 428-0190

Gatlinburg
Mountain Home Veterinary Clinic
1661 E. Parkway, Gatlinburg
• (865) 436-3350

HEALTHCARE AND WELLNESS

Senior Scene

Prominent among the many unusual aspects of living in the Smokies is the size and character of the senior population. Our central location and temperate climate combine to draw a great many visitors who are looking for a place to spend their "golden days," and the natural charm of this place convinces a healthy percentage (no pun intended) of the visitors to make the Smokies their home when they retire. Where the definitive retirees in the Smokies part company with their contemporaries in other parts of the country is what happens when they move to East Tennessee.

LOOK FOR:
• **Retirement Homes and Villages**
• **Senior Information and Assistance**
• **Publications**
• **Organizations**

First, they'd better be in good shape—"retirement" in the Smokies means a lot more than a rocking chair and an occasional stroll down to the shuffleboard courts. There are very few traditional "retirement communities" in the area right now. Additionally, most of the Smokies seniors have chosen this place after careful consideration, have probably purchased property or even a home well in advance of moving here, and usually intend to become part of the mainstream community when they move. Those who choose not to work or even start a new business career when they move to the Smokies are able to stay active by performing volunteer work at local chambers of commerce, visitor's information services, hospitals, and the Great Smoky Mountains National Park. The role of the senior citizen in the Smokies is so firmly entrenched in the community at large that, abundant services notwithstanding, the older members of the Smokies' permanent population are simply regarded as neighbors, and that's about as dignified a status as one can aspire to here.

Naturally, a host of services and organizations provide assistance where it's needed, but the city and county governments have been slow to recognize their retirees as a "special needs" group because the people in question have been reluctant to accept that status. As the population grows exponentially, and the number of retirees seeking a more conventional refuge for their ultimate homes increases, more attention is being given to the elder population's needs.

The recent formation of a citizens task force to address the issue head-on is spurring new approaches to promoting the Smokies as a retirement haven. To that end, more conventional retirement agencies are popping up and promoting local interest in the retired population as an organized group. It is estimated that by 2005, municipal retirement services and facilities in the Smokies will be at parity with services offered in any community of 100,000 permanent population, assuming that the permanent population doesn't actually achieve that figure. Updates of this book will pay close attention to those developments, but it's tough at the moment to tell a "retired" citizen in the Smokies from any other until you get to know them well. Then you learn the biggest difference: The retirees in the Smokies are usually busier, healthier, and generally happier than their counterparts who still work for a living.

The following list of services and organizations will help steer the potential retiree toward the answers to questions they may have about relocating to the Smokies area, beginning with the only true assisted-living facilities in the county dedicated to retired citizens.

Retirement Homes and Villages

Assisted Living

Markhill Village Retirement Community
700 Markhill Dr., Sevierville
• (865) 428-2445

Secluded from the traffic on the Parkway a block away, Markhill Village is a community unto itself. Single-story dwelling units are laid out along the middle prong of the Little Pigeon River across from Sevierville City Park, insuring that commercial incursion won't disturb the residents in the foreseeable future. The Markhill system provides whatever level of care is desired by its residents, from complete freedom to the highest level of assisted care in a non-medical facility. The Markhill residents are generally considered no different from any other residents of Sevierville, except that they're more active than most. Monthly rentals are available.

Wellington Place
1020 Middle Creek Rd., Sevierville
• (865) 774-2221

Convenient to Fort Sanders Sevier Medical Center, Wellington Place is a brand-new assisted living facility that offers its residents a full menu of options. The facility is far enough from any commercial district to consider itself "rural" at the moment, and on a big enough piece of land that privacy will be insured when commercial spread reaches the area south of Dolly Parton Parkway. Wellington Place has 60 units in various configurations, with plans for additional accommodations by the end of the year 2000. On-site services are provided by professional staff and visiting specialists, ranging from special dietary programs to weekly haircuts. Medical and health monitoring services are available on-site, as are housekeeping and laundry services. Transportation can be arranged for trips into Sevierville for shopping or recreation. The beautifully landscaped grounds and communal facilities provide an active social atmosphere for Wellington Place's permanent residents, and the variety of available services make living easy for those unable to travel too far from home.

Independent Living

Douglas-Cherokee Economic Authority
Morristown, TN • (865) 587-4500

The Douglas-Cherokee Economic Authority is the local umbrella organization for most of the federal agencies responsible for government assistance programs. Among a huge number of facilities and programs in its portfolio, Douglas-Cherokee operates two small apartment complexes in Sevierville that are reserved for people aged 62 years and up who meet the federal (HUD) guidelines to qualify for low-income housing. The units are single-family dwellings in single-story apartment-style buildings. Income-based rental rates include standard utilities—cable television and telephone service are available at the tenants' discretion. Part-time maintenance and administration services are provided by the housing authority. Availability of units is practically non-existent now and for the foreseeable future—there's a long waiting list at both sites. The Woodland Park site has land available for further development if money can be found to build more units.

Gateway Village Apartments
120 West Paine St., Sevierville
• (865) 453-1729

Contained within the Gateway complex of low-income and handicapped housing are 16 dwelling units reserved for senior residents. The Gateway complex is next to Sevierville City Park on the east side of the downtown business district, in one of the city's oldest residential neighborhoods. The administrative office is open from 8 AM to noon Monday through Friday.

Woodland Park Apartments
202 Hardin Ln., Sevierville
• (865) 429-6896

With 55 units in operation and more being prayed for, Woodland Park looks like any other suburban apartment complex. The single-story units are laid out on a gently curved road across the Little Pigeon River from the downtown shopping area. The admin-

SENIOR SCENE

istration building includes a community room where residents can get together for social functions. The office is open Monday through Friday from 12:30 to 4:30 PM.

Senior Information and Assistance

Sevier County Senior Citizens Center
750 Old Knoxville Hwy., Sevierville
• **(865) 453-8080**

A full slate of activities and directory services are available Monday through Saturday at the Center, where activities and meals are provided to drop-in guests. Helpful services (shuttles, tax preparation, etc.) are also available by appointment. A new center is under construction nearer to downtown.

Senior Citizens Home Assistance Services
109 Parkway, Sevierville • **(865) 453-6853**

Government and commercial services available to home-bound seniors are coordinated by this office in cooperation with the Senior Citizens Center and local hospitals.

E-Z Access
(865) 453-8080

Originally established as a transportation system for older people unable to drive, E-Z Access has become a dependable public transportation service with no restrictions on age or means. The E-Z Access van will pick up any caller, deliver them to any destination within the county, and return them home for a flat fee of $5. The program is administered by the Sevier County Council on Aging.

Tel-A-Tend
(865) 453-6271

Tel-A-Tend is a computerized system that provides services such as daily monitoring and reminders to take medicine. It raises an alarm if the subscriber doesn't answer the telephone or doesn't respond properly. The service costs $10 per year (waived in most cases). Monies collected are used to offset the cost of additional telephone lines. Tel-A-Tend requires that the subscriber have a touch-tone telephone and touch-tone service on the line, and a friend, neighbor, or relative who will agree to check on any subscriber who doesn't answer a scheduled call. If the secondary number doesn't answer, Tel-A-Tend will automatically call the E-911 service and request that a police unit be sent to the residence.

INSIDERS' TIP

Most of the local real estate firms keep sets of special listings to accommodate retirees. If you're looking for a one-bedroom home or rental property for the special needs of a retired person, be sure to let the realtor know your needs as quickly as possible.

Assistance Hotlines

Local
Ambulance, Fire, and Police 911
Sevier County Ambulance Authority:
    Emergency .... (865) 453-3200
    Business Office, ... (865) 453-3248
Sevier County Office on Aging .... (865) 453-8080

National
Alzheimer's Association .... (800) 621-0379
Arthritis Foundation .... (800) 283-7800
Elder Hotline .... (800) 677-1116
Parkinson's Educational Program .... (800) 344-7872
Security Fraud .... (800) 863-9117

SENIOR SCENE

Publications

The Mountain Press publishes a tabloid-size supplement on the 15th of each month that's dedicated to providing information for citizens 50 years of age or older. "Experienced Living" usually runs about 24 pages in length , and is primarily a compilation of relevant articles gleaned from other sources. Features on prominent local seniors are indicative of the "normal" expectations of senior citizens in the area. Schedules throughout the paper note regular and irregular events of particular interest, and a listing of emergency and assistance hotline numbers is always included. Unfortunately, the only easy way to get a copy of "Experienced Living" is to buy *The Mountain Press* on the 15th of any month. A free copy can be requested by writing Experienced Living c/o The Mountain Press, P.O. Box 4810, Sevierville, TN 37864, or sending an e-mail request to the editor, maryo24@aol.com.

INSIDERS' TIP

Retirees who have time and don't need additional income are welcome to work as volunteers for the myriad civic activities going on in all three of the corridor cities. A call to the chamber of commerce in any one of the three cities will provide enough volunteer work to keep any retiree as busy as they want to be.

Organizations

American Association of Retired Persons (AARP)
Senior Citizens Center, Old Knoxville Hwy., Sevierville • (865) 453-8080
The Sevier County chapter of the AARP meets at noon on the first Wednesday of each month at the Senior Citizens Center. Meetings usually include lunch and guest speakers.

Retired Citizens of Gatlinburg
Gatlinburg Community Center, Mills Park Rd., Gatlinburg • (865) 436-4990
This large energetic group meets on the first Monday of every month at 1 PM for a light luncheon and to plan the activities for the month ahead. These usually include several hikes, a few get-togethers for domestic interests like knitting and sewing, and a field trip to a concert or athletic event. They also have their own informal bowling league that meets for all-comers competition on the Community Center lanes every second and fourth Thursday at 1 PM.

Sevier County Senior Citizens
Senior Citizens Center, Old Knoxville Hwy., Sevierville • (865) 453-8080
The best way for seniors to meet new people in Sevier County is to attend one or two monthly meetings of the Sevier County Senior Citizens. They meet at noon on the third Tuesday of every month for a covered dish luncheon aimed at welcoming newcomers, and hold a special party on the fourth Friday at 11:30 AM to celebrate birthdays and wedding anniversaries. The covered dish luncheon is followed by a musical performance by the Good Time Band. Special holiday parties are also held throughout the year.

Worship

East Tennessee is smack in the center of that portion of middle America that's referred to as the "Bible Belt." Overwhelmingly Christian in orientation, most Sevier County natives continue to practice the old-time religion of their forebears. Meanwhile, non-native residents who couldn't bring themselves to accept the deep fundamental religious attitudes they found here have brought their own more liberal brands of faith with them. When you think about it, you can understand the depth of religion in a place like the Smokies — it's difficult to look at the grandeur of these surroundings and question the existence and the awesome power of a supreme being.

Since the original settlers took their religion seriously, the church was the major center of social life. Church services were the only social activity that operated on a dependable schedule, and the mountain people of the southern end of the county moved quickly to establish chapels instead of hiking 15 or 20 miles to Sevierville or Wear's Fort, usually carrying their shoes. (This was an interesting conceit found among mountain people: They carried their shoes to church and to school so they wouldn't get scuffed and worn out on the dusty, rocky roads, and so they'd look their best during services and classes. It's kind of ironic that one of the few vanities actually practiced by these people was to surrender the protection of their feet so the covering would look good.)

Mostly Presbyterian on arrival, the settlers took to the Baptist faith early on when they found that seminary-trained ministers of other faiths were not exactly standing in line to move to the mountains and work for livestock instead of a salary. In contrast, any member of a Baptist congregation who "felt the calling" could preach if he was approved by the local church board. The Baptist system of home-grown preachers ministering to their own flocks is still in widespread use in East Tennessee, and its effectiveness is proved by the fact that Sevier County alone has a separate Baptist church for about every 75 residents.

The Baptists had another advantage in the early days. They were more tolerant than their Presbyterian and Methodist brethren of some of the mystical practices that bordered on voodoo in the deeper recesses of the mountains, particularly those involving the occasional sacrifice of poultry. The Baptists reasoned that most of these practices were harmless, and nearly all of them were used for medicinal purposes.

As the population of the area increased more by emigration than reproduction, other Protestant faiths took hold. The county today is still more Baptist than anything else, but just about every Protestant denomination currently in practice has a home in the Smokies. Roman Catholicism, unlike the pioneer trends of its missionaries elsewhere in the world, was a latecomer to the scene. The first established Catholic church opened in 1950 in Gatlinburg as a chapel extension of a Maryville church, and St. Mary's Catholic Church was consecrated there in 1953. Forty years later, a second Catholic church was built in Pigeon Forge, and it reaches out to the migrant worker population by celebrating the Mass in Spanish at a special service every Sunday.

There are more than 40 churches of various Christian denominations within three miles of the Smokies corridor, most of them on or in sight of the Parkway. Sevierville's two biggest churches (Baptist and United Methodist) are on the Parkway just south of Dolly Parton Parkway.

The same is true of Pigeon Forge, where the biggest Baptist Church is on the Parkway just north of traffic light #7, and the Methodist church is on River Road just south of the same light.

Gatlinburg has six churches of varying denominations (including Catholic and Church of Christ) in a four-block area of Airport Road and Reagan Drive near the center of town. In keeping with the character of the area, the churches all welcome visitors.

The following list of denominations by city may be helpful in planning your visit to a place of worship: Sevierville has the only congregations of Assembly of God, Church of Jesus Christ of Latter-day Saints, Jehovah's Witnesses, Pentecostal, and Seventh Day Adventist. Pigeon Forge has the county's only Christian Science Society center. Among the rest of the represented faiths, the following numbers apply:

Baptist — 12 churches in Sevierville, two in Pigeon Forge, four in Gatlinburg
Christian Church — one each in Sevierville and Pigeon Forge
Church of Christ — one each in Sevierville, Pigeon Forge and Gatlinburg
Church of God — two in Sevierville, one each in Pigeon Forge and Gatlinburg
Episcopal — two in Sevierville, one in Gatlinburg
Lutheran — one each in Pigeon Forge and Gatlinburg
Presbyterian — two in Sevierville, one in Gatlinburg
Roman Catholic — one each in Pigeon Forge and Gatlinburg

Also, there's an AME Zion church in Strawberry Plains, less than 10 miles west of Sevierville-Goodes Temple. AME Zion church is at 476 Old Dandridge Pike, (865) 933-8099.

Several non-Christian faiths are accommodated in Knox-ville, about 30 miles west of Severville. These include:

Baha'i World Faith, (865) 687-0444
Knoxville Jewish Federation, (865) 693-5837
Muslim Community of Knoxville, (865) 637-8172

This list doesn't include anywhere near all the churches in Sevier County, nor does it mention several Christian denominations whose affiliations are not readily understood by the layman. It does attempt to provide enough of a choice that the visitor can find a house of worship that is close enough to the center of their beliefs to be sufficient while they're away from home.

The only non-Christian religious organization in Sevier County is a Hindu ashram in Sevierville. The local telephone directory yellow pages contain a complete list of churches by denomination, and the Friday edition of *The Mountain Press* has a full page listing the locations and worship services of every church that provides the information.

INSIDERS' TIP

In keeping with the local industrial base, most churches are very liberal when it comes to manner of dress. Anything you'd feel comfortable in at a restaurant is usually OK, but some of the more conservative churches prefer that worshipers not wear shorts to their services.

Index of Advertisers

Index

A

Abrams Creek Campground 260
Acorn Shop, The 223
Adoughable Things/Shucks Y'All 240
Adult Education Program 343
Adventure Golf 176
Adventure Raceway 144, 176
advocacy groups 352
air travel 13–14
Alabama Grill 104, 107–108
Alan Jackson's Showcar Cafe 108–109
Alewine Pottery 240
Alf's 104
Alpine RV Park and Campground 91
Alto Motel 62
American Association of Retired Persons (AARP) 356
American Eagle Weekend 190, 192
American Youth Soccer Organization (AYSO) 277
amusements and attractions
amusement centers 141–144, 146–147, 149–151, 153–155, 157, 160–169, 173–176, 178–184
aquariums 148–149
baseball, professional 135
canoeing 263–265
caves 138–139
Dollywood 160–169, 178–179
gardens 158
Gatlinburg 147–159
go-carts 136–137, 139–147, 171–178, 180
golf 278–282
helicopter rides 135–136
horseback riding 273–275
laser tag 143, 174–175, 177, 183
miniature golf 147–151, 176–181, 183, 184
mining 139, 143
museums 137–138, 141–142, 144–146, 149, 151, 157, 171
Pigeon Forge 140–147
rafting 158–159
Sevierville 135–140
skiing 155–157, 158
skydiving 144–145

theaters, specialty 146, 150, 152, 183–184
tubing 263–265
vineyards 140–141
water parks 141, 173
zoos 138, 172, 182–183
See also nightlife; theaters, music and variety
Anita Bryant's Music Mansion Theater 120–121
Anna Porter Public Library 180–181
annual events. See festivals and annual events
antiques and collectibles stores 205, 213, 220–221, 222
apartments 324–325
Appalachian Attitude, The 235
Apple Tree Inn 110–111
Applewood Farmhouse Restaurant 103–104
Applewood Farms 217–218
aquariums 148–149
Arrowcraft 234–235
Arrow Creek Campground 93
arts, creative and performing 290–294
arts and crafts. See crafts, mountain
Asheville, North Carolina
attractions 315, 317–318
Biltmore Estate 311–315
getting there 311
Atrium Restaurant 113
attractions. See amusements and attractions
Aunt Mahalia's Candies 223
automobile rentals 14

B

Back Home Wedding Chapel 285
Bales Town & Country Motel 60
Balsam Mountain Campground 260
Bankshot Basketball 150–151, 184
Barbara's Real Estate Company 326
Barn Owl, The 213
baseball 135, 275–276
basketball, youth 276
Baskins Square Mall 216
Baxter's Stained Glass 242
Bearland Lodge & General Store 62

INDEX